The Victoria History of the Counties of England

EDITED BY R. B. PUGH, M.A., F.S.A.

A HISTORY OF
LEICESTERSHIRE

VOLUME II

A LEICESTERSHIRE LANDSCAPE: KING'S NORTON FROM THE SOUTH-EAST

THE
VICTORIA HISTORY
OF THE COUNTIES
OF ENGLAND
LEICESTERSHIRE

PUBLISHED FOR

THE UNIVERSITY OF LONDON
INSTITUTE OF HISTORICAL RESEARCH

REPRINTED FROM THE ORIGINAL EDITION OF 1954

BY

DAWSONS OF PALL MALL

LONDON

1969

Published by the
Oxford University Press
in 1954

Reprinted for the University of London
Institute of Historical Research
by
Dawsons of Pall Mall
16 *Pall Mall, London, S.W.* 1
1969
SBN: 7129 0368 2

Reprinted by Stephen Austin and Sons Ltd., Caxton Hill, Hertford

INSCRIBED
TO THE MEMORY OF
HER LATE MAJESTY
QUEEN VICTORIA
WHO GRACIOUSLY GAVE
THE TITLE TO AND
ACCEPTED THE
DEDICATION OF
THIS HISTORY

THE
VICTORIA HISTORY
OF THE COUNTY OF
LEICESTER

EDITED BY

W. G. HOSKINS, M.A., Ph.D.

ASSISTED BY

R. A. McKINLEY, M.A.

VOLUME TWO

PUBLISHED FOR
THE UNIVERSITY OF LONDON
INSTITUTE OF HISTORICAL RESEARCH
REPRINTED BY
DAWSONS OF PALL MALL
LONDON

CONTENTS OF VOLUME TWO

CONTENTS OF VOLUME TWO

LIST OF MAPS AND ILLUSTRATIONS

The air photographs of Grace Dieu Priory and the site of Hamilton were taken by Dr. J. K. St. Joseph and are deposited in Leicester City Museum: they are reproduced by permission of the Museums and Art Gallery Committee of Leicester City Corporation. The photograph of the portrait of Sir Arthur Hazlerigg was taken by K. & S. Photos Ltd. of Leicester: the reproduction is printed by permission of the present Lord Hazlerigg. The air photograph of Kilby was taken by the Royal Air Force and is reproduced by permission of the Air Ministry. Photographs of the engravings of Robert Bakewell and Lord John Manners were supplied by the British Museum, and are reproduced by courtesy of the Trustees. The frontispiece and the photographs of Ulverscroft Priory, Dishley Grange, and the two yeoman's houses were taken by F. L. Attenborough, Esq., M.A., and are reproduced by his permission. The three maps were drawn at the Leicester College of Art and Technology under the supervision of A. E. Christopherson, Esq., A.R.C.A.

EDITORIAL NOTE

VOLUME I of the *Victoria History of Leicestershire* was published in 1907, and was designed as the first of four volumes. Though some material for a second volume was ready by 1908 no further progress was made until 1948, when a group of enthusiasts in Leicestershire came together to form a Leicestershire Victoria County History Committee. Upon this Committee there have sat since that time representatives of the Leicestershire County Council, the Leicester City Council, the Leicestershire Archaeological Society, the Leicestershire Literary and Philosophical Society, the Leicester Chamber of Commerce, the Leicester Branch of the Historical Association, and the Diocese of Leicester. In addition certain individuals have been co-opted. The two local authorities and the two Leicestershire societies subscribed funds for editorial purposes in the period from 1948 to 1953. Since 1953 the Leicestershire Literary and Philosophical Society has been unable to continue its grant, but University College, Leicester, has stepped into its place. The other three bodies continue to subscribe. A valuable donation to the funds was made in 1949 by the Leicester Chamber of Commerce.

The scheme devised in 1948 constitutes a partnership between Leicestershire and the University of London similar to and modelled approximately upon that subsisting between the University and Wiltshire, described in the introductory note to the *Victoria History of Wiltshire*, Volume VII. By such a partnership the local Committee is responsible for preparing and editing the material for the history and the University for publishing it. As the first step in carrying out its share of the enterprise the local Committee appointed as its honorary local editor Dr. W. G. Hoskins, then Reader in English Local History at University College, Leicester, and now Reader in Economic History in the University of Oxford. Both the University of London and Leicestershire were singularly fortunate in attracting to the local editorship a person so deeply immersed in local studies as Dr. Hoskins. He planned the present volume, its successor, and the articles which are to form the history of Leicester City, and edited much of the material submitted. In 1951 he was joined for a time as honorary local editor by Dr. C. H. Thompson, then Archivist to the Leicestershire County Council and now holding a parallel post in Surrey. In 1949 Mr. R. A. McKinley was appointed full-time local Assistant Editor and became local Editor in 1952 when Dr. Hoskins resigned from his post at University College, Leicester.

Everyone interested in local history must be sensible of the debt that is owed to those bodies in Leicestershire who have so generously granted funds to enable this and succeeding volumes to be prepared. Without their subsidies there is no likelihood that the *History of Leicestershire* would have been completed in the present generation. In particular, deep gratitude must be felt, as much by the University of London as by Leicestershire, to Sir Robert Martin, Chairman alike of the Leicestershire County Council and of the local V.C.H. Committee.

EDITORIAL NOTE

His lively interest in the Leicestershire history and powerful local influence have contributed most valuably to the whole enterprise.

There are some points peculiar to this volume which it is desirable to explain. The history of Leicester City is being treated on its own. Most of the general chapters on Leicestershire, therefore, in this and the succeeding volume ignore the City; where they do not, the fact is mentioned in text or footnote. Although the chapter on Ecclesiastical History in Volume I purports to cover the whole history of Christianity in Leicestershire, Roman Catholicism had been less fully treated than the history of either the Church of England or of Protestant Non-conformity. This explains the presence in this volume of a special article on Roman Catholicism. Volume III is designed to include a comprehensive index to the first three volumes of the Leicestershire History; hence there is no index in this one.

Much valuable help has been given both in the preparation and execution of this volume and in the preparation of the volumes that are to follow it by Professor Jack Simmons and by Dr. L. A. Parker and Mrs. A. M. Woodcock, archivists of the county and city of Leicester respectively.

R. B. PUGH

LEICESTERSHIRE
VICTORIA COUNTY HISTORY
COMMITTEE

Where not otherwise stated members have served on the Committee from 1948 until the present time.

ALDERMAN LT.-COL. SIR ROBERT E. MARTIN, C.M.G.,
 T.D., D.L. (Chairman)
ALDERMAN MAJOR T. G. F. PAGET, D.L. (died 1952)
COUNCILLOR MRS. M. E. KEAY, B.E.M. (from 1952)   *Representing Leicester County Council*
COUNCILLOR W. G. COATES
THE REVD. D. A. ADAMS

ALDERMAN C. R. KEENE, C.B.E.
COUNCILLOR P. G. HUGHES (resigned 1949)   *Representing the City of Leicester*
COUNCILLOR A. H. W. KIMBERLIN (from 1949)

C. D. B. ELLIS, ESQ., M.C. . . . . .   *Representing the Leicestershire Archaeological Society*

J. MILNE, ESQ. . . . . . .   *Representing the Leicestershire Literary and Philosophical Society*

S. H. RUSSELL, ESQ. . . . . .   *Representing Leicester and County Chamber of Commerce*

DR. ANNE K. B. EVANS (from 1950)
PROFESSOR J. SIMMONS   *Representing University College, Leicester*

B. ELLIOTT, ESQ. (resigned 1952)   *Representing the Leicester Branch of the Historical Association*
P. A. STEVENS, ESQ.

THE RT. REVD. DR. G. VERNON SMITH, M.C., *formerly*   *Representing the Diocese of Leicester*
 Bishop of Leicester (resigned 1953)

A. TAYLOR MILNE, ESQ. (resigned 1950)   *Representing the Central Committee of the Victoria*
R. B. PUGH, ESQ. (from 1950)   *County History*

Co-opted Members

SIR WILLIAM BROCKINGTON, C.B.E.   DR. J. H. PLUMB

L. H. IRVINE, ESQ., M.B.E.   H. P. R. FINBERG, ESQ. (Co-opted 1952)

PROFESSOR A. HAMILTON THOMPSON, C.B.E., F.B.A.   DR. W. G. HOSKINS (Co-opted 1953)
 (died 1952)

     DR. C. H. THOMPSON (resigned 1951)
     DR. L. A. PARKER   Honorary Secretary

     S. B. BORDOLI, ESQ.   Honorary Treasurer

LIST OF CLASSES OF THE PUBLIC RECORDS

USED IN THIS VOLUME, WITH THEIR CLASS NUMBERS

Chancery
- C 54 Close Rolls
- C 66 Patent Rolls
- C 78 Decree Rolls
- C 132 Inquisitions post mortem, Series I, Hen. III
- C 133   ,,   ,,   ,, Edw. I
- C 134   ,,   ,,   ,, Edw. II
- C 135   ,,   ,,   ,, Edw. III
- C 142   ,,   ,, Series II

Exchequer
- E 25 Acknowledgements of Supremacy
- E 142 Ancient Extents
- E 150 Inquisitions post mortem, Series I
- E 179 Subsidy Rolls
- E 303 Conventual leases
- E 326 Ancient Deeds, Series B
- E 329 Ancient Deeds, Series BX
- E 359 Enrolled accounts, subsidies
- E 377 Recusant Rolls

Home Office
- H.O. 40 Disturbances, Correspondence
- H.O. 41 Disturbances, Entry Books
- H.O. 42 Correspondence, Domestic, Geo. III
- H.O. 50 Correspondence, Military
- H.O. 52 Correspondence, Counties

War Office
- W.O. 4 Out Letters, Secretary-at-War
- W.O. 13 Muster Lists and Pay Books, Militia and Volunteers

Duchy of Lancaster
- D.L. 29 Ministers' Accounts
- D.L. 43 Rentals and Surveys

Justices Itinerant
- Just. Itin. 1 Assize Rolls, Eyre Rolls, &c.

Special Collections
- S.C. 6 Ministers' Accounts
- S.C. 11 Rentals and Surveys (Rolls)
- S.C. 12   ,,   ,, (Portfolios)
- S.C. 13 Seals

State Paper Office
- S.P. 12 State Papers, Domestic, Eliz. I
- S.P. 16   ,,   ,,   ,, Chas. I
- S.P. 41   ,,   ,,   ,, Military

Court of Star Chamber
- Star Cha. 5 Proceedings, Eliz. I

Court of Wards and Liveries
- Wards 5 Feodaries' Surveys

NOTE ON ABBREVIATIONS

Among the abbreviations and short titles used the following may require elucidation:

Assoc. Arch. Soc. *Rep. & Papers*	Associated Archaeological and Architectural Societies' *Reports and Papers*
Cath. Dir.	*Catholic Directory*
Curtis, *Topog. Hist. Leics.*	J. Curtis, *Topographical History of Leicestershire*
Farnham, *Leics. Notes*	G. F. Farnham, *Leicestershire Medieval Village Notes* (6 vols., 1929–33, priv. print., Leicester)
Leic. Boro. Rec.	*Records of the Borough of Leicester*, ed. Mary Bateson and Helen Stocks, 4 vols., 1899–1923
Leic. City MSS.	Leicester City Manuscripts in the Town Hall, Leicester
Leic. City Mun. Room	Leicester City Muniment Room, in Leicester City Museum
L.R.O.	Leicestershire County Record Office
Lincs. N. and Q.	*Lincolnshire Notes and Queries*
Nichols, *Leics.*	J. Nichols, *The History and Antiquities of the County of Leicester*, 4 vols. in 8, 1795–1811
N.R. Rec.	Publications of the North Riding Record Society
T.L.A.S.	Leicestershire Archaeological Society, *Transactions*
White, *Dir. Leics.* (1846)	W. White, *History Gazetteer and Directory of Leicestershire, with Rutland, 1846,* &c.
Wyggeston Hosp. Rec.	*Calendar of Charters and other documents belonging to the Hospital of William Wyggeston*, ed. A. Hamilton Thompson

THE RELIGIOUS HOUSES OF LEICESTERSHIRE[1]

LEICESTERSHIRE has never had any great Benedictine house. From the 7th to the 9th centuries there was at Breedon-on-the-Hill a monastery which was sufficiently important to furnish an Archbishop of Canterbury, but this foundation was apparently destroyed by the Danes in the mid-9th century.[2] At the time of the Norman Conquest the county contained no monasteries, and it was not until English monasticism expanded during the 12th century that religious houses were again founded in Leicestershire. The only Benedictine houses established in the county after the Conquest were the small nunnery of Langley and an alien priory at Hinckley. The Cluniacs of Bermondsey had in the early 13th century a small property at Alderman's Haw, in Charnwood Forest, where there were usually three monks,[3] and the cell apparently still existed in 1278.[4] When, however, Alderman's Haw was inspected subsequently, probably in the late 14th century, it was reported that hardly any trace of the cell remained.[5] The statement that there was a cell of the Cluniac Priory of Lewes at Melton Mowbray[6] seems to be without foundation.[7] A Cistercian abbey was founded at Garendon in 1133; the remaining monasteries of the county all followed some form of the Augustinian rule. No Leicestershire monastery ever became of great importance, and most of them always remained small. Only the abbeys of Leicester and Croxton, with Launde Priory, had a net yearly revenue assessed at over £200 in 1535.[8] Besides these three monasteries, the Hospital of Burton Lazars and the college of secular canons in the Newarke at Leicester were of some note.

The only place in Leicestershire where the friars were established during the Middle Ages was the town of Leicester itself, which at one time in the 13th century probably contained four friaries. The Templars and the Hospitallers each had a house in the county. Apart from the College of the Newarke, which was of a type intermediate between the older collegiate churches of secular canons and the later colleges of chantry priests, the only chantry colleges in Leicestershire were the small foundations at Nosely and Sapcote.

[1] In writing this article, considerable use has been made of an unpublished article written in 1907 by Sister Elspeth, of the Community of All Saints.

[2] F. M. Stenton, 'Medeshamstede and Its Colonies', *Hist. Essays in Honour of James Tait*, 317–18.

[3] *Rot. Hugonis de Welles*, ed. W. P. W. Phillimore, i, 254.

[4] G. F. Farnham, *Charnwood Forest and Its Historians*, 25. See also ibid. 81.

[5] A. Hamilton Thompson, *Abbey of St. Mary of the Meadows, Leicester*, 99. Bermondsey retained land at Alderman's Haw until the Dissolution. Dugd. *Mon.* v, 104.

[6] Nichols, *Leics.* ii, 239; *Leland's Itin.*, ed. Lucy Toulmin-Smith, iv, 19.

[7] References to the Prior of Melton (*Cal. Pat.*, *1258–66*, 81; *Cur. Reg. R., Ric. I–1201*, 42; *Rot. Hugonis de Welles*, i, 257) relate to the Yorks. Priory of Malton.

[8] *Valor Eccl.* (Rec. Com.), iv, 148, 152, 165.

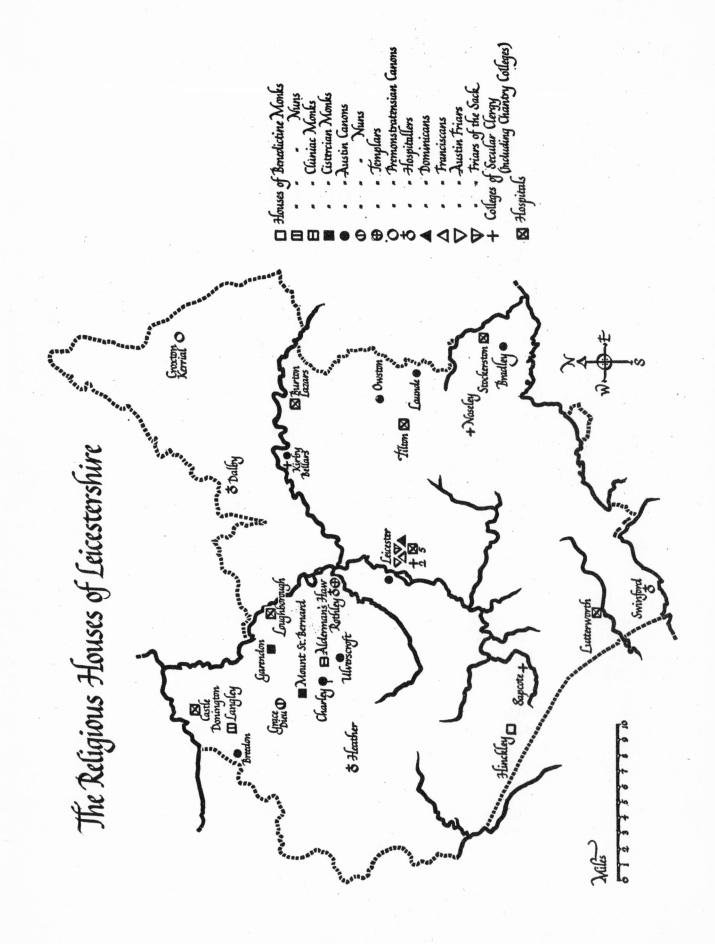

The Religious Houses of Leicestershire

Legend:

Houses of Benedictine Monks ▫
" " " Nuns ⊟
" Cluniac Monks ⊞
" Cistercian Monks ◼
" Austin Canons ●
" " Nuns ⊖
Templars ⊕
Premonstratensian Canons ○
Hospitallers ⊙
Dominicans ◀
Franciscans △
Austin Friars ▷
Friars of the Sack ▽
Colleges of Secular Clergy (including Chantry Colleges) +
Hospitals ⊠

THE RELIGIOUS HOUSES OF LEICESTERSHIRE
HOUSE OF BENEDICTINE NUNS

1. THE PRIORY OF LANGLEY

Langley Nunnery was founded by William Pantulf and his wife Burgia, about the middle of the 12th century.[1] William Pantulf endowed the priory with the Leicestershire churches of Somerby[2] and Little Dalby,[3] and with lands at Somerby, Little Dalby, Langley, and Tonge. Burgia gave lands at Kettleby, and tithes at Tonge and Wilson.[4] The priory also received, before 1205,[5] gifts from other donors of property at Diseworth, Prestwold, Somerby, Burrough, Long Whatton, and Nottingham.[6] Before 1220 the nuns had acquired the advowson of Diseworth (Leics.), which was appropriated with the consent of Bishop Hugh de Welles.[7] During the 13th century Langley received further numerous gifts of land at Diseworth.[8] In 1291 the priory's temporalities in Leicestershire and Nottinghamshire were assessed at £20. 0s. 9d.[9]

The claim of Langley's mother house,[10] Farewell Priory, to exercise a measure of control over Langley led to disputes between the two nunneries. By an agreement concluded in the early 13th century it was provided that the Prioress of Farewell should have the right to participate in the election of prioresses at Langley, while in return the nuns of Farewell renounced their other claims on Langley.[11] The quarrel was subsequently resumed, but in 1248 peace was again established by an arrangement under which Langley agreed to pay the sum of 4 marks to Farewell.[12] Farewell seems to have been a Benedictine house,[13] but in the 12th century, at least, the

nuns of Langley claimed that their lands were exempt from tithe in accordance with the privileges of the Cistercian Order. As Langley lay within the parish of Breedon, these claims led to disputes between the nuns and the canons of Breedon Priory, to which Breedon parish church was appropriated.[14] A document of Pope Alexander III specifically refers to the nuns as Cistercian, and although the nuns' claim to belong to that Order was disputed by the Prior of Breedon, papal judges delegate decided in favour of Langley.[15] The nuns, however, were unable to maintain their claim to the exemption of their possessions from tithe. A later decision by judges delegate provided that the nuns were to pay tithes to Breedon Priory for a carucate of land held and cultivated by them within Breedon parish, though some of their other possessions in the parish were to be free from tithes.[16] An agreement of 1229 between Langley and Breedon Priory laid down that the nuns should give to Breedon a toft, an acre of land, and 7 marks in money, in return for the exemption from tithe of all the lands they held in Breedon parish.[17] In the late 13th century it was agreed that the nuns were to pay 2s. yearly to the canons in composition for tithes from their lands in the parish, and for some other matters, and in 1429 another agreement provided that the nuns should similarly pay 4s. 6d. a year.[18] It therefore seems that the nuns were forced to abandon their claims to Cistercian privileges in connexion with tithe exemption. In the later Middle Ages Langley is mentioned as a Benedictine house.[19]

[1] A document issued by Pope Alexander III, c. 1170–80, orders an inquiry as to whether the nuns of Langley had paid certain tithes for 30 years previously. It might be rash to deduce that Langley had been in existence for 30 years before the issue of this document, but it is certainly implied that the nunnery had existed for some time. For the text of Alexander's mandate, see Dugd. *Mon.* iv, 221, and on its date, see *Regesta Pontificum Romanorum*, ed. P. Jaffé, ii, p. 353, no. 13528. The nuns of Langley came from Farewell Priory, Staffs. (Dugd. *Mon.* iv, 221), which was founded by Roger, Bp. of Chest. 1129–48, probably c. 1140 (Dugd. *Mon.* iv, 110). Langley must have been established before the death, in 1160, of Robert de Chesney, Bp. of Linc., who confirmed the priory's possessions (ibid. iv, 222, no. iii). Langley must therefore have been founded 1129–60, and probably c. 1150.

[2] Appropriated by 1220: *Rot. Hugonis de Welles*, ed. W. P. W. Phillimore, i, 269.

[3] Appropriated 1354. Linc. Reg. Gynewell, Inst., f. 317a; see also *Cal. Pat., 1340–3*, 397.

[4] Dugd. *Mon.* iv, 222; F. M. Stenton, *Doc. Illustrative of Social and Econ. Hist. of Danelaw*, 308.

[5] i.e. before the death of Abp. Hubert Walter.

[6] Dugd. *Mon.* iv, 222.

[7] *Rot. Hugonis de Welles*, i, 251.

[8] *Cat. Anct. D.* i, 331, 333–8; Dugd. *Mon.* iv,

223–4.

[9] *Tax. Eccl.* (Rec. Com.), 66, 339.

[10] Dugd. *Mon.* iv, 221.

[11] Ibid. iv, 112, no. v. The date of the agreement is probably 1210, for the consecration of Hugh de Welles, which took place Dec. 1209, is mentioned, apparently as a recent event.

[12] Dugd. *Mon.* iv, 112, no. vi.

[13] Ibid. 110.

[14] The ch. was described c. 1220 as having been appropriated *ab antiquo*: *Rot. Hugonis de Welles*, i, 252.

[15] Dugd. *Mon.* iv, 221–2; *Regesta Pontificum Romanorum*, ii, 353.

[16] T. Madox, *Formulare Anglicanum* (1702), 23; this doct. may be provisionally dated 1183–8, as of the 2 judges delegate mentioned in it, 'M' Prior of Coventry is probably Prior Moses, elected 1183 (*V.C.H. Warw.* ii, 58), and 'N' Abbot of Stoneleigh is probably Abbot Nicholas, died 1188 (ibid. 81).

[17] Dugd. *Mon.* iv, 222–3. This agreement was witnessed by Mathias, Abbot of Leic., elected 1229 (*Cal. Pat., 1225–32*, 237, 243), and confirmed by the Prior of Nostell in a doct. dated 1229 (Dugd. *Mon.* iv, 222).

[18] John Rylands Libr., Manchester, Latin MS. 222, ff. 57b, 54–55.

[19] *Visitations of Religious Houses in the Dioc. of Linc.* [1420–49], ed. A. Hamilton Thompson, ii, 173; *L. & P. Hen. VIII*, x, p. 497.

Nothing is known of the internal affairs of the house before the 14th century. When Bishop Gynewell visited Langley about 1354 he found the house in good order, and occupied by twelve nuns, but the priory's lands were then barren for lack of cultivation, probably owing to the pestilence.[20] In 1440 the priory was visited by Bishop Alnwick.[21] There were then eight nuns in the house, including the prioress. The priory's revenues had been greatly reduced and it was £50 in debt, so that the convent only supplied the nuns with food and drink, with nothing for their raiment, and not even fuel was provided for them. The nuns maintained separate households in pairs, but ate in the frater daily. A lay boarder, Lady Audely, was the cause of some disturbance, and secular women or girls slept in the nuns' dorter. No serious faults were revealed, though some of the nuns dressed in a way rather unsuitable for religious. It is, however, obvious that the priory was very poor. Its rents were said to be worth only £20 annually, although besides this revenue some lands were evidently being cultivated on behalf of the nuns.[22]

An inventory of 1485 gives a list of the books, vestments, and fittings in the priory church. It shows that the priory's relics then included a piece of the Holy Cross.[23] In 1518 the priory was visited by the bishop's commissary. Some minor faults on the part of several nuns were noted, and the prioress was warned to render account to her sisters yearly, but there were no serious abuses.[24] In 1535 the priory's clear yearly income was assessed at £29. 7s. 4½d. Its possessions at that date included the appropriated rectories of Dalby and Somerby.[25] The appropriated rectory of Diseworth probably also remained in the possession of the priory until the Dissolution.[26] It was reported in June 1536 that the priory, which was dedicated to God and to the Blessed Virgin, contained six nuns besides the prioress, who was very old and impotent. All the nuns desired to continue in religion, and all were virtuous, though one was over 80 and another was feeble-minded. There was a priest attached to the nunnery, and the lay servants consisted of ten men and four women. The priory was small and old but in good repair.[27] Langley was presumably dissolved with the other small religious houses in 1536,[28] though there is no record of the exact circumstances of its suppression.[29] The First Minister's Account shows a total gross revenue of £47. 4s. 2½d., and a net revenue of £42. 10s. 8½d.[30]

PRIORESSES OF LANGLEY

Rose, occurs 1229.[31]

Burgia, elected 1229–30.[32]

Isabel of Leicester, elected 1236–7,[33] occurs 1265.[34]

Juliane of Winchester, appointed 1269.[35]

Alice of Tatyrsal, occurs 1275,[36] died 1275–6.[37]

Margaret of Leicester, elected 1276,[38] occurs 1278–9.[39]

Christine of Winchester, occurs 1284,[40] resigned 1294–5.[41]

Amice de Burgh, confirmed 1295,[42] died 1302.[43]

Alice Giffard, elected 1302.[44]

Elizabeth of Caldwell, elected 1306,[45] occurs to 1332.[46]

Joan of Outheby, occurs from 1333[47] to 1336.[48]

Matanye,[49] occurs 1350.[50]

Maud,[49] occurs 1355.[51]

Margaret de Sulveye,[49] occurs 1355 to 1374.[52]

[20] Linc. Reg. Gynewell, Inst., f. 317a.

[21] Visitations in Dioc. Linc. [1420–49], ii, 173–7.

[22] There were said to be 2, sometimes 3, plough teams at the priory: ibid. 175.

[23] 'Inv. of St. Mary's Benedictine Nunnery at Langley', ed. M. E. C. Walcott, Assoc. Arch. Soc. Rep. and Papers, xi, 201–6.

[24] Visitations in Dioc. Linc., 1517–31, ed. A. Hamilton Thompson, ii, 178.

[25] Valor Eccl. (Rec. Com.), iv, 176.

[26] In 1535 it was noted that Langley possessed a third of the tithes of Diseworth: ibid. As the par. of Diseworth only included part of the village of that name, the rest being in 2 other pars. (Nichols, Leics. iii, 755) this probably indicates that Langley still held the appropriated rectory.

[27] L. & P. Hen. VIII, x, p. 497.

[28] Ibid., p. 515.

[29] It was dissolved before June 1537: Hist. MSS. Com., 8th Rep., App. ii, 21b.

[30] Dugd. Mon. iv, 225–6; S.C. 6 / Hen. VIII / 1825, mm. 28–29.

[31] Ibid. iv, 222–3. On the date see n. 17 above.

[32] Rot. Hugonis de Welles, ii, 312.

[33] Rot. Roberti Grosseteste, ed. F. N. Davis, 393.

[34] Cat. Anct. D. i, B212.

[35] Rot. Ric. Gravesend, ed. F. N. Davis, 149. Her election was quashed, and the appointment made by the bishop.

[36] Cat. Anct. D. i, B1288.

[37] Rot. Ric. Gravesend, 158.   [38] Ibid.

[39] Cat. Anct. D. ii, B3496.

[40] E329/144.

[41] Rosalind Hill, 'Bishop Sutton and the Inst. of Heads of Religious Houses in the Dioc. of Linc.': E.H.R. lviii, 209.

[42] Ibid.

[43] Linc. Reg. Dalderby, Inst., f. 199b.

[44] Ibid.

[45] Cal. Pat., 1301–7, 445.

[46] Cat. Anct. Deeds, ii, B3836.

[47] Ibid. i, B1258.

[48] E. 326/8202; E. 326/12547.

[49] These 3 prioresses may be the same person appearing under varying names. 'Mathama' occurs as the name of the prioress in 1363: Cal. Papal Pet., 1342–1419, 419.

[50] Cat. Anct. D. i, B887.

[51] Ibid. B478.

[52] Ibid. B1246, B423; E. 326/9027.

Margaret Salhowe, occurs 1430.[53]

Margaret Pole, occurs 1441,[54] resigned 1447–8.[55]

Margaret Bellairs, elected 1447–8,[56] resigned 1485.[57]

Anne Shafton, elected 1485.[58]

Dulcia Bothe, occurs from 1507[59] to 1535.[60]

A 12th-century seal[61] of the priory, a pointed oval measuring 1⅞ by 1⅛ in., shows the Virgin Mary seated on a throne, holding the Child on her lap. The legend runs:

SIGILLUM SANCTE MARIE DE LANGELEIA

A 13th-century seal of the same shape,[62] 1¼ by ¾ in., shows the seated figure of the Virgin with the Child on her lap, and bears the legend:

AVE MARIA GRACIA [?] PL . . .

A larger seal[63] of the same shape, measuring 2⅛ by 1¾ in. and belonging to the 15th century, shows the same design, but with the addition of the kneeling figure of a nun in the base of the seal. The legend is:

SIGILL' PRIORISSE ET C . . . . BEATE MARIE DE LANGLEY

HOUSE OF CISTERCIAN MONKS

2. THE ABBEY OF GARENDON

Garendon Abbey was founded in 1133 by Robert, Earl of Leicester.[1] It was in all probability a daughter house of Waverley, the earliest Cistercian monastery to be established in England.[2] The founder endowed the abbey with 5 carucates and 3 virgates of land at Garendon, a burgage tenement at Leicester, and other lands at Dishley, Shepshed, and Ringolthorp.[3] During the 12th century various benefactors granted to the abbey lands at Eastwell,[4] Ibstock,[5] Welby,[6] Burton on the Wolds,[7] and Stanton under Bardon,[8] in Leicestershire, at Costock[9] (Notts.), and at Heathcote[10] (Derbys.). The wild country of Charnwood Forest, in which Garendon lay, gave the monks opportunities for agricultural develop-

ment of the type accomplished by many other Cistercian houses. Before the end of the 12th century granges had been established in the vicinity of the abbey at Garendon itself, Stanton, Dishley, and Ibstock, and farther afield at Burton on the Wolds, Ringolthorp,[11] Goadby, and Welby,[12] in eastern Leicestershire, the Peak,[13] and at Costock and Rempstone (Notts.).[14] The abbey seems to have carried on sheep farming on a considerable scale; in 1225 the abbot obtained permission to export wool to Flanders or elsewhere,[15] and there are references to sheep-folds at the granges.[16] So far as can be discovered from the extant cartulary of the house,[17] Garendon did not in the 12th century acquire such property as tithe, rents, and advowsons.[18] About the middle of the 13th century, however, the abbey was

[53] John Rylands Libr., Manchester, Latin MS. 222, ff. 54–55.

[54] *Visitations in Dioc. Linc.* [1420–49], ii, 174. She was elected less than 6 years before 1441: ibid. ii, 174, n. 3.

[55] Ibid. i, 157, where, however, she is called Margery. [56] Ibid.

[57] *Assoc. Arch. Soc. Rep. and Papers*, xi, 202.

[58] Ibid.

[59] Hist. MSS. Com., *Hastings*, i, 94.

[60] *Valor Eccl.* (Rec. Com.), iv, 176.

[61] B.M. Harl. Chart. 44 F13; D.C. E27, lxvi, 56.

[62] E. 329/205.

[63] B.M. Seals, lxvi, 57.

[1] *Ann. Mon.* (Rolls Ser.), i, 186; ii, 223; B.M. Lansd. MS. 415, f. 35a. Hen. Knighton, *Chron.* (Rolls Ser.), i, 147, gives the date erroneously as 1168–9.

[2] The Waverley Annals, printed *Ann. Mon.* (Rolls Ser.), ii, do not specifically state that Garendon was a dau. of Waverley, but they give many details about Garendon. It was to Waverley that Wm. Gerbertus, who claimed that his father had been unlawfully disseised of Garendon, gave up his claims: Nichols, *Leics.* iii, 814. See also *Statuta Capitulorum Generalium Ordinis Cisterciensis*, ed. D. J.-M. Canivez, i, 299.

[3] Nichols, *Leics.* iii, 791; Dugd. *Mon.* v, 331; B.M. Lansd. MS. 415, ff. 2a, 11.

[4] Ibid., f. 7; Hist. MSS. Com., *Rutland*, iv, 3–7.

[5] B.M. Lansd. MS. 415, f. 2.

[6] Ibid., f. 8b.

[7] Ibid., f. 5a; Nichols, *Leics.* iii, 809.

[8] Nichols, op. cit. iii, 806; B.M. Lansd. MS. 415, f. 12b.

[9] Nichols, op. cit. iii, 806; B.M. Lansd. MS. 415, ff. 3a, 14a; *Pipe R. 1160* (Pipe R. Soc. ii), 43; *Pipe R. 1163* (Pipe R. Soc. vi), 2.

[10] Nichols, op. cit. iii, 812; B.M. Lansd. MS. 415, f. 9b.

[11] Near Scalford, Leics.

[12] 'Alebi' or 'Haleby' in 12th-century docs.

[13] The grange at the Peak, referred to as 'the new grange' in a doc. of Alexander III (Nichols, *Leics.* iii, 813–14), was no doubt established to exploit the pasture rights granted by the Earl of Derby around Heathcote. See John Rylands Libr., Manchester, Latin MS. 222, f. 23a.

[14] Nichols, op. cit. iii, 813–14; B.M. Lansd. MS. 415, ff. 2b, 3a, 5b, 8b, 10b, 11a, 20a. For a list of the abbey's granges, with the number of carucates attached to each, see Nichols, op. cit. iii, 826–7.

[15] *Cal. Pat.*, 1216–25, 522.

[16] Nichols, *Leics.* iii, 806; B.M. Lansd. MS. 415, f. 17b.

[17] B.M. Lansd. MS. 415.

[18] The burgage in Leic., granted to the abbey by its founder, was given for a specific purpose (*ut hospitetur eos*).

granted rents at Anstey.[19] In 1296 the grange at Rempstone was let out to farm,[20] and Swannington grange was farmed out in 1343.[21] In 1341 the abbey was granted the royal chapel or hermitage of Cripplegate, at London, and in 1343 the abbey had licence to acquire 4 messuages in London.[22] The advowson of Dishley was obtained in 1458, and the church was appropriated in the same year.[23]

Two daughter houses were founded from Garendon—Bordesley (1138) and Bittlesden (1147).[24] There are indications, however, that in the late 12th century the Cistercians of Garendon failed to live up to the highest standards of their Order. One of the abbots, Geoffrey, seems to have been a married man,[25] and one of the monks is said to have become a Jew.[26] The resignation of Abbot William in 1195[27] was perhaps due to the displeasure of the general chapter of the Order at the Garendon lay brothers' habit of drinking beer.[28] A serious incident occurred in 1196, when the new abbot, Reynold, was attacked in the infirmary, and gravely wounded, by a lay brother. In consequence the general chapter of Cîteaux ordered all the abbey's lay brothers to be dispersed.[29] The command was not carried out at once, and in 1197 the abbots of two other Cistercian houses were instructed to proceed to Garendon and enforce the will of the general chapter.[30] The abbey continued to contain lay brothers after this incident.[31] In 1219 the conventual church was dedicated by the Bishop of St. Asaph.[32] At the end of the 13th century the finances of the house seem to have been in an unsound condition; in 1295 the king, at the request of the abbot and convent, appointed a special keeper to apply the revenues of the abbey to the relief of its debts, providing reasonable

maintenance for the abbot and monks meanwhile,[33] and two years later the abbot acknowledged that the house owed debts totalling £160.[34] The depredations of a powerful neighbour, John Comyn, Earl of Buchan, may have contributed to the abbey's difficulties at this period.[35] In the middle of the 14th century matters seem to have improved under the rule of Abbot Walter Seint Croys, an especial favourite of Edward III.[36] Nevertheless in 1360 the abbey was in need of reform, and the king appointed several laymen as guardians.[37] In 1368 a monk of the house was said to have harboured robbers and to have assisted them in the commission of various offences,[38] while in 1382 the conventual church was polluted by two monks.[39]

In the 16th century, if not earlier, the Holy Cross at Garendon was an object of pilgrimage locally.[40] In 1535 the clear yearly value of the abbey's revenues was assessed at less than £160.[41] Cromwell's investigators, visiting Garendon in the following year, alleged that five of the monks were guilty of unnatural vice, and that three sought release from religion.[42] The county commissioners, who visited the house in June of the same year, gave a much more favourable report, stating that all the fourteen monks of the house desired to continue in religion, and that twelve of them were priests, of good conversation. Divine service was well maintained, though the large old monastery was partly ruinous. Five children and five impotent persons were maintained by the monks' charity,[43] and there were also two corrodiaries.[44] The abbey, however, was listed amongst the smaller monasteries dissolved in 1536.[45] The abbot obtained a pension of £30.[46] The First Minister's Account shows a net income of £100. 18s. 10½d.[47]

[19] Nichols, *Leics.* iii, 824; B.M. Lansd. MS. 415, f. 26b. The rents were later surrendered: Nichols, op. cit. iii, 824.

[20] Ibid. iii, 830; B.M. Lansd. MS. 415, f. 38b.

[21] Ibid.

[22] *Cal. Pat.*, *1340-3*, 145; *1343-5*, 133.

[23] A. Hamilton Thompson, *Abbey of St. Mary in the Meadows, Leic.* 129-30.

[24] *Ann. Mon.* (Rolls Ser.), i, 186; D. Knowles, *Monastic Order in Engl.* 248; Dugd. *Mon.* v, 367, no. ii; *Stat. Capitulorum Generalium Ordinis Cisterciensis*, iii, 89.

[25] *Chartularium Abbathiae de Novo Monasterio* (Surtees Soc. lxvi), ed. J. T. Fowler, p. xvii, n. 1. It is not quite certain whether the Abbot Geoffrey was the Abbot of Garendon of that name, but it seems probable.

[26] Knowles, *Monastic Order in Engl.* 657, citing Giraldus Cambrensis, *Opera* (Rolls Ser.), iv, 139.

[27] *Ann. Mon.* (Rolls Ser.), ii, 250.

[28] Knowles, *Monastic Order in Engl.* 657; *Stat. Capitulorum Generalium Ordinis Cisterciensis*, i, 202.

[29] *Stat.* i, 202; *Ann. Mon.* (Rolls Ser.), i, 23; ii, 250.

[30] *Stat.* i, 216; cited Knowles, *Monastic Order in Engl.* 657-8. A lay brother of Garendon was a fugitive in Lincs., not later than 1202: *The Earliest Lincs.*

Assize R., ed. D. M. Stenton, 134.

[31] *Cal. Pat.*, *1225-32*, 473.

[32] *Ann. Mon.* (Rolls Ser.), ii, 291-2.

[33] *Cal. Pat.*, *1292-1301*, 154.

[34] *Cal. Close*, *1296-1302*, 118.

[35] B.M. Lansd. MS. 415, f. 33a; Nichols, *Leics.* iii, 827; *Abbrev. Plac.* (Rec. Com.), 230; Farnham, *Leics. Notes*, vi, 356.

[36] *Cal. Pat.*, *1340-3*, 145; *Cal. Close*, *1349-54*, 371, and *1354-60*, 22.

[37] *Cal. Pat.*, *1358-61*, 358.

[38] Ibid. *1367-70*, 121.

[39] B.M. Lansd. MS. 415, f. 32b.

[40] Hist. MSS. Com., *Middleton*, 384; A. Hamilton Thompson, *Hist. of the New Coll. of the Annunciation of St. Mary in the Newarke*, 199; *Valor Eccl.* (Rec. Com.), iv, 173; Nichols, *Leics.* iii, 797; Dugd. *Mon.* v, 336.

[41] *Valor Eccl.* (Rec. Com.), iv, 173.

[42] *L. & P. Hen. VIII*, x, p. 138.

[43] By the will of Ralph Shirley the abbey was bound to maintain 4 poor persons: Nichols, *Leics.* iii, 713.

[44] *L. & P. Hen. VIII*, x, pp. 487, 496.

[45] Ibid. x, p. 515. For a list of the ornaments of the abbey ch., see Nichols, *Leics.* iii, 797-8.

[46] *L. & P. Hen. VIII*, xiii (1), no. 575.

[47] S.C. 6/Hen. VIII/1825, mm. 19-26.

ABBOTS OF GARENDON

Robert, occurs 1144–5.[48]

Geoffrey, occurs 1147.[49]

Thurstan, occurs between 1155 and 1164.[50] Died 1189.[51]

William, elected 1189,[52] resigned 1195.[53]

Reynold, elected 1195,[54] occurs 1196.[55]

Adam, resigned 1219.[56]

William, resigned 1226.[57]

Reynold, elected 1226,[58] resigned 1234.[59]

Andrew, elected 1234.[60]

Simon, occurs 1251.[61]

Robert, occurs 1275.[62]

Roger, occurs before 1281.[63]

Eustace, occurs 1290[64] and 1294.[65]

John, occurs from 1299[66] to 1330.[67]

Walter Seynt Croys, occurs 1340,[68] resigned in, or shortly before, 1350.[69]

John, occurs 1360.[70]

Thomas of Lughtburgh,[71] elected 1361,[72] occurs 1382.[73]

John, occurs 1406.[74]

Richard, occurs early 15th century.[75]

John Scarburghe, occurs 1418.[76]

John of London, occurs 1439.[77]

John Clareborough, occurs 1487.[78]

William Leycestre, occurs 1490.[79]

Thomas, occurs 1513.[80]

Thomas Siston, occurs 1535.[81]

Randolph Arnold, last abbot.[82]

A 13th-century seal[83] of the abbey is a pointed oval, $1\frac{1}{4}$ by $1\frac{3}{16}$ in., showing a hand and clothed arm holding a crosier. The background is powdered with stars. The legend is:

CONTRASIGILL' ABB . . . O . . . DON

A second seal[84] of the same century has the same design of the arm and crosier, but omits the powdering of stars. Its legend reads:

SIGILL' A . . . . ERŌDON IN . . . .

Its dimensions are $1\frac{5}{8}$ by 1 in.

A 14th-century seal,[85] $1\frac{3}{4}$ in. in diameter, of the abbey shows the figure of the abbot within a cusped quatrefoil, with his right hand raised in blessing, and holding a pastoral staff in his left. At the left side of the figure is a shield charged with three stars. Of the legend only the letters . . . REN . . . remain.

A pointed oval 14th-century seal,[86] about $2\frac{1}{4}$ by about $1\frac{1}{2}$ in., shows the Virgin Mary standing beneath a columned canopy with the Child on her left arm. The sides of the field are diapered, and at the bottom under a pointed arch there is the half-length figure of an ecclesiastic praying. Most of the legend is gone but the following letters remain:

. . . VET . . . E . . . EROUDON

Another seal[87] of the house is a small oval, $1\frac{1}{4}$ by $\frac{7}{8}$ in., bearing a figure in a canopied niche.

48 Nichols, *Leics.* iii, 813; *Reg. Antiquissimum of the Cath. Ch. of Linc.*, ed. C. W. Foster, ii, 216.

49 *Reg. Antiquissimum*, iii, 263.

50 Nichols, *Leics.* iii, 805.

51 *Ann. Mon.* (Rolls Ser.), ii, 246.

52 Ibid.

53 Ibid. ii, 250.

54 Ibid. Formerly Abbot of Merevale.

55 Ibid. i, 23; ii, 250.

56 Ibid. ii, 292; he then became Abbot of Waverley.

57 Ibid. ii, 302.

58 Ibid. He is said to have been the tenth abbot (ibid.), so that the names of 2 early abbots must be missing from the list.

59 Ibid. ii, 315.

60 Ibid.

61 B.M. Harl. Chart. 44 D47.

62 *Rot. Ric. Gravesend*, ed. F. N. Davis, 157; Farnham, *Leics. Notes*, ii, 27.

63 i.e. in the lifetime of Margaret, Countess of Derby: Nichols, *Leics.* iii, 824; B.M. Lansd. MS. 415, f. 26*b*.

64 Ibid., f. 36*a*.

65 Farnham, *Leics. Notes*, vi, 356.

66 *Cal. Pat., 1292–1301*, 431.

67 *Cal. Chart. R., 1327–41*, 196.

68 Hist. MSS. Com., *Hastings*, i, 7; *Cal. Chart R., 1327–41*, 472.

69 *Cal. Pat., 1348–50*, 560.

70 Ibid. *1358–61*, 358, 412.

71 i.e. Loughborough.

72 Linc. Reg. Gynewell, Memo., f. 153*b*.

73 *Cal. Pat., 1381–5*, 101.

74 *Cal. Papal Letters, 1404–15*, 79.

75 Hist. MSS. Com., *Hastings*, i, 33.

76 *Visitations of Religious Houses in the Dioc. of Linc.* [1420–49], ed. A. Hamilton Thompson, ii, 126.

77 Ibid. i, 8.

78 Ibid. i, 111.

79 Ibid. i, 40, 111.

80 Nichols, *Leics.* iii, 710.

81 *Valor Eccl.* (Rec. Com.), iv, 173. Possibly the same person as the Thomas who occurs 1513.

82 *L. & P. Hen. VIII*, xv, p. 345.

83 B.M. Harl. Chart. 44 D48.

84 B.M. Seals, lxvi, 51.

85 Ibid., 50.

86 S.C. 13/D. 143.

87 B.M. Seals, lxvi, 51. Another seal of the abbey is illustrated in Nichols, *Leics.* iii, 786, pl. cxi, fig. 5, but the original on which it was based has not been discovered.

HOUSES OF AUGUSTINIAN CANONS

3. THE PRIORY OF BREEDON

Breedon first became the site of a monastery in the 7th century, when a colony of Medeshamstede was established there. Little is known of this ancient religious house, though its presumed importance is shown by the elevation of one of its abbots, Tatwine, to the see of Canterbury in 731. The monastery ceased to exist during the Danish invasions of the 9th century.[1]

At an unknown date under Henry I the parish church of St. Mary and St. Hardulph at Breedon was given to the Augustinian Priory of St. Oswald at Nostell (Yorks.) by Robert de Ferrers, later 1st Earl of Derby.[2] Canons were established at Breedon by 1122.[3] A cell of Nostell was presumably then in existence, so that the date of the foundation of Breedon Priory must lie between the foundation of Nostell, c. 1109–14,[4] and 1122. The endowment of the priory, as given in the earliest charter of which the terms are known, consisted of Breedon church,[5] with its subordinate chapels of Worthington and Staunton Harold, 4 virgates of land, with some other property and tithes, in Breedon parish, revenues from Stapleford (Leics.), Crakemarsh (Staffs.), and West Leake (Notts.), and land at Heathcote, in the Derbyshire Peak.[6] These possessions received no very important additions during the course of the priory's existence. Lands at Cole Orton (Leics.) were granted to the house before 1160,[7] and several minor gifts of land in and near Breedon were made in the 12th and early 13th centuries.[8] The priory was granted pasture rights in the Peak, in augmentation of its original possessions there,

by William, Earl of Derby, about 1200,[9] and by Henry, Earl of Lancaster, in 1333.[10] Land at Saxby (Leics.) was obtained in place of the priory's revenue from Stapleford.[11] In 1291 the spiritualities of the house were assessed at £33. 6s. 8d., and its temporalities at £8. 2s.[12] Another estimate, made apparently at about the same date, put the true value of the priory's spiritualities at £100.[13]

The priory throughout its existence continued to be a cell of Nostell, and always remained very small. About 1220 it was stated that there were five canons at Breedon, with the apparent implication that this was the usual number,[14] and in 1441 the canons numbered only three.[15] A very close connexion was always maintained between Breedon and its mother house in Yorkshire. In the 13th century it was stated that Breedon Priory only contained canons sent there from Nostell.[16] The canons of Breedon were entitled to participate in the conduct of affairs at Nostell,[17] while in the 13th century it was the Prior and Convent of Nostell who presented to the patron of Breedon Priory two canons, from whom the patron chose one to be Prior of Breedon.[18] The Prior and Convent of Nostell, on the other hand, agreed not to remove the priors of Breedon without due cause, and not to disturb the cell's possessions.[19] An attempt by Gervase, Prior of Breedon, to obtain independence from Nostell was a failure, and led to Gervase's resignation in 1244.[20] So far as is known, no canon of Breedon Priory ever held the cure of souls of Breedon parish church.[21] Bishop Alnwick, visiting the priory in 1441, found that it was in debt, while

---

[1] F. M. Stenton, 'Medeshamstede and Its Colonies', *Hist. Essays in Honour of James Tait*, 317–18; A. W. Clapham, 'The Carved Stones at Breedon on the Hill', *Archaeologia*, lxxvii, 219.

[2] John Rylands Libr., Manchester, Latin MS. 222, f. 30a; Nichols, *Leics.* iii, 696.

[3] L. Delisle, *Rouleaux des Morts*, 314; cited D. Knowles, *Religious Houses of Medieval Engl.* 81.

[4] A. Hamilton Thompson, *Bolton Priory*, Introduction, pp. 23–27.

[5] Appropriated by 1220: *Rot. Hugonis de Welles*, ed. W. P. W. Phillimore, i, 252.

[6] Dugd. *Mon.* vi, 97; Nichols, *Leics.* iii, 697; B.M. Cott. MS. Vesp. E. xix, f. 125; John Rylands Libr., Manchester, Latin MS. 222, f. 28a.

[7] John Rylands Libr., Manchester, Latin MS. 222, f. 34b. Confirmed either by Robert, 1st Earl of Derby, or by Robert, 2nd Earl, who died before 1160: ibid., f. 28a; Nichols, op. cit. iii, 697.

[8] See the deeds printed by Nichols, op. cit. iii, 698–701, from John Rylands Libr., Manchester, Latin MS. 222.

[9] Ibid., f. 28b; B.M. Cott. MS. Vesp. E. xix, f. 125a; Nichols, op. cit. iii, 697.

[10] Nichols, op. cit. iii, 698; John Rylands Libr., Manchester, Latin MS. 222, ff. 32a, 32b; B.M. Cott.

MS. Vesp. E. xix, f. 125a.

[11] John Rylands Libr., Manchester, Latin MS. 222, ff. 28a, 28b, 33a, 33b.

[12] *Tax Eccl.* (Rec. Com.), 64, 67, 317.

[13] John Rylands Libr., Manchester, Latin MS. 222, f. 9; W. E. Lunt, *Valuation of Norw.* 148.

[14] *Rot. Hugonis de Welles*, i, 252.

[15] *Visitations of Religious Houses in the Dioc. of Linc.* [1420–49], ed. A. Hamilton Thompson, ii, 40.

[16] *Rot. Roberti Grosseteste*, ed. F. N. Davis, 441.

[17] *L. & P. Hen. VIII*, x, p. 497; see also a MS., now in the custody of the trustees of the late Lord St. Oswald at Nostell, entitled 'De Gestis et Actibus Priorum Monasterii Sancti Oswaldi de Nostell', f. 50a. For a description of this MS., see W. T. Lancaster, 'A 15th Century Rental of Nostell Priory', *Yorks. Arch. Soc. Rec. Ser.* lxi, 108.

[18] Nichols, *Leics.* iii, 697.

[19] Ibid.

[20] *Rot. Roberti Grosseteste*, 424, 440–2; *Cal. Close, 1237–42*, 449.

[21] Nichols, *Leics.* iii, 689, lists Walter de Stokes, later Prior of Breedon, as a vicar of Breedon, but no evidence is cited for Walter's inclusion in the list of vicars.

the church and the priory buildings were dilapidated.[22] One of the three canons then at Breedon was suspended for failing to appear,[23] and some years later another canon was in jail at Leicester awaiting trial.[24] In 1518 Breedon parish church was again in need of repair, though as it was the nave and porch which were dilapidated at this time, the responsibility may have rested on the parishioners rather than on the canons.[25]

In 1535 the clear yearly income of Breedon Priory was estimated at £24. 10s. 4d.[26] In the following year it was reported that there was no convent at Breedon. The priory was apparently then occupied only by the prior, who had a stall at Nostell, and a voice in affairs there.[27] Breedon was surrendered, with Nostell's other possessions, in November 1539.[28] In the First Minister's Account the net yearly value of the priory lands was stated to be £32. 4s. 7d.[29] In 1553 the clear yearly value of the property formerly belonging to the priory in Leicestershire alone was estimated at £31. 3s. 4¼d.[30]

PRIORS OF BREEDON

Elias, occurs between 1153 and 1160.[31]
Thomas, occurs late 12th century.[32]
William, occurs about 1170–80.[33]
Ralph, occurs between 1175 and 1207.[34]
Gervase, presented 1223,[35] resigned 1244.[36]
Walter of Stokes, presented 1245.[37]
T., occurs before 1253.[38]

Thomas of Acomb, occurs 1288,[39] died 1293.[40]
William Wyles, presented 1293,[41] occurs 1299.[42]
Robert of Pontefract, presented 1314,[43] died 1324.[44]
John de Insula, presented 1324,[45] elected Prior of Nostell, 1328.[46]
William Buttrebuske, presented 1328,[47] occurs 1341.[48]
Richard, occurs 1348.[49]
Adam, occurs 1384,[50] elected Prior of Nostell, 1385.[51]
Robert of Qwyxlay, occurs before 1393.[52]
Adam, presented, for the second time, 1393,[53] died 1402.[54]
William of Altofts, presented 1402.[55]
John Amyas, presented 1411.[56]
William Horbury, presented 1422,[57] occurs 1439.[58]
James Byrtby, presented 1439,[59] resigned 1449.[60]
Stephen Melsymby, presented 1449.[61]
William Yorke, presented 1450,[62] died 1472.[63]
John Hyndrewell, presented 1472,[64] died 1495.[65]
John Emley, presented 1495,[66] died 1503.[67]
Richard Bretaynger, presented 1503,[68] died 1513.[69]
John Brydell, presented 1513,[70] died 1524.[71]
Robert Harrop,[72] presented 1524,[73] occurs 1535.[74]

[22] *Visitations in Dioc. Linc.* [1420–49], ii, 40–42.
[23] Ibid.
[24] *Cal. Pat.*, 1446–52, 534.
[25] *Visitations in Dioc. Linc.*, 1517–31, ed. A. Hamilton Thompson, i, 28.
[26] *Valor Eccl.* (Rec. Com.), iv, 177.
[27] *L. & P. Hen. VIII*, x, p. 497.
[28] Ibid. xiv (2), pp. 195, 240. Not in 1540, as Dugd. *Mon.* vi, 91.
[29] S.C. 6 / Hen. VIII / 7313, m. 75.
[30] W. G. D. Fletcher, 'Unpublished Doc. Relating to Leics.', *Assoc. Arch. Soc. Rep. and Papers*, xxiii, 245–8.
[31] *Desc. Cat. of Derbys. Charts.*, ed. I. H. Jeayes, 68, 243.
[32] *Doc. Illustrative of Social and Econ. Hist. of Danelaw*, ed. F. M. Stenton, 310.
[33] Dugd. *Mon.* iv, 221; *Regesta Pontificum Romanorum*, ed. P. Jaffé, ii, p. 353.
[34] Nichols, *Leics.* iii, 866; John Rylands Libr., Manchester, Latin MS. 222, f. 30b.
[35] *Rot. Hugonis de Welles*, ii, 290.
[36] *Rot. Roberti Grosseteste*, 424.
[37] Ibid.; B.M. Cott. MS. Vesp. E. xix, f. 126a.
[38] John Rylands Libr., Manchester, Latin MS. 222, f. 38b.
[39] Ibid., f. 35b.
[40] Rosalind Hill, 'Bishop Sutton and the Inst. of Heads of Religious Houses in the Dioc. of Linc.', *E.H.R.* lviii, 209.
[41] Ibid.
[42] *Cal. Pat.*, 1292–1301, 468.
[43] Nichols, *Leics.* iii, 694.

[44] *Cal. Pat.*, 1321–4, 415.
[45] Ibid.
[46] John Rylands Libr., Manchester, Latin MS. 222, f. 11b.
[47] Ibid.
[48] Ibid., f. 64b.
[49] *Cal. Pat.*, 1348–50, 177.
[50] E. 326/B 8108.
[51] W. Burton, *Mon. Eboracensis*, 311.
[52] 'De Gestis . . . Priorum Monasterii . . . de Nostell', f. 53a. On this MS., see n. 17 above.
[53] Ibid.   [54] Ibid.
[55] R. Somerville, 'D. of Lanc. Presentations, 1399–1485', *Bull. Inst. Hist. Research*, xviii, 66.
[56] *Visitations in Dioc. Linc.* [1420–49], ii, 126.
[57] Ibid. i, 162.
[58] Hist. MSS. Com., *Hastings*, i, 34.
[59] *Bull. Inst. Hist. Research*, xviii, 66.
[60] *Visitations in Dioc. Linc.* [1420–49], i, 162.
[61] B.M. Cott. MS. Vesp. E. xix, f. 126b.
[62] Ibid.
[63] Linc. Reg. Rotherham, Inst., f. 63a.
[64] Ibid.
[65] B.M. Cott. MS. Vesp. E. xix, f. 126b.
[66] Ibid.
[67] Linc. Reg. Smith, Inst., f. 277b.
[68] Ibid.
[69] Linc. Reg. Attwater, Inst., f. 7a.
[70] Ibid.
[71] Linc. Reg. Longland, Inst., f. 128b.
[72] Or Garope.
[73] Linc. Reg. Longland, Inst., f. 128b.
[74] *Valor Eccl.* (Rec. Com.), iv, 176.

Thomas Clarke, occurs 1529[75] and 1536,[76] died 1537.[77]

Henry Huntingdon, presented 1537.[78]

The small oval seal[79] of Prior Adam, measuring $\frac{7}{8}$ by $\frac{3}{4}$ in., depicts a figure in a long robe (possibly St. Peter) holding a pair of keys. The legend is now broken away. According to Dugdale,[80] however, it was once possible to read the words:

S. ADA' PETRI

4. THE PRIORY OF LAUNDE

The Augustinian Priory of St. John the Baptist at Launde was founded by Richard Basset and his wife Maud[1] before 1125.[2] It was endowed by the founders with the village of Loddington (Leics.) and the churches of Weldon, Weston-by-Welland, and Ashby (Northants.), Welham, Holt, Frisby-on-the-Wreak, Oadby, Ab Kettleby, and Witherley (Leics.), Colston Basset (Notts.), Wardley (Rut.), Pattingham (Staffs.), Hathersege (Derbys.), and several others.[3] The grant of Loddington probably included the church of the village, which was certainly in the priory's hands early in the 13th century.[4] Before 1162 Launde also obtained from various benefactors the churches of Tilton, Grimston, and Rotherby (Leics.), and Glaston (Rut.), with the Leicestershire manor of Frisby-on-the-Wreak and some less important endowments.[5] Under Henry II Frisby was seized by the king,[6] but subsequently at the request of the canons of Launde an inquiry was held to discover whether Frisby was part of the royal demesne or whether it belonged to the

priory by the gift of Ralph Basset.[7] In the end the priory seems to have retained Frisby, which it still held at the Dissolution.[8] By the early 13th century the priory had acquired the Leicestershire churches of Peatling Parva, Ashby Folville, and Shoby, with one-half of the advowson of Withcote, and the Northamptonshire churches of Blatherwick, Arthingworth, and Little Bowden.[9] Some of these endowments were later lost. The Templars claimed Grimston church as a chapel of Rothley, apparently with success,[10] and in 1284 the Abbot of Lire secured possession of the church of Witherley.[11] Shoby church had been lost by 1393.[12] The church of Holt, though mentioned in Henry I's confirmation charter, does not appear subsequently amongst the priory's possessions, and probably ceased to exist before the early 13th century.[13]

At the beginning of the 13th century some trouble apparently arose between the priory and its patron, Richard Basset, for in 1201 an agreement made between Basset and the prior provided that the priory should give up all the charters it had obtained from Geoffrey Riddell,[14] retaining only his great confirmation charter and the foundation charter of the earlier Richard Basset. Any charter subsequently brought forward by the priory was to be considered void.[15] Another dispute between the priory and Richard Basset, caused by the convent's action in installing a prior before he had been presented to the patron, was settled by an agreement which provided that presentation to the patron should be duly made.[16] In 1234, the king gave timber to the priory for the building of its church.[17] The Prior of Launde

---

[75] John Rylands Libr., Manchester, Latin MS. 222, f. 1b. It is difficult to explain the appearance of Clarke as prior at a time when Harrop was apparently prior, and it seems that either the date given in Latin MS. 222 must be inaccurate or, less probably, that Harrop was no longer prior when the *Valor Eccl.* was compiled.

[76] *L. & P. Hen. VIII*, x, p. 497.

[77] Linc. Reg. Longland, Inst., f. 144b.

[78] Ibid.

[79] E. 326/B 8108.

[80] Dugd. *Mon.* vi, 97.

[1] Dau. of Geoffrey Ridel: *Complete Peerage*, ii, 1.

[2] *City of London Letter Bk. C*, ed. R. R. Sharpe, 220; cited J. C. Dickinson, *Origins of the Austin Canons*, 121. An early charter of Hen. I confirming the priory's possessions (Dugd. *Mon.* vi, 188, no. I) cannot be considered reliable, as it mentions Alexander, Bp. of Linc., but is witnessed by the chancellor, Ranulph, who died before the death of Alexander's predecessor. See J. H. Round, 'The Spurious Tewkesbury Charter', *Genealogist* (N.S.), viii, 93–94. Another royal charter of confirmation (Dugd. *Mon.* vi, 188–9, no. II) names Ric. and Maud as founders of Launde.

[3] Dugd. *Mon.* vi, 188–9, no. II. The list of chs. confirmed to Launde includes those of 'Pillesleye', 'Tacheham', 'Stantona', 'Brinton', and 'Malucshella'. These 5 places have not been identified. Nichols (*Leics.* iii, 301) identifies 'Tacheham' with Thatcham (Berks.). But see *V.C.H. Berks.* iii, 325. Frisby was appro-

priated from the foundation of the priory, and Welham before c. 1220: *Rot. Hugonis de Welles*, ed. W. P. W. Phillimore, i, 259, 261.

[4] Ibid. i, 259. Loddington was appropriated by c. 1220 (ibid.).

[5] Dugd. *Mon.* vi, 189, no. III. Tilton was appropriated by c. 1220: *Rot. Hugonis de Welles*, i, 258.

[6] *Pipe R. 1182* (Pipe R. Soc. xxxi), 97; and see subsequent Pipe R.

[7] *Pipe R. 1190* (Pipe R. Soc., N.S. i), 44; *Pipe R. 1191–2* (Pipe R. Soc., N.S. ii), 128.

[8] Dugd. *Mon.* vi, 189.

[9] *Rot. Hugonis de Welles*, i, 52, 105, 240, 258, 260, 268; Nichols, *Leics.* iii, 302.

[10] Farnham, *Leics. Notes*, ii, 338; *Rot. Ric. Gravesend*, ed. F. N. Davis, 163.

[11] Farnham, op. cit. v, 425–6.

[12] Ibid. iv, 76.

[13] The ch. is not mentioned in the 'Matriculus' of the Archdeaconry of Leic.: *Rot. Hugonis de Welles*, i, 238–72. See also Nichols, *Leics.* ii, 16.

[14] Unlikely to be Geoffrey Ridel, the father of Maud who was one of the founders of the priory. Possibly Geoffrey Ridel, Bp. of Ely, whose relationship to the earlier Geoffrey, and to the Basset family, has not been ascertained.

[15] B.M. Sloane Chart. xxxi, 4, m. 1, no. 2.

[16] Ibid., no. 4.

[17] *Cal. Close, 1231–4*, 517.

was one of the monastic heads removed by Bishop Grosseteste in 1236,[18] but the cause of his removal is unknown. A later prior was summoned to the Parliament of January 1265.[19] In 1344 the priory obtained licence to appropriate Pattingham church,[20] and in 1368 Ralph Basset, the patron, became a canon of the house.[21] The occurrence of three disputed elections, in 1289,[22] 1300,[23] and 1350,[24] suggests that the priory may have experienced a period of internal dissension, and during the 14th century its condition must have been unsatisfactory. At some date between 1360 and 1366 a complaint was made by some of the canons to the Bishop of Lincoln that the prior, John of Witherington, was showing favouritism to some canons, though he was harsh to others, and that he neglected to sleep in the dormitory or to eat in the refectory.[25] When Prior John resigned, in 1366, there was so much difficulty in electing a new prior that the sixteen canons of the house requested the bishop to nominate one.[26] Some years later serious differences arose between the canons and another prior, Thomas Colman. The canons brought a lawsuit against Colman, and while the action was pending, in 1388, the king, then controlling the patronage owing to the minority of Richard Basset, found it necessary to order the prior to refrain from beating, imprisoning, and expelling the canons, alienating the priory's chattels, and wasting its woods, as information had been received that the prior was committing such acts. The prior was ordered to allow the canons adequate maintenance out of the priory's goods.[27] Before the end of 1388 Colman either resigned or was deprived because of his opposition to a papal provision to the priory's church of Hathersege.[28] His successor was a canon of Dunstable, Walter Baldok.[29] Baldok had deserted his own monastery, and had spent some time at the royal court seeking preferment.[30] No doubt he owed his election to the king's temporary possession of the patronage, and it was probably through Baldok that Richard II was led to consider founding a chantry at Launde in 1393.[31] The chantry was duly established, and endowed by the appropriation of the churches of Ab Kettleby in 1397 and of Wardley and Hathersege in 1398; it was provided that three canons of Launde were to celebrate masses daily for the souls of the king, his parents, and his first queen, Anne, and for the good estate of the king and his second queen, Isabel. Licence was granted for the three churches to be served by suitable canons.[32] In the case of Ashby Folville church, appropriated to Launde a few years earlier, the pope had laid down that the cure of souls was to be exercised by a canon of the house.[33] In 1395 Baldok obtained papal exemption from the jurisdiction of the Bishop of Lincoln, the Archbishop of Canterbury, and other judges ordinary.[34] He proved an unsatisfactory prior, and at some date between 1395 and 1398 he was deprived of his office.[35] His successor, John Henriz, was probably also a supporter of Richard II, for the king employed him on a mission to Rome.[36] After the fall of Richard II Baldok was executed for treasonable activities on behalf of the deposed king.[37]

Before 1404 Thomas Colman had again become Prior of Launde,[38] and he remained in office until 1416 at least.[39] In view of his past record, his rule is unlikely to have been very successful. In 1440 the priory was visited by Bishop Alnwick, and a rather unsatisfactory position was disclosed; the canons numbered only ten, although some time previously there had been eighteen; there were complaints that women were allowed too free access to the choir of the conventual church, that silence was not properly kept, that corrodies were sold without the bishop's licence, and that the prior failed to render a full

---

[18] *Ann. Mon.* (Rolls Ser.), iii, 143.

[19] *Cal. Close, 1264–8*, 86.

[20] *Cal. Pat., 1343–5*, 235.

[21] *Complete Peerage*, ii, 11, and references there cited.

[22] Rosalind Hill, 'Bishop Sutton and the Inst. of Heads of Religious Houses in the Dioc. of Linc.', *E.H.R.* lviii, 209.

[23] Linc. Reg. Dalderby, Inst., f. 196*b*.

[24] Linc. Reg. Gynewell, Inst., f. 316*a*.

[25] Linc. Reg. Buckingham, Memo., f. 144*a*.

[26] Ibid., Inst. i, f. 238*a*.

[27] *Cal. Close, 1385–9*, 519–20.

[28] *Cal. Pat., 1385–9*, 527; *Cal. Papal Letters, 1362–1404*, 435.

[29] *Cal. Pat., 1388–92*, 1.

[30] T. Walsingham, *Hist. Anglicana* (Rolls Ser.), ii, 249.

[31] *Cal. Papal Letters, 1362–1404*, 446.

[32] *Cal. Pat., 1396–9*, 124, 322.

[33] Ibid., *1388–92*, 107; *Cal. Papal Letters, 1362–1404*, 523.

[34] Ibid.

[35] *Cal. Pat., 1396–9*, 413; T. Walsingham, *Hist. Anglicana* (Rolls Ser.), ii, 249.

[36] *Cal. Pat., 1396–9*, 413.

[37] T. Walsingham, *Hist. Anglicana* (Rolls Ser.), ii, 249; *Ypodigma Neustriae* (Rolls Ser.), 393. Other accounts merely state that the Prior of Launde was executed, without giving his name, but Walsingham, who gives more detailed information than the other chroniclers, states that the victim was Baldok, and that he was a former Prior of Launde. For other accounts, see *Eulogium Hist. sive Temporis* (Rolls Ser.), iii, 389, 392–3; *Monumenta Franciscana* (Rolls Ser.), ii, 162; *Chron. of Grey Friars of London* (Camden Soc., 1st ser. liii), ed. J. G. Nichols, 10. Baldok was described as the king's 'secret chaplain' in 1393: *Anglo-Norman Letters and Pet.*, ed. M. D. Legge, 382.

[38] *Descriptive Cat. of Derbys. Charts.*, ed. I. H. Jeayes, 166; *Cal. Close, 1405–9*, 528. In 1392 Colman, who had previously been absolved, had obtained papal dispensation and rehabilitation, so that he could hold any offices of his order: *Cal. Papal Letters, 1362–1404*, 435.

[39] *Cal. Pat., 1416–22*, 14.

account to the canons yearly. In general, the canons seem to have neglected the divine offices in order to attend to business affairs. The bishop ordered these faults to be amended, and warned the prior not to take any important steps without the convent's consent. When Launde was allowed to appropriate Oadby church in 1446, it was stated that the priory was then worth only 400 marks a year, although it had formerly been worth a thousand; bad management and untoward events in the vicinity were said to be the cause of the decline.[40]

Little is known of the priory's history for the rest of the 15th century. In 1528 the house was visited by the chancellor of the diocese.[41] Besides the prior, there were then thirteen in the priory, including four novices. The refectory was reported to be ruinous, and the conventual church was also rather dilapidated, but the prior was making preparations for repair. No serious personal faults were disclosed, though the prior and sub-prior were admonished for failing to treat their brethren with sufficient charity after correction, and one of the canons was said to be causing discord in the house. In 1534 the prior and thirteen others acknowledged the royal supremacy over the church.[42] Launde, being assessed at a clear yearly value of nearly £400 in 1535,[43] was not included amongst the smaller monasteries which were first dissolved.[44] In 1536 an attempt seems to have been made to blackmail the prior by threatening to charge him with immorality.[45] The priory was surrendered in December 1539, the prior receiving a pension of £60, and ten of

the canons pensions ranging from £9 to £5 a year.[46] Thomas Cromwell, who had been interested in the priory's possessions as early as 1528,[47] had marked down the house for himself,[48] and in 1540 he was granted the site of the monastery, together with some of its possessions.[49] In the First Minister's Account the annual gross value of the priory's possessions is given as £517. 8s. 1½d.[50]

PRIORS OF LAUNDE

John, occurs before 1125.[51]
Ralph, occurs about 1160.[52]
Walkelin, occurs 1189[53] and 1201.[54]
Osbert, occurs 1230.[55]
Robert, occurs 1236.[56]
Robert de Martivall, occurs 1240[57] to 1252.[58]
Reynold, died 1273.[59]
Richard de Martivall, elected 1273,[60] died 1289.[61]
William of Somerby, elected 1289,[62] resigned 1300.[63]
John of Kirkby, elected 1300,[64] died 1309.[65]
John de Burgh, elected 1309,[66] died 1319.[67]
Henry of Braunseton, elected 1319,[68] resigned 1334.[69]
John of Peatling, elected 1334,[70] died 1350.[71]
John of Wytherington, elected 1350,[72] resigned 1366.[73]
John of Leicester, elected 1366,[74] died 1369.[75]
John of Rearsby, elected 1369,[76] resigned 1376.[77]
Thomas Colman, elected 1376,[78] deprived or resigned, 1388.[79]

[40] For the record of the visitation, see *Visitations of Religious Houses in the Dioc. of Linc.* [1420–49], ed. A. Hamilton Thompson, ii, 177–83. For the appropriation of Oadby, see *Cal. Papal Letters, 1431–47,* 570; *Cal. Pat., 1441–6,* 392.
[41] *Visitations in Dioc. Linc., 1517–31,* ed. A. Hamilton Thompson, ii, 178–81.
[42] *L. & P. Hen. VIII,* vii, p. 472.
[43] *Valor Eccl.* iv, 165. The priory's possessions included in 1535 the appropriated rectory of Rosthorne (Ches.); ibid. iv, 164. Rosthorne had been granted to Launde in 1507, and appropriated in the same year: *Cal. Pat., 1494–1509,* 535; G. Ormerod, *Hist. of Chester* (2nd ed.), i, pt. 2, 432.
[44] *L. & P. Hen. VIII,* x, p. 515.
[45] Ibid. x, p. 522.
[46] Ibid. xiv (2), p. 256.
[47] Ibid., Addenda, i (1), p. 192.
[48] Ibid. xiv (2), p. 150.
[49] Ibid. xv, p. 285.
[50] S.C. 6 / Hen. VIII / 7312, mm. 60–75.
[51] *City of London, Letter Bk. C,* 220. Cited J. C. Dickinson, *Origins of the Austin Canons,* 121.
[52] F. M. Stenton, *Doc. Illustrative of Social and Econ. Hist. of Danelaw,* 337; *Descriptive Cat. of Derbys. Charts.,* 132.
[53] T. Madox, *Formulare Anglicanum,* f. xiv; cited Nichols, *Leics.* ii, 302.
[54] B.M. Sloane Chart. xxxi, 4, m. 1, no. 2.
[55] Ibid. no. 5; Nichols, *Leics.* iii, 303.

[56] G. F. Farnham, 'The Skeffingtons of Skeffington. App.', *T.L.A.S.* xvi, 106. Possibly Robt. de Martivall.
[57] Hist. MSS. Com., *Rutland,* iv, 131.
[58] *Cal. Close, 1251–3,* 190; *Cal. Chart. R., 1226–57,* 333.
[59] *Rot. Ric. Gravesend,* 154.
[60] Ibid. Elected *per viam compromissi.*
[61] *E.H.R.* lviii, 209.
[62] Ibid.
[63] Linc. Reg. Dalderby, Inst., f. 196b.
[64] Ibid.
[65] Ibid., f. 204a.
[66] Ibid.
[67] *Cal. Fine R., 1319–27,* 9; *Cal. Pat., 1317–21,* 400.
[68] *Cal. Pat., 1317–21,* 405.
[69] Linc. Reg. Bek, Inst., f. 42b.
[70] Ibid.
[71] Linc. Reg. Gynewell, Inst., f. 316.
[72] Ibid.
[73] Linc. Reg. Buckingham, Inst., i, f. 238a.
[74] Ibid.
[75] Ibid. i, f. 246b.
[76] Ibid.
[77] Ibid. i, f. 266a.
[78] Ibid.
[79] *Cal. Pat., 1358–9,* 527; *Cal. Papal Letters, 1362–1404,* 435.

Walter Baldok, elected 1388,[80] occurs 1395,[81] deprived before 1398.[82]

John Henriz, occurs 1398.[83]

Thomas Colman, occurs 1404 to 1416.[84]

William Northampton, elected 1423,[85] occurs 1440.[86]

Thomas Myles, occurs 1458.[87]

Thomas Frisby, occurs 1464[88] to 1478.[89]

Robert Northampton, occurs 1482–3.[90]

John Lancaster, occurs 1509,[91] surrendered the priory 1539.[92]

The very elaborate 15th-century seal[93] of the priory is a large vesica, 2¾ by 1¾ in. It shows St. John the Baptist standing under a canopy, and holding a lamb in his left hand. On the right and left, respectively, of the saint's figure are the figures of a lady and of an armed knight, probably representing the founders, Richard and Maud Basset. In the base is a kneeling canon between two shields, one bearing the arms of Basset of Weldon dimidiating those of Ridel, the other bearing the arms of Basset of Weldon alone. The legend reads:

. . . LL COE . . . IOHIS BAPTISTE DE LANDA.

5. LEICESTER ABBEY

In 1143 an abbey of Augustinian canons was founded at Leicester in honour of the Assumption of the Virgin Mary by Robert *le Bossu*, Earl of Leicester.[1] The abbey was endowed with the possessions of a college of secular canons, usually known as the College of St. Mary *de Castro*, established at Leicester by Robert's father.[2] The new Augustinian house did not altogether replace the college, which continued to exist in a modified form under the control of the abbey.[3] The

endowments which were transferred from the college to the abbey consisted of all the churches of Leicester,[4] the church of Lilbourne (Northants.), the manor of Asfordby,[5] and other property.[6] To these possessions Earl Robert *le Bossu* added the Leicestershire churches of Knaptoft, Stoney Stanton, 'Erdesby',[7] Enderby[8] with the chapel of Whetstone, Cosby, Shepshed with all the churches of the soke of Shepshed, Thurnby, and Illston, the church of West Ilsley (Berks.), and the churches of Brackley and Farthinghoe (Northants.). Earl Robert also gave lands at Stoughton and Pinslade (Leics.), and other property.[9] The manor of Knighton was granted to the abbey by Robert *le Bossu*, who had obtained it from the Bishop of Lincoln.[10] After a complicated series of exchanges, during which the abbey's lands at Asfordby and Segrave were for a time handed over to the bishop, Leicester Abbey finally gave up its claims to Knighton in or before 1218.[11] The abbey's property at Segrave was returned to it, but the lands at Asfordby, with the advowson of the church there, seem to have been permanently lost. Westcotes, near Leicester, which had been given to the abbey by Earl Robert FitzParnell in compensation for the Asfordby and Segrave lands, was retained by the abbey until the Dissolution.[12] The abbey also obtained, before 1162,[13] from various donors the churches of Evington, Humberstone, Thorpe Arnold, Narborough, Langton, Barrow, Billesdon, Blaby, North Kilworth, Husbands Bosworth, Barkby, Hungarton, Easton, Eastwell, Knipton, Harston, Bitteswell, Croft, Wanlip, Theddingworth, Thornton, and Queniborough, all in Leicestershire, Clifton-on-Dunsmore, Cudworth, and Bulkington (Warws.), Adstock and one-half of the church of Chesham (Bucks.), Sharnbrook (Beds.), Eydon, Billing Magna, and

80 *Cal. Pat., 1388–92*, 1.

81 *Cal. Papal Letters, 1362–1404*, 523.

82 *Cal. Pat., 1396–9*, 413; T. Walsingham, *Hist. Angl.* (Rolls Ser.), ii, 249.

83 *Cal. Pat., 1396–9*, 413.

84 *Descriptive Cat. of Derbys. Chart.* 166; *Cal. Close, 1405–9*, 528; *Cal. Pat., 1416–22*, 141; *Cal. Papal Letters, 1404–15*, 335. Colman was still only a canon in 1400 (*Cal. Papal Letters, 1362–1404*, 310), so he must have been re-elected between 1400 and 1404.

85 *Visitations in Dioc. Linc.* [1420–49], i, 164.

86 Ibid. ii, 178.

87 Nichols, *Leics.* iii, 306, citing a deed not now available.

88 *Cat. of the Archives of All Souls Coll. Oxf.*, ed. C. T. Martin, 261.

89 *Cal. Pat., 1476–85*, 84.

90 Ibid. 342; *Cat. Anct. D.* v, A13424.

91 *L. & P. Hen. VIII*, i (2nd ed.), p. 246.

92 Ibid. xiv (2), p. 256.

93 E. 25/72*.

1 A. Hamilton Thompson, *The Abbey of St. Mary of the Meadows*, Leic. 2; Hen. Knighton, *Chron.* (Rolls Ser.), i, 62.

2 Knighton, op. cit. i, 62; Dugd. *Mon.* vi, 463–4.

3 Hamilton Thompson, *Abbey of Leic.* 2. And see account of the Coll. of St. Mary *de Castro*, below, p. 42.

4 Except St. Margaret's, a prebendal ch. of Linc.

5 Probably including the ch. of Asfordby, which came into the abbey's hands before 1162: Dugd. *Mon.* vi, 467.

6 Ibid. vi, 464; Hamilton Thompson, *Abbey of Leic.* 2, 5.

7 Probably Arnesby.

8 'Aldeby.'

9 The list of Earl Robert's donations has been based on Henry II's confirmation charter, printed Dugd. *Mon.* vi, 467–8.

10 Nichols, *Leics.* iv, 235.

11 Ibid.; *Reg. Antiquissimum of the Cath. Ch. of Linc.*, ed. C. W. Foster, iii, 213–17.

12 *Reg. Antiquissimum*, iii, 220, 223–4; Dugd. *Mon.* vi, 468; *Rot. Chart.* (Rec. Com.), i, 145; *Rot. Hugonis de Welles*, ed. W. P. W. Phillimore, i, 256; *Valor Eccl.* (Rec. Com.), iv, 146.

13 i.e. by the date of grant of Hen. II's charter, which is witnessed by Becket as chancellor: Dugd. *Mon.* vi, 468.

Syresham (Northants.), Youlgreave (Derbys.), and Cockerham (Lancs.), with the manors of Cockerham and 'Cawkesberia',[14] and many lesser gifts.[15] Dishley church (Leics.) was obtained from an unknown donor before 1220.[16] Leicester Abbey thus acquired within a relatively short time of its foundation the advowsons of many churches, though seven of them passed out of the abbey's hands before the end of the 13th century.[17] None of the remainder seems to have been regularly served by canons of the abbey, not even those in Leicester itself,[18] though by a papal privilege granted in 1148 the abbey was empowered to present its canons to the cures of parish churches.[19]

The tradition that the founder, Earl Robert le Bossu, spent the last fifteen years of his life as a canon of the abbey[20] is disproved by the known facts about his career,[21] though he may have assumed the habit of a canon at the abbey shortly before his death.[22] Alexander, Bishop of Lincoln, together with Earl Robert, laid down for the abbey certain regulations, which were confirmed by Pope Urban III.[23] By the privilege of 1148, already mentioned, Eugenius III exempted from tithe lands newly brought into cultivation and tilled by the canons themselves, and also exempted the increase of their livestock. The same privilege forbade the use of violence or improper means in the election of abbots, and granted free burial in the monastery to those who left bequests to the house, even if they lay under excommunication or interdict.[24] In 1207 or 1208 a cell, normally occupied by four canons, was established at Cockerham. The cell had ceased to exist by the middle of the 14th century, and probably never became conventual.[25] The great choir of the abbey church was built by Parnel, wife of Earl

Robert ès Blanchemains, the founder's son.[26] Parnel's son, Robert Earl of Leicester, gave the abbey 24 virgates of land at Anstey.[27] The resignation in 1235 of Abbot Matthias Bray was probably due to pressure exercised by Bishop Grosseteste.[28] In 1311 the Bishop of Durham granted lands at Ratby to the abbey,[29] and in 1315 the manor of Lockington (Leics.) was acquired.[30] In October 1326 a violent attack was made upon the abbey by the Earl of Lancaster's followers, who broke in and seized the property of Hugh Despenser the elder deposited there.[31]

Under Abbot William Clowne, elected in 1345,[32] Leicester Abbey enjoyed a period of great prosperity. Clowne's character is described in very favourable terms by a canon of the abbey.[33] In his time canons of Leicester became heads of four other Augustinian houses,[34] while the abbey's endowments were increased by the acquisition of the Leicestershire manors of Ingarsby and Kirby Mallory, with the advowson of Kirby Mallory[35] and other property, and by the appropriation of the churches of Hungarton and Humberstone.[36] Clowne also secured for the abbots of Leicester exemption from attendance at Parliament, to which the heads of the house had been summoned intermittently since 1265.[37] Thanks to his friendly relations with Edward III, Clowne was able to obtain in 1363 for the prior and convent the right of having custody of the abbey with its temporalities during future vacancies.[38] The abbey had previously obtained this privilege at times for particular vacancies,[39] but Clowne secured the right for the whole period of all future voidances. It was also probably during Clowne's abbacy that Henry of Knighton, a canon of Leicester Abbey, began to write his chronicle.[40]

---

[14] Not identified.

[15] Dugd. *Mon.* vi, 467–8; Hamilton Thompson, *Abbey of Leic.* 5–7.

[16] *Rot. Hugonis de Welles*, i, 253.

[17] The chs. of West Ilsley, Knaptoft, Stoney Stanton, Illston, Langton, Knipton, and Wanlip. Hamilton Thompson, *Abbey of Leic.* 8.

[18] Ibid. 4, 5. [19] Nichols, *Leics.* i, 68.

[20] Knighton, *Chron.* (Rolls Ser.), i, 147.

[21] Hamilton Thompson, *Abbey of Leic.* 10; *Complete Peerage*, vii, 529–30.

[22] Thompson, op. cit. 9; B.M. Sloane Chart. xxxii, 22.

[23] Nichols, *Leics.* i (2), App., 68.

[24] Ibid.; Hamilton Thompson, *Abbey of Leic.* 13.

[25] *V.C.H. Lancs.* ii, 152–3.

[26] Hamilton Thompson, *Abbey of Leic.* 10; Knighton, *Chron.* (Rolls Ser.), i, 63.

[27] *Rot. Chart.*, *1199–1216* (Rec. Com.), 145.

[28] *Ann. Mon.* (Rolls Ser.), iii, 143; *Rot. Roberti Grosseteste*, ed. F. N. Davis, 385; *Cal. Close, 1234–7*, 144; *Cal. Pat., 1232–41*, 117–18.

[29] Hamilton Thompson, *Abbey of Leic.* 22, citing *Cal. Pat., 1307–13*, 323.

[30] Thompson, op. cit. 22, citing *Cal. Pat., 1313–17*, 212.

[31] Knighton, *Chron.* (Rolls Ser.), i, 435.

[32] *Cal. Pat., 1343–5*, 558.

[33] Knighton, *Chron.* (Rolls Ser.), ii, 125–7.

[34] Ibid. 126; *Cal. Pat., 1370–4*, 433; Hamilton Thompson, *Abbey of Leic.* 35–36.

[35] Licence was obtained in 1363 to appropriate Kirby Mallory ch. (*Cal. Pat., 1361–4*, 99, 413), but the appropriation was not carried out: Thompson, op. cit. 34, 155–6.

[36] Knighton, *Chron.* (Rolls Ser.), ii, 126; Thompson, op. cit. 30–31, 35; Nichols, *Leics.* i (2), App., 62–63; Farnham, *Leics. Notes*, iii, 156; *Cal. Pat., 1350–4*, 146, and *1361–4*, 99; *Cal. Papal Pet., 1342–1419*, 226. The advowson of Willoughby Waterless seems to have been acquired with the manor of Ingarsby: Nichols, op. cit. i (2), 72. In 1535 Leic. Abbey was receiving a payment of 3s. 4d. from Willoughby ch.: *Valor Eccl.* (Rec. Com.), iv, 145. It is uncertain whether the abbey then held the advowson.

[37] Thompson, op. cit. 31–32; *Cal. Pat., 1350–4*, 230; *Cal. Close, 1264–8*, 86.

[38] *Cal. Pat., 1361–4*, 415.

[39] Ibid., *1266–72*, 460; *Cal. Close, 1343–6*, 615; *Cal. Fine R., 1307–19*, 348. In 1344 the right had been granted to keep the abbey for 4 months after vacancies arose: *Cal. Pat., 1343–5*, 560.

[40] Knighton, *Chron.* (Rolls Ser.), ii, Introduction, *passim*.

After Clowne's death at the beginning of 1378,[41] the abbey entered a difficult period. It is probable that the late 14th century saw a decline in the income derived from the abbey's lands.[42] During the 15th century the abbey, once active in producing corn and wool, leased out most of its demesne lands, so that by 1477 the only property still in the canons' hands for cultivation was the demesne in the immediate vicinity of Leicester, and the demesnes of Stoughton and Ingarsby, not far from the abbey.[43] A canon of the abbey, Philip Repyngdon, became, while studying at Oxford, one of the most notable of Wycliffe's followers, and in 1382 certain of his opinions were declared heretical. Repingdon recanted,[44] and lived to become Abbot of Leicester and eventually Bishop of Lincoln. When Archbishop Courtenay visited Leicester in 1389 during his metropolitical visitation of Lincoln Diocese, he ordered the election of four persons to form a council for the abbot.[45] Repingdon, elected Abbot of Leicester in 1393,[46] became Bishop of Lincoln in 1405. It was perhaps felt that as bishop he was inclined to interfere in the internal affairs of the house, for in 1412 the canons of Leicester Abbey obtained a royal licence permitting them to obtain from the Pope exemption from the Bishop of Lincoln's jurisdiction, so long as Repingdon should be bishop.[47] Such exemption, if ever obtained, was nullified in the following year, when Repingdon obtained from the Pope a declaration that Leicester Abbey should be fully subject to him and his successors.[48]

The state of the abbey as revealed by Bishop Alnwick's visitation in 1440 was not altogether sound.[49] The number of canons had fallen to fourteen, besides the abbot, William Sadyngton, and one other canon who was studying at a university. There had been not long previously as many as thirty or forty canons in the house. Similarly the number of boys in the almonry had been reduced from about twenty-five to only six, and the abbot was accused of having admitted unsuitable boys in return for money. Abbot Sadyngton kept a tight grip on financial affairs, pocketing various minor revenues, keeping the offices of treasurer and cellarer in his own hands, and failing to render account to his canons. He also kept many lay servants, some of whom he favoured excessively, and he was said to indulge in magical practices. The abbot was negligent in

preventing private ownership of property by the canons, and there were features of the abbey's life which must have encouraged this sin. Each canon received a yearly allowance of 5 marks, and it had been customary for the goods of a deceased canon to be divided amongst the most needy of his brethren. The abbot was obviously on bad terms with many of his canons. The general financial position of the abbey was, however, satisfactory. Its net annual revenue was then estimated at £780, while a further £400 or more yearly was derived from what were apparently casual profits. The conventual buildings had been extensively rebuilt. No serious immorality was disclosed by the visitation, a charge of incontinence against the abbot being apparently not sustained, while he was allowed to clear himself by his unsupported oath of the charge of having practised divination. In the injunctions issued after the visitation, Bishop Alnwick ordered that the number of canons should be raised to thirty, and that there should be at least sixteen boys in the almonry. The abbot was ordered to render proper accounts to his brethren, to grant no corrodies without the bishop's licence and the convent's consent, and to take vigorous action to prevent the canons owning private property. The abbot was further enjoined to behave more charitably to his canons.[50]

In or shortly before 1485, the abbey was granted the church of Stoke (Staffs.), with licence to appropriate it,[51] but the grant does not seem to have taken effect, as the church is not amongst the abbey's possessions as listed in 1535.[52] Little is known of the internal affairs of the abbey between 1440 and 1518, when another visitation took place. It was at the end of the 15th century and the beginning of the 16th century that William Charyte, Prior of Leicester, drew up an elaborate record of the possessions of the house.[53] A catalogue of the books in the abbey's library, drawn up by Charyte, lists more than 900 volumes.[54] Many of the faults discovered in 1440 were still to be found when the abbey was again visited in 1518. Abbot Pescall, like Sadyngton, was charged with keeping financial control too much in his own hands. As in 1440, complaints were made about the excessive number of hounds kept in the abbey, and about the failure to educate the boys in the almonry properly. In 1518 it was further said that the prior was too old to perform

41 Ibid. 125; *Cal. Pat.*, 1377–81, 104.
42 R. H. Hilton, *Econ. Development of Some Leics. Estates*, 88.
43 Ibid. 90–91.
44 *Fasciculi Zizaniorum* (Rolls Ser.), 202, 289–90, 296–7, 299, 306, 310, 316–29.
45 Hamilton Thompson, *Abbey of Leic.* 51–52.
46 *Cal. Pat.*, 1391–6, 279.
47 Ibid., 1408–13, 457.
48 *Cal. Papal Letters*, 1404–15, 419.
49 *Visitations of Religious Houses in the Dioc. of Linc.* [1420–49], ed. A. Hamilton Thompson, ii,

206–17.
50 Ibid.
51 *Cal. Pat.*, 1476–85, 541.
52 *Valor Eccl.* (Rec. Com.), iv, 145–8.
53 Nichols, *Leics.* i, App., 53; Hamilton Thompson, *Abbey of Leic.* 73–74. Charyte's compilation is now Bodl. Libr. Laud. MS. 625. A considerable portion of this MS. is printed by Nichols, *Leics.* i, App. xvii.
54 M. R. James, 'The Cat. of the Libr. of Leic. Abbey', *T.L.A.S.* xix, 120. For a transcript of the cat., see ibid. xix, 131–6, 381–435, and xxi, 1–88; see also Thompson, op. cit. 204–30.

his functions properly, and that some canons were in the habit of eating and drinking at unaccustomed hours. Bishop Attwater, in his injunctions, dealt with some of the defects revealed by the visitation.[55] At an unknown date Bishop Longland, who succeeded Attwater in 1521, made his first visitation of Leicester Abbey. There is no record of the visitation itself, but certain injunctions, which probably followed it, have survived.[56] These injunctions show the state of the abbey in a most unfavourable light. The abbot, Pescall, was extremely remiss in his attendance at the divine offices in the conventual church, and when he did enter the church he was often accompanied by his fool, who disturbed the services by his buffoonery. The prior too was evidently unsuitable, for the bishop had to order him to be present at the divine offices and in the refectory. The canons, following the example of their superiors, were also lax in their attendance in choir, so that out of at least twenty-five canons in the house not more than eleven were usually present. The canons were accustomed to roam about outside the monastery, and two of them were suspected of incontinence. The finances of the house were in no less need of reform than its spiritual state. At some time before the issue of the injunctions Bishop Longland had found it necessary, on account of the abbey's indebtedness, to appoint two administrators to control its business affairs, but Pescall had removed the bishop's two nominees. One of the administrators, Richard Lichefeld, had proved unworthy, and the bishop in one of the injunctions removed him from the office of cellarer. The other administrator was reappointed, and together with a new cellarer was given control over the abbey's finances. The bishop forbade the abbot and prior to grant out property at farm without the convent's consent, and ordered that the abbey's common chest should have three keys, to be kept by the abbot, the prior, and one of the two administrators. When in 1528 the abbey was visited by the chancellor of the diocese Pescall's conduct was found to have improved but little. His attendance in choir was still lax, and he had a burdensome habit of taking his meals apart from the canons, at irregular times and in unusual places. Complaints were made about the excessive number and the conduct of the abbot's lay servants. It was further said that the novices, though diligently taught, were unwilling

to learn, and were disrespectful to their seniors. While the prior was commended by his fellow canons for having done much to relieve the abbey's financial position, Richard Lichefelde, who was once again cellarer, was said to be of little use to the house. The canons were still in the habit of going out of the abbey without leave. There were in 1528 twenty-four canons in the house, not including the abbot.[57]

In view of the facts concerning Pescall given in the visitation records, it is hardly surprising that Bishop Longland concluded that the abbot's deposition was essential. Some time elapsed before this could be achieved, and in the interval the bishop seems to have harassed Pescall by constant interference in the internal affairs of the house.[58] Pescall, on the other hand, tried to secure his position by presents to Thomas Cromwell.[59] It was in 1530, while Pescall was still abbot, that Cardinal Wolsey died at Leicester Abbey. Pescall finally resigned at the end of 1533 or the very beginning of 1534.[60] He was granted a pension of £100 a year.[61]

The new abbot, John Bourchier, elected by acclamation in January 1534, was apparently Cromwell's nominee.[62] Bourchier must have had a difficult task, for the house was £1,000 in debt, and Pescall's pension was an additional burden.[63] Bourchier's term of office was, however, to be short. In 1534 with twenty-five canons he acknowledged the royal supremacy over the Church.[64] The abbey's clear yearly income was assessed in the following year at £951. 14s. 5¾d.,[65] making it by far the richest religious house in Leicestershire. The abbey therefore survived the dissolution of the smaller monasteries. Richard Layton, visiting the house in 1535, reported that Bourchier was an honest man, but that the canons were factious, and refused to confess anything. Layton therefore intended to prefer charges of adultery and unnatural vice against them.[66] Bourchier took steps to secure Thomas Cromwell's favour. The canons objected to the proposal to grant Richard Cromwell a lease of Ingarsby, which had been retained as the abbey's demesne, but the abbot sent Thomas Cromwell £100 in 1536, and later a present of sheep and oxen.[67] The abbey was finally surrendered in October 1538 by Bourchier and nineteen canons.[68] Bourchier seems to have reduced the debts of the house considerably, for the money

[55] *Visitations in Dioc. Linc. 1517–31*, ed. A. Hamilton Thompson, ii, 183–6.

[56] For the text of the injunctions, see G. G. Perry, 'Episcopal Visitation of the Austin Canons of Leic. and Dorchester', *E.H.R.* iv, 304–9. On the date, see *Visitations in Dioc. Linc. 1517–31*, ii, 201, and Hamilton Thompson, *Abbey of Leic.* 77.

[57] *Visitations in Dioc. Linc. 1517–31*, ii, 186–95.

[58] *L. & P. Hen. VIII*, vi, pp. 604–5; vii, p. 383.

[59] Ibid. v, pp. 513, 604.

[60] Hamilton Thompson, *Abbey of Leic.* 85.

[61] Ibid. 86.

[62] Ibid. 85.

[63] Ibid. 86; *L. & P. Hen. VIII*, vii, p. 228.

[64] Thompson, op. cit. 88; *L. & P. Hen. VIII*, vii, p. 440.

[65] *Valor Eccl.* (Rec. Com.), iv, 148.

[66] *L. & P. Hen. VIII*, ix, p. 341.

[67] Ibid. x, p. 285; xiii (1), p. 346; Hamilton Thompson, *Abbey of Leic.* 87–88.

[68] Thompson, op. cit. 88; *L. & P. Hen. VIII*, xiii (2), p. 80.

owing in 1538 only amounted to £411. 10s., apart from debts to the king.[69] Bourchier was granted the large pension of £200 a year.[70]

The lands held by the abbey at the Dissolution lay mostly in Leicestershire.[71] Of the churches granted to it at various times, some had been lost.[72] The abbey abandoned the advowson of Adstock in the 15th century,[73] while the advowson of Billing Magna was exchanged for land at Cossington (Leics.).[74] The advowson of Blaby was lost shortly before 1424, after prolonged litigation,[75] but the abbey continued to receive a pension from Blaby church.[76] The church of Dishley was transferred to Garendon Abbey in 1458,[77] and the advowson of Hathern was alienated, in or shortly after 1379, to the college of St. Mary *de Castro*, at Leicester.[78] The advowson of Narborough is listed in the *Matriculus* of the Archdeaconry of Leicester as disputed between Leicester Abbey and Fulk Fitzwarine,[79] and by 1329 the patronage was in lay hands.[80] The abbey continued to possess until the Dissolution[81] the churches of All Saints, St. Leonard, St. Martin, St. Mary *de Castro*, St. Michael, St. Nicholas, and St. Peter, at Leicester. These churches all seem to have been appropriated at an early date, probably in the 12th century.[82] The church of St. Clement at Leicester was also once part of the abbey's possessions, but there is no record of the abbey having presented a vicar later than 1221–2.[83] The other churches which the abbey retained were Barkby,[84] Barrow on Soar[85] with the chapels of Quorndon and Mountsorrel,[86] Queniborough,[87] Shepshed,[88] Bitteswell,[89] Lockington[90] with the chapel of Hemington, Thorpe Arnold[91] with the chapel of Brentingby, Eaton,[92] Hungarton[93] with Baggrave and Ingarsby, Enderby[94] with the chapel of Whetstone, Billesdon[95] with the chapels of Goadby and Rolleston, Thurnby[96] with the chapel of Stoughton, Theddingworth,[97] Thornton[98] with the chapels of Bagworth and Stanton, Cosby,[99] Humberstone,[1] Evington,[2] North Kilworth, Husbands Bosworth, Croft, Harston, Eastwell, and Long Whatton.[3] The last was probably one of the churches of the soke of Shepshed. Besides these churches, all of which are in Leicestershire, the abbey possessed the churches of Bulkington,[4] Clifton-on-Dunsmore,[5] Cudworth,[6] Brackley[7] with the chapel of Halse,[8] Farthinghoe,[9] Clay Coton

---

[69] Ibid., p. 81; Thompson, op. cit. 89.

[70] Thompson, op. cit. 89; *L. & P. Hen. VIII*, xiv (1), p. 598.

[71] *Valor Eccl.* (Rec. Com.), iv, 145–8.

[72] See above, n. 17, for chs. lost before 1300.

[73] Hamilton Thompson, *Abbey of Leic.* 92.

[74] Ibid. 104.

[75] Ibid. 107; Farnham, *Leics. Notes*, v, 38, 41–43.

[76] *Valor Eccl.* (Rec. Com.), iv, 145.

[77] Hamilton Thompson, *Abbey of Leic.* 129–30.

[78] Ibid. 144–5. Hathern was probably one of the chs. of the soke of Shepshed, granted to the abbey by its founder.

[79] Thompson, op. cit. 177; *Rot. Hugonis de Welles*, i, 243; *Cur. Reg. R.*, *1221–2*, 135–6.

[80] Thompson, op. cit. 178.

[81] *Valor Eccl.* (Rec. Com.), iv, 145–6; Thompson, op. cit. 91–203.

[82] *Rot. Hugonis de Welles*, i, 238; Hamilton Thompson, *Abbey of Leic.* 157–72.

[83] Thompson, op. cit. 160; *Rot. Hugonis de Welles*, ii, 286. And see the account of the Dominicans of Leic. below, p. 34.

[84] Appropriated by 1220: *Rot. Hugonis de Welles*, i, 257.

[85] Appropriated by grant of William de Blois, Bp. of Linc. 1203–6: ibid. i, 253; Hamilton Thompson, *Abbey of Leic.* 96.

[86] Woodhouse, which is listed separately in *Valor Eccl.* (Rec. Com.), iv, 145, was in Barrow Par.

[87] Appropriated by 1220: *Rot. Hugonis de Welles*, i, 257. [88] Appropriated by 1220: ibid. i, 254.

[89] Appropriated by 1220: ibid. i, 243; Hamilton Thompson, *Abbey of Leic.* 106–7.

[90] One of the chs. of the soke of Shepshed, granted to the abbey by its founder: Thompson, op. cit. 189; appropriated by 1220: *Rot. Hugonis de Welles*, i, 254.

[91] Appropriated by 1220: ibid. i, 272.

[92] Appropriated by 1220: ibid. i, 271.

[93] Appropriated 1352: Hamilton Thompson, *Abbey*

of *Leic.* 150; *Cal. Papal Letters, 1342–62*, 459.

[94] The ch. of Aldeby, granted by the founder, is said to have been transferred to Enderby under Bp. Sutton: Thompson, op. cit. 134. But the transfer seems to have taken place earlier, as Enderby is listed as if it were a par. ch. in the *Matriculus*: *Rot. Hugonis de Welles*, i, 243. Enderby was appropriated by 1220: ibid.

[95] Appropriated by 1220: ibid. i, 263.

[96] Appropriated by 1220: ibid.

[97] Appropriated by 1220: ibid. i, 266.

[98] Appropriated by 1220: ibid. i, 247.

[99] Appropriated by 1220: ibid. i, 241.

[1] Appropriation was authorized in 1352, and subsequently carried out: Hamilton Thompson, *Abbey of Leic.* 147; *Cal. Papal Letters, 1342–62*, 459.

[2] Appropriated by 1220: *Rot. Hugonis de Welles*, i, 264.

[3] The last 7 chs. in the list were not appropriated. In *Valor Eccl.* (Rec. Com.), iv, 145, the ch. of Newton juxta Clyfton is listed amongst the Leic. chs. appropriated to the abbey, but it was a chapel of the abbey's ch. of Clifton on Dunsmore (Warws.): Nichols, *Leics.* i (2), App., 81; Wm. Dugdale, *Antiquities of Warws.* (1666), 7.

[4] Appropriated by 1229: Hamilton Thompson, *Abbey of Leic.* 113.

[5] Appropriated to the abbey by Bp. Geoffrey Muscamp, 1198–1208: Thompson, op. cit. 119.

[6] Appropriated to the abbey by Bp. Ric. Peche, 1161–82: ibid. 126. This ch. is not listed amongst the abbey's possessions in the *Valor Eccl.* (Rec. Com.).

[7] One of the chs. of the soke of Halse. Appropriated in or before 1224: Thompson, op. cit. 110; *Rot. Hugonis de Welles*, ii, 115.

[8] 'Hatsoo' in *Valor Eccl.* (Rec. Com.), iv, 146.

[9] A ch. of the soke of Halse. It does not seem to have been appropriated. It is not listed as appropriated in 1535 (ibid. iv, 146) and certainly still had a rector at the end of the 13th century: *R. and Reg. of Bp. Oliver Sutton*, ed. Rosalind Hill, ii, 84, 98.

(Warws.),[10] Eydon (Northants.),[11] Rugby[12] with the chapel of Brownsover (Warws.),[13] Lilbourne,[14] Syresham,[15] Chesham (with a moiety of the advowson),[16] Sharnbrook,[17] Youlgreave,[18] and Cockerham.[19] The First Minister's Account lists property with a net annual value of £786. 16s. 1¾d., but this probably does not include all the abbey's endowments.[20]

ABBOTS OF LEICESTER[21]

Richard, elected 1143 or 1144, ruled twenty-four years.[22]

William of Kalewyken, elected 1167–8, ruled ten years.[23]

William of Broke, elected 1177, resigned 1186.[24]

Paul, elected 1186, ruled nineteen years.[25]

William Pepyn, elected 1205, ruled nineteen years.[26]

Osbert of Duntun, elected 1222,[27] died 1229.[28]

Matthias Bray, elected 1229,[29] resigned 1235.[30]

Alan of Cestreham, elected 1235.[31]

Robert Furmentin, elected 1244.[32]

Henry of Rotheleye,[33] elected 1247,[34] resigned 1270.[35]

William of Shepheved,[36] elected 1270,[37] died 1291.[38]

William of Malverne, elected 1291,[39] died 1318.[40]

Richard of Tours, elected 1318,[41] died 1345.[42]

William of Clowne, elected 1345,[43] died 1378.[44]

William of Kereby, elected 1378,[45] died 1393.[46]

Philip of Repingdon, elected 1393,[47] resigned 1405.[48]

[10] Formerly a chapel of Lilbourne: Hamilton Thompson, *Abbey of Leic.* 117.

[11] Not appropriated: Thompson, op. cit. 139–40.

[12] Originally a chapel of Clifton: Thompson, op. cit. 184. 'Rokeby', under Northants. in error, in *Valor Eccl.* (Rec. Com.), iv, 146.

[13] 'Bronesov': ibid.

[14] Appropriated at an early date. A vicarage was ordained by Hugh de Welles: Hamilton Thompson, *Abbey of Leic.* 172. This is apparently the ch. listed as 'Kelborne' in *Valor Eccl.* (Rec. Com.), iv, 146. See ibid. iv, 325.

[15] Originally a chapel of Brackley: Nichols, *Leics.* i, App., 57.

[16] Appropriated by 1221: *Rot. Hugonis de Welles*, ii, 55.

[17] Apparently appropriated by 1226–7: ibid. iii, 13.

[18] Appropriated by Bp. Stavensby, 1224–38. Middleton and Winster, listed as appropriated rectories in *Valor Eccl.* (Rec. Com.), iv, 146, were chapels of Youlgreave: Hamilton Thompson, *Abbey of Leic.* 202.

[19] Appropriated earlier than c. 1290: ibid. 121. For a table giving the values of chs. held by the abbey, as assessed at various dates, see ibid. 202–3.

[20] S.C. 6/Hen. VIII/1825, mm. 33–63.

[21] Lists of abbots are in Lamb. MS. dlxxv, f. 215, and in B.M. Cott. MS. Vitellius F. xvii, f. 46. These 2 lists were conflated by Nichols, who printed a list of abbots in *Leics.* i, 275. This list is not altogether satisfactory. The dates of the abbots' elections are given in two forms, by the years of the Incarnation and by the regnal years of the kings of Engl., but in several cases the two forms of dating do not agree. In view of the lack of more precise information concerning the first 5 abbots, and of the fact that where other evidence is available about the 5 abbots it agrees with Nichols's list, the evidence of the list has been accepted provisionally, as regards the first 5 abbots only.

[22] Nichols, op. cit. i, 275, gives the year as 1144, or alternatively as 8 Steph. But the eighth year of Steph. ran from Dec. 1142 to Dec. 1143. As the abbey was founded in 1143, it is probable that Ric. was elected in that year. See also *Doc. Illustrative of Social and Econ. Hist. of Danelaw*, ed. F. M. Stenton, 251–2, and *Ancient Chart.* (Pipe R. Soc. iv), ed. J. H. Round, 59.

[23] Nichols, op. cit. i, 275, gives the date of election

as 1167, or alternatively as 14 Hen. I, an obvious error for 14 Hen. II. Wm. must therefore have been elected at the very end of the historical year 1167 or in 1168.

[24] Nichols, op. cit. i, 275. See also *Doc. Illustrative of Hist. of Danelaw*, 241.

[25] Nichols, op. cit. i, 275. The alternative date of 8 Ric. I given by Nichols must be an error, as Paul, while abbot, witnessed a charter which is not later than 1195: *Ancient Chart.* (Pipe R. Soc. iv), 101. See also *Rot. Chart.* (Rec. Com.), i, 125–6, and *Cat. Anct. D.* i, B1035.

[26] Nichols, op. cit. i, 275. Abbot Paul is mentioned in the Pipe R. of 1208 and 1209, but the references do not imply that he was alive in those years: *Pipe R. 1208* (Pipe R. Soc., N.S. xxiii), 163; *Pipe R. 1209* (Pipe R. Soc., N.S. xxiv), 20. On Abbot Wm., see *Reg. Antiquissimum of the Cath. Ch. of Linc.* iii, 218–21, 223–4.

[27] *Rot. Litt. Claus.* (Rec. Com.), ii, 508; *Cal. Pat., 1216–25*, 338.

[28] *Cal. Pat., 1225–32*, 235.

[29] Ibid. 243; C66/38, m. 10, where the name is abbreviated Math'.

[30] *Rot. Roberti Grosseteste*, ed. F. N. Davis, 385.

[31] *Cal. Pat., 1232–47*, 118.

[32] Ibid. 446.

[33] i.e. Rothley (Leics.).

[34] *Cal. Pat., 1232–47*, 510, where his name is given as Ric. But it appears as Hen. in *Rot. Roberti Grosseteste*, 429, and *Cal. Pat., 1266–72*, 463. He was blessed by Walter Mauclerc, formerly Bp. of Carlisle, not Wm. Bp. of Carlisle, as stated by Nichols, *Leics.* i, 275.

[35] *Cal. Pat., 1266–72*, 463.

[36] i.e. Shepshed (Leics.).

[37] *Cal. Pat., 1266–72*, 464; *Rot. Ric. Gravesend*, 151, 311.

[38] *Cal. Pat., 1281–92*, 444.

[39] Ibid. 446; Rosalind Hill, 'Bishop Sutton and the Inst. of Heads of Religious Houses in the Dioc. of Linc.', *E.H.R.* lviii, 209.

[40] *Cal. Pat., 1317–21*, 68.

[41] Ibid. 73.

[42] Ibid., *1343–5*, 560.

[43] Ibid. 558.

[44] Ibid., *1377–81*, 104.

[45] Ibid. 124.

[46] Ibid., *1391–6*, 266.

[47] Ibid. 279.

[48] Resigned on becoming Bp. of Linc.: *Cal. Pat., 1405–8*, 2.

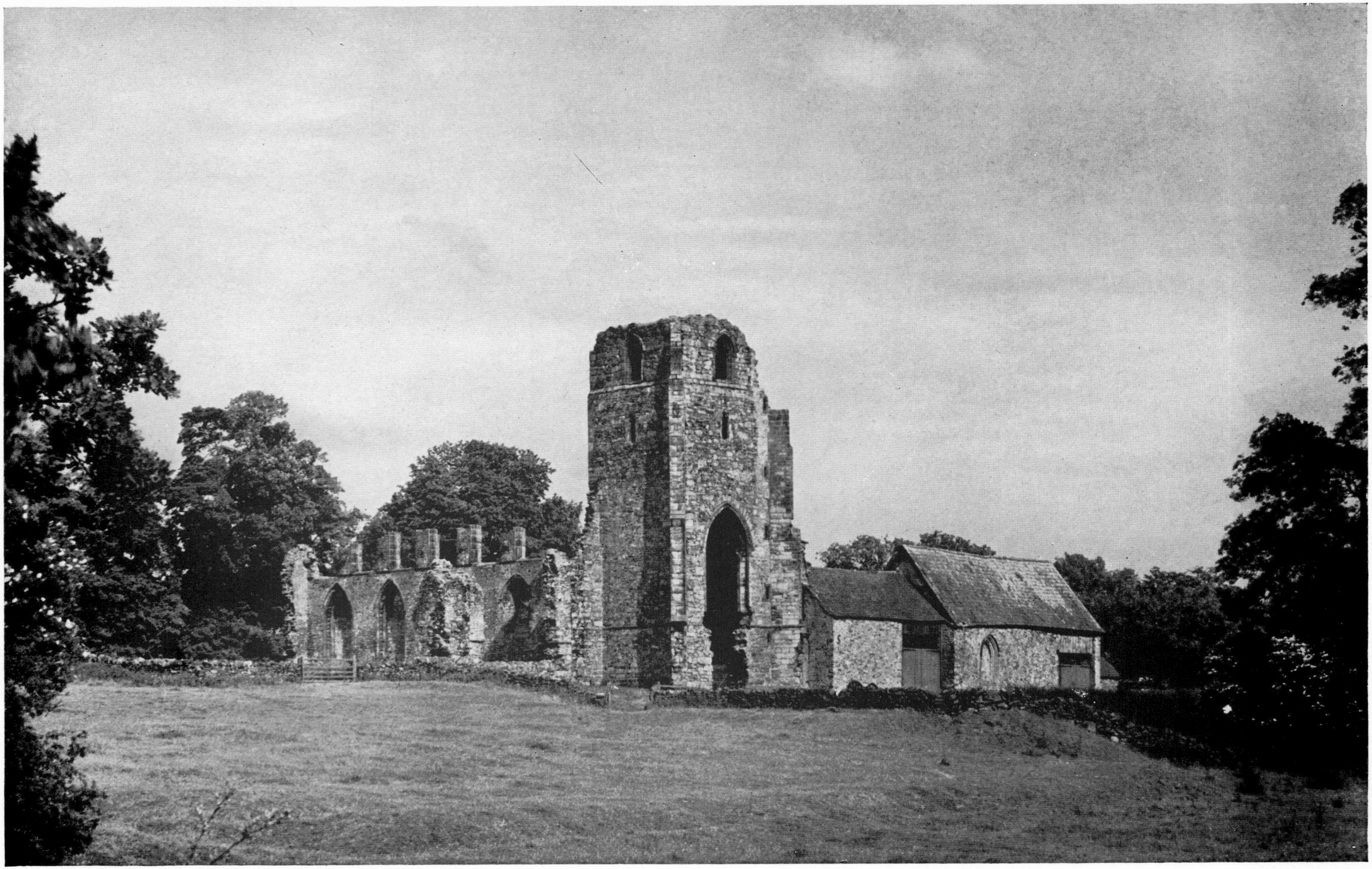

Ulverscroft Priory

Richard of Rothely, elected 1405,[49] resigned 1420.[50]

William Sadyngton, elected 1420,[51] died 1442.[52]

John Pomery, elected 1442,[53] died 1474.[54]

John Sepyshede, elected 1474,[55] died or resigned 1485.[56]

Gilbert Manchestre, elected 1485,[57] died 1496.[58]

John Penny, elected 1496,[59] resigned 1509.[60]

Richard Pescall, elected 1509,[61] resigned December 1533 or January 1534.[62]

John Bourchier, elected 1534,[63] surrendered the abbey 1538.[64]

The 12th-century seal[65] of the abbey is round, 2½ in. in diameter. It shows the Virgin Mary seated on a throne, crowned and holding a sceptre in her right hand, with the infant Jesus, holding a book, on her left knee. The legend is:

SIGILLUM SANCTE MARIE DE PRATIS

The counterseal, a circle 1¾ in. in diameter, shows the half-length figure of an abbot, with a crosier and book, between two ecclesiastics. In the base of the design are three half-length figures of ecclesiastics, under a triple arch.

Another 12th-century seal,[66] 1¾ in. in diameter, has a half-length figure of the Virgin Mary crowned, holding a fleur-de-lis in her right hand, and a book in her left. The legend reads:

SIGILLUM SANCTE MARIE DE PRATO

It is, however, not certain that this seal belongs to Leicester Abbey.

Another seal,[67] on a 16th-century document, is very similar to these two. It is round, 2½ in. in diameter, and shows the Virgin seated beneath a canopy, holding the infant Jesus on her left knee and a fleur-de-lis in her right hand. The legend reads:

SIGILLUM SANCTE . . . DE PRATO.

The counterseal shows the same design as that mentioned above, with the legend:

PONIMUR A TERGO SIGNI TESTES SUMUS ERGO.

A 14th-century seal,[68] apparently used by the proctor of the abbey's revenues, is circular, with a diameter of 1⅛ in. It shows an enthroned abbot, holding a crosier and book, between the heads of four ecclesiastics. All that now remains of the legend is:

S PROCURA . . . . CONVĒCIONŪ ABB'IS ET CONVE . . . . RE .[69]

The counterseal, a circle ⅞ in. in diameter, has the Virgin Mary enthroned, with the Child on her left knee, and a star on either side of the figures. The legend reads:

AVE MARIA GRACIA

A large vesica-shaped seal[70] of the 15th century, 3 by 1¾ in., shows the Virgin standing crowned, between the letters 'T. R.', and surrounded by four angels. The scene is perhaps a representation of the Assumption. In the base is a kneeling abbot, holding his crosier, between two seals each bearing a cinquefoil ermine. Of the legend all that remains is:

SIGILLŪ . . . . IE

A 13th-century seal[71] of the abbey is a large oval, 2 by 1½ in., and shows a full-length figure of an abbot, holding crosier and book. All that can be deciphered of the legend is:

. . . . ABBA . . . . YRCEST . . . .

Another seal[72] of the house, probably of about 1300, is of very similar size and shape to that just described. It shows the figure of the Virgin Mary, seated on a throne in a canopied niche, having on her left knee the Child with His right hand raised in blessing.

6. THE PRIORY OF ULVERSCROFT

The priory of St. Mary at Ulverscroft was founded by Robert, Earl of Leicester,[1] who gave the site on which the house was built.[2] A papal document of 1174, in which the first mention of the monastery occurs, states that Ranulph, Earl of Chester, gave 30 acres in Charnwood Forest to the priory, and it must therefore have been founded before the death of Earl Ranulph *de Gernon* in

[49] Ibid. 8, where his name appears as Rotheby, but see ibid. 11, 33, and *Cal. Pat.*, *1416–22*, 302.

[50] *Cal. Pat.*, *1416–22*, 302.   [51] Ibid.

[52] Ibid. *1441–6*, 64.   [53] Ibid. 82.

[54] Ibid. *1467–77*, 461.   [55] Ibid. 475.

[56] He was still in office in Mar. 1485: *Cal. Pat.*, *1476–85*, 541.

[57] Ibid. *1485–94*, 18.

[58] Ibid. *1494–1509*, 56.

[59] Ibid. Became Bp. of Bangor 1505, and held the abbey *in commendam*: Hamilton Thompson, *Abbey of Leic.* 73.

[60] *Cal. Pat.*, *1494–1509*, 594–5. Resigned on trans. to see of Carlisle.   [61] Ibid.

[62] *L. & P. Hen. VIII*, vi, pp. 604–5, 631; vii, pp. 9, 55.

[63] Ibid. vii, pp. 109–10.

[64] Ibid. xiii (2), p. 80.

[65] B.M. Seals, lxvi, 60, 61.

[66] Ibid. lxxiv, 24.   [67] E. 25/77.

[68] B.M. Seals, lxvi, 62, 63.

[69] Some abbreviations have been extended in transcribing this legend.

[70] B.M. Seals, lxvi, 64.

[71] B.M. Add. Chart. 21402.

[72] B.M. Seals, lxvi, 65.

[1] Almost certainly Robert *le Bossu*.

[2] B.M. Harl. Chart. 111, A6.

1153.[3] The house was described as a hermitage about 1220,[4] but as early as 1174 the Pope ordered the Augustinian rule to be observed there.[5] Before 1174 the priory obtained the church of Stanford on Soar (Notts.).[6] The advowson of Stanford was a source of dispute in the 13th century,[7] and the priory had lost it by 1280.[8] In 1323 William de Ferrers had licence to alienate in mortmain to Ulverscroft 70 acres of waste land at Groby, and the advowson of the church of Syston (Leics.).[9] Licence was granted in 1361 for the appropriation of Syston.[10] The advowson of Bunny (Notts.) was granted to the priory in 1345 by Thomas de Ferrers.[11]

About 1220 the priory contained only three brothers, all priests,[12] but this number was later exceeded. There were eight canons in the house in 1438, when a visitation by Bishop Alnwick revealed an unsatisfactory state of affairs. There were many complaints about the prior's bad management of the monastery's concerns, and it was also said that he was lax in the maintenance of religious discipline. The sub-prior was said to have once been absent from the house for twenty years, and to have been readmitted without the knowledge of the convent. The prior accused the canons of wandering outside the priory, and of possessing private property. Bishop Alnwick provided that the prior should retain control of the priory until the next Michaelmas, when it would be decided whether he should resign, or be assisted by a coadjutor. In fact the prior resigned in 1439.[13]

The small priory of Charley was united with Ulverscroft in, or shortly after, 1465.[14] In 1518 another visitation of Ulverscroft took place, and it was found that one canon had apostatized.[15] The prior and nine canons of the priory acknowledged the royal supremacy over the Church in 1534.[16] In the following year the clear annual income of Ulverscroft was assessed at little more than £83,[17] and the house was therefore listed amongst the smaller monasteries for early dissolution.[18] A report of 1536 gives a favourable picture of the priory. It then contained, besides the prior, 8 canons, of whom 6 were priests; the canons were virtuous and discreet, all desirous of continuing in religion, and skilled at writing, embroidery, and painting. There were 2 old people living in the priory, besides a corrodiary. As servants there were 20 yeomen, 14 children for the chapel, and 3 women for the dairy. The house was in good repair, and much building had been done in the past three years. The priory stood in a wilderness,[19] and refreshed many poor folk and travellers.[20]

Thomas Cromwell was asked to intercede with the king on behalf of the house, which was stated to enjoy a good reputation locally.[21] In 1536 the prior received a grant of continuance, on payment of £166. 13s. 4d.,[22] and it was not until September 1539 that the surrender of Ulverscroft was taken by Dr. London. The priory then contained the prior, six canons, and a novice. The prior was granted a pension of £20 a year, while the canons received pensions of from £6 to £5. 6s. 8d. each, and the novice one of £2.[23] The First Minister's Account shows a total net revenue of £60. 13s. 5½d.[24] The property of the house at the Dissolution included the churches of Syston and Bunny.[25]

PRIORS OF ULVERSCROFT

William, occurs 1174.[26]
Walter, occurs about 1230.[27]
Thomas, resigned 1268.[28]
William of Spondon, admitted 1268,[29] became a Franciscan 1276.[30]
Robert of Gaddesby, admitted 1276,[31] occurs 1288.[32]

---

[3] B.M. Harl. Chart. 111, A6. This document has been printed, not quite accurately, in Nichols, *Leics.* iii, 1085. It implies that Ulverscroft had existed for 40 years before 1174, but this is no doubt a round number.

[4] *Rot. Hugonis de Welles*, ed. W. P. W. Phillimore, i, 255.

[5] B.M. Harl. Chart. 111, A6; Nichols, *Leics.* iii, 1085.   [6] Ibid.

[7] *Cur. Reg. R.*, 1207–9, 158; *Reg. of Walter Giffard* (Surtees Soc. cix), ed. Wm. Brown, 262.

[8] *Reg. of Wm. Wickwane* (Surtees Soc. cxiv), ed. Wm. Brown, 70.   [9] *Cal. Pat.*, 1321–4, 351.

[10] Ibid. *1358–61*, 572. In 1337 licence was granted to Hen. de Ferrers to alienate the advowson of Rothley ('Rothele'), Leics., to the priory, which was licensed to appropriate the ch.: *Cal. Pat.*, 1334–8, 427. Rothley ch., however, was appropriated to the Templars in 1240, and by 1341 was in possession of their successors, the Hospitallers. Ulverscroft can never have obtained the advowson: A. Hamilton Thompson, 'The Vicars of Rothley', *T.L.A.S.* xii, 122–5.

[11] *Cal. Pat.*, 1343–5, 475; G. F. Farnham, *Charnwood Forest and its Historians*, 120.

[12] *Rot. Hugonis de Welles*, i, 255.

[13] *Visitations of Religious Houses in the Dioc. of Linc.* [1420–49], ed. A. Hamilton Thompson, iii, 385–9.

[14] See the account of Charley, p. 23.

[15] *Visitations in Dioc. Linc. 1517–31*, ed. A. Hamilton Thompson, iii, 116.

[16] *L. & P. Hen. VIII*, vii, p. 473.

[17] *Valor Eccl.* (Rec. Com.), iv, 175.

[18] *L. & P. Hen. VIII*, x, p. 515.

[19] Charnwood Forest.

[20] *L. & P. Hen. VIII*, x, p. 496.

[21] Nichols, *Leics.* iii, 1087.

[22] Ibid.; *L. & P. Hen. VIII*, xii (1), p. 144; xiii (2), p. 177.

[23] Ibid. xiv (1), p. 51.

[24] S.C. 6/Hen. VIII/7311, mm. 19–24.

[25] Ibid.; *Valor Eccl.* (Rec. Com.), iv, 174.

[26] B.M. Harl. Chart. 111, A6.

[27] Ibid. 112, C27; Nichols, *Leics.* iii, 1085.

[28] *Rot. Ric. Gravesend*, ed. F. N. Davis, 148.

[29] Ibid.   [30] Ibid. 159.   [31] Ibid.

[32] Farnham, *Charnwood Forest*, 120.

John of Normanton, elected and resigned 1304.[33]

Walter of Evesham, elected 1304,[34] resigned 1315.[35]

Roger of Glen, elected 1315,[36] died 1338.[37]

Roger of Shepshed, elected 1338,[38] occurs to 1367.[39]

Thomas of Lockington, died 1387.[40]

John Ruydyngton, elected 1387,[41] occurs 1395.[42]

John Annesley, occurs 1433,[43] resigned 1439.[44]

John Pollesworth, admitted 1439,[45] occurs 1450.[46]

John Whatton, occurs from 1466 to 1492.[47]

Robert Whaton, occurs 1492 or 1493.[48]

William Shepeston, occurs from 1502 to 1511.[49]

Geoffrey Whalley, occurs 1524.[50]

William Bradebern, occurs 1525.[51]

Edward Dalby, occurs 1534,[52] surrendered the priory, 1539.[53]

Three seals of Ulverscroft Priory are known. The earliest[54] is a circular seal of the 12th century, 2 in. in diameter, showing the Virgin Mary crowned and seated on a canopied throne, holding the infant Jesus on her left knee, and a sceptre in her right hand. On each side of the throne is an angel, and in the base of the design, under an arch, is an ecclesiastic kneeling. The legend reads:

S' CANONICORŪ SCE MARIE DE ULVISCROFT

A 13th-century seal[55] of the priory is of a very similar design, but without angels. This seal is an oval, 1¾ by 1 in. The legend has been broken away.

Another oval seal,[56] measuring 1⅝ by 1⅛ in.,

of the 15th century is of like design. All that remains of the legend is:

SIGILLŪ . . . . DE ULVISCROFT

7. THE ABBEY OF OWSTON

The abbey of St. Andrew at Owston was founded, before 1161,[1] by Robert Grimbald, whose foundation charter provided that the canons of Owston should live according to the rule of Haghmon Abbey (Salop).[2] Haghmon seems to have followed the usual form of the rule of St. Augustine, and there is no reason to suppose that Owston was not an Augustinian house of the usual type.[3] The only endowments mentioned in the foundation charter are the vill and church of Owston.[4] In addition, the abbey acquired before 1166 the churches of Burrough, King's Norton, and Slawston (Leics.), North Witham (Lincs.), and Tickencote (Rut.).[5] Henry II granted the church of Medbourne (Leics.) to the canons of Owston, but the church was only to pass to them on the death of the incumbent. The canons never seem to have been able to exercise their right of presenting to Medbourne, and after Henry III had refused in 1253 to confirm the advowson to them, their rights in the church were lost.[6] A moiety of the advowson of Withcote (Leics.) was given to the abbey by Walter of Norton, probably in the late 12th century.[7] In 1203 the Abbot of Owston laid claim to the advowson of Gumley, but was forced to give way.[8] It seems unlikely that during the 13th century the canons of Owston themselves served any of the parish churches in the gift of the abbey. About 1220

[33] Linc. Reg. Dalderby, Inst., ff. 202a, 210a.

[34] Ibid., f. 210a; Reg. Dalderby, Memo., f. 289a.

[35] Ibid.

[36] Ibid.

[37] Linc. Reg. Burghersh, Inst., f. 154b.

[38] Ibid.

[39] Farnham, Charnwood Forest, 120.

[40] Linc. Reg. Buckingham, Inst. ii, f. 207b.

[41] Ibid.

[42] Farnham, Charnwood Forest, 120.

[43] Ibid. 106.

[44] Visitations in Dioc. Linc. [1420–49], i, 165; iii, 389.

[45] Ibid.

[46] Cal. Close, 1447–54, 244.

[47] Nichols, Leics. iii, 122; Farnham, Charnwood Forest, 121.

[48] Leic. Boro. Rec., 1327–1509, 337–9.

[49] Farnham, Charnwood Forest, 121–2.

[50] L. & P. Hen. VIII, iv (1), p. 195.

[51] G. F. Farnham, 'Rothley; the Descent of the Manor', T.L.A.S. xii, 92.

[52] L. & P. Hen. VIII, vii, p. 473.

[53] Ibid. xiv (2), p. 51.

[54] B.M. Seals, lxvi, 77.

[55] Ibid. 79.

[56] Ibid. 78.

[1] Gifts to the abbey were confirmed by Abp. Theobald of Cant. who died in 1161: Doc. Illustrative of Social and Econ. Hist. of Danelaw, ed. F. M. Stenton, 316–17.

[2] Dugd. Mon. vi, 424; Nichols, Leics. ii, App., 145.

[3] Owston is referred to as an Augustinian house in a charter of Robert de Chesney, Bp. of Linc.: Dugd. Mon. vi, 424.

[4] Ibid.; Nichols, Leics. ii, App., 145.

[5] See the confirmation charter by Robert, Bp. of Linc., in Nichols, op. cit. ii, App., 145, and Dugd. Mon. vi, 424. The grantor must be de Chesney, not Grosseteste, as the wording of the charter implies that it was granted in Grimbald's lifetime. It is uncertain by whom these chs. were granted. There is a copy of a charter of Grimbald granting North Witham ch. to Owston, but Ernald de Bosco also granted half the advowson of North Witham to the abbey: Dugd. Mon. loc. cit.

[6] Cal. Chart. R., 1226–57, 420–1; Abbrev. Plac. (Rec. Com.), 105; Bracton's Note Bk., ed. Maitland, ii, 231; Nichols, op. cit. ii, App., 146.

[7] G. F. Farnham and A. Hamilton Thompson, 'Hist. of the Manor of Withcote', Assoc. Arch. Soc. Rep. and Papers, xxxvi, 130–1; Rot. Hugonis de Welles, i, 268.

[8] Abbrev. Plac. (Rec. Com.), 41.

the church of Owston itself was being served by a secular clerk, who ate at the canons' table.[9]

Owston obtained some modest additions to its early endowments. Slawston church was appropriated before 1258,[10] and the church of King's Norton in 1340–1.[11] The manor of Muston (Leics.) was obtained, probably in or shortly after 1341, as the endowment of a chantry in the conventual church.[12] About the same date Robert de Colville granted the manor of Normanton (Leics.) to Owston in return for the abbey's undertaking to find two secular chaplains to celebrate at Bytham Castle.[13] Despite its rank as an abbey, however, Owston remained one of the smaller and poorer Augustinian houses.

When the abbey was visited by Bishop Alnwick in 1440 no serious faults were disclosed, though one of the fifteen occupants was out of his wits. The poverty of the house is shown by the statement, made at this visitation, that its net revenues amounted to only £40 yearly, and that it was a hundred marks in debt.[14] At another visitation, in 1518, it was said that the canons were in the habit of drinking and gossiping after compline, but no more serious defects were found. At that time it was permissible for Owston parish church to be served either by a secular clerk or by a canon.[15] In 1526, and again in 1530, the parish church was in fact being served by a canon of the abbey.[16] The record of a visitation of 1528 shows that there was then a certain amount of friction amongst the canons, while the abbot complained that women came into the abbey. It was further said that there were only four priests in the house, and the abbot was ordered to increase the number of canons by four.[17]

The Abbot of Owston, with eleven canons, ac-

knowledged the royal supremacy over the Church in 1534.[18] In the next year the abbey's clear yearly income was assessed at only £161. 14s. 2d.,[19] and the house was therefore listed amongst the smaller religious houses.[20] It was reported in 1536 that there were in the abbey only the abbot and six canons, of whom one was very old and one mad. All desired to give up monastic life. The buildings of the house were well constructed but in an unfinished state.[21] The abbey was dissolved in 1536, the abbot receiving a pension of £18.[22] The First Minister's Account shows a total net revenue of £86. 0s. 3¾d.[23]

ABBOTS OF OWSTON

Odo, occurs in or before 1161.[24]

Edward, occurs 1183–4.[25]

Ralph, occurs 1202.[26]

Richard, admitted 1236.[27]

Peter of Leycestre, elected 1241,[28] died 1264.[29]

William of Flamstead, elected 1264,[30] died 1268.[31]

Ivo of Cosseby, elected 1268,[32] resigned 1280.[33]

John Chaumberleyn, elected 1280,[34] resigned 1284.[35]

Ivo of Cosseby, elected 1284,[36] resigned 1286.[37]

Robert of Lincoln, elected 1286,[38] died 1289.[39]

Ernald of Slawston, elected 1289,[40] died 1298.[41]

Richard of Bokesworth, elected 1298,[42] died 1316.[43]

Robert of Staunford, elected 1316,[44] resigned 1322.[45]

William of Braunston, elected 1322.[46]

John of Kibbeworth, occurs 1344,[47] died 1355.[48]

---

[9] *Rot. Hugonis de Welles*, i, 275.

[10] *Reg. Antiquissimum of the Cath. Ch. of Linc.*, ed. C. W. Foster, ii, 103.

[11] *Cal. Pat.*, *1338–40*, 546; *1340–3*, 230.

[12] Nichols, *Leics.* ii, App., 146, no. 12. A doc. concerning the transfer of the manor to Owston is dated 1371: Hist. MSS. Com., *Rutland*, iv, 15–16. It may have been drawn up long after the transfer had taken place. The abbey's lands in Muston were sold in 1493: Nichols, op. cit. ii, App., 146–7.

[13] Ibid. 146; Hist. MSS. Com., *Rutland*, iv, 16.

[14] *Visitations in Dioc. Linc.* [1420–49], ed. A. Hamilton Thompson, iii, 264–5.

[15] *Visitations in Dioc. Linc.*, *1517–31*, ed. A. Hamilton Thompson, iii, 44.

[16] Ibid. iii, 45, n. 4; A. P. Moore, 'Proc. Eccl. Cts. in the Archdeaconry of Leic.', *Assoc. Arch. Soc. Rep. and Papers*, xxviii, 153.

[17] *Visitations in Dioc. Linc.*, *1517–31*, iii, 45–47; in 1528 there were ten in the abbey, including the abbot.

[18] *L. & P. Hen. VIII*, vii, p. 472.

[19] *Valor Eccl.* (Rec. Com.), iv, 158.

[20] *L. & P. Hen. VIII*, x, p. 515.

[21] Ibid., p. 496.

[22] Ibid. xiii (1), p. 575.

[23] S.C. 6/Hen. VIII/1825, mm. 12–17.

[24] *Doc. Illustrative of Hist. of Danelaw*, 316–17.

[25] B.M. Campb. Chart. xv, 2; Add. Chart. 6104(2).

[26] Farnham, *Leics. Notes*, iii, 106.

[27] *Cal. Pat.*, *1232–41*, 151; *Rot. Roberti Grosseteste*, ed. F. N. Davis, 388. Ric. was previously precentor of Oseney.

[28] *Cal. Pat.*, *1232–41*, 256, 259.

[29] *Rot. Ric. Gravesend*, 144.

[30] *Cal. Pat.*, *1258–66*, 387.

[31] Ibid., *1266–72*, 217.

[32] Ibid., 219.

[33] Ibid., *1272–81*, 374; *Cal. Fine R.*, *1272–1307*, 127.

[34] *Cal. Pat.*, *1272–81*, 378.

[35] Ibid., *1281–92*, 146.

[36] Ibid. 147.

[37] Ibid. 229.

[38] Ibid. 230, 234.

[39] Ibid. 312.

[40] Ibid. 314; Rosalind Hill, 'Bishop Sutton and the Inst. of Heads of Religious Houses in the Dioc. of Linc.', *E.H.R.* lviii, 209.

[41] *Cal. Pat.*, *1292–1301*, 364.

[42] Ibid. 372.

[43] Ibid., *1313–17*, 470.

[44] Ibid. 480.

[45] Ibid., *1321–4*, 51.

[46] Ibid. 83.

[47] Ibid., *1343–5*, 214.

[48] Ibid., *1354–8*, 193.

William of Cottesmore, elected 1355,[49] resigned 1401.[50]

Robert of Nouesle, elected 1401,[51] resigned 1421.[52]

William Kilpesham, elected 1421,[53] died 1467.[54]

Robert Kirkeby, elected 1467,[55] resigned 1481.[56]

Henry Medban, elected 1481,[57] occurs 1497.[58]

John Belton, admitted 1504,[59] resigned 1520.[60]

John Slawston, last abbot, elected 1520.[61]

A 13th-century seal[62] of the abbey is a large vesica, $2\frac{5}{8}$ by $1\frac{3}{4}$ in., representing the crucifixion of St. Andrew by two executioners. Above the saint is a hand, in the attitude of blessing, coming out of clouds, between a sun and a moon. In the base an abbot with his crosier kneels before an altar. The legend is:

SIGILL' ECCL'IE SCI A . . . . E APL'I OSOLVESTON'

Of Abbot Nouesle's seal[63] only the upper half has survived. It shows an abbot standing in a niche, holding a crosier and a book. When complete, the seal must have been an oval, measuring about $1\frac{3}{4}$ by $1\frac{1}{8}$ in.

8. THE PRIORY OF CHARLEY

The circumstances of the foundation of the small Augustinian priory at Charley, in Charnwood Forest, are unknown. The first definite mention of the house occurs in 1190, when the Countess Parnel of Leicester gave to the Norman abbey of St. Évroul, Orne, the house of Charley, with a carucate at Anstey, on condition that the prior whom the abbot should appoint to Charley should be left undisturbed while he continued to be of good life.[1] The gift of Charley was confirmed, between 1203 and 1206, to the Prior of Ware,

the subordinate in England of the Abbot of St. Évroul.[2] About 1220 the priory was described as a hermitage where there were usually three brothers. Its patron was the Earl of Winchester,[3] and it was apparently independent.[4] There is no definite evidence that Charley was then an Augustinian house, and it may still have been a hermitage not subject to any definite rule. At a later date it was certainly Augustinian,[5] and its priors were sometimes drawn from other houses of that Order.[6] The priory possessed the advowson of Ratcliffe on the Wreak by about 1220.[7] In 1291 the house's temporalities were valued at only £9. 2s. $9\frac{1}{2}d$.[8] A licence was granted in 1307 for the alienation in mortmain to Charley of the advowson of Markfield (Leics.), and of 30 acres of land near Charley.[9] The title to the advowson was disputed,[10] and in 1327 the Prior of Charley seems to have been forced to abandon his claim to it.[11]

Information concerning the internal life of the priory is scanty. In 1285 the prior and one of the canons were accused of robbery.[12] When the prior, Thomas of Evesham, resigned in 1298 and became a Cistercian, the bishop refused to confirm the election of Robert of Radcliffe as his successor.[13] In 1444 Bishop Alnwick, hearing that the Prior of Charley was neglecting the celebration of the divine offices and spending his time in taverns, while the buildings of the priory were lapsing into ruin, and its resources being wasted, ordered an inquiry into the state of affairs at Charley. The results of the investigation are not recorded, but the prior resigned shortly afterwards.[14] It was stated in 1444 that there was danger of the priory ceasing to exist,[15] and in 1465 Sir John Bourchier and his wife, as patrons, petitioned the Bishop of Lincoln to unite the priory with the adjacent Augustinian house of Ulverscroft.[16] This plan was apparently carried

---

49 Ibid. 201. 50 Ibid., *1401–5*, 18.

51 Ibid. 25, 27.

52 *Visitations in Dioc. Linc.* [1420–49], i, 91–92.

53 Ibid. i, 91–92; iii, 264.

54 *Cal. Pat.*, *1467–77*, 23.

55 Ibid. He is said to have been prior of Kirkeby, and to have been an Augustinian, but cannot have been Prior of Kirby Bellars. See list, p. 26.

56 *Cal. Pat.*, *1476–85*, 280.

57 Ibid. 288. Formerly Prior of Bradley.

58 Hist. MSS. Com., *Rutland*, iv, 15.

59 E. 326/12544.

60 *Visitations in Dioc. Linc.*, *1517–31*, iii, 45; *L. & P. Hen. VIII*, iii, p. 375.

61 *L. & P. Hen. VIII*, iii, p. 375; *Visitations in Dioc. Linc.*, *1517–31*, iii, 45; *Valor Eccl.* (Rec. Com.), iv, 158.

62 B.M. Seals, lxvi, 75. 63 Ibid. 74.

1 *Cal. Doc. France*, ed. Round, 228. The *locus Sanctae Mariae de Charleia* was confirmed to Luffield Priory in 1174: Dugd. *Mon.* iv, 349. If the place concerned was the Leics. Charley, the connexion with Luffield was not permanent.

2 *Cal. Doc. France*, 227.

3 The Earl of Winchester had inherited some of the lands of the Earls of Leic.: L. Fox, 'The Honour of Leicester. Origin and Descent', *E.H.R.* liv, 393.

4 *Rot. Hugonis de Welles*, ed. W. P. W. Phillimore, i, 255.

5 *Chapters of the Augustinian Canons*, ed. H. E. Salter, 102, 271, 277.

6 *Cal. Pat.*, *1381–5*, 157; *Visitations of Religious Houses in the Dioc. of Linc.* [1420–49], ed. A. Hamilton Thompson, i, 163.

7 *Rot. Hugonis de Welles*, i, 259.

8 *Tax. Eccl.* (Rec. Com.), 69.

9 *Cal. Pat.*, *1307–13*, 14.

10 Farnham, *Leics. Notes*, vi, 359, 360.

11 *Cal. Close*, *1327–30*, 80–81.

12 *Cal. Pat.*, *1281–92*, 102.

13 Rosalind Hill, 'Bishop Sutton and the Inst. of Heads of Religious Houses in the Dioc. of Linc.', *E.H.R.* lviii, 290.

14 *Visitations in Dioc. Linc.* [1420–49], iii, 390.

15 Ibid.

16 Linc. Reg. Chedworth, Memo., ff. 80–81.

out shortly afterwards.[17] Mass continued to be celebrated yearly at Charley on Easter Day.[18]

PRIORS OF CHARLEY

William, occurs early 13th century.[19]

Simon, resigned 1264.[20]

Robert of Grimesby, elected 1264,[21] resigned 1272.[22]

John of Bawtry, elected 1272,[23] occurs 1283.[24]

Stephen of Keyham, resigned 1291.[25]

Thomas of Evesham, admitted 1291,[26] resigned 1298.[27]

Robert of Radcliffe, elected 1298, but confirmation refused by the bishop.[28]

John of Bawtry, admitted 1298,[29] resigned 1309.[30]

William of Segrave, elected 1309,[31] died 1318.[32]

William of Leicester, elected 1318.[33]

Henry of Stratford, resigned 1335.[34]

Roger, occurs 1371 and 1386.[35]

Richard Haitlee, presented 1382.[36]

John atte Well, occurs before 1390.[37]

Ralph, occurs 1390.[38]

John Ince, admitted 1414,[39] occurs 1418.[40]

John Botyler, admitted 1422.[41]

John Belton, resigned 1444.[42]

John Whitewyk, admitted 1444.[43]

Thomas Frisby, resigned 1458.[44]

John Zouche, admitted 1458.[45]

No seal is known.

9. THE PRIORY OF BRADLEY

Neither the date nor the circumstances of the foundation of Bradley Priory are known. According to Leland, it was founded by Robert Bundy.[1] The priory is first mentioned in 1233–4, when Robert de Burnebi was the patron,[2] and it is possible that he may have been the founder. The priory is not referred to in the *Matriculus* of the Archdeaconry of Leicester (c. 1220),[3] so that the priory was probably founded between 1220 and 1234. The original endowment has not been recorded, though in 1317 it was stated that a windmill at Holt had belonged to Bradley Priory since its foundation.[4] In 1385 Lord Scrope of Bolton, with Thomas Shepesheved, a former rector of Allexton, granted to the priory the manor of Blaston,[5] and in 1392 Scrope obtained licence to grant some further small items of property to Bradley.[6] Leland describes Scrope as the *fundator modernus* of Bradley,[7] and he seems to have been its principal benefactor. In 1503 John Penny, Abbot of Leicester and from 1505 Bishop of Bangor also, became Prior of Bradley, but after Penny's translation to the see of Carlisle, Lord Scrope, as patron, presented a canon of Bradley, who was admitted as prior at the beginning of 1509.[8] In 1535 the priory's possessions consisted of land in the villages of Blaston, Slawston, Holt, and Holyoak, all adjacent to Bradley. The net yearly income of the house was only just over £20.[9] In 1535 it was reported that there were only two canons at Bradley; both were of virtuous conversation, and desired to continue in religion. The house had five servants, and a child was supported in the almonry. The buildings of the priory were in good repair.[10] Very shortly afterwards the priory was dissolved. The prior was granted a pension of £4 yearly.[11]

Bradley was probably at all times a very small monastery. There seems to be no doubt that it was a house of Augustinian canons of the normal type. In 1535 the prior stated that he and his companions were 'white canons of St. Augustine',[12] but canons of well-known Augustinian houses became priors of Bradley,[13] and one Prior of Bradley became abbot of the Augustinian abbey of Owston.[14] The colour of the habits worn by Augustinian canons

[17] Nichols, *Leics.* iii, 121.

[18] Ibid. 1091.

[19] Ibid. 120; Hist. MSS. Com., *Hastings*, i, 12.

[20] *Rot. Ric. Gravesend*, ed. F. N. Davis, 143.

[21] Ibid.   [22] Ibid. 153.

[23] Ibid.

[24] *Cal. Pat., 1281–92*, 102.

[25] *E.H.R.* lviii, 290.

[26] Ibid.   [27] Ibid.

[28] Ibid.

[29] Ibid. Probably the same person as the prior elected in 1272.

[30] Linc. Reg. Dalderby, Inst., f. 204b.

[31] Ibid.

[32] Ibid. 218a.

[33] Ibid.

[34] Linc. Reg. Burghersh, Memo., f. 291b.

[35] *Cal. Pat., 1370–4*, 140; G. F. Farnham, *Charnwood Forest and its Historians*, 86.

[36] *Cal. Pat., 1381–5*, 157.

[37] Farnham, *Charnwood Forest*, 86.

[38] Ibid.

[39] *Visitations in Dioc. Linc.* [1420–49], i, 163.

[40] *Cat. Anct. D.* iii, D1301.

[41] *Visitations in Dioc. Linc.* [1420–49], i, 163.

[42] Ibid. i, 163; iii, 390.

[43] Ibid. iii, 388, n. 4.

[44] Linc. Reg. Chedworth, Inst., f. 97b.

[45] Ibid.

[1] J. Leland, *Collect.* (1770), i, 74.

[2] *Rot. Hugonis de Welles*, ed. W. P. W. Phillimore, ii, 324–5.

[3] Ibid. i, 238–72.

[4] *Cal. Close, 1313–18*, 502.

[5] Nichols, *Leics.* ii, 446.

[6] *Cal. Pat., 1391–6*, 157.

[7] Leland, *Collect.* (1770), i, 74.

[8] A. Hamilton Thompson, *The Abbey of St. Mary of the Meadows, Leic.* 74.

[9] *Valor Eccl.* (Rec. Com.), iv, 159.

[10] *L. & P. Hen. VIII*, x, p. 496.

[11] Ibid. xiii (1), p. 575.

[12] Ibid. x, p. 496.

[13] *Rot. Ric. Gravesend*, ed. F. N. Davis, 143; Linc. Reg. Repingdon, Inst., f. 180b.

[14] *Cal. Pat., 1476–85*, 288.

seems to have varied.[15] The First Minister's Account shows a net revenue of £9. 14s. 5½d.[16]

PRIORS OF BRADLEY

Robert, elected 1233–4.[17]

Henry, appointed by the Bishop of Lincoln, 1263.[18]

Walter of Drayton, confirmed 1290, resigned 1295.[19]

John of Kirkby, confirmed 1295.[20]

Walter of Drayton, elected 1300,[21] deprived 1302.[22]

John of Quorndon, elected 1302,[23] occurs 1309.[24]

Richard of Brownknave,[25] elected 1381.[26]

Richard Chanon,[25] occurs 1389.[27]

Richard Stokes,[25] resigned 1393.[28]

William Wenge, elected 1393,[29] died 1415.[30]

John Coventry, elected 1415.[31]

Henry Medburn, resigned 1481.[32]

Thomas Leicester, died 1493.[33]

Thomas Horninghold, elected 1493,[34] resigned 1503.[35]

John Penny, Abbot of Leicester, admitted 1503, resigned 1508.[36]

John Oundle, confirmed 1509,[37] last prior.[38]

No seal is known.

10. KIRBY BELLAIRS[1]

The first step towards the foundation of Kirby Bellairs Priory was taken in 1316, when Sir Roger Beler[2] granted 4 messuages, 4 virgates, and certain revenues, all at Kirby Bellairs, to a chaplain, who was with a second chaplain provided by himself to celebrate daily in the chapel of St. Peter at Kirby, for the souls of Roger Beler, his wife Alice, and others.[3] This modest chantry was soon enlarged. In 1318 or 1319 Roger granted to the chantry the manor of Buckminster, the advowson of Kirby Bellairs,[4] and other property.[5] In 1319 the chaplains were granted exemption from aids, tallages, and other royal levies.[6] The chantry also acquired two-thirds of the advowson of Clipston (Northants.)[7] and the advowson of Stapleford (Leics.), with licence to appropriate Stapleford church.[8] As established in 1319 the chantry, with these additional endowments, was to consist of a warden and twelve chaplains.[9] Thirteen separate freehold benefices were created for the warden and chaplains, and the patronage of the benefices was divided between several patrons, of whom the Dean and Chapter of Lincoln were the most important.[10] Careful regulations were made for the common life of the warden and chaplains,[11] and for the celebration of the divine offices.[12] After Roger Beler's murder, in 1326,[13] difficulties arose through the continual changes which took place amongst the chaplains disturbing the orderly celebration of services, and in 1359 the college of secular clergy was transformed into an Augustinian priory, with a prior and twelve canons.[14] The regular canons would, of course, be unable to leave their house in the way that the secular canons had been able to do. Roger Beler's heirs were the patrons of the priory.[15]

The priory was granted licence, in 1363, to transfer its share of the advowson of Clipston to the Hospitallers, and at the same time the priory was authorized to appropriate the church of Buckminster, which was acquired from the

15 Dugd. Mon. vi, 852.

16 S.C. 6/Hen. VIII/1825, m. 1.

17 Rot. Hugonis de Welles, ii, 324–5.

18 Rot. Ric. Gravesend, ed. F. N. Davis, 143.

19 Rosalind Hill, 'Bishop Sutton and the Inst. of Heads of Religious Houses in the Dioc. of Linc.', E.H.R. lviii, 209.

20 Ibid.

21 Linc. Reg. Dalderby, Inst., f. 196a.

22 Ibid., f. 199a.   23 Ibid.

24 Farnham, Leics. Notes, iv, 349.

25 It is possible that these 3 names were all borne by the same person.

26 Linc. Reg. Buckingham, Inst., i, f. 274b.

27 Cal. Pat., 1388–92, 170.

28 Linc. Reg. Buckingham, Inst., ii, f. 266b.

29 Ibid.

30 Linc. Reg. Repingdon, Inst., f. 180b.

31 Visitations of Religious Houses in the Dioc. of Linc. [1420–49], ed. A. Hamilton Thompson, i, 163.

32 He became Abbot of Owston: Cal. Pat., 1476–85, 288.

33 Linc. Reg. Russell, Inst., f. 97b.

34 Ibid.

35 Linc. Reg. Smith, Inst., f. 277b.

36 Hamilton Thompson, Abbey of Leic. 74.

37 Ibid.; Linc. Reg. Smith, Inst., f. 292a.

38 Nichols, Leics. ii, 510.

1 For an account of the coll. of secular clerks at Kirby, see A. Hamilton Thompson, 'The Chapel of St. Peter at Kirkby-upon-Wreak', T.L.A.S. xvi, 130–212.

2 For his career, see D.N.B.

3 Cal. Pat., 1313–17, 438; T.L.A.S. xvi, 153–65.

4 Kirby Bellairs ch. was appropriated almost at once: ibid. xvi, 144, 149, 192–3.

5 Ibid. xvi, 135, 167; Cal. Pat., 1317–21, 392; Farnham, Leics. Notes, iii, 113.

6 Cal. Pat., 1317–21, 340.

7 Ibid., 1321–4, 355.

8 Ibid., 1324–7, 158; Farnham, Leics. Notes, v, 365. Stapleford was appropriated by 1335: Cat. Anct. D. ii, B1927.

9 T.L.A.S. xvi, 143; Dugd. Mon. vi, 512; Cal. Chart. R., 1341–1417, 164–5.

10 T.L.A.S. xvi, 144.

11 Ibid. 171–5.

12 Ibid. 177–80.

13 Cal. Pat., 1324–7, 250, 283; Farnham, Leics. Notes, iii, 117–18.

14 Cal. Chart. R., 1341–1417, 164–5; T.L.A.S. xvi, 150–1, 207–12. The first prior was a former Prior of Owston Abbey: Hen. Knighton, Chron. (Rolls Ser.), i, 432.

15 Cal. Close, 1381–5, 173; ibid. 1389–92, 393; Farnham, Leics. Notes, iii, 123–4, 126.

Hospitallers in exchange for Clipston.[16] The appropriation was duly carried out.[17] In 1392 royal licences were obtained for the alienation to Kirby Bellairs of the advowson of Garthorp, with some other property,[18] and in 1412 licence was similarly granted for the priory to acquire the advowson of Twyford, and to appropriate the church.[19] The rectories of both Twyford and Garthorp were subsequently appropriated.[20]

When visited by Bishop Alnwick in 1440, the priory was found to be in a satisfactory state; the bishop only found it necessary to correct minor faults in the canons' dress and in their celebration of the divine offices. There was then the full number of thirteen canons, including the prior, in the house.[21] In 1511 the prior and convent were authorized to declare indulgences and collect gifts, as their monastery was in great decay and its buildings had been destroyed by fire.[22] When the priory was visited by the bishop's commissary in 1518 the buildings still needed repair. At the same time the sub-prior was found to be possessed of private property, two of the canons were suspected of immorality, and there were complaints about the food provided for the canons.[23] At another visitation, ten years later, it was disclosed that the canons were in the habit of going out of the priory singly to take exercise.[24] In 1536, however, it was reported that the prior and the eight[25] canons of the house were all of good conversation, though two wished to return to secular life, and that the priory buildings were in good repair.[26] As the clear yearly revenue was assessed at little more than £140 in 1535,[27] the priory was dissolved, with the other small monasteries, in 1536; the prior obtained a pension of £17.[28] One of the canons of Kirby Bellairs went to Launde,[29] which as one of the larger religious houses continued to exist for some time. The First Minister's Account shows a total net revenue of £50. 3s. 11½d.[30]

WARDENS OF THE COLLEGE

William Spigurnel, first warden,[31] occurs 1319.[32]
John Cosyn.[33]
John of Kirby, died 1338.[34]
Edmund of Coston, presented 1338,[35] died 1359.[36]
Roger Wiseman, presented and removed, 1359.[37]

PRIORS OF KIRBY BELLAIRS

Roger of Cotes, appointed 1359.[38]
Alexander Thurgarton, occurs 1416, died 1418 or 1419.[39]
Henry Dalby, elected 1419,[40] occurs to 1444.[41]
William Leicester, resigned 1461.[42]
William Burton, elected 1461,[43] died 1480.[44]
William Kirby, elected 1480,[45] died 1488.[46]
Richard Sewstern, elected 1488,[47] died 1526.[48]
Thomas Kirby, elected 1526.[49]
William Kyrkeby, last prior, occurs 1534 and 1535.[50]

Two seals of the priory, both of them vesicas of the 14th century, are known. One[51] shows St. Peter, the patron saint of the house, wearing a mitre and seated on a canopied throne. The saint's right hand is raised in blessing, while in his left he holds the keys. In the lower part of the seal is a shield bearing the arms of Sir Roger Beler, the founder. The seal measures 2½ by 1½ in. The legend reads:

S' ECCLESIE BEATI P . . . KIRKEBI SUPER WRETHEK

The other seal[52] shows a standing figure holding a staff and book, with the legend:

SIGILLUM PRIORIS DE KIRKEBI

The seal measures 1⅜ by 1 in.

[16] *Cal. Pat., 1361–4*, 351.
[17] *Valor Eccl.* (Rec. Com.), iv, 149.
[18] *Cal. Pat., 1391–6*, 140–1, 151.
[19] Ibid., *1408–13*, 409.
[20] *Valor Eccl.* (Rec. Com.), iv, 139.
[21] *Visitations of Religious Houses in the Dioc. of Linc.* [1420–49], ed. A. Hamilton Thompson, ii, 164–8.
[22] *L. & P. Hen. VIII*, i (2nd ed.), p. 473.
[23] *Visitations in Dioc. Linc., 1517–31*, ed. A. Hamilton Thompson, ii, 174–5.
[24] Ibid. 176.
[25] In 1534 there had been 9 canons, besides the prior: *L. & P. Hen. VIII*, vii, p. 473.
[26] Ibid. x, p. 496.
[27] *Valor Eccl.* (Rec. Com.), iv, 149.
[28] *L. & P. Hen. VIII*, xiii (1), p. 575.
[29] Ibid. xiii (2), p. 470.
[30] S.C. 6/Hen. VIII/1825, mm. 3–8.
[31] *T.L.A.S.* xvi, 194.
[32] *Cal. Pat., 1317–21*, 394.
[33] *Cal. Close, 1369–74*, 2; Farnham, *Leics. Notes,*
iii, 121. The dates of this warden's rule are unknown.
[34] *T.L.A.S.* xvi, 194.
[35] Ibid.
[36] Ibid. 195.
[37] Ibid. 195, 209.
[38] Ibid. 209.
[39] *Visitations in Dioc. Linc.* [1420–49], i, 164; Farnham, *Leics. Notes*, iv, 147.
[40] Ibid.
[41] *Cat. Anct. Deeds*, ii, B3241.
[42] Linc. Reg. Chedworth, Inst., f. 100a.
[43] Ibid.
[44] Linc. Reg. Russell, Inst., f. 80b.
[45] Ibid.
[46] Ibid., f. 92a.
[47] Ibid.
[48] Linc. Reg. Longland, Inst., f. 136b.
[49] Ibid.
[50] *L. & P. Hen. VIII*, vii, p. 473; *Valor Eccl.* (Rec. Com.), iv, 149.
[51] B.M. Seals, lxvi, 54.
[52] Ibid. 55.

11. THE PRIORY OF GRACE DIEU

The Priory of Grace Dieu at Belton was founded by Rose de Verdon for Austin nuns between 1235[1] and 1241, and endowed with the manor and advowson of Belton, and the manor of Kirkby in Kesteven.[2] In the early days of the house there was anxiety about both its spiritual state and its material possessions, and the well-known Franciscan, Adam Marsh, intervened on behalf of the priory, writing to the Bishop of Lincoln, the Archdeacon of Leicester, and others.[3] An agreement concluded between John de Verdon, son of the foundress, and the convent, provided that the nuns should not elect a prioress without the patron's licence, and that the patron should have the right of presenting the prioress-elect to the bishop.[4] The life of the nuns at Grace Dieu seems to have had some special features; they were forbidden ever to leave the precincts of the priory,[5] while shortly before the Dissolution they described themselves as 'White Nuns of St. Augustine', and thought that there was no other house of their own Order in England.[6] There is no evidence that Grace Dieu was ever connected with any of the separate congregations which lived under the Augustinian rule, and it seems probable that the peculiarities of Grace Dieu were merely especial customs of the house.

The priory obtained some additions to the endowments originally given by its foundress. Amice de Freschenville gave lands at Staveley Woodthorp (Derbys.), to provide for the nuns' clothing,[7] and in 1306 the Earl of Buchan obtained a licence to grant a hundred acres at Whitwick to Grace Dieu.[8] Belton church was appropriated to the priory before 1270.[9] The priory also obtained the manors of Houghton (Northants.), Great Limber (Lincs.), and Harby (Notts.).[10]

There is some information about the state of the nunnery during the 15th century. A surviving account book of the priory for the years from 1414 to 1418 gives some insight into the life of the nuns.[11] There were at that time fourteen nuns at Grace Dieu, besides several daughters from local families lodging there. The nuns were each allowed 6s. 8d. a year for clothing. The priory possessed a considerable quantity of live-stock, though much of its land at Belton was evidently rented out. The accounts mention the names of twenty-two male and eight female servants. A less attractive picture of the priory is given in the record of Bishop Alnwick's visitation at the beginning of 1441.[12] The prioress was accused of favouritism, and of failing to render account of the convent's affairs to the other nuns. The cellaress was said to be too familiar with the convent's chaplain, to be very lax in her attendance in choir, and to manage all the priory's affairs without consulting others. The infirmary was in a bad state of repair. The priory had previously been £48 in debt, and in 1441 it was still in debt for £38. The bishop issued injunctions designed to remedy the faults disclosed. In 1441 the number of nuns was again fourteen. Grace Dieu was visited by the bishop's commissary in 1518, when complaints were made by several nuns about minor defects in the management of the house.[13] At a visitation by the chancellor of the diocese in 1528 there were again fourteen nuns present. Nothing requiring correction was found.[14]

The clear yearly income of the house was assessed at about £92 in 1535.[15] In the following year Dr. Legh and Dr. Layton reported that the nuns reverenced the girdle and part of the tunic of St. Francis, and accused two of the nuns of incontinence.[16] A commission of the local gentry, however, visiting the convent in the same year, stated that the fifteen nuns there were virtuous and all desired to continue in religion. Nine persons were supported by the priory's charity.

---

[1] It was evidently established during Grosseteste's episcopate: *Monumenta Franciscana* (Rolls Ser.), ed. J. S. Brewer, i, 115, 130.

[2] *Cal. Chart. R., 1226–57*, 265. There is no proof that Kirkby was given by Rose de Verdon, but as it belonged to her fee, and was in possession of the nuns by about 1243 (*Bk. of Fees*, ii, 1110), it is highly probable that she was the donor.

[3] *Monumenta Franciscana* (Rolls Ser.), i, 115, 119, 130, 197–8, 403–4.

[4] *Eccl. Doc.* (Camden Soc., 1st ser. viii), ed. Joseph Hunter, 66–67. John de Verdon inherited his mother's lands in 1247: *Excerpta e Rot. Fin.* (Rec. Com.), ii, 7, 11. He died in 1274: *Cal. Inq. p.m.* ii, p. 58. On the patron's rights during a vacancy of the priory, consisting only of the power to appoint a porter, see *Cal. Inq. Misc.* ii, p. 307, and *Cal. Close, 1318–23*, 35.

[5] *Cal. Pat., 1232–47*, 290–1; *1247–58*, 153.

[6] *L. & P. Hen. VIII*, x, p. 497.

[7] Nichols, *Leics.* iii, 651–2.

[8] *Cal. Pat., 1301–7*, 441. For some lesser gifts to the convent, see ibid. *1391–6*, 120, and Nichols, op. cit. iii, 652.

[9] *Rot. Ric. Gravesend*, ed. F. N. Davis, 151.

[10] *Valor Eccl.* (Rec. Com.), iv, 175. Great Limber was in the hands of the nuns by the late 14th century: B.M. Harl. Chart. 44 A2; *Cal. Inq. p.m.* vii, p. 356.

[11] See the description in F. A. Gasquet, *Engl. Mon. Life* (1904), 158–76.

[12] *Visitations in Dioc. Linc.* [1420–49], ed. A. Hamilton Thompson, ii, 119–29.

[13] *Visitations in Dioc. Linc., 1517–31*, ed. A. Hamilton Thompson, ii, 158–9.

[14] Ibid. ii, 159–60.

[15] *Valor Eccl.* (Rec. Com.), iv, 175.

[16] *L. & P. Hen. VIII*, x, p. 138; Nichols, *Leics.* iii, 652.

The buildings were in good repair, though not stately. There were twenty-seven male and nine female servants, about the same number as in the early 15th century.[17] The priory would have been suppressed with the other small religious houses,[18] but in August 1536 the prioress obtained a licence for the nunnery to continue its existence.[19] The priory was finally surrendered in October 1538.[20] An inventory of the convent's possessions, taken immediately after the surrender, shows that to the end some of the priory's land was being farmed under the direct control of the nuns. The same inventory mentions the church, cloister, and chapter house, with other buildings.[21] The First Minister's Account shows a gross income of £73. 11s. 8d.[22]

PRIORESSES OF GRACE DIEU

Mary of Stretton, elected 1242–3.[23]

Agnes of Gresleye, occurs 1268–9,[24] died 1286.[25]

Agnes, died 1318.[26]

Joan of Hastings, elected 1318,[27] died 1330.[28]

Joan Meinwaryng, elected 1331,[29] died 1349.[30]

Cicely of Strawley, elected 1349.[31]

Margaret of Twyford, resigned 1400.[32]

Margaret Rempston, elected 1400,[33] died 1418.[34]

Alice Dunwich, elected 1418,[35] occurs 1441.[36]

Elizabeth Shirburne, occurs 1485.[37]

Margaret Zouche, occurs 1493,[38] died 1524.[39]

Agnes Liderland, elected 1524,[40] surrendered the priory, 1538.[41]

The 13th-century seal[42] of this priory is a vesica, $2\frac{1}{8}$ by $1\frac{1}{4}$ in., having a figure of our Lord seated on His throne, blessing with His right hand, and holding a book in His left. In the base is a female figure, probably representing the priory's foundress, kneeling and holding a charter. All that remains of the legend are the words

SIGILL' CONVENT' . . . . . ALIV DE GRATIA . . .

A seal[43] of Prioress Agnes of Gresleye has a representation of the Virgin Mary on a throne, holding the infant Jesus on her left knee. The sun and moon are on either side of her head, and in the base of the seal is a kneeling nun, probably representing the prioress.. The legend has been wholly broken away. When complete, the seal would have been about $1\frac{1}{2}$ by 1 in.

HOUSE OF PREMONSTRATENSIAN CANONS

12. THE ABBEY OF CROXTON KERRIAL

The founder of the Abbey of St. John the Evangelist at Croxton was William, Count of Boulogne and Mortain,[1] who gave a site for the building of the abbey, and endowed it with the church of Croxton Kerrial,[2] and lands and pasture rights there.[3] Count William also confirmed grants to the abbey by his vassals of the Derbyshire churches of Lowne and Ault Hucknall,[4] a carucate at Nether Broughton (Leics.), and other less important possessions.[5] Although these grants must have been made before Count William's death in 1159, it seems likely that canons were not established at Croxton until 1162.[6] The new

---

[17] L. & P. Hen. VIII, x, p. 497.
[18] Ibid., p. 515.
[19] Ibid. xi, p. 156.
[20] Ibid. xiii (2), p. 268.
[21] Nichols, Leics. iii, 653.
[22] S.C. 6/Hen. VIII/7311, mm. 25–29.
[23] Rot. Roberti Grosseteste, ed. F. N. Davis, 420.
[24] Descriptive Cat. of Derbys. Chart., ed. I. H. Jeayes, 51.
[25] Rosalind Hill, 'Bishop Sutton and the Inst. of Heads of Religious Houses in the Dioc. of Linc.', E.H.R. lviii, 208.
[26] Cal. Pat., 1317–21, 134. Probably Agnes Gordon, who appears under Edw. I: Hist. MSS. Com., Hastings, i, 29.
[27] Cal. Pat., 1317–21, 136.
[28] Ibid. 1330–4, 19.
[29] Ibid. 33.
[30] Linc. Reg. Gynewell, Inst., f. 303a.
[31] Ibid.
[32] Linc. Reg. Beaufort, Inst., f. 74a.
[33] Ibid.
[34] Eccl. Doc. (Camden Soc., 1st ser. viii), 67.
[35] Ibid.
[36] Visitations in Dioc. Linc. [1420–49], ii, 119.
[37] Farnham, Leics. Notes, vi, 98.

[38] Hist. MSS. Com., Hastings, i, 33.
[39] Linc. Reg. Attwater, Inst., f. 31b.
[40] Ibid.
[41] L. & P. Hen. VIII, xiii (2), p. 268.
[42] B.M. Seals, lxvi, 53; B.M. Harl. Chart. 44, D51.
[43] B.M. Wolley Chart. vi, 28.
[1] Count from 1154 to his death in 1159.
[2] Not known as Croxton Kerrial until the 13th cent. About 1220 it was said that Croxton ch. had been appropriated since the foundation of the abbey: Rot. Hugonis de Welles, ed. W. P. W. Phillimore, i, 267.
[3] Nichols, Leics. ii, App., 77; Hist. MSS. Com., Rutland, iv, 175.
[4] Ault Hucknall ch. was lost in the early 13th century: H. M. Colvin, White Canons in Engl. 96; Cal. Papal Letters, 1198–1304, 50; A. Hamilton Thompson, 'Newstead Priory', Trans. Thoroton Soc. xxiii, 59.
[5] Nichols, Leics. ii, App., 77; Hist. MSS. Com., Rutland, iv, 175. Lowne ch. was appropriated during the episcopate of Geoffrey, Bp. of Coventry and Lich., 1198–1208: Nichols, op. cit. ii, App., 82.
[6] Colvin, White Canons in Engl. 92–93; Collect. Anglo-Premonstratensia (Camden Soc., 3rd ser. x), ed. F. A. Gasquet, ii, 153.

GRACE DIEU PRIORY FROM THE AIR

monastery was a daughter of the Premonstratensian Abbey of Newhouse.[7] Croxton Abbey was granted further lands at Croxton Kerrial, and at Sedgbrook (Lincs.), by William and Hugh, the sons of Ingram, *portarius de Liuns*.[8] Other important additions to the abbey's possessions[9] were the church of Sproxton (Leics.), of which one-third was given by Hugh of Boby and two-thirds by Achardus of Sproxton,[10] one-half of the advowson of South Croxton (Leics.),[11] and the advowsons of Tunstall[12] and Mellinge (Lancs.).[13] Early in the 13th century Philip D'Aubigny granted the manor of Waltham-on-the-Wolds (Leics.) to the abbey.[14]

Croxton was the mother house of the abbeys of Blanchland (Northumb.), founded in 1165, and Cockersand (Lancs.), founded *c.* 1180.[15] A cell of Croxton was established at Hornby (Lancs.) before 1212,[16] and this offshoot remained subject to the mother house.[17] When King John lay dying at Newark he summoned the Abbot of Croxton to hear his last confession and to embalm his body for burial.[18] The king's heart was buried in the abbey church,[19] and Henry III, in memory of his father, bestowed a number of gifts upon Croxton.[20] In 1217 the king granted to the abbey a hundred *solidatae* of land at Finedon (Northants.),[21] but the abbey either never obtained seisin of the property or was obliged to return it, for in 1229 the king ordered the Exchequer to pay 100s. yearly to Croxton in place of the land

that had been assigned at Finedon.[22] In 1227 the abbey obtained a grant of a market and yearly fair at Waltham,[23] and in 1231 the king gave it revenues from Twyford, Skeffington, Tilton, and Rothley in place of the 100s. yearly from the Exchequer.[24] King Henry made frequent gifts of timber to Croxton,[25] and in 1244 he presented a chasuble to be used in the conventual church for celebrating the anniversary of King John's death.[26] In the reign of Henry III Hubert de Burgh, who had obtained possession of the manor of Croxton, appears to have claimed some right to nominate canons to vacancies in the abbey.[27]

In the 14th century a series of misfortunes fell upon Croxton. In June 1326, through a plumber's carelessness, the abbey church and the cloister, with some other buildings, were burnt down, and one canon died in the fire.[28] The abbey suffered further loss through Scottish devastation of its possessions in the north of England.[29] Its resources were, however, increased by the acquisition of the manor of Croxton Kerrial, in or after 1335,[30] and of the advowson of Finedon in 1346.[31] Finedon was appropriated by 1350.[32] At about the same time Croxton received several gifts of less importance.[33] Despite these benefactions, the house was £2,000 in debt in 1348,[34] presumably because of the heavy cost of rebuilding after the fire. The abbey also suffered severe losses through pestilence, which carried off all its senior canons save the abbot and prior.[35] Novices were brought

[7] Ibid. i, 102–4, 223; ii, 153.

[8] Nichols, *Leics.* ii, 151; ii, App., 77–78; Hist. MSS. Com., *Rutland*, iv, 177, 180. Wm.'s gifts were confirmed by Ric. I: Nichols, op. cit. ii, App., 77. The grants of both Wm. and Hugh must be later than 1176, when their father obtained both Croxton and Sedgbrook: Hist. MSS. Com., *Rutland*, iv, 175.

[9] Tugby ch. was in possession of the abbey of 'Crokeston' *c.* 1220 (*Rot. Hugonis de Welles*, i, 258), but the monastery in question was Crokesden (Staffs.), not Croxton: *Valor Eccl.* iii, 125.

[10] Nichols, *Leics.* ii, App., 82. Croxton was in possession of part of the advowson of Sproxton before 1209 (*Rot. Hugonis de Welles*, i, 73) and apparently of the whole advowson by about 1220: ibid. 267. One-third of Sproxton ch. had been appropriated by *c.* 1220 (ibid.), and licence to appropriate the remaining ⅔ was obtained in 1310: *Cal. Pat., 1307–13*, 281.

[11] The abbey was granted the whole advowson in the late 12th century, but the grant was disputed, and eventually the abbey only obtained half: Nichols, op. cit. ii, App., 82. Licence to appropriate half of South Croxton ch. was obtained in 1310: *Cal. Pat., 1307–13*, 281.

[12] Nichols, op. cit. ii, App., 82. The grant of the advowson was confirmed by Roger, Abp. of York, d. 1181: ibid. Tunstall was appropriated before 1230: *V.C.H. Lancs.* ii, 160.

[13] Granted to Hornby Priory: ibid. ii, 160; Nichols, op. cit. ii, App., 83. Licence to appropriate Mellinge was obtained in 1310: *Cal. Pat., 1307–13*, 229.

[14] Nichols, op. cit. ii, App., 96; *Cal. Inq. p.m.* i,

p. 257.

[15] *V.C.H. Lancs.* ii, 154; Colvin, *White Canons in Engl.*, 98–99, 139; *Collect. Anglo-Premonstratensia*, i, 96, 224; ii, 89, 95, 111. An undated list of Premonstratensian houses (ibid. i, 224) mentions Blanchland as a dau. of Newhouse, but see the other references cited. [16] *Bk. of Fees*, i, 219.

[17] See *V.C.H. Lancs.* ii, 160, for an account of Hornby.

[18] Matt. Paris, *Chron. Majora* (Rolls Ser.), ii, 668–9.

[19] *Cal. Chart. R., 1226–57*, 463.

[20] See instances given below.

[21] *Cal. Pat., 1216–25*, 41.

[22] Ibid., *1225–32*, 264–5; *Cal. Lib., 1226–40*, 24, 76, 109, 126.

[23] *Cal. Chart. R., 1226–57*, 65.

[24] Ibid. 131.

[25] *Cal. Close, 1227–31*, 181, 273; *1234–7*, 139; *1242–7*, 209.

[26] *Cal. Lib., 1240–5*, 250.

[27] Colvin, *White Canons in Engl.* 95, citing *Cat. Anct. D.* ii, A3264.

[28] Hen. Knighton, *Chron.* (Rolls Ser.), i, 433.

[29] *Cal. Papal Reg. Pet., 1342–1419*, 128.

[30] *Cal. Pat., 1334–8*, 125.

[31] *Cal. Papal Letters, 1342–62*, 252.

[32] *Cal. Pat., 1350–4*, 18.

[33] Ibid., *1334–8*, 237; ibid., *1330–4*, 556; ibid., *1338–40*, 206; ibid., *1340–3*, 33; Farnham, *Leics. Notes*, v, 135.

[34] *Cal. Close, 1346–9*, 595. The debt was later paid off: ibid.

[35] *Cal. Close, 1349–54*, 335–6.

in,[36] and in 1363 the abbot obtained a papal dispensation permitting the ordination of twelve canons of Croxton and Cockersand at the age of 21, to compensate for the losses caused by the plague.[37] The abbey seems to have made a good recovery from its losses by fire and pestilence; its abbot acted as visitor of the Premonstratensian houses of England in 1362,[38] and in or shortly after 1363 Sir Andrew Louterel granted to the abbey the Leicestershire manors of Saltby and Bescaby, as the endowment for two secular clerks who were to celebrate mass daily in the conventual church.[39] The lay brothers of the house are mentioned in the 14th century, though not subsequently.[40]

At the end of the 14th century difficulties seem to have arisen at Croxton,[41] and it is possible that one abbot may have been deposed,[42] but the records of a series of visitations show that in the late 15th century Croxton was in an exemplary state.

Richard Redman, Bishop of St. Asaph, when he visited the abbey in 1482 in his capacity as general visitor of the Premonstratensian Order in England, found affairs in a very satisfactory state both spiritually and materially, and it was only necessary to order minor corrections in the canons' dress and chanting. There were at the time the abbot and 15 canons at Croxton, besides the prior of the cell at Hornby, and another 7 canons resident outside the monastery.[43] In 1484 there were besides the abbot 25 canons in all, including 3 at Hornby. There were also 3 novices. The vicarages of Croxton, Mellinge, and Tunstall were then being served by canons,[44] and it is probable that several of the canons mentioned two years earlier as residing outside the house were serving the abbey's appropriated churches. In 1484 three canons were engaged in serving chantries established in the conventual church.[45] In 1488 Bishop Redman again found the house in a praiseworthy condition. Three canons were acting as vicars of Croxton, Tunstall, and Mellinge,[46] as was still the case three years later.[47] Visiting the abbey in 1491, Redman found it necessary to punish one of the canons for apostasy,[48]

but when he came again in 1494 everything was in an excellent state, and the abbey was particularly well provided with grain and livestock.[49] In 1497 the position was equally satisfactory; there were then twenty-three canons, including the abbot, the Prior of Hornby, and four canons acting as vicars of Croxton, Sproxton, Mellinge, and Tunstall. There were also two novices.[50] In 1500 the same four churches were being served by canons, and the abbey had thirty canons in all, including the Prior of Hornby and one canon there.[51] At the same date Bishop Redman again found that the house was in a satisfactory condition; the chapel of St. Mary had been rebuilt, and lost revenues had been recovered.[52]

No later visitation records of the abbey are available. Tunstall and Mellinge were being served by canons of Croxton in 1527.[53] The election of Thomas Greene, the last Abbot of Croxton, was marked by a violent conflict with the abbey's patron, Lord Berkeley. After the death, early in March 1534, of the abbot, the canons of Croxton agreed under pressure from Thomas Cromwell to defer the election of a successor, though claiming that they had always previously held elections without any licence from the patron.[54] Later, however, Lord Berkeley arrived at the abbey with a body of retainers and refused to allow the election to proceed until his demand for £500 had been satisfied. The canons refused, and eventually Berkeley allowed the election to take place. The new abbot was, however, forced to pay Berkeley £160 in cash, and to give a bond for the payment of another £160.[55]

The clear yearly revenues of Croxton Abbey, including those of the cell at Hornby, were assessed at £485. 0s. 10¾d. in 1535,[56] and the abbey in consequence survived the dissolution of the smaller monasteries.[57] Croxton was surrendered in September 1538 when there were, besides the abbot, eighteen canons at Croxton, with a prior and two canons at Hornby.[58] Shortly afterwards all were pensioned, the abbot being granted £80 a year, and the canons an average of about £5 each.[59] The First Minister's Account shows a total net revenue of £320. 2s. 2½d.[60]

---

36 *Cal. Close, 1349–54*, 335–6.

37 *Cal. Papal Letters, 1362–1404*, 32.

38 *Cal. Pat., 1361–4*, 177.

39 Ibid. 395; *Cal. Close, 1364–8*, 358–9; Farnham, *Leics. Notes*, v, 342.

40 *Cal. Pat., 1358–61*, 301; Colvin, *White Canons in Engl.* 361 n.

41 Colvin, op. cit., 389–90; *Collect. Anglo-Premonstratensia*, i, 53–56.

42 *Collect. Anglo-Premonstratensia*, i, 53–56, 230–2. The nature of this incident is obscure. Gasquet (loc. cit.) gives the date as *c.* ? 1336, but John of Grantham, who is mentioned in this connexion, occurs as abbot in 1398: Farnham, *Leics. Notes*, v, 137. See also Colvin, op. cit. 389–90, 401.

43 *Collect. Anglo-Premonstratensia*, ii, 152–3.

44 Ibid. ii, 155. Tunstall and Mellinge were prob-

ably being served by canons in the first half of the 14th century: Colvin, *White Canons in Engl.* 144 n.

45 *Collect. Anglo-Premonstratensia*, ii, 155.

46 Ibid. 156–7. 47 Ibid. 160.

48 Ibid. 159. 49 Ibid. 160–1.

50 Ibid. 162–3.

51 Ibid. 163–4.

52 Ibid. 164. For a list of lands and rents regained at this time, see Nichols, *Leics.* ii, App., 103.

53 *V.C.H. Lancs.* ii, 160.

54 *L. & P. Hen. VIII*, vii, pp. 129, 156.

55 Ibid. vii, App., p. 635.

56 *Valor Eccl.* (Rec. Com.), iv, 152.

57 *L. & P. Hen. VIII*, x, p. 515.

58 Ibid. xiii (2), p. 502.

59 Ibid. xiv (1), p. 598.

60 S.C. 6/Hen. VIII/1827, mm. 20–32.

ABBOTS OF CROXTON KERRIAL[61]

Alan, translated to Blanchland, 1165.[62]
William, occurs 1177.[63]
Adam, occurs from 1202[64] to 1221.[65]
Elyas, occurs from 1228[66] to 1231.[67]
Ralph of Lincoln, restored 1230–1,[68] occurs 1240.[69]
Geoffrey, elected 1241–2,[70] occurs 1268.[71]
William of Graham, elected 1274,[72] occurs 1280–1.[73]
William of Huntingdon, occurs 1285.[74]
William of Brackleye, occurs 1319.[75]
William, occurs from 1342 to 1348.[76]
Thomas of Loughtburgh, occurs from 1351[77] to 1374.[78]
John Grantham, occurs 1398.[79]
John of Skotyltorp, occurs 1401 and 1402.[80]
William, occurs 1408–9.[81]

William Overton, occurs 1417.[82]
Adam of Berforthe, elected 1421.[83]
John Eston, occurs from 1425[84] to 1444.[85]
Robert, occurs 1448.[86]
John Arghume, elected 1473,[87] died 1491.[88]
Elias Atterclyff, elected 1491,[89] occurs to 1529.[90]
Thomas Greene, elected 1534,[91] surrendered the abbey, 1538.[92]

The 13th-century seal[93] of Croxton Abbey is a pointed oval, measuring 2½ by 1⅝ in. It depicts the Virgin Mary enthroned, with the infant Jesus on her left arm. Her foot rests on an eagle (the symbol of St. John the Evangelist) which holds a scroll with the word 'JOH'ES'. Of the legend there remains:

. . . IGILL' CŌVĒT SCI JOH'IS . . . DE VALLE DE CROXT . . .

HOUSE OF KNIGHTS TEMPLARS

13. PRECEPTORY OF ROTHLEY

The Knights Templars already possessed land at Rothley in 1203, when King John confirmed to them 5 librates of land there, given by John de Harecurt.[1] A further 10 librates of land at Rothley were given to the Templars by John de Harecurt some years later, probably in 1218–19,[2] but it is unlikely that a preceptory of the Order of the Temple was established at Rothley until Henry III, in 1231, granted the manor and advowson of Rothley to the Templars in free alms.[3] The church of Rothley, a large parish with five dependent chapels, was appropriated in 1240.[4] A rental of c. 1250 gives the yearly revenue of Rothley Bailwick as £62. 10s. 5d., besides a rent

---

[61] See the list given in Colvin, *White Canons in Engl.* 400–1, which differs in some details from that given here.
[62] Ibid. 400.
[63] *Doc. Illustrative of Social and Econ. Hist. of Danelaw*, ed. F. M. Stenton, 209, 215.
[64] *Earliest Lincs. Assize R.*, ed. D. M. Stenton, 52, 85.
[65] Colvin, *White Canons in Engl.* 400.
[66] Nichols, *Leics.* ii, App., 93.
[67] Ibid. 94; Farnham, *Leics. Notes*, ii, 193.
[68] *Rotuli Hugonis de Welles*, ii, 316.
[69] Farnham, *Leics. Notes*, ii, 193. In the list in Dugd. *Mon.* vi (2), 876, an Abbot John is given as occurring in 1241, but no authority is cited.
[70] *Rot. Roberti Grosseteste*, ed. F. N. Davis, 416.
[71] Farnham, *Leics. Notes*, i, 214. In the list in Dugd. *Mon.* vi (2), 876, Abbot Wm. of Houghton is listed as having died in 1274, but no authority is cited.
[72] *Rot. Ric. Gravesend*, ed. F. N. Davis, 156.
[73] *Cal. Pat., 1272–81*, 413, 467.
[74] Nichols, *Leics.* ii, App., 89.
[75] *Cal. Pat., 1317–21*, 393. Wm., Abbot of Croxton, occurs several times between 1285 and 1319, but it is impossible to say which abbot is meant. See Colvin, *White Canons in Engl.* 401; Farnham, *Leics. Notes*, ii, 378; v, 133; *Collect. Anglo-Premonstratensia*, i, 3.
[76] Farnham, op. cit. ii, 197; Nichols, *Leics.* ii, App., 100; Hist. MSS. Com., *Rutland*, iv, 14.
[77] Farnham, op. cit. v, 135.
[78] Hist. MSS. Com., *Rutland*, iv, 122. The reference to Thomas, Abbot of Croxton, in *Collect. Anglo-*

Premonstratensia, ii, 148–9, which has been tentatively assigned to 1279 by the editor, should probably be dated 1379. See Colvin, *White Canons in Engl.* 390.
[79] Farnham, *Leics. Notes*, v, 137.
[80] *Cat. Anct. D.* iv, A9030; *Cal. Pat., 1401–5*, 75.
[81] Hist. MSS. Com., *Rutland*, iv, 181. Perhaps Wm. of Sleforde; *Collect. Anglo-Premonstratensia*, i, 230.
[82] Farnham, *Leics. Notes*, v, 137.
[83] *Visitations of Religious Houses in the Dioc. Linc.* [1420–49], ed. A. Hamilton Thompson, i, 122.
[84] Farnham, *Leics. Notes*, v, 137.
[85] Colvin, *White Canons in Engl.* 401.
[86] *Cal. Pat., 1446–52*, 129.
[87] A. Hamilton Thompson, *Premonstratensian Abbey of Welbeck*, 96.
[88] *Collect. Anglo-Premonstratensia*, i, 102–4.
[89] Ibid. i, 102–4. Elected *per viam inspirationis*. On the date, see Colvin, *White Canons in Engl.* 389.
[90] *L. & P. Hen. VIII*, iv (3), p. 2,698. Elias was probably the abbot who died in Mar. 1534: ibid. vii, p. 129.
[91] Ibid. vii, App., p. 635.
[92] Ibid. xiii (2), p. 502.
[93] B.M. Seals, lxvi, 59.
[1] *Rot. Chart., 1199–1216* (Rec. Com.), 104.
[2] *Rott. Lit. Claus., 1224–7* (Rec. Com.), 402.
[3] *Cal. Chart. R., 1226–57*, 135.
[4] *Rot. Ric. Gravesend*, ed. F. N. Davis, 162–4; cited by A. Hamilton Thompson, 'The Vicars of Rothley', *T.L.A.S.* xii, 122–3. The appropriation was to take effect when the rectory became vacant.

of 5 marks from the Rothley mills.[5] The revenue from Rothley was used to furnish a pittance for the Templars at Acre.[6] Early in the 14th century the Templars had granges at Baggrave and Gaddesby, where they themselves carried on farming.[7]

In 1308 Rothley was seized by the Crown, together with the Templars' other possessions in England.[8] An inventory of the Templars' goods at Rothley, drawn up in 1309, mentions the hall and chapel of the preceptory, and lists the live-stock, including more than 350 sheep and lambs,

belonging to it.[9] The preceptory of Rothley thus came to an end, though its lands were later transferred to the Hospitallers.[10]

PRECEPTORS OF ROTHLEY

Stephen of Todmershe.[11]
John Feversham.[12]
Walter of Ewenightewith.[13]
William of Wald.[14]
Alexander *blundus*.[15]
William of Colewell, occurs 1271.[16]

No seal is known.

HOUSE OF KNIGHTS HOSPITALLERS

14. THE PRECEPTORY OF DALBY AND HEATHER

Lands at Dalby on the Wolds[1] are said to have been given to the Hospitallers by Robert *le Bossu*, Earl of Leicester, in exchange for other property.[2] The Hospitallers were certainly in possession of land at Dalby by 1206, when there seems to have been a preceptory established there.[3] They had acquired lands at Swinford, Isley Walton, Heather, and Ravenstone before 1199.[4] About 1220 they also possessed the advowsons of Swinford, Ashby Parva, Dalby on the Wolds, and Buckminster; of these, Dalby and Heather at least had been in the hands of the Order for some time.[5] In 1274 the Hospitallers had a view of frankpledge and the assize of bread and beer in Ashby Parva.[6] It is uncertain how far these

Leicestershire possessions of the Order were included in the preceptory of Dalby. In 1338 the bailiwick[7] of Dalby[8] included, besides land at Dalby and the appropriated church[9] there, pro-perty at Peatling,[10] Heather, Grimston,[11] and Beaumont Leys.[12] There were then at Dalby the preceptor and one other brother, while the vicar of Dalby lived in the preceptory and acted as chaplain.[13] In 1377 there were again only two Hospitallers at Dalby.[14] The yearly revenue from the Dalby property was little more than £60 in 1338.[15] At the same date the Hospitallers' lands at Swinford, with the appropriated rectory there, were administered by a bailiff as a separate *camera*,[16] which had existed since at least 1225.[17] Rothley, which after the suppression of the Templars had in 1313 been handed over to the Hospitallers,[18] was accounted for separately in

[5] G. T. Clark, 'Customary of the Manor and Soke of Rothley', *Archaeologia*, xlvii, 96.

[6] *Cal. Pat.*, *1272–81*, 159; cited by G. F. Farnham, 'Rothley. The Descent of the Manor', *T.L.A.S.* xii, 44.

[7] *T.L.A.S.* xii, 45.

[8] Ibid. 45.

[9] T. H. Fosbrooke, 'Rothley. The Preceptory', *T.L.A.S.* xii, 32–34. The inventory is also printed in Nichols, *Leics.* iii, 947–8, where the date 1293 is assigned to it in error.

[10] See the account of Dalby and Heather, below.

[11] *Customary of the Manor and Soke of Rothley* (1881), ed. G. T. Clark, 13. The dates and order of the first 5 preceptors are unknown.

[12] Ibid. 14.

[13] Ibid. 17.

[14] Ibid. 38.

[15] *A Cal. of Chart. and Other Doc. belonging to the Hosp. of Wm. Wyggeston*, ed. A. Hamilton Thompson, 542.

[16] Ibid. 545.

[1] Also known as Old Dalby.

[2] Nichols, *Leics.* iii, 244. No evidence is quoted for this statement; lands at Dalby were in the earl's hands in 1124–9: *V.C.H. Leics.* i, 348.

[3] *Pipe R. 1206* (Pipe R. Soc., N.S. xx), 8. The Master of the Hosp. of Dalby is mentioned. See also *Cur. Reg. R.*, *1207–9*, 219, 311, and *Descriptive Cat. of Derbys. Charts.*, ed. I. H. Jeayes, 351.

[4] Dugd. *Mon.* vi, 809; *Rot. Chart.*, *1199–1216* (Rec. Com.), 16.

[5] *Rot. Hugonis de Welles*, ed. W. P. W. Phillimore, i, 242–3, 247, 256, 267.

[6] *Rot. Hund.* (Rec. Com.), i, 239.

[7] *bajulia*.

[8] *Knights Hospitallers in Engl.* (Camden Soc., 1st ser. lxv), ed. L. B. Larking, 63–65.

[9] Dalby ch. was appropriated before c. 1220: *Rot. Hugonis de Welles*, i, 256. The ch. of Dalby on the Wolds has been confused (ibid. i, 269) with that of Dalby Parva, held by the nuns of Langley. See ibid. ii, 291, and *Rot. Ric. Gravesend*, ed. F. N. Davis, 158, for evidence that Dalby Parva was the ch. held by Langley.

[10] The Hospitallers were already holding land at Peatling in 1205: Farnham, *Leics. Notes*, iii, 306.

[11] Grimston was a chapelry of Rothley, and the Hospitallers presumably obtained their property there when Rothley passed to them after the suppression of the Templars.

[12] Acquired by the Hospitallers from Simon de Montfort: *Rot. Hund.* (Rec. Com.), i, 238.

[13] *Knights Hospitallers in Engl.* 64–65.

[14] Farnham, *Leics. Notes*, v, 143.

[15] *Knights Hospitallers in Engl.* 65.

[16] Ibid. 63–65.

[17] *Rot. Hugonis de Welles*, ii, 297.

[18] G. F. Farnham, 'Rothley. The Descent of the Manor', *T.L.A.S.* xii, 46.

1338, though it does not seem to have formed an independent preceptory.[19] The Hospitallers' lands at Melton Mowbray and Stonnesby were also not included in the accounts of the Dalby preceptory.[20] In 1346 the Hospitallers, who had long held one manor at Dalby on the Wolds, acquired a second manor there by exchanging it for their manor at Thrumpton (Notts.).[21] By 1371 Dalby and Rothley certainly formed a single preceptory,[22] and they remained united until the seizure of the Hospitallers' lands in England under Henry VIII. In 1338, and again in 1371, the Hospitallers were themselves cultivating their lands at Dalby, while the manor of Heather, and various outlying properties in the county, were rented out.[23] Beaumont Leys, near Leicester, was exchanged for the rectory of Boston in 1482.[24]

In the 16th century the Preceptor of Dalby and Rothley sometimes also held the bailiwick of the Eagle (Linc.).[25] From 1500, if not earlier, Dalby, Rothley, and Heather[26] were farmed out.[27] In 1535 the clear yearly revenue of the preceptory of Dalby, Rothley, and Heather was assessed at £231. 7s. 10d.[28] The lands of the preceptory passed to the Crown in 1540 with the suppression of the Hospitallers in England. The last preceptor, Sir Henry Poole, was granted a pension of 200 marks.[29] The First Minister's Account gives a net revenue of £167. 10s. 9¾d.[30]

PRECEPTORS OF DALBY

Robert of Sutton, occurs under Henry III or Edward I.[31]

Robert Cort, occurs 1326.[32]

John Larcher, occurs 1338.[33]

John Dingley, occurs 1363 and 1371.[34]

John Langstrothyr, occurs 1448.[35]

Thomas Newport, occurs 1503,[36] died 1522.[37]

Henry Babbington, occurs 1525.[38]

John Babbington, died 1534.[39]

Henry Poole, became preceptor 1535–6[40] and remained in office until 1540.[41]

No seal is known.

FRIARIES

15. THE FRANCISCAN FRIARS OF LEICESTER

The date of foundation of the Franciscan friary at Leicester is unknown, but the house was already in existence by 1230.[1] It is most unlikely that it can have been founded by Simon de Montfort, as has been stated,[2] for Simon did not obtain the lands of the Earldom of Leicester until 1231.[3] According to Stow, the founders were Gilbert Luenor and his wife Ellen,[4] but the basis for this statement is unknown. John Pickering is also said, by Francis Peck, to have been either the founder, or an early benefactor, of the friary, but no evidence has been cited in support of this view.[5]

The Leicester Franciscan house was dedicated to St. Francis, and was included in the Custody of Oxford.[6] The chapel of the Leicester Franciscans is first mentioned in 1255.[7] In 1349 a licence was granted for the alienation in mortmain to the Franciscans of a dwelling-house at Leicester, for the enlargement of their dwelling-place.[8]

The sympathies of the Leicester Franciscans for Richard II brought serious consequences upon the friary in 1402. A Franciscan declared to Henry IV that he and ten other friars of the house at Leicester, together with a master of divinity, had conspired in favour of the deposed Richard. In consequence eight Franciscans of Leicester, with the master of divinity, were

---

[19] *Knights Hospitallers in Engl.* 176–7. For an extent of Rothley drawn up in 1331, see *T.L.A.S.* xii, 47.

[20] *Knights Hospitallers in Engl.* 178.

[21] *T.L.A.S.* xii, 48–49.

[22] Nichols, *Leics.* iii, 245.

[23] Ibid. 245–6; *Knights Hospitallers in Engl.* 63.

[24] *Rot. Parl.* vi. 210.

[25] Nichols, *Leics.* iii, 246; *L. & P. Hen. VIII*, vii, p. 620; *T.L.A.S.* xii, 77.

[26] Heather is referred to in 1534 as if it were a separate preceptory (Farnham, *Leics. Notes*, vi, 333), but there is no record of its having had a separate preceptor, and it is only mentioned in connexion with Dalby.

[27] Ibid. v, 148–9; vi, 333–4; *T.L.A.S.* xii, 69–92.

[28] *Valor Eccl.* (Rec. Com.), iv, 165.

[29] *L. & P. Hen. VIII*, xvi, p. 177.

[30] S.C. 6/Hen. VIII/7272, mm. 1–10.

[31] Hist. MSS. Com., *Hastings*, i, 35.

[32] B.M. Add. Chart. 11225.

[33] *Knights Hospitallers in Engl.* 65.

[34] Hen. Knighton, *Chron.* (Rolls Ser.), ii. 119; Nichols, *Leics.* iii, 245.

[35] *Cal. Papal Letters, 1447–55*, 26; he was Preceptor of Balsall in 1454: ibid. 161.

[36] Nichols, *Leics.* iii, 246.

[37] *T.L.A.S.* xii, 77.

[38] Ibid. xii, 92.

[39] *L. & P. Hen. VIII*, vii, p. 620.

[40] Farnham, *Leics. Notes*, v, 148–9; *L. & P. Hen. VIII*, vii, p. 620.

[41] Ibid. xv, pp. 231–2.

[1] A. G. Little, *Studies in English Franciscan History*, 5; *De Adventu Fratrum Minorum in Angliam* (1951), ed. A. G. Little, 38.

[2] Nichols, *Leics.* i, 297; Dugd. *Mon.* vi (3), 1513.

[3] L. Fox, 'The Honour of Leicester; Origin and Descent', *E.H.R.* liv, 395–6.

[4] Nichols, *Leics.* i, 297; Dugd. *Mon.* vi (3), 1513.

[5] Ibid.

[6] *Monumenta Franciscana* (Rolls Ser.), i, 580.

[7] *Cal. Close, 1254–6*, 244.

[8] *Cal. Pat., 1348–50*, 296.

arrested and brought to London for trial. The remaining two friars escaped. After two juries had failed to convict, a third jury found the prisoners guilty, and they were executed. Two other Franciscans from Leicester, presumably the two who had at first escaped, were executed at Lichfield about the same time.[9] In 1402, at a general chapter of the Franciscans held at Leicester, it was forbidden to any of the Order to speak against the king.[10]

Apart from this grim incident, practically nothing is known of the history of the Leicester Franciscans. Richard III was buried in the friary church after his death at Bosworth.[11] In 1538 the house was surrendered by the warden and six others.[12] The possessions of the friary consisted of little else save the house itself, with its precincts.[13] The First Minister's Account shows a net revenue of only £1. 2s.[14]

WARDENS OF THE FRANCISCANS

Walter, occurs 1253.[15] No longer warden in 1279.[16]

Henry Tykesor, occurs 1378–9.[17]

John Holcote, occurs 1393.[18]

Richard, occurs 1479.[19]

Alan Bell, occurs 1520.[20]

William Gyllys, occurs 1538.[21]

The 14th-century seal of the Franciscans at Leicester is a small vesica, $1\frac{1}{2}$ by $\frac{7}{8}$ in. It depicts St. Mary Magdalene kneeling in the garden before the risen Christ. Of the broken legend all that can be deciphered is

'S' FRATRṼ . . . LEICEST' NOLI M' TANGERE.'[22]

16. THE DOMINICAN FRIARS OF LEICESTER

The house of the Dominican friars at Leicester is said to have been founded by an Earl of Leicester under Henry III.[1] The first reliable reference to the Dominicans at Leicester relates to 1284, when an inquisition was held concerning the proposed grant to them of two plots of land in the borough.[2] Their friary stood on an island formed by two arms of the River Soar.[3] According to Nichols[4] the Dominicans obtained the parish church of St. Clement, at Leicester, as their conventual church. Such an arrangement would have been very unusual,[5] and the evidence for it seems to be inadequate.[6] A 15th-century seal of the house bears the figure of St. Clement,[7] and the friary church is said to have been dedicated to the saint,[8] but these facts are hardly sufficient to prove that the friars acquired possession of a parish church.

In 1291 Queen Eleanor's executors gave £5 to the Leicester Dominicans,[9] and in 1301 they received a royal gift of seven oaks from Rockingham Forest, for house building.[10] Provincial chapters of the order were held at the Leicester house in 1301, 1317, and 1334.[11] Royal gifts of money to thirty Dominicans at Leicester in 1328–9, and to thirty-two in 1334–5,[12] indicate the size of the convent in the 14th century. The garden and cemetery of the friary are mentioned in 1336.[13] During the 14th and 15th centuries the Dominicans received many minor gifts and bequests.[14] In 1489 Henry VII ordered oaks to be delivered to the Dominicans of Leicester for the rebuilding of their dormitory.[15]

[9] J. de Trokelowe and H. de Blaneforde, *Chron. et Annales* (Rolls Ser.), 341; *Eulogium Hist. sive Temporis* (Rolls Ser.), iii, 389–94; *Chron. of the Grey Friars of London* (Camden Soc., 1st ser. liii), ed. J. G. Nichols, 10; *An Engl. Chron. of the Reigns of Ric. II, Hen. IV, Hen. V, and Hen. VI* (Camden Soc., 1st ser. lxiv), ed. J. S. Davies, 23, 26; *Cal. Close, 1399–1402*, 528.

[10] *Eulogium Hist. sive Temporis* (Rolls Ser.), iii, 389.

[11] J. Gairdner, *Hist. of the Life and Reign of Ric. III*, 245, and references there cited.

[12] *L. & P. Hen. VIII*, xiii (2), 307.

[13] Nichols, *Leics.* i, 298.

[14] S.C. 6/Hen. VIII/7311, m. 67.

[15] *The Gt. Reg. of Lich. Cath.* (Wm. Salt Arch. Soc., 1924), ed. H. E. Savage, 67.

[16] Ibid. 120.

[17] *Leic. Boro' Rec., 1327–1509*, 176.

[18] *Cal. Pat., 1391–6*, 396.

[19] E. 326/8037.

[20] *Cal. of Chart. and other Doc. Belonging to the Hosp. of Wm. Wyggeston at Leicester*, ed. A. Hamilton Thompson, 52.

[21] *L. & P. Hen. VIII*, xiii (2), 791.

[22] B.M. Seals, lxvi, 67. The illustration given by Nichols, *Leics.* i, pl. xvii, fig. 9, appears to be an inaccurate reproduction of an impression of the same seal.

[1] Dugd. *Mon.* vi (3), 1486; T. Tanner, *Notitia*

Mon. (1744), 245, note b, quoting a brief of Innocent IV, states that the Dominicans were already established at Leic. by 1252. The brief in question is, however, apparently that printed in *Gt. Reg. of Lich. Cath.* (Wm. Salt Arch. Soc., 1924), ed. H. E. Savage, 69–70. The Dominicans mentioned in this brief are those of London, not of Leic.

[2] C. F. R. Palmer, 'The Friars Preachers or Black Friars of Leicester', *T.L.A.S.* vi, 46–47.

[3] *Leland's Itin.*, ed. Lucy Toulmin-Smith, i, 16.

[4] *Leics.* i, 295.

[5] C. J. Billson, *Medieval Leic.* 70.

[6] The licence for the foundation of a chantry in St. Clement's in 1331 makes no mention of the Dominicans: *Cal. Pat., 1330–4*, 156.

[7] B.M. Seals, lxvi, 66.

[8] Dugd. *Mon.* vi (3), 1486.

[9] *T.L.A.S.* vi, 47.

[10] *Cal. Close, 1296–1302*, 434.

[11] *T.L.A.S.* vi, 49.

[12] Ibid. 47.

[13] *Cal. Pat., 1334–8*, 278.

[14] *T.L.A.S.* vi, 43–53; *Leic. Boro. Rec., 1103–1327*, 295; *John of Gaunt's Reg.* (Camden Soc., 3rd ser. xxi), ed. S. Armitage-Smith, ii, 322.

[15] *Materials for the Hist. of Hen. VII* (Rolls Ser.), ii, 458.

The friary was surrendered in November 1538 by the prior and nine others.[16] Part of the property of the house was being leased, in 1538, for a yearly rent of £2, and the remainder was valued at only 1s. 8d. The net yearly income, as given in the First Minister's Account, was only £1. 19s. 8½d.[17]

PRIORS OF THE DOMINICANS

John Garland, occurs 1394.[18]
William Ceyton, occurs 1505.[19]
Ralph Burrell, occurs 1538.[20]

The 15th-century seal of the Leicester Dominicans is a large oval, 2⅛ by 1⅜ in.; it depicts St. Clement standing under a canopy, his right hand raised in blessing, and his left holding a cross. The legend is:

'SIGILLŪ COMUNE FRATRŪ PREDICATORŪ CŌVENTU LEYC'.[21]

17. THE AUGUSTINIAN HERMITS OF LEICESTER

The house of the Augustinian hermits of Leicester is first mentioned in 1304, when Thomas, Earl of Lancaster, obtained a licence to alienate in mortmain 3 messuages in a suburb of Leicester to the Augustinian hermits for the enlargement of their dwelling-place.[1] The date of foundation of the friary, and the name of the founder, are both unknown. The house is said to have been dedicated to St. Catherine.[2] The church of the Augustinian friars at Leicester is first mentioned in 1306,[3] and in 1372 a general chapter of the Order was held at Leicester.[4] Thomas Ratcliffe, a friar of this house in the late 14th century, is said to have obtained renown as a preacher.[5] The house was surrendered in

November 1538 by the prior and three others.[6] At the surrender the property of the friary consisted only of the house itself and a few small items of property in Leicester. The total net yearly value is given as £1 in the First Minister's Account.[7]

PRIOR OF THE AUGUSTINIAN HERMITS

Richard Preston, occurs 1538.[8]

No other priors are known.

A seal[9] occurs on a 16th-century deed of surrender. It is a pointed oval 2½ by 1½ in., and shows St. Catherine standing crowned, with her wheel beside her, beneath a panelled canopy. The surviving part of the legend reads:

HOSPITALIS . . . VILLE . . .

18. THE FRIARS OF THE SACK OF LEICESTER

The Friars of the Order of the Penitence of Jesus Christ, commonly known as the Friars of the Sack, first reached England in 1257.[1] In 1274 the Council of Lyons provided for the gradual suppression of the Order, but some of its houses survived for many years.[2] The Prior of the Friars of the Sack at Leicester is mentioned in 1283.[3] The house of the Order at Leicester ceased to exist before 1295, when Bishop Sutton forbade the conversion of the site of the friary to secular uses.[4]

PRIOR OF THE FRIARS OF THE SACK.

Richard, occurs 1283.[5]

No other priors and no seal of the house are known.

---

[16] L. & P. Hen. VIII, xiii (2), p. 307; T.L.A.S. vi, 51.
[17] Nichols, Leics. i, 296; S.C. 6/Hen. VIII/7311, m. 66.
[18] Gibbons, Early Linc. Wills, 53.
[19] Leic. Boro. Rec., 1327–1509, 375.
[20] L. & P. Hen. VIII, xiii (2), p. 307.
[21] B.M. Seals, lxvi, 66.

[1] Cal. Pat., 1301–7, 268.
[2] Nichols, Leics. i, 300.
[3] Leic. Boro. Rec., 1103–1327, 371.
[4] John of Gaunt's Reg. (Camden Soc., 3rd ser. xxi), ed. S. Armitage-Smith, ii, 74.
[5] Nichols, Leics. i, 300.

[6] L. & P. Hen. VIII, xiii (2), 306.
[7] Nichols, Leics. i, 300; S.C. 6/Hen. VIII/7311, mm. 66–67.
[8] L. & P. Hen. VIII, xiii (2), 306.
[9] E. 322/124.

[1] A. G. Little, 'The Friars of the Sack', E.H.R. ix, 121, citing Matt. Paris, Chron. Majora (Rolls Ser.), v, 612, 621.
[2] E.H.R. ix, 121; J. Emery, 'The Friars of the Sack', Speculum, xviii, 327–8.
[3] Nichols, Leics. i, 302; Dugd. Mon. vi (3), 1607.
[4] D. Knowles, Religious Houses of Medieval Engl. 118.
[5] Nichols, Leics. i, 302; Dugd. Mon. vi (3), 1607.

19. THE HOSPITAL OF BURTON LAZARS

So far as can be learnt, the hospital of Burton Lazars was founded by Roger de Mowbray, who granted to the lepers of St. Lazarus of Jerusalem 2 carucates of land at Burton, with a messuage and the site of a mill.[1] The date of Roger's grant is unknown, but it is unlikely to have been earlier than 1138, when Roger was still a very young man,[2] and must have been before 1162.[3] Roger de Mowbray participated in the Second Crusade in 1147,[4] and it was probably during his stay in Palestine that he became acquainted with the Order of St. Lazarus. According to Nichols[5] the foundation of the hospital was partly financed by a general collection throughout England, but there seems to be no authority for this statement.

After Roger de Mowbray, the most important benefactor of the hospital was William Burdet, who before 1184[6] gave to it a hospital at Tilton, land at Cold Newton, the churches of Loseby[7] and Galby (Leics.), and the church of Haselbech (Northants.) after the death of Robert Burdet.[8] Under Henry II the hospital was also given by Simon, Earl of Northampton, and his wife, Adelicia de Gant, the Lincolnshire churches of Great Hale, Heckington, and Threckingham.[9] Before 1184 the hospital further obtained the

reversion of the church of Spondon (Derbys.), after the death of the existing incumbent, by the gift of William, Earl of Derby,[10] and the grant of the church of Castleford (Yorks.), by the gift of Henry de Lacy.[11] Henry II granted the hospital 30 marks yearly, to be paid until lands or churches of the equivalent value should be assigned.[12] In 1200 this grant was confirmed by King John,[13] who at the same time exempted the hospital, its lands, and its men from aids, tallages, and other royal levies.[14] The house continued to enjoy such exemption for many years.[15]

The Hospital of Burton Lazars was subject to the Augustinian rule,[16] and originally formed part of the Order of St. Lazarus of Jerusalem. The head of the house was sometimes referred to as the prior[17] or preceptor,[18] but seems to have been generally known as the master. The relationship of the Master of Burton Lazars to the other houses of the same Order in England before the 13th century is not clear, but in a charter of 1249 or 1250 Philip *de Insula*, then master of the hospital, is styled *Magister et Generalis* of the Order in England.[19] Subsequently the Master of Burton Lazars appears as proctor-general in England of the Order,[20] or as master of the Order in England.[21] In the 14th century, at least, the Master of Burton Lazars visited the lesser English houses to correct faults.[22] There seems to be no

[1] Roger's charter is printed in Dugd. *Mon.* vi (2), 632, from the copy in B.M. Cott. MS. Nero C. 12, f. 1*a*. Roger's grant is the first charter copied in Cott. MS. Nero C. 12, which is a cartulary of the hosp. There is no statement in the MS. that this grant is the foundation charter.

[2] *Complete Peerage*, ix, 369, citing *Chron., Steph., Hen. II, and Ric. I* (Rolls Ser.), iii, 182–3. Roger's charter is witnessed by 2 of his sons: Dugd. *Mon.* vi (2), 632.   [3] *Pipe R. 1162* (Pipe R. Soc. v), 2.

[4] *Complete Peerage*, ix, 370.

[5] *Leics.* ii, 272.

[6] His gifts were confirmed by Hen. II in a charter not later than 1184. See *Cal. Chart. R., 1327–41*, 77, where details of Hen.'s charter are given, and Dugd. *Mon.* vi (2), 634.

[7] Loseby was apparently appropriated by 1232: *Rot. Hugonis de Welles*, ed. W. P. W. Phillimore, ii, 320.

[8] Nichols, *Leics.* ii, App., 128–9; Dugd. *Mon.* vi (2), 633; B.M. Cott. MS. Nero C. 12, ff. 98*a*, 100. The hosp. never seems to have obtained the advowson of Haselbech: Dugd. *Mon.* vi (2), 633; *Rot. Hugonis de Welles*, ii, 98. The hosp. at Tilton was still in existence in 1345: *Cal. Close, 1343–6*, 631.

[9] See the confirmation charters by Hen. II (Nichols, *Leics.* ii, App., 129; Dugd. *Mon.* vi (2), 634; *Cal. Chart. R., 1327–41*, 77) and John (*Rot. Chart., 1199–1216* (Rec. Com.), 67).

[10] Nichols, *Leics.* ii, App., 129; Dugd. *Mon.* vi (2), 634; *Cal. Chart. R., 1327–41*, 77; B.M. Harl. MS. 3868. Spondon was appropriated to Burton Lazars in

or shortly after 1286: *Descriptive Cat. of Derbys. Charts.*, ed. I. H. Jeayes, 275; B.M. Harl. MS. 3868, ff. 11*b*–17.

[11] *Early Yorks. Chart.*, ed. W. Farrer, iii, 156–7; *Cal. Chart. R., 1327–41*, 77. By 1270 the advowson of Castleford had reverted to the Lacy family: *Reg. of Walter Giffard*, ed. Wm. Brown, 31.

[12] Nichols, *Leics.* ii, App., 129.

[13] *Rot. Chart., 1199–1216* (Rec. Com.), 67. The money continued to be paid under Hen. III and Edw. I: *Cal. Lib., 1240–5*, 182, 285; *1245–51*, 44, 115, 178, 232, 283, 384; *Cal. Close, 1279–88*, 100.

[14] *Rot. Chart., 1199–1216* (Rec. Com.), 67.

[15] *Cal. Close, 1330–3*, 187; *1333–7*, 32, 44; *1385–9*, 218; *1447–54*, 449; *Cal. Pat., 1343–5*, 224; *Cal. Fine R., 1452–61*, 38.

[16] *Cal. Papal Letters, 1447–55*, 72.

[17] Farnham, *Leics. Notes*, i, 252.

[18] *Cal. Pat., 1216–25*, 443; *Cal. Papal Letters, 1417–31*, 181.

[19] B.M. Harl. MS. 3868, f. 16*a*.

[20] *Cal. Pat., 1307–13*, 344; *1313–17*, 1, 394; *1317–21*, 394, 571; *1377–81*, 290; *1422–9*, 268; *Cal. Chart. R., 1341–1417*, 165.

[21] B.M. Add. Chart. 33635; *Cal Pat., 1361–4*, 253. In 1371 Nicholas of Dover described himself as 'governor, warden, and master of the conventual house of Burton Lazars, and lieutenant and vicar-general in spiritualities and temporalities of the General Master of the Order of St. Lazarus in England and Scotland': *Cal. Pat., 1370–4*, 418. See also ibid., *1377–81*, 290.

[22] *Cal. Pat., 1345–8*, 414; *1354–8*, 43.

reason to doubt that Burton Lazars was fully subject to the master of the whole Order of St. Lazarus.[23] From 1439 onwards, however, attempts were made to obtain fresh papal bulls regulating the election of masters of the hospital,[24] and in 1450 the Pope, on the petition of the master and brethren of the house, took Burton Lazars under his especial protection, exempted it from all episcopal jurisdiction, and provided that for the future the master, when elected by the brethren, should be the undoubted head of the house without any confirmation being required.[25] The effect must have been to make Burton Lazars an independent house, and after 1450 there is no indication of its having been subject to any lesser authority than the papacy.[26]

While the Master of Burton Lazars seems to have exercised a measure of control over all the English establishments of the Order of St. Lazarus, the Burton hospital also obtained direct possession of a group of lesser houses. The acquisition of the hospital at Tilton has already been noted. At an unknown date, probably in the 12th century, an agreement was made between Ralph de Amundevill and the brothers of the Order of St. Lazarus, providing that the brothers were to maintain and clothe four lepers in the hospital at Carleton in Moreland (Lincs.), to which lands at Carleton belonged.[27] It is not known how long the hospital at Carleton remained in existence, but Burton Lazars retained the manor of Carleton until the Dissolution.[28] In 1299 the Hospital of St. Giles, outside London, was granted to Burton Lazars in place of the pension of 40 marks yearly previously received from the king.[29] The possessions of St. Giles included the rectory of Feltham, Middlesex.[30] Under Richard II Burton Lazars was deprived of

St. Giles,[31] which was granted to Mountgrace Priory, but after a lawsuit[32] Burton Lazars regained its rights.[33] St. Giles was retained by Burton Lazars until 1537, when it was exchanged for the manor of Burton Lazars.[34] In 1347 the then Master of Burton Lazars became also Preceptor of La Maudelyne, a house of the Order of St. Lazarus at Locko (Derbys.).[35] La Maudelyne had been previously dependent on a French house.[36] Since there is no further reference to the preceptory at Locko after 1351,[37] and since at the Dissolution Burton Lazars was possessed of the manor of Locko,[38] it seems probable that the possessions of the preceptory passed to Burton Lazars. Another hospital whose lands were acquired by Burton was that at Choseley, near Wymondham (Norf.). A hospital of the Order of St. Lazarus was in existence there in 1291,[39] but by 1428 the hospital had ceased to exist,[40] and at the Dissolution its lands were in the possession of Burton Lazars.[41] In 1456 the king granted to William Sutton, Master of Burton Lazars, the Hospital of the Holy Innocents, outside Lincoln, after the death of the existing holder.[42] The grant was apparently due to the unsatisfactory condition of Holy Innocents Hospital while it was independent.[43] Sutton seems to have obtained the Lincoln hospital in 1461.[44] A condition of the royal grant was that three lepers from the king's household or, failing such, from amongst the king's tenants, should be maintained in the Hospital of the Holy Innocents.[45] Burton retained possession of the Lincoln hospital until the Dissolution.[46]

Very little is known of the internal life of Burton Lazars hospital. There are references to the chapter, with the consent of which the master acted.[47] A dispute for the mastership

---

[23] In 1353 a member of the Order from Burton obtained the king's protection for a journey overseas to treat with the Master Superior of the Order: *Cal. Pat., 1350–4*, 502.   [24] Ibid., *1436–41*, 362.

[25] *Cal. Papal Letters, 1447–55*, 81; for other papal privileges bestowed on the hospital in the 15th century, see *Leic. Boro. Rec., 1327–1509*, 386–7.

[26] In 1457 a brother of Burton was referred to as belonging to the Order of the *Cruciferi* (*Cal. Papal Letters, 1455–64*, 126), but this term was used to denote several different bodies living under the Augustinian rule (D. Knowles, *Religious Orders in Engl.* 203), and it is unlikely that Burton Lazars was attached to any of the Orders known as Friars of the Cross.

[27] B.M. Cott. MS. Nero C. 12, ff. 116a–117b; Nichols, *Leics.* ii, 275. The agreement is dated 'in the year in which the young King of France was married'. If the king in question was Louis VII, the year would be 1137, when Louis first married. If the king meant is Philip II, the year similarly would be 1180. But see above on the date of Burton's foundation. The agreement was confirmed by Wm., Count of Aumale, and the last English Count Wm. died in 1260.

[28] Dugd. *Mon.* vi (2), 634; *Valor Eccl.* (Rec. Com.), iv, 153.

[29] *Cal. Pat., 1292–1301*, 404.

[30] Dugd. *Mon.* vi (2), 635–6.

[31] *Cal. Pat., 1401–5*, 120.

[32] *Cal. Close, 1399–1401*, 450–1; *1402–5*, 16.

[33] *Cal. Pat., 1413–16*, 248.

[34] Dugd. *Mon.* vi (2), 635.

[35] *Cal. Close, 1346–9*, 338, 382.

[36] *Cal. Pat., 1345–8*, 408.

[37] *V.C.H. Derbys.* ii, 78.

[38] Ibid.; Dugd. *Mon.* vi (2), 634.

[39] *Tax. Eccl.* (Rec. Com.), 94.

[40] J. Tanner, *Notitia Mon.* (1744), 358.

[41] *Valor Eccl.* (Rec. Com.), iv, 152. See also *Tax. Eccl.* (Rec. Com.), 94. Lands at Choseley are said to have been given to Burton Lazars by Wm. de Albini, before 1146 (*V.C.H. Norf.* ii, 453; Nichols, *Leics.* ii, 273), but there seems to be no reliable evidence for this.

[42] *Cal. Pat., 1452–61*, 359.

[43] *V.C.H. Lincs.* ii, 231.

[44] *Cal. Pat., 1461–7*, 123.

[45] Ibid.

[46] *Valor Eccl.* (Rec. Com.), iv, 152; Dugd. *Mon.* vi (2), 634.

[47] *Cal. Pat., 1416–22*, 310–11; B.M. Add. Chart. 33635.

between Nicholas of Dover and Geoffrey of Chaddesden[48] was finally settled, after several years of controversy,[49] in 1372, when Geoffrey gave up his claims in return for a pension.[50] In 1404 the master ordered the cartulary of the house to be drawn up.[51] Not long before the Dissolution there were at the hospital the master and eight brothers, and it was described as 'a very fair hospital and collegiate church'.[52] In 1535 only one poor person was being maintained at Burton, though there were fourteen poor in the subordinate hospital of St. Giles, London.[53] Burton's possessions in 1535 included the appropriated rectories of Loseby, Spondon, Threckingham, and Feltham. In the same year its clear yearly revenues, which included offerings made before the image of St. Lazarus at the hospital, were assessed at £265. 10s. 2½d.[54]

By 1536 Dr. Thomas Legh had determined to secure the hospital for himself,[55] and in the following year he obtained a reversion of the mastership.[56] He seems to have become master in the same year,[57] and in 1540 he was still in office.[58] The hospital was surrendered before 1544.[59]

MASTERS OF BURTON LAZARS[60]

Walter *de Novo Castro*.[61]
William, occurs 1208.[62]
Heincius, occurs 1222.[63]

Roger of Reresby, occurs 1246.[64]
Philip de Insula, occurs 1250 and 1251.[65]
Robert of Tarington, occurs 1252.[66]
Richard Bustard, occurs 1264.[67]
John of Horbeling, occurs in or before 1278[68] and in 1281.[69]
Robert of Dalby, occurs 1268.[70]
Terry of Almain (*Alamannus*), occurs late 13th century.[71]
John Crispyng, occurs 1316.[72]
Richard of Leighton, occurs 1319.[73]
William Daumenyl, occurs 1321.[74]
William of Ty, occurs from 1324[75] to 1327.[76]
William Daumenyl, occurs again, 1331.[77]
Hugh Michel, occurs from 1336[78] to 1339.[79]
Richard, occurs 1345.[80]
Hugh Michel, occurs again, August 1347.[81]
Thomas of Kyrkeby, occurs October 1347.[82]
Geoffrey of Chaddesden, occurs 1354.[83]
Robert Haliday, occurs 1358.[84]
Nicholas of Dover, occurs from 1364[85] to 1383.[86]
Richard Clifford, appointed 1389.[87]
Walter Lynton, occurs 1401,[88] resigned 1421.[89]
Geoffrey Schriggely, collated 1421.[90] Occurs to 1445.[91]
William Sutton, occurs from 1450[92] to 1482.[93]
George Sutton, occurs from 1484[94] to 1492.[95]
Thomas Honyter, occurs 1506.[96]
Thomas Norton, occurs from 1512[97] to 1524.[98]

[48] Geoffrey had been master at an earlier date: *Cal. Pat., 1354–8*, 43.
[49] The dispute was in progress in 1369: *Cal. Pat., 1367–70*, 259.
[50] *Cal. Close, 1369–74*, 432.
[51] Nichols, *Leics.* ii, App., 129; B.M. Cott. MS. Nero C. 12, f. 1*a*.
[52] *Leland's Itin.*, ed. Lucy Toulmin-Smith, iv, 19; J. Leland, *Collect.* (1770), i, 72.
[53] *Valor Eccl.* (Rec. Com.), iv, 152.
[54] Ibid. 152–3.
[55] *L. & P. Hen. VIII*, xi, p. 114.
[56] Ibid. xii (1), p. 35.
[57] B.M. Harl. Chart. 80, F26.
[58] *Descriptive Cat. of Derbys. Charts.*, ed. I. H. Jeayes, 79–80.
[59] *L. & P. Hen. VIII*, xix (1), p. 371.
[60] An incomplete list is given in Farnham, *Leics. Notes*, i, 269.
[61] B.M. Cott. MS. Nero C. 12, ff. 3*a*, 34. The date of this master's rule is unknown.
[62] Farnham, *Leics. Notes*, i, 252.
[63] Ibid. i, 269. Heincius occurs in a fine dated Hil., 6 Hen. III. Farnham, op. cit. i, 269, gives the date as 1221, but Hil., 6 Hen. III, falls in Jan. 1221–2, i.e. in the historical year 1222.
[64] *Cal. Lib., 1245–51*, 44.
[65] B.M. Harl. MS. 3868, ff. 15*b*, 16*a*.
[66] Farnham, *Leics. Notes*, i, 269.
[67] B.M. Cott. MS. Nero C. 12, f. 31.
[68] Farnham, *Leics. Notes*, iii, 109.
[69] Ibid. i, 255.
[70] *Cal. Close, 1279–88*, 418.
[71] B.M. Add. Chart. 33635; Cott. MS. Nero C. 12,

f. 33. The position of this master in the list is uncertain. He may be the same person as Ric. Germin', who was master about the same period: B.M. Cott. MS. Nero C. 12, ff. 3*b*, 61*a*.
[72] Ibid., f. 52*a*.
[73] *Cal. Pat., 1317–21*, 394.
[74] *Cal. Close, 1318–23*, 498.
[75] B.M. Cott. MS. Nero C. 12, f. 47*a*.
[76] Farnham, *Leics. Notes*, i, 258.
[77] *Cal. Close, 1330–3*, 327.
[78] B.M. Cott. MS. Nero C. 12, f. 37*a*.
[79] *Cal. Close, 1339–41*, 148.
[80] Farnham, *Leics. Notes*, i, 259.
[81] *Cal. Close, 1346–9*, 382.
[82] *Cal. Pat., 1345–8*, 414.
[83] Ibid., *1354–8*, 43.
[84] *Cal. Close, 1354–60*, 498.
[85] Farnham, *Leics. Notes*, i, 269.
[86] Ibid. On the dispute for the mastership between Nicholas and Geoffrey of Chaddesden, see above, pp. 37–38.
[87] *Cal. Pat., 1388–92*, 117.
[88] Ibid., *1399–1401*, 434; *Cal. Close, 1399–1402*, 450–1.
[89] *Cal. Papal Letters*, vii, 181.
[90] Ibid.
[91] *Cal. Close, 1441–7*, 343.
[92] Farnham, *Leics. Notes*, i, 262; *Cal. Papal Letters, 1447–55*, 81.
[93] Farnham, op. cit. i, 269.   [94] Ibid.
[95] B.M. Harl. Chart. 43 A13.
[96] Hist. MSS. Com., *Middleton*, 125.
[97] Farnham, *Leics. Notes*, i, 269.
[98] *L. & P. Hen. VIII*, iv (1), p. 332.

Thomas Ratcliff, occurs from 1526[99] to 1536.[1]
Thomas Legh, occurs from 1537[2] to 1540.[3]

A 14th-century seal[4] of the hospital is circular, 2¼ in. in diameter. It shows a half-length figure of St. Lazarus in a sexfoil, holding in his right hand a trident, the instrument of his martyrdom, and in his left a book. On either side of the saint is a shield of arms, that on his left bearing a cross, that on his right a lion. The legend is:

S' COMUNE ORDINIS MILICIE HOSPITALIS SCI
LAZARI DE BORTONE

Four seals of the 15th century,[5] all vesica-shaped and of various sizes, have full-length figures of the saint in the attitude of blessing, and holding a crosier. These seals bear the legend:

SIGILLUM FRATERNITATIS SANCTI LAZARI
JERUSALEM IN ANGLIA.[6]

A large 16th-century seal,[7] 2½ by 1½ in., shows a standing figure of St. Lazarus, holding a trident and crosier. The legend reads:

SIGILL' DE INDULGENCIA DE BORTO' SCI.
LAZARI JR . . . L'M.

A second 16th-century seal,[8] 2¼ by 1⅛ in., shows a seated figure, probably St. Lazarus, holding a crosier. Below is a religious person in prayer. The legend is:

SIGILLŪ DOM' BORTŌ SANCTI LAZARI

20. THE HOSPITAL OF CASTLE DONINGTON

The Hospital of St. John the Baptist at Castle Donington is traditionally stated to have been founded by John, Constable of Chester and Baron of Halton.[1] The tradition is supported by the statement in the *Matriculus* of the archdeaconry of Leicester that the hospital was founded by J.,

formerly Constable of Chester,[2] and it may well be true. If the account given in the *Matriculus* is correct, the founder must have been John, Constable of Chester, who died in 1190.[3] It was further noted in the *Matriculus*[4] that the hospital ought to have contained thirteen brothers, with a number of sisters; that the brothers had no regular habit, and lived under no rule; and that the hospital received a tithe of nine-tenths of the sheaves of the constable's demesne at Donington,[5] besides the tithe of all the hay from the demesne. In the 13th century the hospital was receiving payments from the Cheshire manors of Halton and Runcorn.[6] It was stated in 1311 that the hospital held the tithes of the Earl of Lincoln's[7] demesne at Donington, with a little property there, in return for finding a chaplain to celebrate daily in the chapel of Donington Castle, and for maintaining twelve poor persons in the hospital.[8]

Nothing is known of the internal affairs of the hospital. In 1535 its clear yearly income was estimated at only £3. 13s. 4d.[9] The certificate returned under Henry VIII's Chantry Act[10] gives the hospital's annual income as £3, and states that though the hospital was founded to sustain certain poor men, none was then in residence.[11] The hospital was dissolved under the Chantry Act of Edward VI.[12]

WARDENS OF CASTLE DONINGTON HOSPITAL

Elias, occurs before 1190.[13]
Umfridus, occurs about 1220.[14]
Henry of Leycestre, appointed about 1315, ejected 1322.[15]
John of Wodeford, appointed 1322,[16] resigned 1343.[17]
John of Heselarton, appointed 1343.[18]
John of Maderseye, appointed 1347.[19]
Richard of Helpryngham, appointed 1348, but appointment revoked in the same year.[20]
Thomas le Moigne, appointed 1348.[21]

[99] Farnham, *Leics. Notes*, i, 265.
[1] *L. & P. Hen. VIII*, x, p. 81.
[2] B.M. Harl. Chart. 80 F26.
[3] *Descriptive Cat. of Derbys. Charts.*, ed. I. H. Jeayes, 79, 80.
[4] B.M. Seals, lxvi, 47.
[5] Ibid. lxvi, 48A, 48B; B.M. Add. Chart. 19864; B.M. Wolley Chart. viii, 13.
[6] The form of the legend given in the 4 seals varies slightly.
[7] B.M. Seals, xxxv, 169.   [8] B.M. D.C., H. 37.

[1] Nichols, *Leics.* iii, 780, citing the Donington Town Bk. of 1634.
[2] *Rot. Hugonis de Welles*, ed. W. P. W. Phillimore, i, 252.
[3] *Complete Peerage*, vii, 677.
[4] Compiled *c.* 1220.
[5] i.e. the hosp. obtained ⅒ of all sheaves remaining after the normal parochial tithe had been taken.
[6] *Rot. Hugonis de Welles*, i. 252. See also *Cal. Close, 1237–42*, 223, 411; and *Cal. Lib., 1245–51*, 245.

[7] The earl was the descendant of the Constables of Chest.: *Complete Peerage*, vii, 677.
[8] G. F. Farnham and A. Hamilton Thompson, 'Castle Donington', *T.L.A.S.* xiv, 49; *Cal. Inq. p.m.* v, 156.
[9] *Valor Eccl.* (Rec. Com.), iv, 179.
[10] 37 Hen. VIII, c. 4.
[11] A. Hamilton Thompson, 'The Chant. Cert. for Leics.', *Assoc. Arch. Soc. Rep. and Papers*, xxx, 505.
[12] For the sale of the hosp.'s lands, see ibid. xxx, 534–6.
[13] Nichols, *Leics.* iii, 780.
[14] *Rot. Hugonis de Welles*, i, 252. Ric. of Stavensby, said to have been warden in 1226 (Nichols, op. cit. iii, 780), was the parson of the par. ch. of Donington: *Rot. Hugonis de Welles*, ii, 305.
[15] *T.L.A.S.* xiv, 50.
[16] *Cal. Pat., 1321–4*, 95.
[17] Ibid., *1343–5*, 33. He exchanged benefices with his successor.   [18] Ibid.
[19] *Cal. Pat., 1345–8*, 266.
[20] Ibid., *1348–50*, 87, 101.   [21] Ibid. 101.

John Lucas, resigned 1409.[22]

William Pollard, appointed 1409.[23]

Robert Lowes, appointed 1415.[24]

Thomas Lyserisc, resigned 1444.[25]

Richard Haysnape, appointed 1444.[26]

John Menaude, appointed 1474, resigned 1482.[27]

John Boteler, appointed 1482,[28] occurs 1485.[29]

Thomas Burgoyn, occurs 1535.[30]

No seal is known.

21. THE HOSPITAL OF ST. JOHN THE BAPTIST AND ST. JOHN THE EVANGELIST, LEICESTER

Both the date of the foundation of the Hospital of St. John the Baptist and St. John the Evangelist[1] at Leicester and the founder's name are unknown. The hospital is mentioned in 1200, when its master was involved in a plea concerning land at Holwell, near Melton Mowbray.[2] In a charter of about the same date Richard Basset confirmed a gift to the hospital of 1 virgate at Cosby (Leics.).[3] The hospital must have been already old in 1200, for in an early 13th-century document the monthly revenue of corn which the hospital enjoyed from the lands of the earls of Leicester is said to have been granted by the 2nd earl.[4] Both the brothers and the sisters of the hospital are mentioned about 1235[5] and subsequently.[6] In the 15th century, and probably at other periods as well, the master of the hospital lived under the Augustinian rule,[7] and it may be presumed that his subordinates did the same. There is no evidence about the functions fulfilled

by the hospital during the Middle Ages,[8] but the mention c. 1200 of the poor of the hospital,[9] suggests that it sheltered the destitute rather than the sick. A master of the hospital, Thomas of Bretford, was removed from his office at the end of the 13th century for unspecified offences, but was later restored to his position,[10] while in 1361 the master and all save two of the brethren were carried off by the pestilence.[11]

No full account of the hospital's property at any period during the Middle Ages has survived. About 1200 the hospital was granted land at Lubbesthorpe (Leics.),[12] and in 1212 it possessed 4 virgates at Cosby.[13] Lands at Frisby by Galby (Leics.) were granted to the hospital by the Prior and convent of Trentham in 1255.[14] In 1355 the hospital possessed $\frac{1}{16}$ of a knight's fee in Hungarton and Barkby (Leics.),[15] and grants of property in and near Leicester itself were made to the hospital in 1349 and 1355.[16] The hospital possessed, besides its own church, the chapel of St. John in the eastern suburbs of Leicester.[17]

In 1479 St. John's Hospital passed into the possession of the College of the Newarke at Leicester, through the instrumentality of William, Lord Hastings.[18] The exact means by which this was effected are unknown, and it may have been Edward IV who gave the hospital to the college.[19] St. John's continued to exist separately, and in 1491 it was under the supervision of the Treasurer of the Newarke.[20] After the suppression of the College of the Newarke in 1547 the hospital still survived, and in 1548 it contained six poor women,[21] but subsequently it seems to have ceased to exist.[22] In 1589 Queen Elizabeth granted the lands of St. John's Hospital to the Corporation of Leicester.[23] In the 17th century the hospital was

[22] R. Somerville, 'D. of Lanc. Presentations, 1399–1485', Bull. of Inst. of Hist. Research, xviii, 74.

[23] Ibid.   [24] Ibid.

[25] Ibid.   [26] Ibid.

[27] Ibid.   [28] Ibid.

[29] Rot. Parl. vi, 373.

[30] Valor Eccl. (Rec. Com.), iv, 179.

[1] On the full invocation of the hosp., see Leic. Boro. Rec., 1327–1509, 282–3, 425, and Hist. MSS. Com., Hastings, i, 59.

[2] Cur. Reg. R., Ric. I–1201, 164.

[3] Leic. Boro. Rec., 1103–1327, 9.

[4] Hist. MSS. Com., Hastings, i, 336, 341. The earl in question is presumably Robert le Bossu, styled earl in 1119, d. 1168. The hosp.'s revenue of 13 small quarters of corn probably issued from the earl's property in Leic.

[5] Rot. Roberti Grosseteste, ed. F. N. Davis, 390–1.

[6] Hist. MSS. Com., Hastings, i, 59; A. Hamilton Thompson, Hist. of the Hosp. and New Coll. of the Annunciation of St. Mary in the Newarke, 215; Cal. of Chart. and other Doc. Belonging to the Hosp. of Wm. Wyggeston at Leic., ed. A. Hamilton Thompson, 17; Leic. Boro. Rec., 1327–1509, 100–2, 282–3; Reg. of Hen. Chichele, Abp. of Cant., ed. E. F. Jacob, i, 326–8.

[7] Reg. Chichele, i, 326–8. The hosp. chapter house is mentioned in 1424: ibid. i, 328.

[8] It has been stated that Hen. de Lacy, Earl of Linc., gave property to St. John's Hosp., Leic., for the maintenance there of 12 poor persons: Dugd. Mon. vi (2), 765. It was to the hosp. at Donington that the earl made this benefaction: Cal. Inq. p.m. v, p. 156.

[9] Hist. MSS. Com., Hastings, i, 58.

[10] Linc. Reg. Dalderby, Inst., ff. 196a, 200a.

[11] Linc. Reg. Gynewell, Inst., f. 334b.

[12] Hist. MSS. Com., Hastings, i, 58.

[13] Cur. Reg. R., 1210–12, 378.

[14] Cat. Anct. D. ii, B3823.

[15] Cal. Close, 1354–60, 151.

[16] Cal. Pat., 1348–50, 421; Leic. Boro. Rec., 1327–1509, 100–2.

[17] Ibid., 1327–1509, 283; 1509–1603, 251; Cal. Close, 1447–54, 422; Leland's Itin., ed. Lucy Toulmin-Smith, i, 17.

[18] R. Somerville, 'D. of Lanc. Presentations, 1399–1485', Bull. Inst. Hist. Research, xviii, 75.

[19] Leland's Itin., ed. Lucy Toulmin-Smith, i, 14.

[20] A. Hamilton Thompson, Hist. of Hosp. of the Annunciation in the Newarke, 131.

[21] Ibid. 215; Char. Com. Rep. [163], p. 41, H.C. (1839), xv.

[22] Char. Com. Rep. (1839), p. 41; Leic. Boro. Rec., 1509–1603, 63.

[23] Ibid.

revived in the form of an almshouse for poor widows, but its later history cannot be dealt with here.[24]

MASTERS OF ST JOHN'S HOSPITAL

Gervase, occurs 1236.[25]

Robert, occurs 1265.[26]

Thomas of Bretford, admitted 1292,[27] deprived before 1300.[28]

Peter of Quorndon, admitted 1300,[29] resigned 1302.[30]

Thomas of Bretford, admitted 1302,[31] resigned 1315.[32]

Peter of Quorndon, admitted 1315.[33]

Robert of Ravenstone, admitted 1353.[34]

John of Northburgh, occurs 1355 and 1361.[35]

Robert of Clapthorn, admitted 1361,[36] died 1367.[37]

Adam of Oadby, admitted 1367.[38]

William of Gaddesby, occurs 1378–9[39] and 1385.[40]

William Hylle, admitted 1424,[41] occurs 1434.[42]

John Peckleton, died 1436.[43]

John Swaffield, admitted 1436,[44] resigned 1452.[45]

John Dane, admitted 1452.[46]

Thomas Cloreley, resigned 1460.[47]

John Willoughby,[48] admitted 1460,[49] resigned 1461.[50]

John Rodgeford, admitted 1461,[51] resigned 1466.[52]

Lawrence Aylvesmere,[53] admitted 1466,[54] resigned 1467.[55]

Richard Nicholas,[56] admitted and resigned, 1467.[57]

Thomas Leche,[58] admitted 1467,[59] resigned 1471.[60]

Robert Sileby, admitted 1471,[61] occurs 1478.[62]

A broken 12th-century seal[63] of the hospital, which would have been an oval about 2½ in. long by 1¾ in. wide when complete, shows the eagle of St. John the Evangelist rising. Between its claws is what appears to be a scroll bearing the letters:

.. AN .. ELIS

Of the legend there remains only:

... S LEGREC ...

Two other seals of the hospital occur amongst the Hastings manuscripts.[64] One of these, closely resembling the seal first described, is a vesica, measuring 2¼ by 1⅝ in., and bearing an eagle rising and carrying a scroll. This seal is of 13th-century date also. Of the legend all that remains is:

SECRET .... ANNIS LEI ...

The remaining seal, which dates from the late 15th century, is also a vesica, measuring 2⅛ by 1⅝ in. It shows the eagle of St. John the Evangelist rising, with the letter R above its head, a cinquefoil beneath its right wing, and another object, perhaps a thistle head, beneath its left wing. The surviving portion of the legend reads:

SIGILLU' COM' HOSPITAL' S'CORUM ... PTISTE ET ... ANGELISTE LEYCEST ...

22. THE HOSPITAL OF ST. LEONARD, LEICESTER

According to Henry of Knighton, the founder of the Hospital of St. Leonard at Leicester was William the Leper, son of Robert ès Blanchemains, Earl of Leicester.[1] Knighton wrote long after the hospital's foundation, but he may well have had reliable information about the origins of an institution which stood close to the abbey where he was himself a canon. It is not known what the

---

[24] For the later history of the hosp., see *Char. Com. Rep.* (1839), pp. 68–72.
[25] *Rotuli Roberti Grosseteste*, ed. F. N. Davis, 390–1.
[26] *Cat. Anct. D.* ii, B3823.
[27] Rosalind Hill, 'Bishop Sutton and the Inst. of Heads of Religious Houses in the Dioc. of Linc.', *E.H.R.* lviii, 209.
[28] Linc. Reg. Dalderby, Inst., f. 196a.
[29] Ibid.
[30] Ibid., f. 200a.   [31] Ibid.
[32] Ibid., f. 210b.
[33] Ibid.
[34] Linc. Reg. Gynewell, Memo., f. 45a.
[35] *Leic. Boro. Rec., 1327–1509*, 100–2, 399.
[36] Linc. Reg. Gynewell, Inst., f. 334b.
[37] Linc. Reg. Buckingham, Inst., i, f. 240a.
[38] Ibid.
[39] *Leic. Boro. Rec., 1327–1509*, 177.
[40] *Cat. Anct. D.* ii, B3845.
[41] *Reg. Chichele*, i, 326–8.
[42] Hist. MSS. Com., *Hastings*, i, 64.
[43] Linc. Reg. Gray, Inst., f. 147a.
[44] Ibid.
[45] Linc. Reg. Chedworth, Inst., f. 89a.

[46] Ibid.
[47] Ibid., f. 99b.
[48] Alias John Dawes.
[49] Linc. Reg. Chedworth, Inst., ff. 99b, 100b.
[50] *Bull. Inst. Hist. Research*, xviii, 75.
[51] Ibid.   [52] Ibid.
[53] Or Ayllemere.
[54] *Bull. Inst. Hist. Research*, xviii, 75.
[55] Ibid.
[56] Or Niclos.
[57] *Bull. Inst. Hist. Research*, xviii, 75.
[58] Or Leige.
[59] *Bull. Inst. Hist. Research*, xviii, 75.
[60] Ibid.
[61] Ibid.
[62] Hist. MSS. Com., *Hastings*, i, 59.
[63] E. 336/6747.
[64] See the descriptions in Hist. MSS. Com., *Hastings*, i, 59. It has not been possible to inspect these two seals.
[1] Hen. Knighton, *Chron.* (Rolls Ser.), i, 62, 64. The Wm. in question is probably Wm. of Breteuil, the earl's eldest son, who died 1189–90: *Complete Peerage*, vii, 533.

original endowment of the hospital was. Simon de Montfort granted to it an annual rent from the honour of Leicester, and in exchange the hospital gave up its rights to a revenue of £3 previously paid to it from the bailiwick of Hinckley.[2] As Hinckley formed part of the honour of Leicester,[3] a rent from it may have been granted by William of Breteuil, the eldest son of an Earl of Leicester. In 1308 a licence was granted to the Earl of Lancaster to alienate to St. Leonard's 3 messuages, with 4 acres and 1 rood of meadow.[4] The king, in 1330, granted his protection to the masters and brethren of the hospital, collecting alms.[5] In the next year Philip Danet granted to the hospital 5 messuages and 7½ virgates in Whetstone, Croft, and Frisby by Galby (Leics.), in return for which the hospital was to maintain a chaplain to celebrate masses in St. Clement's church, Leicester, for the souls of Philip and others.[6]

There were both brothers and sisters at St. Leonard's Hospital, at least in the 14th century.[7] They were under the control of a master, who wore a black habit bearing a red crescent and star,[8] but it is not known whether they lived under any rule. The hospital is said to have been founded to succour lepers,[9] but there is no evidence for this statement. Under the terms of an agreement of March 1396–7 for free access to the parish church of St. Leonard, which was probably adjacent to the hospital, the master of the hospital paid a yearly rent of 10s. to the Abbot and convent of Leicester, to whom the parish church was appropriated.[10] The Abbot of Leicester visited the hospital in 1397, and again in 1406.[11]

In or before 1472 St. Leonard's Hospital was bought from the king[12] by William, Lord Hastings, who granted it to the College of the Newarke at Leicester.[13] The hospital apparently continued to exist, as in 1491 it was under the supervision of the college's treasurer.[14] When the College of the Newarke was suppressed under Edward VI's Act for the Dissolution of Chantries, St. Leonard's Hospital presumably shared its fate.[15]

MASTERS OF ST. LEONARD'S HOSPITAL

John of Barrow, occurs 1367.[16]

Thomas Thornton, occurs 1392.[17]

Richard Mannefeld, occurs from 1397 to 1405.[18]

Robert Matfeyn, occurs 1438,[19] died 1445.[20]

Thomas Lughtburgh, presented 1445.[21]

Richard Ednam, presented 1461.[22]

John Kery, presented 1464.[23]

William Est, presented 1466.[24]

A 12th-century seal[25] of the hospital is a very large vesica, 3 by 1¾ in., showing St. Leonard, abbot, seated and blessing. The legend is broken away.

Another of the hospital's seals,[26] of the 15th century, is 2½ by 1 9/16 in. It shows a full-length figure of St. Leonard standing in a niche, holding fetters in his right hand and a crosier in his left. Below is a priest in prayer. The legend reads:

SIGILLŪ COMMUNE MAGISTRI ET FRATRUM HOSPITAL' SCĪ LEONARDI LACESTRIE

23. THE HOSPITAL OF LUTTERWORTH

The Hospital of St. John the Baptist[1] at Lutterworth was built in or shortly before 1219,

---

[2] *Rot. Parl.* i, 390, where the rent granted by Simon is given as £6. 19s. 1d., and *Cal. Close, 1318–23,* 622, where the rent is given as £7. 19s. 1½d.

[3] L. Fox, 'The Honour of Leicester. Origin and Descent', *E.H.R.* liv, 390.

[4] *Cal. Pat., 1307–13,* 75.

[5] Ibid., *1330–4,* 11.

[6] Ibid., *1330–4,* 156. Nichols, *Leics.* i, 324, wrongly states that this grant was made to St. John's Hosp., Leicester.

[7] *Cal. Pat., 1330–4,* 156; *Rot. Parl.* i, 390.

[8] *Visitations in the Dioc. of Linc.* [1420–49], ed. A. Hamilton Thompson, ii, 190.

[9] Nichols, *Leics.* i, 321; T. Tanner, *Notitia Mon.* (1744), 242.

[10] Nichols, op. cit. i, 322, citing Bodl. Libr., Laud MS. 625.

[11] Nichols, op. cit. i, 322.

[12] The patronage of the hosp. was by 1445 in the hands of the D. of Lanc. (R. Somerville, 'D. of Lanc. Presentations, 1399–1485', *Bull. Inst. Hist. Research,* xviii, 75) to which many of the lands of the earls of Leicester had passed (*E.H.R.* liv, 396–9).

[13] *Cal. of Chart. and Other Doc. Belonging to the Hosp. of Wm. Wyggeston at Leic.,* ed. A. Hamilton Thompson, 89. In 1465 the next presentation to the mastership of the hosp. was granted to Hastings: *Bull. Inst. Hist. Research,* xviii, 75.

[14] Hamilton Thompson, *Hist. of the Hosp. of the Annunciation in the Newarke,* 131.

[15] The 'messuage called Saynt Leonarde's' granted away in 1550 (*Cal. Pat., 1549–51,* 122) may have been St. Leonard's Hosp.

[16] *Leic. Boro. Rec., 1327–1509,* 401.

[17] Ibid. 408.

[18] Nichols, *Leics.* i, 322, citing Bodl. Libr., Laud MS. 625; *Cal. of Chart. of Hosp. of Will. Wyggeston,* ed. A. Hamilton Thompson, 325.

[19] Nichols, op. cit. i, 322; *Cal. Papal Letters, 1431–47,* 69.

[20] *Bull. Inst. Hist. Research,* xviii, 75. A grant, dated 1461, of the custody of the hosp., void by Matfeyn's death, to John Walter occurs on the Pat. R. (*Cal. Pat., 1461–7,* 46), but this entry does not agree with the continuous series of presentations recorded in the D. of Lanc. rec., the evidence of which has been preferred here.

[21] *Bull. Inst. Hist. Research,* xviii, 75.

[22] Ibid. [23] Ibid. He was a Franciscan.

[24] Ibid. Also a Franciscan.

[25] B.M. Seals, lxvi, 69.

[26] B.M. D.C., F46, xxxv, 66.

[1] It is described as the hosp. of SS. John and Antony in 1436 (*Cal. Papal Letters, 1431–47,* 553), but this is the only reference to St. Antony in connexion with the hosp.

when Bishop Hugh of Lincoln permitted divine offices to be celebrated at the newly erected hospital.[2] Its foundation has been attributed to Rose de Verdon[3] and her son Nicholas,[4] but there seems to be no reliable evidence for this statement. Under Henry VIII the founder was said to have been Nicholas de Verdon,[5] and although not proved, this may well be true. About 1220 the hospital was receiving a yearly pension of 4 marks from the parish church of Lutterworth,[6] but in 1221 or 1222 the pension was only 3 marks.[7] The hospital is said to have obtained a grant of seven yardlands from Nicholas and Rose[8] de Verdon.[9]

Very little is known of the internal affairs of the hospital. Early in the 14th century Bishop Dalderby drew up regulations for the hospital, ordaining that the brethren there should obey the Augustinian rule, and that no women should be admitted as sisters without the consent of himself or his successors.[10] The altar of St. Mary in the hospital church is mentioned in 1350.[11] In 1436 it was said that there had been no brethren at the hospital for fifty years, and that the revenues had so declined that they amounted to not more than £20 a year. The Pope decreed in consequence that the mastership of the hospital might be held with any other benefice.[12] It seems probable that by 1400 at the latest the hospital had ceased to relieve the poor or sick, and that the office of master had become a benefice with few duties attached to it. In 1518 it was found that the master was not serving the hospital as he should.[13] The clear yearly income of the hospital was assessed at £29. 9s. 5d. in 1535. A sum of £4 was distributed in alms annually for the founder's soul.[14] In the certificate returned under Henry VIII's Act for the Dissolution of Chantries the hospital's net yearly revenue is given as £33. 7s. 4d., derived from lands at Lutterworth, two water-

mills there, and property at Bitteswell, Cadeby, Aston Flamville, Sharnford, Shawell, Frowlesworth, Cottesbach, and Walcote (Leics.), Long Itchington and Hillmorton (Warws.), and Haselbech (Northants.). The hospital was said to have been founded to maintain a priest and six poor men, and to provide hospitality for poor wayfarers, but in 1546 there were no poor in the hospital, the master was not resident, and the buildings, including the chapel, were greatly dilapidated.[15]

The hospital survived the seizure of chantry lands by the Crown, and in 1556 its net annual revenue was estimated to be £26. 9s. 5d. The master at that time was an absentee. He should have provided a priest for the hospital, but had not done so for three years before 1556. There were then no poor in the hospital, and the buildings were again said to be ruinous.[16] A master was presented as late as 1672.[17] It is not known when the hospital came to an end. It seems probable, however, that its property was disposed of by the Crown, to which the patronage had fallen,[18] and that the institution thus ceased to exist.

MASTERS OF LUTTERWORTH HOSPITAL

Simon of Asfordby, occurs 1218–19.[19]
Peter of Stanford, admitted 1242–3.[20]
G., resigned 1262–3.[21]
Hugh, admitted 1262–3.[22]
Geoffrey, resigned 1275.[23]
Godfrey, admitted 1275.[24]
John of Hathern, died 1299.[25]
Robert of Billesdon, admitted 1299,[26] resigned 1319.[27]
Adam of Bagworth, admitted 1319,[28] died 1321.[29]
William of Cotgrave, admitted 1321,[30] died 1329.[31]

[2] *Rot. Hugonis de Welles*, ed. W. P. W. Phillimore, i, 152.
[3] D. in or before 1216: *Rot. Lit. Claus., 1204–24* (Rec. Com.), 184.
[4] Nichols, *Leics.* iv, 259; J. Tanner, *Notitia Mon.* (1744), 243; Dugd. *Mon.* vi (2), 765; Rotha M. Clay, *Medieval Hosp. of Engl.* 301.
[5] A. Hamilton Thompson, 'The Chant. Cert. for Leics.', *Assoc. Arch. Soc. Rep. and Papers*, xxx, 498.
[6] *Rot. Hugonis de Welles*, i, 243.
[7] Ibid. ii, 284, 287.
[8] Possibly Nicholas's dau. and heiress, who d. 1247: *Excerpta e Rot. Fin.* (Rec. Com.), ii, 7, 11. But possibly his mother.
[9] W. Burton, *General Description of Leics.* (1777), 169.
[10] Linc. Reg. Dalderby, Memo., f. 140b; Linc. Reg. Buckingham, Memo., f. 197a.
[11] *Cal. Pat., 1348–50*, 552.
[12] *Cal. Papal Letters, 1431–47*, 553.
[13] *Visitations in Dioc. Linc., 1517–31*, ed. A. Hamilton Thompson, i, 17.
[14] *Valor Eccl.* (Rec. Com.), iv, 184.
[15] The identification of Sharnford and Shawell,

amongst the places where the hosp. held property, is uncertain: *Assoc. Arch. Soc. Rep. and Papers*, xxx, 496–8.
[16] Nichols, *Leics.* iv, 261, citing the return made by the Bp. of Linc. to Cardinal Pole, 1556.
[17] *Cal. S.P. Dom., 1671–2*, 138.
[18] Nichols, *Leics.* iv, 260–1; *Assoc. Arch. Soc. Rep. and Papers*, xxx, 498. The hosp. mills had been granted away in fee farm by 1631: Nichols, op. cit. iv, 253.
[19] *Rot. Hugonis de Welles*, i, 152.
[20] *Rot. Roberti Grosseteste*, ed. F. N. Davis, 419; *Mon. Franciscana* (Rolls Ser.), i, 173, 254.
[21] *Rot. Ric. Gravesend*, ed. F. N. Davis, 142.
[22] Ibid. [23] Ibid. 158.
[24] Ibid.
[25] Rosalind Hill, 'Bishop Sutton and the Inst. of Heads of Religious Houses in the Dioc. of Linc.', *E.H.R.* lviii, 209.
[26] Ibid.
[27] Linc. Reg. Dalderby, Inst., f. 220a.
[28] Ibid.
[29] Linc. Reg. Burghersh, Inst., f. 114a.
[30] Ibid. [31] Ibid., f. 126a.

Robert of Newbold, admitted 1329,[32] died 1331.[33]

Thomas of Lutterworth, admitted 1331,[34] died 1335.[35]

John of Rokeby, admitted 1335,[36] died 1338.[37]

Thomas of Peatling, admitted 1338.[38]

Thomas of Schrugton, died 1349.[39]

John of Lutterworth, admitted 1349,[40] resigned 1377.[41]

William Odde, admitted 1377,[42] deprived 1379.[43]

Elias of Wythyford, admitted 1380,[44] resigned 1386.[45]

William Wandesford, admitted 1386,[46] resigned 1390–1.[47]

Robert Leche, admitted 1391,[48] resigned 1392.[49]

Thomas Basford, admitted 1392,[50] died 1412.[51]

Stephen Brackley, admitted 1412,[52] resigned 1414.[53]

John Cryspe, admitted 1414,[54] died 1431.[55]

William Vesey, admitted 1431.[56]

Simon Smith, admitted 1434,[57] resigned 1454.[58]

Richard Wolsi, admitted 1454,[59] resigned 1475.[60]

Hugh Lewys, admitted 1475,[61] resigned 1504.[62]

Stephen Curteys, admitted 1504,[63] resigned 1510.[64]

Humphrey Knottesford, presented 1510,[65] died 1536.[66]

Robert Broke, presented 1536,[67] occurs 1546.[68]

William Rustat, presented 1577.[69]

Michael Hudson, presented 1640.[70]

William Hoare, presented 1672.[71]

No seal is known.

24. THE HOSPITAL OF ST. MARY MAGDALENE AND ST. MARGARET, LEICESTER

In 1312 Bishop Dalderby issued a licence for an oratory to be built for the leprous brethren in the parish of St. Margaret at Leicester,[1] and in the same year he granted an indulgence to them.[2] The brothers to whom these grants were made were almost certainly those of the Hospital of St. Mary Magdalene and St. Margaret. In 1334 the king granted protection to the leprous men of the Hospital of St. Mary Magdalene and St. Margaret at Leicester, and their messengers, collecting alms for their house, which was stated to depend on charity.[3] As no other institution in Leicester is certainly known to have succoured lepers, references in the early 13th century to the leper brothers of Leicester[4] may perhaps apply to this hospital, but such a suggestion is conjectural. Henry of Knighton refers to a leper house existing near St. John's Chapel in 1382;[5] this house may have been the Hospital of St. Mary Magdalene and St. Margaret, since the site indicated would have been within St. Margaret's parish as it later existed.[6] The leper house in St. Margaret's parish, mentioned in 1550,[7] is probably also the same foundation as this hospital. No seal is known.

[32] Linc. Reg. Burghersh, Inst., f. 126a.
[33] Ibid., f. 135a.
[34] Ibid.
[35] Ibid., f. 143b.
[36] Ibid.
[37] Ibid., f. 152d.
[38] Ibid.
[39] Linc. Reg. Gynewell, Inst., f. 334b. Possibly the same person as Thomas of Peatling.
[40] Ibid.
[41] Linc. Reg. Buckingham, Inst., i, f. 268a.
[42] Ibid.
[43] Ibid., f. 272a; Linc. Reg. Buckingham, Memo., f. 196a. Deprived for non-residence.
[44] Linc. Reg. Buckingham, Inst., i, f. 272a.
[45] Ibid. ii, f. 202b.
[46] Ibid.
[47] Cal. Pat., 1388–92, 373–4. Resigned on exchange of benefices.
[48] Ibid.
[49] Cal. Pat., 1391–6, 125. Resigned on exchange of benefices.
[50] Ibid.
[51] Linc. Reg. Repingdon, Inst., f. 171b.
[52] Ibid.
[53] Market Harborough Par. Rec., to 1530, ed. J. E. Stocks and W. B. Bragg, 125. Resigned on exchange of benefices.
[54] Ibid.
[55] Linc. Reg. Gray, Inst., f. 37b

[56] Ibid.
[57] Linc. Reg. Alnwick, Inst., f. 145a.
[58] Linc. Reg. Chedworth, Inst., f. 92b.
[59] Ibid. He was also Bp. of Down and Connor.
[60] Linc. Reg. Rotherham, Inst., f. 69b.
[61] Ibid.
[62] Linc. Reg. Smith, Inst., f. 281a.
[63] Ibid.
[64] Ibid., f. 296b.
[65] Ibid., f. 297b. Wm. Shepeston, Prior of Ulvescroft, is stated in another entry (ibid. 296b) to have been admitted as master, but this is probably an error.
[66] Linc. Reg. Longland, Inst., f. 144a.
[67] Ibid.
[68] Assoc. Arch. Soc. Rep. and Papers, xxx, 498.
[69] Rymer, Foedera (3rd ed., 1740), iv (4), 176.
[70] Cal. S.P. Dom., 1639–40, 532.
[71] Ibid. 1671–2, 138.
[1] Linc. Reg. Dalderby, Memo., f. 236a.
[2] Ibid., f. 221b.
[3] Cal. Pat., 1334–8, 32.
[4] They are said to have received a charter from the 1st Earl of Leicester, i.e. probably Robert de Beaumont, who d. 1118: Hist. MSS. Com., Hastings, i, 336; Pipe R. 1209 (Pipe R. Soc., n.s. xxiv), 26.
[5] Hen. Knighton, Chron. (Rolls Ser.), ii, 182.
[6] See map in Leic. Boro. Rec., 1103–1327, facing p. 1.
[7] Cal. Pat., 1549–51, 122.

25. THE HOSPITAL OF ST. EDMUND

In the 13th century Geoffrey, Abbot of Croxton,[1] granted certain lands in Galby and Frisby on the Wreak to the house of St. Edmund, Archbishop and Confessor, at Leicester, and to the poor brethren there.[2] The house cannot have been founded before the death of St. Edmund Rich in 1240. Nothing further is known concerning this foundation, and no seal has been found.

26. THE HOSPITAL OF ST. BARTHOLOMEW, LEICESTER

In 1322 Bishop Burgersh granted an indulgence to the infirm of St. Bartholomew's Hospital, Leicester.[1] No other record of this hospital has been discovered, and no seal is known.

27. THE HOSPITAL OF LOUGHBOROUGH

There was a hospital for the sick at Loughborough in 1301, when Bishop Dalderby allowed alms to be collected for it.[1] No seal is known.

28. THE HOSPITAL OF STOCKERSTON

In 1466 licence was granted to Sir John Boyville to found by the church at Stockerston a perpetual almshouse, for one chaplain and three poor persons, and to grant it funds in mortmain to the value of £10 yearly.[1] Boyville died before the hospital could be founded, and in 1468 his executors obtained a licence to found an almshouse for three poor persons, with a chantry chaplain. The almshouse was to be dedicated to the Virgin Mary, and the chaplain was licensed to obtain for himself and the three poor lands with a yearly value of up to £12.[2] In 1535 the hospital was still in existence, and it was then noted that the three poor persons were paid £3. 11s. yearly, while the gross yearly income of the hospital was £12. 3s.[3] The subsequent fate of the hospital is unknown, but it may have been the institution at Stockerston dissolved by Thomas Waldron shortly after 1535.[4]

CHAPLAIN OF STOCKERSTON HOSPITAL

William Warton, occurs 1536.[5]

No seal is known.

COLLEGES

29. THE COLLEGE OF ST. MARY DE CASTRO

The College of St. Mary *de Castro* at Leicester is traditionally said to have existed before the Norman Conquest, when it is stated to have been destroyed,[1] but there is no reliable evidence for this. A college for a dean and twelve secular canons was established at St. Mary's church at Leicester by Robert de Beaumont,[2] in honour of the Virgin Mary and in veneration of All Souls, and for the souls of William I, his queen Maud, and his son William II, and in the future for the souls of Henry I, his wife and children, and for the souls of the founder and his relatives. Robert de Beaumont endowed the college with the churches of All Saints and St. Peter at Leicester, the churches of the sokes of Shepshed (Leics.) and Halse (Northants.), with various lands near Leicester, and with revenues worth £6 yearly from the town of Leicester itself. Ralph *pincerna* gave the college the church of St. Martin at Leicester, and the church of Lilbourne (Northants.). The date of foundation is said to have been 1107.[3]

The college of secular canons existed until 1143, when all its endowments were transferred by the founder's son, Robert *le Bossu*, Earl of Leicester, to the canons of the new Augustinian abbey at Leicester.[4] The new abbey, however, did not altogether replace the old college of secular canons. At some date before 1167 the Abbot and

---

[1] Occurs from 1241–2 to 1268: *Rot. Roberti Grosseteste*, ed. F. N. Davis, 416; Farnham, *Leics. Notes*, i, 214.
[2] Hist. MSS. Com., *Rutland*, iv, 180.

---

[1] Linc. Reg. Burghersh, Memo., f. 52a.

---

[1] Linc. Reg. Dalderby, Memo., f. 37b.

---

[1] *Cal. Pat.*, *1461–7*, 486.
[2] Ibid., *1467–77*, 113.
[3] *Valor Eccl.* (Rec. Com.), iv, 162.
[4] It was stated in 1547 that a chantry at Stockerston had been dissolved by Waldron 12 or 13 years earlier. This may have been the hosp., but it is to be noted that in 1535 there was another chantry at Stockerston,

besides the hosp.: *Valor Eccl.* (Rec. Com.), iv, 162; A. Hamilton Thompson, 'The Chant. Cert. for Leics.', *Assoc. Arch. Soc. Rep. and Papers*, xxx, 528.
[5] *Valor Eccl.* (Rec. Com.), iv, 162.

---

[1] Nichols, *Leics.* i, 303; Dugd. *Mon.* vi (3), 1456. The account given by Hen. Knighton, *Chron.* (Rolls Ser.), i, 62, seems to indicate that a coll. existed before the Conquest, for Knighton speaks of Robert de Beaumont restoring lands and chs. to the canons.
[2] Probably the 1st Earl of Leicester.
[3] Dugd. *Mon.* vi (1), 466–7; Nichols, *Leics.* i, App., 53; A. Hamilton Thompson, *Abbey of St. Mary of the Meadows, Leicester*, 1, 2.
[4] Dugd. *Mon.* vi (1), 466–7; Knighton, *Chron.* (Rolls Ser.), i, 62.

convent of Leicester agreed to provide for the service of St. Mary's church eight clerks, consisting of a sacrist, a chaplain, and six others, who were all to be appointed, and if necessary removed, solely at the will of the abbot and convent. The Abbot of Leicester, or one of his canons appointed for the purpose, was to preside over the chapter of the collegiate church. The eight clerks were to receive all the offerings of St. Mary's parish, and most of the tithes, with a revenue of 20s. given by Robert de Beaumont for the lamps and other needs of the church. The sacrist and clerks of the college had to serve in person, and were not allowed to appoint vicars to act in their places.[5] About 1220 there were seven clerks, including presumably the sacrist, serving at St. Mary's, with two chaplains, instead of only one as originally provided.[6] The college existed in obscurity for the rest of the Middle Ages. In 1379 the Abbot and convent of Leicester had licence to alienate the advowson of Hathern to the sacrist and canons of St. Mary's, on condition that the grantees should provide a chaplain to celebrate daily for the souls of the king, his mother, Robert *le Bossu*, and others.[7] The alienation was carried out within the next few years.[8] The college's clear yearly income, as assessed in 1535, was only £23. 12s. 11d., of which the dean[9] had a stipend of £4. 19s. 2d., and the prebendaries £2. 9s. 7d. each.[10] The certificate returned in 1546 under Henry VIII's Chantry Act[11] states that one of the prebends was then vacant. It also mentions that a dwelling-house was provided for the college's clergy.[12] The college was dissolved under the Chantry Act of Edward VI.[13]

SACRISTS[14] OF THE COLLEGE OF ST. MARY DE CASTRO

Richard de Tuttebury, resigned 1376.[15]

John de Hemyngburgh, collated 1376,[16] died 1382.[17]

Simon Bache, collated 1382,[18] occurs 1390.[19]

James Whistones, died 1512.[20]

John Yong, collated 1512.[21]

Thomas Darby, occurs 1534.[22]

Richard Fowler, occurs 1535,[23] resigned before 1546.[24]

Ralph Cowley, occurs 1546.[25]

A 14th-century seal,[26] a pointed oval about 2 by 1¼ in., shows the Virgin Mary, crowned, seated beneath a canopy, holding the infant Jesus on her left knee. Both Mother and Child have their right hands raised in benediction. All that remains of the legend is:

... CESTRIE ...

30. THE COLLEGE OF NOSELEY[1]

The first step towards the foundation of a chantry college at Noseley was taken in 1274, when Anketin de Martivall granted to God and to the chapel of St. Mary at Noseley, and the chaplains there celebrating the divine offices, a messuage at Noseley, a messuage and a virgate at Slawston, 5 acres at Hallaton, and 4 virgates at Houghton, with the villeins occupying the tenements concerned.[2] Anketin's grant was confirmed by his son and heir, Roger de Martivall, in 1276,[3] but it is not known how the chantry thus endowed was constituted, or even whether a chantry was in fact established at this time. In 1303 it was reported that it would not be to the king's damage if licence was granted to Roger de Martivall to alienate 3 messuages, 6¼ virgates, and 8 marks rent at Noseley, Stretton, and Gilmorton to four chaplains, who were to celebrate the divine offices in Noseley chapel for the souls of Roger and his ancestors,[4] and in 1304 the patrons of the parish church at Noseley gave their consent to Roger and his successors having a free chapel there.[5] In June 1306 Anketin's gift of property at Slawston, Hallaton, and Houghton was confirmed by royal letters patent, and licence was

---

[5] *Ancient Chart.* (Pipe R. Soc. x), ed. J. H. Round, 59–63; Nichols, *Leics.* i, 303.

[6] *Rot. Hugonis de Welles*, ed. W. P. W. Phillimore, i, 238.

[7] *Cal. Pat.*, *1377–81*, 371.

[8] Hamilton Thompson, *Abbey of Leic.* 145.

[9] The head of the coll., originally styled the sacrist, was frequently known as the dean, at least from the 14th century onwards: *Cal. Pat.*, *1374–7*, 339; *1292–1301*, 524; *Cal. of Chart. and Other Doc. Belonging to the Hosp. of Wm. Wyggeston at Leicester*, ed. A. Hamilton Thompson, 320.

[10] *Valor Eccl.* (Rec. Com.), iv, 172.

[11] 37 Hen. VIII, c. 4.

[12] A. Hamilton Thompson, 'The Chant. Cert. for Leics.', *Assoc. Arch. Soc. Rep. and Papers*, xxx, 492–3.

[13] For particulars of sale of an item of the coll.'s property, see ibid. xxx, 544.

[14] Or deans; see n. 9 above.

[15] *Cal. Pat.*, *1374–7*, 339. Resigned on exchange of benefices.   [16] Ibid.

[17] *Cal. of Chart. of Hosp. of Wm. Wyggeston*, 320.

[18] Ibid.

[19] Hamilton Thompson, *Abbey of Leic.*, 145.

[20] *L. & P. Hen. VIII*, i, p. 459.

[21] Ibid.

[22] Hamilton Thompson, *Abbey of Leic.*, 146.

[23] *Valor Eccl.* (Rec. Com.), iv, 172.

[24] *Assoc. Arch. Soc. Rep. and Papers*, xxx, 493.

[25] Ibid.; he was the last sacrist (*Char. Com. Rep.* [163], p. 42, H.C. (1839), xv).

[26] D.L. 25/317.

[1] The account of Noseley Coll. given by A. Hamilton Thompson and G. F. Farnham, in 'The Manor of Noseley', *T.L.A.S.* xii, 233–57, has been followed here.

[2] Ibid. 233–4; H. Hartopp, 'Unpublished Doc. Relating to Noseley', *Assoc. Arch. Soc. Rep. and Papers*, xxv, 448.

[3] *Assoc. Arch. Soc. Rep. and Papers*, xxv, 450.

[4] *T.L.A.S.* xii, 234–5.

[5] *Assoc. Arch. Soc. Rep. and Papers*, xxv, 453.

granted for the alienation by Roger de Martivall of 2 messuages and 8 marks of rent in Noseley and Stretton to three chaplains, who were to celebrate divine services daily in Noseley chapel.[6] An agreement concluded in August of the same year between Roger de Martivall and the rector of Noseley specified in detail what ceremonies might be performed in the free chapel, and how offerings were to be divided between the chapel and the parish church. The rector gave up all claim to the advowson of the chapel, and Roger granted to the rector a messuage and a virgate at Noseley.[7] This agreement was confirmed by the patrons of Noseley parish church, and by the Bishop and Chapter of Lincoln.[8] Roger de Martivall laid down the regulations for the chantry in a document of October 1306. It was provided that the head of the free chapel was to have the power to remove his subordinates at will, and to replace them by others; arrangements were made for the payment of the clergy of the chantry, and it was provided that if any surplus profits arose they were to be used to support further priests and clerks; the services to be celebrated in the chapel were briefly described.[9]

Noseley chantry, one of the earliest chantry colleges to be founded, survived until the general suppression of chantries under Edward VI, but though the college obtained some further endowments it never became important. In 1334 licence was granted for the alienation to the college of one-third of the manor of Garthorpe (Leics.).[10] About 1336 the college was granted the advowson of Noseley parish church,[11] which was appropriated in 1338.[12] The parochial cure of souls was transferred to the warden of the college, and the ordinary services were probably celebrated after this date in the chantry chapel rather than in the parish church.[13] In 1369 one-half of the advowson of Hallaton (Leics.) was granted to the college,[14] and in the same year licence was given for the alienation to the college of the manor of Caldecote (Warws.).[15] In 1370 the college obtained a manor at Blaston (Leics.),[16] and some property in Noseley was conveyed to it in 1375.[17]

In 1526 there were in the college three priests,[18] two deacons, an organist, two other clerks, and a curate, who was presumably engaged in parochial duties,[19] but in 1530 only the warden, the curate, and one other clerk are mentioned.[20] Leland, visiting Leicestershire some years later, noted that there were then in the college three priests, two clerks, and four choristers.[21] Shortly before the college was suppressed its gross yearly revenue was estimated at £24. 13s. 9½d. Out of this, the two chaplains each had a yearly stipend of £2. 13s. 4d., and two clerks each had a stipend of £1. 6s. 8d.[22] Another document of about the same date, however, gives the warden's stipend as £6. 13s. 4d., that of one of the chaplains as £5. 6s. 8d., and those of two deacons as £3. 13s. 4d. each.[23] The college was dissolved under Edward VI's Act for the Dissolution of Chantries, the last warden being granted a pension of £6.[24]

WARDENS OF NOSELEY COLLEGE[25]

Miles of Leycestre, occurs 1306.[26]
William of Carleton, resigned 1315.
Robert Benet, presented 1315.
Ralph, resigned 1330.
Roger of Ryngested, presented April 1330, resigned 1330.
John Pere, presented October 1330.
John of Ilneston of Gothemundele,[27] resigned 1343.
John of Ilneston,[27] presented 1343, died 1349.
William of Humberston, presented June 1349, resigned 1349.
Ralph de Peek, presented August 1349, died 1375.
William of Rothewell, presented 1375.
John of Bolton, presented 1397.
Richard Gaytecote, presented 1398, resigned 1402.[28]
John Bale, presented 1402, resigned 1407.[28]

---

6 Ibid. 456–8; xxvi, 277; *Cal. Pat., 1301–7*, 444; *T.L.A.S.* xii, 237–8.

7 *T.L.A.S.* xii, 238–41; *Assoc. Arch. Soc. Rep. and Papers*, xxvi, 281–5.

8 *T.L.A.S.* xii, 241–2; *Assoc. Arch. Soc. Rep. and Papers*, xxvi, 276–81, 288–9.

9 *T.L.A.S.* xii, 242–8; *Assoc. Arch. Soc. Rep. and Papers*, xxvi, 292–9.

10 *T.L.A.S.* xii, 249; *Cal. Pat., 1330–4*, 516.

11 *T.L.A.S.* xii, 249.

12 Ibid. 250–1.

13 Ibid. 251–2.

14 Ibid. 253; *Cal. Pat., 1367–70*, 24, 107–8.

15 *Cal. Pat., 1367–70*, 246. The alienation was subsequently carried out. *Valor Eccl.* (Rec. Com.), iv, 160.

16 *Cal. Close, 1374–7*, 75, where the donor's charter is recited.

17 *T.L.A.S.* xii, 253.

18 Listed as chaplains.

19 *Subsidy Collected in Dioc. of Linc. in 1526*, ed. H. E. Salter, 118.

20 'Proc. of the Eccl. Ct. in the Archdeaconry of Leic.', ed. A. P. Moore, *Assoc. Arch. Soc. Rep. and Papers*, xxviii, 152.

21 *Leland's Itin.*, ed. Lucy Toulmin-Smith, i, 14.

22 A. Hamilton Thompson, 'The Chant. Cert. for Leics.', *Assoc. Arch. Soc. Rep. and Papers*, xxx, 509–10.

23 Ibid. 532.

24 Ibid.; *T.L.A.S.* xii, 256–7.

25 The list given by A. Hamilton Thompson, 'The Rectors of the Chapel and Par. Ch. of Noseley', *T.L.A.S.* xiii, 74–77, has been reproduced here, as except for the first warden it is complete.

26 *T.L.A.S.* xii, 243–7.

27 The names of the two successive wardens are given thus, possibly in error, in the bishop's reg. (cited ibid.).

28 Resigned on exchange of benefices.

Lawrence Blakesle, presented 1407, resigned 1408.

John Amore, presented 1408, resigned 1419.

John Billesfeld, presented 1419, resigned 1425.[28]

Thomas Rydell, presented September 1425, resigned 1425.[28]

John Boneyamy, presented October 1425, resigned 1433.

William Brocket, presented 1433, resigned 1440.

Robert Gybbes, presented 1440, resigned 1461.

William Attekyns, presented 1461, died 1462.

John Geby, presented 1462,[29] died 1500.

Thomas Chapman, presented 1550, died 1503.

Christopher Rosyndale, presented 1503, resigned 1509.

Richard Alkeborowe, presented 1509, resigned 1513.

Roger Worthington, presented February 1513, resigned 1513.

Richard Wodd, presented July 1513, resigned 1520.

Roger Worthington, presented 1520, died 1527.

Denis Morison, presented 1527. Last warden.

No seal is known.

31. THE COLLEGE OF THE ANNUNCIATION OF ST. MARY IN THE NEWARKE, LEICESTER[1]

In April 1330, Henry, Earl of Lancaster, obtained a royal licence to establish a hospital at Leicester, and in the following January the earl by letters patent founded the hospital in honour of the Annunciation of St. Mary, for a warden, four chaplains, fifty poor and infirm folk, and five women attendants.[2] The building of the hospital seems to have been begun in 1330.[3] The founder's regulations of January 1331 provided that the warden and chaplains, though secular clerks, were to lead a common life, and to wear a habit marked with a white crescent and star. The warden was to be elected by the chaplains, and then presented by the patron to the bishop. Of the fifty poor folk, twenty were to be permanent inmates of the hospital, living in a house beside the hospital's church, while the remaining thirty, who were to be admitted temporarily, were to be housed on

beds in the body of the church.[4] In 1334 the hospital obtained papal licence for the celebration of all the sacraments in its chapel, and for the burial of those attached to the house in its cemetery.[5] The original endowment consisted of the site of the hospital, 4 carucates at Leicester, and the advowson of Irchester (Northants.), with certain common rights in the founder's woods around Leicester.[6] In 1331 Earl Henry added the advowson of Duffield (Derbys.) to the hospital's possessions.[7] The rectories of Irchester and Duffield were both appropriated to the hospital when they fell vacant.[8]

After the death of Henry of Lancaster the patronage of the hospital passed to his son Henry, created Duke of Lancaster in 1351, who munificently enlarged his father's foundation. In 1353 the duke obtained the Pope's permission for the transformation of the hospital into a college with a dean and canons.[9] In 1354 the duke provided that there should be in the enlarged foundation a dean, 12 canons, 13 vicars, 3 other clerks, a verger, 100 poor folk, and 10 women attendants to care for the poor,[10] but it was not until the following year that the endowment was increased by the grant of the manors of Inglesham (Wilts.), Wollaston (Northants.), Kempsford (Gloucs.), Chedworth (Gloucs.), and Hannington (Wilts.), with the advowsons of Edmonthorpe (Leics.), Wymondham (Leics.), Higham Ferrers (Northants.), Raunds (Northants.), and Hannington (Wilts.). The college was authorized to appropriate the churches.[11] The churches of Llandyfaelog and Pembrey in Carmarthenshire were added to the college's possessions in 1356, in exchange for the advowsons of Edmonthorpe and Wymondham, which were restored to the Duke of Lancaster.[12] The college's regulations, as drawn up by Duke Henry and revised by Bishop Gynewell,[13] provided that the dean, canons, and vicars should all be priests; the poor folk were all to live together in one house, containing a chapel where masses were to be said daily for the poor; when the office of dean fell vacant, the canons were to nominate two persons to the duke, to his lieutenant if he should be abroad, or to the duke's heirs after his death, and one of the two was to be chosen for presentation to the bishop; new canons were to be chosen by the duke or his heirs, and presented to the bishop for institution; the dean, canon, and vicars were to be allowed to be absent

---

[28] Resigned on exchange of benefices.

[29] For some unknown reason Geby was presented for a second time in 1478.

[1] This account is almost entirely based on A. Hamilton Thompson's *Hist. of the Hosp. and New Coll. of the Annunciation of St. Mary in the Newarke*.

[2] Hamilton Thompson, op. cit. 12, 13.

[3] Ibid. 12, n. 5.   [4] Ibid. 17–19.

[5] *Cal. Papal Letters, 1305–42*, 398.

[6] Hamilton Thompson, *Hist. of Hosp. of the Annunciation in the Newarke*, 13–14.

[7] Ibid. 20.

[8] Ibid. 21, 22.

[9] Ibid. 26.

[10] Ibid. 27.

[11] Ibid. 26–27.

[12] Ibid. 31–32.

[13] For a transl. of the rules, with an account of the various additions and revisions made to them, see ibid. 41–81. For the full Latin text, see A. Hamilton Thompson, 'Notes on Coll. of Secular Canons in Engl.', *Arch. Jnl.* lxxiv, 200–39.

for up to two months every year, provided that no more than three canons and three vicars were absent at any one time; the canons and vicars were not to celebrate yearly masses or trentals for the souls of deceased persons, but were to rest content with their stipends; the dean and canons were each to have a separate house, and each vicar was to dwell in the house of one of the canons.

As established by Duke Henry the college was adequately endowed, and the regulations carefully provided for the maintenance of the morals of its clergy and the due celebration of the divine offices.[14] Duke Henry died in 1361, but John of Gaunt, who after a short interval succeeded to the Duchy of Lancaster, proved to be a generous patron of the college. In 1363 a licence was obtained for the alienation to the college by John and his wife of the church of Llanelly, in Carmarthenshire.[15] The building of the college church continued, and in 1374 John of Gaunt granted 100 marks yearly, payable from the honour of Tutbury, to pay for its completion.[16] It was, however, not finished until after 1414.[17] By his will John provided for the establishment of a chantry with two chaplains in the college church,[18] though it was not until 1410 that the chantry was endowed by the grant to the college of the Warwickshire manors of Draycote and Bourton.[19] At about the same period other chantries were founded in the college church:[20] in 1401 a licence was issued for the foundation of a chantry, endowed with the advowson of Arnold (Notts.), for the soul of John Elvet;[21] in 1406 Mary Hervey gave to the college two manors at Southrop (Gloucs.), for the establishment of a chantry for the souls of her husband, William Hervey, of Alexander Dalby, and of herself after her death;[22] and Thomas, Duke of Clarence, provided in his will for the establishment of a chantry in the collegiate church, though his wishes do not seem to have been carried out.[23] Other important additions to the college's possessions were the manor and advowson of Cransley (Northants.), granted by Simon Symeon in 1380,[24] the advowson of Preston in Amounderness (Lancs.), granted by

Henry IV in 1400,[25] and the advowson of Bradford (Yorks.), granted by Henry V in 1416.[26]

Despite these rich endowments and the detailed system of rules, the internal affairs of the college were in a very unsatisfactory state by 1440, when Bishop Alnwick visited the house.[27] Several canons were accused of immorality,[28] and one was deprived of his prebend for unnatural vice.[29] The poor folk of the college complained that a plot of land originally assigned to them as a garden had been used as a site for a stable, and that certain payments due to them had been selfishly withheld by the canons,[30] while on the other hand it was said that sick people who had been received into the almshouse remained there after their recovery, and worked for gain.[31] There were also complaints regarding the celebration of the divine offices in the collegiate church.[32] Though there were some complaints about the handling of business affairs by the provost,[33] to whom the management of the college's goods was entrusted, there is no indication that the college was in serious pecuniary difficulties.

For a considerable period after the visitation of 1440 there is little evidence about the internal state of the college. The deans, during the later 15th century, were mostly men who held important preferments outside Leicester.[34] The provision that the dean should be chosen from amongst the canons[35] was at first evaded by the practice of admitting the persons selected as deans to canonries for a qualifying period of a few days, before their advancement to the deanery.[36] Later, from 1485 onwards, the deans seem to have been chosen merely at the will of the Crown as patron, without election, and usually without having previously obtained a canonry in the college.[37] Under Edward IV, the college was fortunate in gaining the friendship of William, Lord Hastings, who bestowed on it the Hospital of St. Leonard, at Leicester, in return for an annuity of £20 for life, and for the keeping of the obits of himself and of his wife Katherine after his death.[38] Hastings also obtained St. John's Hospital, at Leicester, for the college.[39] In 1491 the college was provided

[14] Hamilton Thompson, *Hist. of Hosp. of the Annunciation in the Newarke*, 55–57, 59, 61–63, 71.

[15] Ibid. 72, 82.   [16] Ibid. 83.   [17] Ibid. 96.

[18] Ibid. 72, 89, 90.   [19] Ibid. 95.

[20] The establishment of chantries in the ch. was specifically allowed by the rules enacted when the coll. was first founded: A. Hamilton Thompson, op. cit. 74.

[21] Ibid. 91.   [22] Ibid. 93–94.

[23] Ibid. 96–97.

[24] Ibid. 84. The coll. appropriated Cransley ch. in 1385. Ibid. 87.

[25] Ibid. 91. Hen. of Grosmont, in 1355, had obtained a licence to alienate Preston ch. to the coll., but did not actually grant the ch.: ibid. 27–28.

[26] Ibid. 96.

[27] The record of the visitation is printed in *Visitations in the Dioc. of Linc.* [1420–49], ed. A. Hamilton Thompson, ii, 187–206.

[28] Ibid. 188–94.   [29] Ibid. 197.

[30] Ibid. 196.

[31] Ibid. 192–3.

[32] Ibid. 190, 192, 198–9.

[33] Ibid. 189, 192–3.

[34] Hamilton Thompson, *Hist. of Hosp. of the Annunciation in the Newarke*, 117–19, 136.

[35] Ibid. 48.   [36] Ibid. 139.

[37] Ibid. 139–40.

[38] Ibid. 118; *Cal. of Chart. and other Doc. Belonging to the Hosp. of Wm. Wyggeston at Leicester*, ed. A. Hamilton Thompson. 89.

[39] Hamilton Thompson, *Hist. of Hosp. of the Annunciation in the Newarke*, 118, citing Nichols, *Leics.* i, 333, states that Hastings granted the revenues and advowson of St. John's to the coll. But the exact means by which the coll. obtained St. John's seems doubtful. See the account of St. John's Hosp., Leic., p. 40.

with new statutes issued by John Russell, Bishop of Lincoln, one of a commission appointed by the Pope in 1488 with powers to revise and add to the rules of the house.[40] Some minor relaxations were allowed by the new regulations. The number of months yearly during which the dean and canons were allowed to be absent from the college was increased from two to three and, in addition, the dean was allowed to be absent for a further two months, for recreation, and every canon beneficed elsewhere for a further month. Vicars were still allowed only two months' leave of absence yearly.[41] The rule which forbade canons and vicars, while in residence, to sleep outside the college was also to some extent relaxed.[42] In 1513 William Wigston founded a chantry in the college church. Wigston paid 100 marks to the college, and gave it the manor of Chester-by-the-Water (Northants.); in return the college agreed to pay the two chaplains of the chantry a yearly stipend of £7 each, and to celebrate Wigston's obit annually.[43]

The record of the episcopal visitation of the college in 1518 reveals no such serious faults as had come to light in 1440, but does show that in some ways the state of the college was not good. It was reported that the canons and vicars did not attend the divine offices as they should, that the canons frequented taverns, and that women were received into the college without licence.[44] The canons complained of the arbitrary conduct of the dean, George Grey.[45] No serious delinquency was revealed, and there is no evidence that the college's finances were in an unsatisfactory state. A more detailed account of the college's affairs is provided by a visitation of 1525, carried out by Bishop Longland.[46] It is evident from the record of the visitation that there had been constant friction between the dean and Lady Hungerford, who with her second husband was living within the college precincts, and various scuffles had taken place in the college between the servants of the two parties. The dean was evidently also on bad terms with some of the canons. The visitation gives little evidence of any immorality in the college, though one of the canons was accused of

incontinence. The bishop's injunctions suggest that in 1525 the college's finances were not altogether sound.[47] As in 1518, there were complaints about the irregular attendance of canons and vicars in choir, while, as in 1440, it was stated that people were allowed to remain in the almshouse after they had recovered from their sickness. It was further revealed that many of the poor had been admitted through bribery. The bishop in his injunctions endeavoured to remedy the faults revealed in the visitation, and especially to establish good relations between the dean and canons.[48] His efforts were apparently successful, for when the college was visited in 1528 by the chancellor of the diocese the dean and canons seem to have been on good terms.[49] No serious faults were disclosed in 1528, though complaints were made about the vicars' lax attendance in choir, and one of the canons was continually absent from the college.[50]

The college for some time survived the great religious changes of the 16th century. In 1534 the dean and thirty of the college clergy acknowledged the royal supremacy over the Church,[51] and Dr. Layton, visiting the college in the following year, reported that it was occupied by honest men, and that there were £300 in the treasury.[52] There seems at one time to have been a possibility that the college might be changed into a cathedral.[53] The clear yearly income of the college was assessed in 1535 at £595. 7s. 4d.[54] In 1544 the college was visited by the bishop's representative; the surviving records of this visitation mention no major faults, though it seems that some of the college clergy were in the habit of frequenting taverns.[55] In 1545, however, by the first Act for the Dissolution of Chantries the college, and the chantries associated with it, were placed in the king's hands. The certificate drawn up under this Act gives the total yearly income of the college as just over £850.[56] Henry VIII was apparently unwilling to destroy a religious house so closely connected with his Lancastrian ancestors,[57] but after his death the college was suppressed under Edward VI's Act for the Dissolution of Chantries, which provided that all chantry foundations should

---

[40] Hamilton Thompson, *Hist. of Hosp. of the Annunciation in the Newarke*, 120.

[41] Ibid. 125.

[42] Ibid. 129. Compare the earlier rule: ibid. 62.

[43] Ibid. 137. See also S. H. Skillington, 'The Chant. House in the Newarke', *Assoc. Arch. Soc. Rep. and Papers*, xxxi, 431–4, and *Cal. of Chart. of Hosp. of Wm. Wyggeston*, 2–16.

[44] *Visitations in Dioc. Linc., 1517–31*, ed. A. Hamilton Thompson, iii, 13. [45] Ibid. iii, 2, 3.

[46] For details of the visitation, see ibid. iii, 123–238.

[47] Ibid. iii, 239, 249.

[48] For the injunctions, see ibid. iii, 239–49.

[49] Hamilton Thompson, *Hist. of Hosp. of the Annunciation in the Newarke*, 197.

[50] Ibid. 197; *Visitations in Dioc. Linc., 1517–31*, iii, 56.

[51] Hamilton Thompson, *Hist. of Hosp. of the Annunciation in the Newarke*, 205.

[52] Ibid. 204. T. Wright, *Three Chapters Relating to the Suppression of the Mon.* (Camden Soc., 1st ser. xxvi), 93.

[53] Hamilton Thompson, *Hist. of Hosp. of the Annunciation in the Newarke*, 205; *L. & P. Hen. VIII*, xiv (2), p. 152.

[54] *Valor Eccl.* (Rec. Com.), iv, 171.

[55] 'Leics. Doc. in Linc. Episcopal Reg.', in *Assoc. Arch. Soc. Rep. and Papers*, xxii, 117–19.

[56] A. Hamilton Thompson, *Hist. of Hosp. of the Annunciation in the Newarke*, 206. For full text of the cert., see A. Hamilton Thompson, 'The Chant. Certs. for Leics.', *Assoc. Arch. Soc. Rep. and Papers*, xxx, 515–27.

[57] *L. & P. Hen. VIII*, xx (1), p. 609.

cease to exist at Easter 1548, their property passing to the king.[58] The dean received a pension of £20 a year, the canons pensions of £10 each, and the vicars and chantry priests pensions of £6 each.[59]

The College of the Newarke thus ceased to exist in its original form, and the collegiate church was before long demolished.[60] The subsequent history of the hospital attached to the college cannot be dealt with here.

WARDENS OF THE HOSPITAL OF THE ANNUNCIATION OF ST. MARY[61]

Thomas of Burthyngbure, presented 1331, resigned 1332.

John of Horncastre, presented 1332, resigned 1336.

Hugh of Scaldeforde, presented 1336.

John of Eydone, occurs 1348, died 1349.

William of Knighton, presented 1349.

DEANS OF THE COLLEGE OF THE NEWARKE.[62]

Richard of Hamslape, presented 1356, died 1361–2.

John Porter, presented 1362, died 1369.

Peter of Kellisheye, presented 1369, died 1383.[63]

Thomas Brightewell, presented 1383,[64] died 1390.

William Chuseldene, presented 1390, died 1396.

Richard Elvet, presented 1396, died 1431.

William Walesby, presented 1431, resigned 1450.

Richard Andrews, presented 1450.

William Witham, died 1472.

William Dudley, presented 1472, resigned 1476.

William Chauntre, presented 1476, died 1485.

John Morgan, presented 1485, resigned 1496.[65]

Robert Middleton, presented 1496, died 1499–1500.

William[66] Stokedall, presented January 1500, died 1500.

James Whitston, presented November 1500, died 1512–13.

John Yong, presented 1513, resigned 1515.

William Knyght, presented 1515, resigned 1517.

George Grey, presented 1517, resigned 1530.

Robert Bone, presented 1530.

A 14th-century seal[67] of the college is a vesica, 2¼ by 1⅜ in., showing the Virgin Mary seated on a throne under a canopy, with the infant Jesus on her knee. Both have the right hand raised in the attitude of blessing. All that remains of the legend is:

S' CAP . . . ULI . . . . . ESTRIE

The large and very beautiful 15th-century seal[68] of the college represents the Annunciation. The archangel Gabriel is depicted holding a scroll bearing the letters A.M.G., while the Virgin holds a scroll inscribed ECCE AN. DO. Below is a shield bearing the arms of England differenced with a label. The seal is about 2½ by 1½ in. The legend reads:

S' C̄OE. DECANI. ET. CAPL'I. NOVE. ECCL. COLL. BĒ. MAR'. LEYC . . . ĒR. DUCE LAN̄C. FŪDATE.

32. THE COLLEGE OF SAPCOTE

The small college of chantry priests at Sapcote was founded in or shortly after 1361, when licence was granted to Ralph Basset to alienate in mortmain 11 messuages, 10 virgates of land, and 20 acres of meadow at Sapcote and Stoney Stanton to two chaplains, who were to celebrate the divine offices in Sapcote church in accordance with Basset's ordinance.[1] In 1372 Basset was planning to increase the endowment and to raise the number of chaplains to three.[2] By 1376 the third chaplain had been established,[3] and in the same year Basset obtained a licence for the alienation to the chantry college of property at Sapcote.[4] The chantry priests performed their office in the chapel of St. Mary, on the north side of Sapcote church.[5] The chapel was described in 1377 as newly erected,[6] and it was probably built by Basset for this chantry. The chantry college was known as the chapel of St. Mary,[7] and was under the control of a warden,[8] who was presumably one of the three chaplains.

In the certificate returned under Henry VIII's

---

[58] Hamilton Thompson, *Hist. of Hosp. of the Annunciation in the Newarke*, 209.

[59] Ibid. 220–1.

[60] Ibid. 230.

[61] The following list is based on that given by Hamilton Thompson, op. cit. 20.

[62] The following list is based on that given by Hamilton Thompson, op. cit. 231–3.

[63] *John of Gaunt's Reg., 1379–83* (Camden Soc., 3rd ser. lvi), ed. Eleanor C. Lodge and R. Somerville, i, 5.

[64] Ibid.

[65] Resigned on consecration as Bp. of St. David's:

Hamilton Thompson, *Hist. of Hosp. of the Annunciation in the Newarke*, 232.

[66] In the notice of his successor's appointment, however, Stokedall's first name is given as John: ibid.

[67] B.M. Seals, lxvi, 171.

[68] B.M. Add. Chart. 10655.

[1] *Cal. Pat., 1361–4*, 20.

[2] Ibid., *1370–4*, 232.

[3] Farnham, *Leics. Notes*, v, 349.

[4] *Cal. Pat., 1374–7*, 379.

[5] Farnham, *Leics. Notes*, v, 349.

[6] Ibid.

[7] Ibid. 352–3.

[8] Ibid. 352.

Act for the Dissolution of Chantries the net yearly income of the college was given as £16. 10s. 5d.[9] The chantry college was suppressed under Edward VI. Its possessions at the time of dissolution included property in Sapcote, Stoney Stanton, Leire, Frolesworth, and Sharnford.[10]

WARDENS OF SAPCOTE COLLEGE

William Gerbot, presented 1381.[11]
John Wignall, occurs 1526.[12]
Richard Frampton, occurs 1535.[13]
John Borough, occurs about 1547.[14]

No seal is known.

ALIEN PRIORY

33. THE PRIORY OF HINCKLEY

The details of the foundation of Hinckley Priory are obscure. In the *Matriculus* of the Archdeaconry of Leicester it is stated that Hinckley church was given to the Benedictine Abbey of Lire by William *filius Roberti Osberti*;[1] the person meant is probably William Fitz Osbern, founder of the Abbey of Lire (Eure).[2] It seems, however, that Hinckley church was given to Lire not by William Fitz Osbern but by Robert *le Bossu*, Earl of Leicester. A charter granted by Henry II to Lire describes the church of Hinckley as having been given to the abbey by Robert, Earl of Leicester, and a charter of Robert *ès Blanchemains*, Earl of Leicester, describes Hinckley as the gift of his father, Robert *le Bossu*.[3] Property confirmed to Lire by Robert *ès Blanchemains* included tithes from the earl's soke of Hinckley, and a revenue of 2 marks from the township of Hinckley.[4] It is not known when a cell of Lire was established at Hinckley, but it must have been before 1209, when a Prior of Hinckley is mentioned.[5] About 1220 there were two monks only at Hinckley,[6] and the cell was probably always a small one. An agreement made in 1283 between the Abbot of Lire and the vicar of Hinckley stated that the mortuaries of the inhabitants of Hinckley and of the dependent chapelries of Dadlington and Wykin were to be the perquisite of the Prior of Hinckley, together with the Candlemas offerings from Hinckley and

Dadlington. The agreement also mentions the priory's barn.[7]

As an alien priory Hinckley was repeatedly seized by the king during the later years of its existence, though while in the king's hands it was frequently granted at farm to its own prior.[8] In March 1399 Hinckley Priory was granted to the Carthusian house of Mountgrace, and licence was given to Lire to alienate the priory to Mountgrace. This grant, however, was vacated later in the same year,[9] and in the following May Hinckley was granted to Mountgrace for the duration of the war with France only.[10] In January 1400 Hinckley was handed back to its prior,[11] presumably because of the truce with France concluded soon afterwards. In 1409 revenues arising from the priory were granted to Queen Joan for life,[12] and in 1414, by a second grant, a slightly larger income from the priory was secured to the queen.[13] In 1415, though the queen was still alive, Hinckley Priory was finally granted to Mountgrace.[14] A pension continued to be paid to Queen Joan.[15] The possessions of Hinckley Priory seem to have consisted of little save tithes from the parish of Hinckley, with its dependent chapelries, and a little land in the vicinity.[16] Nothing is known of the internal life of this small cell.

PRIORS OF HINCKLEY

Richard, occurs between 1209 and 1211.[17]
Richard de Capella, admitted as administrator[18] 1224–5.[19] Resigned 1230–1.[20]

[9] A. Hamilton Thompson, 'The Chant. Cert. for Leics.', *Assoc. Arch. Soc. Rep. and Papers*, xxx, 506.
[10] Ibid. 554–7. [11] *Cal. Pat.*, *1381–5*, 13.
[12] *Subsidy Collected in Dioc. of Linc. in 1526*, ed. H. E. Salter, 102.
[13] *Valor Eccl.* (Rec. Com.), iv, 182.
[14] *Assoc. Arch. Soc. Rep. and Papers*, xxx, 532.
[1] Sic. *Rot. Hugonis de Welles*, ed. W. P. W. Phillimore, i, 248.
[2] Dugd. *Mon.* vi (2), 1092.
[3] *Cartae Antiquae* (Pipe R. Soc., N.S. xvii), ed. L. Landon, 117; Dugd. *Mon.* vi (2), 1030.
[4] Dugd. *Mon.* loc. cit.
[5] *Pipe R. 1209* (Pipe R. Soc., N.S. xxiv), 26.
[6] *Rot. Hugonis de Welles*, i, 248.
[7] H. J. Francis, *Hist. of Hinckley*, 33.
[8] *Cal. Close*, *1327–30*, 19; *1337–9*, 162, 337; *1341–3*, 361; *Cal. Pat.*, *1350–4*, 106; *1358–61*, 561; *1370–4*, 254; *1374–7*, 173; *1381–5*, 299, 342; *1388–92*, 302; *1396–9*, 319, 332; *Cal. Fine R.*, *1337–47*, 30, 262;

1369–77, 16, 25, 286; *1383–91*, 300–1, 304; *1377–83*, 17; *1391–9*, 204, 256.
[9] *Cal. Pat.*, *1396–9*, 497.
[10] Ibid. 570.
[11] *Cal. Pat.*, *1399–1401*, 71. See also *Cal. Fine R.*, *1399–1405*, 241.
[12] *Cal. Pat.*, *1408–13*, 86–87.
[13] Ibid., *1413–16*, 165; *Cal. Close*, *1413–19*, 154.
[14] *Cal. Pat.*, *1413–16*, 355; *Cal. Close*, *1413–19*, 225.
[15] *Cal. Close*, *1422–9*, 20. Payment of the pension may have ceased during the period when Joan was in disfavour with Henry V, after 1418. Thomas, Duke of Exeter, bequeathed £40 to Mountgrace, to be paid so long as the pension to Queen Joan was payable from Hinckley: Nichols, *Leics.* iv, 681.
[16] For an extent of the priory's property, of 1380, see Nichols, *Leics.* iv, 680.
[17] *Cat. Anct. D.*, iii, A5785. [18] *Sic*.
[19] *Rot. Hugonis de Welles*, ii, 300.
[20] Ibid. ii, 315–16.

John de Capella, presented 1230–1,[21] resigned 1233–4.[22]

Richard de Paceio, presented 1233–4,[23] resigned 1236–7.[24]

Peter Lumbardus, presented 1236–7,[25] resigned 1244–5.[26]

William de Aquila, presented 1244–5,[27] resigned 1246–7.[28]

Hugh of Winchester, presented 1246–7.[29]

Gilbert, died 1265.[30]

Adam de Trungey, presented 1265,[31] resigned 1268.[32]

Richard de Audreia, presented 1268,[33] resigned 1271.[34]

Nicholas Bynet, presented 1271.[35]

William de Arena, resigned 1289.[36]

Hervey de Alneto, presented 1289.[37]

Reyner de Sarieta, died 1310.[38]

Matthew de Puteio, presented 1310.[39]

Michael, resigned 1333.[40]

Nicholas de Gaynario, presented 1333.[41]

John Pepyn, occurs 1342 and December 1347.[42]

John Morelli, occurs 1348,[43] died 1367.[44]

John de Ponte, appointed 1367,[45] resigned 1368.[46]

Ralph de Gorin,[47] presented 1368,[48] died 1375.[49]

Michael Aufri, presented 1375,[50] occurs 1404.[51]

The seal[52] of Prior John Morelli is a small vesica, 1¼ by 1 in. Its subject is the coronation of the Virgin Mary. Below is a figure kneeling in prayer. The legend is:

S' PR̄S JOH'IS MORELL PRI' D' HINKL'

It is not proposed to describe all the Roman Catholic religious houses that have arisen in Leicestershire since the time of Henry VIII.[1] The following short history of Mount Saint Bernard Abbey, however, seems called for in view of the monastery's particular importance and of the especial interest attaching to it as the first Cistercian house for monks to be permanently established in England since the Dissolution.[2]

THE CISTERCIAN ABBEY OF MOUNT SAINT BERNARD[3]

The Abbey of Mount Saint Bernard owes its origin to the generosity of Ambrose Phillipps de Lisle,[4] a Roman Catholic gentleman living at Grace Dieu, who in 1835 offered to purchase an estate in Charnwood Forest and to present it to the Cistercian Order. The offer was accepted, and De Lisle bought 222 acres of land with the aid of a loan from Dr. Walsh, the Vicar Apostolic of the Midland District.[5] Only 35 acres of the land were then under cultivation.[6] Before the end of 1835 six monks, led by Father Odilo

Woolfrey as Superior, were established at Mount Saint Bernard. The mother house of the new monastery was the Irish abbey of Mount Melleray.[7] At first the monks lived in a four-roomed cottage, but before long temporary domestic buildings and a chapel were constructed. The chapel was consecrated in 1837 by Dr. Walsh.[8] De Lisle's resources were largely exhausted by the initial expense of establishing the monastery, and work on the permanent buildings was delayed for lack of money.[9] With the assistance of the Earl of Shrewsbury,[10] who gave £3,000, and of other benefactors, the most essential domestic buildings and the church were completed, at a cost of over

21 Ibid.
22 Ibid. ii, 334.
23 Ibid.
24 *Rot. Roberti Grosseteste*, ed. F. N. Davis, 392, where the name is given as Ralph de Paceio.
25 Ibid.
26 Ibid. 423.
27 Ibid.
28 Ibid. 427.
29 Ibid.
30 *Rot. Ric. Gravesend*, ed. F. N. Davis, 145.
31 Ibid.
32 Ibid. 148.
33 Ibid.
34 Ibid. 152.
35 Ibid.
36 Rosalind Hill, 'Bishop Sutton and the Inst. of Heads of Religious Houses in the Dioc. of Lincoln', *E.H.R.* lviii, 209.
37 Ibid.
38 Lincoln Reg. Dalderby, Inst., f. 204b.
39 Ibid.
40 Lincoln Reg. Burghersh, Inst., f. 142a.
41 Ibid.
42 *Cal. Fine R.*, 1337–47, 262; ibid., 1347–56, 61.
43 Ibid. 95.
44 Lincoln Reg. Buckingham, Inst. i, f. 240b.
45 Ibid.
46 Ibid., f. 241a.

47 Or de Cornuti: *Cal. Fine R.*, 1369–77, 25.
48 Lincoln Reg. Buckingham, Inst. i, f. 241a.
49 Ibid., f. 264a.
50 Ibid.
51 *Cal. Fine R.*, 1399–1405, 241.
52 B.M. Seals, lvii, 4.
1 Other modern religious houses will be dealt with in the topographical sections of *V.C.H. Leics.*
2 A Cistercian house was established at Lulworth Park, Dors., in 1794, but in 1817 the monks of Lulworth returned to France, and at the time when Mount Saint Bernard was founded no monastery of Cistercian monks existed in England: J. Morson, *Cistercian Monks of Mount Saint Bernard Abbey*, 15–16.
3 This account is largely based on Morson's book.
4 Originally named Ambrose Phillipps, he assumed the surname of de Lisle. See *D.N.B.*
5 Morson, *Cistercian Monks of Mount St. Bernard*, 16; E. S. Purcell, *Life of Ambrose Phillipps de Lisle*, 66.
6 White, *Leics. Dir.* (1846), 367.
7 Morson, *Cistercian Monks of Mount Saint Bernard*, 16; Purcell, *Life of de Lisle*, 66.
8 J. Morson, op. cit. 16; Purcell, op. cit. 75.
9 Purcell, op. cit. 74, 76.
10 The 16th earl: *Complete Peerage*, xi, 726.

£5,000, by 1844,[11] when the church was solemnly blessed and the new buildings were occupied.[12] Local stone was used for the monastery, and the buildings were designed by A. W. N. Pugin.[13] The monks, who by 1846 numbered more than thirty, themselves assisted in the building of the monastery, and were also busy in cultivating the land given by de Lisle.[14] In 1848 the monastery became an abbey, with Dom Bernard Palmer as its first abbot.[15] The new abbey obtained in 1849 a papal brief uniting it with the Cistercian congregation in France.[16]

The abbey continued to experience difficulties. The rule of the second abbot, Dom Bernard Burder, who was elected in 1853, led to various misunderstandings, and Dom Bernard resigned in 1858.[17] Under his successor progress was resumed, and various buildings, including the chapter house, were completed.[18] The abbey continued to suffer from financial difficulties, and from a lack of recruits to the community, for the rest of the 19th century.[19] Both difficulties were eventually overcome. Under Father Louis Carew, who was the Superior from 1910 to 1927, the material position of the abbey was much improved, and under his successor, Dom Celsus O'Connell, the number of monks was increased to more than seventy.[20] A visible sign of the monastery's progress was the building between 1935 and 1939 of the enlarged abbey church. The old church completed in 1844 became the choir of the new building,[21] and a nave, transepts, and a great tower above the crossing were added.[22] Although the new church was finished in 1939, it was not until 1945 that the church was consecrated by the Bishop of Nottingham.[23]

ABBOTS AND SUPERIORS OF MOUNT SAINT BERNARD

Odilo Woolfrey, appointed Superior 1835.[24]

Bernard Palmer, appointed Superior in succession to Odilo Woolfrey,[25] became Abbot 1848,[26] died 1852.[27]

Bernard Burder, elected Abbot 1853, resigned 1858.[28]

Bartholomew Anderson, appointed provisional Superior 1859,[29] elected Abbot 1862,[30] died 1890.[31]

Wilfrid Hipwood, elected Abbot 1890,[32] died 1910.[33]

Louis Carew, appointed provisional Superior 1910,[34] died 1927.[35]

Celsus O'Connell, appointed Superior 1927,[36] elected Abbot 1929,[37] became Abbot of Mount Melleray 1933.[38]

Malachy Brasil, elected Abbot 1933.[39]

---

[11] White, *Leics. Dir.* (1846), 367; Purcell, *Life of de Lisle*, 77–78; on the benefactions of the Earl of Shrewsbury to other foundations, see M. Trappes-Lomax, *Pugin*, 100–1. It is sometimes stated that the sum given by the earl was £2,000, but the total amount given by him was £3,000. See Purcell, op. cit. 77–78.

[12] Purcell, op. cit. 82; Morson, *Cistercian Monks of Mount Saint Bernard*, 18.

[13] Purcell, op. cit. 77–78; Morson, op. cit. 18; White, *Leics. Dir.* (1846), 367.

[14] Purcell, op. cit. 75; White, op. cit. 367.

[15] Morson, *Cistercian Monks of Mount Saint Bernard*, 18.

[16] Purcell, *Life of de Lisle*, 86.

[17] Morson, *Cistercian Monks of Mount Saint Bernard*, 18–19.   [18] Ibid. 19–20.

[19] Ibid.   [20] Ibid. 20.

[21] The old ch. had originally been intended for the nave of the completed structure. W. White, *Leics. Dir.* (1846), 367.

[22] Morson, *Cistercian Monks of Mount Saint Bernard*, 21.   [23] Ibid. 22.   [24] Ibid. 16.

[25] Ibid.   [26] Ibid. 18.   [27] Ibid.

[28] Ibid.   [29] Ibid. 19.   [30] Ibid.

[31] Ibid.   [32] Ibid.   [33] Ibid. 20.

[34] Ibid.   [35] Ibid.   [36] Ibid.

[37] Ibid.   [38] Ibid.

[39] Ibid. Formerly Prior of Mount St. Joseph, Roscrea, co. Tipperary.

ROMAN CATHOLICISM

THE Acts of Supremacy and Uniformity of 1559 required Englishmen to conform to certain standards in religious matters, and penalized those who refused to do so. In studying Roman Catholicism in Leicestershire and elsewhere we are consequently seeking a proscribed people. Underground movements are necessarily difficult to trace. As little as may be is committed to writing—it is, for example, very unusual to find Roman Catholic baptismal registers before 1750—and every effort is made to dissemble even internal convictions. A host of stratagems grew up from the elaborately contrived hiding-place to minute chalices and small portable altar-stones. Lawyers invented methods of concealing the ownership and inheritance of land. The priests were, of course, especially vulnerable. Disguise of costume was essential. False names were often used. Their calling might be concealed under the guise of tutor, steward, or gardener. Even when suspicion had been allayed by such subterfuges there remained the problems of an income on which to live, since the priest seldom had private means, and of a roof under which to sleep and say mass. All three difficulties were best solved when a layman of sufficient means volunteered to harbour, if only for some weeks, a priest in his house, and this was in fact the solution most generally adopted in country districts. It is necessary, then, to identify the Roman Catholic families in Leicestershire in order to ascertain the centres of Roman Catholic worship.

The initial attack was not, however, directed against the laity but against the clergy, who between 1560 and 1574 were required to accept the Acts of Supremacy and Uniformity under pain of deprivation. Seven institutions to benefices are known within the period. In 1561 Anthony Nubie of Queniborough was deprived 'because he is certificated amongst the recusants'.[1] In 1561–2 Baldwin Norton of Lutterworth and in August 1570 John Bowserre of Langton were deprived, but in neither case is the cause of deprivation stated.[2] In 1561, 1565–6, 1567–8, and 1569 presentments were made to Hungarton, Withcote, Fenny Drayton, and Arnesby respectively, all of which benefices are described as vacant by resignation.[3] While in Nubie's case only is the reason of the vacancy specifically said to be recusancy, it is probable that Norton and Bowserre were deprived for the same cause, and possible that it also led to the resignation of the other four incumbents. Even so, only some 3 per cent. of the parish priests—for there were some 200 parishes and chapelries—can have refused the oaths. While it is possible that some benefices were vacant, and probable that some incumbents signed against their consciences, and that others, while using the Anglican service in church, 'said mass in their parlour chambers',[4] it is clear that few adhered to the old ways.

[1] C. W. Foster, 'Inst. to Benefices in Dioc. of Linc., 1547–1570', *Assoc. Arch. Soc. Rep. and Papers*, xxv, 491.
[2] Ibid. 471, 469.
[3] C. W. Foster, 'Inst. to Benefices in Dioc. of Linc. in the 16th Cent.', *Lincs. N. & Q.* v, 180, 195, 196, 200.
[4] S.P. 12/169 no. 19 (a Norfolk instance).

Some of the seven deprived and resigning priests may be assumed to have remained in Leicestershire to minister to adherents of the old religion—a work in which they may have been joined by some surviving monks from the dissolved monasteries[5] and by other priests who had been deprived under Edward VI and not been given incumbencies under Mary. Such a one was perhaps John Benchskynne, who was chaplain to Francis Shirley at Staunton Harold in 1571.[6] In 1568 seminaries began to be established on the Continent to train priests for the English ministry. Their *alumni* replaced the generation of pre-Reformation priests and monks. To discover how these invaders fared in Leicestershire we must turn to the homes of the wealthier Roman Catholics of the county.

John Palmer of Kegworth was excommunicated in 1592 for recusancy.[7] A spy's report dated 3 February 1595 relates how 'Mr. Palmer's house at Kegworth always has a priest whether Palmer be there or not. On 29 January last Launcelot Blackburn,[8] seminary priest, was there. Nicholas Wade alias Icke (or Jake)[9] a seminary priest often at Mr. Palmer's though he lived at Mr. Merry's house, in Barton Park,[10] who married Palmer's sister.'[11] John Palmer appears in the Recusant Rolls from 1599 to 1605 and in 1607.[12] Of the twenty-two recusants reported in the Deaneries of Goscote and Akeley in 1603 four were in Kegworth parish.[13] Palmer's house is said to have had a priest's hide.[14] Kegworth was the birthplace of Robert Sutton, a layman, who was executed at Clerkenwell on 5 October 1588.[15]

On 6 April 1580 Arthur Faunt S.J., a younger son of William Faunt of Foston (d. 1559), wrote from abroad to his eldest brother Anthony at Foston, '. . . I pray you, good brother, to have a care of your soul and faith which our father did teach us in . . .'.[16] The anxious tone suggests perhaps that Anthony was weakening. On his death in 1588 Foston certainly ceased to be a Roman Catholic centre.

Staunton Harold was intermittently a Roman Catholic centre until 1633. Francis Shirley, who was in possession from 1517 to 1571, took his wife from the staunchly recusant family of Giffard of Chillington (Staffs.), married his daughter Anne to Sir Basil Brooke of Madeley (Salop), one of the most prominent Roman Catholics of the day, and left by his will, dated 1571, a black gown

[5] Robert Buckley O.S.B. (d. 1610) was perhaps the last of them. In this article there have been added to the names of priests who were regulars the initial letters of their orders (O.S.B. for Benedictine, S.J. for Jesuit, O.P. for Dominican, and O.F.M.Rec. for Franciscan Recollect). Seculars are distinguished by the abbreviation Revd.

[6] See below, p. 57.

[7] *State of the Ch.*, ed. C. W. Foster, p. lxxv. He was buried at Kegworth in 1614.

[8] He left Rheims for Engl. 10 Nov. 1576, was imprisoned before 16 Dec. 1576, but freed before 2 Mar. 1577. He was a secular: T. F. Knox, *Rec. of the Engl. Caths. under the Penal Laws; Douay Diaries*, 5, 7, 25, 113, 116, 260, 289.

[9] Unidentified.

[10] Two miles south of Alkmonton, Derbys.

[11] J. Morris, *Life of Father John Gerard*, 11–13; H. Foley, *Rec. of the Engl. Province*, v. 470.

[12] E. 377/8–15.

[13] A. P. Moore, 'Leics. Livings in the Reign of James I', *Assoc. Arch. Soc. Rep. and Papers*, xxix, 144–58.

[14] G. Squiers, *Secret Hiding Places*, 59.

[15] 'Doc. Relating to the Engl. Martyrs', ed. J. H. Pollen, *Cath. Rec. Soc.* v, 290. The only other person born in Leicestershire who was executed for recusancy was Antony Turner or Ashby S.J., son of the vicar of Little Dalby. He suffered at Tyburn, 20 June 1679 (Foley, *Rec. of the Engl. Province*, vii, 786). His elder brother Edw. also became a Jesuit. Both were received into the Roman Cath. ch. by Michael Griffith or Alford S.J., the chaplain at Nevill Holt (see below), as well as their mother (Foley, op. cit. vii, 789). Edw. was arrested in Leics. in 1678 or 1679 (Foley, op. cit. v, 473).

[16] Foley, op. cit. ii, 289. For his career and writings see *D.N.B.*

and 40*s*. to 'my chaplain Sir John Benchskynne'.[17] Francis's grandson Sir George Shirley 1st Bt., who succeeded him in 1571, was a Roman Catholic between 1581 and 1587. This is proved by the account which his sister Elizabeth, who lived with her brother at Staunton Harold during that period, gave to the superior of the Augustinian convent at Louvain on entering that house in 1596: 'the more her brother or any of her kindred, both priests and others, would seek to persuade her [to become a Roman Catholic] the more perverse she remained . . .'.[18] That Sir George's first wife, Frances Berkeley, was a Roman Catholic is proved by the account which her third son Thomas wrote of her death in 1595,

struck with a deadly disease lying in childbed . . . [she] sends for a famous and holy priest, whom she had honoured for his learning, innocency and sanctity of life, to assist with his prayers at her last hour. . . . Most earnestly desiring her husband that he would have a care that her children might be instructed and brought up in the Catholic religion. . . . Having made a general confession of her whole life, she received the most blessed sacrament of the altar. . . .[19]

In 1603 three recusants were reported in the parish of Breedon, in which Staunton Harold lies.[20] Sir George was keeping an Anglican chaplain in 1618–19 at Astwell (Northants.), but 'died in the bosom of his mother the Roman Catholic Church at Staunton Harold'[21] in 1622. Sir Henry, the heir, was brought up a Roman Catholic, as was Thomas his brother, but unlike Thomas lapsed before 1625, when he was Sheriff of Leicestershire. In his last illness, however, he 'provided himself with a learned Catholic spiritual guide' and died a Roman Catholic in 1633.[22] With his death the connexion between Roman Catholicism and Staunton Harold closes. There is said to have been a priest's hide in the hall[23] and there was certainly a domestic chapel.

On 18 August 1581 Francis Hastings reported that he had searched the house of Mrs. Beaumont.[24] This was Elizabeth Beaumont whose house, Gracedieu, came into her possession on the death of her husband John Beaumont shortly after 1552. It is very probable that Anne Pierrepont, the wife of Francis Beaumont, her eldest son, was a Roman Catholic, for her brothers Sir Henry Pierrepont of Holme Pierrepont (Notts.), and Gervase were the befrienders of Edmund Campion S.J. in 1580.[25] Anne's eldest son, Sir Henry Beaumont, who owned Gracedieu from 1598 to 1605, married the possibly Roman Catholic daughter of Anthony Faunt of Foston (see p. 56). Her second son, John, who owned Gracedieu from 1605 to 1627, lost two-thirds of his property at Gracedieu for recusancy in 1607[26] and occurs with his wife in the Recusant Roll of 1609.[27] He later became a Puritan, but his widow was still a recusant in 1634, for she and eleven other inhabitants of Belton parish, in which Gracedieu lies, were then presented.[28] While there is no certain indication of the religious opinions of his eldest son, the royalist, who was killed in action at Gloucester in 1643, his third son Sir Thomas Beaumont 3rd Bt. was a Roman

---

[17] E. P. Shirley, *Stemmata Shirleiana*, 54.
[18] A. Hamilton, *Chron. of the Engl. Augustinian Canonesses of St. Monica's at Louvain, 1548–1625*, i, 202.
[19] Shirley, *Stemmata Shirleiana*, 66.
[20] *Assoc. Arch. Soc. Rep. and Papers*, xxiv, 147.   [21] Shirley, *Stemmata Shirleiana*, 67–68.
[22] Ibid. 88.   [23] Squiers, *Secret Hiding Places*, 59.
[24] S.P. 12/150, no. 6. Francis Hastings's report makes it certain that he searched the house because its owner was a Roman Catholic.
[25] B.M. Lansd. MSS. 30 N. 78.
[26] E. 377/16.   [27] E. 377/17.
[28] A. P. Moore, 'Metropolitan Visitation of Archbishop Laud', *Assoc. Arch. Soc. Rep. and Papers*, xxix, 509.

Catholic during the Interregnum[29] and in 1680.[30] In 1683 the Roman Catholic life of Gracedieu ended with its sale to the Anglican Sir Ambrose Phillipps of Garendon—but not for ever, for in 1827 Ambrose Lisle March-Phillipps became a Roman Catholic and in 1834 rebuilt Gracedieu Manor and provided himself with a domestic chapel and chaplain. He was a munificent patron of Roman Catholic interests, founding Mount St. Bernard Abbey in 1835, Whitwick mission in 1837, and Shepshed mission in 1840. The Gracedieu chaplaincy ended about 1888, but the Roman Catholic life of the house has been reborn with the foundation of a Roman Catholic school in 1933. The old house is said to have had a priest's hide.[31]

In January 1606, on the death of her husband Sir George Villiers, Mary Beaumont[32] inherited Goadby, and in 1622 was received into the Catholic Church by John Percy alias Fisher S.J., who was given permission to 'live on parole' under her protection. He did so until her death in April 1632, and though Wallingford House, her London residence, was his usual abode, it is probable that he accompanied her when she chose to visit Goadby.[33]

On 12 January 1607 Joyce Roper,[34] wife of Walter Hastings[35] of Kirby Bellars, was convicted of recusancy,[36] as was Dorothy Huddleston, wife[37] of her eldest son Sir Henry Hastings of Braunston, who had harboured John Gerard S.J. about 1601,[38] and asked him shortly before the discovery of the Gunpowder Plot to 'provide him a priest who could join in society publicly and without suspicion'.[39] Two of Dorothy's sons, Walter and Edmund, entered the English College, Rome, in 1623, when the latter informed its Rector that his mother was 'a faithful Catholic' and that his four brothers and seven sisters all professed Roman Catholicism, but that his father was 'a schismatic and time-server, alarmed by the persecution of the times'.[40] This picture of a Roman Catholic wife running a Roman Catholic home[41] with the connivance of a husband intent on preserving the family property by conformity is very typical. By 1634 Sir Henry had openly declared himself a Roman Catholic, for he and his wife and daughters were reported to be recusants in that year.[42] Walter, the eldest son, inherited Braunston in September 1649, but sold it next year, when its connexion with Roman Catholicism ends.

Margaret, wife of Richard Bowes of Humberstone, was excommunicated for recusancy in 1588.[43] Jane Bowes, widow, of Humberstone, was convicted

---

[29] *Cal. of the Ctee for Compounding*, pp. 109, 1988.
[30] Hist. MSS. Com., *11th Rep.*, *App. ii, Ho. of Lords, 1678–88*, 236.
[31] Squiers, *Secret Hiding Places*, 59. This house fell to ruin *c.* 1750.
[32] Dau. of Antony Beaumont of Glenfield, Leics.; created Countess of Buck., 1618.
[33] H. R. Williamson, *Geo. Villiers, First Duke of Buck.*, 112, 118; Foley, *Rec. of the Engl. Province*, i, *passim*; vii, 586. For his writings and career see *D.N.B.*, under Fisher.
[34] Dau. of Wm. Roper of Well Hall, Eltham, Kent, and St. Dunstan's, Cant., by his wife Margaret, dau. of Sir Thomas More, Lord Chancellor.
[35] Sixth son of Francis, 2nd Earl of Huntingdon, by Catherine Pole, granddaughter of Margaret, Countess of Salisbury. [36] E. 377/14.
[37] Dau. of Sir Edmund Huddleston, of Sawston, Cambs.
[38] Morris, *Life of Fr. Gerard*, 309. [39] Ibid. 381.
[40] Foley, *Rec. of the Engl. Province*, v, 494; vi, 301, 303. 'Schismatic' is the term applied by Roman Catholics to those who, while not necessarily abandoning the tenets of Roman Catholicism, conformed exteriorly by attending their par. chs. These 'Church Papists', as they were popularly termed, were numerous during the last decade of the 16th cent. and as late as 1640.
[41] In 1634 2 members of the Hastings family, the bailiff, and 7 others were presented for recusancy: *Assoc. Arch. Soc. Rep. and Papers*, xxix, 496.
[42] Ibid. xxix, 512.
[43] *State of the Ch.*, ed. C. W. Foster, p. lxxxv. She was a dau. of Hen. Keble of Humberstone.

of recusancy from 1594 to 1599,[44] and Richard Bowes, late of Humberstone, in 1604.[45] Richard's son John sold the property.

Jane, wife of Richard Everard of Shenton, was convicted of recusancy in 1600,[46] and Ralph Layton of Shenton in 1606.[47]

Margaret Harcourt, late of Newton Linford, wife of Anthony, was convicted of recusancy in 1607.[48] Henry Harcourt or Beaumont S.J., who was born in Leicestershire about 1611, was probably of this family.

In 1631 Rowland Eyre of Hassop (Derbys.), a Roman Catholic, bought land in Eastwell parish and built a house upon it which remained in the possession of his descendants, all of whom were Roman Catholics—Thomas Eyre of Eastwell occurs in the 1680 list of prominent Leicestershire Roman Catholics[49]—until sold about 1795. If the family's practice of maintaining resident chaplains in its other homes[50] may be taken as a guide, there can be little doubt that Eastwell always had a priest, though the earliest of whom record survives is the Revd. Richard Downes alias Haskett, who was here from 1720 to 1726.[51] By his will dated 1788 Thomas Eyre left money to build a church at Eastwell which replaced the chapel in the hall on its sale. The Revd. Robert Beeston, who was at Eastwell from 1775 to his death in 1832, left a plot of land in the parish to support a priest.[52] About 1790 six out of the eighteen families in the parish were Roman Catholic.[53] The Revd. John Bick was here from 1832 to at least as late as 1844.[54] The mission was abandoned in 1936.

In a letter dated 28 August 1609 William Uvedale wrote: 'William Wright the Jesuit is now at Holywell in Wales[55] but returneth shortly to the Countess of Rutland. . . .'[56] She was Elizabeth daughter of Sir Philip Sidney, the poet. She married before 15 March 1599 Roger Manners, 5th Earl of Rutland, and died in the same year, 1612, as her husband. William Wright S.J. escaped from a London prison in 1607 and made his way into Leicestershire.[57] It would seem that Belvoir Castle was his refuge.

Francis Manners, 6th Earl of Rutland (d. 1632), owner of Belvoir, had a recusant wife by 1616[58] and was himself a Roman Catholic by 23 March 1624.[59] In 1633 the Revd. Richard Broughton[60] dedicated his book, *The Ecclesiastical Historie of Great Britaine*, to the earl's widow and daughter,[61] and describes himself as their 'sometime secretarie'.[62] Some letters to him are still at Belvoir.[63] It may reasonably be inferred that he had been harboured in the castle.

44 E. 377/3-8.   45 E. 377/12.   46 E. 377/6.
47 E. 377/14.   48 E. 377/15.
49 Hist. MSS. Com., *11th Rep., App.* ii, *Ho. of Lords, 1678-88*, 236.
50 Hassop (Derbys.), Bury's Hall (Norf.), and Warkworth (Northants.).
51 J. Kirk, *Biographies of Engl. Caths., 1700 to 1800*, 66.   52 Ibid. 15, 16.
53 Nichols, *Leics.* ii, 167.   54 *Cath. Dirs.*
55 St. Winifrid's Well at Holywell was a well-known place of Roman Catholic pilgrimage in the 17th and 18th centuries.
56 B.M. Lansd. MS. 153, f. 24.
57 Foley, *Rec. of the Engl. Province*, ii, 275-86; vii, 871-4. See below for his later career in Leics.
58 *Complete Peerage*, xi, 261.   59 Ibid.
60 He was ordained priest at Rheims in 1592, and laboured in the Engl. mission from 1593 until his death in 1635.
61 She was Catherine, a Roman Catholic until her marriage in 1620 to Geo. Villiers, and probably still one at heart after it: Williamson, *Geo. Villiers, First Duke of Buck.*, 112.
62 R. Webster, 'Ric. Broughton', *Downside Rev.* liv, nos. 160, 506.
63 Ex inf. Librarian at Belvoir Castle. The suggestion that Ric. Rous was a priest and chaplain to the Earl of Rut. made in Hist. MSS. Com., *12th Rep., App.* iv, *Rut.*, vol. i, xix, 468, 471-3, 480, 481, is thus confirmed.

Aston Flamville Hall probably became a Roman Catholic house when George Turville inherited it in 1616, for his wife[64] had been convicted of recusancy in 1606.[65] It was reported at the Metropolitical Visitation of 1634 that George Turville and his son-in-law Mr. Berry and all his household were recusants or thought to be recusants.[66] Their eldest son Henry married three wives, of whom two probably and the third certainly were Roman Catholics, for he and the third were presented by the churchwardens of Aston Flamville as convicted recusants in 1662.[67] William, who succeeded to Aston Flamville on Henry's death in 1671, was a Roman Catholic in 1680, as was William's younger brother John.[68] It is possible that there were Jesuit chaplains in the later 17th century, since two of William's sons became Jesuit priests.[69] The earliest chaplain of whom record survives is John Clarkson O.P., who arrived about Christmas 1734 and was succeeded in 1747 by Robert (Pius) Bruce O.P.[70] Bruce was followed about 20 January 1748 by Nicholas (Hyacinth) Leadbitter O.P., who remained until 1754.[71] A secular called Canton was here from 1754 to 1757.[72] John Clarkson O.P. returned on 24 September 1757 and on 11 November 1757 moved the mission into Sketchley, 2 miles away.[73] Aston Flamville was without a resident priest until July 1759, when Matthew (Thomas) Norton O.P. arrived, but on 9 August of the same year he too moved into Sketchley.[74] In 1746 Carrington Francis Turville sold the property, and in 1749 left £5,000 to the Dominican Order to endow the Aston Flamville mission and gave the library, vestments, and chapel furniture from Aston Flamville Hall.[75] Among the documents which once belonged to this chaplaincy is an undated certificate in the following terms: 'I, the undersigned, take my oath that AB is a Catholic and may be safely admitted to the sacraments and other Catholic devotions.'[76] This vividly illustrates the insecurity in which Roman Catholics long lived.

The Sketchley mission was served by John Clarkson O.P. from 11 November 1757 to August 1758[77] and by Matthew (Thomas) Norton O.P. from 9 August 1759 to the spring of 1765, when Norton abandoned Sketchley in favour of Hinckley.[78] He said his first mass in Hinckley on Easter Sunday 1765 and two years later built a chapel behind his house.[79] He was followed in November 1767 by John Kearton O.P., who remained to October 1771,[80] but Norton came back before the end of 1771 and remained to 1774.[81] Robert (Peter) Robson O.P. was here from May 1774 to midsummer 1777, when he

---

[64] Ann, dau. and co-heiress of John Martin of Poole House, Leics. Her father is probably identical with John Martin of Earl Shilton whose wife Mary was excommunicated for recusancy in 1602 (*State of the Ch.*, ed. Foster, p. lxxxvi) and convicted of recusancy in 1606 (E. 377/14).

[65] E. 377/14.

[66] *Assoc. Arch. Soc. Rep. and Papers*, xxix, 512.

[67] Ibid. 493. Hen. had been similarly presented at Earl Shilton in 1634: ibid.

[68] Hist. MSS. Com., *11th Rep.*, App. ii, *Ho. of Lords, 1678–88*, 236.

[69] Hen. (1674–1714) and Chas. (1681–1757): Foley, *Rec. of the Engl. Province*, vii, 789–91. While there is no evidence that either of them lived as priests at Aston Flamville, the fact that the Jesuit school at St. Omer was chosen for them very strongly suggests Jesuit influence.

[70] C. F. R. Palmer, *Obituary Notices of Friars-Preachers*, 17.   [71] Ibid. 18.

[72] E. Henson, 'Cath. Reg. of Aston Flamville, Leics., 1759–1767', *Cath. Rec. Soc.* xxv, 253.

[73] Palmer, *Obit. Notices of Friars-Preachers*, 17.   [74] Ibid. 21.

[75] *Catholic Rec. Soc.* xxv, 253.

[76] *Holy Cross Mag.* July 1934.

[77] Palmer, *Obit. Notices of Friars-Preachers*, 17.   [78] Ibid. 21.

[79] Ibid. 21; ex inf. Reginald Ginns O.P.

[80] Palmer, *Obit. Notices of Friars-Preachers*, 20.   [81] Ibid. 21.

went to live in Leicester, whence he supplied at Hinckley until September 1779.[82] John (Bernard) Smith O.P. was at Hinckley from September 1779 to October 1780,[83] when Norton returned.[84] In 1785 Norton was forced to leave in order to escape arrest as a priest and went into Yorkshire. The year of his return is not known, but he died at Hinckley on 7 August 1800 and was buried at Aston Flamville, where his tombstone may still be seen.[85] His poverty was such that he supported himself by selling halfpenny worths of vegetables from his garden, and, unable to afford to keep or hire a horse, had to walk the 26 miles into Coventry and back to attend the dying. He won prizes with his pamphlets *On raising Wool*, *On the Use of Oxen as Beasts of Draught*, and *On raising Bees*.[86] He was assisted from July 1787 to August 1795 by James (Vincent) Sharp O.P.,[87] and succeeded in August 1800 by John (Benedict) Atkinson O.P., who left in July 1801.[88] From then until October 1813 Hinckley was served from Leicester,[89] but since that date the succession of Dominican friars at Hinckley has been unbroken. In August 1814 a Novitiate was opened[90] and in 1825 a boys' school.[91] Hinckley is the oldest Dominican mission in England.

The Byerley family of Leicester acquired property in Belgrave between 1622 and 1653.[92] On 20 January 1667 Thomas (Bernardine of St. Clare) Smith O.F.M.Rec. died at Belgrave in the house of Charles Byerley,[93] who occurs with his eldest son in the 1680 list of prominent Leicestershire Roman Catholics.[94] Since the Franciscan authorities in 1637 decided to appoint a Guardian of Leicester on the grounds that some of the Order were 'labouring in the district of Leicester',[95] it is very probable that William Byerley of Belgrave, who died in 1653, was harbouring a Franciscan before 1637. Bernardine de Senis O.F.M.Rec. was Guardian of Leicester from 1637 to 1640[96] and may well have lived at Belgrave. In 1704 Bonaventure Parry O.F.M.Rec., the Provincial, reported that 'at Mr. Byerley's near Leicester there are Mr. Gervase Cartwright's books, which I recommended to Mr. Augustine Hickins either to be sold or brought to Mr. Neville's of Holt, where the said Mr. Hickins at present resides'.[97] Two inferences may be made, first that Cartwright, who was a Franciscan and who was lodged in Leicester jail on his arrest in 1689, had lived with the Byerleys, possibly from his arrival in England in or soon after 1677,[98] and secondly that the Franciscans had ceased to live in Belgrave by 1704. It is probable that they were succeeded by Jesuits, since a list of Jesuit addresses for 1727–34 contains two entries relating to Belgrave.[99] It may be inferred that Giles Poulton or Palmer S.J., who did not reach England before 1722,[1] was

82 Ibid. 19. 83 Ibid. 22. 84 Ibid. 21.

85 Ibid.; A. H. Kimberlin, *Return of Catholicism to Leic., 1746–1946*, photograph facing p. 16.

86 Kimberlin, op. cit. 15; Palmer, *Obit. Notices of Friars-Preachers*, 21.

87 Palmer, op. cit. 21. 88 Ibid. 25.

89 Ibid. 24. 90 Ibid. 23. 91 Ibid. 25.

92 Nichols, *Leics.* iii, 178, where a Byerley pedigree describes John Byerley (d. *c*. 1622) as of Leic., but his son Wm. (d. 1653) as of Belgrave.

93 'Necrology of the Engl. Province of Friars Minor of the Order of St. Francis', ed. R. Trappes-Lomax, *Cath. Rec. Soc.* xxiv, 267. Smith was in Brussels in 1654: ibid. xxiv, 142.

94 Ho. of Lords MSS., 321, c. 65.

95 Thaddeus (a Franciscan friar), *Franciscans in Engl. 1600–1850*, 56.

96 Ibid. 302. 97 Ibid. 158.

98 Ibid. 76, 209. Cartwright spent 2 years and 4 months in Leic. jail. His death sentence was commuted to banishment by Wm. III.

99 R. Trappes-Lomax, 'Addresses of Stations in Engl. served by Jesuit Fathers, 1727–34', *Cath. Rec. Soc.* xiii, 186, 188. 1 H. Foley, *Rec. of the Engl. Province*, vii, 622.

succeeded between 1727 and 1734 by Owen Joseph Kingsley S.J. A late limit for Kingsley's stay is set by his death abroad in January 1739.[2] Thomas Gerard S.J. was here in 1744.[3] A succession of Dominicans supplied here from Aston Flamville, Sketchley, and Hinckley from about 1746 until midsummer 1777, when the last of them transferred the mission into Leicester.[4] Some years later Nicholas wrote: 'The Catholic chapel is in a large garret; the altar separated at the east end by oak balustrades. The mats on which the worshippers used to kneel yet remain. . . .'[5]

The Leicester Roman Catholics were probably served by the Franciscan chaplains at Belgrave before the middle of the 17th century.[6] In October 1692 William Bentney or Bennet S.J. died in Leicester jail.[7] The first resident priest of whom record survives is Thomas Busby or Roberts S.J., whose address within the period 1727-34 was 'at the Globe in Leicester'.[8] He was still in this part of England in 1741,[9] very possibly in the town. Thomas Maire S.J. died in Leicester on 3 December 1752,[10] but he had only recently arrived.[11] The existing Dominican mission dates from 1777.[12] It was served by Robert (Peter) Robson O.P., who occupied a room in Causeway Lane until September 1779.[13] From then until October 1780 John (Bernard) Smith O.P. supplied from Hinckley: in that month he went to live in Leicester and was succeeded in May 1783 by Edward Leadbitter or Burgis O.P., who remained until October.[14] From October 1783 to August 1785 Matthew (Thomas) Norton O.P. supplied from Hinckley.[15] In September 1785 Henry (Francis Xavier) Chappell O.P. took up residence in the town and in 1798 bought the house in Causeway Lane.[16] In that year there were some sixty Roman Catholics in the town.[17] Chappell was succeeded in October 1815 by Charles (Benedict) Caestryck O.P., who opened in 1819 the church of Holy Cross,[18] which an unbroken succession of Dominicans has served to the present day.

About 1793 a French *émigré* priest named Dobler settled in the town.[19] He had left by 1824, when he was at Old Dalby, where he remained until 1829.[20] His patron appears to have been Frances Duncombe,[21] who inherited Old Dalby Hall jointly with her sister in 1763 and became sole owner in 1788. Her husband, John Bowater, died in 1810 and she in 1827.

Husbands Bosworth Hall was bought in 1630 by Grace Manners, widow of Sir Francis Fortescue of Salden (Bucks.). She had become a Roman Catholic about 1598 and had harboured Jesuits at Salden.[22] She probably did as much

---

[2] H. Foley, *Rec. of the Engl. Province*, vii, 420.   [3] Ibid. v, 479; vii, 297.

[4] C. F. R. Palmer, *Obituary Notices of the Friars-Preachers*, 17, 18, 19; W. Lescher, *Priory Ch. of Holy Cross, Leic., passim*.

[5] Nichols, *Leics.* iii, 176.   [6] See above, p. 61.

[7] Foley, *Rec. of the Engl. Province*, vii, 53.   [8] *Cath. Rec. Soc.* xiii, 178.

[9] Jesuit Archives, Annual Cat. for 1741 (now at Farm Street, London, W.1).

[10] Foley, *Rec. of the Engl. Province*, vii, 481.   [11] See below, p. 63.

[12] See the preceding paragraph.

[13] Palmer, *Obit. Notices of Friars-Preachers*, 19.   [14] Ibid. 19, 22.

[15] Ibid. 121.

[16] Ibid. 24. Lescher, *Priory Ch. of Holy Cross, Leic., passim*.

[17] Lescher, op. cit., *passim*. In 1841 these were about 105.

[18] Palmer, *Obit. Notices of Friars-Preachers*, 27.

[19] *D.N.B.* under Wm. Gardiner.

[20] *Cuddon's Pocket Book* (1824); *Cath. Dirs.* for the appropriate years.

[21] Dau. and co-heiress of Antony Lord Feversham.

[22] J. Morris, *Life of Father John Gerard*, 335-7. She was reported as a recusant in 1634; A. P. Moore, 'The Metropolitical Visitation of Archbishop Laud', *Assoc. Arch. Soc. Rep. and Papers*, xxix, 489.

at Bosworth until her death in 1634. The hall contains a priest's hide,[23] and since it is improbable that such places were built after the Oates Plot (1678) it may be inferred that priests were harboured before that date. Charles Fortescue of Husbands Bosworth occurs in the 1680 list.[24] In 1753 Mary Alethea Fortescue, the owner, left £1,000 to the Jesuit Provincial 'for the maintenance of a Jesuit to serve the flock at Bosworth'.[25] The presence of this congregation postulates the presence of a priest for some years previously, for Roman Catholic groups did not spring up suddenly in the 18th century. The bequest to the Jesuit Provincial suggests that they had been Jesuits. Thomas Maire S.J. describes himself as of Husbands Bosworth in his will dated 1752.[26] Edward Scarisbrick or Neville S.J. was here from about 1756 to not later than 1764,[27] James Le Motte or Lancaster S.J. from about 1765 to about 1767,[28] John Royall S.J. from 1768 to his death in 1770,[29] James Jenison S.J. from 1770 or 1771 to 1772,[30] and Robert Dormer S.J. from 1772 to probably 1780.[31] The first secular priest was Thomas Potts, who arrived at least as early as 1783, probably in 1780 or 1781, and remained to at least as late as 19 August 1790.[32] The Revd. Rowland Davies arrived between 13 January 1792 and 28 September 1794[33] and remained to his death on 16 March 1797.[34] The Husbands Bosworth Roman Catholic register is then signed by the Revd. Edward Peach (27 Feb. 1798–15 Dec. 1805), Revd. Henry Le Sage (3 Feb. 1808–31 Aug. 1809), Desmoulin, a French *émigré* priest (19 Nov. 1810–11 Sept. 1811), Revd. John Sanderson (17 May 1812–3 June 1812), and Jean Dubosq, a French *émigré*, on 2 June 1813. The Revd. William Hayes supplied from King's Cliffe (Northants.) between 6 January 1814 and 6 November 1816 and again from 25 July 1818 and 13 June 1821. The Revd. C. H. Blake signs on 13 February 1816 and the Revd. Thomas Witham from 2 April 1817 to 5 July 1818. Louis Saintpierre, a French *émigré*, was here by 7 April 1822 and remained to his death, 2 September 1824.[35] Charles (Benedict) Caestryck O.P. supplied from Leicester in July 1820 and September 1824 and the Revd. William Foley from Northampton in August 1824 and August 1825. The Revd. J. F. Ross signs from 25 September 1826 to 14 October 1827, the Revd. R. Bagnall from 5 March 1829 to 18 April 1830, the Revd. James F. Jones from 19 September 1830 to 19 December 1848, and the Revd. Edward Whitehouse from 29 April 1849 to 3 December 1865. There has been a succession of resident or supplying priests since that date until now. Since September 1841 the priest at Market Harborough has been in charge.

Although that mission was not established on a permanent footing until 1859,[36] there had been a priest in the town before the end of the 18th century,

---

23 G. Squiers, *Secret Hiding Places*, 57–59.

24 Hist., MSS. Com., *11th Rep., App.* ii, *Ho. of Lords, 1678–88*, 236.

25 MS. at Husbands Bosworth Hall, Leics.

26 MS. at Stonyhurst Coll.

27 Foley, *Rec. of the Engl. Province*, v, 489; vii, 688; Jesuit Archives, Annual Cat. (now at Farm Street, London, W.1).

28 Foley, op. cit. vii, 451; Jesuit Archives, Annual Cat. for 1764 and 1769.

29 Foley, op. cit. iv, 563; Jesuit Archives, Annual Cat. for 1768 and 1769.

30 Jesuit Archives, Annual Cat. for 1769 and 1772.

31 Foley, *Rec. of the Engl. Province*, v, 489; T. Agius, *Map of Engl. Province*, 120.

32 MSS. at Husbands Bosworth Hall, Leics.

33 MSS. at Husbands Bosworth Hall, Leics.; Husbands Bosworth Roman Catholic Reg.; *N.R. Rec.* viii, 154.

34 Gravestone in Husbands Bosworth par. churchyard (Leics.).   35 Ibid.

36 See the table below, p. 70.

for on 17 April 1787 the Revd. Thomas Potts, then chaplain at Husbands Bosworth, wrote to his patron Francis Fortescue Turville abroad that a Mrs. Porter had lately settled in Harborough and that James Jenison S.J. 'is her aumonier; and a very agreable well bred man I find him. . . .'[37] The Dominicans of Leicester said mass in the house from about 1825.[38] Mrs. Flint had a private chapel in her house in the town in 1849,[39] and Francis Dent O.P. supplied from Hinckley from 1850 to 1851.[40]

While it is probable that Sir Thomas Neville of Nevill Holt (d. 1569) and Mary (d. 1593) his daughter and heiress were Roman Catholics, as were also Mary's son and grandson, who were in possession to 1612, no evidence survives of the presence of a chaplain at Nevill Holt until the ownership of Sir Thomas Neville (1612–37). Michael Alford or Griffith S.J. was there from c. 1629[41] and probably from 1622, when he came into Leicestershire.[42] He was still there in 1640[43] and almost certainly until 1652.[44] The house contained three priest's hides.[45] Henry Neville of Holt occurs in the 1680 list of prominent Leicestershire Roman Catholics.[46] Augustine Hickins O.F.M.Rec. was there in 1704,[47] and John Musson S.J. from 1724 probably until 1726.[48] The address of Richard Levinge S.J. at some time within the period 1727–34 was Holt[49] and he died, probably at Holt, on 5 January 1746.[50] At this perod Holt was the residence of the superior of the Jesuits working in Derbyshire, Nottinghamshire, and Leicestershire, since Levinge was appointed to that office in 1738[51] and Thomas Gerard S.J. held it when he was there from at least as early as 1750 to at least as late as 1754[52] and Edward Scarisbrick or Neville S.J. during his stay there from 1764 to 1768.[53] Nathaniel Elliott S.J. succeeded Scarisbrick in 1769 and died at Holt on 10 October 1780.[54] The Revd. Matthew Burgess came in or soon after 1782 and had left by 25 August 1784.[55] Peter Jenkins S.J., who was at Holt in 1786 and signs the register from 13 April 1789 to 23 August 1790, was the last Jesuit.[56] The chapel was then served from Hinckley and Leicester until the arrival of the Revd. B. O'Brien, who signs from 30 September 1802 to 20 March 1808.[57] It is, however, possible that the

[37] MSS. at Husbands Bosworth Hall, Leics.
[38] Dominican Rec., formerly at Holy Cross Priory, Leic.
[39] B.M. Add. MS. 34565 (Neville Holt Reg.).
[40] Palmer, *Obit. Notices of Friars-Preachers*, 30.
[41] Foley, *Rec. of Engl. Province*, v, 489.
[42] Jesuit Archives, Annual Cat. for 1622 (now at Farm Street, London, W.1).
[43] Foley, *Rec. of Engl. Province*, ii, 306.
[44] Ibid. vii, 321. The article on Alford in *D.N.B.* is unsatisfactory. For an accurate account of Alford, and his book *Annales Ecclesiastici et Civiles Britannorum, Saxonum et Anglorum*, see *Studies*, for Sept. 1942. Alford spent the years 1641–52 on this book. Its great merit is that though written in an age of controversy it is a work based on original sources, with the object of relating historical facts.
[45] For a description, see Squiers, *Secret Hiding Places*, 54–57.
[46] Hist. MSS. Com., *11th Rep.*, App. ii, *Ho. of Lords, 1678–88*, 236.
[47] D. 1710 (Thaddeus, *Franciscans in Engl., 1600–1800*, 252); see above, p. 61.
[48] Foley, *Rec. of Engl. Province*, vii, 535.
[49] *Cath. Rec. Soc.* xiii, 184.
[50] Foley, *Rec. of Engl. Province*, vii, 455.
[51] Ibid.
[52] Ibid. vii, 297; Jesuit Archives, Annual Cat. for 1750 and 1754. His will, dated 1752, describes him as of Nevill Holt. MS. at Stonyhurst Coll.
[53] Jesuit Archives, Annual Cat. for 1764, 1768, and 1769.
[54] Ibid., Annual Cat. for 1769 and 1771; Foley, *Rec. of Engl. Province*, v. 472; vii, 223.
[55] MSS. at Husbands Bosworth Hall (Leics.); ex inf. Engl. Convent, Bruges; *St. Francis Mag.* (N.S.), no. 38, 132–4.
[56] Foley, *Rec. of Engl. Province*, v, 489; vii, 402; B.M. Add. MS. 34565.
[57] B.M. Add. MS. 34565.

Revd. John R. Liot, who signs on 13 July 1795, was resident.[58] The Revd. Robert Tindal succeeded O'Brien and signs from 5 October 1808 to 15 October 1809.[59] The French *émigrés* Jean Desmoulin and Christopher Louvel sign respectively from 28 April 1811 to 12 March 1814 and from 23 March 1815 to 28 May 1819.[60] The Revd. William Hayes supplied from King's Cliffe (Northants.) in 1820.[61] The French *émigré* Nicolas Malvoisin signs from 10 December 1821 to 9 November 1845.[62] He probably left in 1846 and was the last resident chaplain.[63] Francis (Aloysius) Dent O.P. supplied from Hinckley from 1845 to 1851.[64] The Holt chapel was closed when the Market Harborough mission was permanently established in 1859.

John Mordaunt[65] of Medbourne, 2 miles from Holt, occurs in the 1680 list,[66] but no doubt he used the Holt chaplains and did not incur the expense of maintaining a chaplain of his own.

John Wildman of Burton on the Wolds occurs in the same list.[67] He had inherited the property about 1658 and married a daughter of the recusant Christopher Roper, 4th Lord Teynham.[68]

The last of the thirteen names in the list is Lord Brudenell. He is Francis Brudenell, who used the style of Lord Brudenell, being the son and heir of the Roman Catholic peer, Robert, 2nd Earl of Cardigan. He married in 1668 and died in 1698 in the lifetime of his father. In 1680 his father was occupying the main family home at Deene (Northants.) and Francis was presumably living in Leicestershire. The family owned property at Stonton Wyville, but it was in 1680 occupied by a younger branch. The residence of Lord Brudenell remains unknown, but it is probable that he harboured a chaplain, since his father certainly did so at Deene.

The Smith family provided three mass centres, at Ashby Folville Hall, Brentingby Hall, and Queniborough Hall. On 18 August 1581 Francis Hastings reported that 'the house of Mr. Smith of Ashby Folville, whose wife is most obstinately settled in Popery', ought to be searched.[69] She was Elizabeth, daughter of Sir Thomas Brudenell of Deene (Northants.) and second wife of Francis Smith, whose first wife had brought him Ashby. She was excommunicated for recusancy in 1588,[70] and convicted of that offence in 1600.[71] Francis Smith died in 1605 and was succeeded by his son George, whose religious convictions as well as those of his wife are described below. George was succeeded in 1607 by his son Sir Francis, who 'ever kept a priest in his house as also entertained others when they came'.[72] About 1624 his chaplain was a Jesuit.[73] Charles Smith, 1st Viscount Carrington, who succeeded his father Sir Francis in 1629, received a certificate of conformity to the established

---

[58] Ibid.   [59] Ibid.   [60] Ibid.

[61] Ibid.   [62] Ibid.

[63] *Cath. Dir.* He was so sensitive about his surname that he persuaded his host to call him Voisin: M. F. Roskell, *Memoirs of Francis Kerril Amherst*, 50.

[64] B.M. Add. MS. 34565.

[65] Grandson of Hen., 4th Lord Mordaunt of Turvey (Beds.) and Drayton (Northants.).

[66] Hist. MSS. Com., *11th Rep., App.* ii, *Ho. of Lords, 1678–88*, 236.

[67] Ibid.

[68] Coll. of Arms MSS., Leic., K. 2 L., f. 114.

[69] S.P. 12/150, no. 6. Another house to be searched was that of 'one Conyers that dwelleth near me'. The letter was written from Market Bosworth (Leics.). Conyers and his house have not been identified.

[70] *State of the Ch.*, ed. C. W. Foster, p. lxxxv.

[71] E. 377/6.

[72] A. Hamilton, *Chron. of Engl. Augustinian Canonesses of St. Monica's at Louvain, 1625–44*, ii, 21.

[73] Ibid. 24.

religion on 7 June 1642, but reverted to his ancestral faith before July 1646, when he was one of the fifteen Roman Catholic Royalists who were exempted by name from pardon in the Parliamentary proposals of that month and was fined for recusancy from 1649 to 1654. It was reported at the Metropolitical Visitation of 1634 that his wife 'and her followers' were recusants and that 'they bury recusants there [i.e. at Ashby Folville] in the night'.[74] That the 2nd Viscount was a Roman Catholic is proved by his endowing three annual masses for his father's soul, and it was during his ownership that in 1676 twenty-two Roman Catholics were reported in Ashby Folville parish, by far the largest group in the county.[75] His younger brother John became a Jesuit in 1663,[76] which suggests the continued influence of Jesuit chaplains at Ashby Folville. The 2nd Viscount died in 1701 and left Ashby Folville to his widow,[77] who registered the Ashby Folville property as a Roman Catholic Non-Juror under the Act of 1715,[78] and survived until 1748. Next year the property was sold to a Protestant and its connexion with Roman Catholicism ended.

Brentingby Hall was occupied during Francis Smith's lifetime by his eldest son George. In October 1564 George was described as 'an adversary of the True Religion'. In 1588 his wife[79] was excommunicated for recusancy.[80] On 10 October 1600 his younger son John made the following statement on entering the English College, Rome:

... I was born at Ashby Folville [in 1580]. I have five brothers and five sisters, all Catholics, together with my mother. My father and grandfather are schismatics. . . . Both [my grandfather's] wives were Catholics. . . . About three years ago, while I was spending my Oxford vacation at home [i.e. at Brentingby], my mother introduced me to the priest who afterwards reconciled me to the Church. . . . Not long after this a certain priest arrived, named I think Mush[81] . . . Seeing me so ignorant, he deferred my reconciliation till his next visit. . . . But before his return I had gone back to Oxford where the first named priest finding me reconciled me. His name was I think Sewell.[82] . . .[83]

George Smith, dying in 1607, left Brentingby to his widow, who in the following year lost two-thirds of the manor of Brentingby for her recusancy.[84] On her death the property reverted to Sir Francis Smith of Ashby Folville, who left it to his younger son Sir Thomas, who was a Roman Catholic during the Interregnum[85] and no doubt in the reign of Charles I. He sold Brentingby in 1637 and went to live at Sproxton. His widow[86] with three of her children was imprisoned in 1679 in Nottingham jail for recusancy.[87]

Queniborough Hall was bought by Francis Smith of Ashby Folville in 1587 and was inherited by George Smith, second son of George Smith (d. 1607). It remained in the possession of his descendants, all of whom were Roman Catholic, until its sale about 1765. Edmund Smith of Queniborough occurs in

---

74 A. P. Moore, 'Metropolitical Visitation of Archbishop Laud', *Assoc. Arch. Soc. Rep. and Papers*, xxix, 515. Recusants, being excommunicate from the Anglican Communion, were denied burial in their par. graveyards. Hence such stratagems as burial at night.

75 Archbishop Sheldon's Visitation of 1676. MS. in the Wm. Salt Libr., Stafford.

76 H. Foley, *Rec. of Engl. Province*, vii, 117.

77 Lady Anne Herbert, dau. of Wm., 1st Marquess of Powis.

78 E. E. Estcourt and J. O. Payne, *Engl. Cath. Non-Jurors of 1715*, 156.

79 Anne, dau. of Sir Thomas Giffard of Chillington, Staffs.

80 *State of the Ch.*, ed. Foster, xxiii, p. lxxxv.

81 He is either Wm. or John Mush (or Ratcliffe), both secular priests, and both working in Engl. at the time.

82 The secular priest Robert Sewell, who left Rheims for Engl. in 1580.

83 Foley, *Rec. of Engl. Province*, iv, 18, 19.   84 E. 377/16.

85 *Cal. of the Ctee. for Compounding*, 111, 3169.

86 Mary, dau. of the recusant Thos. Waterton, of Walton, Yorks.

87 Foley, *Rec. of Engl. Province*, v, 493.

the 1680 list of prominent Leicestershire Roman Catholics.[88] John Gardiner S.J. was chaplain there from probably 1701 until shortly before 1727[89] and was succeeded by Giles Poulton S.J., who left in or before 1737.[90]

It was the Brooksby family which probably made the most important, if indirect, contribution to the survival of Roman Catholicism in the county, for, as is shown below, it was they who harboured William Wright S.J. after he had left the Countess of Rutland and it was he who founded the Jesuit 'Leicestershire mission'.[91] The family was, indeed, playing a valuable role before the arrival of Wright, as is fully proved by the 1603 return of recusants. Out of the twenty-two recusants reported in the county in that year no fewer than fourteen were living in parishes in which the Brooksbys owned property; namely, four at Grimston, eight at Frisby, and two in Saxelby.[92] In the year beginning Michaelmas 1605 no fewer than four members of the family were convicted for recusancy.[93] In 1634 sixteen persons were presented for recusancy at Grimston.[94] Robert Brooksby (b. *c.* 1526) inherited Shoby in Saxelby parish, Great Ashby, and Grimston in 1552. He did not die until December 1615, outliving both his eldest son Edward (d. 1580 or 1581) and the latter's eldest son William (d. 1606). He is almost certainly identical with the 'Mr. Brooksby, a gentleman in Leicestershire', who, the Bishop of Lincoln informed the Government in 1557, 'had for a long time not come to his parish church nor received the Sacrament'.[95] On 18 August 1581 Francis Hastings wrote to the Earl of Leicester that 'the house of one Mr. Bruxby of Sholby' ought to be searched, as also 'the house of Mistress Bruxby, daughter to the Lorde Vaux and wife of Bruxby's sonne but now a widow'.[96] This is Eleanor Vaux, who had married Edward Brooksby about 1577. The house she was living in was almost certainly Great Ashby Hall, for it was settled on her as her jointure and her brother Henry Vaux was buried at Great Ashby in 1587.[97] In June 1580 her husband met in London the first Jesuit priest to land in England, Robert Parsons S.J.,[98] and probably Edmund Campion S.J.[99] This meeting was the beginning of a long and close association between the Brooksby family and the Society of Jesus. Henry Garnet S.J., the Jesuit Provincial, who reached England in 1586, made the family's acquaintance by 1589, probably in 1587. From then until his arrest in 1606 Eleanor Brooksby and her even more famous sister Anne Vaux devoted themselves to providing a succession of houses for Garnet[1] and it was probably Garnet who introduced William Wright S.J. to the sisters. That Wright had left the Countess of Rutland and gone to Eleanor Brooksby before 1615 may be inferred from the following circumstance. In 1636 Edward Thimelby[2] entered the English College at Rome and gave this account

[88] Ho. of Lords, MS. 321, c. 65.

[89] Foley, *Rec. of Engl. Province*, v, 494; vii, 287. R. Trappes Lomax, 'Addresses of the Stations in Engl. served by the Jesuit Fathers, 1727–34', *Cath. Rec. Soc.* xiii, 179.

[90] Foley, op. cit. v, 494; vii, 622; *Cath. Rec. Soc.* xiii, 179.

[91] Foley, op. cit. vii, 872. The Leics. Mission covered Leics., Derbys., and Notts.

[92] *Assoc. Arch. Soc. Rep. and Papers*, xxix, 129–60.   [93] E. 377/14.

[94] *Assoc. Arch. Soc. Rep. and Papers*, xxix, 499.   [95] S.P. 12/117, no. 13.

[96] S.P. 12/150, no. 6.

[97] Gt. Ashby Par. Reg., 19 Nov. 1587.

[98] R. Simpson, *Edmund Campion*, 173.

[99] Campion was executed at Tyburn, 1 Dec. 1581.

[1] For a search of one of these houses in Oct. 1591, see H. Morris, *Life of Fr. John Gerard*, 108–16.

[2] He was a younger son of Thos. Thimelby of Irnham, Lincs., by his wife Mary, dau. of Edw. and Eleanor Brooksby, and was b. at Irnham in 1615.

of himself: 'Immediately after my birth I was carried by my grandmother Eleanor Brooksby into Leicestershire. She took care that I should be instructed in the Catholic faith by Father William Wright and on her death [about 1625] left me in charge of her sister Anne Vaux and under the guardianship of the said Father.'[3] Now by 1615 Great Ashby had been sequestered for Eleanor's recusancy and she was homeless. She and Anne had probably gone to live at Shoby with Robert Brooksby, who died in 1615, aged 89. That they did so is supported by the fact that in 1627 Anne Vaux appears among the eleven recusants in Saxelby parish.[4] Eleanor does not appear in the list, for she had died about 1625, leaving Edward Thimelby in the charge of her sister and under the guardianship of William Wright S.J., who had previously instructed him. Wright therefore was probably harboured at Shoby Hall from some date between August 1609[5] and 1615 until at least as late as 1625 and very possibly until his death on 18 January 1639 in the Jesuit Derbyshire District, which included Leicestershire. From Shoby, then, Wright founded and organized the Jesuit mission in the counties of Derby, Leicester, and Nottingham. By 1621 he had collected eight of his fellow Jesuits to help him, by 1628 twelve, and by 1633 fifteen.[6] While it is not possible to say what proportion of these totals of nine, thirteen, and sixteen were stationed in Leicestershire, it is certain that Ashby Folville and Nevill Holt and probable that Husbands Bosworth and Aston Flamville had Jesuit chaplains before 1639.[7] In December 1615 Shoby was inherited by Winifred Brooksby, a girl of 13. She married the Roman Catholic Sir Francis Englefield 2nd Bt.[8] and was buried at Saxelby in June 1672.[9] Anthony Englefield of Shoby occurs in the 1680 list.[10] Not long after, the Roman Catholic story of Shoby, as of Great Ashby, closed with their sale to a Protestant.[11] Shoby Hall, partly rebuilt and called Priory Farm, still stands, and a ruinous stone building next the kitchen is still called the chapel.

Frisby and Birstall were owned by Bartholomew Brooksby before 10 July 1600, when he was convicted of recusancy,[12] and passed on the death of Gregory Brooksby, who was living in 1641, to Gregory's daughter Ann, who married Thomas Gifford. Their son Sir Henry Gifford 1st Bt. (d. 1664) and his son Sir John (d. 1736) were Roman Catholics. Sir Henry's younger brother Maurice became a Dominican and was working in England from before 1672 until 1692.[13] It was possibly through him that the Dominicans became established in Leicestershire.[14]

This survey of Roman Catholic centres may be compared with the reports on the numbers of papists which the incumbents of parishes submitted at Archbishop Sheldon's visitation of 1676,[15] and at the enumerations of 1767 and 1780,[16] and the numbers reported by the county authorities in 1829.[17] The figures are tabulated as follows:

3 Foley, *Rec. of Engl. Province*, v, 599.   4 E. 377/35.
5 See above, p. 59.
6 Jesuit Archives, Annual Cat. for 1621, 1628, and 1633.   7 See above, pp. 60, 63, 64, 65.
8 He and 'all his household' were recusants in 1634: *Assoc. Arch. Soc. Rep. and Papers*, xxix, 516.
9 Saxelby Par. Reg., 5 June 1672.
10 Hist. MSS. Com., *11th Rep.*, App. ii, *Ho. of Lords, 1678–88*, 236.
11 Nichols, *Leics.* ii, 402; ex inf. 10th Earl of Aylesford.   12 E. 377/6.
13 C. F. R. Palmer, *Obit. Notices of Friars-Preachers*, 6.
14 See above, p. 60.
15 W. G. D. Fletcher, 'Religious Census of Leics. in 1676', *T.L.A.S.* vi, 296–303.
16 Ho. of Lords, Main Papers; Returns of Papists, 1767 and 1780.
17 Leics. County Rec. Office, Return of Papists, 1829.

ROMAN CATHOLICISM

Roman Catholics in Leicestershire, 1676–1829

Parish	1676	1767	1780	1829	Parish	1676	1767	1780	1829
Ashby de la Zouch	1	..	..	..	Leire	..	1	..	..
Ashby Folville	22	1	..	..	Loughborough	2	..	4	..
Ashby, Little	..	1	..	..	Medbourne with Holt[21]	8	31	33	48
Aston Flamville[18]	7	21	22	..	Melton Mowbray	..	1	3	..
Barkestone	..	1	..	..	Mountsorrel	..	5	..	..
Barwell	1	3	..	..	Norton juxta Twycross	1	..	..	..
Belgrave	5	..	..	..	Queniborough	2	..	5	..
Belton	9	..	..	..	Saxelby	5	..	..	..
Bosworth, Husbands	8	28	18	80	Scalford	..	1	..	..
Breedon	16	..	..	..	Sheepy	..	..	1	..
Carlton Curlieu with Ilston	2	..	..	..	Shepshed	6	..	..	..
Claxton alias Long Clawson	..	1	..	..	Shilton, Earl	3	..	..	..
Coston	2	6	10	..	Syston	..	1	..	..
Dalby, Great	2	..	..	..	Stapleford	1	..	..	..
Diseworth	1	..	..	..	Stathern	..	3	2	..
Dishley	4	..	1	..	Stoke Golding	..	..	1	..
Donington, Castle	..	1	6	..	Thurcaston	..	..	1	..
Eastwell	13	29	35	25	Tilton	1	..	..	..
Eaton	2	10	5	4	Twycross and Orton on the Hill	2	..	..	..
Enderby	1	..	..	..	Twyford with Hungarton[22]	..	1	1	..
Frisby	1	..	..	..	Waltham	..	1	..	..
Glen Magna	..	..	4	..	Whitwick	5	..	..	..
Hallaton[19]	..	1	1	..	Witherley	..	1	..	..
Higham on the Hill	..	3	2	..	Wycomb and Chadwell	..	3	..	..
Hinckley	4	18	8	40	Wymeswold[23]	2	11	..	..
Hose	1	2	4	5	Wymondham	3	..	..	..
Kibworth	..	1	1	..	Totals	148	218	211	602 to 702
Kimcote	..	2	..	..					
Kirby Bellars	1	..	..	..					
Knaptoft	..	5	4	..					
Laughton with Mowsley	..	..	2	..					
Leicester[20] (including St. Leonards)	4	24	37	400 to 500					

It has been shown that from the reign of Elizabeth I onwards there was a number of families of position who probably or certainly opened their doors to Roman Catholic priests. No doubt, too, there were humbler folk who did the like. Thus it was in the homes of both small and great that the Roman communion was harboured for more than two centuries. It has been shown, too, how during the long years of proscription families dropped out of the struggle, through impoverishment as with the Hastingses of Braunstone, through the failure of male heirs as with the Beaumonts, through apostasy as with the Shirleys, or through a voluntary sale as with the Eyres.

By 1740 only Ashby Folville, Aston Flamville, Belgrave, Eastwell, Husbands Bosworth, Nevill Holt, and Queniborough remained; by 1780 only Eastwell, Husbands Bosworth, and Nevill Holt, though Hinckley and Leicester had

[18] The totals for 1767 and 1780 include Burbage.
[19] The 1767 figure is for North and South Hallaton.
[20] The 1767 total is shown by parishes: All Saints—15, St. Leonard—1, St. Margaret—1, St. Martin—2, St. Mary—5.
[21] The 1829 total is for Holt and Bradley.
[22] The 1767 figure is for Hungarton only.
[23] The Metropolitical Visitation of 1634 notes under Wymeswold 'many Papists there': *Assoc. Arch. Soc. Rep. and Papers*, xxix, 516.

replaced Aston Flamville and Belgrave. Thus the long rearguard action which began in 1559 reached its last and weakest position and was to hold it for another fifty years, for in 1830 the Roman Catholic centres remained the same five as in 1780.[24] The year 1833, with the foundation of the Loughborough mission, marks the start of the recovery.

Religious orders of men and women have appeared in the county; the Cistercians at Mount St. Bernard,[25] the Institute of Charity (Rosminians) at Birstall, Loughborough, Whitwick, Gracedieu, and Ratcliffe, the Fathers of the Blessed Sacrament at Leicester and the Priests of the Sacred Heart at Earl Shilton, Dominican nuns at Hinckley and Leicester, Franciscan nuns at Leicester and Melton Mowbray, Sisters of St. Joseph at Leicester and Rearsby, Sisters of the Nativity of the Blessed Virgin Mary at Leicester, Poor Clares at Coalville, and Sisters of Providence at Loughborough and Whitwick. An asylum for the aged poor and destitute children, a babies' home, a home for girls, and three nursing homes have been provided.[26] A public school for boys has been founded at Ratcliffe with a preparatory school at Gracedieu Manor, and convent schools for girls at Coalville, Evington Hall, Hinckley, Loughborough, and Melton Mowbray. Primary schools have been built at Earl Shilton, Hinckley, Loughborough, Market Harborough, Measham, and Leicester, which has four, of which one dates from 1824 and one was only started in 1950.

Administrative changes within the Church have made their contribution. Whereas up to 1840 Leicestershire was one of fifteen counties under the rule of the Vicar Apostolic of the Midland District, from 1840 to 1850 it shared a Vicar Apostolic with seven other counties, and since 1850 it has been ruled by the Bishop of Nottingham, who has only four other counties in his charge. This reduction in the size of episcopal jurisdictions has made possible better planning, closer supervision, and more vigorous action.

The Irish immigration, which began about 1826 and increased rapidly from about 1840, has contributed to the number of Roman Catholics in the county. The most obvious and important manifestation of all this is found in the creation of Mass centres. In consequence there has been both an absolute increase in Roman Catholic numbers from some 800 about the year 1830 to over 22,000 in 1950, and an increase relative to the county's population from just over 0·4 to 3·5 per cent. in the same period.

Roman Catholicism in Leicestershire after 1833

Mass centre	Founded	Notes
Loughborough . . .	1833	
Gracedieu Manor . .	1834	The 1834 foundation ended about 1888. It was refounded in 1933.
Mount St. Bernard Abbey	1835	
Whitwick . . .	1837	
Barrow-on-Soar . .	1839	Served from Birstall since 1947.
Shepshed . . .	1840	
Lindley Hall . . .	1840 or soon after	This was a domestic chapel of the Eyre family. It was served from Nuneaton until about 1889 and from then until it was closed between 1915 and 1921 from Hinckley.
Melton Mowbray . .	1842	
Ratcliffe College . .	1844	

[24] The brief-lived chaplaincy at Old Dalby Hall is ignored here.
[25] For a full account of the abbey see above, p. 53.
[26] They are not necessarily situated in Leics. but in the Nott. Dioc., and serve the county.

Mass centre	Founded	Notes
Ashby-de-la-Zouch . .	1850	The 1850 foundation ended in 1870. It was refounded in 1893.
Leicester, St. Patrick .	1854	This church was replaced in 1922 by a church dedicated to St. Patrick and Our Lady of Good Counsel.
Market Harborough . .	1859	
Swinford . . .	1869	It was closed 1875. It was served from Rugby and Mount St. Bernard Abbey.
Lutterworth . . .	1874	It was served until 1880 by the Earl of Denbigh's chaplain at Monks Kirby (Warws.).
Coalville . . .	1875	The 1875 foundation ended in 1876. It was refounded in 1897.
Normanton Hall . .	1875	This was a domestic chapel of the Worsley-Worswick family. It was served from Hinckley to 1900, from Leicester to 1907, by a resident chaplain in 1907 and 1908, and from Earl Shilton from 1908 until closed between 1915 and 1921.
Sileby	1877	Served from Birstall since 1947. The date 1877 is that of the building of the church. The Fathers of Charity from Ratcliffe College were working in Sileby in 1850 and had established a school in it by 1865.
Stanford Hall . .	1880	This was a domestic chapel of the Lords Braye. It is served from Lutterworth.
Measham. . . .	1881	
Leicester, Sacred Heart .	1882 or 1883	
Willesley Hall . . .	1883	This was a domestic chapel of the Countess of Loudoun. It was served from Measham until it was closed in 1900.
Leicester, St. Peter . .	1896	
Hathern . . .	1899	Served from Shepshed.
Syston	1899	The 1899 foundation ended in 1901. It was refounded in 1921. It has been served from Birstall since 1943.
South Wigston . .	1905	
Earl Shilton . . .	1908	
Aylestone . . .	1915	
Rothley	1922	Served from Birstall since 1941.
Market Bosworth . .	1931	Served from Earl Shilton.
Kibworth Beauchamp .	1935	Served from Market Harborough.
Castle Donington . .	1935	Served from Melbourne (Derbys.).
Braunstone . . .	1935	
Blaby	1936	Served from S. Wigston.
Leicester, St. John Bosco .	1937	Served from Aylestone.
Birstall	1938	
Leicester, St. Joseph . .	1938	
Kirby Muxloe . . .	1939	Served from Leicester, St. Peter.
Oadby	1940	Served from South Wigston.
Knighton . . .	1941	
Burbage	1943	Served from Hinckley.
Port House . . .	1943	Served from Hinckley until 1951, when it was closed.
Billesdon	1945	Served from Leicester, St. Joseph.
Rearsby	1946	Served from Hinckley.
Narborough . . .	1946	Served from Braunstone.
Ellistown	1948	Served from Coalville.
Lindley Estate . . .	1949	Served from Hinckley.
Stoke Golding Lodge .	1949	Served from Hinckley.
Leicester, Stadium . .	1950	Served from Leicester, St. Patrick and Our Lady of Good Counsel.
Hinckley, Sacred Heart .	1951	It replaced Port House. Served from the original Hinckley mission of 1765.

The fortunes of Roman Catholicism in the county are vividly manifest in the numerical decline of its supporters from 1559 to the early 19th century and in their subsequent increase. Not that exactness is possible, since the only religious census took place in 1851.[27] A further difficulty lies in the fact that Roman Catholics were at pains to conceal their religion until at least as late as

---

[27] *Census Returns*, 1851 [1690], H.C. (1852–3), lxxxix.

1750. It is uncritical to assume that lists of recusants[28] are a reliable guide to the number of Roman Catholics. A recusant was a Roman Catholic who had been detected, reported to the authorities, taken into court, and convicted of the crime of recusancy. Increasingly, as time went on, he might be a Protestant Dissenter and at all times his offence might be only neglect of churchgoing. Not all members of underground movements are discovered. Not all the members of the Roman Catholic underground movement, even after discovery, were reported;[29] not all, even when reported, were proceeded against;[30] not all who were proceeded against were convicted. It is equally uncritical to believe that presentments at Quarter Sessions give a true picture of the Roman Catholic population, since as a general rule those only were presented who had already been convicted. Unfortunately the Minute Books of Leicestershire Quarter Sessions do not begin until 1693 and the indictments at an even later date. They therefore throw no light on the number of recusants.

The total of 148 provided for Archbishop Sheldon in 1676 is too small because it included only convicted recusants over sixteen.[31] The total number of Leicestershire Roman Catholics at that date was probably about 1,100.[32]

[28] e.g. in Oct. 1577 the Bp. of Linc., in reply to a request for a list of recusants in his dioc., names only 1 person in Leics. P. Ryan, 'Diocesan Returns of Recusants for Engl. and Wales, 1577', *Cath. Rec. Soc.* xxii, 52. 'A Note of the Papists and Recusants in the several shires of Engl.' of Mar. 1588 gives only 2 Leics. names. J. H. Pollen, 'Recusants and Priest, Mar. 1588', *Cath. Rec. Soc.* xxii, 125. In 1601 the commissary of the Archd. of Leic. reported that 6 persons had been decreed excommunicate for recusancy: *State of the Ch.*, ed. Foster, p. lxxxv. A list of recusants of 1603 has only 33 in Leics.: ibid. 445.

[29] Many motives operated, such as reluctance to harm one's neighbour or to offend one's landlord, and the reluctance of the Anglican clergy to incur the reflection upon them implied by the presence of Roman Catholics in their parishes.

[30] The Government was as much concerned to win revenue as to enforce conformity. It was useless to harry the indigent.

[31] That those under 16 were excluded is established: *Assoc. Arch. Soc. Rep. and Papers*, xxix, 159; 'The Religious Census of 1676', *Trans. Soc. of Cymmrodorion*, 1925–6, Supplem. 14–16. That the numbers of papists returned in 1676 were much less than the true numbers, and probably only included those actually convicted of recusancy, is clear from a comparison between the 1676 returns and a series of reports made between 1632 and 1696 by persons in touch with the rulers of the Roman Catholic ch. in Engl. and Wales. In 1637 the Revd. Gregorio Panzani, who was Papal Agent in Engl. 1634–7, reported the number of Roman Catholics as 150,000 (Barberini Libr., Rome, MS. LVI, 136/A, no. 2450). In 1632 Bp. Ric. Smith, Vicar Apostolic in Engl. 1625–31, stated there were 200,000 Roman Catholics, excluding those who made an appearance of conforming: P. Hughes, *Rome and Counter-Reformation in Engl.* 414. In 1662 Patrick Con, confidential agent in Engl. of the Cardinal in charge of Propaganda, gave the number of Roman Catholics as 200,000 (see his letter of 24 Apr. 1662, in the Archives of St. Mary's Coll., Blairs). A memorial drawn up in 1669 by the agent in Rome of the Engl. secular clergy also gives the number of Roman Catholics as 200,000 (W. M. Brady, *Annals of the Catholic Hierarchy*, 107) and in 1677 the same agent again gave the figure as 200,000 (M. V. Hay, *The Jesuits and the Popish Plot*, 89). About 1696 the Procurator in Rome of the Engl. Vicars Apostolic reported the number of Roman Catholics as 100,000 (Westm. Archives, MS. xxxvi, f. 176). This consensus of opinion that the Roman Catholics numbered 100,000 to 200,000 in the 17th century cannot be set aside. The decline reported at the end of the cent. is explained by the failure of Jas. II and the widespread discouragement which followed. Yet the total numbers reported to Sheldon in 1676 were only 11,871 in the Province of Cant., and 2,252 in the diocs. of York and Carlisle: Bodl. Libr., Tanner MSS. 149, ff. 1–4; 150, ff. 27–38, 129 et seq. The returns for Durham and Chester diocs. are lacking, but making a liberal allowance for the missing returns, the number of Roman Catholics reported in 1676 can hardly have exceeded 25,000. An addition of 50 per cent. must be made to allow for those under 16, giving a total Roman Catholic population on the basis of the 1676 returns of perhaps 37,000, or only about ⅕ the figure indicated by the estimates given above. Evidence that only about ⅕ of the Roman Catholic population were convicted as recusants can be obtained from the comparison of a list of recusants convicted in 22 counties in 15–22 and 26, 28, and 29 Chas. II (*Cath. Rec. Soc.* vi, 75–326), and the lists of the more prominent papists prepared by counties for the Ho. of Lords in 1680 (Hist. MSS. Com., *11th Rep. App.* ii, *Ho. of Lords, 1678–88*, 236). The former includes 33 persons described as 'esquires', but the latter, for the same 22 counties, 159 esquires, i.e. about 5 times as many. It is difficult to see how incumbents in 1676 could have used for their returns any other basis than conviction for recusancy, the only certain indication available to them. Sheldon's instructions made it clear that he did not wish the number of Dissenters, Catholic or Protestant, to appear very great, for his object was to prove them so negligible that his policy of repression would succeed (*Trans. Soc. of Cymmrodorion*, 1925–6, Supplem., 4, 5).

[32] For the calculations on which this figure is based, see n. 31, above.

ROMAN CATHOLICISM

The list of 1680 has thirteen Leicestershire names, but it covers only peers, baronets, esquires, and gentlemen.[33] The list compiled under the Papists' Estates Act of 1715[34] gives thirty-three names, but it is concerned only with freeholders, annuitants, and the tenants of the Roman Catholic freeholders, provided they were themselves Roman Catholics, and from the total of thirty-three, sixteen must be deducted since they did not live in the county.[35] The inquiries ordered by the House of Lords in 1767 and 1780 were designed to arrive at the exact numbers of Roman Catholics of all ages, and an examination of the returns proves that the incumbents of parishes did in fact include children, however young. Apart, then, from the failure of some incumbents to make any return at all, and the difficulties which others admitted in counting heads, the numbers reported in 1767 and 1780 may be taken to be as reasonably accurate as the circumstances under which the inquiries were carried out permitted. They probably erred on the low side in the case of Leicestershire, since in 1773 the Vicar Apostolic of the Midland District, which included the county, reported to Rome that it contained 330 Roman Catholics.[36] Since this total should be increased by about 25 per cent.[37] for those under 7 years of age, the full figure would be over 400. A return made to the House of Commons in 1829 gave a total of between 602 and 702 Leicestershire Roman Catholics.[38] The Religious Census of 1851 states that on Sunday, 30 March, of that year, 1,893 persons were present at mass in the county. The number of Roman Catholics about 1875, based on the reports of Visitations, was given as 5,586. In 1920 the Nottingham Diocesan Year Book gives 9,917 and in 1950, 22,263.

[33] Hist. Com., *11th Rep.*, *App.* ii, *Ho. of Lords, 1678–88*, 236.
[34] I Geo. I, c. 55.
[35] Estcourt and Payne, *Engl. Cath. Non-Jurors of 1715*, 156–60.
[36] W. M. Brady, *Annals of Cath. Hierarchy*, 212.
[37] The justification for this 25 per cent. addition is that, whereas the returns of 1767 and 1780 give 67,916 and 69,401 respectively as the Roman Catholic totals for Engl. and Wales, the 4 Vicars Apostolic whose territories covered all Engl. and Wales told Rome in 1773 that they had 56,475 Roman Catholics under their charge: Brady, op. cit. 169, 212, 263, 301. There is no doubt that the Vicars Apostolic reckoned only those who had reached the 'age of reason', about 7, required for the reception of certain sacraments. A 25 per cent. addition for those under 7 brings the Vicars' Apostolic total to 70,594, which agrees well with the necessarily rather under-estimated totals of 1767 and 1780.
[38] Leics. County Rec. Off.

MEDIEVAL POLITICAL HISTORY

LITERARY sources give little information about the Anglian invasion of the territories now included in the county of Leicester, so that any attempt to reconstruct the stages by which the region was settled must depend on archaeological evidence, supplemented by such deductions as can be made from place-names and from the geography of the area. The circumstances attending the decline of Roman rule in this area are not known, though no doubt the district experienced the same collapse of Roman authority during the first half of the 5th century as did the rest of Britain. Extensive Anglian settlement does not seem to have taken place until the late 6th century, but there is some evidence of earlier penetration. The earliest traces of the Germanic invaders' presence have been found at Peatling Magna, where grave-gear assigned to the period of about A.D. 500 has been discovered.[1] Rather later than Peatling, probably in the first half of the 6th century, Leicester itself was occupied,[2] and at Glen Parva, about 3 miles from Leicester, Anglian burials dating from early in the same century have been found.[3] The known preference of the Anglo-Saxon invaders for using navigable waterways[4] makes it probable that the settlers at Leicester travelled by the Trent and the Soar, and Peatling Magna, which stands on a small stream running into the Sence, a tributary of the Soar, was probably occupied by the same route. It is possible that Peatling was occupied by an advance over land from one of the north-bank tributaries of the Welland, but it seems more probable that the settlement here should be linked with the other early settlements in the neighbourhood of Leicester, and that all were reached through the continuous water route provided by the Trent and Soar. The settlement at Rothley, not far from the Soar and near a tributary stream, may have been first established in the early 6th century,[5] and if this is so it would be further evidence that the Trent–Soar route was in use at an early date. Traces of Anglian occupation found at Oadby and Wigston Magna[6] may indicate etwo further settlements made at the same period as those near by at Leicester and Glen Parva.

Further Anglo-Saxon occupation of Leicestershire does not seem to have taken place before the second half of the 6th century, when several settlements were established in the upland country of eastern Leicestershire, lying between the valleys of the Soar, the Trent, and the Welland.[7] The Welland valley to the south had been occupied considerably earlier, in the later 5th century,[8] and the unattractive nature of the east Leicestershire countryside, which is mostly covered by a thick stratum of boulder clay, was probably responsible for the fact

---

[1] W. G. Hoskins, 'Further Notes on the Anglian and Scandinavian Settlement of Leics.', *T.L.A.S.* xix, 95. The name 'Peatling' is of a form generally associated with early settlements.

[2] *Anglo-Saxon Leics. and Rut.* (Leic. City Mus.), 11, 12.   [3] Ibid. 19, 20.

[4] E. T. Leeds, *Archaeology of the Anglo-Saxon Settlements*, 18.

[5] *Anglo-Saxon Leics. and Rut.* (Leic. City Mus.), 20.

[6] Ibid. 19; W. G. Hoskins, 'Anglian and Scandinavian Settlement of Leics.', *T.L.A.S.* xviii, 121.

[7] *T.L.A.S.* xviii, 120.   [8] Ibid. 119.

that this area was not colonized earlier.[9] The situation of most of the known settlements of the pagan period[10] on the Soar and the Wreak, or their tributaries, makes it probable that the settlers in eastern Leicestershire made use of the Trent and the Soar, though some settlements near the south-eastern border of the county, such as that at Medbourne,[11] were no doubt occupied from the nearby River Welland. The relative scantiness of the evidence for settlement during the heathen period in the lower Soar valley itself[12] cannot be held to prove that the obvious river route was not used, for the fragmentary nature of the existing evidence about the Anglo-Saxon settlement makes any deductions based on the absence of evidence more than usually dangerous.[13] West of the Soar valley no traces of Anglo-Saxon occupation at such an early date have been found, except on the south-western border of the county near Watling Street.[14] The period between the conversion of the Anglian inhabitants of Leicestershire to Christianity in the middle of the 7th century[15] and the Danish invasions of the 9th century must have seen the gradual extension of the Anglian settlement into western Leicestershire, but there is no evidence that would allow the process to be described in detail. The difficult country of Charnwood Forest remained virtually unoccupied until a much later period.

The new inhabitants of the present county of Leicester, or at least of most of it, formed part of the Middle Angles.[16] The name of this people suggests that they were at one time an independent race, and the terms in which they are referred to by Bede[17] seem to imply this also, but there is no record of the Middle Angles' history before they fell under the domination of the Mercian kings. The lands of the Middle Angles cannot have coincided even approximately with the modern Leicestershire, for their territory appears to have included several more southerly counties,[18] and it is unlikely that any subdivision of the race can have occupied the same area as the present shire; in the 9th century, part of north-west Leicestershire lay in the territory of the Tomsaetan, a Mercian folk whose lands must have included much of Warwickshire,[19] and it has been suggested that the Herefinna, a folk listed in the 'Tribal Hidage', may have inhabited the later Framland wapentake, as well as Kesteven in Lincolnshire.[20] Although there is evidence that some of the Celtic inhabitants survived the Anglian occupation of Leicestershire,[21] no details of the struggles which presumably attended the conquest are known, and it is not until 586, when the districts ruled by Credda, King of Mercia, are said to have included Leicester-

[9] Ibid. 115.

[10] i.e. before c. 650. For a map showing the location of such settlements, see *Anglo-Saxon Leics. and Rut.* (Leic. City Mus.), 12–13.

[11] *T.L.A.S.* xviii, 120.

[12] The only sites attributed to the pagan period are those at Rothley (see above) and Loughborough: *Anglo-Saxon Leics. and Rut.* (Leic. City Mus.), 21.

[13] The fact that the burials at Saxby probably date from the early 6th century (ibid. 15) is further evidence for use of the route via the Soar and Wreak.

[14] Ibid. 19.   [15] Bede, *Hist. Eccl.* iii, 21.

[16] The see of Leic. is mentioned by Bede as the bishopric of the Middle Angles: ibid. iv, 23.

[17] Ibid. i, 15.

[18] F. M. Stenton, *Anglo-Saxon Engl.* (2nd ed.), 42.

[19] Birch, *Cart. Sax.*, nos. 454, 455; Stenton, op. cit. 40–41, and 'Medeshamstede and its Colonies', *Hist. Essays in Honour of James Tait*, 318. The name of the present village of Markfield, 7½ miles north-east of Leic., may perhaps indicate where the boundary between the Tomsaetan and the Middle Angles ran. I owe this information to a suggestion made orally by Sir Frank Stenton.

[20] J. Brownbill, 'The Tribal Hidage', *E.H.R.* xl, 49. But see another article by the same writer ('The Tribal Hidage', *E.H.R.* xxvii, 638), where a different position is assigned to the Herefinna.

[21] *T.L.A.S.* xviii, 128.

shire,[22] that more precise information is available. In 653 the Middle Angles were under the rule of Peadda, who had been set over them by his father, King Penda of Mercia.[23] From this time onwards Leicestershire formed part of Mercia, and little further of its political history is recorded until the Danish invasions of the 9th century.[24]

The Scandinavian settlement in England, which produced important changes in the population and social structure of Leicestershire, was preceded by a period of devastation, and although Leicestershire, as an inland county, probably escaped the earlier Danish attacks, at a later stage it must have suffered severely. In the winter of 873–4 the Danes wintered at Repton, not far across the Derbyshire border, and in 874 King Burhed of Mercia was expelled by the invaders, who set up Ceolwulf as king.[25] The Danish settlement of the east midlands may have been begun at this time.[26] In 877 the Danes and King Ceolwulf divided Mercia between them,[27] and while the frontiers of the Danish territory as then established are unknown, Leicester and the surrounding country certainly lay within them. After 877 Leicester became part of the confederation known as the 'Five Boroughs',[28] and the adjacent territory was settled by the Danes, who here as elsewhere seem to have retained their military organization.[29] The exact extent of territory seized by the Danish army of Leicester is unknown, but Watling Street, later the border of the Danelaw, may well have already formed the boundary on the south-west, and to the south-east the Welland was, early in the 10th century, the northern frontier of the Northampton Danes.[30] The existence of other Danish groups with centres at Stamford, Lincoln, Nottingham, and Derby indicates roughly the borders of the Leicester army's lands in other directions. It is evident that the area held by the Danes of Leicester was approximately the same as the later shire. For the first time, so far as is known, the region formed a political unit, and it is in the territory connected with the Danish borough of Leicester that the origin of the later county is to be found. The four original wapentakes of Leicestershire,[31] three of which have boundaries meeting at Leicester,[32] probably came into existence at this time, although there is no evidence concerning them before the Norman Conquest. Two of the wapentakes, Framland and Gartree, have names of Scandinavian origin,[33] and the use of the term 'wapentake' rather than 'hundred' is an additional reason for supposing that these four divisions were first created by the Danes.[34] The evidence of place-names shows that within the area controlled by the army of Leicester the Anglian inhabitants were not by any means exterminated,[35] nor were the Danish settlers evenly distributed. The

---

[22] Matt. Paris, *Chron. Majora* (Rolls Ser.), i, 252.

[23] Bede, *Hist. Eccl.* iii, 21.

[24] The statement that the Britons were defeated at Leic. by Aethelfrith of Northumbria (Symeon of Dur., *Hist. Works* (Rolls Ser.), i, 345; Gaimar, *Lestorie des Engles* (Rolls Ser.), ii, 44) is obviously a reference to Aethelfrith's victory at Chester.

[25] *Angl. Sax. Chron.* (Rolls Ser.), i, 143.

[26] R. H. Hodgkin, *Hist. of the Anglo-Saxons*, ii, 559.

[27] *Angl. Sax. Chron.* (Rolls Ser.), i, 146.   [28] Ibid. 208, 209.

[29] The Danish army of Leic. is referred to several times: ibid. 188–9, 192–4.

[30] Ibid. ii, 83.

[31] Framland, Gartree, Goscote, and Guthlaxton.

[32] The cause of the curious arrangement of the wapentake boundaries on the eastern border of the county is unknown. It already existed in 1086.

[33] *T.L.A.S.* xviii, 132.

[34] Stenton, *Anglo-Saxon Engl.* (2nd ed.), 497; the divisions are referred to as wapentakes in 1086: *V.C.H. Leics.* i, 304.   [35] *T.L.A.S.* xviii, 129.

Wreak valley and the north-west corner of Leicestershire seem to have been the areas where the Danes settled most densely.[36]

Although the period immediately after the Danish settlement must have been of great importance for Leicestershire history, when the Danish and English inhabitants began to settle down together into a new order which was to leave an enduring mark on the social structure of the county, nothing is recorded of the Danish army of Leicester for more than thirty years after 877. It is known, however, that a number of fortified posts was established in the county.[37] The slowness of the Danes to abandon either their military organization or their marauding habits was shown in 913, when the Danes of Leicester and Northampton made two raids into English territory, the second of which was defeated.[38] In 917 the Leicester and Northampton armies, with Danes from the north, attacked the English stronghold at Towcester, and being repulsed there raided as far south as Buckinghamshire.[39] The defeat at Towcester, and the fall of the neighbouring Danish strongholds of Derby and Northampton in the same year, together with the steady advance of Edward the Elder, must have dispirited the Leicester Danes, for in 918 Aethelflaed, Edward's sister, peacefully obtained possession of the borough of Leicester, and the greater part of the Danish army there submitted to her.[40] Whether or not an English garrison was placed in Leicester is unknown, but the Danish element in the population of the area certainly remained very strong, and even in the 11th century the east midlands seem to have been ready to welcome a Danish invasion. After the reconquest of 918 the Leicester region developed into a shire of the same general type as those in other parts of England, but the Danish population retained a large measure of autonomy.[41]

The death of Edward the Elder's successor Athelstan in 939, and the succession of his young brother Edmund, gave an opportunity for the invasion of English territory by the Norwegians. Having taken York in 939, the Norwegians advanced southwards in 940, penetrating as far south as Northampton and Tamworth, and devastating the countryside. King Edmund's counterattack on the Norwegians, under their leader Olaf Guthfrithson, at Leicester was unsuccessful, the Norwegians escaping from the town by night, and the peace which was then arranged through the mediation of the Archbishops of Canterbury and York was extremely disadvantageous to the English. Watling Street was established as the northern boundary of English territory, so that all the Danish Five Boroughs, including Leicester, remained under Norwegian rule.[42] It was presumably during the period of Norse domination after 940 that there were established in Leicestershire a few Norwegian settlements, whose existence is attested by place-names.[43] In 942 Edmund regained the Five Boroughs, and the poem which records their recovery shows that twenty years after Edward the Elder's conquests the Danes of the east midlands could

---

[36] Ibid. 131, 133. These two areas were particularly easily accessible by river, the Wreak valley through the Trent and the Soar, and the north-west of the county directly from the Trent.

[37] *T.L.A.S.* xix, 101–8.

[38] *Angl. Sax. Chron.* (Rolls Ser.), i, 188–9. On the chronology, see M. L. R. Beaven, 'The Beginning of the Year in the Alfredian Chron.', *E.H.R.* xxxiii, 328–42.

[39] *Angl. Sax. Chron.* (Rolls Ser.), i, 194; on the date, see Stenton, *Anglo-Saxon Engl.* (2nd ed.), 323.

[40] *Angl. Sax. Chron.* (Rolls Ser.), i, 192–3.   [41] F. M. Stenton, *Danes in Engl.* 45.

[42] *Angl. Sax. Chron.* (Rolls Ser.), ii, 89; Symeon of Dur., *Hist. Works* (Rolls Ser.), ii, 93. On the chronology, see M. L. R. Beaven, 'King Edmund I and the Danes of York', *E.H.R.* xxxiii, 39.

[43] *T.L.A.S.* xviii, 134.

consider the Norwegians as oppressive invaders and the English king as their natural lord.[44] It is the same poem which makes the earliest mention of the Five Boroughs, a Danish confederation formed by Leicester, Lincoln, Stamford, Nottingham, and Derby, with the adjacent districts where the Danish armies had settled. The political organization of the Five Boroughs is unfortunately obscure, but the Wantage code of Aethelred II shows that there was a general assembly, possessing judicial powers, with below it separate courts for boroughs and for wapentakes; the same code shows that Scandinavian law and Scandinavian methods of reckoning currency were dominant in the area within which Leicestershire lay.[45]

Edmund's recovery of the Five Boroughs in 942 was followed by a lengthy peace, which for Leicestershire remained undisturbed until the renewed Danish attacks of the next century. The raids which disturbed the early years of Aethelred II did not, so far as is known, touch Leicestershire at any time, but when in 1013 King Swein of Denmark sailed up the Trent and landed at Gainsborough, the whole of the Danelaw, including the Five Boroughs, accepted him as king, and gave up hostages from every shire.[46] The Danish districts of England supplied Swein with horses and provisions, and the fact that Swein allowed no ravaging north of Watling Street[47] shows that he considered the lands of the Five Boroughs to be friendly territory. Swein was soon in possession of all England, but his sudden death in the following year, and the withdrawal of his son Cnut led to a temporary recovery of the Danelaw by King Aethelred. It was soon lost again through the treacherous murder in 1015 of Sifirth and Morcar, two leading thegns connected with the Five Boroughs,[48] by Eadric Streona, whose Mercian ealdormanry possibly included Leicester. Edmund, Aethelred's son, abducted Sifirth's widow and, taking possession of the murdered thegns' property, was accepted as king by the inhabitants of the Five Boroughs.[49] The dangers created by the internal divisions of the country and the treacherous conduct of leading men were made plain when a new Danish army, invading the country under Cnut, was joined by Eadric Streona. None of the fighting which followed Cnut's invasion took place in Leicestershire, so far as the existing evidence shows,[50] and peace returned when the successive deaths of Aethelred II and Edmund Ironside left Cnut the ruler of all England.

Under Cnut and his successors Leicestershire probably formed part of the Mercian earldom. In 1017 Eadric Streona was made earl, but later in the same year he was murdered,[51] and the subsequent history of his earldom is obscure. His successor may have been Leofric, who was made an earl after Eadric's death,[52] and was Earl of Mercia under Edward the Confessor. From this

---

[44] *Angl. Sax. Chron.* (Rolls Ser.), i, 208–9; A. Mawer, 'The Redemption of the Five Boroughs', *E.H.R.* xxxviii, 551–7; Stenton, *Anglo-Saxon Engl.* (2nd ed.), 354.

[45] Stenton, op. cit. 503, quoting Leibermann, *Gesetze der Angelsachsen*, i, 288–33.

[46] *Angl. Sax. Chron.* (Rolls Ser.), i, 270–1.   [47] Ibid.

[48] The *Angl. Sax. Chron.* (Rolls Ser.), i, 274–5, states that they were the chief thegns of the 'Seven Boroughs', which are not mentioned in any other connexion, but which presumably included the 'Five Boroughs' of the Danelaw: Stenton, *Anglo-Saxon Engl.* (2nd ed.), 383.   [49] *Angl. Sax. Chron.* (Rolls Ser.), i, 274.

[50] The ravaging of Salop, Staffs., and Leics. in 1016 mentioned by Howden (R. de Houedene, *Chron.* (Rolls Ser.), i, 80) is presumably a reference to the ravaging of Salop, Staffs., and Chester recorded in the Angl. Sax. Chron. (*Angl. Sax. Chron.* (Rolls Ser.), i, 79; ii, 121).

[51] *Angl. Sax. Chron.* (Rolls Ser.), i, 284–5.

[52] Ibid.; Symeon of Dur., *Hist. Works* (Rolls Ser.), ii, 155. It seems to be implied, however, that Leofric was the successor of his own brother, and not of Eadric.

time until 1066 Leicestershire may have been included in the earldom of Mercia held successively by Leofric, his son Alfgar, and his grandson Edwin, but the boundaries of the pre-Conquest earldoms are very imperfectly known.[53]

The Norman Conquest brought great changes, and probably some devastation, to the county. The Domesday survey of Leicestershire suggests that part of the county was ravaged at some time during the reign of William I, probably in 1068, when the Conqueror must have passed through Leicestershire on his march from Warwick to Nottingham.[54] Further fighting followed when the men of Leicestershire, or more probably the Normans established in the county, took part in the pursuit of Hereward, then a fugitive in the great forest of the Bruneswald.[55] By 1086 Leicestershire had been divided between a number of Norman lords, amongst whom Hugh de Grentemesnil held the most extensive lands in the county.[56] Hugh was almost certainly Sheriff of Leicestershire, and may also have been the keeper of Leicester castle.[57] Whatever his exact position, he must have been the man upon whom the Conqueror relied for the maintenance of his rule in Leicestershire. The Countesses Godeva and Alveva, wives of two former earls of Mercia, retained lands in Leicestershire after 1066,[58] but none of the pre-Conquest nobility still possessed fiefs of any importance at the time of the Domesday survey. The sub-tenants recorded in 1086, however, include a considerable number of men whose Anglo-Saxon or Scandinavian names suggest that they were survivors of the native landholding class.[59]

Hugh de Grentemesnil, thus established as the most powerful feudal lord in the county, rebelled against William Rufus in 1088, and ravaged Leicestershire and Northamptonshire.[60] The revolt was a failure, but Hugh retained his lands. His son Ivo, who inherited his father's English possessions, and was the Sheriff of Leicestershire,[61] as his father may have been, joined the rising against Henry I in 1102, and once again the countryside was devastated.[62] For his participation in the unsuccessful rebellion Ivo was punished by a heavy fine.[63] Not long afterwards, preparatory to setting out on Crusade for the second time, Ivo pledged his lands for fifteen years to Robert, Count of Meulan, as security for a loan of 500 marks. In return the Count promised to give his niece in marriage to Ivo's son and to reconcile Ivo with the king. Ivo died on Crusade, and his son was unable to recover his inheritance in England.[64] Robert of Meulan, who by thus adding the extensive fiefs of the Grentemesnil family[65] to the lands already held by him in Leicestershire became the most important lord in the county, was a prominent adviser of Henry I,[66] and by virtue of his wide possessions on both sides of the Channel was one of the greatest Anglo-Norman nobles.

[53] See, for a discussion, E. A. Freeman, *Norman Conquest* (3rd ed.), ii, 573–4, and Stenton, *Anglo-Saxon Engl.* (2nd ed.), 408–9. [54] *V.C.H. Leics.* i, 284.

[55] Gaimar, *Lestorie des Engles* (Rolls Ser.), i, 392. [56] *V.C.H. Leics.* i, 290.

[57] Ordericus Vitalis, *Hist. Eccl.* (ed. le Prévost), iii, 13, 270. For discussions of Hugh's position, see F. M. Stenton, *First Century of Engl. Feudalism*, 334–5, and W. A. Morris, *Medieval Engl. Sheriff*, 49.

[58] *V.C.H. Leics.* i, 313.

[59] See ibid. 286–98 for a detailed discussion of the Leics. fiefs, as recorded in Dom. Bk.

[60] *Angl. Sax. Chron.* (Rolls Ser.), i, 357; Robert of Glouc., *Metrical Chron.* (Rolls Ser.), ii, 569.

[61] Ordericus Vitalis, *Hist. Eccl.* (ed. le Prévost), iv, 169.

[62] Ibid. 168. [63] Ibid.

[64] Ibid. 168–9.

[65] He had also obtained some at least of the Leics. lands which had been held by Aubrey de Couci: *V.C.H. Leics.* i, 290.

[66] Wm. Malmesbury, *De Gestis Regum* (Rolls Ser.), i, 483.

At some time before his death in 1118 Robert seems to have been created Earl of Leicester. He never used the style, however, perhaps because he already held the title of Count of Meulan.[67] There is no contemporary evidence that he held the 'third penny' of the county, though in 1181 it was stated that the predecessors of the 3rd earl had received the 'third penny' under Henry I.[68] Robert's descendants in the male line held the earldom of Leicester for the rest of the 12th century, and until 1204 were by far the strongest feudal lords in the shire. Besides the disappearance from Leicestershire of the important house of Grentemesnil, the reign of Henry I saw the establishment as a tenant in chief in the county of a trusted royal official, Ralph Basset, whose descendants were for centuries prominent members of the Leicestershire baronage. The extensive possessions held by Ralph's son, Richard, who was also prominent in the king's service, are revealed by the 'Leicestershire Survey' of 1124–9.[69] Ralph Basset himself was the leading actor in a grim scene at Huncote in December 1124, when forty-four thieves were hanged and six men were mutilated.[70]

During the disturbances of Stephen's reign Leicestershire seems to have suffered less than some other parts of the country. Robert, 2nd Earl of Leicester, with his relatives the Earl of Northampton and the Count of Meulan, was at first a supporter of Stephen,[71] but never seems to have taken a very active part in the struggles of the period. So far as Leicestershire is concerned, he is chiefly to be remembered as the founder of Leicester Abbey. The chief aim of Earl Robert, as of the other great lords of the midlands,[72] seems to have been the preservation of his own lands. The treaty concluded at some date between 1147 and 1153 by Earl Robert and Ranulf, Earl of Chester, whose vast possessions extended into northern Leicestershire, shows how the magnates ensured the security of their own territories without any reference to the royal authority. By this treaty[73] the Earls of Leicester and Chester agreed to assist each other against anyone save their respective liege lords;[74] neither earl was to erect any castle between Hinckley and Coventry or Hartshill, between Donnington and Coventry or Leicester, between Belvoir and Oakham or Kinoulton, or between Oakham and Rockingham, nor was any castle to be built at Gotham or Kinoulton; if any third party were to erect a castle in these areas, the two earls were to unite in destroying it. Mountsorrel Castle was to be held by the Earl of Leicester from the Earl of Chester. Ravenstone Castle[75] was to be destroyed by the Earl of Leicester, and if anyone attempted to hold it the Earl of Chester was to assist in its destruction. Whitwick Castle was left in the hands of the Earl of Leicester. It was further agreed that if either party was called upon to assist his liege lord against the other, he should do so with not more than twenty knights, and any booty taken in such a case was to be restored. Neither earl was to take hostile action against the other unless he had defied him fifteen days in advance. By

[67] Complete Peerage, vii, 525.

[68] Pipe R., 1181 (Pipe R. Soc. xxx), 79. The Count of Meulan may have obtained the third penny of the mint at Leics., which had been received by Hugh de Grentemesnil: V.C.H. Leics., i, 306.

[69] J. H. Round, Feudal Engl. 212; V.C.H. Leics. i, 344–54.

[70] Angl. Sax. Chron. (Rolls Ser.), ii, 221.

[71] Complete Peerage, vii, 528, and references there cited.

[72] H. W. C. Davis, 'The Anarchy of Steph.'s Reign', E.H.R. xviii, 639.

[73] Printed, F. M. Stenton, First Century of Engl. Feudalism, 285–8, where the dates 1147–53 are assigned to it.

[74] The Earl of Leic. was not to be compelled to give aid against the Earl of Northampton, nor the Earl of Chest. against the Earl of Derby.

[75] The terms of the treaty seem to imply that Ravenstone Castle was held by Wm. de Alneto.

this pact the building of fortifications was forbidden over a large area round the borders of Leicestershire, and military operations between two of the greatest lords in England were virtually prevented. Such an agreement, though it ignores the royal authority, must have done something to secure peace in the midlands, especially since the Earls of Derby and Northampton, though not themselves parties to the treaty, were apparently the allies of the Earls of Chester and Leicester respectively.

In 1153 the Earl of Leicester and his son Robert wisely came to terms with Henry of Anjou, obtaining from him charters by which the earl's retention of his lands was secured, and he was granted the Stewardship of England and Normandy, a hereditary office which his successors continued to hold.[76] The earl's efforts to preserve his own territories do not seem to have been wholly successful in preventing devastation in Leicestershire, for early in Henry II's reign more than half the Danegeld due from Leicestershire had to be remitted because the countryside was lying waste.[77] It is not clear to what extent the impoverished condition of Leicestershire was due to actual warfare,[78] but the county's rapid recovery in the early years of Henry II's reign[79] shows that the losses must have been due to the disturbed conditions prevailing under Stephen.

Until his death in 1168 Earl Robert II was one of the most important royal ministers, but his son and successor, Robert III, took part in the revolt of the king's sons in 1173, with the result that Leicestershire saw a good deal of fighting. Other rebel leaders were the Earl of Derby, whose honour of Tutbury included considerable fiefs in Leicestershire, Robert de Mowbray, lord of Melton, and in the early stages of the revolt the Earl of Chester.[80] The king's supporters included Bertram de Verdon, Sheriff of Warwickshire and Leicestershire, who had a quarrel of his own against the Earl of Leicester.[81] In the early stages of the revolt the earl was on the Continent, where his lands were extensive, but in England the castles of Leicester, Groby, and Mountsorrel[82] were held for him by his vassals under the Constable of Leicester Castle, Anketil Mallory,[83] and William de Diva.[84] In July 1173, at the king's orders, the justiciar, Richard de Lucy, and the Earl of Cornwall laid siege to Leicester. Much of the town was burnt, and the inhabitants treated for peace, which they obtained for a fine of 3,000 marks; the town walls were dismantled. The earl's knights in the castle held out, and the justiciar, who was needed to defend the north against the Scots, made a truce with them to last until Michaelmas.[85] In

---

[76] G. W. Watson, *Genealogist* (N.S.), x, 12; Vernon Harcourt, *His Grace the Steward*, 58 (cited *Complete Peerage*, vii, 529); Gervase of Cant., *Hist. Works* (Rolls Ser.), i, 152.

[77] *Pipe R., 1155–8* (Rec. Com.), 45; *E.H.R.* xviii, 640.

[78] There is no definite record of any fighting in Leics., but the county may have been affected in 1147, when the Earl of Chest. besieged Coventry, and Steph. attacked some of the earl's castles: *Chrons. of Steph., Hen. II, and Ric. I* (Rolls Ser.), iii, 126–7; *E.H.R.* xviii, 640. It has also been conjectured (K. Norgate, *Engl. under Angevin Kings*, i, 316) that the Earl of Glouc.'s army passed through Leics. on its march to Linc. in 1141.

[79] There was no allowance for waste in Leics. when Danegeld was levied in 1161–2: *Pipe R., 1162* (Pipe R. Soc. v), 2.

[80] *Chrons. of Steph., Hen. II, and Ric. I* (Rolls Ser.), i, 171, 176, 180; iii, 282, 284, 299.

[81] *Gesta Regis Hen. II* (Rolls Ser.) i, 51; *Chrons. of Steph., Hen. II, and Ric. I* (Rolls Ser.), iii, 298; *Pipe R., 1174* (Pipe R. Soc. xxi), 39, 142.

[82] *Gesta Regis Hen. II*, i, 48.

[83] A local kt. who had previously been active in the earl's affairs: R. de Houedene, *Chron.* (Rolls Ser.), ii, 58; Farnham, *Leics. Notes*, iii, 148; *Pipe R. 1174* (Pipe R. Soc. xxi), 142.

[84] A vassal of the earl: *Rot. de Oblatis et Finibus* (Rec. Com.), 320.

[85] R. de Wendover, *Chron.* (Rolls Ser.), i, 94; R. de Diceto, *Opera Hist.* (Rolls Ser.), i, 375; *Chrons. of Steph., Hen. II, and Ric. I* (Rolls Ser.), i, 177; *Ann. Mon.* (Rolls Ser.), iii, 21, 35; R. de Coggeshall, *Chron. Anglicanum* (Rolls Ser.), 18.

the autumn, probably about the time that the truce was due to expire,[86] the Earl of Leicester landed in Suffolk with a force of mercenaries from France and the Netherlands.[87] After gaining some successes in East Anglia, Earl Robert resolved to march to Leicester, prompted perhaps by his ally, Hugh Bigod, who found the presence of the Flemish mercenaries burdensome.[88] At Fornham, near Bury St. Edmunds, the way was barred by the royal forces. In the ensuing battle the rebels were routed, and Earl Robert, with his countess, was captured and sent to Normandy.[89]

Despite their lord's capture, Earl Robert's knights continued to hold out at Leicester, Groby, and Mountsorrel. With David, the Scots Earl of Huntingdon, as their leader, and joined by many desperate characters, they devastated the country around their strongholds.[90] Led by Earl David and Anketil Mallory, the garrison of Leicester Castle, after Whitsuntide 1174, attacked Northampton and defeated the burgesses.[91] In another raid, which was led by the Earl of Derby, the garrison captured and burnt Nottingham, though it was held for the king by Reynold de Lucy.[92] These activities were brought to an end by the appearance in the summer of 1174 of Henry II, bringing with him the Earl of Leicester, who was placed in custody immediately on arrival in England.[93] To prevent harm to their lord, whom the king threatened to starve to death,[94] Anketil Mallory and William de Diva surrendered Leicester, Groby, and Mountsorrel castles. David of Huntingdon returned to Scotland,[95] while the Earl of Derby and Roger de Mowbray made their peace with the king.[96] Although taken back to Normandy as a prisoner, the earl was later released.[97] The castles of Leicester and Groby were demolished in 1176,[98] and Mountsorrel, the only one of the earl's castles in England to be left standing, was retained by the king[99] when Earl Robert recovered his lands in 1177 or later.[1]

During the revolt the Earl of Leicester, though absent from his own territories, seems to have had the support of many of his vassals. At his landing in Suffolk he was accompanied by foreign mercenaries, and Flemings were included in the garrison of Leicester Castle,[2] but the two men who are named as commanding the earl's forces in Leicestershire were both of the locality, and the list of lands taken into the king's hands[3] shows that several Leicestershire knights

---

[86] The chroniclers disagree about the exact date of the earl's landing. Diceto, op. cit. i, 376, gives 29 Sept., but in *Gesta Regis Hen. II* (Rolls Ser.), i, 60, the date is given as 18 Oct. The earl is said to have been at Gisors on 25 Sept.: Houedene, *Chron.* (Rolls Ser.), ii, 54.

[87] Diceto, op. cit. i, 377; *Chrons. of Steph., Hen. II, and Ric. I* (Rolls Ser.), i, 178; iii, 271; *Ann. Mon.* (Rolls Ser.), iv, 35.

[88] Diceto, op. cit. i, 377.

[89] *Chrons. of Steph., Hen. II, and Ric. I* (Rolls Ser.), i, 179; iii, 294, 296; Houedene, *Chron.* (Rolls Ser.), ii, 55; Diceto, op. cit. i, 377; *Gesta Regis Hen. II* (Rolls Ser.), i, 61.

[90] *Chrons. of Steph., Hen. II, and Ric. I* (Rolls Ser.), i, 180; iii, 296.

[91] Ibid. iii, 298; Houedene, *Chron.* (Rolls Ser.), ii, 58; *Gesta Regis Hen. II* (Rolls Ser.), i, 68.

[92] *Gesta Regis Hen. II*, i, 69; Houedene, op. cit. ii, 58.

[93] *Gesta Regis Hen. II*, i, 72.

[94] *Chrons. of Steph., Hen. II, and Ric. I* (Rolls Ser.), i, 195.

[95] Jordan Fantosme states that David surrendered Leic. on hearing of the capture of his brother, the King of Scots: ibid. iii, 372.

[96] Ibid. i, 194; R. de Wendover, *Chron.* (Rolls Ser.), i, 101; Diceto, *Opera Hist.* (Rolls Ser.), i, 384; Houedene, *Chron.* (Rolls Ser.), ii, 65; *Gesta Regis Hen. II* (Rolls Ser.), i, 73.

[97] *Chrons. of Steph., Hen. II, and Ric. I* (Rolls Ser.), i, 195, 197.

[98] Houedene, *Chron.* (Rolls Ser.), ii, 101; *Pipe R., 1176* (Pipe R. Soc. xxv), 179; *Pipe R., 1177* (Pipe R. Soc. xxvi), 29.

[99] Houedene, op. cit. ii, 101; *Gesta Regis Hen. II* (Rolls Ser.), i, 134.

[1] *Gesta Regis Hen. II*, i, 134; *Pipe R., 1180* (Pipe R. Soc. xxix), 105.

[2] *Pipe R., 1176* (Pipe R. Soc. xxv), 184.   [3] *Pipe R., 1174* (ibid. xxi), 143.

were involved in the revolt. A number of amercements levied in the years immediately following the royal victory probably represents the king's vengeance on the rebels. Anketil Mallory, whose lands remained in the king's hands for several years,[4] was heavily amerced for unjust disseisin,[5] and William de Diva was put under pledge.[6] Ernald de Bosco, who was Earl Robert's steward,[7] thought it advisable to pay a fine of 100 marks to secure the king's good will.[8] The military operations due to the rebellion must have caused considerable damage in the county. Destruction due to war prevented the collection of revenues from lands held by the king at Rothley and Medbourne,[9] so that payments due at Michaelmas 1174 were not paid until 1176.[10] The increment on the farm of the county for the years 1173-4 and 1174-5 was not paid until 1176.[11]

For the rest of his life Earl Robert was naturally distrusted by Henry II, and when a new revolt broke out in 1183 the earl's lands were taken into the king's hands.[12] Robert died in 1190, and his successor was a strenuous supporter of Richard I and John. On the death of the 4th earl in 1204 without male heirs the great possessions of the earls of Leicester were divided between his two sisters, Amice, wife of a nobleman of northern France, and Margaret, wife of Saher de Quency. The task of dividing so great an inheritance was long and arduous, and rendered more so by the claims of the Countess Parnel, mother of the late earl.[13] The partition was carried out by commissioners,[14] whose clerks worked in the chapel of St. Mary de Castro at Leicester,[15] and the period between the death of Earl Robert and the completion of the division must have been a time of uncertainty for many Leicestershire tenants.[16] Saher de Quency was created Earl of Winchester and obtained his share of the inheritance by 1207,[17] though only on payment of enormous fines to the king.[18] The lands acquired by Saher were in future known as the honour of Winchester, a term which continued in use for long after the partition of the lands concerned in 1264.[19] Simon de Montfort, son of Earl Robert's elder daughter Amice, obtained recognition as Earl of Leicester,[20] and was granted certain lands by King John.[21] Since, however, Simon was a vassal of the French king, with whom John was at war, it was impossible to allow him control of a great fief in England, and in February 1207 all Simon's English lands were entrusted to Robert de Roppeley, who became Sheriff of Warwickshire and Leicester-

[4] *Pipe R., 1177* (ibid. xxvi), 35.   [5] *Pipe R., 1176* (ibid. xxv), 181.

[6] *Pipe R., 1177* (ibid. xxvi), 29.

[7] *Pipe R., 1180* (ibid. xxix), 105; L. Fox, 'The Honor and Earldom of Leicester', *E.H.R.* liv, 390.

[8] *Pipe R., 1177* (Pipe R. Soc. xxvi), 29; a special aid was levied from Earl Robert's kts. after the earl's capture at Fornham: *E.H.R.*, liv, 390; *Red Bk. of the Exch.* (Rolls Ser.), ii, pp. ccli, 768-9; *Pipe R. 1209* (Pipe R. Soc., n.s. xxiv), 16.

[9] *Pipe R., 1174* (Pipe R. Soc. xxi), 140.   [10] *Pipe R., 1176* (ibid. xxv), 180.

[11] Ibid. 179.

[12] *Pipe R., 1184* (ibid. xxxiii), 50. The lands must have been returned before Mich. 1184.

[13] *Rot. Litt. Claus., 1204-24* (Rec. Com.), 16; *Rot. de Oblatis et Finibus* (Rec. Com.), 226, 320. See also F. M. Powicke, 'Loretta, Countess of Leicester', *Hist. Essays in Honour of Jas. Tait*, 255-6, and *E.H.R.* liv, 392-3.

[14] See, for the commissioners' names, and some details of the partition, Hist. MSS. Com., *Hastings*, i, 334-5.

[15] *Pipe R., 1209* (Pipe R. Soc., n.s. xxiv), 25-26.

[16] See, for an example of the difficulties caused by such a situation, *Pipe R. 1206* (Pipe R. Soc., n.s. xx), 9.

[17] Vernon Harcourt, *His Grace the Steward*, 95.

[18] *Rot. de Oblatis et Finibus* (Rec. Com.), 320; *Pipe R., 1207* (Pipe R. Soc., n.s. xxii), 197.

[19] See, for examples of later references to the honour or fee of Winchester, Nichols, *Leics.*, i, pp. civ, cx; *Feud. Aids*, iii, 99; *Cal. Inq. p.m.* vi, p. 377.

[20] *Pipe R., 1206* (Pipe R. Soc., n.s. xx), 9, 107; *Complete Peerage*, vii, 538.

[21] *Rot. Litt. Claus., 1204-24* (Rec. Com.), 74.

shire a few months later.[22] Two knights of the honour of Leicester were to supervise the receipt of the revenues from the sequestered lands.[23]

The struggle which broke out between King John and the barons in 1215 again made Leicestershire the scene of conflict. The magnates who opposed the king included Saher de Quency, who, though he was apparently still loyal to the king in January 1215,[24] was amongst the insurgent barons at Stamford in the following April, together with the lord of Belvoir, William de Albini, who in 1201 had been forced to give up his son to John as a hostage,[25] and the lord of Melton, William de Mowbray.[26] De Quency, Albini, and Mowbray were all amongst the twenty-five barons who swore to take action against the king if he should commit a breach of Magna Carta.[27] The Letters Patent sent from Runnymede to inform the counties of Leicestershire and Warwickshire that peace had been made between the king and his magnates were entrusted to Saher de Quency.[28] When, late in 1215, the settlement made at Runnymede broke down, de Quency, Albini, and Mowbray were all excommunicated by the Pope for their revolt against John.[29] William de Albini was captured when Rochester Castle, which he was commanding on behalf of the rebel barons, was taken.[30] In December 1215, after the fall of Rochester, John moved north, passing through Melton[31] on his way to Nottingham, where he spent Christmas.[32] John's northward march is said to have been accompanied by widespread ravaging,[33] and the rebels' lands in eastern Leicestershire probably suffered severely. Immediately after Christmas John moved to Langar,[34] whence he called on the garrison of Belvoir to surrender, threatening that unless they did so William de Albini would be starved to death. William's son, Nicholas, who with two knights was holding the castle, surrendered on condition that the king should deal leniently with William, and that the garrison, retaining their horses and arms, should remain in the king's peace. On 27 December John himself came to Belvoir, took oaths of fealty from the garrison, and committed the castle to two Poitevins.[35] The royal Constable of Belvoir, like the Constable of Sauvey, subsequently levied special contributions from the surrounding countryside.[36] Mountsorrel Castle was one of the few places in the north and midlands holding out against the king,[37] and at the end of January 1216 John offered safe conduct to all men of Warwickshire and Leicestershire who wished to come into the king's peace and whom William de Cantilupe, sheriff of the two counties, could persuade to resume their allegiance to the king.[38]

[22] *Rot. Litt. Pat., 1201–16* (Rec. Com.), 74.
[23] Ibid. 68. The share of the inheritance allotted to Simon de Montfort was later known as the honour of Leicester.
[24] Rymer, *Foedera* (1745 ed.), i (1), 66; *Rot. Chart, 1199–1216* (Rec. Com.), 204.
[25] Houedene, *Chron.* (Rolls Ser.), iv, 161.   [26] Wendover, *Chron.* (Rolls Ser.), ii, 114.
[27] Matt. Paris, *Chron. Majora* (Rolls Ser.), ii, 604–5.
[28] *Rot. Litt. Pat., 1201–16* (Rec. Com.), 180.   [29] Rymer, *Foedera* (1745 ed.), i (1), 71.
[30] Wendover, *Chron.* (Rolls Ser.), ii, 150.
[31] *Rot. Litt. Claus., 1204–24* (Rec. Com.), 243.
[32] Matt. Paris, *Hist. Anglorum* (Rolls Ser.), ii, 171; Wendover, *Chron.* (Rolls Ser.), ii, 164; *Rot. Litt. Pat., 1201–16* (Rec. Com.), 162.
[33] Wendover, op. cit. ii, 162.
[34] *Rot. Litt. Claus., 1204–24* (Rec. Com.), 243.
[35] Wendover, *Chron.* (Rolls Ser.), ii, 164; *Rot. Litt. Pat., 1201–16* (Rec. Com.), 162.
[36] *Rot. Litt. Claus., 1204–24* (Rec. Com.), 249, 261; *Rot. Litt. Pat., 1201–16* (Rec. Com.), 167–8.
[37] Wendover, *Chron.* (Rolls Ser.), ii, 167. In June 1215 the king had ordered that Mountsorrel Castle should be handed over to Saher de Quency: *Rot. Litt. Pat., 1201–16* (Rec. Com.), 145. Early in 1216, however, the castle seems to have been in the king's hands: ibid. 162; *Rot. Litt. Claus., 1204–24* (Rec. Com.), 249.
[38] *Rot. Litt. Pat., 1201–16* (Rec. Com.), 164. The offer was repeated in Aug.: ibid. 194.

The arrival in England of Louis, son of the French king, with considerable forces, and the death of John in October 1216 for a time caused a great improvement in the prospects of the rebellious party. The greater part of the midlands, however, was under the control of William Marshal,[39] who ruled the kingdom in the name of the young Henry III, and the royalist position in Leicestershire must have been strengthened by the return to his allegiance of William de Albini, who was ransomed and, after doing homage to Henry III, was entrusted with Sleaford Castle.[40] A further step to strengthen the king's hold on the midlands was taken after Easter 1217, when a royal army led by the Earls of Chester and Derby, the Count of Aumale, William de Cantilupe, and others laid siege to Mountsorrel, which was defended by Henry de Braibroc with ten knights and many men-at-arms.[41] Braibroc and the garrison, who had earlier attempted to plunder the countryside,[42] were soon hard pressed, and appealed for aid to their lord, Saher de Quency. In response, Saher left London with a force of English and French, commanded by Robert Fitzwalter and the Count of Perche. On the approach of the relieving force the Earl of Chester and the other royalists burnt their siege engines and fell back, without fighting, to Nottingham. The baronial forces, having relieved Mountsorrel in May, marched on to Lincoln through the Vale of Belvoir, which was plundered by the French infantry.[43] Though Mountsorrel had thus survived a siege, its fate was decided by the baronial defeat at Lincoln. In the absence of Henry of Braibroc[44] the garrison of Mountsorrel lost heart, and fled immediately after the battle.[45] The castle was handed over to the Earl of Chester and destroyed.[46]

No further clashes of importance took place in Leicestershire before the conclusion of peace in September 1217. For some years after the agreement of 1217, however, trouble continued to be caused by the question of the custody of the royal castles, many of which had been handed over to various magnates during the course of hostilities. Sauvey Castle,[47] on the eastern border of Leicestershire, had, together with Rockingham Castle, been committed in 1216 to William, Count of Aumale.[48] In February 1218 the earl was commanded to hand over the castles, which had only been granted to him until he should regain his own lands.[49] The earl retained the castles, and nothing further seems to have been done until November 1219, when the barons, knights, and free tenants of Leicestershire and Rutland, together with those of the three northern counties of Yorkshire, Lancashire, and Cumberland, where the bulk of Aumale's lands lay, were informed that the earl was fortifying the castles which he held in the

[39] Kate Norgate, *Minority of Hen. III*, 17. [40] Wendover, *Chron.* (Rolls Ser.), ii, 200.

[41] Ibid. 208.

[42] Ibid. 205.

[43] Ibid. 209, 211; Walter of Coventry, *Memoriale* (Rolls Ser.), ii, 237; *L'Histoire de Guillaume le Marechal*, ed. Mayer, ii, 216.

[44] He was present at the battle of Linc., from which, according to one source, he fled to London: *Ann. Mon.* (Rolls Ser.), iii, 49. Another version states that he was captured at Linc.: Gervase of Cant., *Opera Hist.* (Rolls Ser.), ii, 111. The first version appears to be correct: *Rot. Litt. Claus., 1204–24* (Rec. Com.), 321.

[45] The castle was in the hands of the royalists 3 days after the battle: *Cal. Pat., 1216–25*, 64.

[46] Wendover, *Chron.* (Rolls Ser.), ii, 219, where it is stated that the castle was entrusted to the Sheriff of Notts. for destruction. The Dunstable Annals state that it was destroyed by the Earl of Chest.: *Ann. Mon.* (Rolls Ser.), iii, 50. Mountsorrel Castle was certainly handed over to the earl: *Cal. Pat., 1216–25*, 64.

[47] The importance of Sauvey Castle is shown by John's acquisition of the adjacent manor of Withcote: G. F. Farnham and A. Hamilton Thompson, 'Notes on the Hist. of the Manor of Withcote', *Assoc. Arch. Soc. Rep. and Papers*, xxxvi, 131.

[48] *Cal. Pat., 1216–25*, 13; Wendover, *Chron.* (Rolls Ser.), ii, 167.

[49] *Cal. Pat., 1216–25*, 136.

king's name, and were ordered not to assist him in fortifying Sauvey, but to be ready to take action against him.[50] Despite the issue of these orders, no action was taken against Aumale, and the matter was allowed to rest until June 1220, when the king, arriving at Rockingham on his way north to meet the King of Scots, found the castle gates closed to him.[51] When Rockingham was besieged Aumale gave way, and surrendered both Rockingham and Sauvey into the king's hands. Stephen de Segrave was appointed Constable of Sauvey,[52] which for the future was commanded by a royal official.[53]

During the disturbances which troubled the last years of John and the beginning of his successor's reign there was no Earl of Leicester. The lands of the earldom,[54] with all the resources and influence attached to them, had been in the king's hands from 1204[55] until 1215, when at the instance of the Pope[56] they were committed to the Earl of Chester, to hold to the use of Simon de Montfort.[57] The lands continued to be held by the Earl of Chester[58] until 1231. On the death of the elder Simon de Montfort in 1218 his claims on the Leicester earldom passed to his eldest son, Amauri, who as a vassal of the French king was no more acceptable as the holder of an English earldom than his father had been. In consequence Amauri, having failed to obtain the earldom for himself,[59] in 1229 granted all his father's lands in England to his younger brother Simon.[60] Simon, who no longer held any land from the King of France, came to England, and in February 1230 Henry III acknowledged that he was bound to deliver to Simon all the lands of the honour of Leicester held by Simon's father, with 'third penny' of the county and the stewardship of England, as soon as the lands should be given up by the Earl of Chester.[61] In 1231 the king took Simon's homage, and the sheriffs were ordered to give him seisin of all his lands of the the honour of Leicester.[62] In 1239 Simon was formally invested as Earl of Leicester.[63]

A matter which at the time may have seemed of more importance to the men of Leicestershire than the succession of a Frenchman to the earldom was the exemption of the complete county from the forest law. The Forest Charter of 1217 had promised that those areas, outside the royal demesne, which had been made part of the royal forest for the first time under Henry II should be disafforested, if the afforestation had been to the detriment of the tenants.[64] In accordance with this provision some areas in Leicestershire should have been

---

[50] *Cal. Pat., 1216–25*, 258.
[51] Walter of Coventry, *Memoriale* (Rolls Ser.), ii, 245.
[52] Letters Patent were issued declaring that Aumale had given up the castles freely: *Cal. Pat., 1216–25*, 240.
[53] *Assoc. Arch. Soc. Rep. and Papers*, xxxvi, 133–4.
[54] Except those held by the earls of Winchester.
[55] The lands allotted in dower to the Countess Loretta, wife of the 4th earl, were outside Leics.: F. M. Powicke, 'Loretta, Countess of Leicester', *Hist. Essays in Honour of Jas. Tait*, 256–7.
[56] Simon's activities as a Crusader against the Albigensians were presumably the cause of the Pope's intervention.
[57] *Rot. Litt. Pat., 1201–16* (Rec. Com.), 150; Harcourt, *His Grace the Steward*, 75.
[58] In 1218, after the death of the elder Simon de Montfort, the lands were again in the king's hands (*Cal. Pat., 1216–25*, 163), but in 1220 they were restored to the Earl of Chest. on his return from Crusade (ibid. 254; *Rot. Litt. Claus. 1204–24* (Rec. Com.), 393, 431).
[59] Harcourt, *His Grace the Steward*, 108.
[60] In return, Simon quitclaimed his own inheritance in France to Amauri: C. Bémont, *Simon de Montfort* (1884), 5.
[61] *Cal. Pat., 1225–32*, 325.
[62] *Close R., 1227–31*, 543, 560; *Excerpta e Rot. Fin.* (Rec. Com.), i, 217; *E.H.R.* liv, 395.
[63] Matt. Paris, *Chron. Majora* (Rolls Ser.), iii, 524; *Hist. Anglorum* (Rolls Ser.), iii, 278.
[64] W. Stubbs, *Select Chart.* (9th ed.), 345; see below, p. 266.

disafforested.[65] In 1227 a Leicestershire jury charged with the perambulation of the forest stated that Henry II had afforested a considerable area on the eastern border of the county.[66] The king held that the district had formed part of the royal forest before Henry II's reign, and the jurors were forced to admit that in their perambulation they had trespassed against the king.[67] Disafforestation was apparently not obtained until 1235, when the men of Leicestershire, acting through the Abbot of Owston and the Prior of Launde, made fine with the king for the disafforestation of all the royal forest in the county.[68] The charter embodying this concession was ordered to be read in full county court.[69] It would be interesting to know more about the corporate action which seems to have been taken on this occasion, and especially to know whether it was agreed in the county court that the two monastic heads should act on behalf of the shire.

This early example of joint action by the men of Leicestershire is of particular interest because of the constitutional developments which took place during the 13th century. There is unfortunately little evidence concerning the attitude of the county's inhabitants during the series of political changes which began in 1258. The names of the knights who were presumably sent from Leicestershire, as from other counties, to the Parliament at Oxford in June 1258 are unfortunately unknown. The results of the proceedings at Oxford began to be felt locally with the appointment in August, in Leicestershire as elsewhere, of four local knights to inquire into trespasses and injuries committed in the county.[70] In the Parliament of October 1258 Leicestershire was apparently represented by four knights, who may have been the same as those commissioned in August to carry out the inquiry.[71] One of these knights, Anketil de Martival,[72] was appointed to keep the counties of Warwick and Leicester in the form provided by the king and council,[73] so that local administration came under the control of a baronial nominee. Martival was not eligible to serve as sheriff for a second year,[74] and from 1259 to 1261 the Sheriff of Warwickshire and Leicestershire was William Bagod,[75] who, though originally appointed sheriff through baronial influence, in the later stages of the contest between the king and the reforming party was an active royalist. In July 1261, when Henry III had regained the initiative and was strengthening his hold over the country,

[65] *Rot. Litt. Claus., 1224–7* (Rec. Com.), 26. The district which formed part of the royal forest lay on the eastern border of Leics.: ibid. 207. It did not include the area known as Leic. Forest, or Charnwood Forest: L. Fox and P Russell, *Leic. Forest*, 13, 21 G. F. Farnham, *Charnwood Forest and its Historians*, 3–5.

[66] *Rot. Litt. Claus., 1224–7* (Rec. Com.), 207. The boundaries of the forest area are given.

[67] The king remitted his indignation against the jurors: *Cal. Pat., 1225–32*, 110; *Rot. Litt. Claus., 1224–7* (Rec. Com.), 169. See comments by C. Petit-Dutaillis, *Studies . . . Supplementary to Stubbs's Constitutional Hist.* (1915), i and ii, 215.

[68] Withcote, a manor of the royal demesne, was excluded from the disafforestation in accordance with the forest charter of 1217: *Close R., 1234–7*, 304. Launde Priory lay within the royal forest in Leics., and so probably did Owston Abbey.

[69] *Close R., 1234–7*, 51; *Cal. Chart. R., 1226–57*, 193. An *inspeximus* and confirmation of this charter was obtained as late as 1450: *Cal. Chart. R., 1446–52*, 400.

[70] *Cal. Pat., 1247–58*, 646. The fact that in 1252 Philip Marmioun found it necessary to pay the large sum of 8 marks of gold to obtain pardon for trespasses committed while sheriff (ibid. 128) indicates that there were serious abuses in the county administration.

[71] Helen Cam, 'Parl. Writs De Expensis of 1258', *E.H.R.* xlvi, 630–1.

[72] In 1261 he was a steward of Simon de Montfort: G. F. Farnham, 'Extracts from the Cur. Reg. R.', *Assoc. Arch. Soc. Rep. and Papers*, xxxv, 180.

[73] *Cal. Pat., 1247–58*, 654. His bailiwick probably included Rut. See R. F. Treharne, *Baronial Plan of Reform*, 121, and *31st Dep. Kpr's Rep.*, App. iv, 332.

[74] *Cal. Pat., 1247–58*, 655–6; *Royal Letters, Hen. III* (Rolls Ser.), ii, 132.

[75] *31st Dep. Kpr's Rep.*, App. iv, 351.

Bagod was ordered to hand over the two shires, together with the custody of Sauvey Castle, to the Earl of Warwick,[76] who as a great magnate would be better able to enforce respect for the royal authority, should there be any opposition.

An armed clash was averted in 1261, and it was not until 1263 that, with the renewal of tension between the king and the reforming party led by Simon de Montfort, open resistance to the king showed itself in Leicestershire, where, as in the midlands generally,[77] the baronial partisans seem to have had the upper hand. From the summer of 1263 onwards the sheriff, William Bagod, was unable to perform the duties of his office. The county revenues were taken by Thomas de Estleye[78] and Roger de Kalford until Michaelmas 1263, while from that date until the following July Ralph Basset of Sapcote held the county and took its issues. Bagod himself was outlawed.[79] Roger de Somery, the royalist[80] farmer of Goscote wapentake, was prevented after 1 November 1263 from collecting the wapentake revenues, which were received instead by Peter Bastard and by Stephen de Nevill, steward of the baronial leader Nicholas de Segrave.[81] The lands of those suspected of royalist sympathies were seized.[82] With the failure of Louis IX's arbitration open war broke out early in 1264. Henry III, having collected an army at Oxford, defeated the forces of the opposition at Northampton, after which, on his way north to Nottingham, he passed through Leicester, defying an old superstition which forbade the king to enter the town.[83] Henry's defeat and capture at Lewes in May 1264 changed the whole situation, and the reforming party was able to secure its position in Leicestershire. The extensive lands of the royalist Earl of Winchester, who had died shortly before Lewes, were committed to one of the king's clerks, Richard de Shyreburn,[84] who must have been acceptable to de Montfort's supporters. Robert de Tateshale, another prominent royalist with lands in Leicestershire, was captured at Lewes, and subsequently detained in prison;[85] his manor of Breedon, it was later alleged, was forcibly occupied by Ralph Basset of Drayton, the baronial keeper of Shropshire and Staffordshire.[86] Early in June Ralph Basset of Sapcote was appointed keeper of Leicestershire on behalf of the reforming party.[87] A new sheriff, Richard Barrington, was appointed[88] for the last quarter of the Exchequer year ending at Michaelmas 1264,[89] and probably held office from July when William Bagod lost control of the county.[90] During the period between the battles of Lewes and Evesham Simon de Montfort and his supporters must have been in full control of the county administra-

---

[76] *Cal. Pat., 1258–66*, 164.

[77] R. F. Treharne, *Baronial Plan of Reform*, 336.

[78] He was baronial *custos* of Leics. in 1264: Rymer, *Foedera* (3rd ed., 1745), i (2), 89. For his lands in Leics., see *Cal. Inq. Misc.* i, p. 235–6.

[79] *Close R., 1268–72*, 350.

[80] Rymer, *Foedera* (1745 ed.), i (2), 83; *Cal. Pat., 1258–66*, 357.

[81] E. F. Jacob, *Studies in Period of Baronial Reform and Rebellion*, 269.

[82] e.g. in Leics., the lands of Philip Marmioun and Robert de Tateshale. See Jacob, op. cit. 224; Rymer, *Foedera* (1745 ed.), i (2), 83; *Cal. Pat., 1258–66*, 305; Farnham, *Leics. Notes*, v, 69; *Assoc. Arch. Soc. Rep. and Papers*, xxxv, 186, 194.

[83] *Ann. Mon.* (Rolls Ser.), iv, 144, 146.

[84] *Cal. Pat., 1258–66*, 320. In Aug. 1264 a provisional grant of lands from the Winchester inheritance was made to one of the heiresses, the mother of the rebel Earl of Derby: *Close R., 1261–4*, 358.

[85] Farnham, *Leics. Notes*, v, 71; *Cal. Pat., 1258–66*, 319.

[86] Rymer, *Foedera* (1745 ed.), i (2), 89; Farnham, op. cit. v, 71.

[87] Rymer, *Foedera* (1745 ed.), loc. cit.

[88] *ut custos.*

[89] *31st Dep. Kpr's Rep.*, App. iv, 352.

[90] *Close R., 1268–72*, 350.

tion, although they were not sufficiently strong to prevent some disorders directed against themselves.[91] Leicestershire sent knights of the shire to the Parliaments held under Earl Simon's control in June 1264 and in January 1265,[92] but their names are unknown.

The defeat and death of Simon de Montfort at Evesham in August 1265 did not immediately bring peace to England, and for another two years disturbances continued in Leicestershire. After Evesham there were widespread seizures of rebels' lands by the king's supporters, and some who were not rebels inevitably suffered loss.[93] The Earl of Gloucester, who after the royalist victory took immediate steps to occupy rebels' lands in many parts of the country, seized lands and rents in Sileby, Diseworth, Hathern, Kegworth, and Loughborough, acting through his attorney, Peter Picot.[94] Robert de Tateshale, whose own lands had been seized when Earl Simon was in power, took lands belonging to Basset of Drayton, who had been killed at Evesham. Others who took part in occupying the lands of Leicestershire rebels were the Marcher lords Roger Mortimer, Roger de Clifford, and Hamo Lestrange.[95] Before long an attempt was made to bring this process of indiscriminate confiscation by individual magnates under the king's control, and in September 1265 William Bagod, the sheriff, and Robert de Grendon were ordered to seize and extend the lands of rebels in Warwickshire and Leicestershire and to appoint two suitable men in each hundred to collect the revenues.[96] Some royal grants of rebels' lands followed, of which the most important was the concession to the king's son Edmund of the earldom and honour of Leicester, the stewardship of England, and all the lands of the late Earl Simon save royal demesnes, together with all the lands of another prominent Leicestershire rebel, Nicholas de Segrave.[97] But disorders continued. From November 1265 until June 1267, William Bagod, appointed sheriff once again shortly after Evesham,[98] was prevented by the rebels holding out in Kenilworth and Ely from collecting the county revenues.[99] The case of Roger Godberd, who in the autumn of 1266 stole charters from the Abbot and convent of Garendon, and later obtained a charter of acquittance from them by force,[1] shows the lack of good order. Godberd was pardoned late in 1266,[2] but resumed his activities as a bandit, and was not taken until 1272.[3] The Earl of Derby, who with a number of other leading rebels kept up resistance in the north midlands until captured at Chesterfield in May 1266, extended his activities into Leicestershire.[4] The resistance of Kenilworth Castle, where the rebels held out under Henry de Hastings[5] until the end of 1266, must have done much to prolong the disturbed conditions in Leicestershire. Bagod's presence at the siege prevented him from appearing at the Exchequer to render his account as sheriff at Michaelmas 1266,[6] and eventually

[91] The manor of Garthorp, held by one of Earl Simon's most loyal friends, Peter de Montfort, was raided by night, apparently early in 1265: *Cal. Pat., 1258–66*, 479.

[92] Rymer, *Foedera* (1745 ed.), i (2), 88–9, 93.

[93] See, for an example, *Rot. Selecti* (Rec. Com.), 178.

[94] *Cal. Inq. Misc.* i, p. 235.

[95] Ibid., pp. 234–6.

[96] *Cal. Pat., 1258–66*, 490.

[97] Ibid. 470. After Evesham, Earl Simon's lands were at first in the hands of the Lord Edw.: *Cal. Inq. Misc.* i, pp. 235–6. Record of most of the grants made at this time has apparently been lost. For another concerning Leics., see *Rot. Selecti* (Rec. Com.), 247.

[98] *Cal. Pat., 1258–66*, 456.

[99] *Close R., 1268–72*, 350.

[1] Ibid., *1264–8*, 353.

[2] *Cal. Pat., 1266–72*, 16.

[3] Ibid. 623; F. M. Powicke, *Hen. III and the Lord Edw.* ii, 530.

[4] *Cal. Inq. Misc.* i, p. 236.

[5] Hen. held land in Barwell, Burbage, and Nailstone: ibid. i, p. 236.

[6] *Close R., 1264–8*, 213.

he had to account for three consecutive years[7] together, a most unusual occurrence.[8]

The *Dictum* of Kenilworth of October 1266, by providing a means whereby rebels could redeem their lands, helped to end a struggle which had been prolonged by the policy of disinheriting the supporters of the losing cause.[9] Many insurgents, or heirs of dead rebels, regained their possessions under the terms of the *Dictum*, and families like the Segraves, the Despensers, and the Bassets, though closely connected with de Montfort's cause, thus survived as important landholders in the county.[10] Some important changes in the distribution of Leicestershire fiefs did, however, take place about this time. Simon de Montfort's lands and rights, including the earldom of Leicester, passed to Henry III's son Edmund, Earl of Lancaster, who also through a piece of legal trickery[11] obtained the Earl of Derby's honour of Tutbury, with its considerable lands in Leicestershire. These acquisitions founded the great territorial strength of the earls, and later the dukes, of Lancaster in the county. A further notable change was the partition, after the death of Roger de Quency in 1264, of the honour of Winchester between three heiresses and their husbands.[12]

Throughout his struggle against Henry III Simon de Montfort was supported by a number of Leicestershire landholders who, although not magnates of the first rank, must have been men of weight and influence in the county. Hugh Despenser, who held the manors of Loughborough and Freeby, with lands at Donnington, Hucklescote, and Leire, was the reformers' justiciar.[13] Other leading members of the reforming party were Peter de Montfort,[14] Ralph Basset of Drayton,[15] Henry de Hastings,[16] Nicholas de Segrave,[17] Robert de Ros, lord of Belvoir,[18] and Richard de Grey of Evington.[19]

The political sympathies of men of lesser rank are more difficult to gauge. Many Leicestershire vavasours certainly supported Earl Simon,[20] but it is impossible to say what proportion of Leicestershire knights espoused his cause actively. The clergy, in Leicestershire as elsewhere, probably tended to favour Simon, and the fact that the Abbots of Leicester, Owston, and Croxton, with the Priors of Belvoir and Launde, were summoned to the Parliament of January 1265[21] shows that these prelates were not expected to be hostile to the reformers. Of the views held by the mass of the population nothing can be said with certainty.[22]

---

[7] Exch. years 50, 51, and 52 Hen. III.

[8] M. H. Mills, 'Adventus Vicecomitum, 1258–72', *E.H.R.* xxxvi, 487.

[9] For an example of the operation of the *Dictum* in Leics., see the arrangements for valuing the lands of the rebel Hugh Gobyun at Knaptoft, which the king had given to Hugh Turbervill: *Cal. Inq. Misc.* i, p. 122.

[10] For lands retained by the 3 families mentioned, see *Cal. Inq. p.m.* i, p. 109; ii, p. 71; iii, p. 192; viii, p. 326, 330.

[11] See the account by Powicke, *Hen. III and the Lord Edw.* ii, 524–6.

[12] For details of the division, see Hist. MSS. Com., *Hastings*, i, 323–34.

[13] *Cal. Inq. Misc.* i, pp. 234–5.

[14] See the account in *Complete Peerage*, ix, 124–6, and references there cited; see also N. Denholm-Young, 'Doc. of the Barons' Wars', *E.H.R.* xlviii, 566.

[15] *Cal. Pat.*, 1258–66, 411, 426; Rymer, *Foedera* (1745 ed.), i (2), 89; *Close R.*, 1264–8, 86, 122.

[16] *Complete Peerage*, vi, 345–6.   [17] *Cal. Inq. Misc.* i, p. 234.

[18] *Ann. Mon.* (Rolls Ser.), iv, 166; *Cal. Pat.*, 1258–66, 398, 627; *Close R.*, 1264–8, 86.

[19] *Cal. Inq. Misc.* i, p. 235; *Ann. Mon.* (Rolls Ser.), i, 447, 453; iii, 210, 225; *Cal. Pat.*, 1258–66, 19, 271.

[20] *Cal. Inq. Misc.*, i, pp. 107, 234–6.   [21] Rymer, *Foedera* (1745 ed.), i (2), 93.

[22] An incident which occurred at Peatling Magna after Evesham suggests that there was considerable popular sympathy for de Montfort's cause. See *Select Cases of Procedure Without Writ* (Selden Soc.), 42–45, and comments by Powicke, *Hen. III and the Lord Edw.* ii, 509–10.

MEDIEVAL POLITICAL HISTORY

The upheavals which marked the days of the great Earl Simon were followed by a period in which Leicestershire enjoyed as much tranquillity as the endemic violence of medieval life permitted. In considering the medieval history of a county much space is inevitably devoted to such exceptional events as civil wars and political crises, while little stress is laid on the routine administration of the shire, which for long periods functioned without serious interruption. At the head of the county administration, as in other counties, stood the sheriff. When evidence concerning individual sheriffs first becomes available the shrievalty of Leicestershire does not seem to have been united with that of any other county, for Hugh and Ivo de Grentemesnil, the only two sheriffs whose names have been preserved for fifty years after the Conquest,[23] were not, so far as is known, sheriffs of any other county at the same time. In the later years of Henry I's reign Leicestershire was at times under the same sheriff as Northamptonshire,[24] and it is possible that the two counties were held by one sheriff from the departure of Ivo de Grentemesnil until the beginning of Stephen's reign at least. The position of the shrievalty under Stephen is unknown. In the early years of Henry II Leicestershire had the same sheriff as Warwickshire,[25] though in 1163–4 the two counties had, exceptionally, different sheriffs.[26] From this time onwards the two counties remained under a single sheriff for the rest of the Middle Ages.[27] In the 12th and early 13th centuries the Sheriff of Leicestershire and Warwickshire seems to have been in possession of Kenilworth Castle, which was at times used as a prison.[28] A royal jail existed at Rothley from 1166 to 1233, and at Leicester from 1243 at the latest, until at least 1285,[29] but between 1261 and 1282, and perhaps over a longer period, Leicestershire prisoners were from time to time detained in Warwick jail.[30] In the late 13th century the jail at Leicester seems to have fallen into disuse, for Leicestershire prisoners were detained at Warwick. The trouble and expense of escorting Leicestershire prisoners to Warwick was evidently too great, for about 1300 permission was obtained from Thomas, Earl of Lancaster, for a prison to be built at Leicester, and money was collected from the men of the county to pay for it. In February 1301 the sheriff was ordered to inquire who was in possession of the funds raised, to buy land at

[23] Ordericus Vitalis, *Hist. Eccl.* (ed. le Prévost), iii, 13, 270; iv, 169.

[24] Hugh *de Legrecestria* accounts on the extant Pipe R. of Hen. I for the joint farm of the 2 shires, for a year prior to 31 Hen. I: *Pipe R., 1130* (Rec. Com.), 81. Hugh is known to have been Sheriff of Leics. at some time before 1120 (J. E. Morris, *Medieval Engl. Sheriff*, 78, citing B.M. Cott. MS. Vespasian E. xvii, f. 17*b*) and was probably Sheriff of Northants. before 1109 (Morris, op. cit. 78; Dugd. *Mon.* vi, 1273). He may have been the same person as Hugh de Warelville, who held the same 2 counties in 1130, and was to have held them for 5 years: *Pipe R., 1130* (Rec. Com.), 85. Possibly Hugh of Leic. held the 2 shires together from the departure of Ivo de Grentemesnil. The position of the sheriffs during the Exch. year 31 Hen. I (when Ric. Basset and Aubrey de Vere accounted for the joint farm of the 2 shires) was exceptional: Morris, op. cit. 86–87.

[25] *Pipe R., 1156–9* (Rec. Com.), 44–45, 86–87, 183.

[26] *Pipe R., 1164* (Pipe R. Soc., vii), 28–29.

[27] For 1163–4 Leics. and Warws. had separate sheriffs (ibid.). There were also separate sheriffs for 6 months under Ric. I: *Pipe R., 1194* (Pipe R. Soc., n.s. v), 43.

[28] *Pipe R. 1173* (Pipe R. Soc., xix), 178. *Cal. Pat., 1232–47*, 50, 143; ibid., *1216–25*, 418; *Rot. Litt. Pat. 1201–16* (Rec. Com.), 74. The appointment in 1230 and 1231 of justices to deliver the jail at Kenilworth shows that prisoners were then detained there: *Cal. Pat., 1225–32*, 366, 445; and see ibid. 512. Hen. III granted Kenilworth Castle to Simon de Montfort and his wife Eleanor: *Cal. Pat., 1247–58*, 250.

[29] *Pipe R., 1166* (Pipe R. Soc. ix), 67; *Close R., 1231–4*, 215 (Rothley). *Close R., 1242–7*, 96, 205; *1256–9*, 95; *1259–61*, 43, 57, 135; *1261–4*, 85; *1264–8*, 10, 152, 164–5; *1268–72*, 19, 22, 73, 155, 375; *1272–9*, 157, 160, 171, 211, 260, 271, 280, 373, 376, 394–5, 523; *Cal. Pat., 1247–58*, 356; *1266–72*, 380, 397; *1281–92*, 160, 209 (Leicester).

[30] See e.g. *Close R., 1259–61*, 341; *1279–88*, 167.

Leicester, and to erect a jail.[31] The work evidently went on slowly, for in 1306 a new investigation was ordered, to discover how much money had been collected for the construction of Leicester jail, how much had been expended, and what had been done, as the prison was still unfinished.[32] The work does not seem to have been completed until 1309, when the sheriff was ordered to send all Leicestershire prisoners to Leicester instead of Warwick, as the jail at Leicester was complete and secure.[33] Edward II ordered that a hall should be built near the jail for the holding of pleas, and money was levied on the county for this purpose. The work was delayed by the mismanagement or corruption of those charged with collecting funds, for in April 1332, when two commissioners were appointed by the king to audit the collectors' accounts, to distrain for arrears, and to complete the building of the hall next to the prison, it was stated that the collectors had retained in their own hands much of the money raised, and that the incomplete hall was standing unroofed.[34] In 1344 a further inquiry was ordered into the improper retention of funds by the collectors, but the hall for the county court was apparently completed, as inquiry was to be made about the cost of its repair.[35] The county hall, and the prison which adjoined it, apparently stood on Gaol Lane, off Northgate Street, Leicester.[36]

The safe custody of prisoners was only one amongst the many duties of a medieval sheriff, and the rolls of the royal Chancery preserve numerous records of the execution of military, financial, and legal business by the Sheriff of Warwickshire and Leicestershire. In these respects the activities of the sheriff do not seem to have differed substantially from those in other shires, and consequently they do not call for description here. It should, however, be noted that there were considerable areas within the county which lay largely outside the range of normal administrative action by the sheriff; the honours of Leicester, Winchester, Huntingdon, and Peverel, with the lands of the Abbot of Peterborough, regularly possessed by the late 13th century the franchise of 'return of writ',[37] and within these liberties many of the sheriffs' duties were performed by the lords' bailiffs.[38]

Below the county as administrative units come the wapentakes, of which Leicestershire in 1086 contained four.[39] Except for the subdivision of Guthlaxton and Goscote, the boundaries of the wapentakes, as revealed in Domesday Book, have survived substantially unchanged to the present day.[40] Between 1284[41] and 1300[42] the western part of Guthlaxton was formed into the separate

[31] *Cal. Close, 1296–1302*, 428.

[32] *Cal. Pat., 1301–7*, 477.

[33] *Cal. Close, 1307–13*, 167. The prison may have been already completed by Feb. 1307, when mention is made of surrendering to Leicester jail as a condition of removing outlawry: *Cal. Pat., 1301–7*, 508. By 1329 the prison was in urgent need of repair: *Cal. Close, 1327–30*, 490.

[34] *Cal. Pat., 1330–4*, 292.   [35] Ibid., *1343–5*, 404.

[36] C. J. Billson, *Medieval Leic.*, 44; Nichols, *Leics.* i, 326.

[37] *Rot. Litt. Pat., 1201–16* (Rec. Com.), 58; *Rot. Hund.* (Rec. Com.), i, 237, 240.

[38] For an account of the exercise of franchisal rights in an honour, see L. Fox, *Administration of Honor of Leic.*, esp. 64–70.

[39] Goscote, Guthlaxton, Framland, and Gartree (*V.C.H. Leics.* i, 306 et seq.). For the 'hundreds' into which the wapentakes were divided in the 12th century, see ibid. i, 340–2.

[40] Ibid. i, 338. In the 11th century, Barrow may have been temporarily attached to Guthlaxton: ibid. i, 293.

[41] Just. Itin. 1/457, m. 47, where Guthlaxton is shown to have been still undivided in 1284. A later doc. seems to show that Guthlaxton was still undivided in 1294–5, but the date of this record is uncertain: Just. Itin. 1/465, small membrane now between mm. 2 and 3.

[42] *Leic. Boro. Rec., 1103–1327*, pp. xii, 233, 235.

wapentake of Sparkenhoe. By 1347,[43] and probably from the creation of the new wapentake, the boundary between Guthlaxton and Sparkenhoe was formed by the Fosse Way and the River Soar.[44] The reason for dividing Guthlaxton was probably its size, and especially its extent from north-west to south-east. Goscote is often, though incorrectly, stated to have been divided into the separate wapentakes of East and West Goscote in 1346,[45] but the division actually appears to have taken place under Elizabeth I.[46]

The *Dictum* of Kenilworth, though not at once accepted by all those who were in arms against the king, led in time to the restoration of peace, and Leicestershire enjoyed a period of freedom from civil war under Edward I. One of the early acts of the new king was the searching inquiry of 1274 into local administration. In Leicestershire, though the sheriff and bailiffs were accused of taking bribes to conceal crimes or to allow indicted persons to escape[47] and past sheriffs were charged with having imprisoned men and forced them to accuse the innocent,[48] the worst abuses seem to have been absent. Apart from the perennial misdeeds of local officials, the reign of Edward I was uneventful for Leicestershire. The king's wars in Wales, Scotland, and on the Continent seem to have affected the county very little, though it had to provide grain for the king's army in Wales,[49] and the sheriff had to provide transport for Welsh and Scottish prisoners.[50] Edward's seizure of wool in 1297 for the purposes of war finance, however, must have caused some unsettlement in Leicestershire, an important wool-producing district.[51]

The growth of Parliament at this period is of more significance for local history than Edward's wars, but, though the names of some Leicestershire knights of the shire are known from 1290 onwards, there is no evidence of their activities in connexion with Parliament or of the circumstances which under Edward I attended their election. Apart from Leicester itself the county contained no boroughs,[52] so that the commons of Leicestershire, outside the county town, were represented only by the two knights of the shire. Amongst the Leicestershire representatives under Edward I appear members of such established local families as Wyvill, Burdet, and Turville,[53] whose names are in some cases still preserved in the place-names of the county.

The good order which generally prevailed under Edward I contrasts strongly with the disturbances of his successor's reign. The new king's troubles with his magnates, which began shortly after his accession, led in March 1311 to the setting up with the king's consent of a baronial committee to draw up

---

[43] Nichols, *Leics.* i, pp. cvii–cix.

[44] A deanery of Sparkenhoe was in existence *c.* 1220: *Rot. Hugonis de Welles*, ed. W. P. W. Phillimore, i, 246. It did not coincide exactly with the later wapentake of Sparkenhoe, the eastern part of which lay in the deanery of Guthlaxton: ibid. i, 243–5.

[45] *V.C.H. Leics.* i, 338; Nichols, *Leics.* iii, 1. Nichols bases his statement on a reference to the Aid of 20 Edw. I, but the returns for this aid, which are printed by Nichols elsewhere (*Leics.* i, pp. civ–cvi) show Goscote as a united wapentake.

[46] Goscote was divided by 1570: *Cal. S.P. Dom., 1547–80*, 423. It appears as a single wapentake in 1554: *Cal. Pat., 1553–4*, 296. Wm. Burton, *Description of Leics.* (1st ed.), 1 (published in 1627), says that Goscote was divided 'now of later times'.

[47] *Rot. Hund.* (Rec. Com.), i, 234, 240.

[48] Ibid. 240.

[49] *Cal. Pat., 1272–81*, 219.

[50] *Cal. Close, 1288–96*, 425, 480.

[51] *Cal. Pat., 1292–1301*, 300.

[52] Hinckley has sometimes been referred to as a borough (Nichols, *Leics.* iv, 69), but there is no evidence that it ever returned members to Parliament.

[53] *Return of Members of Parl.*, H.C. 69 (1878), lxii (1), pp. 3, 5, 7, 11, 14, 16, 22.

ordinances for reform. The dispatch in the following July of the Abbot of Leicester and the king's confessor, John de Linham, to communicate certain things to the Sheriff of Leicester on the king's behalf[54] was probably connected with the tension between Edward II and the Ordainers. During the unhappy years which followed the enactment of the baronial Ordinances in 1311 Leicestershire was free from the Scottish raids which devastated much of northern England, but the county had to supply provisions for the royal forces,[55] and in 1315, when the Scots attacked Carlisle, the Sheriff of Leicestershire, with those of the other counties south of the Trent, was ordered to cause everyone in his bailiwick to have arms as laid down in the Statute of Winchester and to be ready to set out against the enemy.[56] Leicestershire provided troops in 1316.[57] At the same time dissensions continued between the king and many of his magnates, led by Earl Thomas of Lancaster, whose vast possessions included the earldom of Leicester. Some Leicestershire families of knightly rank, such as the Trussels of Peatling[58] and the Cuillys of Gilmorton and Ratcliffe Culey,[59] were consistent supporters of Earl Thomas. The reconciliation on a bridge near Hathern in 1318 between the king and Thomas of Lancaster[60] failed to bring about any settlement of the country's internal differences. A new crisis developed in 1321 with the clash between the royal favourites, the two Despensers, and a group of magnates who included Earl Thomas of Lancaster and John de Mowbray. The magnates were at first successful; the lands of the Despensers, which included five manors in Leicestershire, were seized by their enemies, and crops and chattels were carried off;[61] the Despensers themselves were expelled from the country. No permanent settlement was achieved and civil war broke out again in October 1321. In November four lords, one of whom was Ralph Basset of Drayton, a known supporter of the Despensers,[62] were commissioned by the king to assemble forces to resist the rebels in Leicestershire and in the adjacent counties of Warwick and Stafford;[63] on the same day the same four commissioners were ordered to join the king with horse and foot.[64] When, after a successful campaign in the Welsh Marches, the king prepared to move north against Earl Thomas, orders were again issued, on 7 February 1322, for the assembly of forces in Leicestershire and other midland counties,[65] and four days later the sheriff was ordered to bring up the Leicestershire levies to join the king at Coventry.[66] On 23 February the Sheriff of Warwickshire and Leicestershire was ordered to pursue some leading rebels[67] who were reported to have entered his bailiwick. Lancaster enjoyed some support in Leicestershire, and on 9 March the sheriff was ordered to arrest a number of local men, presumably as rebels.[68] On 11 March the king, from Tutbury,

[54] *Cal. Close, 1307–13*, 275.

[55] *Cal. Pat., 1307–13*, 499; *Cal. Close, 1313–18*, 125, 181, 256.

[56] *Cal. Close, 1313–18*, 306.   [57] Ibid. 292; *Cal. Pat., 1313–7*, 460.

[58] *Cal. Pat., 1317–21*, 229; *Cal. Close, 1318–23*, 421, 486; *Cal. Pat., 1313–7*, 21–2; *Leic. Boro. Rec., 1103–1327*, 328.

[59] *Cal. Pat., 1313–7*, 24; *1317–21*, 230; *1321–4*, 216; *Cal. Close, 1318–23*, 572, 587.

[60] Matt. Westm., *Flores Hist.* (Rolls Ser.), iii, 185; Hen. Knighton, *Chron.* (Rolls Ser.), i, 412; *Chrons. Edw. I and Edw. II* (Rolls Ser.), i, 283; ii, p. lxxxii, and references there cited.

[61] *Cal. Close, 1318–23*, 507.   [62] Ibid. 493.

[63] *Cal. Pat., 1321–4*, 39.   [64] *Cal. Close, 1318–23*, 507.

[65] *Cal. Pat., 1321–4*, 69.   [66] *Cal. Close, 1318–23*, 521.

[67] Ibid. 519. The rebels concerned included several Marcher lords, and were presumably those who fled from the Welsh Marches when resistance there collapsed.

[68] *Cal. Close, 1318–23*, 421. For Leics. men who supported Lancaster's revolt, see ibid. 572, 587, 594; *Cal. Close, 1323–8*, 12; *1327–30*, 22; *Cal. Pat., 1321–4*, 81; *Cal. Inq. Misc.* ii, pp. 200–1, 203.

appointed two commissioners to detain rebels surrendering in Leicestershire,[69] while writs of aid were issued in favour of those charged with arresting various insurgents in the county.[70] It was probably because Lancaster, besides his ally John Mowbray,[71] held considerable lands in Leicestershire that knights and squires of the royal household were sent through the county as the king advanced north against the rebels.[72] The royal forces did considerable damage to Lancaster's property at Leicester and at Castle Donnington.[73] The officials of the honour of Leicester, and of the other Lancastrian fiefs in the county, do not seem to have been enthusiastic in their support of Earl Thomas. Richard le Foun, steward of the honour, took some part in attempting to secure armed aid for the earl from the borough of Leicester,[74] but after his death in captivity it was stated that he had not been an adherent of the Earl of Lancaster except in so far as he was steward of the honour.[75] The appointment of two former Lancastrian officials, Roger Beler[76] and Robert of Gaddesby,[77] to keep the lands of the defeated rebels,[78] shows that others who might have been expected to adhere to Earl Thomas were at least not seriously compromised by the revolt.[79] The defeat of the Earl of Lancaster at Boroughbridge and his subsequent execution virtually brought the revolt to an end, though William Trussel, who had been sent to obtain aid for the rebels from Leicester, continued to cause disturbance in the county for several months.[80] The lands of the rebels in Leicestershire were ordered to be surveyed,[81] and in April the king committed the forfeited lands of Earl Thomas and of other rebels in Leicestershire to Roger Beler.[82] The sheriff was ordered to bring to the king all jewels belonging to the Earl of Lancaster or other insurgents which might be found in his bailiwick.[83] Some of the lesser rebels soon regained their lands,[84] but it was only in 1324 that the earldom and honour of Leicester were restored to Henry, brother and heir of Earl Thomas.[85] Until then, the honour of Leicester remained in the king's hands, and the vassals of Earl Thomas, like those who held lands of other rebels, had to do homage to the king.[86] Meanwhile the interminable war with the Scots had to be carried on. One thousand infantry were ordered to be raised in Leicestershire for the summer campaign of 1322,[87] and later, in accordance with a decision made at a Parliament held at York in May of the same year that every township should provide one armed man, Hugh de Prestwold and Ralph Malore were ordered to raise forces in the county and

[69] *Cal. Pat., 1321–4*, 79. [70] Ibid. 81.

[71] Executed for his share in the revolt: Knighton, *Chron.* (Rolls Ser.), i, 422, 425.

[72] *Leic. Boro. Rec., 1103–1327*, 331.

[73] L. Fox, 'Mins. Accts. of the Honor of Leicester', *T.L.A.S.* xix, 209–11; xx, 87, 109.

[74] *Leic. Boro. Rec., 1103–1327*, 328–30.

[75] *Cal. Close, 1318–23*, 589.

[76] Made bailiff and steward of the town and liberty of Stapleford by Earl Thomas (*Cal. Inq. p.m.* vi, p. 444) and in 1318 was pardoned for aiding the earl: *Cal. Pat., 1317–21*, 228.

[77] Receiver of the honour of Leicester in 1318 (*Leic. Boro. Rec., 1103–1327*, 326) and was later steward of the honour (ibid., 353).

[78] See below.

[79] Cf. *T.L.A.S.* xix, 205–6.

[80] *Cal. Close, 1318–23*, 586; *Leic. Boro. Rec., 1103–1327*, 328–9.

[81] *Cal. Pat., 1321–4*, 85.

[82] *Cal. Close, 1318–23*, 432. Robert of Gaddesby later appears as the keeper of the lands in Leics. of all rebels save Earl Thomas: ibid. 455. [83] Ibid. 441.

[84] Ibid. 472, 594, 604; *Cal. Close, 1323–8*, 12.

[85] *Cal. Fine R., 1319–27*, 268; *Parl. Writs and Writs of Military Summons* (Rec. Com.), ii (1), 381–2.

[86] *Cal. Close, 1318–23*, 540; *1323–8*, 140.

[87] *Cal. Pat., 1321–4*, 97.

bring them to Newcastle.[88] Fresh levies were ordered for the next year,[89] but in 1323 a thirteen years truce was made with the Scots.

Edward's triumph over Lancaster, though it restored the king's personal authority, did not bring back good government. In Leicestershire the murder of Roger Beler, who had been made a baron of the exchequer,[90] by members of the Folville and Zouche families,[91] and the subsequent escape of these murderers of an important royal official,[92] reveals the prevalent lack of security. The overthrow of Edward II in 1326 led to further disorders. Henry, Earl of Leicester, though he had supported the deposition of Edward II and obtained his brother's earldom of Lancaster, soon quarrelled with Queen Isabel and her paramour, Roger Mortimer.[93] In consequence the queen and Mortimer, collecting an army of English and Welsh, attacked Earl Henry's lands. Arriving at Leicester on 6 January 1328[94] the royal forces spent a week ravaging the neighbourhood of the town.[95] Henry of Lancaster collected an armed force and marched northwards to meet Mortimer, but being deserted by his supporters was forced to submit.[96] Henry's lands were handed back to him,[97] and with a few exceptions[98] his followers, who included a number of Leicestershire men, also regained their possessions,[99] though in some cases only on undertaking to pay substantial sums to the king.[1]

After this stormy beginning the long reign of Edward III proved to be a time of internal peace, but in the provision of men and supplies for the king's foreign wars Leicestershire had to play its part. For the campaign of 1333 in Scotland, for example, 1,000 infantry, mostly archers, were levied in Warwickshire and Leicestershire;[2] the sheriff had to provide 1,000 quarters of wheat, 500 quarters of beans, and 500 quarters of oats from Leicestershire alone,[3] besides paying the wages of John of Enderby, who was appointed by the king to supervise the purveying of victuals.[4] The contract between the king and Nicholas 'Lenginour' of Blaby, by which Nicholas undertook to manufacture by Easter 1337 30 springalds for the king's use, shows that Leicestershire supplied munitions also. The siege machines were evidently constructed at Blaby, as the sheriff was ordered to provide adequate transport thither for workers and materials.[5] Demands for men and supplies continued throughout the reign.[6] The requirements of war finance led not only to repeated interference with the wool trade by the king, whose actions naturally had repercussions in wool-producing areas such as Leicestershire,[7] but to the men of the county gaining some further experience in state affairs, for Leicestershire merchants were amongst those summoned to treat with the king's council about

---

[88] *Cal. Pat., 1321–4*, 97.

[89] Ibid. 212, 216; *Cal. Close, 1318–23*, 645. [90] *Cal. Pat., 1321–4*, 182.

[91] *Cal. Pat., 1324–7*, 250, 283; G. F. Farnham, *Leics. Medieval Pedigrees*, 41.

[92] Farnham, op. cit. 41.

[93] Knighton, *Chron.* (Rolls Ser.), i, 447; Adam Murimuth, *Chron.* (Rolls Ser.), 58.

[94] Knighton, *Chron.* (Rolls Ser.), i, 450; *Cal. Close, 1327–30*, 353.

[95] Ibid. 354, 424–5; Knighton, op. cit. i, 450.

[96] Knighton, op. cit. i, 450–1. [97] *Cal. Close, 1327–30*, 433.

[98] Among those excepted was Hen. de Beaumont (Knighton, *Chron.* (Rolls Ser.), i, 451), who held the manors of Whitwick and Loughborough, which he regained in 1330: *Cal. Close, 1330–3*, 79, 86.

[99] *Cal. Close, 1327–30*, 429, 437, 439–40. [1] Ibid. 530.

[2] *Cal. Pat., 1330–4*, 419. [3] *Cal. Close, 1333–7*, 25.

[4] Ibid. 40. [5] Ibid. 724–5.

[6] e.g. *Cal. Pat., 1334–8*, 131; *1350–4*, 161; *Cal. Close, 1341–3*, 370; *1349–54*, 294, 304; *1360–4*, 97, 101, 103, 340.

[7] e.g. *Cal. Pat., 1338–40*, 291–2, 294–5, 473; *1340–3*, 15, 59, 61.

financial matters. In March 1347, for example, the Sheriff of Leicestershire, with those of some other counties, was required to order four or six merchants of the shire to come before the council at Westminster, there to treat concerning the affairs of the realm.[8] In May another batch of merchants was called before the council,[9] and in June a further summons was issued to various individuals, including men from Harborough, Loughborough, Mountsorrel, and Barrow.[10] Those summoned were reluctant to appear, and further writs had to be issued in July, August, and September, ordering the sheriff to attach those who failed to attend.[11] The participation of Leicestershire merchants in such business under Edward III must have helped to increase their experience of public affairs. At the same time Leicestershire of course continued to send knights of the shire to successive Parliaments. To some extent the parliamentary representation of the county in the 14th century reflects the local importance of the powerful earls and dukes of Lancaster,[12] though there seems to be no evidence that any special efforts were made to secure the return of representatives likely to have Lancastrian sympathies.[13] Throughout the reigns of Edward III and Richard II the house of Lancaster[14] continued to be of great territorial importance in Leicestershire, and Leicester Castle served as an administrative centre for a large section of the Lancastrian lands in the midlands.[15] On the death of Henry of Grosmont, 1st Duke of Lancaster, in 1361,[16] his lands were partitioned between his two daughters,[17] but on the death of the elder daughter in 1362 the Lancastrian possessions were reunited in the hands of the surviving daughter, Blanche, and her husband, John of Gaunt, who was created Duke of Lancaster.[18] In Leicestershire, if the attitude of a local chronicler can be taken as an indication of the general feeling,[19] John of Gaunt was popular. The revolt of 1381, during which Gaunt was one of the chief objects of the rebels' hatred, did not cause any extensive risings in Leicestershire, although there was some disturbance on the Hospitallers' manors of Rothley and Wartnaby.[20] Despite the absence of serious trouble in the county the alarm caused by the rising was so great that the Abbot of Leicester dared not admit into the abbey wagons carrying Gaunt's property.[21] The incidents attending the accession to the throne of Gaunt's son, as Henry IV, by which the Duchy of Lancaster was merged in the Crown, do not seem to have given rise to any disturbances in Leicestershire. The absence of any drastic changes in the commission of the peace for the county after Richard II's deposition indicates that the crisis of 1399 had few local repercussions.[22]

---

[8] *Cal. Close, 1346–9*, 257. [9] Ibid. 180.

[10] Ibid. 361–2. [11] Ibid. 360, 376, 391.

[12] Several officials of the honour of Leic. repeatedly sat for the county, e.g. Simon Pakeman, who became steward of the honour in 1362 (L. Armitage Smith, *John of Gaunt's Reg.* (Camden Soc., 3rd ser. xx), i, 109), frequently sat for Leics. (*Return of Members of Parl.* H.C. 69 (1878), lxii (1)), and John of Gaunt's retainers frequently appear as the county's representatives: C. J. Wedgwood, 'John of Gaunt and the Packing of Parl.', *E.H.R.* xlv, 623–4. [13] *E.H.R.* xlv, 625.

[14] The title of Duke of Lanc. was bestowed in 1351: *Cal. Pat., 1350–4*, 60.

[15] See, on this subject generally, L. Fox, *Administration of Honor of Leicester in 14th Century*, esp. 17–18.

[16] *Cal. Pat., 1361–4*, 25. [17] *Cal. Close, 1358–61*, 201–11.

[18] *Rot. Parl.* ii, 273. [19] Hen. Knighton, *Chron.* (Rolls Ser.), ii, p. xcix.

[20] C. Oman, *The Gt. Revolt of 1381* (1906), 41, citing A. Reville, *Le Soulèvement des Travailleurs en 1381*, App., 252. [21] Knighton, *Chron.* (Rolls Ser.), ii, 143.

[22] Compare the list of J.P.s under Ric. II (*Cal. Pat., 1396–9*, 238) with that at the beginning of the next reign (ibid. 560). The only notable absentees from the second list, of those named in the first, are the deceased John of Gaunt, and Hereford. There are 2 important new-comers in the second list, Ferrers of Groby and Grey of Codnor. Neither seems to have been an enemy of Ric. II, though Ferrers was one of those who agreed to

The first fifty years of the new dynasty's rule were uneventful for Leicestershire, though the county had to contribute to the loans and levies necessitated by the wars of the period.[23] Under Henry VI, however, the magnates who held land in the county, and with them their numerous dependants, were divided between the factions of York and Lancaster. When the tension between the rival parties first became acute, in 1450, it might have been expected that Lancastrian influence would be predominant in Leicestershire. Apart from the great territorial importance locally of the Duchy of Lancaster, the county contained lands held by some important supporters of the Lancastrian cause. Amongst these were James Butler, Earl of Wiltshire,[24] John, Viscount Beaumont,[25] Thomas Lord Ros,[26] John Lord Lovel,[27] and Sir Edward Grey of Groby.[28] On the other side, amongst the great Yorkist magnates the only one with very extensive possesssions in Leicestershire was the Duke of Norfolk, whose inheritance included the lands of the Mowbrays and Segraves in the county.[29] William Hastings, though he rose to a position of great authority through his devotion to the Yorkist cause, cannot have been a person of very great note in the earlier stages of the struggle.[30] His political sympathies were no doubt due to his family connexion with Richard, Duke of York,[31] and perhaps also to his possession of lands in Yorkshire.[32] There is some evidence that Leicestershire was, in fact, predominantly Lancastrian in sympathy. The adjournment of the stormy Parliament of 1449–50 to Leicester in March 1450[33] is evidence that the town was regarded by Henry VI and his advisers as a place where Lancastrian influence would be predominant. Robert Staunton, one of the knights of the shire in the predominantly Yorkist Parliament of November 1450, was, to judge by his subsequent activities, a Lancastrian.[34] The king's summons, issued in 1445 for a Great Council to meet at Leicester,[35] and again the summons of April 1459 to possible supporters of Henry VI to meet at Leicester,[36] further suggest that Leicestershire was considered as an area likely to be sympathetic to the Lancastrians. On the other hand, in the Parliament of 1455, which met after the Yorkist victory at St. Albans, both the Leicestershire representatives were Yorkists,[37] although by no means all the Commons belonged to the victorious party.[38] If, as these facts seem to show, the county was on the whole Lancastrian before 1460, it would seem to have undergone a change later, perhaps due to the growing influence of William Hastings.

Richard's imprisonment: *Rot. Parl.* iii, 426–7. Both belonged to families who later supported the Lancastrian side.

[23] e.g. *Cal. Pat.*, *1399–1401*, 357; *1436–41*, 505; *1441–6*, 430; *P.C. Proc. and Ords.*, *1386–1410* (Rec. Com.), 186.
[24] *Cal. Pat.*, *1461–7*, 103–4.
[25] *Cal. Pat.*, *1452–61*, 371, 603; *1461–7*, 103–4; *Rot. Parl.* v, 477.
[26] *Rot. Parl.* v, 477; *Cal. Pat.*, *1452–61*, 657; *1461–7*, 30, 103–4.
[27] *Cal. Pat.*, *1452–61*, 534; *1461–7*, 43; *Cal. Inq. p.m.* (Rec. Com.), iv, p. 356.
[28] *Rot. Parl.* v, 282–3.
[29] For the Leics. lands of John, Duke of Norf. (d. 1461), see *Cal. Inq. p.m.* (Rec. Com.), iv, pp. 315–16.
[30] For the lands which Wm. inherited from his father, see ibid. iv, p. 271.
[31] Hist. MSS. Com., *Hastings*, i, 580.
[32] *Cal. Inq. p.m.* (Rec. Com.), iv, p. 271.
[33] *Rot. Parl.* v, 172.
[34] C. J. Wedgwood and A. D. Holt, *Hist. of Parl.*, *1439–1509*; *Biographies*, 802, and references there cited.
[35] *Rot. Parl.* v, 280; *Reg. Quorundam Abbatum Mon. S. Albani* (Rolls Ser.), i, 166.
[36] *Paston Letters*, ed. Gairdner (1904), i, 443.
[37] Wedgwood and Holt, *Hist. of Parl.*, *1439–1509*; *Reg.* 236. They were Leonard Hastings, a retainer of the Duke of York (Wm. Dugdale, *Baronage*, i, 580; Hist. MSS. Com., *Hastings*, i, 158, 300), and Thomas Palmer: Wedgwood and Holt, op. cit.; *Biographies*, 658–9, and references there cited.
[38] J. H. Ramsay, *Lanc. and York* (1892), ii, 185.

The earlier episodes of the civil wars, up to the Yorkist triumph in 1461, did not directly involve Leicestershire in any major conflict, although even in periods of nominal peace there was sometimes disorder.[39] During the crisis of 1459–60 the chief Lancastrian leader in the shire seems to have been John, Viscount Beaumont, who headed the commission of array issued against York and his supporters in December 1459[40] and who was in 1460 the chief of those commissioned to muster the men of Leicestershire and lead them in opposition to the expected Yorkist landing.[41] The Yorkist triumph of 1461 was, of course, followed by measures against the Lancastrians in Leicestershire. Amongst those attainted for fighting on the Lancastrian side at Wakefield and Towton were Lord Ros, holder of the honour and castle of Belvoir, William, Viscount Beaumont,[42] and several lesser men.[43] After Towton, steps were taken to secure the lands of the defeated party. In May 1461 William Hastings and four others were empowered to take possession of Viscount Beaumont's lands, and of the lordship and castle of Belvoir.[44] In July a new commission of the peace for Leicestershire was issued, headed by the Bishop of Lincoln, the Earl of Warwick, and William Hastings.[45] In 1462 a large grant of forfeited lands was made to Hastings, including the Leicestershire lands of the Earl of Wiltshire, Viscount Beaumont, and Lord Ros.[46] The possession by Hastings of these extensive lands within the shire and of several locally important offices,[47] with the consequent increase of his local influence, must have greatly strengthened the Yorkist faction in Leicestershire, and other grants to rather less prominent Yorkists, such as those to Lord Ferrers of Chartley[48] and to Richard Hastings,[49] must have had the same effect. The long antagonism between the Greys of Groby and the Hastings family may have originated at this time in the rivalry between William Hastings and the relatives of Edward IV's queen,[50] although the choice of different sides in the struggle between York and Lancaster by two neighbouring families such as the Hastingses of Kirby Muxloe and the Greys of Groby[51] may have led to a development of the feud at an earlier date.

The results of the increase in the local influence of William Hastings, a man whose feelings of personal loyalty to Edward IV were very strong, were shown when differences arose between the king and his mighty adherent, the Earl of Warwick. Leicestershire seems to have played no part in the rebellion which broke out in the neighbouring county of Lincoln early in 1470, although Leicester was the place at which Warwick and his ally Clarence had arranged to unite with the Lincolnshire insurgents.[52] When Edward IV was driven from

[39] e.g. *Cal. Pat., 1452–61*, 371.   [40] Ibid. 560.   [41] Ibid. 603.

[42] His father had been slain at Northampton: *Engl. Chron. of Reigns of Ric. II–Hen. VI* (Camden Soc., 1st ser. lxiv), ed. P. Davies, 97.

[43] *Rot. Parl.* v, 477; for the lands of those involved, see ibid. 580, 585, and *Cal. Pat., 1461–7*, 103–4.

[44] Ibid. 30.

[45] Ibid. 566. The bp. had apparently become a Yorkist. See *Rot. Parl.* v, 571, and *D.N.B.* under 'Chedworth'.   [46] *Cal. Pat., 1461–7*, 103–4.

[47] Hist. MSS. Com., *Hastings*, i, 302; *Complete Peerage*, vi, 371.

[48] *Rot. Parl.* v, 580; *Cal. Pat., 1461–7*, 153.

[49] *Rot. Parl.*, loc. cit.; *Cal. Pat., 1461–7*, 187, 362.

[50] Sir Thomas Moore, *Engl. under Ric. III* (1870), 194; *Three Bks. of Polydore Vergil's Engl. Hist.* (Camden Soc., 1st ser. xxix), ed. Ellis, 175.

[51] Sir John Grey, son of Lady Ferrers of Groby, and first husband of Queen Eliz., was a Lancastrian commissioner of array in Leics. (*Cal. Pat., 1452–61*, 560, 603) and was killed at the second battle of St. Albans on the Lancastrian side (*Complete Peerage*, v, 361, and authorities there cited).

[52] *Chron. of the Rebellion in Lincs., 1470* (Camden Soc., 1st ser. xxxix), ed. J. G. Nichols, 10, 18; *Recueil des Chroniques, par Jehan de Waurin* (Rolls Ser.), v, 590.

England in 1470, William Hastings was one of his few companions. During the Lancastrian revival in 1470 and 1471 Hastings's power was naturally in eclipse. His name, with those of several supporters, was omitted from the two commissions of the peace for Leicestershire issued in December 1470, though he was a Justice of the Peace in the county both before and after Henry VI's brief period of restoration.[53] When Edward returned in 1471 the extent of Hastings's influence in Leicestershire was demonstrated. Advancing from York to Nottingham and thence to Leicester, Edward is said to have been joined by some 3,000 men, most of them Hastings's followers.[54] The final triumph of Edward IV naturally secured to Hastings a high position in the state. In 1474 he obtained permission to crenellate his manors of Ashby-de-la-Zouch, Bagworth, Thornton, and Kirby,[55] and subsequently he began the building of Kirby Muxloe Castle and considerably altered that at Ashby.[56] A document of 1474–5 shows how, in accordance with the usual methods of the time, Hastings secured, through indentures, the armed assistance of numerous lesser men in return for extending to them the protection of his vast influence.[57] This numerous body of retainers was naturally well represented in the Parliaments of Edward IV's later years; both the Leicestershire representatives in the Parliament of 1478 and one of those in the Parliament of 1472–5 were Hastings's retainers.[58] The political career of Hastings, who must after 1471 have been the most influential magnate in Leicestershire, was brought to an end by his summary execution in 1483, caused apparently by his unwillingness to fall in with the plans of Richard of Gloucester to usurp the throne.[59]

The troubles of Richard III's reign began early in Leicestershire, for it was at Leicester that the king's supporters were ordered to concentrate their forces in October 1483, when the revolt led by the Duke of Buckingham was about to break out.[60] Buckingham's rising was suppressed, and it was not until 1485 that the final overthrow of Richard III took place on Leicestershire soil. The campaign of Bosworth, however, was an event of national rather than local history, and as such it does not merit a detailed description here.[61] The men of Leicestershire do not seem to have played any notable part in the battle, though amongst those who fell was Lord Ferrers of Chartley,[62] a Yorkist who had obtained large grants of Lancastrian lands, including some in Leicestershire.[63]

[53] *Cal. Pat., 1466–7*, 618. Those who were omitted from the commissions of Dec. 1470, but who were named as J.P.s on the immediately preceding and following commissions, were Wm. Sutton, Thomas Palmer, and Wm. Moton. On the connexions of the three with Wm. Hastings, see Hist. MSS. Com., *Hastings*, i, 19, 295–7, and Dugdale, *Baronage*, i, 583.

[54] *Holinshed's Chron.* (London, 1807–8), iii, 306; *Recueil des Chroniques par Jehan de Waurin* (Rolls Ser.), v, 650; *Three Bks. of Polydore Vergil's Engl. Hist.* (Camden Soc., 1st ser. xxix), 140. Warkworth, *Chron. of the First 14 Years of King Edw. IV* (Camden Soc., 1st ser. x), ed. J. O. Halliwell, 13–14, states that Warwick took refuge from Edw. IV at Leic., but the other authorities state that this occurred at Coventry.

[55] *Cal. Chart. R., 1427–1516*, 242.

[56] On Hastings's work at Ashby, see W. D. Simpson, *The Castles of Dudley and Ashby-de-la-Zouch* (1940), 155–8, and T. H. Fosbrooke, *Ashby-de-la-Zouch Castle*, 9.

[57] Printed Dugdale, *Baronage*, i, 583–4.

[58] Dugdale, *Baronage*, i, 583–4; Wedgwood and Holt, *Hist. of Parl., 1439–1509*; *Reg.* 414, 438. The names of the Leics. M.P.s for the Parliament of Jan. 1483 are unknown.

[59] *Three Bks. of Polydore Vergil's Engl. Hist.* (Camden Soc., 1st ser. xxix), 179.

[60] *Stonor Letters and Papers* (Camden Soc., 3rd ser. xxx), ed. C. L. Kingsford, 163.

[61] For descriptions of the Bosworth campaign, see J. H. Ramsay, *Lanc. and York*, ii, 542–51, and the older account by W. Hutton, *Battle of Bosworth Field*; see also A. H. Burne, *Battlefields of Engl.* 137–55, for a recent description of the battle of Bosworth.

[62] *Three Bks. of Polydore Vergil's Engl. Hist.* (Camden Soc., 1st ser. xxix), 224.

[63] *Cal. Pat., 1461–7*, 153.

For some time after the great battle the county was in a disturbed state, so that Robert Throckmorton, who had been appointed sheriff by Henry VII immediately after Bosworth, was unable to collect the county revenues.[64] As a result of Henry's victory, some Leicestershire Lancastrians recovered their lands.[65] The lands and offices of the Yorkist William Hastings, however, were confirmed to his son and heir, Edward,[66] so that the Hastings family retained their importance in the county.[67]

With the end of the Wars of the Roses peace settled upon the county. It is true that old animosities, such as the feud between the two families of Hastings and Grey,[68] persisted into the 16th century and even longer. The county was also called upon to supply forces for the overseas expeditions of Henry VII[69] and Henry VIII,[70] and for the Flodden campaign.[71] Interest in the political history of Leicestershire, however, now shifts, for the time at least, to Westminster.

The two knights of the shire for Leicestershire in the Reformation Parliament of 1529 were Sir William Skeffington and Sir Richard Sacheverell.[72] Both were landowners in the county.[73] Skeffington was an important royal servant, who was Lord Deputy of Ireland from 1530 to 1532 and again from 1534 until his death at the end of 1535. He also served as Master of the Ordnance.[74] It seems unlikely that such a man would have been opposed to the royal policy, and it is known that Skeffington was anxious to obtain certain monastic lands in Leicestershire.[75] Sir Richard Sacheverell was a less prominent man, but he, too, seems unlikely to have been against the religious changes of Henry VIII's reign. Sacheverell was closely linked with the powerful Hastings family,[76] whose head, the 1st Earl of Huntingdon, was a favourite of Henry VIII, and took a leading part in the suppression of the Pilgrimage of Grace.[77] In 1530 Sacheverell signed a petition to the Pope praying him to agree to the divorce of Catherine of Aragon.[78] Sacheverell died in 1534.[79] Such were the representatives of Leicestershire in the Reformation Parliament.

---

[64] Ibid., *1485–94*, 55.

[65] e.g. the Acts of Attainder and Forfeiture on 2 members of the Beaumont family were repealed: *Rot. Parl.* vi, 328–9.

[66] *Materials for Hist. of Reign of Hen. VII* (Rolls Ser.), i, 593.

[67] Of other Yorkists who held land in the county, Ferrers of Chartley was attainted (*Rot. Parl.* vi, 276), but the attainder was later reversed (ibid. vi, 414–15).

[68] On the disputes between these 2 families over Leic. Forest under Hen. VIII, see L. Fox and P. Russell, *Leic. Forest*, 77 et seq.

[69] *Cal. Pat., 1485–94*, 280.

[70] *L. & P. Hen. VIII*, i (2nd ed.), nos. 1804 (28), 1804 (30), 2392.

[71] Ibid., nos. 2330 (3), 3408 (37).

[72] *Return of M.P.s.*

[73] On the Skeffington family and their possessions, see G. F. Farnham, *Leics. Medieval Pedigrees*, 93, and S. H. Skillington, 'The Skeffingtons of Skeffington', *T.L.A.S.*, xvi, 74–103. On Sacheverell's lands, see Nichols, *Leics.* iii, 508.

[74] *D.N.B.*; *Handbk. of Brit. Chronology*, ed. F. M. Powicke, 115; *L. & P. Hen. VIII*, iv, pp. 85, 2272, 2919; v, p. 528; vi, p. 424; vii, p. 412; S. H. Skillington, op. cit. 98–99.

[75] *L. & P. Hen. VIII*, vii, p. 427.

[76] *Complete Peerage*, vi, 375, 623; Nichols, *Leics.* iii, 508.

[77] *Complete Peerage*, vi, 655; *D.N.B.*

[78] *L. & P. Hen. VIII*, iv, p. 2930.

[79] *Complete Peerage*, vi, 375, 623.

POLITICAL HISTORY, 1530–1885

FROM the Reformation to the last quarter of the 19th century the political history of Leicestershire maintained, except at times of national crisis, a constant pattern. Political activity was confined almost entirely to parliamentary elections when broad issues of national policy were rarely debated. Elections were very largely settled by arrangement between the leading families, aristocratic and gentle, and when contests took place they were as much the result of family feuds and quarrels as of differences on political issues. It was natural that the families with the greatest influence at Court, or in the 19th century in the Government, should dominate local politics. Until the Civil War the Hastingses, earls of Huntingdon, and from the Civil War to the end of the 19th century the Mannerses, dukes of Rutland, had the dominating voice in Leicestershire politics.[1] But in this the political history of Leicestershire differs very little from that of other midland counties. The political power of the dukes of Devonshire in Derbyshire and of the dukes of Newcastle in Nottinghamshire was commensurate with that of the Rutlands in Leicestershire.

The Reformation had singularly little effect upon Leicestershire politics; the great families, whatever their differences with each other, moved conformably with the times. Even Edward Hastings, Lord Hastings of Loughborough, the ardent supporter of Queen Mary and her executor, took the Oath of Supremacy, after a taste of the Tower, and died a Protestant.[2] The upshot of this was to add to the political tranquillity of the county, and recusancy never became a problem in Leicestershire.

The Parliament called in 1536 was vital for the development of Thomas Cromwell's attack on the monasteries and care was taken to secure Members of Parliament who 'for their worship and qualities be most meet for the purpose'.[3] The writs for Leicestershire have been lost, but William Ashby of Quenby was certainly one of the members. He wrote effusively to Thomas Cromwell, thanking him for his letters of recommendation to the Earl of Huntingdon and others, and he assured Cromwell that he would do his best to serve the king.[4] He was appointed Commissioner to survey the monasteries of Leicestershire on 24 June 1536 along with Sir John Nevell, John Beaumont, George Gyfford, Robert Burgoyn, and Roger Ratclyff.[5] And he did not fail in his duty. The writs for the Parliaments of 1539 are also missing,[6] but for the penultimate Parliament of Henry VIII summoned on 16 January 1542, Sir Richard Manners, the brother of Thomas, the 1st Earl of Rutland, was elected as the senior Knight of the Shire. The powerful influence of his brother at court, strengthened by the active part he played in defeating the insurrection of the

---

[1] Between 1547 and 1628 7 members of the Hastings family represented Leics. From 1807 to 1888 a Manners represented the county: *Return of Members of Parl.*, H.C. 69 (1878), lxii (1).
[2] *D.N.B.*
[3] *L. & P. Hen. VIII*, x, p. 344.
[4] Ibid., p. 345.
[5] Ibid., p. 495.
[6] *Return of M.P.s.*

northern rebels in 1536, would have made his election certain. He was the first of his family to represent Leicestershire.[7] The Christian name, Thomas, alone survives of the junior Knight of the Shire, but he may well have been Thomas Hastings, who represented the county in 1553 and 1554 (twice),[8] the second son of George, 1st Earl of Huntingdon, who, like the Earl of Rutland, was a great favourite of Henry VIII and was instrumental in helping to defeat the Pilgrimage of Grace.[9] The names of the representatives of Leicestershire in the last Parliament of Henry VIII's reign are not known, but for the first Parliament of Edward VI, called in 1547, Sir Edward Hastings was the senior Knight and Sir Ambrose Cave the junior. They also represented the county in Edward VI's second Parliament.[10]

Unlike most of his family, Sir Edward, afterwards Lord Hastings of Loughborough, was a strong Catholic. He took part in the invasion of Scotland with Protector Somerset in 1547, but his political triumph came with Queen Mary's accession; apart from his religious convictions, it was natural enough for him to support her, for the hereditary enemies of the Hastingses, the Greys, were deeply involved in Northumberland's bid to obtain the crown for Lady Jane Grey. Their defeat was Hastings's triumph. In spite of his opposition to Mary's marriage with Philip II, offices were showered on him. He became a Privy Councillor, Master of the Horse, and finally Lord Chamberlain (1557). Honours and land came his way as well as office. He was made Knight of the Garter in 1555 and Lord Hastings of Loughborough in 1558: the manors of Market Bosworth, Loughborough, and Creech St. Michael (Som.) were bestowed on him. Nevertheless, he remained 'given to melancholy': justified, as events turned out, for at the accession of Elizabeth I he was disgraced, imprisoned, and made to abjure his religion. But when such a man was proposed for the county, backed as he was by the weight of Hastings's family, there was nothing for the gentry to do but accept him. In the political circumstances of the time opposition was inconceivable.[11]

His colleague, Sir Ambrose Cave, was far closer to their kind. The Caves, who were to play an important role in Leicestershire politics for the next three centuries, were more typical of those Leicestershire gentry of the 16th century who were making money fast out of monastic lands. His brother, Sir Thomas, had purchased the manor of Stanford (Northants.), belonging to Selby monastery (Yorks.), for £1,194. 3s. 4d.[12] Sir Ambrose's father had married into the Fieldings of Newnham Paddox, afterwards earls of Denbigh, the most powerful family just across the Warwickshire border. In such ways they built up their territorial influence until they completely dominated south-west Leicestershire. Sir Ambrose himself was wise and discreet. He hitched his wagon to Burleigh's star. Burleigh brought him into the Queen's Privy Committee and no doubt was responsible for making him Chancellor of the Duchy of Lancaster in 1563. The alliance was cemented, as Tudor alliances were wont to be, by marriage, for Sir Ambrose's nephew, Roger, married Burleigh's sister.[13] Nevertheless, Sir Ambrose Cave may be regarded as truly representing the gentry of Leicestershire. Although the writs for Mary's reign are defective, it is clear that the

[7] D.N.B.; Nichols, *Leics.* ii, 67. [8] Nichols, op. cit. iii, 577; *Return of M.P.s.*
[9] D.N.B.
[10] Hist. MSS. Com., *12th Rep., App.* iv, *Rut.,* i, 32; *Return of M.P.s.*
[11] D.N.B.; *Complete Peerage,* vi, 384–5. [12] Nichols, *Leics.* iii, 290.
[13] Ibid. iv, 351–2.

gentry managed to retain their hold on at least one seat. The junior representatives in her four Parliaments were Henry Poole of Countesthorpe, George Turpin of Knaptoft, William Skeffington of Skeffington, and George Sherrard of Stapleford.[14] Of these, all but Poole came of families long established in Leicestershire, and all, including Poole, were deeply concerned in accumulating land, tolerant of inclosure, tolerant of depopulation, men in whom the Leicestershire gentry and yeomanry could put their trust.[15] In the last of Mary's Parliaments the gentry managed to capture both seats, for George Vyncent of Peckleton, a new-comer to the county, was surprisingly enough elected as Senior Knight of the Shire. But for the other Parliaments of Mary for which the returns exist, a Hastings held the senior seat.[16]

These years required great circumspection, for Leicestershire gentry were involved in more dramatic political activity than the choice of parliamentary representatives. Throughout the forties and fifties of this century the country was involved in war, rebellion, and threats of invasion, all of which touched the lives and fortunes of Leicestershire men. In 1544 Henry VIII called on Leicestershire to provide him with 54 carriages, 8 ox-wagons, and 340 horses.[17] For the projected invasion of France 2,534 men were mustered, and the list of gentlemen responsible reads like a roll from a Tudor Debrett—Villiers, Grey, Haslerigg, Digby, Skeffington, Vyncent, Turvill, Shirley, Cave, Beaumont— all are there and their status can be judged by what is demanded of them. Sir John Villiers undertook the heavy burden of providing 4 horsemen and 106 foot, completely furnished with arms.[18]

The next year the same demands were made and by June 1545 500 Leicestershire men had been sent to Boulogne.[19] In 1546 another group of 400 was dispatched to Dover, to be followed later in the year by similar groups.[20] Kett's rebellion in 1549 aroused but slight sympathy amongst the Leicestershire peasantry, and the Council thanked Henry, Marquess of Dorset, for the quietness of the shire.[21] Yet some sympathy there was, for in September 1549 the Earl of Huntingdon had been hanging peasants in Rutland for intended rebellion and he proposed to deal subsequently with the men from Leicestershire.[22]

On the death of Edward VI in 1553, Leicestershire was involved in more spectacular events. Henry Grey, 3rd Marquess of Dorset, whose wife was a granddaughter of Henry VII, was made steward of the manors and lordships in Leicestershire belonging both to the Crown and to the duchy of Lancaster, and in the same year was created Duke of Suffolk.[23] His daughter, Lady Jane Grey, who was born at Bradgate in 1537, was married on 21 May 1553 to Guildford Dudley,[24] and on 10 July 1553 entered the Tower as queen. Warrants were issued in her name to her followers to 'assemble muster and levie all the povere that ye can possible make',[25] but the men of Leicestershire waited on

[14] Nichols, *Leics.* iv, 351–2; *Return of M.P.s.*
[15] For Turpin, cf. W. G. Hoskins, *Essays in Leics. Hist.*, 86, 100.
[16] *Return of M.P.s.*
[17] *L. & P. Hen. VIII*, xix (1), 146. Only 2 counties, Hants and Suss., were called on to provide fewer ox-wagons, whereas the demand on horses from Leics. was very high indeed, only 3 other counties providing more.
[18] Ibid. xix (1), 157–8.
[19] Ibid. xx (1), 516, 527, 633, 650.
[20] Ibid. xxi, 177, 313, 317.
[21] *Cal. S.P. Dom., 1547–80*, 21.
[22] E. Lodge, *Illustrations of Brit. Hist.* i, 134. This information is conveyed in a letter from the Earl of Huntingdon to the Earl of Shrewsbury.
[23] J. Strype, *Eccl. Mem.* (1822), ii (1), 435, 499.
[24] *D.N.B.*, under Lady Jane Dudley.
[25] Nichols, *Leics.* iii, 670.

events. It was enough for the Hastingses to know that the Greys were involved with Northumberland; that alone made certain that they would support Mary as soon as they were able. Sir Edward Hastings, brother of the Earl of Huntingdon, ignored Jane's commission but responded at once to Queen Mary's appeal.[26] A further reason is to be found in the fact that Cardinal Pole, Mary's closest adviser, was a relative of the Hastings family and it is to him that their success in her reign is due.[27]

Northumberland's attempt quickly failed and Mary had little difficulty in securing her throne, but it was more seriously jeopardized by her proposal to marry Philip of Spain. Wyatt's rebellion of 1554 presented Suffolk with an opportunity to re-establish his position. He dashed into Leicestershire with his brothers and issued a proclamation calling people to take up arms against the foreigner.[28]

The men of Leicestershire gave him no support; he fled to Warwickshire where, ironically enough, he was captured by the Earl of Huntingdon.[29] Death and disgrace followed for his family; he himself, his brother Lord Thomas Grey, his daughter Lady Jane, and her husband Dudley were all executed.[30] Had it not been for this last act of folly it is unlikely that his daughter would have lost her life. By all reports she was a young woman of singular intelligence and accomplishment: she had spent almost all her life at Bradgate, which will always be associated with her name.[31]

The accession of Elizabeth I did little to upset the balance of political forces in Leicestershire. Catholicism was not strong, and the Hastings family quickly swung back to its natural alliance with puritanism. The Greys therefore failed to make much capital out of the religious revolution, although one small triumph was the capture of the senior seat for the young husband, Adrian Stokes, of Suffolk's widow. The junior knight was Francis Cave, a relative of Sir Ambrose Cave.[32] But the political history of Leicestershire in this reign is largely the history of the Hastings family.[33] By 1584 Henry, 3rd Earl of Huntingdon, had secured a dominant position in the politics of the county, or rather had re-established the Hastings interest, which had weakened during the reigns of Edward VI and Mary, at the expense of the gentry, but not, it would seem, without a struggle. Evidence is scant but the names of the members elected indicate a contest for power. Nicolas Beaumont of Coleorton and George Turpin of Knaptoft were elected Knights of the Shire in 1562.[34] In the short Parliament of 1571 they were not returned; Francis Hastings, 'the meanest beagle of the House of Huntingdon',[35] younger brother of the earl, and Adrian Stokes sat in place of them.[36] This has every appearance of an alliance between the great families of Hastings and Grey to keep out the gentry.

[26] Strype, *Eccl. Mem.* iii (2), 171–2. Hen., the 3rd earl, was married to the sister of Lady Jane's husband. He did homage to Jane as queen, but deserted her as soon as he could: *Complete Peerage*, vi, 656–7.

[27] See letters of Cardinal Pole to his niece, Catherine Countess of Huntingdon, in Hist. MSS. Com., *Hastings*, ii, 3–7.

[28] Nichols, *Leics.* iii, 670; *Cal. S.P. Dom., 1547–80*, 58.

[29] R. Holinshed, *Chron.* iii, 1095.

[30] Ibid. iii, 1099–1101, 1117.

[31] R. Ascham, *Scholemaster* (ed. Mayor), 33.

[32] *Return of M.P.s.*; Nichols, *Leics.* iii, 144–5. Francis Cave was an executor of Sir Ambrose Cave in 1568: ibid. iv, 351.

[33] J. E. Neale, *Elizabethan Ho. of Commons*, 39–42.

[34] *Return of M.P.s.*

[35] H. N. Bell, *Huntingdon Peerage*, 57. The Jesuit, Fr. Parsons, so described him. See also T. Fuller, *Worthies of Engl.*

[36] Neale, *Eliz. Ho. of Commons*, 40.

At the next election, in 1572, the gentry reappear in the persons of Nicholas Beaumont and Sir George Turpin. But it was a short-lived triumph. From 1584 until the end of James I's reign the gentry could never be certain of holding even one seat, and this is an extremely rare situation in county politics. In those counties whose social and political life was dominated by a great family, it was usual for that family to share the representation with the gentry. Certainly the stranglehold of the Hastingses bred resentment, but the resentment was never strong enough to become effective.[37]

The head of the Hastings family was Henry, the 3rd earl, an ardent and devout Puritan, although his mother was the niece of Cardinal Pole. Through her he had a claim to the succession, and had Elizabeth's attack of smallpox in 1562 proved fatal he would have been, as Professor Neale has pointed out, the ardent Protestants' candidate.[38] He was Lord-Lieutenant of Leicestershire in 1559 and of Rutland in 1569, Knight of the Garter in 1570, and Lord President of the Council in the north in 1572.[39] As Lord President he was responsible for the custody of Mary, Queen of Scots, whose joint guardian he had been made in 1569, and for a time his castle at Ashby was considered a suitable place for her imprisonment.[40] He had raised forces in Leicestershire to help suppress the rising of the northern earls in Mary's favour and this had probably helped him to his Garter.[41] His position in the county was further strengthened by his brothers, all active men, all Puritans, all resident in Leicestershire. His two deputy-lieutenants were his brothers.[42] His influence in Leicester, of which his family held the stewardship, was also very great, and his nominees sat for the borough.[43] In Leicestershire no one could compare with the earl in social prestige or political influence; there was no one, even, strong or powerful enough to make capital when, for a short time, he fell out of favour with the queen.[44] Election followed election and the Hastings monopoly was not challenged; the gentry took their seats when the Hastingses did not want them both, and a Turpin, a Beaumont, or a Skeffington was occasionally seen at Westminster. But in 1601, at the election for Elizabeth's last Parliament, a challenge was made. It would seem that there was a growing faction in the county which disliked the Hastings monopoly, for the earl's influence was directly challenged in Leicester itself. There George Belgrave managed by guile and chicanery to gain a seat, although he was described as a noted enemy of the earl.[45] Belgrave was the heir of William Stokes, the brother of Adrian, and so distantly con-

---

[37] See below, p. 109.

[38] *D.N.B.*; *Complete Peerage*, vi, 656–7; Neale, *Elizabethan Ho. of Commons*, 39. M. M. Knappen, *Tudor Puritanism*, 411, quotes a rather extravagant eulogy, *The Crie of the Poor*, on his death in 1595. The least happy stanza from a Leics. point of view was the following:

'No groves he enclosed nor felled no wood,
No pastures he paled to do himself good;
To commons and county he lived a good friend,
And gave to the needy what God did him send.'

[39] *Complete Peerage*, vi, 656–7.

[40] Nichols, *Leics.* iii, 610; W. Kelly, *Royal Progresses and Visits to Leic.* 290; Hist. MSS. Com., *Hastings*, ii, 8–9.

[41] *Cal. S.P. Dom., Add. 1566–74*, 125–6.

[42] Hist. MSS. Com., *15th Rep., App.* v, *Foljambe*, 25.

[43] Neale, *Eliz. Ho. of Commons*, 171–4; *Leic. Boro. Rec., 1509–1603*, 208–10; J. Thompson, *Hist. of Leic.*, 256, 274–5.

[44] Hist. MSS. Com., *Hastings*, ii, 15.

[45] Star Cha. 5 A 54/2, cited Neale, *Eliz. Ho. of Commons*, 176; for the election in general, cf. Thompson, *Hist. of Leic.*, 300–1; *Leic. Boro. Rec., 1509–1603*, 336–7; and Neale, op. cit. 174–6.

nected with the Greys.[46] In the county itself the challenge came from Sir John Grey, who wrote asking for the help of the Earl of Rutland, whose brothers he had befriended when in his custody after the rising of the Earl of Essex.[47] But it was to no avail. As yet Rutland's power in Leicestershire was negligible.

The strongest protest against the Hastings influence came in the election of 1621. Once again both seats were demanded, this time for Sir George Hastings and Sir Henry Hastings. The election was held at Leicester Castle and 1,200 freemen declared for the two Hastingses but, although they had a clear majority, the sheriff, Sir Alexander Cave, took legal advice, and refused to return Sir George Hastings on the ground that he was a non-resident and returned Sir Thomas Beaumont, the defeated candidate, in his stead.[48] Naturally the Hastingses petitioned the House of Commons against this decision, and as the legal question involved—the right of a non-resident to represent a county—raised important constitutional issues, the case was extensively debated in the House.[49] Sir Thomas Beaumont was allowed to be represented by counsel. Inevitably his petition was dismissed, for its acceptance would have led to the unseating of many members.[50] Sir Thomas Beaumont was so infuriated by the result that he threatened to sue Cave for damages and he was only saved by the protection of the House of Commons.[51] This result so encouraged the Earl of Huntingdon that, in 1625, he was writing about the county as an 18th-century peer might have written about a pocket borough. 'I pray you speak', he wrote to Thomas Wright from St. Albans, 'to the freeholders of Leicestershire to vote for my brother, Sir George Hastings, at the election on May 5. At my coming home you shall know who I desire should be the other Knight of the Shire.'[52] But times were not so easy for the Hastingses; one seat went to Sir Wolstan Dixie of Bosworth, who was closely related to the Beaumonts, and Sir George had to be content with the Hastings seat at Leicester itself. The senior county seat went to the earl's son Ferdinand, Lord Hastings, who, since he is not mentioned in the letter of 5 May, must have been rushed in at the last minute. This was done perhaps to still criticism about the non-resident Sir George and to make certain that at least one county seat was procured for the family, for the earl's son and heir had almost a prescriptive right.[53] Although the Hastings family maintained a hold on the senior seat until 1640, they never again monopolized both, and the stand taken at Leicester Castle in February 1621 by a Beaumont and a Cave seems to have effectively rallied the Leicestershire gentry. Nevertheless, from the Reformation to the Civil War, the political life of Leicestershire was dominated by the earls of Huntingdon; there was no power comparable to theirs, and their relatives and clients represented both county and borough almost continuously in Parliament.

We must, however, return to Elizabeth's reign. National events had their repercussions in Leicestershire; the threat of a Spanish armada rendered more acute differences in religion. From 1585 commissions to take recusants were issued to the leading gentlemen of the shire, and George Shirley of Staunton and

---

[46] Hist. MSS. Com., *12th Rep., App.* iv, *Rut.* i, 360.   [47] Nichols, *Leics.* iii, 146.

[48] W. Notestein, F. H. Relf, and H. Simpson, *Commons Debates, 1621* (Yale, 1935), ii, 41–42; iv, 22.

[49] Ibid. ii, 49, 50–51. Sir Geo. Hastings was said to have had an annuity of £300 a year, which some argued was the equivalent of a freehold. Sir Edw. Coke took a large part in the debate on the constitutional issue.

[50] Ibid. ii, 50–51; iv, 29–30.   [51] Ibid. ii, 53; vi, 361; *C.J.* i, 516.

[52] Hist. MSS. Com., *Hastings*, ii, 67.

[53] *Return of M.P.s.* Sir Wolstan Dixie married Frances, dau. of Sir Thomas Beaumont of Stoughton, and his son was married into the Beaumonts of Gracedieu: Nichols, *Leics.* iv, 506.

Robert Brooksby were taken into custody. In February 1588 the sheriff, William Cave, proceeded against Roman Catholic women and youths but complained that some had fled from their habitations before the arrival of his officers.[54] Compared with other counties, however, the amount of recusancy in Leicestershire seems to have been small and caused little trouble to the local authorities.[55] The fear of a Spanish invasion was more alarming and the military resources of the country were strained to the utmost. In December 1587 the Lord-Lieutenant, Henry, Earl of Huntingdon, was ordered to 'select and equip 500 men in Leicestershire to be in readiness to serve on any sudden occasion'.[56] The full force of those liable for service was called out and sent to Tilbury; in addition to the 500 footmen raised according to his instructions,[57] the earl gathered together a band of 500 private soldiers which was maintained by his family for many years.[58]

The foreign policy of Elizabeth's latter years made further demands for soldiers from Leicestershire. She supported the French Huguenots with troops and in 1591 150 able-bodied men from the shire were ordered to be sent to Normandy for the succour of the French king.[59] They were soon recalled, 'the Queen not being minded that they should be out of the realm above 2 months', but in the following year more Leicestershire men had to do a term of service overseas.[60]

Provision of men for the army in Ireland, however, was to prove a more severe strain than help to the French. The hardships of guerrilla warfare made constant reinforcements necessary; in 1595 thirty-five men were ordered from Leicestershire for service in Ireland 'furnished with coates of good stuf and to be lined to preserve them better this winter season'.[61] Further men were called for in April and more contingents, fully furnished with arms, were required in 1596 and 1597 to fill up the decayed bands already in Ireland.[62] So desperate was the resistance of the Irish that Elizabeth, 'fynding her gracyous dispocycon to reduce the rebells of Ireland by some peaceable means to obedyence doth not take effecte', ordered fresh levies in 1598 and 1599.[63] Money was collected in the county for the relief of the sick and disabled who returned.[64] Their tales of suffering in Ireland made it very difficult to obtain any but undesirable men for the service, and the Council complained to the Earl of Huntingdon in 1600 that the Leicestershire levies 'have and do contyneuallie either runne awaie before they comme to embarque, or abandon their service very soone after their comming into Ireland'.[65] The defeat of Tyrone by Mountjoy in 1603 put an end to this strain on the county's military resources.

But peace may have been a dubious blessing, for at least the Irish war had been one way of getting rid of the violent and the discontented, who seem to have been particularly rife in the early years of the 17th century. There was a fierce riot at Cotesbach in 1607, a part of the bitter and widespread midland

---

[54] Cal. S.P. Dom., 1581–90, 275, 463; 1591–4, 21.
[55] A. L. Rowse, Engl. of Eliz. 446–56. [56] Cal. S.P. Dom., 1587–90, 442.
[57] Bell, Huntingdon Peerage, 77; Acts of P.C., 1588, 171.
[58] Cal. S.P. Dom., 1625–6, 387. [59] Acts of P.C., 1591, 220–1.
[60] Ibid. 352; 1613–14, 135; Cal. S.P. Dom., 1591–4, 266, 281, 284.
[61] Acts of P.C., 1595–6, 47–48.
[62] Ibid. 262–3; 1596–7, 164; 1597, 27.
[63] Acts of P.C., 1597–8, 584–6, 659; 1598–9, 97, 312–15, 577; Bell, Huntingdon Peerage, 86–87.
[64] Hist. MSS. Com., 8th Rep., App., pt. 1, sect. ii, 433; Acts of P.C., 1598–9, 155–6; 1599–1600, 317.
[65] Ibid. 413 et seq.

protest against inclosure.[66] In 1606 fears of peasant discontent had led the Earl of Huntingdon to order two barrels of gunpowder to be used to 'compel the inhabitants to desist from assembling to lay open enclosed ground'. A gibbet which had been erected *ad terrorem* had been demolished by a turbulent mob and the chamberlain and the mayor, Robert Herrick, were confined to their houses by the order of the Earl of Huntingdon.[67] This was rough treatment, since the Herricks had been lending the Hastingses money.[68] Not only the peasantry but the gentry were restless. Henry, 5th Earl of Huntingdon, was very conscious of the great political power which he wielded in the county and he did not hesitate to use it in the most forthright manner. The tone of his letters is always peremptory and often aggressive. This in itself cannot have endeared him to the Leicestershire gentry,[69] some of whom, moreover, may have been alienated by his rabid puritanism and somewhat tyrannical handling of county elections.[70] Whatever the cause, there was considerable plain speaking about his character in 1628 and two Leicestershire gentlemen, Sir Henry Shirley and Sir Anthony Faunt, were severely punished for their aspersions; Shirley was imprisoned in the Fleet by the House of Lords and Faunt was heavily fined in the Star Chamber.[71] But this, together with the fact that after 1621 the Hastingses were never able to dominate the county elections and occasionally found the town itself intractable,[72] shows that their political domination was far less secure than it had been in Elizabeth's reign. The jealousies and animosities of the gentry towards them were to be more important in the political crisis which led to the Civil War than the violent and sporadic outbursts of the peasantry.

Indeed, the personal and family feuds were notorious; Leicestershire was described as 'like a cockpit, one spurring against another'.[73] Clarendon believed that the whole county was violently divided between Greys and Hastingses, 'a notable animosity' without the addition of any other quarrel.[74] The personal nature of the quarrel may have had an important bearing on the strategy of the war, owing to the reluctance of Henry, Earl of Stamford, to move his forces from Leicestershire and so leave the county at the mercy of the Hastingses.[75] From the lists of parliamentarians and royalists, compiled from the State Papers, it is possible to discover the allies of these great houses amongst the gentry.[76]

A rough geographical division is discernible. The bulk of the royalists were drawn from the country lying to the north and west of the Fosse Way with the addition of the spur of highland which runs up to Belvoir, an outlying bastion of royalist strength. Most of Grey's supporters, on the other hand, were

[66] Cf. L. A. Parker, 'The Agrarian Revolution at Cotesbach, 1501–1612', *T.L.A.S.* xxiv, 72–73; E. F. Gay, 'The Midland Revolt and the Inquisitions of Depopulation of 1607', *Trans. R. Hist. S.* (2nd ser.), xviii, 195–237; J. Stow, *Chron.*, 889.

[67] Bell, *Huntingdon Peerage*, 108.   [68] Ibid. 76, 98.

[69] Hist. MSS. Com., *8th Rep.*, *App.*, pt. 1, sect. ii, 434–5; *Hastings*, ii, 54–55.

[70] Cf. *ante*, p. 107.

[71] Bell, *Huntingdon Peerage*, 112–13, 114; *L.J.* iii, 822, 842, 849, 877.

[72] Hist. MSS. Com., *Hastings*, ii, 63.

[73] B.M. Pamphs., E. 108 (16), *Terrible News from Leicester*.

[74] Clarendon, *Hist. of Rebellion*, vi, 275.

[75] J. Buchan, *Oliver Cromwell*, 139; W. C. Abbot, *Letters and Speeches of Oliver Cromwell*, i, 228.

[76] Information about Leics. parliamentarians and royalists is derived from *Cal. S.P. Dom.*, *Acts and Ord. of Interr.* (ed. Firth and Rait); *C.J.* for parliamentarians, *Cal. of Proc. of Committee for Compounding, 1643–60*, for royalists.

drawn from the south and east of the county. The parliamentarians had a clear majority of the leading families amongst the gentry. Behind Henry, Earl of Stamford, were ranged the following families: Ashby of Quenby, Babington of Rothley, Cave of Stanford, Dixie of Bosworth, Faunt of Foston, Hartopp of Buckminster, Hazlerigg of Noseley, Herrick of Beaumanor, Packe of Prest-wold, Palmer of Wanlip, Pochin of Barkby, Smith of Edmundthorpe, Villiers of Brooksby, Winstanley of Braunstone. Many of these were relatively new families. Some, like the Caves, Babingtons, and Ashbys, had done particularly well out of monastic land; others, like the Herricks and Dixies, had made their money as merchants and had then turned landowners; but the Faunts and the Villierses were old-established families, as old as any on the royalist side. In general the royalists were more impressive in lineage than wealth. Shirleys, Turvilles, Skeffingtons, Turpins, Skipwiths, Poulteneys, and the Beaumonts of Gracedieu had deep roots in Leicestershire and were not unprosperous, but the majority of royalists were small squires such as Farnham of Quorn or Wright of Barlestone.[77] Nor had the royalists, apart from the leading families, the same experience of politics and administration, for, apart from the Hastingses, only one royalist family, Staresmore of Frolesworth, had produced a Knight of the Shire since the great disputed election of 1621, whereas a Hazlerigg, a Hartopp, and a Dixie had sat in the Commons. At the two critical elections of 1640, the Hastingses failed to retain their hold on the county and both seats went to sup-porters of Parliament's cause—Sir Arthur Hazlerigg and Lord Grey of Ruthin.[78]

There were three major strategic points in Leicestershire—the town itself and the castles of Ashby-de-la-Zouch and Belvoir.[79] Belvoir, with Newark, was a serious threat to the communications of the parliamentary forces in East Anglia and Yorkshire. Ashby was extremely important, not only as a strong-hold for guerrilla raids but also as a fortress protecting the royalist communica-tions between the south-west and the Duke of Newcastle in Yorkshire; in consequence the skirmishes in Leicestershire were of considerable importance to both sides, and it was not by chance that the decisive battle of the war was fought at Naseby on the borders of Leicestershire.

The first real trial of strength came in March 1642 in the struggle between Stamford and Henry Hastings, the militant royalist son of the Earl of Hunting-don, to obtain control of the militia and of the magazine, kept at the Newarke, Leicester. The Commons were determined to put an end to the king's control over the militia, which he exercised through the appointment of the Lord-Lieutenant, and to this end, on 5 March 1642, both Houses of Parliament nominated Stamford Lord-Lieutenant of Leicestershire.[80] He was also em-powered to call together all His Majesty's subjects in Leicestershire 'that are meet and fit for the wars, and them to train, exercise and put in readiness, and them . . . from time to time to cause to be arrayed and weaponed and to take muster of them'. Power to appoint deputy-lieutenants and officers was also conferred on him, and he used his forces 'for the suppression of all rebellions,

[77] *Cal. of Proc. of Committee of Compounding,* iii, 2295 (Shirley); iv, 2433 (Turville); ii, 1515 (Turpin); ii, 1553 (Skipwith); iii, 1818 (Poultney); iii, 1998 (Beaumont); ii, 941 (Farnham); iii, 1651 (Wright). For Skeffington, cf. H. Symonds, *Diary,* 182–3.

[78] *Return of M.P.s*; *Complete Peerage,* vi, 175–6, for Grey of Ruthin. His father Anthony, 9th Earl of Kent, was rector of Aston Flamville (with Burbage), 1590–1643. He was 82 when he succeeded his distant cousin Hen., 8th Earl of Kent. His son had no right to the title Grey of Ruthin, which he used: *C.J.* ii, 2.

[79] Belvoir Castle became a royalist stronghold in Jan. 1643, although the 8th Earl of Rut. was a parlia-mentarian. See p. 113, and Nichols, *Leics.* ii, 51.　　　　　　　　　　　　　[80] *C.J.* ii, 425.

insurrections and invasions that may happen, according as they . . . shall receive directions by his Majesty's authority, signified unto them by the Lords and Commons assembled in Parliament'.[81]

The king could not agree, for such an act would have destroyed the whole basis of his military power, but the Parliament passed the Militia Bill as an 'ordinance of Parliament' and the lord-lieutenants were directed to act according to its provisions. In response, the king issued a proclamation forbidding the raising of levies except by his express command.[82] To counter this the two Knights of the Shire, Sir Arthur Hazlerigg and Lord Grey of Ruthin, were sent by Parliament to Leicester to see the Militia Ordinance put into force, and Stamford was given authority to call out the trained bands for June.[83] Stamford had an enthusiastic welcome in Leicester and an attempt, probably by Hastings, to stop him executing his warrant was brushed aside.[84]

The royalists had not been idle under these provocations and Leicestershire was the first county to receive a commission of array from the king (12 June). Hastings issued warrants for assembling the trained bands of foot and free-holders' bands on 22 June but he was so doubtful of Leicester that he appointed the Raw Dykes as the place of assembly and persuaded the Mayor of Leicester, Thomas Rudyard, to ignore Stamford's order and not call out the town bands.[85] It was Hastings's intention to seize the magazine of the county at the Newarke, but in this he was frustrated by Stamford, who removed most of it to Bradgate.[86] Stamford, however, either had second thoughts or the royalist forces were strong enough to compel him to change his mind, for by 7 July Charles was complimenting Hastings on its return to Leicester. Hastings had been appointed High Sheriff on 25 June in place of Archdale Palmer, who was a parliamentarian, and he was instructed to use the magazine 'as there shall be occasion'.[87] In addition, Hastings's royalists were preventing considerable numbers of men from obeying Stamford's summons, particularly in north Leicestershire.[88] It was doubtless because of the success of Leicestershire royalists that Hastings, Sir Richard Halford, Sir John Bale, and John Bate were impeached by the Commons, on the grounds that by acting under the king's commission of array they had disturbed the peace of the kingdom and betrayed the liberties of the subject.[89] The Commons wished to intimidate royalists in other counties from following the prompt and energetic action of Hastings, who had arrested the parliamentary commissioner sent down to declare his actions illegal, and who was taking great pleasure in harrying his old enemy Stamford at Bradgate.[90]

Nevertheless, Stamford, Hazlerigg, and Grey of Ruthin were doing what they could to rally the parliamentary forces and they reported excellent response at Broughton Astley, where appeared on 14 June 'above 100 volunteers and trained and private men'. The next day Kibworth made 'a good appearance' and further recruiting meetings were held at Copt Oak, Melton Mowbray, and

[81] *L.J.* iv, 625.   [82] Nichols, *Leics.* iii, App. iv, 19.

[83] *C.J.* ii, 604, 434; *L.J.* iv, 589–90.

[84] Nichols, *Leics.* iii, App. iv, 19; Hist. MSS. Com., *Hastings*, ii, 84.

[85] *L.J.* v, 147–9.   [86] Hist. MSS. Com., *Hastings*, ii, 84.

[87] Ibid. ii, 85; *C.J.* iv, 78; Clarendon, *Hist. of Rebellion*, v, 417.

[88] *L.J.* v, 132–3.

[89] Hist. MSS. Com., *Hastings*, ii, 85; *C.J.* ii, 632; *L.J.* v, 150.

[90] *C.J.* ii, 641, 646, 649, 654–5; B.M. Pamphs., E. 154 (4), E. 134 (43), for the commissioners' report of their treatment at Leic.: *L.J.* v, 193, 195, 202, 203, 208; Nichols, *Leics.* iii, App. iv, 26.

Queniborough, where the appearance was considered particularly good 'considering how many great Papists and ill-affected people live there-about'. But much as the parliamentary propagandists made of this response,[91] it was far less spectacular and heartening than the forays of Hastings. Charles decided to visit Leicester himself in order to consolidate the admirable effect which the royalists were having.[92]

The king entered the town on 22 July and was received with warm expressions of loyalty by 'ten thousand of the gentry and better sort of inhabitants of that county'. Charles appealed for help, if help were needed, but the king hoped that such help would not be necessary as he thought that Parliament could not reasonably refuse his latest proposals. But if occasion should arise, 'I know you will bring horses, men, money and hearts, worthy of such a cause'.[93] Apart from an offer to raise and maintain six-score horses and horsemen, the appeal did not receive much response;[94] for, as Clarendon realized, 'if the King were loved there as he ought to be, Parliament was more feared than he'.[95] Indeed, the king was promptly presented with a petition which expressed regret at his long estrangement from his 'highest and safest council of Parliament', complained of Hastings's actions and of the honours bestowed on him, and requested the king to leave the magazine and militia in the hands of the Earl of Stamford—a bold demand, since the king had already declared Stamford a traitor.[96] But worse was to follow on the next day, when a further petition was presented which called for an immediate settlement of the question of the control of the magazine. Three demands were made that the magazine might be distributed to the several hundreds of the county, that it might never be 're-assumed' but by a legal power, and that the keepers of it might have liberty and protection for discharging their trust.[97] No doubt the Mayor and Corporation, caught between the conflicting demands of Hastings and Stamford, felt their position to be invidious and desired protection. None was forthcoming; the king merely replied that if the keepers of the magazine had done what was warrantable they needed no protection but the law. It was, however, decided to distribute the magazine through the six hundreds of the county.[98] The king left Leicester on 26 July but returned for a night on 18 August before proceeding to Nottingham, where he set up his standard on 22 August 1642.[99]

The declaration of war spurred Hastings to increased patrol activity, in which he was helped by Prince Rupert, who was quartered at Leicester with 800 of the king's horse. They found each other congenial company and they attacked Bradgate, carrying off some of the arms stored there by Stamford. They scared the household and had boisterous fun with the chaplain, for they took away his clothes and spoilt them.[1] But Rupert overstepped his instructions in September when, short of ready money, he roughly demanded £2,000 in the king's name from the Mayor and Corporation of Leicester, threatening in his postscript to appear before the town with horse, foot, and cannon to teach them that it was safer to obey than to refuse the king's demands. The town

91 B.M. Pamphs., E. 154 (4).   92 Hist. MSS. Com., *Hastings*, ii, 85.
93 *Cal. S.P. Dom.*, *1641–3*, 359; Nichols, *Leics.* iii, App. iv, 28.
94 *Cal. S.P. Dom.*, *1641–3*, 362.   95 Clarendon, *Hist. of Rebellion*, v, 417.
96 B.M. Pamphs., E. 108 (20); Hist. MSS. Com., *Hastings*, ii, 84.
97 B.M. Pamphs., E. 154 (43).   98 Ibid. E. 108 (20).
99 *Somers Tracts*, v, 264 (*Iter Carolinum*); W. Kelly, *Royal Progresses*, 407; Clarendon, *Hist. of Rebellion*, vi, 1.
1 Clarendon, loc. cit.; Nichols, *Leics.* iii, App. iv, 30.

hurriedly provided £500. They did not, however, have to find the rest, for the king heard of Rupert's rash action, disowned it, and discharged the Corporation from obedience to Rupert's demands on the ground that he only wished for voluntary loans from his subjects.[2] It is not known whether the Corporation took this broad hint, but it does not appear that the money paid was returned. Fortunately for Leicestershire Rupert was called away to the west: Hastings accompanied him and fought with great bravery at Edgehill on 23 October.[3]

During the winter Parliament took measures to strengthen its position in Leicestershire and the Committee for the Safety of the Kingdom received orders in April 1643 to provide Lord Grey with 6 guns, 1,000 muskets, and ammunition.[4] During this winter the parliamentary forces seem to have obtained a secure grip on Leicester itself. But the royalists continued to consolidate their position, and their most striking victory during the winter was the taking of Belvoir Castle in January 1643 by Colonel Gervase Lucas, High Sheriff of Lincolnshire. Lucas was made governor of the castle and had the revenues of Framland hundred for his support, 'which Lord Loughborough takes ill'.[5] In February it was rumoured that the parliamentarians intended to recapture Belvoir but no action resulted.[6] Throughout the county conditions were anarchic and Hastings attempted to secure some sort of order by declaring that he would use his utmost endeavour to prevent the plundering of those who had obeyed the ordinance of Parliament for the militia, upon a similar promise from Lord Grey to those who had appeared for the king.[7] It is not known whether Lord Grey responded to his request.

Both Ashby and Belvoir were exceptionally strong and well-fortified, both admirable bases for marauding raids on Roundhead territory, and many skirmishes took place between the Ashby and Belvoir royalists and the Roundheads from Leicester during the next two years.[8] Indeed, the strength of Ashby and the riotous royalism of its soldiers became topics of the London press. It was reported that there are as 'debased wicked wretches there as if they had been raked out of hell' and that 'they have three malignant priests there, such as will drink and roar . . . and swear and domineer so as it would make ones heart ache to hear the country people to relate what they heard of them'.[9]

Fear of Lord Loughborough at Ashby and Colonel Lucas at Belvoir immobilized Lord Grey of Groby, who was unwilling to move his forces. Oliver Cromwell's plan to unite his own forces with Grey's and with those of Sir John Gell, the Roundhead leader of Nottingham and Derby, was thus completely frustrated, and he was unable to go to the relief of the Fairfaxes, hard pressed by the Duke of Newcastle in Yorkshire. 'Believe it', Cromwell wrote, 'it were better, in my poor opinion, Leicester were not, than that there should not be an immediate taking of the field.' He persuaded Grey to go as far as Nottingham but no farther. In consequence of this and of Hotham's treachery the Fairfaxes were decisively defeated by Newcastle at Adwalton Moor.[10]

[2] Ibid. iii, App. iv, 30–31. [3] J. F. Hollings, *Civil War in Leics.* 24.

[4] *C.J.* iii, 47.

[5] Nichols, *Leics.* ii, 51; *Cal. S.P. Dom., 1644,* 285. Hastings was raised to the peerage as Lord Loughborough, Oct. 1643. [6] Hist. MSS. Com., *Hastings,* ii, 89.

[7] Ibid. 87–88. [8] Clarendon, *Hist. of Rebellion,* vi, 275.

[9] Nichols, *Leics.* iii, App. iv, 39.

[10] W. C. Abbot, *Letters and Speeches of Oliver Cromwell,* i, 228. 'I perceive Ashby-de-la-Zouch sticks much with him', wrote Cromwell.

Grey had little ability, 'a young man of no eminent parts', as Clarendon described him,[11] and the initiative in Leicestershire remained with the royalists. In November 1643 Colonel Lucas, in command of a strong force from Belvoir and acting in concert with a troop of horse from Newark, caught the Roundheads unawares at Melton Mowbray, and took 300 prisoners, three members of the Leicester Committee among them. Much valuable booty—300 horses and 400 weapons—was also taken, a loss which had to be made good by a parliamentary vote of £500 and 400 arms on 7 December 1643.[12] But some relief was given by the aggressive action of Sir John Gell, who later in the winter captured 120 horses belonging to Hastings, together with some prisoners.[13] Further sharp skirmishing took place round Hinckley church in March 1644. Loughborough, returning from a successful ambush of Covenanters on the way to Leicester, had locked up his prisoners in the church. A relief party was summoned partly from Leicester and partly from Bagworth. The prisoners were rescued, but most of the Cavaliers escaped safely to Ashby.[14]

These minor successes, however, did little to allay the concern which Parliament felt for the military situation in Leicestershire.[15] In July 1644 the principal parliamentarian inhabitants of the county were formed into a new Committee for the Militia whose duties were to 'raise forces, suppress the enemy, to assess taxes, to pay the troops, to appoint officers and suppress revolt'.[16] But the new committee was soon at loggerheads with Lord Grey,[17] and the 'gentlemen, freeholders, and best affected of Leicestershire' petitioned Parliament to compose their differences and complained that the best men of the county were left out of the new committee. They wanted 'the now disheveled soldiers' to be collected under the command of Lord Grey so that 'we may be able again to give limits to the now unbounded enemy'.[18] Attempts were made throughout the summer of 1644 to destroy or to reduce the marauding forces of Ashby and Belvoir, and, although some success was achieved, it was insufficient to repress the royalists; the Roundheads' most important achievement was the victory of the parliamentary forces under General Fairfax and Colonel Gell in the Vale of Belvoir,[19] but the expected consequence—the fall of Belvoir—did not ensue. Moreover, this success was quickly overshadowed by a brilliant royalist cavalry victory at Melton Mowbray, where Sir Marmaduke Langdale, on his way north to relieve Pontefract Castle, overcame Colonel Rossiter, who tried to intercept him.[20]

As yet no serious warfare had touched Leicestershire and there is a very amateur air about the skirmishes and ambushes between the Hastingses and the Greys, but in 1645 more serious events were at hand. It was suspected that the royalists were planning an attack on Leicester itself, the state of whose defences gave cause for alarm. Colonel George Booth wrote to Lord Grey from Leicester in April 1645, stressing the weakness of the garrison and the inability of the town to withstand a siege—'500 resolute well-managed soldiers could at any

---

[11] Clarendon, *Hist. of Rebellion*, vi, 275.
[12] Nichols, *Leics.* ii, 51; *C.J.* iii, 333; Hist. MSS. Com., *Hastings*, ii, 109.
[13] B. Whitelocke, *Mem. of Engl. Affairs* (1682), 78.
[14] Nichols, *Leics.* iii, App. iv, 34; J. Vicars, *God's Ark*, 169–70.
[15] *L.J.* vi, 144.   [16] *Cal. S.P. Dom., 1644*, 229.
[17] *C.J.* iii, 618.
[18] Nichols, *Leics.* iii, App. iv, 36–39; Whitelocke, *Mem. of Engl. Affairs* (1682), 105.
[19] Nichols, op. cit. iii, App. iv, 38; Whitelocke, op. cit. 105; *C.J.* iii, 682.
[20] *Mercurius Aulicus*, 2–9 Mar., 1645; *Moderate Intelligencer*, 27 Feb.–6 Mar. 1645.

time make themselves masters of this town'. The defenders consisted of ill-disciplined men; the townsfolk were dissatisfied with the Government, for the 'Grand Masters' (presumably the members of the Leicester Committee) fortified their own houses in the Newarke but left the rest of the town undefended. This letter provoked the Committee of both Kingdoms to advise the Leicester Committee to put their defences in order.[21] This they tried to do but time was denied them.[22] Charles was forced to take action in order to draw off Fairfax, who had begun to besiege Oxford, and having joined his army with Rupert's he was strong enough to tackle Leicester. On 27 May the king was at Ashby, on the 28th he spent the night at Cotes, the home of Sir Henry Skipwith, on the 29th he was at Aylestone, and the siege began.[23] The royalist forces numbered about 5,520.[24] There is no very reliable figure for the garrison, but probably it was fewer than 2,000.[25]

On Thursday 29 May the main body of the king's army approached and a skirmish took place, but the Leicester forces had to withdraw to the town.[26] On Thursday night or Friday Rupert set up a battery of six guns directed on the weak places in the defences. These were pointed out by royalists who had escaped from Leicester during the night.[27] On the same day Rupert sent in generous conditions of surrender, considering the disparity of the forces.[28] While the Leicester Committee were still discussing their answer the time allowed by Rupert ran out, and he commenced the bombardment of the town at three o'clock on Friday, 30 May.[29] By night wide breaches were made in the walls, 'which by the industry of the men and women of the town were some of them made up again with Wool-packs and other materials'.[30] The repairs were inadequate; the breach considered practicable; at midnight twenty companies of the Royalist infantry advanced against the town. A desperate defence of great valour was conducted by Sir Robert Pye and Major Innes at the Newarke, Captains Babington and Hacker at the West Bridge, and Colonel Grey and Lieutenant-Colonel Whitbrooke at Eastgates and St. Margaret's churchyard.[31] The resistance was finally concentrated at the Newarke breach. Here, as one of the defenders afterwards wrote,

'was the fiercest assault, the enemy there comming to push off Pike, four times they attempted and were as often repulst, our men taking two of their Colors from them. Captain Hacker and Captain Babington with their horse and a cannon from a corner of the wall made a miserable slaughter of them; amongst the rest Colonell St. George in a bravery came up to our cannon, and was by it shatter'd into small parcels, and with him many more, for after the manner of the Turks, the horse forced on the foot to fight, they being beaten upon by our Musketteers, great slaughter was made of them.'[32]

About the same time the royalists by use of hand grenades forced an entrance at the Eastgates and 'the horse being come in they rid with a full career in a body of about 600 up the streets, clearing them as they went, and so to the Newarke, and coming upon the backs of our forces there, they fighting gallantly and defending the breach, there was no way left but to submit upon quarter, which they did'.[33]

[21] B.M. Pamphs., E. 261 (3); *Cal. S.P. Dom., 1644–5*, 434.
[22] B.M. Pamphs., E. 289 (6). [23] *Somers Tracts*, v, 271 (*Iter Carolinum*).
[24] H. Symonds, *Diary*, 182. [25] Ibid., loc. cit.; B.M. Pamphs., E. 289 (6).
[26] B.M. Pamphs., E. 289 (6) ('Narration of the seige and taking of the town of Leicester').
[27] Ibid., E. 288 (4) ('Perfect Relation of the taking of Leicester'); Symonds, *Diary*, 179.
[28] B.M. Pamphs., E. 289 (6), loc. cit. [29] Symonds, *Diary*, 179.
[30] B.M. Pamphs., E. 288 (4), loc. cit. [31] J. F. Hollings, *Civil War in Leics.* 46.
[32] B.M. Pamphs., E. 289 (6), loc. cit. [33] Ibid.

In the heat of victory the royalists sacked the town, and exaggerated reports of the carnage were rapidly circulated. Charles I, in one account, was described as urging his troops on to greater bloodshed,[34] and Whitelocke wrote that 'they gave no quarter but hanged some of the committee and cut others in pieces. Some letters say the kennels ran down with blood'.[35] One newspaper, however, reported that it was the Irish who were the most desperate assailants, though, it was added, they did no more hurt than 'what was done in a heat'.[36] Also, a Puritan pamphleteer wrote, 'give the divell his due, there was indeed many slaine at the first enterance and some that made little resistance and some women and children amongst the multitude, by the rabble of common souldiers, but I cannot learne of any such order to destroy all, as is said by some'.[37] Nevertheless carnage there was, for Clarendon reports that it was 'exceeding regretted' by Charles.[38]

The plunder was vast; 140 cartloads of goods were sent off to Lichfield, Belvoir, and Newark, and at their own estimate the parliamentarians admitted losing 9 pieces of ordnance, 1,000 muskets, 400 horses, and about 50 barrels of powder.[39] The king was elated, for the prestige of the victory was very great, and, much to the consternation of Parliament, the parliamentary garrisons at Bagworth, Coleorton, Kirby Bellars, and Burghley House promptly deserted their posts.[40] Recriminations of prophetic intensity were hurled at the wretched Leicester Committee.[41] Fairfax promptly abandoned the siege of Oxford, and strengthened by the addition of Cromwell with 600 horse marched north to engage the king.[42]

The decisive battle of the war was nearly fought in Leicestershire. Having reprovisioned Oxford, the king occupied a strong defensive position on carefully chosen ground at Market Harborough. When Rupert's scouts, however, reported that Fairfax, who was encamped 6 miles away at Gilsborough, was retreating, Charles incautiously moved into Northamptonshire, to find himself at a disadvantage of ground at Naseby. Parliament's victory was total, and 'magnanimous Lieutenant General Cromwell pursued their horse with a full carrier about 12 or 13 miles at least, even within 2 or 3 miles of Leicester, the longest pursuite that ever was since this unhappy Warre began'.[43] According to tradition the king and Prince Rupert stopped in their flight at Wistow Hall, the home of Sir Richard Halford, in order to obtain plain saddles which would not betray their rank. They left their richly decorated ones behind, to be a memento in the Halford family of faithful service and loyal hospitality. The king made a short stop at Leicester to see that the wounded were being cared for and then made his way to the Welsh border.[44]

The parliamentary forces rapidly overran south Leicestershire and invested the town, whose royalist governor, Lord Loughborough, had done all in his power to strengthen the defences. But he had only been in command for a fortnight, and, apart from enlisting 400 recruits from the county for garrison work, little had been done.[45] On 16 June Fairfax demanded the surrender of

[34] Nichols, *Leics.* iii, App. iv, 42.
[35] Whitelocke, *Mem. of Engl. Affairs* (1682), 143.
[36] *Moderate Intelligencer*, 5 June 1645.
[37] B.M. Pamphs., E. 288 (4).
[38] Clarendon, *Hist. of Rebellion*, ix, 33.
[39] B.M. Pamphs., E. 288 (4).
[40] *Cal. S.P. Dom., 1644–5*, 551; Nichols, *Leics.* iii, App. iv, 54.
[41] B.M. Pamphs., E. 261 (3).
[42] C. H. Firth, *Cromwell*, 126.
[43] J. Vicars, *Burning Bush not Consumed*, 162.
[44] Clarendon, *Hist. of Rebellion*, ix, 42; W. Gardiner, *Music and Friends*, i, 189.
[45] Nichols, *Leics.* iii, App. iv, 54.

the town but Hastings resolutely refused.[46] Fairfax proceeded to use the siege guns which he had captured at Naseby and bombarded the Newarke.[47] On 17 June Hastings realized that the position was hopeless and asked for a parley. Colonels Rainborough and Pickering were sent in to treat and Hastings accepted their terms.[48] On Wednesday, 18 June, Hastings marched out at the head of his force, but only the cavalry officers were allowed to take out their arms.[49] Hastings was bitterly criticized for surrendering all the guns, arms, ammunition, and provisions at Leicester,[50] an act which led to great rejoicing in Parliament, who voted a day of public thanksgiving, observed on the 19th. A collection was ordered in London churches for the relief of those people of Leicester who had suffered most from the ravages of the royalists.[51]

Although the king's cause was lost, neither Ashby nor Belvoir tamely surrendered to Parliament. Both Lord Loughborough and Colonel Lucas, with their gallant garrisons, were determined to fight to the last. In October Belvoir was besieged by Colonel Pointz.[52] On 21 November he summoned the castle to surrender, but Lucas replied tersely: 'I was not placed here by the King to surrender to rebels. I will not give one inch of ground I am able to maintain with my sword.' The garrison responded to the bravery of its commander. They defended themselves with great courage, and only after a bitter battle were they forced to give up the stables and outworks. 'The works were the strongest I have seen in England', wrote one of the attackers, 'and gallantly defended, and our men at first discouraged so much that the General, myself, and some other officers were fain to keep the men at the works with our swords.'[53] In January 1646 Lord Loughborough made a sortie from Ashby and attempted to relieve Belvoir. Although he surprised the parliamentarians he was unable to break their hold on the castle. After the loss of his outworks and his freshwater supply, it was only a matter of weeks before Colonel Lucas was forced to parley with the envoys from Parliament, one of whom was, naturally enough, the Earl of Rutland. His presence probably secured the honourable terms which were allowed to Lucas in order to avoid the destruction which a final assault would have caused.[54]

Only Ashby remained. With the county very largely under parliamentary control, it became very difficult for the garrison to secure supplies. The castle was closely besieged from September 1645,[55] and, although it was reinforced by 600 royalists in October, its fall was only a matter of time.[56] Loughborough finally surrendered to Colonel Needham, the governor of Leicester, on 2 March 1646. The fall of Ashby marks the close of the Civil War in Leicestershire.[57] That was obvious to all men.

What was less obvious was that it also marked the fall of a great family. The surrender terms demanded that the castle was to be 'slighted' and stripped of all means of defence, which was carried out later, in or after 1648.[58] Never again was Ashby to be the seat and stronghold of the Hastings family. Even

[46] Whitelocke, *Mem. of Engl. Affairs* (1682), 146.
[47] Nichols, *Leics.* iii, App. iv, 57; Vicars, *Burning Bush*, 171.
[48] Vicars, *Burning Bush*, 172.
[49] Nichols, *Leics.* iii, App. iv, 57.
[50] Whitelocke, *Mem. of Engl. Affairs* (1682), 146.
[51] *C.J.* iv, 175.
[52] *Cal. S.P. Dom. 1645*, 177.
[53] Nichols, *Leics.* ii, 56.
[54] Ibid. ii, 57–58.
[55] Ibid. iii, App. iv, 65.
[56] Ibid. 65–66.
[57] *Cal. S.P. Dom., 1645–7*, 352; H. N. Bell, *Huntingdon Peerage*, 124–5, for the articles of surrender.
[58] Nichols, *Leics.* iii, 611–12.

before the Civil War that family had begun to live more frequently at Donnington Park and afterwards they lived there permanently.[59] Although Loughborough prevented the sequestration of both his own estates and those of his brother, Lord Huntingdon, yet the wealth of both was seriously diminished by subsequent fines.[60] But more than all of this was the loss of prestige. Many of their followers were not so lucky and their estates were lost, and further support of Hastings held out little hope of recovery or reward.[61] It was natural that the Hastingses should be proud of their devotion to the royalist cause and so develop a tradition of uncritical loyalty to the Stuarts. Theophilus, the 7th earl, was imprisoned for his Jacobite sympathies.[62] This attachment to a lost cause resulted in a steady decline in their political prestige in Leicestershire, and after the Civil War no member of the Hastings family ever represented either the county or the borough of Leicester in Parliament, both of which had been almost their private preserves for a century. Yet in political structure the century which followed the Civil War differed little from that which went before. Aspiring men needed the patronage of a great man or family. The men of Leicestershire turned naturally to the Greys, earls of Stamford, the successful rivals of the Hastingses, and also, and more effectively, to the Mannerses, earls of Rutland, who, after the Civil War, devoted far more time to their Leicestershire interests. In 1668 Belvoir Castle was reconstructed and became their chief home, and from that time they began to exercise a power nearly as extensive as that wielded previously by the Hastingses.

The shape of things to come was indicated in August 1648, when Lord Grey of Groby was made Governor of Ashby Castle during the scare caused by the Second Civil War, which did not touch Leicestershire.[63] Later he was granted £1,500 out of Crown lands because he had been 'very zealous in forwarding Parliamentary interests' in Leicestershire.[64] Another £1,500 was granted to the Earl of Rutland to recompense him for the demolition of Belvoir.[65]

The invasion of Charles II in 1651 made great demands on the military resources of the midland counties. Lord Grey was ordered to raise volunteers in Leicester, Nottingham, and Rutland to march against Charles.[66] They were quickly raised and they fought under him at the battle of Worcester, for which Grey received the thanks of the Council of State.[67]

Leicestershire was undisturbed by royalist plots or insurrections during the Commonwealth, and a loyal address was sent to Richard Cromwell from the 'well-affected inhabitants of the county of Leicester' on the death of Oliver Cromwell.[68] But as the Commonwealth dissolved in anarchy, conditions in Leicestershire became more turbulent. In August 1659, when 300 volunteer horse had left Leicester to tackle the rising of the royalists in Cheshire, the Earl of Stamford declared for the king, and Major Babington of Rothley Temple, another Roundhead who had changed his principles, gathered together two or three hundred men in arms. These, however, were easily dispersed by the militia and he himself was taken prisoner.[69] Stamford and Babington had been

[59] Hist. MSS. Com., *Hastings*, ii, 70, 141.
[60] *Cal. Committee for Compounding*, 1043; Hist. MSS. Com., *Hastings*, ii, 138.
[61] Hist. MSS. Com., *Hastings*, ii, 138.
[62] Hist. MSS. Com., *Hastings*, ii, 211–12.
[63] *C.J.* v, 692.
[64] Ibid. vi, 248.
[65] *Cal. S.P. Dom.*, *1649–50*, 180.
[66] Ibid. *1651*, 323.
[67] Ibid. *1651–2*, 39, 98.
[68] Nichols, *Leics.* iii, App. iv, 68–69.
[60] *Cal. S.P. Dom.*, *1659–60*, 77, 114, 120, 125.

wise only a little before their time and in less than twelve months (12 May 1660) Charles II was proclaimed in Leicester. The county celebrated wholeheartedly; at Melton Mowbray an ox was roasted in the streets; and 'ringing of bells, volleys of shot, bonfires, music and dancing and all the usual ways of expressing so great a joy continued three days'.[70] But there were few who lost, or gained, by the change. Sir Arthur Hazlerigg, excluded from the Act of Oblivion, died in the Tower.[71] Lord Loughborough was restored to the lord-lieutenancy of the county in 1661 but to little else, and on his death it passed to the Earl of Rutland, in whose family it remained with scarcely a break for the next 200 years.[72]

After the Restoration the pattern of Leicestershire politics was soon made clear. Lord Roos, the eldest son of the Earl of Rutland, was returned for the county with George Faunt of Foston.[73] This division of representation between the aristocracy and the gentry was usual for the next 150 years, and electoral peace was only disturbed when the aristocracy tried to secure both seats for themselves or on those rarer occasions when party or personal feelings ran so high that a contest became inevitable. In the election of 1679 Lord Roos joined with Lord Sherrard, but they were immediately opposed by Sir John Hartopp of Rotherby. Hartopp had married the daughter of General Fleetwood: he was a known friend of Nonconformists and his whiggery was far more ardent than that of Sherrard or Roos: indeed, the latter was associated with the Court. Nevertheless, in Hartopp's opposition there was a social as well as a political protest, an expression of the resentment felt by the smaller gentry at the prospect of both seats going to sons of the nobility. The sheriff was cautious and returned Roos and Sherrard, but Hartopp's supporters petitioned against the return. In the House of Commons Roos's election was declared void by 116 to 78 and a new election ordered.[74] The Commons did not bother to consider a counter-petition against Hartopp,[75] who was returned, presumably unopposed, at the subsequent election.[76] Sherrard and Hartopp continued to represent the county throughout the Exclusion Parliaments. The crisis about the succession, and the fears aroused by the Popish plot, appear to have touched Leicestershire but little.

The defeat of Shaftesbury and the Whig débâcle which followed the exposure of the Rye House Plot brought a slight change in political forces. The earls of Rutland moved quietly and discreetly with events. They were regarded for a time as loyal by James II,[77] but the earls of Stamford lost face and their position was taken by the earls of Huntingdon, who enjoyed a brief Indian summer of political influence.[78] At the election of 1685 Hartopp was dropped

[70] J. Thompson, *Hist. of Leic.*, 419; Nichols, *Leics.* ii, 246.

[71] *D.N.B.*; 12 Chas. II, c. 11.

[72] *Cal. S.P. Dom.*, *1667*, 452; Hist. MSS. Com., *12th Rep.*, *App.* v, *Rut.* ii, 14, 54.

[73] *Return of Members of Parl.*, H.C., 69 (1878), lxii (1). The Faunts had played a discreet part in the Civil War. In 1660 Geo. Faunt was worth more than £2,000 p.a. and was a prospective Kt. of the Royal Oak: Nichols, *Leics.* iv, 170. He was also a commissioner of the Leics. militia in 1660: *Acts and Ord. of Interr.*, ed. Firth and Rait, ii, 1434.

[74] *C.J.* ix, 577, 596–7, 598; *Cal. S.P. Dom.*, *1679–80*, 120. Voting was: Lord Sherrard 2,585, Lord Roos 2,389, Sir John Hartopp 1,831.

[75] Ibid. 616.

[76] *Return of M.P.s.*

[77] Hist. MSS. Com., *8th Rep.*, *App.*, pt. 1, sect. ii, 440.

[78] Theophilus, 7th Earl of Huntingdon, was made Captain of the Band of Gentlemen Pensioners 27 June 1682, and a Privy Councillor 28 Feb. 1683; Hist. MSS. Com., *Hastings*, ii, 349, 173; *Hastings*, iv, 220. Cf. also *D.N.B.* In 1685 the Huntingdon influence once more made itself powerfully felt in Leic.: Leic. City MSS., Hall Bks. xix, Nos. 197, 200, 202.

and his place taken by a young Tory lawyer, John Verney, the son of Sir Richard Verney of Allexton who afterwards on his son's advice claimed and obtained the dormant barony of de Broke.[79] Passionately royalist as the Parliament of 1685 was, it was nevertheless not royalist enough for James II, who began to develop the political revolution started by his brother. Both Charles II and James II realized that they could never secure complete toleration for Roman Catholics until the control of local government was in the hands of their supporters. Borough after borough was made to forfeit its charters—Leicester's went in 1684—and the new ones issued usually reserved considerable powers of appointment to the Crown and the right of election of a Member of Parliament restricted to the corporation, which was easier to control.[80] The turn of county government followed; the method employed was to remove strong Whig justices of the peace and replace them by Roman Catholics or Protestant dissenters. The same was done with the deputy lieutenants. In order to facilitate this process in Leicestershire, the Earl of Rutland, the Whig tradition of whose family made him unreliable, was dismissed from the lord-lieutenancy and replaced by the Earl of Huntingdon, an uncompromising royalist.[81] By the spring of 1688 the process was considered to have gone far enough for James to call a new Parliament, but he was determined to be certain of his members on the issue of toleration. The lord-lieutenants were instructed to question all their deputies and justices as to whether they would support the repeal of the Test and Penal Laws. If they answered unfavourably they were to be dismissed from office and every step taken to prevent their election to Parliament. Huntingdon carried out this investigation for Leicestershire in February 1688 and made his return to James.[82] His deputy lieutenants, Sir Thomas Burton of Stockerston, Sir Henry Beaumont of Stoughton, Sir William Holford of Welham, Richard Roberts of Thorpe Langton, and Henry Nevill of Holt, all carefully chosen for their loyalty, agreed, but apart from one justice, Dr. William Foster, little other support was forthcoming from the county gentry. Many such as the Abneys, Verneys, Noels, and Packes were discreetly absent from the county during the inquiry; but Sherrards, Babingtons, Hazleriggs, Boothbys, de la Fontaines, and others flatly refused. There could be no doubt that the most powerful political families in the county were steadfastly opposed to James's policy.[83]

It was the removal of so many country gentlemen from the bench and the militia which made the Revolution of 1689 inevitable and success easy for William III. Stamford, Rutland, Ferrars, and Sherrard all attended in November 1688 on the Princess Anne as she passed through Leicestershire on her way to join the northern lords at Nottingham.[84] In the county the Revolution was accomplished easily but not without incident. Fears of the Irish put the county in a state of alarm on 12 December 1688,[85] and so disturbed were conditions in January 1689 that soldiers had to accompany the collectors of customs and

---

[79] *Return of M.P.s*; *Complete Peerage* (1896 ed.), 152. The Earl of Rut. was asked by the king to manage the county election: Hist. MSS. Com., *12th Rep.*, *App. v, Rut.*, ii, 85–86.

[80] Chas. II was so certain of Leic. that the franchise was in fact widened: cf. R. W. Greaves, *Corp. of Leic.*, *1689–1836*, 8.

[81] Sir Geo. Duckett, *Penal Laws and Test Act*, i, 95; Hist. MSS. Com., *Hastings*, iv, 220.

[82] The replies for Leics. are printed by Duckett, op. cit. 98–107.

[83] Ibid.

[84] Hist. MSS. Com., *Hastings*, ii, 211.

[85] Ibid.; *Leic. Boro. Rec., 1603–88*, 593–5.

excise.[86] After James II's flight, William called a Convention which after his acceptance of the Crown declared itself to be a Parliament. Elections to this assembly had been rushed and many men were returned who would have been returned had James called a Parliament. This was partly true of Leicestershire. Sir Thomas Halford, an ardent Tory, was returned for the county, along with Bennet, Lord Sherrard. Halford, with Babington, one of the members for the town, refused to vote for the motion offering the Crown to William and Mary.[87]

The Revolution of 1689 opened a new era in Leicestershire politics. From this date Parliaments have met every year, and one of the easiest ways to social and political success has been through service in the House of Commons. The control of membership added greatly to the prestige of the aristocracy, who cultivated parliamentary electors as carefully as their pheasants. This attempt to dominate completely the political life of the county bred resentment amongst the lesser gentry. By mutual support they became powerful enough to win one county seat and to maintain their hold on it. As Leicestershire was poorly provided with seats in Parliament, the borough representation was quickly dominated by the leading county families and the parliamentary politics of the borough were very largely an extension of those of the county. As the king's agent phrased it in February 1688: 'there are none of the Members of the Corporation of Leicester proper to stand for Parliament men, either for quality, fortune or interest, especially in a County where there are so few Elections.'[88] But the corporation did not suffer: members of county families were as attentive to the special interests of Leicester as any corporation member would have been. They were always ready to present petitions on behalf of the town.[89] In the same way, of course, the county members looked after any matter which touched the life of the county, and in return they expected the county to make loyal addresses when the occasion arose so that they themselves would not seem to be lacking in loyalty.[90]

For much of the 18th century the politics of Leicester followed a placid course, members and electors pursuing harmoniously their mutual interests, but there were occasions when there was a sudden flare-up of political strife and this was very common from 1689 to 1722. In 1695 the peace of the county was disturbed, for the Duke of Devonshire considered setting up his son as a candidate.[91] On the other hand Thomas, Earl of Stamford, was confident that he had secured complete control of both the county and the town.[92] Events proved otherwise. Stamford secured a seat for one of his clients, George Ashby of Quenby, but Rutland was powerful enough to keep his hold on the other for the Hon. John Verney. Devonshire had to place his sons elsewhere.[93] Stamford, although defeated, was determined in 1698 to try once more. 'I find my

---

[86] Hist. MSS. Com., *12th Rep., App.* ii, *Earl Cowper*, ii, 345.

[87] K. Feiling, *Hist. of Tory Party, 1660–1714,* 497. T. Babington's politics were rather unstable. He had been Huntingdon's candidate in 1685 (Leic. City MSS., Hall Bks., xix, no. 202); in Feb. 1688 he refused to support the repeal of the Test Act (Duckett, *Penal Laws,* i, 104), yet a year later he supported Jas. II; but once more, in 1690, he turned militant Whig and voted for the Sacheverell Clause. He lived at Rothley Temple and was the ancestor of Lord Macaulay.　　　　　　　　　　　　　　　[88] Duckett, op. cit. i, 105.

[89] Greaves, *Corp. of Leic., 1689–1836,* 90–91; *Cal. S.P. Dom., 1700–2,* 596.

[90] On 2 May 1721 the county presented a petition demanding punishment of the South Sea directors: *C.J.,* ix, 533; whereas in 1753 the county members were very attentive over the Ashby Turnpike Bill: *C.J.* xxvi, 531, 536, 543, 597, 622, 633.

[91] Duke of Rut. MSS., at Belvoir Castle, vol. xxi, Duke of Devonshire to Earl of Rut., 19 Sept. 1695.

[92] Hist. MSS. Com., *Downshire,* ii, 560.

[93] *Return of M.P.s;* Duke of Rut. MSS., at Belvoir Castle, vol. xxi, John Verney to Earl of Rut., 25 May 1698.

Ld. Stamford', wrote Verney to the Earl of Rutland, 'is resolved to have a poll in Leicestershire again for Mr. Bird and Mr. Ashby will stand. I am sorry I am like to be the occasion of more trouble to your Lordship having given you more than all my services to you can ever deserve.'[94] At this election the gentry were not prepared to stand by and watch Stamford and Rutland fight it out. They had their own candidate in John Wilkins of Ravenstone, a Tory squire, related through his wife to the Caves and the Villierses, both powerful families among the independent gentry. Rutland managed to secure the election of Verney but Stamford failed with Ashby and Bird.[95] The gentry succeeded with Wilkins. Stamford did not take kindly to his eclipse, and in the next election the county was threatened with a further contest, but in the end the same members were returned.[96] This Parliament lasted but a few months and the county was plunged into a violent contest in which old friends were parted and new alliances made. The trouble began with Lord Roos, Rutland's eldest son. The removal of the family home from Haddon Hall to Belvoir Castle had lowered Roos's interest in Derbyshire, and he was so frightened of defeat that he insisted on his father backing him for Leicestershire.[97] At the mayor's feast at Leicester on 18 November Roos declared his intention of standing for the county and joined with Lord Sherrard, a young man of 24, who had just succeeded his father and was already Lord-Lieutenant of Rutland.[98] This was an outrageous action on the part of the aristocracy and aroused great anger among the gentry. Verney immediately deserted his patron, the Earl of Rutland, and set up in opposition. He joined with Sir George Beaumont, a sound Tory; Wilkins too was a candidate.[99] The loss of Verney and his friends to the Rutland interest was offset by the gain of George Ashby and Bird, who now became ardent supporters of Lord Roos.[1] Yet so complex were the political alignments of this time that many of Rutland's supporters in the county were very strongly opposed to his choice for the town, James Winstanley.[2] But Rutland was overwhelmingly triumphant; the two lords were returned for the county, and both his clients, James Winstanley and Lawrence Carter, secured the representation of the town. It was the most complete victory ever achieved by the Rutlands, equalling the triumphs of the Hastingses in the days of Elizabeth, but it was never repeated. This aristocratic domination was bitterly resented, and as soon as William III died Verney and Wilkins were busily canvassing the county. Once more Roos joined with Sherrard, but the resentment felt by the squirearchy was too strong for them and Verney and Wilkins were returned.[3] Roos did not venture to contest the county again until 1710 and Verney remained a member until his death in 1707.[4] In 1702 the Rutland

[94] *Return of M.P.s.:* Duke of Rut. MSS., at Belvoir Castle, vol. xxi, John Verney to Earl of Rut., 25 May 1698.

[95] *Return of M.P.s.* Wilkins was married to Rebecca, dau. of Wm. Wollaston of Shenton, whose mother was a Cave and whose grandmother was the widow of a Villiers: Nichols, *Leics.* iv, 541. Wilkins was one of the first to exploit the Leics. coalfield on a large scale: ibid. iii, 932–3, 1125.

[96] *Return of M.P.s*; Hist. MSS. Com., *12th Rep., App.* ii, *Earl Cowper*, ii, 408, 419.

[97] Duke of Rut. MSS., at Belvoir Castle, vol. xxi, Lord Roos to Earl of Rut., 13 Nov. 1701.

[98] Hist. MSS. Com., *13th Rep., App.* ii, *Portland*, ii, 181; *Complete Peerage*, vi, 295.

[99] Hist. MSS. Com., *12th Rep., App.* ii, *Earl Cowper*, ii, 440; Duke of Rut. MSS., at Belvoir Castle, vol. xxi, Ambrose Phillipps to Earl of Rut., 18 Nov. 1701.

[1] Duke of Rut. MSS., at Belvoir Castle, vol. xxi, letters of Geo. Ashby to Earl of Rut., 17–19 Nov. 1701. Ashby received half a doe from Rutland on 19 Nov.

[2] Duke of Rut. MSS., at Belvoir Castle, vol. xxi, letters of Ambrose Phillipps to Earl of Rut., 18 Nov. 1701, and Geo. Ashby to Earl of Rut., 19 Nov. 1701. Probably because Winstanley had Tory leanings.

[3] *Return of M.P.s.*   [4] *Complete Peerage* (1896 ed.), 152.

interest was partly defeated at Leicester itself, Sir George Beaumont of Stoughton Grange, a firm Tory, capturing a seat from Lawrence Carter.[5] At the by-election which followed Verney's death George Ashby was returned unopposed,[6] but this was because Parliament had almost completed its three years. At the general election of 1708 Ashby joined with Sir Gilbert Pickering, Bt., another Whig, related to the important clan of Wortley Montagu. Although Pickering was successful, Ashby was defeated and Geoffrey Palmer of Carlton Curlieu, a sound Tory, was elected in his place. A petition attacking Palmer for bribery and corruption was presented by Ashby's supporters, but the House of Commons refused to take cognizance of it.[7] In 1710 Lord Roos, by that time Marquess of Granby, decided to quit his pocket borough of Grantham and stand once again as Knight of the Shire for Leicestershire. In order to facilitate his election Pickering stood down, the Tories were not challenged for the other seat, and the county was spared an election contest.[8] Granby, however, spent only a few months in the Commons, for his father died in 1711 and he removed to the Upper House as the 2nd Duke of Rutland. The Tories decided that there was a chance of obtaining the second seat and they pressed Sir Thomas Cave of Stanford to accept nomination. He did so only to find that another Tory, Captain Tate, was already in the field. 'I must confess', wrote Sir Thomas, ''twould be unhappy to have the Church interest once divided which would be difficult to unite.' Fortunately for Sir Thomas, Tate realized that he lacked influential backing and withdrew.[9] In 1713 the Tories retained their hold, Lord Tamworth, the eldest son of Earl Ferrers, who had been a strong supporter of Cave in 1711, taking the other seat.[10] The Tories had taken advantage of the violent revulsion from the Whigs, caused by the Sacheverell trial, and also of the preoccupation of the Duke of Rutland with his family affairs. But it was inconceivable to the Whigs that the Tories should be allowed to control both seats and a determined challenge was made to defeat them in 1715. Tamworth had succeeded his father as Earl Ferrers and Sir Thomas Cave was joined with Sir Geoffrey Palmer. The Whigs adopted George Ashby and Thomas Bird, who was strongly backed by the Duke of Rutland and Lord Sherrard.[11] The election took place at Leicester Castle on 14 February 1715. The sheriff, Sir John Meeres, was a Whig. He prevaricated and made the election as difficult as possible for the Tories and then refused to make a return on the ground that it was not possible to conclude the election owing to 'tantas riotas, routas, affraias, tumultus, et perturbationes'.[12] The sheriff's refusal caused a great stir in London and filled the newspapers.[13] To try and strengthen their position the Whigs petitioned the Commons, maintaining that William Baresby, the under-sheriff and a Tory, had refused over 600 of their votes.[14] Eager as the House of Commons was in 1715 to secure the return of Whig members, the behaviour

[5] Immediately afterwards, no doubt out of pique, the Earl of Rut. refused to recommend Beaumont for a deputy-lieutenancy: *Cal. S.P. Dom., 1702–3*, 339.

[6] If we are to believe his memorial tablet in Hungerton ch., he was elected 'without any expence to himself or family'. [7] *C.J.* xxi, 22.

[8] *Return of M.P.s*; Hist. MSS. Com., *12 Rep., App.* v, *Rut.*, ii, 190.

[9] Margaret, Lady Verney, *Verney Letters of 18th Century*, i, 323–4.

[10] Ibid., loc. cit.

[11] Ibid. i, 325. 'Bird is supplied from above, for to be sure he has not of his own, his interest is the Duke of Rutland's and Lord Sherrard's so they must support him.' [12] *C.J.* xviii, 21–22.

[13] Lady Verney, *Verney Letters*, i, 329. Cf. also 'A True State of the Proc. at the Leics. Election', B.M. Historic Tracts, T. 1700 (1), probably written by Cave: Verney, loc. cit.

[14] *C.J.* xviii, 21–22.

of the sheriff had been so outrageous and the evidence for Cave and Palmer so strong that the best that they could do for Ashby and Bird was to order a new writ for a fresh election.[15] The Tories hoped to avoid a new contest, but Ashby and Bird demanded a poll, which lasted three days. Lord Keeper Wright stayed in Leicester throughout the contest 'lest tricks should be played'. He was an ardent Tory who 'protests to spend his blood and estate before this country shall be nos'd by any Duke in Christendom'.[16] The county agreed with Wright, and, when the poll was cast up, there were 2,251 votes for Sir Geoffrey Palmer, 2,203 for Sir Thomas Cave, 1,639 for Bird, and 1,630 for Ashby.[17] Undoubtedly the desire of the Duke of Rutland and Lord Sherrard to dominate Leicestershire politics caused widespread resentment. But it was difficult for the Tories to maintain this success. The great Whig nobleman had a great attraction for the ordinary freeholder. The nobleman could oblige the freeholder in a hundred and one different ways. He could also be a dangerous enemy.[18] When Sir Thomas Cave suddenly died in 1719, Lord William Manners was put up to represent the Rutland interest. To oppose him was a more audacious act than to oppose candidates merely supported by the Duke of Rutland. In consequence the Tories failed against him and although they petitioned the Commons on behalf of Francis Mundy, accusing the deputy-lieutenants, justices of the peace, and the sheriff of corrupt, arbitrary, and illegal proceedings, they had so little faith in their own case that they asked the Commons to allow them to withdraw their petition.[19]

At the election of 1722 a curious situation arose. Between 1689 and 1705 Leicester borough elections had been partly controlled by the great county families, but the decision of the Commons in 1705 to allow non-resident freemen a vote increased the electorate considerably and made the elections more difficult to manage. Until 1768 the town returned ardent Tories, unsympathetic to the Whig aristocratic families.[20] Leicester, of course, had many freeholders who had a vote in the county, and in 1722 they put up their own Tory candidate, James Wigley, in opposition to Lord William Manners and Edmund Morris. Wigley only had backing from the town and the sheriff refused a poll, probably on the ground that the issue of the election was clear from a view of the voters. The sheriff's refusal resulted in a petition by the corporation's most ardent Tories—Gabriel Newton, Samuel Bull, and Thomas Johnston—but it is interesting that none of the Tory gentlemen of standing in the county supported them.[21] The gentry had been content to divide the representation with the Whigs, for Morris was a Tory. No doubt it was resentment at this deal which had caused the Tories of the borough to run their own candidate.

Amicable arrangements between Whig and Tory, alternating with attempts by one side or the other to capture both seats—this represents the

---

[15] C.J. xviii, 22. Sir Thomas Cave's account of the election is to be found in Margaret, Lady Verney, *Verney Letters*, i, 327–30.   [16] Verney, op. cit. 332–3.   [17] Ibid. 333.

[18] Hist. MSS. Com., *14th Rep., App.* i, *Rut.*, iii, 1. 'Sir Thomas Cave interceding for Mr. Wright of Eaton says that he is to be discharged from the lands he holds of the Duke because he would have voted for Cave at the last election': 19 Dec. 1771.

[19] C.J. xix, 217, 251; Hist. MSS. Com., *12th Rep., App.* v, *Rut.*, ii, 193. The contest was extremely close. Manners polled 2,691, Mundy 2,684: Leics. County Rec. Off., *Poll Bk. of 1719*.

[20] Greaves, *Corp. of Leic.*, 100, 104.

[21] C.J. xx, 39. Wigley obtained his revenge in 1737 when he was elected for Leic., defeating the Whig aristocrat's candidate, T. Ruding of Westcotes: Greaves, op. cit. 101.

LORD JOHN MANNERS

SIR ARTHUR HAZLERIGG

pattern of Leicestershire politics until the end of the century. There were contested elections in 1734 and 1741; at the latter an Ashby still forlornly battled against a Cave.[22] After that there was peace until the by-election of 1775 when the Duke of Rutland and the Earl of Huntingdon ran opposing candidates—William Pochin, Whig, and John Hungerford, Tory. A bitter contest ensued but the Tory finally carried the day.[23] For the general election of 1780 the Duke of Rutland made great efforts to secure agreement between the parties in order to avoid the expense of an election. This was done, and Pochin and Hungerford were returned.[24]

But times were changing. Throughout the 18th century the Whig aristocracy and the Tory squirearchy had used the grievances and prejudices of the working class for their own purposes.[25] Very frequently the Rutlands, Stamfords, and Harboroughs had allied themselves with the stocking-frame knitters against the Tory corporation of Leicester.[26] In fact this had become the tradition of Leicestershire politics. It was broken in the first place by the French Revolution; according to a contemporary, 'the Whig families and landowners of this county soon surrendered all their former notions of liberty, and joined the Tories in supporting the old governments in their abuses'.[27] But an equally important factor in breaking up this traditional pattern of politics was the change caused in the balance of social forces by the widespread development of stocking-frame knitting[28] and the increased exploitation of the Leicestershire coalfield. These two factors created industrial villages in the county and gave rise to a class of capitalists, bankers, merchants, and manufacturers such as the Pagets, Pareses, Frewens, or Coltmans. This new class looked to liberalism and radicalism, to free trade and Free Church, to solve the problems of the dangerous social ferment of the early 19th century.[29]

The first effect of the change in county elections was to make both the aristocracy and the squirearchy unwilling to allow their differences to go to the length of a disputed election, and a contest did not take place until 1818. During these years the military history of the county is of greater interest than its parliamentary politics.

The fears of an invasion from France in the Seven Years War led to a revival and reorganization of the national militia, which had been neglected during the long period of peace. The new militia law of 1757 fixed a quota of 560 men for Leicestershire to be raised by ballot.[30] After a reluctant start the militia by 1760 was fully constituted and formed into two companies under the command of the lord-lieutenant, the Duke of Rutland.[31] But the fears of the French Revolution and of Napoleon led to far greater military activity in the

[22] Lady Verney, *Verney Letters*, ii, 253. The poll was: Smith 2,722, Cave 2,536, Ashby 1,744. In 1734 2 Tories were returned, Lord Wm. Manners being defeated. No doubt this was because of his support of Walpole and excise. For the election, cf. Leic. City Mun. Room, Hastings MSS., Bundle 18, Ambrose Phillipps to the Earl of Huntingdon, 9 Dec. 1733.

[23] *Memoirs of the Late Contested Election for the County of Leicester*; *Return of M.P.s.* The voting was: Hungerford 2,715, Pochin 2,595: Leics. County Rec. Off., *Poll Bk. for 1775.*

[24] Hist. MSS. Com., *14 Rep., App.* i, *Rut.*, iii, 25.

[25] W. Gardiner, *Music and Friends*, i, 207.   [26] Greaves, *Corp. of Leic.*, 101.

[27] Gardiner, *Music and Friends*, i, 209.

[28] There was only one stocking-frame in the town to every 6 in the county: cf. W. Felkin, *Hist. of Machine Wrought Hosiery and Lace Trade*, 177.

[29] C. J. Billson, *Leic. Memoirs*, 19–34; Gardiner, *Music and Friends*, 73–82.

[30] 30 Geo. II, c. 25, s. 16.

[31] S.P. 41/30, ff. 369–70; S.P. 41/31, ff. 13, 25; W.O. 4/759, ff. 16–21. In 1758 and 1759 Rutland received insufficient support in Leics. to create a militia regiment.

county.[32] During the invasion scare of 1803–4 there was very great enthusiasm for the Volunteers. The Leicestershire Yeomanry was formed. The Duke of Rutland offered to raise a corps of infantry, 'The Belvoir Castle Volunteers', consisting of 4 companies of 100 men.[33] Not only did Leicester and the main market towns raise companies of infantry but many smaller villages such as Earl Shilton did likewise.[34] In case the Volunteers should be called away to the coast, the Mayor of Leicester wished to form a local corps for the 'preservation of peace' in the thickly populated districts.[35] The mayor was far-sighted, for the training acquired during these years was to be of great value to the gentlemen of Leicestershire during the turbulence of the Luddite and Chartist agitations.

Leicestershire came comparatively lightly out of the Luddite riots. Conditions throughout the Napoleonic wars had been getting steadily worse for the working classes. The high price of food and the unstable conditions of the stocking-frame trade had led to very frequent distress. In 1800 the Duke of Rutland and the Earl of Stamford were making large donations for the relief of the Leicestershire poor; soup kitchens were opened in Hinckley, but this did not prevent serious riots, in which bakers' shops were attacked.[36] It was these scenes of turbulence, as much as the fear of Napoleon, that encouraged the middle class to volunteer for the yeomanry. By 1812 conditions had deteriorated badly in the midlands. Changes in fashion, over-production, particularly of shoddy goods, and excess labour created conditions of great difficulty in the hosiery trade, and serious frame-breaking manifested itself in Nottinghamshire.[37] It did not spread seriously in Leicestershire, though a few frames were broken, and a correspondent of the *Leicester Journal* boasted that 'in several large village halls the stockingers themselves have come to a resolution that they will have no Ludd's men'.[38] The main activity of the Luddites in Leicestershire was the extortion of money for the support of their cause. In December 1811 collectors were active in Osgathorpe, Hugglescote, and Ibstock.[39] Often the Luddites protected themselves by forcing the sale of copies of the Framework Knitters Act.[40] At the assizes in March 1814 David Walker, Thomas Thorne, and William Plant were found guilty of extorting money in aid of frame-breakers and transported.[41] The secretary of the Committee of Framework Knitters, Thomas Allsop, sent a letter to a leading manufacturer, threatening him with death in the name of Ned Ludd.[42] And finally on 14 May 1812 there was a considerable riot at Loughborough, arising out of a protest about food prices. Only the prompt action of Colonel Boot and the militia prevented serious destruction. The yeomanry was called out until this part of the county

---

[32] There were 15 recruiting centres in Leics. for the volunteer forces between 1794 and 1812; Leicester (1794–1812); Leicester West (1803–8); Allexton (1803–5); Appleby (1803–9); Ashby-de-la-Zouch (1803–5); Belvoir Castle (1803–6); Coleorton (1803–6); Donnington Park (1803–6); Gt. Glen and Gt. Stretton (1803–12); Market Harborough (1803–9); Ibstock (1803–9); Loughborough (1803–8); Melton Mowbray (1803–6); Scraptoft (1803–8); Shepshed and Garendon (1803–6): W.O. 13/4426–7.

[33] H.O. 50/77, Rutland to Home Sec. 27 Aug. 1803.

[34] Ibid. Rutland to Home Sec. 25 and 26 Aug. 1803; Winstanley to Home Sec. 13 Sept. and 10 Oct. 1803.

[35] Ibid. Samuel Smith to John King 6 Nov. 1803.

[36] *Leic. Jnl.* 10 Jan. 1800; 31 Jan. 1800; 14 Feb. 1800; 9 May 1800.

[37] For conditions in the hosiery trade, cf. Felkin, *Hist. of Machine Wrought Hosiery*, and F. O. Darvall, *Popular Disturbances and Public Order in Regency Engl.*

[38] *Leic. Jnl.* 7 Feb. 1812.

[39] Darvall, *Popular Disturbances in Regency Engl.* 71–72.

[40] Ibid.

[41] *Leic. Jnl.* 24 Mar. 1812.

[42] Ibid. 12 and 18 June, 1812.

was peaceful again. Colonel Keck, M.P. for the county, commanded the yeomanry. With the prospect of an election before him, he used the opportunity to address his men on the state of the country and the necessity of maintaining law and order, if need be by force.[43]

For the next four years Leicestershire was free from any serious trouble,[44] but on 29 June 1816 a grave disturbance occurred in Loughborough, at the factory of Heathcote and Bodenz, important bobbin-lace manufacturers. The employees at this factory, whose wages had recently been greatly reduced, suggested to the Loughborough committee of the stockingers that the factory should be attacked. The Loughborough committee borrowed £40 from the 'Warp Lace Committee' of Nottingham, in order to hire what was in effect a semi-professional team of frame-breakers.[45] At one o'clock in the morning,

'The large Bobbin Lace Manufactory of Mr. Heathcote at Loughborough in this county was beset by about 100 men, armed with blunderbusses. One of the six watchmen by which the place was guarded snapped his pistol at them and was immediately shot through the neck; the ball, however, is extracted and he is considered out of danger. They then secured the remainder of the watchmen and compelled 10 men who were at work in the factory to lie down with their faces towards the ground, whilst they destroyed upwards of 50 frames in the short space of 40 minutes. The damage, including the lace cut and burnt, is upwards of £5,000, independent of the loss of business and above 300 hands, in consequence, out of employ.'[46]

This was the most daring and destructive outrage of 1816. The Government acted promptly; dragoons were sent to Loughborough and a reward of 500 guineas offered for the apprehension of any of the Luddites.[47] The ringleaders were quickly arrested. They included James Towle, who had previously been acquitted on a charge of frame-breaking at Nottingham. Towle was extremely popular among the framework knitters and the authorities took great care at his trial at the summer assizes at Leicester. There were threats of disturbances and it was reported that ten men were paid to attempt to kill the judge.[48]

Towle was condemned and, later in the year, executed. His death did nothing to stop the Luddites; indeed, his brother William organized destruction for revenge. But he too was caught and he followed James to the gallows. With him were executed four other Luddites, and three others were transported for life.[49] This mass execution proved a grim and effective warning and it marks the end of Luddite activity in Leicestershire. Trade was improving and at the same time there was a growing hope that conditions would be improved through more orthodox methods of political agitation and negotiation.[50]

At first the new spirit in politics did not touch the county elections. Those of 1790, 1796, 1802, 1806, 1807, and 1812 were decided according to the old pattern—a client or relative of Rutland taking one seat, a Tory the other. In October 1812 there is a letter from Lord Robert Manners to his fellow candidate, George Anthony Leigh Keck of Stoughton Grange, which discusses the election in purely 18th-century terms. Lord Robert writes that the only possible danger to either candidate is that his father may have to put up Pochin, because the Duke is obliged him to for the part he has played in recent considerable sales of

---

[43] Ibid.

[44] In 1814 a few frames were broken at Castle Donnington: ibid. 2 May 1817.

[45] F. O. Darvall, *Popular Disturbances in Regency Engl.*, 184; W. Felkin, *Hist. of Machine Wrought Hosiery*, 237 et seq.   [46] *Leic. Jnl.* 5 July 1816.

[47] Ibid.; Darvall, *Popular Disturbances in Regency Engl.*, 157, citing H.O. 42/152.

[48] Darvall, op. cit. 186. For the elaborate precautions taken at Leic., where 2,000–3,000 special constables were enrolled, cf. *Leic. Jnl.* 17 Aug. 1816.   [49] Ibid. 30 Mar. 1817.

[50] Darvall, *Popular Disturbances in Regency Engl.*, 159.

property. Lord Robert intends to send his freeholders into Leicester—'if you have no objection, to give these freeholders a dinner and supper in a plain way at Stephenson's'. Also his two sons will be there for canvassing; they should have 'some weight with the ladies at heart, being both very tall and very handsome youths'.[51] The dinner and the youths were both unnecessary, for both candidates were returned unopposed.[52] In the correspondence and in the letters of thanks published by the newly elected members there is no mention of the growing turbulence of the county and of the difficulties which faced the lower classes.[53]

In 1818 the election did not run so smoothly. Naturally Keck and Manners stood for re-election. Thomas Babington of Rothley Temple, who had represented the borough for fourteen years, was also adopted. But unexpectedly C. M. Phillipps of Garendon Park was nominated. His supporters were the Pagets, which indicated that his attitude to politics was likely to be independent and liberal.[54] Shortly before the election Keck withdrew on grounds of ill health. Nevertheless a spirited election, 'as determined a contest as the County has ever witnessed', was expected.[55] The election started on the Saturday, and on Monday, 28 June, 'carriages of every description from the elegant barouche to the humble dung cart were put in requisition and came rattling in from all quarters'[56] to Leicester Castle. During the weekend, however, Babington thought better of it and decided to retire from the contest. Anti-Catholic feeling was extremely strong in the county and Babington's vote in favour of the admission of Roman Catholics was held against him.[57] It is true that Phillipps was a Whig, but he was believed to be sound on the Catholic issue.[58] At the chairing of the successful candidates there were scenes of considerable violence. 'The populace', it was said, 'appeared to be seized with a fit of revolutionary frenzy, and upon Lord Robert Manners appearing in the Chair, commenced a most brutal attack upon his person, by a discharge of almost every species of missile accompanied with the most furious gestures and diabolical language.'[59] By the time Lord Robert reached his committee room he was battered, bleeding, and coated with filth.[60] It was one of the few ways open to the unenfranchised to express their attitude to Lord Robert's reactionary opinions. Phillipps regarded his election as a portent, which in some ways it was. He said at the hustings: 'man is no longer the same passive machine he once was; ignorant, unlettered, uninformed. He has begun to think, reflect and reason; and what is knowledge but power? Woe to those who shut their ears to the popular expression of the public voice!' His election cry was 'vox populi, vox dei'.[61] The election of 1818 indicates that the structure of Leicestershire politics was changing. Old rivalries were giving way to new, and coveys of freeholders could not be driven so easily to the polls to vote for their landlord's choice. Even though Phillipps did not feel strong enough to contest the elections of

[51] Leic. City Mun. Room, 109/30/43, Letters to Geo. Anthony Leigh Keck from Lord Robert Manners, 11 Oct. 1812.

[52] *Leic. Jnl.* 13 Oct. 1812. [53] Ibid.

[54] Ibid. 13 June 1818; 24 June 1818. [55] Ibid. 26 June 1818.

[56] Ibid.; Leics. County Rec. Off., *Poll Bk. for 1818.* The poll, on the Saturday night, stood at: Lord Robert Manners, 391; C. M. Phillipps, 307; T. Babington, 257. [57] *Leic. Jnl.* 3 July 1818.

[58] Ibid.; this was before his son became an ardent Roman Catholic: cf. G. B. Pagani, *Life of Revd. Aloysius Gentili,* 192–7.

[59] *Leic. Jnl.*, 3 July 1818. [60] Ibid.

[61] Ibid.

1820 and 1826 against Keck,[62] now recovered in health, nevertheless both Keck and Lord Robert Manners could no longer ignore the working classes as they had done in the past. In their election addresses they went out of their way to express sympathy with the distress which was, at this time, the unhappy lot of manual workers.[63]

With the mounting excitement occasioned by the question of parliamentary reform, the radicals decided once more to attack the county seat. At the election of 1830 Thomas Paget was the candidate but he was unsuccessful against the two die-hard Tories, Keck and Manners, both supported strongly by the Duke of Rutland.[64] Nevertheless Lord Robert Manners's bitter and determined opposition to any reform of the constitution whatsoever lost him considerable support throughout 1831. After thirty-two years in Parliament Keck did not fancy a violent contest in which, owing to the agitation for reform, his chances of success were slender and he retired. Phillipps was nominated in his place, and on Manners's withdrawal the second seat went to another Liberal, Paget.[65] The demand for parliamentary reform was widespread—7,000 persons in Leicestershire signed a petition in favour of the Reform Bill. Meetings of thanksgiving were also held when the Bill was before Parliament.[66] But Leicestershire was largely free from the disturbances which were common in the rest of the country during the passing of the Reform Bill. In October 1831 there was a riot at Loughborough which had to be suppressed by the yeomanry. This led to active recruiting of the yeomanry and to the building up of armament at Belvoir in case of further trouble; but none materialized.[67]

The Reform Act divided the county into two parliamentary constituencies, North and South—a division which lasted until 1885.

Leicestershire returned two Tories, Lord Robert Manners and Henry Halford, and two independents, Charles March Phillipps and Edward Dawson, to the first reformed Parliament. Of the two independents Dawson was the more radical and was the first to go in 1835; he retired from the contest on the advice of his district committees—the first hint we have of Liberal organization in the county. It was almost certainly *ad hoc* and not permanent.[68] Phillipps, although in favour of the Reform Bill, was far less radical than Dawson and he was completely sound on the Church issue, which was one of the most burning political questions in the county. In his election address in 1835, Phillipps made it quite clear that he would not vote for any further change in Church or State, and particularly stressed his disapproval of Lord Althorp's Church Rate Bill and of the suggestion to allow dissenters into the universities.[69] Nevertheless he did not last and in 1837 he was replaced by another Tory, C. W. Packe. Leicestershire continued to return four Tory members for more than twenty years. This was partly due to the superior organization of the Tory party; a permanent conservative society was established in the southern division of the county, where the Liberal danger was greatest. The society held monthly meetings and paid great

---

[62] Ibid. 18 Feb. 1820.   [63] Ibid. 23 June 1826.

[64] Ibid. 13 Aug. 1830; C. J. Billson, *Leic. Memoirs*, 32–33; *Return of Members of Parl.*, H.C. 69 (1878), lxii (1). The voting was: Keck 3,517; Lord Robert Manners 3,000; Paget 2,203: Leics. County Rec. Off., *Poll Bk. for 1830*.

[65] *Leic. Jnl.* 13 May 1831.   [66] Ibid. 1 Apr. 1831; 13 May 1831.

[67] H.O. 52/14, C. G. Mundy to Home Sec. 16 Oct. 1831; Lt. Edwards to Home Sec. 15 Nov. 1831; Rut. to Melbourne 15 Dec. 1831.   [68] *Leic. Jnl.* 16 Jan. 1835.

[69] Ibid. Lord Althorp's Ch. Rate Bill proposed to abolish ch. rates in return for a charge of £250,000 on the land tax: E. L. Woodward, *Age of Reform*, 492.

attention to the register.[70] But the main Tory strength was derived from the hatred of free trade which was naturally widespread in a community which believed that the Corn Laws were the bulwark of agrarian prosperity.[71] Moreover, there is no doubt that many freeholders in Leicestershire voted consistently Tory because of their fear that a Liberal government was bound to undermine the established Church. They had a real horror of both Roman Catholicism and Protestant Dissent and could not tolerate the idea of any concessions to either party. In July 1847 a public meeting of freeholders and parliamentary voters was held at Melton Mowbray at which the following resolutions were passed:

'1. That payment of public money to Roman Catholic clergy, Jesuits &c. ought not to be allowed.
2. That Roman Catholicism subverts souls and the Pope is a foreign ruler not to be obeyed.
3. That the Crown takes oaths to protect Protestants and to abjure Popery.
4. That if Britain tolerates Roman Catholicism she will fall as a nation.
5. That the displeasure of God will be incurred.
6. That all reasonable toleration for Roman Catholics was allowed by previous legislation.'[72]

At the same time the *Leicester Journal* strongly criticized the votes given by Lord Charles Manners and Sir Henry Halford, two of the county members, in favour of the Maynooth Grant, which they considered to be an unwarrantable concession to Roman Catholics.[73] One of the reasons for the bitter opposition to Roman Catholicism was the fact that north Leicestershire, where Roman Catholic parishes were already established at Shepshed, Whitwick, and elsewhere, was one of the most fruitful fields for Roman Catholic missionary enterprise.[74]

Both the Corn Laws and the Roman Catholic question agitated politics of mid-19th-century Leicestershire, but the most critical political issue lay just outside formal politics. This was the question of the Charter and Chartism. Throughout the thirties the peace of the county was frequently disturbed by riots caused by the wretchedness of the conditions of life of the working class, particularly the stockingers.[75] At each general election in the thirties disturbances were expected at Hinckley, Loughborough, Shepshed, and other centres of frame-work knitting, and special constables were enrolled and regular troops temporarily quartered there.[76] In 1837 a detachment of the 10th Hussars was sent for, post-haste, from Nottingham, in order to quell a serious riot at Loughborough, where trouble seems to have arisen from the detestation in which the working class held the new Poor Law.[77]

The Chartist agitation itself falls into two distinct periods: from 1839 to 1840 and from 1848 to 1849. In the former period the industrial villages of the county were more disturbed than the town; in the latter period the town

[70] *Leic. Jnl.* 23 Jan. 1837.
[71] B.M. Add. MS. 40522, f. 15. Duke of Rut. to Robert Peel 1 Jan. 1843. His son, the Marquess of Granby, resigned his post in the Prince Consort's Household as a protest against the repeal of the Corn Laws. He was M.P. for the Northern Division at the time: B.M. Add. MS. 40583, f. 217.
[72] *Leic. Jnl.* 23 July 1847.　　　　　　　　　　　　　　　[73] Ibid.
[74] For the growth of Roman Catholicism in north Leics., cf. Pagani, *Life of Gentili*, 178, 182, 192–4, 197, and *Dublin Rev.* xxxi, 381–2.
[75] For the condition of the stockingers in the 30's and 40's, cf. T. Cooper, *Life of Thomas Cooper written by Himself*, 133–42. Also H.O. 52/24.
[76] H.O. 52/26. Magistrates of Leic. to Home Sec. 13 Jan. 1835, stating that 70 special constables were sworn in for preservation of peace during the election for the southern division of the county. Also Revd. J. Dyke to Home Sec. 5 Jan. 1835.
[77] H.O. 52/34. E. Dawson to Russell, 6, 7, 8, and 16 Dec. 1837.

was the centre of the agitation. In January 1839 Loughborough was in a very unsettled condition. Inflammatory leaflets were being distributed, and early in February it was reported that arms for Chartists were being made at Shepshed as well as at Loughborough.[78] The wealthier inhabitants became thoroughly alarmed and besought the Home Secretary to send metropolitan police officers, or to permit them to form an armed association for the protection of life and property. Finally, they sent a deputation to the Home Office to stress the expediency of stationing a permanent military force at Loughborough in a new barracks to be built for the purpose.[79] Apart from Loughborough the most serious disturbances, or threats of disturbance, were in the Hinckley district, which, after Leicester and Loughborough, was the most important centre of the hosiery trade. The first signs of political activity on the part of the Chartists occurred in June, when they distributed handbills in Earl Shilton and Hinckley calling for a mutiny. The magistrates were immediately alarmed and sent for cavalry from Coventry. This, or lack of success, intimidated the Chartists, who postponed their meeting for a month. During the summer several demonstrations and meetings were held, but there was no physical violence, only impassioned and inflammatory language.[80] Throughout the winter of 1839–40 Chartists' meetings were held in the industrial villages, creating alarm of an almost hysterical intensity amongst the magistrates and the manufacturers, some of whom remembered the Luddite outrages.[81] The reason, of course, for their fear was the almost complete absence of a police force. The Hinckley magistrates pointed out to the Home Secretary in August 1839 that they had no police force at all.[82] The only method they had of keeping law and order was by intimidation, by the ostentatious use of the yeomanry and militia. There is no doubt that the lack of police made the whole situation more dangerous, but Home Office agents also magnified the danger of Chartist agitation.[83] In fact the Chartist leaders in Leicestershire, Smart, Skevington, and Cooper, were cautious men and their following was small.[84] After 1840 the agitation died away and the county authorities were less concerned about public order, but occasionally there was a clash. In 1842 a meeting of Chartists at Mowmacre Hill was roughly broken up by the police and this fracas achieved some notoriety in Chartist circles as the 'Battle of Momecker Hill'. But with growing demand for the repeal of the Corn Laws and for the Ten Hour Act, the support for Chartism dwindled and faded; dissensions among the Chartists themselves were also responsible for their temporary eclipse.[85]

In 1848 there was a sharp revival of Chartist activity. Again Loughborough was a focal point and the Chief Constable of Leicestershire was worried by Chartist meetings held there on 3 April.[86] The Home Office immediately took steps to provide Loughborough with arms and ammunition in case the

[78] H.O. 40/44. C. M. Phillipps to Lord John Russell 30 Jan. 1839; Leaflet of 24 Jan. 1839; C. M. Phillipps to Lord John Russell 9 Feb. 1839.

[79] Ibid., B. Brock to Lord John Russell 27 Feb. 1839; Lord John Dudley to Lord John Russell 16 May 1839; Thomas Cradock to C. M. Phillipps 23 July 1839.

[80] H.O. 40 (No. 44). Magistrates of Earl Shilton Petty Sessions to Home Sec. 13 June 1839; Duke of Rut. to Lord John Russell 28 June 1839; Clerk to Hinckley magistrates to Home Sec. 6 May 1839.

[81] Ibid., various letters from magistrates to Home Sec.

[82] Ibid., clerk to Hinckley magistrates to Home Sec. 6 Aug. 1839.

[83] Darvall, *Popular Disturbances in Regency Engl.*, 274–99.

[84] T. Cooper, *Life*, 135; *Leic. Jnl.* 21 May 1839; 18 Aug. 1839.

[85] Cooper, op. cit. 181, 227.

[86] H.O. 41/19. Denis Le Marchant to F. Goodyer 5 Apr. 1848.

civil authorities should have to be strengthened with army pensioners.[87] A troop of dragoons was also sent to the town. A largely attended meeting was immediately followed by a parade of the dragoons through the principal streets, followed by extensive drill in the market-place. Skevington, the Chartist leader, refused to be provoked and acted with elaborate courtesy towards the commanding officer.[88] A Chartist camp, to last several days, was set up at Loughborough on Sunday, 9 April, and Chartists from Leicester and Nottingham and their surrounding villages poured into the town. The civic authorities took elaborate precautions but there was no danger until a rumour spread that twenty Chartists had been arrested. A protest meeting was called and quarrymen from Mountsorrell, armed with their hammers, rushed into the town, but the magistrate, C. M. Phillipps, persuaded Skevington to put an end to the meeting. This he did after a few skilful sarcasms about the past liberalism of Phillipps, who had been an ardent supporter of the Reform Bill.[89] During the next few weeks rallies, meetings, and canvassing campaigns were held in the district; Feargus O'Connor was cheered as he passed through the railway station on his way to Nottingham.[90] In May Chartists at Loughborough were being enrolled in the National Guard.[91] But elsewhere, apart from Leicester itself, the county was quiet and Chartist agitation at Hinckley and Wigston was not very effective.[92] At Loughborough, however, the authorities were sufficiently worried to ban a meeting of Feargus O'Connor and elaborate precautions were taken in case of trouble; dragoons were brought into the town and army pensioners enrolled; as it turned out the protest meetings and processions were broken up without disorder.[93] Later in the summer Chartist meetings became more numerous and widespread. There were riots at Countesthorpe, and at Earl Shilton Chartists were thought to be drilling at night and to be in possession of pikes. There was also trouble at Stoney Stanton and Sapcote.[94] By the end of September the county was quiet.

For the next thirty years the political life of Leicestershire is concerned with formal politics, with the struggle between ever-growing Liberalism and the traditional Tory attitude of the county, and this struggle is focused on the general elections. As the number of voters grew the representation of the county ceased to be a matter for arrangement between the leading families and the gentry, and there developed a need for party organization, for committees, local societies, and election agents. Members themselves were forced to state their attitude on a far greater variety of topics than would have been considered decent by their forerunners in the 18th century. But after years of uncontested elections, the first contest which took place in the Northern Division of the county in 1857 was more typical of 18th-century politics. C. H. Frewen, who had a highly developed sense of the value of independence, objected to the hold of the Manners family and so set himself up in opposition. He was easily defeated.[95] In 1859 E. B. Farnham, who had represented his division since 1837,

[87] H.O. 41/19. Denis Le Marchant to magistrates at Loughborough 6 Apr. 1848.
[88] *Leic. Jnl.* 7 Apr. 1848.   [89] Ibid. 14 Apr. 1848.
[90] Ibid. 28 Apr. 1848.   [91] Ibid. 5 May 1848.
[92] Ibid. 2 June 1848; 9 June 1848.
[93] Ibid. 16 June 1848; H.O. 41/19. C. M. Phillipps to Sir Geo. Grey 17 June 1848.
[94] H.O. 41/19. Clerk to Leic. County magistrates to Sir Geo. Grey 21 Aug. 1848; magistrates of Market Bosworth Division to Grey 28 Aug., 4 Sept. 1848.
[95] Leics. County Rec. Off., *Poll Bk. for 1857*; the voting was: Lord John Manners 1,787; E. B. Farnham 1,733; C. H. Frewen 1,250.

decided to retire, and his brother-in-law, E. B. Hartopp of Little Dalby, was promptly nominated in his place, possibly to exclude Frewen.[96] Hartopp was a fanatical Anglican, bitterly opposed both to Rome and to Protestant Dissent.[97] But more important than these personal objections was the feeling that no notice was being taken of the opinions of the electors. A meeting of Liberals was held at Melton Mowbray and strong denunciations were made of the influence of the Manners family; as a protest it was decided after all to run C. H. Frewen as an independent candidate. Frewen was not a Liberal, but a somewhat eccentric Conservative. His major support, however, came from radical and advanced circles and at the ensuing election, which he lost, it is interesting to note that he polled more votes than his opponents at Loughborough and Syston only.[98] There was no doubt too that he had some sympathy amongst the gentry, who disapproved of the high-handed way in which nominations were made, but the serried ranks of the Rutland tenantry carried the day.[99] But this election is still remote from modern political conflicts.

The first county election which has, in any way, a modern air is the by-election for South Leicestershire in 1867. At the general election of 1865 the borough had returned two Liberal members, and this encouraged the Liberal party to challenge the Tory hold on South Leicestershire when C. W. Packe died.[1] The Liberal party chose Thomas Tertius Paget of Humberstone Hall, an important Leicester banker, as their candidate.[2] The Conservatives put forward Sir Henry Halford's son-in-law, Albert Pell, an owner of extensive property in East London.[3] A fierce campaign ensued. Central headquarters of both parties were in Leicester; there was door-to-door canvassing in villages; the candidates toured the countryside, or, as Paget put it, 'the whole energy of the Tory party has been called forth from Burbage Wood to Easton's lonely vale'.[4] But the Liberals caught the Tories by surprise. Their party organization was far superior, and this undoubtedly gave Paget his narrow margin of victory. He beat Pell by 39 votes.[5]

This seriously disturbed the Conservatives. They blamed their own apathy, their defective register of voters, and grumbled because residents in Leicester had a vote in the county, a fact which to them seemed unjust. Immediately after the defeat they set to work to prepare for the next election.[6] They had not long to wait, for the parliamentary reform carried through by Disraeli in 1867 necessitated a speedy election. The county occupation franchise was lowered to the £12 limit,[7] but voting was still open and many tenants-at-will were frightened to vote against the wishes of their landlords.[8] Paget lost his seat after a hard-fought contest. The final figures of the poll were: Lord Curzon

[96] *Return of M.P.s*; *Leic. Jnl.* 15 Apr. 1859.

[97] Cf. his election address, printed ibid., loc. cit. 'I should oppose with a watchfulness and jealous resistance the unbounded pretensions of the Church of Rome', also ibid. 29 April 1859, where Hartopp is described by the Revd. E. Stevenson as 'a religious tyrant'.

[98] *Leic. Advertiser*, 19 Sept. 1868; *Leic. Jnl.* 29 Apr. 1859; Leics. County Rec. Off., *Poll Bk.* The voting was: Lord John Manners 2,220; Hartopp 1,954; Frewen, 1,433.

[99] Ibid.   [1] *Return of M.P.s*.

[2] For Paget, see C. J. Billson, *Leic. Memoirs*, 33.

[3] *Leic. Advertiser*, 9 Nov. 1867.   [4] Ibid.

[5] Ibid.; Leics. County Rec. Off., *Poll Bk. for 1867*.

[6] *Leic. Advertiser*, 14 Nov. 1867. Paget had twice as many votes in Leic. itself: cf. Leics. County Rec. Off., *Poll Bk. for 1867*: Paget 1,160, Pell 504.

[7] 30 and 31 Vic. c. 102.

[8] Cf. Paget's speech at Kibworth in June 1870, reported in *Leic. Advertiser*, 4 June 1870: 'The £12 voters did not give their own votes but their landlords', as they were tenants at will.'

3,223, A. Pell 3,111, and T. T. Paget 2,839.[9] In the Northern Division Frewen again challenged Lord John Manners, who was joined by S. W. Clowes, Hartopp having been discreetly dropped. Frewen, however, only polled 1,751 votes against 3,290 cast for Manners and 3,095 for Clowes.[10] In 1870 Lord Curzon succeeded his father as Earl Howe. This caused a vacancy in South Leicestershire. Paget stood once more and the Conservatives put forward W. U. Heygate, a member of an old Leicestershire family with large agricultural and industrial interests.[11] Heygate had a majority of 712 and Paget's poll declined to 2,570, the most considerable fall being in Leicester itself.[12] This was the last open-voting election to be held in Leicestershire, for in 1872 the ballot box was introduced. The change was expected to reduce the influence of the landlord. Perhaps because of this, at the general election in 1874, the Liberals decided to fight both constituencies; Henry Packe challenged Lord John Manners and S. W. Clowes, and Paget stood once more for South Leicestershire.[13] But Leicestershire naturally followed the wave of popular opinion which swept Disraeli into power, and all four Conservatives were elected.[14] In 1880 both divisions of Leicestershire remained loyal to their traditional politics. In 1885 there was a further modification of the franchise. Householders in the county were given a vote and the parliamentary divisions reorganized. North and South Leicestershire, which had been in existence since the Reform Act of 1832, were abolished and replaced by four single-member divisions: Melton, Loughborough, Bosworth, and Harborough.[15]

This reorganization marks the end of the old political structure of Leicestershire, for no longer were there any Knights of the Shire; with the coming of the ballot, too, the direct influence of the great landed families disappeared. The strong party organizations, by now well rooted in the market-towns of Leicestershire, brought an end to the unopposed elections which had been such a feature of Leicestershire politics for centuries. Gradually the names of the great political families—Curzon, Cave, Halford, even Manners—disappear, and are replaced by those of semi-professional politicians. By 1885 the political life of Leicestershire had ceased to be the intimate, personal affair of the nobility and gentry from which the working classes were excluded. It had become impersonal, democratic, a cog in the vast national party machinery in which local issues were frequently submerged. But, perhaps, most important of all was that the working classes, organized in trade unions and possessing a vote, exerted for the first time a powerful political influence.

[9] *Leic. Advertiser*, 21 Nov. 1868.
[10] Ibid.
[11] For the Heygates, see Billson, *Leic. Memoirs*, 21–22.
[12] *Leic. Advertiser*, 11 and 18 June 1870.
[13] Ibid. 14 Jan. 1874.
[14] Ibid. 31 Jan. 1874.
[15] 48 and 49 Vic. c. 23, sched. 7.

POLITICAL HISTORY, 1885–1950

AT the general election of 1885 the newly enlarged electorate in the four county constituencies of Leicestershire, following the general trend in the English counties, swung decisively towards the Liberal party. In 1880 Leicestershire had returned four Conservatives to Parliament; in 1885 the three constituencies of Harborough, Bosworth, and Loughborough elected Liberals, and only the Melton division, which was to remain a Conservative stronghold for the rest of the century, returned a Conservative.[1] It is with the four county constituencies of Leicestershire, as established by the Redistribution of Seats Act (1885),[2] that this article will be concerned, the political history of Leicester itself being left for consideration in a later volume. The four constituencies were not by any means exclusively agricultural, though the borough of Leicester was not of course included in them.[3] The growing suburbs of Leicester spread beyond the boundaries of the borough constituency into the four county parliamentary divisions, while the two western divisions, Loughborough and Bosworth, included a considerable population employed in the hosiery industry, besides many boot and shoe operatives, miners, and quarrymen. It was these two constituencies that contained the main strength of the Liberals in Leicestershire during the late 19th century, and the same areas were later to be the chief local support of the Labour party. Of the members returned for Leicestershire in December 1885, T. T. Paget, a well-known local man who had already had a long political career, belonged to the less Radical section of the Liberal party. In 1885 he declared himself against Home Rule for Ireland; and although he favoured in principle both universal free education and Disestablishment, his attitude on these two questions was very cautious.[4] Paget was elected for the Harborough division by a majority of only 166, out of a total poll of nearly 11,000.[5] J. E. Ellis, a Quaker quarry-owner,[6] who was returned for Bosworth by a substantial majority of over 2,500,[7] was a man of much more advanced opinions. He criticized the foreign policy of the previous Liberal administration as not having been sufficiently Radical,[8] and strongly advocated free education for all.[9] He was, however, at this time against Home Rule.[10] J. E. Johnson-Ferguson, elected as a Liberal for the Loughborough division by a majority of just over 1,000,[11] did not express any distinctive views during the 1885 election,[12] and in the political crisis of 1886 his attitude was to be uncertain. The only Conservative returned by the Leicestershire county

[1] *Leic. Chron. and Leics. Mercury,* 5 Dec. 1885, pp. 5, 6; 12 Dec. 1885, p. 6.
[2] On the provisions of this Act as regards Leics., see above, p. 134.
[3] On the exact boundaries of the constituencies, see 48 & 49 Vic., c. 43, schedule 7.
[4] *Leic. Chron. and Leics. Mercury,* 17 Oct. 1885, p. 4; 31 Oct. 1885, p. 6; 7 Nov. 1885, pp. 5, 6.
[5] Ibid. 5 Dec. 1885, p. 5.
[6] Ibid. 28 Nov. 1885, p. 6.
[7] Ibid. 12 Dec. 1885, p. 6.
[8] Ibid. 3 Oct. 1885, Supplement, p. 3.
[9] Ibid. 14 Nov. 1885, p. 4.
[10] Ibid. 3 Oct. 1885, Supplement, p. 3; 14 Nov. 1885, p. 4.
[11] Ibid. 12 Dec. 1885, p. 6.
[12] Ibid. 19 Sept. 1885, Supplement, p. 3; 14 Nov. 1885, p. 6.

constituencies was Lord John Manners, elected by the Melton division with a majority of over 1,200.[13] Lord John, who was personally much respected, even by his political opponents,[14] was Postmaster-General in Lord Salisbury's administration formed in June 1885.[15]

During the political crisis of 1886 most Leicestershire Liberal organizations seem to have been in favour of Gladstone's policy regarding Home Rule for Ireland. Those of the local Liberal associations and clubs which expressed any definite views on the issue all declared in favour of Home Rule.[16] Of the Leicestershire representatives in Parliament, Paget and Ellis both supported Gladstone.[17] Johnson-Ferguson, though in favour of a measure of self-government for Ireland, stated that he was not prepared to endanger Imperial unity, and in accordance with these views he was at first opposed to parts of Gladstone's Home Rule Bill, particularly its original provision for the exclusion of Irish members from the Westminster Parliament.[18] Eventually, however, he decided in favour of Home Rule.[19]

In the general election of July 1886, brought about by the rejection of Gladstone's Home Rule Bill, Liberalism in Leicestershire, as elsewhere, suffered a defeat. The only Liberal representative returned by the four county constituencies was J. E. Ellis, who was re-elected for Bosworth by a majority of more than a thousand, out of a total vote of about 8,000,[20] although his Conservative opponent, Harrington Hulton, made a special appeal to dissident Liberals, and was also said to have great influence with the miners who formed an important part of this electorate.[21] In the Loughborough division, Johnson-Ferguson was defeated by Edwin de Lisle, a local Conservative, who, however, had a majority of only 135.[22] The worst Liberal defeat was in the Harborough division. There the sitting member, Paget, retired in 1886 because of age and ill health.[23] He was replaced as Liberal candidate by Harris Saunders, who suffered from the disadvantage of being a stranger to the district,[24] though in his support of Gladstone he had the unanimous approval of the constituency's Liberal Association.[25] The Conservative candidate was Thomas Tapling, a London business man who had contested the seat in 1885.[26] Tapling was elected with a majority of over 1,100.[27] The Tory success was perhaps partly due to the fact that just before the election a new party organization had been established in the constituency.[28] Lord John Manners was again returned for the Melton division,[29] and he became Chancellor of the Duchy of Lancaster in the new Conservative administration.[30]

The defeat suffered by the Leicestershire Liberals in 1886, at a time when their party was confused and divided by the Home Rule issue, was not per-

[13] *Leic. Chron. and Leics. Mercury*, 12 Dec. 1885, p. 6.
[14] Ibid. 17 Oct. 1885, p. 6.
[15] Ibid. 4 July 1885, p. 3; *Leic. Daily Post*, 4 July 1885, p. 3.
[16] *Leic. Chron. and Leics. Mercury*, 24 Apr. 1886, pp. 5, 7; 24 Apr. 1886, Supplement, p. 2; 1 May 1886, p. 7; 8 May 1886, p. 7; 15 May 1886, pp. 7, 8; 5 June 1886, p. 8.
[17] Ibid. 1 May 1886, p. 8.
[18] Ibid. p. 3; 15 May 1886, p. 6.
[19] Ibid. 26 June 1886, pp. 5, 6.
[20] Ibid. 17 July 1886, p. 5.
[21] Ibid. 3 July 1886, p. 5; 17 July 1886, p. 5.
[22] Ibid. 17 July 1886, p. 6.
[23] Ibid. 26 June 1886, p. 4.
[24] He was a country gentleman from Herts.; ibid. 26 June 1886, p. 6.
[25] Ibid. 26 June 1886, p. 5.
[26] Ibid. 28 Nov. 1885, p. 6.
[27] Ibid. 17 July 1886, p. 6.
[28] Ibid. 5 June 1886, p. 8.
[29] Ibid. 17 July 1886, p. 3.
[30] C. Whibley, *Lord John Manners and his Friends*, ii, 241; *Complete Peerage*, xi, 273.

manent, and during the following years Leicestershire shared in the revival of Liberal strength which was experienced in the country as a whole. In 1888 Lord John Manners became Duke of Rutland, but he was succeeded as member for Melton by his son, the Marquess of Granby.[31] A more important change took place in 1891, when at a by-election caused by Tapling's death a Liberal, J. W. Logan, was returned as member for Harborough, with a majority of about 500.[32] Logan, a railway contractor who lived in the constituency,[33] was a supporter of Irish Home Rule.[34] In the general election of 1892 Logan was re-elected with a slightly increased majority,[35] while in the Bosworth division another supporter of Gladstone, C. B. B. McLaren, was elected to replace Ellis, who retired.[36] In the Loughborough division Johnson-Ferguson, standing as a believer in Home Rule,[37] defeated Edwin de Lisle,[38] who had held protectionist views[39] and was advocating the payment of a bounty to British farmers.[40] The Marquess of Granby was returned unopposed for Melton.[41] During the 1892 election an early example of political action by the local trade unions occurred when the Leicester Trades Council sent a circular to all candidates for election in the county, asking them to declare their views on certain specific points. Logan's reply was the most satisfactory, and the Trades Council decided to support him.[42] In the 1895 general election all the three Liberal members for the county were re-elected, despite the general reduction of the Liberal vote throughout the country, though in the Loughborough division Johnson-Ferguson had a majority of less than 400.[43] In the Melton division Lord Edward Manners was returned as a Conservative, the Marquess of Granby having retired, but on this occasion the constituency had a Liberal candidate who obtained more than a third of the votes cast.[44] During this election the executive committee of the Coalville and District Miners Association interviewed the candidates for the Bosworth and Loughborough constituencies, in which the Leicestershire coalfield lay, and questioned them about their attitude on certain issues of special interest to miners.[45] Similar action was taken by local trade unions at subsequent elections.[46] In 1906 the Independent Labour Party addressed a questionnaire to the candidates for the Leicestershire constituencies.[47] It was not until 1918 that Labour candidates appeared in the four county divisions, though in 1906 the Labour leader, Ramsay MacDonald, had been elected as one of the members for the borough of Leicester. In 1895 the

[31] *Complete Peerage*, xi, 272–4.

[32] *Whitaker's Almanac* (1892), 137; *Leic. Chron. and Leics. Mercury*, 16 July 1892, p. 2.

[33] Ibid. 9 July 1892, p. 2.

[34] Ibid. 2 July 1892, p. 4. For a brief account of Logan, see *Leics. and Rut. at the opening of the 20th century*, ed. W. Scarff and W. T. Pike, 85.

[35] *Leic. Chron. and Leics. Mercury*, 16 July 1892, p. 2.

[36] Ibid. 25 June 1892, p. 4; *Leic. Daily Post*, 16 July 1892, p. 5. McLaren was M.P. for Stafford, 1880–6; *Leics. and Rut. at the opening of the 20th century*, ed. Scarff and Pike, 84.

[37] *Leic. Chron. and Leics. Mercury*, 25 June 1892, p. 5.

[38] Ibid. 16 July 1892, p. 2; *Leic. Daily Post*, 11 July 1892, p. 5.

[39] *Leic. Chron. and Leics. Mercury*, 17 July 1886, p. 8.

[40] *Leic. Daily Post*, 5 July 1892, p. 5; 7 July 1892, p. 5.

[41] *Leic. Chron. and Leics. Mercury*, 9 July 1892, p. 3.

[42] Ibid. 9 July 1892, Supplement, p. 2; *Leic. Daily Post*, 6 July 1892, p. 7.

[43] Ibid. 22 July 1895, p. 5; 25 July 1895, p. 5; 29 July 1895, p. 5.

[44] Ibid. 3 July 1895, p. 5; 18 July 1895, p. 5.

[45] Ibid. 11 July 1895, p. 8; 17 July 1895, p. 8.

[46] Ibid. 11 Jan. 1906, p. 7; 14 Jan. 1910, p. 7; *Leic. Chron. & Leics. Mercury*, 6 Jan. 1906, p. 9; 13 Jan. 1906, p. 11.

[47] *Leic. Daily Post*, 8 Jan. 1906, p. 5.

Liberal candidate in the Bosworth constituency, McLaren, had the support of the local Labour leaders.[48]

Several Leicestershire units took part in the South African War, which broke out in 1899. The first battalion of the Leicestershire Regiment had been in South Africa since 1895.[49] It was involved in some of the first fighting of the war, in Natal, and formed part of the force besieged in Ladysmith.[50] The second battalion of the county regiment was in Egypt during most of the war.[51] The third battalion, which was a militia unit, was embodied in 1900 to replace regular troops, and sent to Ireland. A draft of militia reservists was sent out to the first battalion, but the third battalion, though it volunteered for active service, was returned to England and disembodied.[52] In 1902 the third battalion was again embodied, and in March of that year it embarked for South Africa,[53] where it was employed in manning blockhouses.[54] The unit returned to England in October 1902.[55] The Leicestershire Yeomanry, though it did not go overseas as a complete unit, provided two companies of Imperial Yeomanry for active service,[56] while the Volunteer battalion of the Leicestershire Regiment furnished two Service companies, which joined the first battalion of the regiment in South Africa.[57] The results of the 'Khaki' election of 1900, brought about at a time when the war seemed to be virtually over, were on the whole encouraging to the Liberals in Leicestershire. The Liberal sitting member, McLaren, was returned unopposed for Bosworth, his Conservative opponent having retired through ill health.[58] Logan was re-elected as a Liberal for Harborough with an increased majority,[59] and though the Melton division was won by the Tory candidate, Lord Cecil Manners, it was by a much reduced majority.[60] The only check to the Liberals occurred in the Loughborough division, where a Liberal was elected, but with a majority reduced to less than seventy.[61] The decline of the Liberal strength at Loughborough may have been due to the rifts which existed in the local Liberal Association,[62] and to the fact that the Liberal candidate, Maurice Levy, was attacked by the Leicester Trades Council as a bad employer.[63] A by-election in the Harborough division in 1904 resulted in the return of the Liberal candidate, P. J. Stanhope.[64] The general election of the next year marks the climax of Liberal strength in the county constituencies of Leicestershire. For the first time all four seats were secured by the Liberal candidates, who all had substantial majorities.[65] In considering the Liberal success it must be remembered that the two divisions of Harborough and Melton, once largely rural, included by 1906 large parts of Leicester itself. The municipal borough of Leicester had been enlarged in 1891,[66] but the boundaries of the parliamentary constituencies had not been changed. In the Melton division,

---

[48] *Leic. Daily Post*, 11 July 1895, p. 5.
[49] E. A. H. Webb, *Hist. of the Services of the 17th (the Leics.) Regiment, 1688–1910*, 206.
[50] Webb, op. cit. 209–10; A. Conan Doyle, *The Great Boer War*, 84, 88, 109, 112.
[51] Webb, op. cit. 211.   [52] G. H. D. B., *Leics. Militia in South Africa*, 1.
[53] Ibid. 6.   [54] Ibid. 17 et seq.   [55] Ibid. 94.
[56] G. R. Codrington, *Outline of the Hist. of the Leics. Yeomanry*, 21–4.
[57] Anon., *Leics. Regiment, 1688–1938*, 5.
[58] *Leic. Daily Post*, 4 Oct. 1900, p. 5; *Leic. Chron. and Leics. Mercury*, 6 Oct. 1900, p. 2.
[59] Ibid. 13 Oct. 1900, pp. 5, 8.   [60] *Leic. Daily Post*, 5 Oct. 1900, p. 4.
[61] *Leic. Chron. and Leics. Mercury*, 13 Oct. 1900, p. 7.   [62] Ibid.
[63] Ibid. 29 Sept. 1900, p. 3; *Leic. Daily Post*, 27 Sept. 1900, p. 4.
[64] *Whitaker's Almanac* (1905), 140.
[65] *Leic. Chron. and Leics. Mercury*, 20 Jan. 1906, p. 6; 27 Jan. 1906, pp. 6, 8, 9.
[66] Leicester Extension Act, 1891.

out of a total of 15,815 voters on the register, 7,256, or nearly half, lived in the suburbs of Leicester.[67] These figures explain the decline of the Conservative strength in the division, so long a centre of the influence of the Manners family. Similarly, in 1906 the Harborough division, out of a total electorate of 17,227, contained 4,162 voters living in the suburbs of Leicester and 2,596 electors who voted in the division as the owners of property in Leicester.[68] The Liberal candidates for these two divisions were both men of advanced views. Henry Walker, who was elected for Melton, described himself as 'a pretty advanced Radical',[69] while R. C. Lehmann, the new member for Harborough, was a man of similar opinions.[70] In the Bosworth and Loughborough divisions the sitting members, McLaren[71] and Levy, were returned.[72] Of the Conservatives, Dixon and Du Pré, the candidates for Harborough and Loughborough, were both strongly in favour of Tariff Reform,[73] while Allen Stoneham, who appeared at a late stage as the Conservative candidate for Bosworth, supported the same policy.[74] Sir Arthur Hazlerigg, the Conservative candidate for Melton, was considered to be a supporter of Balfour, and his attitude towards Tariff Reform was felt to be uncertain.[75] This feeling may have cost Hazlerigg votes, as Tariff Reform was said to have some support in the Leicester part of his constituency.[76] Thus in the Liberal 'landslide' the Leicestershire Liberals succeeded in obtaining all the four county seats.

Of the important measures passed by the Liberal Government which took office in December 1905, only the Territorial and Reserve Forces Act (1907) can be dealt with here. Under this Act the Volunteer battalion of the Leicestershire Regiment was transformed in 1908 into two infantry battalions for the new Territorial Force, the fourth and fifth battalions of the regiment.[77] The county's Yeomanry also became part of the Territorial Force.[78] The Act provided for the eventual disappearance of the Militia,[79] which had hitherto provided the third battalion of the county regiment. After 1908 the third battalion became a Reserve unit.[80]

In the general election of January 1910, the most important single issue in Leicestershire, as elsewhere,[81] was the conduct of the House of Lords in rejecting the 1909 Budget, but there was also much discussion of Tariff Reform.[82] The Liberals succeeded in retaining all the four county seats, but in each constituency the Liberal majority was considerably reduced.[83] This general election was the first during which suffragettes were active on an important scale in the

[67] *Leic. Chron. and Leics. Mercury*, 6 Jan. 1906, p. 9.
[68] Ibid. p. 8.
[69] Ibid. p. 6.
[70] Ibid. p. 8; 8 Jan. 1910, p. 9.
[71] Created a bt. 1902: *Leics. and Rut. at the opening of the 20th century*, ed. Scarff and Pike, 84.
[72] *Leic. Chron. and Leics. Mercury*, 20 Jan. 1906, p. 6; 27 Jan. 1906, p. 9.
[73] Ibid. 6 Jan. 1906, pp. 4, 9; 13 Jan. 1906, p. 9; *Leic. Daily Post*, 1 Jan. 1906, p. 3; 2 Jan. 1906, p. 5; 9 Jan. 1906, p. 7.
[74] *Leic. Chron. and Leics. Mercury*, 6 Jan. 1906, p. 9; 13 Jan. 1906, pp. 7, 9.
[75] Ibid. 6 Jan. 1906, p. 9. For details of his views on tariffs, see his answers to questions submitted by the Leics. Chamber of Agriculture. *Leic. Daily Post*, 1 Jan. 1906, p. 3.
[76] *Leic. Chron. and Leics. Mercury*, 6 Jan. 1906, p. 9.
[77] Anon., *Leics. Regt., 1688-1938*, 6.
[78] Codrington, *Outline Hist. of Leics. Yeomanry*, 25.
[79] J. K. Dunlop, *Development of the British Army, 1899-1914*, 272-3.
[80] *Whitaker's Almanac* (1909), 241.
[81] R. C. K. Ensor, *Engl., 1870-1914*, 417.
[82] *Leic. Chron. and Leics. Mercury* and *Leic. Daily Post* for Jan. 1910, *passim*.
[83] *Leic. Chron. and Leics Mercury*, 22 Jan. 1910, p. 12; 29 Jan. 1912, pp. 3, 9, 12; *Leic. Daily Post*, 20 Jan. 1910, p. 5; 22 Jan. 1910, p. 5; 26 Jan. 1910, p. 5; 28 Jan. 1910, p. 5.

county constituencies of Leicestershire. Their action was concentrated in support of the Unionists in the Loughborough division, where the Liberal candidate, Sir Maurice Levy, was thought to be especially hostile to them.[84] A number of turbulent meetings was held in the division by the Women's Social and Political Union, and such prominent suffragette leaders as Emmeline Pankhurst and Dorothy Pethick-Lawrence spoke against Levy. A house-to-house canvass was also carried out.[85] In the election of December 1910 three Liberals, H. D. McLaren, Sir Maurice Levy, and J. W. Logan, were returned for the Bosworth, Loughborough, and Harborough divisions,[86] but at Melton, where Walker had retired because of ill health,[87] the seat fell to the Conservative candidate, Colonel Yate, by a small majority.[88]

The four county constituencies of Leicestershire thus seemed on the whole to be dominated by the Liberals. Three of the seats were in their hands, and the other had only been lost by a few hundred votes. The outbreak of the First World War naturally brought political controversy on normal lines to an end. The first battalion of the Leicestershire Regiment went to France early in September 1914 as part of the Sixth Division, and with this division the battalion remained in France for the whole of the war.[89] The second battalion of the Leicestershire Regiment was in India when hostilities began, and went to France as part of the Meerut Division, going into action for the first time in October 1914.[90] At the end of 1915 the battalion was transferred to Mesopotamia,[91] where it remained until January 1918.[92] For the rest of the war the battalion served in Egypt and Palestine.[93] The two original Territorial battalions of the Leicestershire Regiment, the fourth and fifth battalions, were mobilized at the outbreak of war, and went to France in February 1915 with the Forty-Seventh (North Midland) Division. Both battalions remained in France until after the Armistice.[94] Two more Territorial battalions of the regiment, the 2/4th and 2/5th battalions, were raised in September 1914,[95] and as the war went on a further two Territorial battalions of the regiment and nine Service battalions were raised.[96] The Leicestershire Yeomanry went to France in November 1914,[97] and remained there until January 1918, when the unit was broken up to provide reinforcements for several cavalry regiments.[98] Second and third line units of the Leicestershire Yeomanry were raised for the duration of the war.[99]

Under the Representation of the People Act (1918) the four county

[84] *Leic. Daily Post*, 5 Jan. 1910, p. 4.

[85] Ibid. 5 Jan. 1910, pp. 4, 7; 8 Jan. 1910, p. 2; 11 Jan. 1910, p. 8; 19 Jan. 1910, p. 7; 20 Jan. 1910, p. 7; 24 Jan. 1910, p. 5; 25 Jan. 1910, p. 7; *Leic. Chron. and Leics. Mercury*, 8 Jan. 1910, p. 10; 15 Jan. 1910, p. 4; 22 Jan. 1910, p. 10. The first public suffragette meeting in Loughborough was held in Jan. 1909: *Leic. Daily Post*, 23 Jan. 1909, p. 5.

[86] Ibid. 10 Dec. 1910, p. 5; 14 Dec. 1910, p. 7; 16 Dec. 1910, p. 5.

[87] *Leic. Chron. and Leics. Mercury*, 5 Mar. 1910, p. 9; 12 Mar. 1910, p. 3.

[88] *Leic. Daily Post*, 8 Dec. 1910, p. 5.

[89] H. C. Wylly, *First and Second Battns. of Leics. Regt. in the Great War*, 5–90.

[90] Ibid. 106, 108.   [91] Ibid. 146.

[92] Ibid. 147–85; Edw. J. Thompson, *Leicestershires Beyond Bagdad*, passim.

[93] Wylly, op. cit. 186–97.

[94] John Milne, *Footprints of the 1/4th Leics. Regiment*; J. D. Hills, *Fifth Leics.*; and R. E. Priestley, *Breaking the Hindenburg Line*, passim.

[95] J. P. W. Jamie, *177th Brigade, 1914–18*, 9. The activities of these two battalions during the war are described herein.

[96] Anon. *Leics. Regt., 1688–1938*, 6.

[97] Codrington, *Outline Hist. of Leics. Yeomanry*, 27.   [98] Ibid. 39.

[99] Ibid. 27–28.

constituencies of Leicestershire continued to exist, but the whole borough of Leicester, as enlarged in 1891, was brought outside their boundaries.[1] Some other changes of less importance took place in the boundaries of the constituencies, and the electorate was greatly enlarged.[2] The general election of 1918 showed that the political position of the Liberal party in the county constituencies was much weaker than it had been before the war. The situation was complicated by the existence of a coalition between the Conservatives and the Lloyd George Liberals, and in Leicestershire the Conservatives and the Coalition Liberals co-operated in 1918. In the Melton division the Conservative, Colonel Yate, was returned unopposed, a Liberal candidate having withdrawn.[3] In Loughborough similarly the Conservative candidate withdrew in favour of Major Guest, a Coalition Liberal, who had the support of both Conservatives and Liberals, and was elected with a substantial majority over the Labour candidate.[4] In the Bosworth division, H. A. McLaren, the Liberal sitting member, was the official Coalition candidate, and he also was elected. He was opposed only by a Labour candidate, a Conservative having withdrawn.[5] In Harborough the position was more complicated, for the sitting member, D. A. Harris,[6] was a Liberal of rather uncertain allegiance. He had voted against the Coalition Government in the division on the 'Maurice debate' in May 1918, and such action was usually held to mark a member as being a follower of Asquith,[7] but on the other hand Harris declared himself a supporter of the Coalition Government.[8] A Conservative, Sir Keith Fraser, was put forward as the official Coalition candidate for the Harborough division, and was elected with a large majority.[9] The Harborough seat thus passed from the Liberals to the Conservatives. Much more ominous for the future of the Liberal party in the county was the substantial number of votes cast for the Labour candidates, standing in 1918 for the first time in any of the Leicestershire county constituencies. At Harborough the Labour candidate, Walter Baker, obtained over 4,000 votes, while the Labour candidates in the Loughborough and Bosworth divisions obtained more than 6,000 votes each.[10] At the 1922 election, brought about by the disruption of the coalition between the Conservatives and a large section of the Liberal party, the full weakness of the Liberals' position in the county was revealed. Colonel Yate and Sir Keith Fraser held the Melton and Harborough divisions for the Conservatives, while the Bosworth division elected another Conservative, Major Paget.[11] At Bosworth the retiring member, McLaren, who was a supporter of Lloyd George,[12] polled fewer votes than did the Labour candidate,[13] while at Harborough J. W. Black, an Independent Liberal,[14] only obtained about the same number of

[1] 7 and 8 Geo. V, c. 64, Schedule 9, pt. ii.

[2] Ibid.; and compare 48 and 49 Vic., c. 43, Schedule 7. See *Leic. Daily Post*, 30 Dec. 1918, p. 1, for the number of voters in the four constituencies in 1918, as compared with 1915.

[3] *Leic. Daily Post*, 9 Dec. 1918, p. 1.

[4] Ibid. 3 Dec. 1918, p. 1; 11 Dec. 1918, p. 2; 30 Dec. 1918, p. 1.

[5] Ibid. 3 Dec. 1918, p. 1; 4 Dec. 1918, p. 2; 30 Dec. 1918, p. 1.

[6] Returned at a by-election in 1916; *Whitaker's Almanac* (1918), 195.

[7] D. Lloyd George, *War Memoirs* (2nd ed.), ii, 1786–7; W. S. Churchill, *World Crisis* (2nd ed.), ii, 1290; *Leic. Daily Post*, 9 Dec. 1918, p. 1.

[8] *Leic. Daily Post*, 3 Dec. 1918, p. 1; 12 Dec. 1918, p. 3.

[9] Ibid. 10 Dec. 1918, p. 1; 5 Dec. 1918, p. 3; 30 Dec. 1918, p. 1.

[10] Ibid. 30 Dec. 1918, p. 1.

[11] *Leic. Daily Post*, 16 Nov. 1922, p. 1; 17 Nov. 1922, p. 3.

[12] Ibid. 30 Oct. 1922, p. 5; 3 Nov. 1922, p. 7.

[13] Ibid. 16 Nov. 1922, p. 1.

[14] Ibid. 17 Oct. 1922, p. 16.

votes as were cast for Labour, although he was well known as a county councillor and had been actively working in the constituency for three years previously.[15] The only Liberal to be elected in any of the county constituencies was Brigadier-General Spears, who was returned unopposed for Loughborough.[16] Spears, however, was supported by the local Conservative Association, and declared his willingness to co-operate with a Conservative Government, should one take office.[17]

After the general election of 1922 the Liberals never regained their dominant position in Leicestershire politics. Since 1885 they had held the three constituencies of Harborough, Loughborough, and Bosworth, except during the few years after the Liberal split over Home Rule in 1886. The Bosworth division had returned an unbroken succession of Liberal members from its creation in 1885 until 1922. Even in the Melton division the Liberals had by the end of the 19th century built up a strong position, and were able to win the seat on two occasions. The Liberal decline in Leicestershire was of course only part of the general weakening of the party in the whole country.

At the 1923 election, however, the Liberals were able to recover temporarily some of the lost ground. Spears, who had some Conservative support,[18] was re-elected at Loughborough.[19] Both Bosworth and Harborough were regained by the Liberals,[20] and even in the Melton division the Conservative, Colonel Yate, had a majority of only forty-four over his Liberal opponent.[21] In the Bosworth and Loughborough constituencies, where there were Conservative and Labour candidates, the Liberals, though successful, polled considerably less than half the total votes cast,[22] while in the Melton and Harborough constituencies, where there were no Labour candidates, the votes were fairly evenly divided.[23] Less than a year after the 1923 election the defeat of the Labour Government, which had taken office without having a majority in the House of Commons, led to another general election in October 1924. In all four of the Leicestershire county constituencies the Conservative candidates were elected, Colonel P. L. Winby for Harborough, W. L. Everard for Melton, Captain R. Gee, V.C., for Bosworth, and F. G. Rye for Loughborough.[24] A particularly notable change of political opinions took place in the Harborough division, where the Conservative candidate, Winby, obtained over 13,000 votes against fewer than 6,000 polled by Liberal sitting member, J. W. Black.[25] In the previous year, when Black had been elected, there had been no Labour candidate, but in 1924 the Labour candidate, J. S. Hyder, obtained rather more votes than Black.[26] Winby had been selected by the Harborough Conservatives as a man likely to rally a large vote against the Labour party, and the former Conservative member, Fraser, had been abandoned in circumstances that gave rise to some resentment.[27]

With the votes of the more Radical section of public opinion in the county

---

[15] *Leic. Daily Post*, 8 Nov. 1922, p. 12.
[16] Ibid. 4 Nov. 1922, p. 1. Owing to an accident no Labour candidate was nominated for Loughborough.
[17] Ibid. 30 Oct. 1922, p. 7.   [18] *Leics. Mercury*, 8 Dec. 1923, p. 12.
[19] Ibid. 7 Dec. 1923, p. 2.
[20] Ibid.; 8 Dec. 1923, p. 13. The Labour candidate at Bosworth, Emrys Hughes, perhaps lost some votes because of his pacifism: ibid. 24 Nov. 1923, p. 13.
[21] Ibid. 8 Dec. 1923, p. 3.   [22] Ibid. 7 Dec. 1923, p. 1; 8 Dec. 1923, p. 13.
[23] Ibid.   [24] Ibid. 30 Oct. 1924, p. 1; 31 Oct. 1924, p. 5.
[25] Ibid. 30 Oct. 1924, p. 1.   [26] Ibid.
[27] Ibid. 11 Oct. 1924, p. 7; 21 Oct. 1924, p. 5.

fairly evenly divided between the Labour and Liberal parties[28] the Conservatives in Leicestershire, as in the whole country, were in a strong position, though at a by-election in 1927 Sir William Edge, a Liberal, was elected for the Bosworth division.[29] The 1924 election was followed by five years of Conservative government. During the general strike of 1926 the situation in the county remained quiet,[30] though the miners of the Leicestershire coalfield were on strike,[31] and local transport services were much interrupted.[32] In the 1929 election the Labour party made considerable gains in Britain as a whole. G. E. Winterton, who was elected for the Loughborough division with a majority of over 2,000, was the first Labour representative to be elected for any of the four county constituencies of Leicestershire.[33] Sir William Edge, aided by some Conservatives who were anxious to defeat the strong Labour candidate, John Minto,[34] was again returned for Bosworth,[35] while two Conservatives, W. L. Everard and Earl Castle Stewart,[36] were elected for Melton and Harborough respectively.[37] This election was the first at which the three main political parties each contested all the four county constituencies. In each of the four constituencies the successful candidate obtained fewer than half of the total number of votes cast.[38] In Leicestershire, as in the rest of Britain, the 1931 general election ended in a very marked success for the National Government. During the weeks before the election much negotiation took place between the local political organizations. In the Bosworth division the Conservative candidate, Captain Pollen, was withdrawn in favour of Sir William Edge, who as a follower of Sir John Simon ranked as a National Liberal.[39] Pollen's withdrawal was hotly discussed amongst the local Conservatives, and in the end the executive of the Conservative party in the division decided by a majority of only one vote not to contest the seat.[40] In the Melton division the Liberals, who were short of funds, took a similar decision,[41] while at Loughborough the Liberal candidate, Leslie Hale, retired after the Conservative candidate, Lawrence Kimball, had agreed not to vote in favour of any tax on food. A National Labour candidate who at one time proposed to contest the seat also withdrew.[42] The Harborough Liberals failed to bring forward any candidate, so that in all the four constituencies the contest was between the Labour party and the supporters of the National Government. The National Government candidates were all elected by large majorities. Sir William Edge, elected for the Bosworth division, was a National Liberal, but the other three county members, Kimball for Loughborough, Earl Castle Stewart for Harborough, and W. L. Everard for Melton, were all Conservatives.[43] The Labour party's defeat was due less to any fall in the Labour vote, which only declined slightly compared

---

[28] On the votes cast in the four county divisions, see ibid. 30 Oct. 1924, p. 1; 31 Oct. 1924, p. 5. In the Melton division, the only one of the four in which there was no Labour candidate, an Independent Liberal was heavily defeated by a Conservative.

[29] *Whitaker's Almanac* (1928), 188.

[30] *Leic. Mail*, 5 May 1926, p. 1; 6 May 1926, p. 1.   [31] Ibid. 3 May 1926, p. 3.

[32] *Leic. Mail* and *Leics. Mercury*, 3 May 1926 to 13 May 1926, *passim*.

[33] Winterton was opposed by both Liberal and Conservative candidates, and polled fewer than half the total votes cast. *Leics. Mercury*, 31 May 1929, p. 6.

[34] Ibid. 18 May 1929, p. 7.   [35] Ibid. 1 June 1929, p. 14.

[36] An Irish peer.

[37] *Leics. Mercury*, 31 May 1929, p. 16; 1 June 1929, p. 14.   [38] Ibid.

[39] Ibid. 6 Oct. 1931, p. 5; 12 Oct. 1931, p. 1.   [40] Ibid. 12 Oct. 1931, p. 4.

[41] Ibid.   [42] Ibid. 16 Oct. 1931, p. 7.

[43] Ibid. 28 Oct. 1931, p. 9; 29 Oct. 1931, p. 7.

with 1929,[44] than to the combination of the Liberal and Conservative parties. The supporters of the National Government remained predominant in the Leicestershire constituencies until the outbreak of war in 1939. A by-election in the Harborough division in 1933 resulted in the return of the Conservative candidate, Ronald Tree, by a considerable majority.[45] At the general election of 1935 Sir William Edge was again elected as a National Liberal for the Bosworth division; in the other three constituencies of the county the successful candidates were all Conservatives.[46] Of the four constituencies, only Loughborough was contested by the independent Liberals.[47] The majorities of the National Government candidates were substantially reduced in all four divisions.[48]

During the period from 1885 to 1939 the county constituencies of Leicestershire neither returned any very notable members to the House of Commons nor displayed any distinctively local features in their political life. On the contrary, the voting of the county electors followed the general trends of public opinion throughout Britain fairly closely. This is no doubt what might have been expected from the nature and situation of the constituencies, for being situated almost in the centre of England, and containing several expanding industries, they could not remain unaffected by general changes in public opinion. On the other hand, the area lacked any special conditions likely to give rise to extreme political views.

The period covered by this article comes to an end with the outbreak of war in 1939, but the results of the three general elections which have been held between the end of the war and the present date[49] may be briefly noted. In 1945 the Labour party was victorious in the Bosworth, Harborough, and Loughborough divisions, but the Conservatives succeeded in retaining Melton. The Liberals fought all the county constituencies except Bosworth, but in all three cases the Liberal candidate came at the bottom of the poll.[50] In 1950 the Conservatives again held Melton, and succeeded in regaining Harborough, but the Bosworth and Loughborough divisions remained in the hands of the Labour party. The Liberals fought all the county constituencies except Loughborough, but with little success.[51] In 1951 the seats were again evenly divided, the Conservatives retaining Harborough and Melton and the Labour party retaining Loughborough and Bosworth. On this occasion the Liberal party, once so strong in the county, only contested the Harborough division.[52] Both in 1950 and in 1951 the Labour and Conservative parties polled a substantial number of votes in each of the four constituencies. None of the county constituencies could be considered to be overwhelmingly in favour of any one political party.

[44] In the Melton division the Labour candidate polled more votes in 1931 than in 1929, when there was a Liberal candidate: ibid. 1 June 1929, p. 14; 29 Oct. 1931, p. 7.
[45] *Whitaker's Almanac* (1935), 273.
[46] *Leics. Mercury*, 15 Nov. 1935, p. 15; 16 Nov. 1935, p. 13.
[47] Ibid.
[48] Ibid.
[49] 1952.
[50] *Whitaker's Almanac* (1946), 329.
[51] Ibid. (1952), 347.
[52] Ibid., Supplement, p. xxiii.

MEDIEVAL AGRARIAN HISTORY

I. Early Settlement. II. The Domesday Survey. III. The Medieval Village and its Fields. IV. Medieval Cropping. V. Meadow and Pasture. VI. Peasant Farming. VII. Landlord Farming. VIII. Estate Administration. IX. Agrarian Change in the Later Middle Ages. X. Social Changes in the Later Middle Ages. XI. Medieval Inclosures for Pasture. XII. The Dissolution.

MEDIEVAL agriculture, in Leicestershire as elsewhere, was much more primitive and more uniform in character than it is today. The principal reason for variety in modern times is the development of production for the market; and the search in a capitalist society for the most profitable type of agricultural production has enhanced the importance of physical variations. In medieval agriculture, however, the market did not determine the character of production. The sustenance of the farmer and his family was the main objective. Even the urban demand was unspecialized, and hence there was comparatively little specialization in production. Everyone had to produce (on the whole) the same type of grain crop and tend the same sort of domesticated animals for meat, wool, and pulling power. Variations in the quality of the land are therefore rarely referred to in medieval documents. A remark in 1345 by those surveying the lands of the deceased Geoffrey Lutterel at Saltby that the arable was not worth more because it was poor and stony, is unusual.[1]

Leicestershire contains little of the very best land such as is found in the Fens or the Vale of Evesham. Much of its land is, however, good. East of the River Soar most of the land is boulder clay overlying the Lias. It is fertile but mostly heavy; and in some parts (the Vale of Belvoir and the south-east) a high water-table makes the land liable to flooding. There are some important minor variations in this eastern half of the county. A belt of lighter marlstone loam runs north-east from Scalford to Knipton, forming a sort of downland whose northern edge is the escarpment overlooking the Vale of Belvoir. Another small but significant variation is a belt of light fertile soil on a limestone spur running north and south along the Lincolnshire border from Croxton Kerrial to Sproxton. West of the Soar the land varies more over short distances. For the most part it is also land of reasonable quality, much of it heavy boulder clay, but interspersed with lighter and more easily worked soils derived from sandstones and gravels, especially in the extreme west (the Mease basin). Set in this region, however, is a large area of which the soils are derived from pre-Cambrian rocks. These are of poor quality, stony, and badly drained. This is the Charnwood Forest area. It repelled all but a few settlers throughout the Middle Ages, and at the beginning of the 17th century was still described as 'that vast and decayed Forest of Charnwood'.[2]

Finally, the agricultural land of the principal river valleys, those of the Soar

[1] C 135/77/4.
[2] Wm. Burton, *Description of Leics.* (1622), 2.

and Wreak, occupies an important place. On the banks of both are considerable deposits of alluvium, and farther away from the banks themselves are older alluvial deposits and gravel terraces. The nearer alluvial banks are liable to flood and are therefore unsuitable for arable farming, but make good meadow land. The higher alluvium is better drained, and the gravel terraces in the region of Syston, Cossington, and Sileby, and, to the north-west, near Loughborough, provide the most fertile soils in the county.

The drainage system of the county was of great importance to medieval farmers. In this respect the eastern and western halves of the county differed considerably. That part of Leicestershire lying to the east of the Soar contains many small streams. These flow westwards and southwards from the uplands and the wolds, mainly to the Soar or to its tributary the Wreake, or southwards towards the Welland. Far fewer streams reach the Soar from the west. The main streams are those which flow from the western edge of the Charnwood Forest area towards the Mease and the Anker. The factors which determined settlement were complex, but access to drinking-water was fundamental.

EARLY SETTLEMENT

It is not until the 11th century that anything can be said about the specific agrarian conditions of Leicestershire. Earlier than that only inferences can be drawn from agricultural conditions in England as a whole.

Anglian settlers began to penetrate the English Midlands from the east before the end of the 5th century. It was they who laid the authentic base for the future development of agriculture in Leicestershire.[3] We know this first of all from the archaeological evidence of pagan Anglian cemeteries. There are some thirty of these sites, dated by archaeologists between the end of the 5th and the middle of the 7th century. Most of them lie beside the upland streams east of the Soar valley; about nine are in or near the Welland, Avon, and Soar valleys; only two have been found in the west of the county.[4] They are characteristic Anglo-Saxon achievements and should be placed in the general setting of a determined attempt, in the Midlands in particular, to advance beyond existing settlement areas and to bring under cultivation hitherto untouched land. The other evidence, which supplements the archaeological, is that of place-names. This confirms the picture we derive from the material remains of the early settlers. It seems probable that, as in other parts of the country, the Angles penetrated the damp oak and ash forest of the Midlands by following the rivers. Those landing in the Wash found their way up the Welland and so northwards, possibly up the Eye Brook to the high ground round Tilton. Others, possibly a little later than those coming up the Welland, entered Leicestershire from the Trent valley, coming up the Soar and down the Wreak. The almost complete absence of the earlier type of place-names (ending in -ing and -ingham) suggests that the most determined and lasting settlement came late in the 6th century,

---

[3] For most of what follows, see W. G. Hoskins, 'Anglian and Scandinavian Settlement in Leics.', *T.L.A.S.* xviii, 110–36, and 'Further Notes on the Anglian and Scandinavian Settlement in Leics.', ibid. xix, 93–109. The uncertainty of the subject is emphasized by Dr. Hoskins's self-criticism in the second article of what he wrote in the first. See also *Anglo-Saxon Leics. and Rut.* (Leic. City Mus.).

[4] Cemeteries or evidence of burial at Knipton, Saxby, Melton Mowbray, Twyford, Lowesby, Beeby, Shawell, Stoke Golding, Wigston Magna, Glen Parva, Rothley, Loughborough, Bensford Bridge, Sysonby, Queniborough, Barkby, Baggrave, Ingarsby, Keythorpe, Medbourne, Husbands Bosworth, Harston.

although some very early (early 6th century) finds have been made at Saxby, Bensford Bridge, and Glen Parva.[5]

From this initial settlement period until the turmoil of the Danish invasions, colonization, primarily of the eastern half of the county, went on steadily. Like much of the so-called 'Midland Triangle' the soil was mostly that heavy clay which was not immediately attractive to the lightly equipped settler. Consequently most of the earliest settlements were made on the glacial gravels which capped the boulder clay, or on the river-gravel terraces. These soils were lighter to work and better drained than the clay, but were usually small in area. Thus while the village settlement itself did not extend beyond the limits of the gravel, the increasing population soon forced the settlers to extend cultivation to the more intractable lands beyond. A detailed analysis of such a village has been made.[6] The medieval fields of Wigston Magna stretched far beyond the gravel over the clay, but the village stopped short at the edge of the gravel.

It is the evidence of place-names, again, which is our principal source for the nature of the settlement of the Danish invaders of the 9th and early 10th centuries. The village names show that the most intense settlement was in the north-west of the county, and in the north-east, in the valley of the Wreak.[7] But field names also reveal Danish influence and these (though not yet sufficiently analysed) seem to suggest a wider spread of Danish settlement than that revealed by village names alone.[8] Since Leicester, in the centre of the county, was one of the five Danish boroughs it is more than likely that Danish farmers (whether lords or peasants) would settle in a wide radius around it.[9] Whether the Danes actually created new settlements, and in so doing brought more land into cultivation, cannot be proved. It would seem natural that this should be so, but the predominance of Danish names in an area may mean the loss of identity of pre-existing settlements rather than the creation of new settlements. In some instances we know that this was so, but it is also likely that they founded some entirely new villages. Whatever may be the answer to the problem, the fact remains that the Danish occupation was of great importance for the social structure of the county, as we shall see from an analysis of Domesday Book, compiled two centuries later. The social significance of this settlement was that the tendencies towards the creation of a sharp division between territorial lords and servile peasants, an inevitable consequence of both economic development and war, were retarded by the very people responsible for the war. For Danish society was more primitive than English. It was less developed away from tribal forms and towards feudalism. Free Danish tribesmen were not reduced to such a subordinate social position as was becoming the fate of the English ceorls. Just as the successive settlements of the semi-tribal Slavs in the territory

---

[5] None, it will be noticed, in the main area of concentration east of Soar and south of Wreak.

[6] W. G. Hoskins, 'The Fields of Wigston Magna', *T.L.A.S.* xix, 163–97; cf. also his 'Galby and Frisby' in *Essays in Leics. Hist.* 25.

[7] F. T. Wainwright in *Derbys. Arch. Jnl.* (1947).

[8] The word 'wong' from Scandinavian 'vangr', for furlong, is a field-name element found in many villages with purely English names, such as Bottesford, Stathern, Potters Marston, Drayton, Burrough, Easton, Long Whatton, Burton on the Wolds, Stoughton. The Scandinavian 'gate', for road, is found at Belvoir and Bottesford. 'Thorp', for outlying settlement, is found in Waltham on the Wolds. The word 'wong', however, became a generally accepted dialect word amongst the English as a word for furlong or flat, *P.N. Northants.* (E.P.N.S.), 270–1; cf. *Introd. to Surv. of Engl. P.N.* (E.P.N.S.), i, 89, for Scandinavian field names in villages with Engl. names. For 'wong' as furlong see *P.N. Notts.* (E.P.N.S.), 292.

[9] Leics. Forest is referred to in Dom. Bk. as 'Hereswode', the wood of the army, i.e. of the settled Danish army; F. M. Stenton, *Danes in Engl.*, 6 n.

of the Byzantine Empire renewed the declining forces of its free peasantry, so the Danes in eastern England bolstered up the free elements of peasant society which the evolution of feudalism was always tending to eliminate.[10]

Little more can be said about the specific features of the agrarian life of pre-Conquest Leicestershire, at any rate on the basis of written evidence.[11] For some English counties there is a wealth of land books from which conclusions can be drawn about land tenure and social conditions. Other facts about agricultural life which apply to England as a whole can be derived from Anglo-Saxon literary sources. There is, however, only one extant land charter[12] which refers to Leicestershire and that tells us nothing that is useful for the present purpose. We are brought therefore to the first important document for the understanding of medieval Leicestershire agrarian conditions—Domesday Book.

THE DOMESDAY SURVEY

By 1086 there were in Leicestershire nearly 300 named settlements, varying in size from considerable villages to mere hamlets. For example, on the generally heavy clays of the Vale of Belvoir, at the foot of the escarpment, were five settlements of considerable size, Bottesford (110 recorded inhabitants), Barkestone (52), Harby (47), Hose (49), and Long Clawson (70).[13] These settlements were in many respects favoured by geography. Their fields became well known later as amongst the best corn-yielding soils of Europe. The villages were situated on the spring line at about the 150-foot contour and (as the old parish boundaries show) the village territories combined the flat arable lands of the Vale with the grazing lands of the escarpment. Large villages are also frequently found in the eastern part of the county, especially in the Wreak valley. They are also to be found in the Soar valley. But there are very few large villages west of the Soar. There, conditions of settlement were less attractive, and settlers moving up Watling Street to the Soar, the Trent, or the Avon tended to bypass the area. Newbold Verdon, for instance, had only 5 recorded inhabitants. Kirby Muxloe had 5, Kirkby Mallory 17. There were, of course, more populous villages than these in the same area. Hinckley, with 69 recorded inhabitants, was perhaps already becoming a local market centre. Sibson (now only a hamlet) had 48 recorded inhabitants. But most settlements lay in the eastern half of the county, and they were, on the whole, much larger than those in the west.

Settlement means clearance. The dense settlement in the east, the lighter settlement in the west, are likely to be reflected in the information we have in Domesday Book about the distribution of woodland. This in general is true. When references to woodland are plotted on the map the principal wooded area is seen to be west of the Soar. The extreme western portion of the county, however—the area whose streams drain into the Mease and the Anker—was not

---

[10] M. V. Levtchenko, *Byzance des origines à 1453*, 119, 130; Stenton, *Danes in Engl.* 14, and *Anglo-Saxon Engl.* 508.

[11] 'Amongst all the five shires [of the Northern Danelaw] there is not one of which the early history is involved in such utter obscurity as that which attends the condition, before the Conquest, of the county of Leicester.' Stenton, *Types of Manorial Structure in Northern Danelaw*, 77.

[12] Birch, *Cart. Sax.*, no. 1283, cited Stenton, op. cit. 78.

[13] The Bottesford entry almost certainly included other settlements, and must be interpreted in this light. J. C. Russell, *Brit. Medieval Population*, 38, suggests that the number of recorded inhabitants should be multiplied by 3½ to arrive at the actual population, but there is no agreement over this figure.

wooded, nor was the south-western tip. These were in fact more heavily settled and more economically advanced areas than the central portion west of the Soar. The core of the Charnwood Forest area itself did not stand out as heavily wooded. Its rock outcrops did not permit the growth of trees worth recording by the Domesday commissioners.[14] The north-eastern and central eastern portions of the county, areas of earliest settlement by the Old English, have practically no recorded woodland. But the south-eastern corner of the county, adjoining what became Rutland, was as heavily wooded as western Leicestershire. It was an extension into the county of the Forest of Rutland and Leicestershire. With its headquarters at Oakham, this was the only royal forest in Leicestershire throughout the Middle Ages.[15] Nevertheless, this south-eastern corner was, in spite of the survival of much woodland, by no means so lightly populated as the Charnwood and Leicester Forest areas. The coincidence of a woodland area with a fair degree of settlement is not very surprising. The Domesday figures, even for those parts where forest seems to be most dense, in fact describe only scattered and not very large stretches of woodland. While we need not challenge the existence of woodland at places where Domesday Book describes it, it may well be that more wood actually existed than was recorded. For example, the total woodland in 1086 at Ashby-de-la-Zouch was 1 league by 4 furlongs; but a single charter of 1316 refers to a sale of 200 acres of wood there. Similarly in 1306 William de Roos, lord of Belvoir, was seeking permission to inclose 100 acres of spinney at Redmile, where no wood is mentioned in 1086.[16] These later references must be added to the general picture given by the Domesday figures. Out of a sample of 47 miscellaneous references to woodland from 13th- and 14th-century manorial and legal sources, only 7 relate to villages where no wood appears on the Domesday map, 2 relate to villages in the south-east forest area, and the rest relate to places west of the Soar, precisely where the principal wooded areas of 1086 are recorded.

The other Domesday evidence for economic development mainly concerns the distribution of agricultural equipment (chiefly mills and ploughs), assessments for taxation, and estimates of manorial values. Something can also be said about the distribution of meadow land, though statements that meadow land was deliberately cultivated at this period should be regarded with caution.[17] Meadow land was naturally mainly dependent on water-supply. The upper valley of the Soar was rich in meadow, even as compared with the lower Soar, but the lands to the west were very deficient, except for the western tip where the few streams of this area drain into the Mease and the Anker. East of the Soar there was meadow land in the valleys, especially those of the upper Wreak and the Welland. But even away from the main valleys meadow was abundant in the east. This no doubt was due to the innumerable small streams of the uplands. Meadow land was precious. At all times in the Middle Ages its rental value was much higher than that of arable, a reflection of the acute shortage of animal feeding-stuffs. The abundance of meadow in the east of the county was therefore an important economic asset.

---

[14] D. Holly, 'Domesday Geography of Leics.', *T.L.A.S.* xx, 180. This article contains an analysis of most of the Domesday geographical data, which has been independently checked for the present purpose.

[15] The Leics. portion was officially disafforested in 1235 ;*Cal. Chart. R. 1226–57*, 193; see also above, p. 87, and below, p. 266.

[16] Hist. MSS. Com., *Hastings*, i, 6; Nichols, *Leics.* ii, App., 16.

[17] Cf. *T.L.A.S.* xx, 180.

The exact signification of various phrases in *Domesday Book* stating the numbers of ploughs that there had been or could be on a manor continues to puzzle historians.[18] A strange feature of some Leicestershire manors is that there appear to be more ploughs employed than there was land for them. The conclusion might be drawn that there was 'overstocking'.[19] On the other hand, the extremely low technical level of medieval agriculture should make us hesitate to conclude that the 11th-century farmers were over-equipped either with plough-beasts or with ploughs. At the risk of evading the problem it is best for a general survey of conditions simply to consider how many ploughs there were in 1086, for this is precisely ascertainable.

The highest concentration of plough-teams is found in the valleys of the Soar, Wreak, and Welland, in the Eye Brook valley and the Vale of Belvoir; the lowest in the Charnwood and Leicester Forest areas. As far as the western half of the county is concerned, however, the extreme west and south-western parts seem to be rather more advanced. The same is true of the distribution of mills, the other important technical equipment of medieval farming. The construction of water-mills was one of the most important advances made by early medieval peoples beyond the level of technical advance of the ancient world.[20] The Anglo-Saxons were not behind the peoples of the Continent in this. But the use of the water-mill naturally requires water-power, and, as we have seen, the eastern half of the county was, in this respect, more favoured than the west. Taking these natural conditions in conjunction with the denser population and other symptoms of economic advancement (for a surplus is necessary to build a mill), it need not surprise us to find that most Leicestershire water-mills in 1086 were on the Soar and the streams to the east of it.

These economic conditions were inevitably reflected in the Domesday manorial valuations and figures of national taxation. The manors of the east (and especially of the north-east) were valued more highly than those in the west. The tax valuations (though not coinciding precisely with manorial values) were also higher in the east than in the west. Here again the west was not uniformly backward. The Mease and Anker basins were more advanced than the central area with Charnwood Forest as its core. Similarly the southwest (roughly the Leicester–Hinckley–Lutterworth triangle) stands out as a more favoured area. The higher values of the east were reflected generally in a higher assessment to taxation.

The foregoing remarks give a general idea of the variations in the level of agrarian technique in Leicestershire. They by no means exhaust the use of Domesday Book, for we can also reach some important conclusions about the proportions of various classes of the population, the extent of landlord farming, and the wealth (at any rate in terms of ploughs) of the peasantry.

As is well known, the Domesday manor was not necessarily coincident with the village. Some villages contained within them more than one manor, some were coextensive with one manor; and in some cases the manor might contain several villages, hamlets, or subdivisions of villages and hamlets. Ashby-de-la-Zouch was a village which was organized as the manor of one man, Ivo, who

[18] It is important not to compare the information concerning ploughs and plough-lands as real, potential, or past agrarian units with the fiscal units also called plough-lands (*carucati*) for which every Domesday manor was assessed.

[19] *T.L.A.S.* xx, 186, 198; F. W. Maitland, *Dom. Bk. and Beyond*, 427.

[20] M. Bloch, 'Avènement et conquêtes du moulin à eau', *Annales d'histoire économique et sociale* (1935).

had it from Leicestershire's greatest magnate, Hugh of Grantmesnil. Ashby had a recorded population of 21 and an equipment of 7 ploughs. Its taxation assessment was 14 carucates. Hose, a village in the Vale of Belvoir, provides a marked contrast, since it contained four separate manors. Two of these were held by tenants of Robert de Todeni; the other two by tenants of Robert the usher (*hostiarius*). The recorded population was, however, only a little more than twice that of Ashby (49). There were 15½ ploughs all told in these 4 manors, and the assessment was 14½ carucates. Each of the Hose manors, as an economic organism, was therefore on a smaller scale than the single manor of Ashby. The manor of Barrow-on-Soar which Earl Hugh of Chester held from the king is an example of the third type. In Barrow itself there was a recorded population of 27, in one manorial organism. The village was equipped with 15 ploughs and 3 mills. It is probable that the mills did not serve only the comparatively small population of Barrow, for the manor had appendages in 13 other villages. Directly subordinate to the earl in these outlying villages were 4 knights and 42 peasants of varying status. In their turn the knights had under them 15 peasants. In each of the 13 outlying villages[21] these manorial appendages of Barrow formed only part of the total village population and economy. At Castle Donington, for example, the Countess Alveva had a large manor with a recorded population of 46 and an assessment of 22½ carucates, while the Barrow appendage was only assessed at 5 carucates. The greater part of Frisby on the Wreak was occupied by an appendage, assessed at 8 carucates, of the royal manor of Rothley, while the Barrow appendage was assessed at 1½ carucates.

The large manor consisting of a central organization with scattered members was not uncommon in the northern Danelaw. It has been suggested that its origins are to be found in the jurisdictional control by a lord over scattered groups of followers of free status owing him rent and suit of court, but in other ways not burdened with manorial obligations such as labour service.[22] Such conditions would seem to fit in with the settlement of free Danish warrior farmers in the Anglian villages of Leicestershire. It should, however, be noted that the peasants living in the outlying members of Barrow were not obvious descendants of free Danes. Out of the 57 only 4 belonged to the class usually assumed to be the descendants of the Danes, the sokemen. The rest were villeins and bordars, and one was a serf. There were, however, three other large 'sokes' or federal manors like Barrow in Leicestershire in whose outlying members sokemen preponderated among the peasantry. Two of these were royal manors, Great Bowden and Rothley. In Great Bowden itself there was the king's manor, with a recorded population of 37, and a manor held by Robert de Buci from the Countess Judith. But appendant to the royal manor were members in 10 villages in south-eastern Leicestershire,[23] containing a recorded population of 78, of whom 60 were sokemen. Rothley village was entirely in the king's hands with a recorded population of 48. The dependent population was

---

[21] Castle Donington, Cossington, Hoton, Seagrave, Sileby, Rearsby, Brooksby, Frisby on the Wreak, Frisby by Galby, Prestwold, Charley, Gaddesby, and Rotherby. Most of these villages are close enough to Barrow for us to be able to presume economic as well as purely jurisdictional ties between the manorial centre and the outlying members.

[22] Stenton, *Manorial Structure of Northern Danelaw*, 44–46; *V.C.H. Leics.* i, 287.

[23] Medbourne, Cranoe, Shangton, Carlton Curlieu, Illston, Galby, King's Norton, Stretton, Smeeton, Foxton. There were also men in Blaston and Theddingworth holding of mesne tenants but still with jurisdictional ties with Great Bowden.

distributed among 22 villages[24] and totalled 455, of whom 204 were sokemen. The third large federal manor belonged to Geoffrey de Wirce. The manorial centre was at Melton Mowbray, which was entirely in Geoffrey's hands, with a recorded population of 40. The outlying members of the manor lay in 7 villages.[25] These contained a recorded population of 123, of whom 100 were sokemen.

While the territorial possessions of the great Leicestershire nobles at the time of Domesday have already been described,[26] the extent of demesne farming on their lands has not. One of the chief features underlying agricultural organization on the great estates of western Europe in the Middle Ages was the direct exploitation by estate owners of manorial demesnes. In this way the great church estates of Carolingian Gaul ensured the regular supply of food, clothing, and other goods to the monks and clergy. In order to ensure the cultivation of demesne lands, compulsory labour services were demanded from both free and servile peasantry in the villages. A similar system was being elaborated on the big estates in England at least as early as the 10th century. As far as economic arrangements were concerned, the Norman nobles who took over the estates of the expropriated English could not have been faced with any novelties for them, and are not likely to have introduced any. In order to fulfil their military obligations, however, they subinfeudated substantial portions of their newly acquired lands to military tenants. In so doing they ceased to exercise control over the economic life of the subinfeudated villages. Hugh de Grantmesnil, Leicestershire's greatest landowner, kept in hand only about a third of the manors which he held of the king. Henry de Ferrers, on his smaller estate, kept about the same proportion in hand. The Count of Meulan kept about a quarter of his manors in hand and subinfeudated the rest.

Owing to the virtual non-existence of wage labour, and to the insignificance of slavery in its classical sense, much of the labour on the lords' demesnes was done by peasants as part of their rent. The larger the demesne, the greater tended to be that part of peasant rent rendered in the form of labour services. This had important social consequences. The enforcement of labour services implied a much more coercive relationship between lord and peasant than the demand for money rent, as is shown by the development by the Norman lawyers of the concept that the performance of certain types of labour service proved servile status.

The Domesday figures of ploughs on the demesne and tenants' ploughs may be used to gain a rough idea of the ratio of demesne to tenant farming. It would, however, be dangerous to attempt to calculate the area of demesne from the number of demesne ploughs. The amount of land with which the ploughs could deal varied considerably from place to place according to the character of the soil.[27] For the county as a whole the ratio of demesne to tenant ploughs seems to have been somewhat more than 1 : 3; that is, the average demesne might have been a little larger than one quarter of the total arable. This indi-

[24] Allexton, Barsby, Seagrave, Sileby, Tugby, Skeffington, North and South Marefield, Halstead, Caldwell and Wycomb, Tilton, Asfordby, Keyham, Wartnaby, Twyford, Somerby, Frisby, Saxelby, Grimston, Baggrave, Gaddesby.
[25] Frisby, Wyfordby, Burton Lazars, Eye Kettleby, Sysonby, Eastwell, Goadby Marwood.
[26] V.C.H. Leics. i, 286 et seq.
[27] Cf. the variations in the amount of land ploughable daily on various manors of the Bp. of Worc. in the 13th century; Red Bk. of Worc. (Worc. Hist. Soc.), s.v. Alia Extenta.

cates only a moderate level of demesne farming, less than on the big church estates of the Carolingian period, where demesnes were a third to a half of the total land of the manor (or *villa*). It is also probably a little less (as an average) than obtained on the estates of lay tenants-in-chief in Leicestershire at the end of the 13th century.[28] The Domesday average conceals, however, important variations. In some manors there was no demesne land, in others very little. On the other hand, in more than a third (117) of the manors, the number of demesne ploughs exceeded a third of the total ploughs, and in one-sixth (51) exceeded one-half of the manorial total. Demesne farming was therefore firmly entrenched in 11th-century Leicestershire.

Another way of estimating the importance of demesne farming is to calculate how many peasants were involved in the demesne economy. Domesday Book tells us nothing about labour services owed by peasants on the demesne, but from the description of manors it emerges clearly whether the manor consisted of a number of tenants grouped around a demesne, or of a group of men connected with their lord by suit of court and payment of rent in money or kind only. Of the total number of Domesday tenants of all grades, 73 per cent. dwelt on manors of the traditional type, that is, containing both demesne and tenant land. The remainder were unattached to manorial demesnes. There were about 190 of these unattached groups, as against 260 manors containing both demesne and tenant land. It should be noticed that about 40 per cent. of the peasants who were unattached belonged to the three federal manors of Great Bowden, Melton Mowbray, and Rothley, and nearly 30 per cent. to Rothley alone. Outside these rather special organizations, therefore, the number of peasants unattached to manorial demesnes was comparatively small. The 'normality' of at least one important element in the county's social and economic structure is worth stressing in view of the emphasis which has been placed on the peculiarities of this and other counties of the northern Danelaw.

What was the economic status of the peasants of Domesday Leicestershire?[29] This is a difficult question to answer, more difficult even than the better-known problem of their legal status. The principal peasant groups in 1086 were the sokemen, the *villani*, the *bordarii*, and the *servi*.[30] The large number of sokemen distinguishes Leicestershire, together with other Danelaw counties, from the rest of midland and southern England. They formed 30 per cent. of the peasant population. As we have seen, many of them were attached to their lords by obligations which were no doubt much lighter than those owed by peasants attached to a demesne. But though as much as one-sixth of the population of sokemen was attached to the three sokes already described, many of the rest were associated with *villani* and *bordarii* in manors of the ordinary type. The *villani*, who formed 41 per cent. of the peasant population in Leicestershire, were mainly the descendants of the Anglo-Saxon ceorls, now well on the way to economic and social servitude, though their legal status was probably not yet precisely defined. The *bordarii*, 21 per cent. of the recorded population, have been assumed to be a peasant group similar to the *villani* but probably holding small tenements, *bordarius* being the Norman equivalent of the *kotsetlas* or cottar of the *Rectitudines Singularum Personarum*. The *servi*, 6·5 per cent. of

[28] Judging by the Inq. p.m. of Edw. I's reign. But the 13th-cent. average figure also conceals great variations.

[29] See *V.C.H. Leics.* i, 305, for figures of the Domesday population. I have checked these figures.

[30] The 8 freemen and 41 priests have been ignored.

the recorded population, were usually counted as part of the demesne, and therefore differed from the rest. They were unfree landless servants—perhaps even slaves, as their name implies.

However speculative most statements about Domesday classes may be, there is one set of figures which permits us to say something definite about the economic resources of these peasants. On each manor tenants and ploughs are numbered. Unfortunately, in almost all cases the number of ploughs is given for the total manorial population, so that no precise figures can be given for the equipment of the different peasant groups. We can, however, get some idea of how many peasant families had to share in order to make up a plough-team. The average figure for the county as a whole is 4·8 peasants to each plough. This figure is of considerable significance, because it tells us also, by implication, something about the average size of peasant holdings, as well as emphasizing a vital aspect of medieval farming.

We do not know what the size of the Domesday plough-team was. It is clear that those who compiled the record assumed a conventional team of 8 oxen, but this may not have corresponded with reality. The number of oxen pulling medieval ploughs undoubtedly varied greatly from place to place even within the same village. On a heavy soil a heavier plough requiring more oxen would be used. On the whole Leicestershire soils were heavy, and a large plough-team was to be found in the 13th century. At Swannington, for instance, in 1289 we find a team of 8 oxen, in Thorp Satchville in 1284 a team of 4 oxen and 2 horses.[31] Now corresponding to the conventional 8-ox plough-team was the unit of tenure characteristic of the northern Danelaw known as the plough-land (or carucate). This represented the amount of arable land which a plough-team was capable of cultivating throughout the year.[32] It was subdivided into 8 oxgangs, which in Leicestershire contained generally about 12 acres of arable land, though it could vary from village to village. The oxgang, as its name implies, was the amount of land which one ox could plough in a year. The individual holder of one or two oxgangs did not plough with one or two oxen. He contributed his animals to the plough-team in which he shared with others.[33] Now if the average ratio of tenants to ploughs in the county was 4·8: 1, we may perhaps also say that the average peasant holding was something between one oxgang and two. Such an average perhaps tells us very little, but it emphasizes that the 11th-century peasant family was economically in a much lower position than the family holders of complete hides or plough-lands at an earlier period. By 1086 there were also quite considerable differences in peasant economic resources, as the ratios of tenants to ploughs on particular manors will show. Such ratios show differences between village and village, though not differences *within* the village, except in so far as a large number of poor peasants with little or no share in the common plough affect the ratio for the village as a whole.

[31] Farnham, *Leics. Notes*, iv, 192, 246, quoting KB27/120, m. 3, and Just. Itin. 1, 458, m. 17.

[32] It was assumed by the Normans to be equivalent to the Anglo-Saxon hide, which was the land capable of keeping one family, and which was subdivided into 4 yardlands (or virgates). Both measures are found in Leics. I see no reason for assuming that the substitution of plough-land for hide represents anything more than a change in nomenclature (Stenton, *Anglo-Saxon Engl.* 506–7). The original hide was the land supporting the large family of several generations, a plough-owning social unit no doubt, and therefore similar to the ploughland. When the tribal family disintegrated into the two-generation family the typical peasant holding became divided also.

[33] These statements are, of course, a generalized account of a reality, which may never have corresponded exactly to it, but which probably fluctuated around it.

MEDIEVAL AGRARIAN HISTORY

The existence of considerable variations of economic status among the peasantry is illustrated by the sokemen, that peasant aristocracy whose members have been assumed to have been 'as a general rule wealthier than the villein'.[34] Some of them undoubtedly were. A sokeman of Sysonby had a whole plough-team to himself. At Walcote two sokemen shared a plough. In the outlying members of the manor of Melton Mowbray 100 out of 123 peasants were sokemen, and the ratio of tenants to ploughs was low—2·9 : 1. But there are sharp contrasts. On a Bottesford manor 7 sokemen, 2 villeins, and 13 bordars had 2 ploughs between them, some, we are told, had nothing at all. These would probably be some of the bordars. In Gilmorton, where there were 24 sokemen out of a population of 28 (the other 4 being Frenchmen), the tenant-to-plough ratio was 5·6—considerably higher than the average. General statements about the relative position of sokemen as a group are therefore difficult to make, though where a direct comparison is possible between groups of sokemen and groups of other peasants in the same village, the sokemen sometimes seem to have the advantage. In Croxton Kerrial, for instance, 30 sokemen had 8 ploughs, whilst 22 villeins and 2 bordars had only 2½ ploughs. At Wigston Magna a group of 38 sokemen and free tenants of various sorts (there were 31 sokemen in all) had 8 ploughs, whilst a group in the same manor of 32 villeins, 12 bordars, and a priest had only 3 ploughs between them. Similar variations occur as between the *villani* and *bordarii*. At Barrow-on-Soar, on the one hand, where there were only villein and bordar tenants, the peasants were well equipped with ploughs. The tenant-to-plough ratio was 2·2. At Cadeby, on the other hand, there was only 1 plough between 7 villeins, 3 bordars, and a priest. The scale of equipment varies between these two extremes throughout the county.

THE MEDIEVAL VILLAGE AND ITS FIELDS

We do not find in Domesday answers to more than a few of the many questions we should like to ask about medieval agrarian conditions. It is not until the 12th and 13th centuries that we can draw a detailed picture of how the fields were worked, what crops were sown, what livestock was kept, and what equipment and buildings were at the disposal of the medieval farmer. This was the great period of the economic expansion of feudalism, and with it went an elaboration of social and political organization. This organizational development resulted in a vast increase in documentation. For the 13th century we have an ever-increasing wealth of conveyancing instruments, together with the annual accounts of manorial officials and the records of manorial courts. The intensified activity of the feudal state further increases our evidence, especially by providing us with the records of the central and itinerant royal courts in which many pleas of land were determined. When we give a general picture of the workings of medieval Leicestershire agriculture, it is therefore drawn mainly from 12th- and 13th-century evidence. But we must also remember, when speaking of the field-systems of this period, that most if not all of their features had come into existence long before the Norman Conquest.

In discussing Domesday Book we have spoken mainly of the manor, the basic unit of seigniorial economic and political power. It has been said that,

34 *V.C.H. Leics.* i, 300.

especially in the northern Danelaw, the geographical coincidence of manor and village was rare. The village preceded the manor. It was the creation of a peasant community, not necessarily socially homogeneous even at the time of the English invasions, but not yet subordinated to a territorial aristocracy. The manors created by the English and, later, Norman nobility were superimposed on the natural economic units, the villages and hamlets, without destroying their essential unity. Hence, even in the 15th century and later, we find that arrangements for the pasturing of animals on stubble fields and wolds had to be made by the village as a whole. Regulations were drawn up for these purposes in Wymeswold about the year 1425, in the presence of two manorial lords and the proctor of a third, but with the necessary common assent of the whole village.[35] Fines for a breach of regulations did not go to the lord but to the Church, and amends were made to him whose corn might be damaged by strays.

The fields, woods, and pastures belonged, then, to the village originally. The village economy was closely integrated. Conflicting property claims between owners of manors could not break up this economic unity, the strength of which was largely due to the fact that most agricultural operations had to be carried on collectively. This created a strong sense of social cohesion among the villagers which expressed itself in village custom. Custom governed a great range of village activity, from forms of inheritance and the property rights of widows to practical details about ploughing. These customs often appear in documents as 'manorial' customs, because the manorial organization was the only one capable of producing written records. Nevertheless what was called 'manorial' custom was for the most part village custom. The only defence the peasants had against the superior economic, political, and military strength of their lords was organization, based on the common routine of a semi-collective agriculture and expressed as custom. It was against custom that the lords had to fight when they sought to increase rents; and they themselves recognized its importance when they tried to justify their actions also on the grounds of custom.

The earliest cultivated plots that were taken in from the wood and waste were won by joint action by the members of the early village communities. This does not mean that there was at this time common appropriation of the crops or of the land. Anglo-Saxon laws of the 7th century make it clear that there were considerable elements of private (that is family) property in land within the framework of an agriculture which was dominated by collective practices. But as we have seen from Domesday Book the ratio of tenants to ploughs implies that most cultivators had to share the plough-teams. It has been convincingly shown that the actual field system arose naturally from common ploughing, and common ploughing must have followed joint action in the clearance of the wood.[36]

These conditions existed in Leicestershire, and every piece of evidence about the predominating form of field layout in the county emphasizes that it had all the features of the traditional open-field system of the Midlands. The Leicestershire evidence, however, reinforces that from other parts of the Midlands in showing that the picture of the Midland open-field system has in the past perhaps been too simply drawn.

[35] *Statutum de Wymundswold*, printed Hist. MSS. Com., *Middleton*, 106–9.
[36] C. S. and C. S. Orwin, *Open Fields*, 36–41.

MEDIEVAL AGRARIAN HISTORY

We are accustomed to think of the cultivated land of the old agricultural system as being subdivided into two or three great open fields in order to permit a two- or three-course rotation of crops and fallow. In fact the village fields were much more complex than this. The first clearing that was made in the settlement period must have been of a size capable of being ploughed, sown, and harrowed by, say, three or four ploughs during the first season of settlement. Ploughing side by side, the cultivators created a bundle of adjacent 'strips', 'lands', or 'selions', each about a furlong in length, varying in width with the quality of the soil, but usually between one-quarter and one-third of an acre in area. The block of land thus ploughed became known as a 'furlong', 'shot', 'flat', or 'wong', according to local speech. Both the words 'flat' and 'wong' are Scandinavian and found in the Danelaw. 'Wong' was a very common name in Leicestershire. In the Latin documents the word used is usually *cultura*. As the years passed and as the village population grew, wong would be added to wong until the complex system, like a patchwork quilt, which we can see on pre-inclosure maps, was created. Each wong was different in layout and size, according to the lie of the land. Each had a characteristic name,[37] usually from some local topographical peculiarity. Many of the names were carried over when the wongs had been made into inclosed fields, so that they still survive. The number of wongs or furlongs which make up the open cultivated land of the village naturally varied considerably according to the size of the settlement. The late-14th-century accounts of Kirby Bellars manor show that the arable demesne was scattered over 113 furlongs. An early-14th-century deed concerned with the assignment of land at Hoby in dower shows that the land was distributed over 141 furlongs. At King's Norton in 1360 the demesne of Owston Abbey was spread over 71 furlongs.[38] There may well have been other furlongs in these three villages, in which there was no demesne or dower land. The figures, then, are minimum figures, and show how intricate the typical open-field system could be.

Most wongs or furlongs were shared between several tenants, each of whom would hold a few strips in a number of wongs to make up his total holding. Deeds of transfer show that throughout the Middle Ages farm-holdings were much fragmented. This was true even of the demesnes of the manorial lords, who had greater opportunities than the peasants of consolidating their strips by exchange and purchase. In the 15th century the demesnes of Leicester Abbey at Barkby, in all about 148 acres, lay in 231 separate parcels. Only 34 of these parcels were as large as 1 acre or more. A very large number (122) were less than ½ acre in size. The numerous small land transfers among free tenants which are transcribed in the Wyggeston Hospital records show a similar fragmentation of the open-field holdings. Ten acres of land transferred at Oadby in the 14th century lay in 25 separate parcels, only 2 of which exceeded ½ acre in area. A holding of 23 acres at Great Bowden in 1507 was split up into 59 parcels of similar size. An early-15th-century transfer at Bottesford was of 14

---

[37] A large collection of furlong names could be made from printed sources alone. An example of some field names at Bottesford from an agreement about tithes in 1250 is given in Nichols, *Leics.* ii, App., 11–12, from B.M. Peck MS. 4936: *Toftis, Milnecroft, Redwong* (possibly rye wong), *Sandwong*, and so on. The word 'ridding' (a clearing) is found at Breedon in 1441: *Arable Ryding, Dame Emma Ryding*, as is the other Danish word for wong mentioned above, *Angelle Flat* (Hist. MSS. Com., *Hastings*, i, 35). An example of a wong named after a crop is *Barlihul* at Husbands Bosworth (B.M. Add. MS. 28639—12th century).

[38] R. H. Hilton, *Econ. Development of Some Leics. Estates*, App. III; Hist. MSS. Com., *Hastings*, i, 84–85; S.C. 11/386.

scattered parcels of land, 10 of which consisted of single strips of probably not more than ⅓ acre in size.[39] The conventional acre strip is almost a myth of the textbooks.

Tendencies towards subdivision as land changed hands by sale, gift, and inheritance could, of course, go hand in hand with the opposite tendency towards consolidation. Both tendencies are observable towards the end of the medieval period. On the other hand, as one would expect, in the earlier Middle Ages fragmentation had not gone so far. Land was taken into cultivation not only by groups of peasants sharing one common plough, and dividing up the land according to their contribution, but also by individuals. These would mostly be lords, but could also include the more substantial free tenants. Land assarted by them would, at first at any rate, be held as one piece: in individual ownership as far as arable cultivation was concerned, even if subject to common pasture rights after the harvest. An example of this process can be discerned in some deeds about Swannington. This village is on the western edge of Charnwood Forest, and there seems to have been a wide stretch of moor and woodland available for cultivation in the 13th century. According to a local jury, which testified in a suit of 1293, it was lawful for each freeman of Swannington to take in land from the waste and to cultivate it, according to the size of his existing freeholding. This 'approvement of the waste' was apparently going on apace, since the suit arose because of a clash between two substantial freeholders, each of whom claimed to be chief lord of the village and therefore to have exclusive rights over the waste.[40] One of these was named Roger Godeberd. According to the cartulary of Garendon Abbey, Roger[41] possessed an assart which was known as 'Godebertes Ryding'. He granted the whole of this to Garendon Abbey with permission to cultivate and use it at pleasure. Clearly this was what we should call a grant in severalty. Yet at some later date it seems to have become divided in ownership. This is shown by a reference in the same cartulary to an exchange of 4 acres held *in* Godebertes Ryding by a third person, for a piece of land in front of the abbot's gate. Furthermore, in this deed Godebertes Ryding is described as a *cultura*.[42] The sequence of events seems to have been that the land was taken into cultivation from the forest in severalty, and later subdivided as a result of some process of alienation by sale, lease, or gift. In the process it must have become indistinguishable from other *culture* of the village open-field system.

There are many references in the Leicestershire charters to wongs or furlongs held in single ownership, particularly in demesne. They varied considerably in size. At Breedon in the 13th century, belonging to Breedon Priory, was Burnagh flatte of 16 acres, and two other furlongs, called Byry and Barley croft, of 8 acres. A furlong was given by Roger Mowbray to Garendon Abbey in Thorp Arnold about the mid-13th century, in exchange for 32 acres belonging to the Abbey. It was assumed that Roger's furlong contained at least 32 acres, as the abbey was to retain anything in the furlong above that figure. Croxton Abbey had a number of complete furlongs in the East and West Fields of Croxton Kerrial varying from 3 to 152 acres. Some of these furlongs may

---

[39] B.M. Cott. MS. Galba E. III (*Liber de Terris Dominicalibus*); *Wyggeston Hosp. Rec.*, 183, 417; Farnham, *Leics. Notes*, vi, 214.

[40] Farnham, op. cit. iv, 192–3.

[41] Or his father, another Roger Godeberd.

[42] Nichols, *Leics.* iii, 836–7, citing a cart. of Garendon Abbey.

KILBY FROM THE AIR, SHOWING THE PATTERN OF INCLOSURE AND TRACES OF THE MEDIEVAL FIELD SYSTEM

have become divided, as at Swannington, so that with their strips in mixed ownership they would be quite indistinguishable from the other units of the open fields. Others might remain in severalty and eventually be inclosed, provided the rights of other tenants to pasture on the fallow could be bought out or got rid of in some way. John Botiler, lord of two-thirds of the village of Eaton in 1396, in a dispute about hay from the uncultivated boundary strips, or balks, in the open fields, claimed to 'have divers wongs in the fields of the said town lying contiguous, and divers balks enclosing those wongs'.[43]

MEDIEVAL CROPPING

The importance of the furlong as a unit is immediately apparent when the cropping system is studied. As is well known, the crop-rotation system of medieval agriculture required that every three years a field should be sown first with a winter crop and secondly with a spring crop, and in the third year allowed to lie fallow.

The method by which a constant supply of grain was ensured is equally familiar. The arable land of the village was divided into three main sectors, so that at any given time part of the land lay fallow, part was mainly under spring crops, and part was mainly under winter crops. In so far as the rotational pattern became fixed, two or three large open fields could be permanently maintained as the units of crop rotation. Thus the 113 furlongs which were the basic units of the arable at Kirby Bellars were grouped into three fields called Westfield, Eastfield, and Middlefield. At Wigston Magna there were also three fields—a north, a west, and an east field—but they were described according to landmarks on the parish boundaries towards which they stretched: the 'field towards Mucklow'; 'towards two brokes'; and 'towards Dry thorn hill'.[44] At Croxton Kerrial there were two main fields known as the West and the East Field.[45] On the other hand there are many surveys or terriers of lands in Leicestershire medieval villages which make no reference to this broad division. Such surveys describe land only according to the furlong or wong in which it was situated. A survey of the demesne possessions of Leicester Abbey at Lockington[46] locates the forty-three separate parcels of strips into which the arable was grouped within the various furlongs, but does not mention 'fields'. What does this divergence of practice mean? Where the two or three main fields remained outstanding features of the arable land, the practice must have originally been to crop one of two, or two of three fields, annually. In the case of the two-field system the proportion of winter and spring corn on the cropped field could vary. But half of the available area had to remain uncropped. In the case of the three-field system the fallow area was reduced, but if the system was to work at full efficiency an equal amount of spring and winter corn would have to be sown annually and in successive years. The evidence that is available suggests, however, that there was no such equal division between spring and winter crops, so that, however significant the main field divisions may once have been, the actual cropping system, by the late 13th century, had come to be more flexible than would be possible in a rigid three-field system. A spill-over

[43] John Rylands Libr., Latin MS. 222, f. 23. Nichols, op. cit. ii, App., 135; Farnham, *Leics. Notes*, ii, 198.
[44] W. G. Hoskins, 'The Fields of Wigston Magna', *T.L.A.S.* xix, 170.
[45] Nichols, *Leics.* ii, App., 81.   [46] B.M. Cott. MS. Galba E. III (*Liber de Terris Dominicalibus*).

of spring crops into the winter field was inevitable where the arable was organized in three fields. It is not surprising therefore that in some villages field divisions were ignored, and the furlong regarded as the basic unit for purposes of cropping.

The earliest satisfactory evidence for the cropping of the open fields in Leicestershire dates from the middle of the 13th century. The bailiffs' accounts for Barton-in-the-Beans, Stretton-in-the-Field, and Cold Overton—all manors of the Lord Edward—have been preserved for the harvest year 1256-7 together with an account for Stretton alone for 1257-8.[47] Records of the demesne sowings appear in the grange accounts and are tabulated below.

Demesne Sowing on Four Manors, 1256–8

Date	Place	Wheat				Rye				Barley				Oats			
		ac.	r.	qr.	bs.	ac.	r.	qr.	bs.	ac.	r.	qr.	bs.	ac.	r.	qr.	bs.
1256-7	Barton	43	1	11	6½	4	..	1	2	1½	..	½	1	33½	1	20	5
,,	Cold Overton	80½	..	19	6	3	3	1	..	4½	1½	1	2½	120	..	65½	½
,,	Stretton	35	..	9	7	..	..	..	..	3	1	..	7	53	1	28	..
1257-8	Stretton	43	..	9¼	2	..	..	..	..	2½	..	..	6	34	..	16½	..

As will be seen, there was no careful equality between spring and winter crops. Indeed, except for Barton in 1256-7 and Stretton in 1257-8, there was a marked preponderance of oats: and this was the more significant in that the greater variety of spring crops found on these and other manors in the 14th century (see below) was yet to appear. It is noteworthy that apart from some internal consumption of barley, rye, and oats for the farm servants and the cattle, the bulk of the grain was sold. The preponderance of spring crops may have been due to a changing market demand. But internal consumption within the manor, by the community and its beasts, no doubt played its part. Possibly, too, the change was partly a reflection of the growing shortage of pasture as the arable area extended, and of the need for other animal feeding-stuffs.

Some accounts and surveys of a number of villages in the 14th century[48] suggest that the preponderance of spring crops, which was beginning in the mid-13th century, became more marked as time went on. Certainly, these documents are too few in number for any but tentative conclusions. However, out of fifteen 14th-century accounts or surveys, in only two do we find more winter than spring crops, and for the most part spring crops comprise about three-quarters of the total crop. Furthermore, new crops appear: beans, peas, maslin, and dredge. The first two, though used indeed for human consumption, were primarily fed to animals in winter. Incidentally the extensive use of these leguminous crops may have marked something of a technical advance in another respect, since they replace the nitrogen in the soil which the white-grain crops exhaust. The other two crops are not really new, since maslin was simply a mixture of wheat and rye, and dredge of barley and oats.

The evidence from these documents is reinforced by figures of cropping from some twenty-five places on the Leicester Abbey estates, which show

[47] S.C. 6/1094/11. One bailiff (Wm. of Willoughby) accounts for all 3 manors in conjunction with the reeve of each.

[48] Rothley, Gaddesby, and Baggrave, 1309: E. 142/105; Broughton Astley and Lutterworth, 1322: S.C. 6/1146/17; Lindridge, 1323: S.C. 6/1147/8, and 1324: S.C. 6/1148/5; Stapleford, 1322: E. 142/67; Hallaton, Lutterworth, and Newbold Verdon, 1333: S.C. 6/1109/24; Norton, 1357 and 1358: S.C. 6/908/36; Owston, 1363, 1386, and 1387: S.C. 6/908/41 and 1108/23; Knossington, 1386 and 1387: S.C. 6/1108/23.

that at five different dates in the 14th and 15th centuries (1363, 1393, 1399, 1401, 1470) the proportion of winter crops never exceeded 23 per cent. of the total, while the proportion of peas, which was 17 per cent. in 1363, had risen to about 30 per cent. by the end of the century, and remained at about that level throughout the 15th century.[49]

These figures show that, from the point of view of agricultural practice, it was of little moment whether a village was run on the two-field system or the three-field system. This is vividly illustrated by the village of Kirby Bellars, already quoted as an example of a typical three-field system. In 1395 the demesne in the West Field was sown with 17 acres of wheat and 25 of barley; in the Middle Field with 6 acres of wheat, 88 of peas, and 34 of oats; while the East Field was fallow. In 1399 the demesne in the West Field was sown with 117 acres of peas; in the East Field with 70 acres of wheat, 56 of barley, and 10 of oats; while the Middle Field was fallow. In 1406 the East Field was fallow again; the demesne in the West Field was sown with 16 acres of wheat, 22 of barley, and 9 of oats; and the Middle Field with 64 acres of peas.[50] It may also be mentioned that the inquisitions *post mortem* in so far as they describe the arable demesne (beyond a statement of its acreage) do not speak in terms of 'fields'. They do, however, often say how much of the demesne lies fallow and in common. In such cases (affecting the outlook of lords with their own separate pastures) the royal officials consider the fallow part of the demesne to be without value.

MEADOW AND PASTURE

The arable lands were the most important part both of peasants' holdings and lords' demesnes. In a relatively unspecialized agriculture, in which subsistence needs were predominant, grain production was of fundamental importance. But the cultivation of the arable would not have been possible without plough and draught animals. These animals had to be fed, so that pastures and meadow land for hay were essential components of the village economy. Meadow land varied in extent according to natural conditions. In Leicestershire, according to Domesday Book, as we have seen, it was most abundant in the river valleys and in the eastern part of the county. But it is not easy to supplement the general picture one derives from Domesday Book of the relative amounts of meadow in different parts of the county with later figures of the ratio of meadow to other types of land. One class of evidence which may be used for this purpose consists of the inquisitions *post mortem*. The tenants-in-chief who form the subject of these inquiries were not likely to have been less favoured with meadow land than the peasants. The inquisitions covering roughly the late 13th and early 14th centuries form a reasonably sufficient sample. The surveys usually give a brief description of what land was held in demesne. Unfortunately the acreages given in these inquisitions cannot be relied upon as accurate, since the heirs (or the escheators) attempted to deceive the Crown about the value of the lands of the deceased. The amount of land in demesne was underestimated, and, naturally enough, the most valuable land—

---

[49] See Hilton, *Econ. Development of Some Leics. Estates*, 63. The figures include some manors outside Leics. but not enough of them to make a significant difference to the figures.

[50] Ibid. 152–6. In the last year, just over an acre of the Westfield and 54 acres of the Middlefield were described as pasture; while 47 acres of the one and 7 acres of the other field were leased out.

the meadow—was most undervalued. Consequently the apparently useful comparative figures for arable and meadow land in desmesne which (for lack of other evidence) we must use, must be understood as minimizing the amount of meadow.[51] Moreover, the extent of meadow land cannot in all cases be calculated as a fraction of the arable. For instance, the demesne of Fulk de Penebruge at Aylestone in 1296 was estimated at 8 yardlands.[52] But, as we shall see, a yardland (or oxgang) implied the existence of some meadow with the arable. Therefore, the meadow is not given separately. But in most surveys the demesne is described in acres, whether of arable or meadow. These surveys, during the period mentioned, give us information about the situation in fifty-five Leicestershire villages and hamlets.

In some of these villages, according to the inquisitions, there was very little demesne meadow. The survey for Newbold Verdon in 1317 says quite specifically that there was none.[53] There was none at Hallaton in 1331, though in 1280 there had been 2 acres to an arable demesne of 4 carucates (probably more than 400 acres).[54] The inquisitions of 1290 on John of Kirby's manors of Holt and Kirby Bellars describe the demesnes in terms of yardlands, but show that the only meadow in demesne was that in the headlands in the arable fields.[55] Most demesne, however, had some meadow, little though it might be. At Knaptoft in 1301 there were in demesne 9 acres of meadow, but this was with a demesne arable of 360 acres.[56] A ratio of only 1 : 40 between meadow and arable was not common, but there were nevertheless 20 out of the 55 villages where the ratio was 1 : 20 or more. Few demesnes had really considerable stretches of meadow. In only three or four cases was the meadow more than one-fifth the size of the arable. At Evington, for example, in 1336 there were

---

[51] A comparison of figures for meadow and arable drawn from inquisitions *post mortem* and manorial accounts:

Place and date					Meadow (acres)	Arable (acres)
Bagworth						
Inq. p.m. (1310)	.	.	.	.	10	120
account (1324)	.	.	.	.	40	80
Broughton Astley						
Inq. p.m. (1300)	.	.	.	.	10	160
account (1322)	.	.	.	.	31	230
Hallaton						
Inq. p.m. (1331)	.	.	.	.	headlands only	120
account (1333)	.	.	.	.	20	200
Lutterworth						
Inq. p.m. (1317)	.	.	.	.	6½	100
account (1322)	.	.	.	.	40	340
Newbold						
Inq. p.m. (1317)	.	.	.	.	none	57
account (1333)	.	.	.	.	30	210

Since there is no exact coincidence between dates of Inq. p.m. and of accounts, variations could be explained by changes in the situation between the dates concerned. But a change in arable demesne of 240 acres as at Lutterworth in 5 years, though by no means impossible, seems unlikely.

[52] C 133/75/1.
[53] C 134/56/1. But see n. 51 above.
[54] C 135/17/12; C 133/57/2, but see n. 51 above, for the evidence of the accounts.
[55] C 133/57/9, 'nec est pratum ibi nisi capita selionum quod jacet in predictis virgatis'.
[56] C 133/101/2.

100 acres of meadow to 400 acres of arable.[57] Apart from these, and from 16 or 17 villages where the demesne meadow was between one-fifth and one-tenth the size of the arable, meadow was at the most only one-tenth as extensive as the arable and in very many cases a good deal less than that.

Meadow land, like arable and pasture, could be held in severalty or be allotted to each villager annually in accordance with the size of his arable holding. There were varying degrees of holding in severalty. In some cases a landholder would have more or less complete control over a separate piece of meadow; in other cases, whilst always retaining the same piece of meadow year after year (instead of receiving a different annual allotment), he might have to allow the other villagers to exercise common pasture rights on his meadow after the hay was cut and removed. Some meadow land which was interspersed among the arable fields was subject to even greater limitations, being only mowable every third year when the field lay fallow and in common.[58] But mostly the meadows were separate from the arable, usually by the river or stream. A common Leicestershire term used in medieval documents to describe meadow was 'holm', which comes from a Scandinavian word meaning a piece of land by a stream, just as the word 'sike' (from Old English *sic*, stream) is found to be used for both stream and meadow.[59] In any case, the meadow had scarcity value and therefore the amount to which each villager had a right was carefully regulated. In many documents it is assumed that the amount of meadow appurtenant, say, to an oxgang, is locally known. Thus a man transferring land to Croxton Abbey in Croxton Kerrial itself gives an oxgang and 'as much meadow as pertains to an oxgang'. Another donor in the same village is more specific, granting 11 acres of arable and an acre of meadow, the whole lot counting as an oxgang (*que jacent pro una bovata terre*).[60] Sometimes the grant can be equally specific without stating quantities. A late-13th- or early-14th-century grant of meadow in Worthington to Breedon Priory defines the meadow as being the amount appurtenant to a yardland, and locates it precisely 'in le Dolemedu' as between the meadow of two other named persons.[61] This grant, however, illustrates another point of some importance. Although the meadow land had once, no doubt, been subject to periodical reallotment, as the name implies, by this date each man's possession had become fixed. Having become fixed, the appurtenance could be alienated if necessary from the parent arable holding. The component parts of the organic agrarian unit were becoming negotiable—an important aspect of the disintegration of the traditional peasant tenements.[62]

The careful allotment of meadow was matched by the care with which peasants' claims for grazing pastures were regulated. Stock could be put to

[57] C 135/43/12. Yet in 1272 there had been only 40 acres of meadow to a demesne arable of 40 oxgangs (stated in the surv. as equivalent to 600 acres), while in 1309 the demesne was described as containing 20 oxgangs with meadow and pasture appurtenant, but not measured; C 132/42/3, and C 134/8/20.

[58] As at Nailstone where, though meadow on the south fields was mowable annually, that in the north and east fields was mowable only once every 3 years; D.L. 43/14/3, mm. 54–65 (extent of lands of John Hastings, Earl of Pembroke, 15 Ric. II).

[59] Nichols, *Leics.* ii, App., 111, quotes from the Seagrave Cart. a reference to one dole (i.e. allotment) of meadow in Sileby *in holmo molendini*. One acre of meadow 'que jacet super Munitelandes et extenditur usque in Sicham de Wimundewolde' and another 'que jacet in Horensicha' are mentioned in an early-13th-century charter concerning Burton on the Wolds; ibid. iii, 826.

[60] Ibid. ii, App., 79.   [61] John Rylands Libr., Latin MS. 222, f. 48b.

[62] Cf. Hilton, *Econ. Development of Some Leics. Estates*, 56, where evidence for the same sort of 'negotiability' of meadow land on the Leic. Abbey estates is discussed.

graze on different types of land. First, the arable when fallow and the meadows when the hay was cut were thrown open to the beasts of the community—a right which could only be exercised in an open-field system where there were no permanent fences. The demesne pasture rights at Nailstone could only be exercised, according to the survey of 1392, every third year in certain specified parcels of land in the Eastfield, since they would only lie fallow once every three years.[63] The villagers of Diseworth, in a suit in 1371, claimed pasture rights together with the men of Belton on certain fields where the boundaries of the two townships joined, to be exercised when those fields were fallow.[64] In some cases (more particularly with meadow) the exact dates when the fields were thrown open to common pasture were specified. At Waltham in the Wolds all the meadows (*holmi*) were inclosed (*solebant poni in defensione*) from 2 February to 1 August. Then the date of inclosure was delayed until 25 March in order to give more grazing to the sheep of the Abbot of Croxton.[65] At Waltham in 1342 the period during which a certain field called Baneholm was open as common pasture extended from 3 May until 11 November. Between November and May it was claimed as the lord's severalty. Here it was not a question of the restoration of fences in the summer to allow the grass to grow, but of a division of interest between lord and community. The severalty was for agistment, not for hay.[66] At Wymeswold about 1425 the by-law already quoted laid down with care at what dates certain beasts were to be allowed pasture on the open fields and for how long. For a week after 14 September certain fields were allotted for the village cattle, then one of the wheat fields for another week. After Michaelmas, however, the wheat fields were forbidden. Horses were allowed in the pease field until Ascension Day. Naturally there were strict rules against the introduction either of the common or of private herds into the wheat and pease fields before the sheaves were gathered in.[67]

Since pasture was generally insufficient and limited in area, the number of beasts had to be stinted by regulation. A fixed number of each type of animal was allowed according to the nature of the holding. In 1245 it was stated by a jury at Croxton Kerrial that one yardland could sustain 40 sheep with their offspring until July; and 2 oxen, 1 cow with offspring; 1 boar, 1 sow with offspring until the end of September, when the offspring no longer had any pasture rights and had to be removed. At Bescaby in 1256 the yardland could maintain 2 horses, 4 oxen and cows with offspring, 30 sheep, 4 pigs and 5 geese all with offspring. At Hose, some forty or fifty years earlier, the yardland had pasture rights for 4 oxen, 2 horses, 30 sheep, a boar and 2 sows with offspring, and 10 geese. These villages were in sheep country, but at Skeffington too in 1257 the yardland could pasture 4 oxen, 2 draught animals, and 2 cows with their offspring, 30 sheep with their offspring, a sow with its offspring, all until July, and 6 geese.[68] Limitations such as these naturally resulted in infringement. The action of the Bescaby tenant who in 1256 overcharged the

---

[63] D.L. 43/14/3, mm. 54–55. This was not the only pasture in demesne. There was also pasture in 'Wythgus' wood.

[64] Farnham, *Leics. Notes*, v, 159.

[65] Nichols, *Leics.* ii, App., 97.

[66] Farnham, *Leics. Notes*, v, 412.

[67] Above, p. 156. Dr. Hoskins suggests that these regulations also imply that cattle could graze on the winter wheat for a period; Hoskins, *Essays in Leics. Hist.* 174, n. 1.

[68] Nichols, *Leics.* ii, App., 80, 85, 87. The limiting dates seem to be those after which young animals beyond the permitted number could no longer be sustained.

pasture by 57 sheep is only an early example of a problem which grew more acute as time went on.[69]

Stint of pasture applied not only to the fallows. It applied also to pasture rights in separate closes and to the rough grazing on moor or in forest within the township boundary. On the Baneholm pasture at Welham, already referred to, the yardlanders were limited to 8 great beasts each (that is, horses or cattle). Those who escaped the limitations of the stint were, of course, those with their own pasture in severalty, normally (at this early period) the lords of manors. Hence the jury which laid down the stint for Croxton in 1245 excluded from its regulations the separate pastures belonging to the abbey manor ('salva severali pastura dicti abbatis de manerio'). Then there were parts of the county in which pasture was abundant because of their previous economic backwardness. The intensive early settlement and relatively dense population of the eastern part of the county contrasted with the sparse settlement of the Leicester and Charnwood Forest areas. But the more barren west had the compensating advantage of extensive forest pasture. We have, it is true, many cases of conflict over pasture rights in the forest, but comparatively little evidence of stint. The conflicts seem to have been due rather to the eagerness of lords to assert their exclusive property rights with the object of emparking or in other ways profiting from their control than to the same sort of pressure on restricted pastures as in the east. Consequently we find that in the 12th century the lords of the forest areas were making lavish grants of pasture and pasture rights to religious houses. Ranulf, Earl of Chester, granted to Garendon Abbey common of pasture for all its beasts of all kinds in his forest appurtenant to his fee of Barrow-on-Soar, not to speak of a daily cartload of firewood. Robert, Earl of Leicester, at the same period, besides giving to the monks of St. Évroul (Orne) all manner of tithes from demesne possessions in his forest of Leicester, also allowed them pannage for 100 pigs.[70] By the 13th century, when the spate of monastic foundations was over, such grants are no longer found, but deeds of transfer still show what an important economic asset the West Leicestershire forests were as pastures for all types of animals (especially pigs), and as sources of timber for building and fuel. A bailiff of Shepshed manor in 1324, accounting for the sums received from tenants for pasture rights, actually refers to the 'plenitude of pasture in Charnwood Forest'.[71]

PEASANT FARMING

The features of the Leicestershire medieval village which have been described were common to peasants and lords. It is now necessary to make some distinction between peasant and landlord farming. During the Middle Ages peasant farming was always the more important quantitatively, and it must be considered first. It is not an easy subject to discuss. Most documents which illustrate farming practice are inevitably by-products of the activity of landlord estates. It was natural that peasants should have few written records of their own. We can only trace their activities in the main through references in the archives of their landlords or of the Government.

The two-roomed house of timber, wattle, and daub in which the peasant

[69] Ibid. ii, App., 85.

[70] Ibid. i, App., 14; iii, 822. Garendon Abbey's pigs in Charnwood Forest are referred to in a case of 1293: *Abbrev. Plac.* (Rec. Com.), 230.   [71] S.C. 6/1148/5.

and his family lived was the central feature of his holding.[72] It stood in its own land, separate from other houses in the village, and would have its yard for stacks, for poultry, with an outhouse perhaps for beasts. The land on which the house stood was often called the toft. It was a separate, possibly inclosed plot which could also be used, as the peasant wished, for pasture, as an orchard, or as a vegetable garden. Tofts were of variable size. One in Diseworth in about the year 1250 measured 8 by 4 perches (44 × 22 yards). An early 14th-century toft in Illston-on-the-Hill was irregular in shape, its longer sides being 80 and 65 yards, and the shorter ones 42 and 44 yards.[73] Like the other component parts of peasant holdings, tofts were often alienated—indeed most charter evidence about them shows them as detached entities. Normally, however, they were associated with a holding, so that a mid-13th-century survey of some lands in Baggrave actually speaks of two peasant holdings as being 'without toft' as though that were unusual.[74] Another type of property which was often associated with the peasant holding (though less often than the toft) was the croft. This is a more mysterious element in the field system. Often it was clearly a piece of land held in severalty by an individual, and as likely as not used for pasture—not very different from a toft. In fact, a 12th-century charter concerning land in Plungar refers to a grant of a plough-land and 'with a toft which is called Middelcrofte'.[75] But just as assarts could be taken from the wood at first in severalty and subsequently be divided, so, it appears, could crofts. Crofts were as likely to consist of arable land as of pasture. A deed in the Segrave Cartulary refers to a *cultura* called Michelcroft. A place from which beasts were impounded as distraint in 1287 in Swannington was called Whetecroft by one party in the lawsuit and Whetewong by the other.[76] At Burton-on-the-Wolds an early-13th-century charter tells us a certain croft contained 2 selions—undoubtedly implying arable. Another 13th-century charter records the transfer of a croft in Lubbesthorpe containing 6 selions. The way in which arable land was worked in strips made alienation easy, so we find at Shoby at the end of the 13th century a grant of four selions in a croft together with common of pasture there—showing that the croft must have become, or was becoming, like other furlongs of the open fields, in divided ownership and subject to communal routine.[77]

Inventories of peasant movable property are unusual in the 12th, 13th, and 14th centuries. Consequently it is not easy (as it is for manorial property) to show what live and dead stock the average holder of yardland or oxgang possessed. There is a rare survey of peasant stock in the village of Stathern, made for taxation purposes probably in 1225.[78] The movable goods of twenty-four peasants are valued in this document, i.e. their grain and their livestock. Implements and household goods do not enter into the valuation. The total number of beasts was 24 horses, 29 oxen, 28 cows, 2 heifers, and 163 sheep, a low total which emphasizes what has been said about the shortage of livestock as the principal defect of medieval agriculture. The individual dis-

[72] W. G. Hoskins, 'Galby and Frisby', *Essays in Leics. Hist.* 55.

[73] John Rylands Libr., Latin MS. 222, ff. 56a, 56b; *Wyggeston Hosp. Rec.*, 261.

[74] 'Consuetudines et Servicia de Manerio de Rol' et soka in comitatu Leic.', ed. G. T. Clarke, *Archaeologia*, xlvii, 107–8.

[75] Nichols, *Leics.* ii, App., 6. [76] Ibid. 111; Farnham, *Leics. Notes*, iv, 191.

[77] Nichols, *Leics.* iii, 826, from a cart. of Garendon Abbey; Farnham, op. cit. iv, 73; Hist. MSS. Com., *Hastings*, i, 59.

[78] S.C. 11/531; this was probably a surv. for a fortieth.

tribution of the beasts shows two interesting features. First there was a fairly even distribution of *grossa animalia*. If we take the oxen and horses to be the draught animals we find that five peasants had none. One of these peasants was a craftsman (a cobbler), one was probably a widow, and the other three were probably cottagers. Only two peasants had 1 draught animal; seven had 2; five had 3; two had 4; two had 5; and one had 6. Inequality was not gross, since conditions were primitive. The figures also show that for the majority common ploughing would have been essential. On the other hand, significant differences of resources appear, not in the amounts of grain held, for that reflected the level of arable farming in a similar fashion to the draught animals, but in the number of sheep held. The largest flock is of 24 sheep; 5 peasants have flocks of 15 each; only 2 others have more than 10 sheep (actually, 12 each).

It may be dangerous to use this single document as general evidence of peasant resources. Perhaps Stathern was particularly unprosperous. It will be noticed, for instance, that the animals possessed by these peasants were much fewer than those allowed on the common pasture appurtenant to a yardland as quoted above. It may also be that the tax assessment does not account for the true total. Fragments of evidence later in the 13th and in the 14th centuries show that the stock of some peasants had risen considerably above the highest level at Stathern in 1225. But from what we know in general about the stratification of the peasantry during this period, this is not surprising. The legal records give us incidental information about some of the free tenants. In 1284 a tenant of 5 wongs in Thorp Satchville was distrained for arrears of rent by his plough-team, namely 4 oxen and 2 horses. The same number of beasts in 1287 was taken as distraint by the Prior of the Hospitallers from the holder of an oxgang in Swannington. In 1293 a tenant of Hugh Barcolf at Billesdon had the unfortunate experience of being distrained for Hugh's arrears of service to his feudal lord. The impounded cattle of this tenant amounted to 33 oxen, 1 cow, 1 horse, and 1 steer.[79] Finally, a much later document may be quoted here, though it illustrates another phase in the process of peasant accumulation which has yet to be discussed. It is the valuation of the goods of John Smyth of Kirby Bellars who was hanged at Leicester in 1375. His own livestock consisted of 8 horses, 8 'great beasts' (probably oxen), and 3 pigs. He also had another 13 oxen, but these were said to have been obtained by theft. Other chattels consisted of an iron-bound cart for 6 horses, 2 saddles, a bridle, 5 lead pans, 2 brass pots, a brass dish, 7 pitchers, 3 vats, a hair cloth, and a tablecloth. An unspecified quantity of corn in the sheaf was also confiscated. It is true that John was no ordinary peasant, but one of the 'new rich' among the peasantry, for he also had debts amounting to £28 owed to him by eight persons in Kirby and elsewhere. Nevertheless his wealth and his sideline in usury were quite characteristic.[80]

Between Domesday and the last quarter of the 13th century there had been considerable changes in the status of the Leicestershire peasants. A survey of villages made in the year 1279 is still available to us,[81] though it covers only

[79] Farnham, *Leics. Notes*, iv, 246, 191; vi, 116.   [80] *Cal. Inq. Misc.* iii, p. 376.
[81] It was transcribed by the early-17th-century Leics. antiquary Wm. Burton, and is in his MS. collection, Bodl. Libr., Rawlinson MS. B. 350. It is printed in part by Nichols, *Leics.* i, pp. cx–cxxi; cf. R. H. Hilton, *Econ. Development of Some Leics. Estates*, 7–10, and 'Kibworth Harcourt', in *Studies in Leics. Agrarian Hist.*, ed. W. G. Hoskins, 19–20.

the two hundreds of Guthlaxton and Gartree. The subdivisions of the peasantry by 1279 were less complicated—in nomenclature at any rate—than they were in 1086. Only free tenants, *villani*, and cottagers are mentioned in the 1279 survey. The term 'sokeman' has disappeared (at any rate from official terminology), being merged into the more comprehensive term 'free tenant'. A simple comparison of Domesday percentages of peasant groups might lead us to conclude that the 30 per cent. of sokemen of 1086 had grown to make the 1279 figure of 39 per cent. free tenants; that the 1279 figure of 55 per cent. *villani* included not only the descendants of Domesday *villani*, but of *servi* and some of the *bordarii* as well; for only 6 per cent. of the tenants in 1279 were classified as cottagers. But a closer comparison of figures village by village shows that it was not a simple process of expansion and absorption, but often an overturning of the old social structure.

For the purposes of strict comparison between the situation in 1086 and 1279, only thirty-eight villages may be taken. Yet even within this narrowed focus interesting results emerge. First, the population increase is most striking—an increase in the recorded population (i.e. heads of families) of two-thirds (647 to 1109). The percentage figures of the different peasant groups are only slightly different from those calculated from the full data. They are, for the thirty-eight villages, as follows:

1086		1279	
	%		%
Sokemen	24	Free tenants	37
Villani	46	*Villani*	53
Bordarii	24	Cottagers	10
Servi	6		

In some villages there may have been some continuity in peasant status. In Cosby, for example, 26 out of the Domesday population of 35 were sokemen; in 1279, 24 out of a population of 39 were free tenants. Walton (near Kimcote) was in 1086 a small settlement of 10 sokemen; in 1279, out of a total population of 32, 23 were free tenants. At Huncote in 1086 there were only 2 sokemen; the remainder (31) were serfs, villeins, and bordars; and in 1279, too, only 5 out of 32 were free tenants. Market Bosworth in 1086 had only 7 sokemen compared with 25 serfs, villeins, and bordars; in 1279 there were 7 free tenants, 25 villeins, and 9 cottagers.

But these examples of continuity are in a minority. More typical is Arnesby, which in 1086 had a population of 17 villeins and 5 bordars, but in 1279 had 39 free tenants out of a total population of 51. Mowsley is another typical example. Its Domesday population was 1 serf, 5 villeins, and 2 bordars, but by 1279 there were 35 free tenants and no one of villein status. Cadeby in 1086 had 7 villeins and 3 bordars; in 1279, 11 free tenants. But an increase in the number of free tenants was not invariable. At Aylestone the 5 sokemen in the Domesday population of 43 disappeared, so that there was in 1279 a population of 60 villeins. At Ashby Magna, where in 1086 there had been 13 sokemen out of a population of 29, there were in 1279 only 2 free tenants to 11 villeins. Blaby in 1086 had 28 sokemen out of a total population of 37, but in 1279 there were 21 villeins and 8 cottagers to 16 free tenants. At Dunton Basset in 1086 there had been 9 sokemen to 11 villeins and bordars; by 1279 there were only 2 free tenants in a total population of 31. These two contrary tendencies reflect two historical trends of the 12th and 13th centuries, trends characteristic not merely of Leicestershire, or even of England, but of Europe. The tendency which produced the increased number of free tenants was the colonization of the woodland and waste, an activity which was partly due to rural overpopulation, partly to seigniorial initiative. It is well known that men who came to do this work had often left their ancestral settlements precisely in order to escape servile tenure.[82] On the other hand, the tendency which depressed the original free peasantry was the result of increasing seigniorial demand for rent and labour services, a demand which was reaching its peak in England after the middle of the 13th century. It was to the lord's interest to overcome the resistance of peasants by defining their status (with the willing help of the lawyers) so that they held as villeins at his will rather than as free men with the right of appeal to the royal courts.[83]

Before examining landlord farming, and the demands made by landlords on the peasants in the form of rents and services, we must add to our survey of peasant farming some words on the arable holdings from which the peasant family subsisted, and to which brief reference has been made in connexion with Domesday Book. It is not until we are in possession of detailed land surveys that we can confidently estimate peasant holdings. Even then we must be cautious. From the point of view of the landlord, a tenant might be holding and paying rent for an oxgang or a yardland. But a study of such documents as the Hundred Rolls of 1279 and manorial court rolls shows us that by the 13th century both free and villein tenants were leasing, buying, and selling land among themselves, often illegally. Hence the holdings actually worked by the peasant might well be greater or smaller than the one for which he was held responsible in the manorial survey. Evidence which would tell us about this peasant land-market is, however, not abundant for Leicestershire, and we must rely mainly on manorial surveys. The earliest large-scale survey after Domesday Book itself dates from before the middle of the 13th century. It is a description of those parts of the great royal soke of Rothley which were granted in 1231 to the Templars.[84] It describes peasant tenements, even the smallest, in great detail. In the case of the Rothley lands the official survey probably gives a reasonably true picture of holdings actually worked. For according to the custom of the soke (written down at the end of the survey) land was freely alienable *within* the soke provided the transfer was registered. It is true that there were registration fees of about 7*d.* or 8*d.*, but apart from this there was no reason to conceal transfers of land between peasant and peasant.

In the 15 villages which at this time contained lands belonging to the soke there were some 360-odd holdings of land, and the general picture is of peasant agriculture on a small scale. It is true that there was a large minority of men (82) holding a yardland (say 24 acres) or more. A small part of these were even substantial cultivators with 50 acres or so. But 131 holdings were something between an oxgang and a yardland (12–24 acres) in size, and 153 were less

[82] For similar events in Warws. see R. H. Hilton, *Social Structure of Rural Warws. in the Middle Ages* (Dugdale Soc. Occasional Papers, ix).

[83] See below, p. 179.

[84] *Archaeologia*, xlvii. It includes tenures in Rothley, Barsby, Gaddesby, Baggrave, Tilton, North and South Marefield, Somerby, Grimston, Saxelby, Wartnaby, Chadwell, Keyham, South Croxton, and excludes the old soke lands in Seagrave, Sileby, Tugby, Skeffington, Halstead, Asfordby, and Frisby.

than an oxgang, many of them being mere tofts or small plots outside the open fields themselves. Conditions varied from village to village. There were very few tenants of the cottager type at Wartnaby and Baggrave, whilst at Chadwell they outnumbered the holders of yardlands and oxgangs. At Rothley itself, while there was a large number of toft- and acre-holders, the intermediate group of tenants of oxgangs was small, and nearly half the land-holding population had a yardland or more. Another phenomenon, however, emphasizes both the small-scale character of the Leicestershire peasant agriculture at the period and the tendencies towards disintegration already noticed. This phenomenon is the significant number of partnerships in peasant land-holding. At Rothley 11 holdings were held in partnership,[85] at Gaddesby 10, at Grimston 6. This means that holdings held in partnership would be supporting not one but two or more peasant families. These partnerships undoubtedly represent an attempt by the peasants to counter the tendencies towards subdivision. According to Rothley custom, holdings were divisible between heirs, and it is significant that many of the partnerships were between brothers, or brothers and sisters,[86] or, as in two cases in Rothley itself, between a named tenant's 'heirs'. Yet the large number of extremely small holdings shows that many heirs had succumbed to the temptation to take their share of the ancestral holding for their own, rather than maintain it intact in partnership with coheirs.

Conditions on the Rothley soke must not be taken as typical, nor must the element of disintegration be overstressed. On the soke most tenants still held the traditional yardland or oxgang. In so far as disintegration was beginning, it is to be explained by the comparative freedom of alienation enjoyed by the privileged sokemen of this ancient demesne manor.[87]

LANDLORD FARMING

In Leicestershire, as in many other counties, the big estates of the Norman lords described in Domesday Book were much reduced in size, as agrarian units, in the 12th and 13th centuries. The 13th-century honour of Leicester was much smaller than the 12th-century estate of the earls of Leicester had been. It comprised a tangle of feudal rights, claims to rents, and profits of jurisdiction extending over some sixty-five villages in the county,[88] but was more impressive as a political than as an agrarian organization. Simon de Montfort, Earl of Leicester, at his death in 1265 held in demesne only the borough of Leicester and the manors of Hinckley, Earl Shilton, Bagworth, Thornton, and Desford. These (less Bagworth and Thornton, and with the later addition of the de Lacy manor of Castle Donington) remained the only demesne manors of the honor when it was in the possession of Simon's Lancastrian successors.[89] Other landlords at the end of the 13th century, such as the Verdons, the Segraves, the Belers, whatever the extent of their feudal jurisdictions, were holding no more

[85] Mostly of 2 partners, but 2 of 3, 1 of 4, and 1 of 5.

[86] According to the statement of custom at the end of the Rothley Surv. (see n. 84 above) holdings were divisible between several sons and daughters, but not between one son and one daughter. If there was one son and several daughters the son took all. Cf. G. C. Homans, 'Partible Inheritance of Villagers' Holdings', *Econ. Hist. Rev.* vii, 48 et seq.

[87] For ancient demesne privileges, see P. Vinogradoff, *Villeinage in Engl.*

[88] L. Fox, 'Account R. of the Honour of Leicester', *T.L.A.S.* xix, 201.

[89] *Cal. Inq. Misc.* i, pp. 234–6; C 133/81/5 (Edmund Earl of Lanc.); C 135/160/5 (Hen. Duke of Lanc.). The accounts ed. by L. Fox, cited n. 88 above, give the situation under Thomas of Lanc. See also L. Fox, *Administration of the Honour of Leic.*

than 4 or 5 demesne manors. And it was only in these that they had a direct concern with agriculture—that is, with demesne production, labour problems, marketing problems, and tenants' rents and services.

On the other hand, while the big lay estates were shrinking in the 12th and 13th centuries, a number of ecclesiastical estates were growing in size and importance. There had been no great church properties in Leicestershire at the time of Domesday Book such as one finds in East Anglia, the West of England, and elsewhere. But the 12th century saw the foundation in Leicestershire of some quite important estates, particularly of the Order of Augustinian canons. Some of them became considerably more important as large-scale agrarian organizations than the lay estates. Outstanding among these was the estate of the Augustinian abbey of Leicester (founded in 1143), which by 1254 possessed eleven manors with demesne farms, besides a considerable income from rents and tithes in many other villages. The receipts of the honor of Leicester over fifteen months in 1322 and 1323 amounted to a cash total of nearly £400, while Leicester Abbey's income from its Leicestershire properties in 1341 was about £980.[90]

The structure of the ecclesiastical estates was rather different from that of the lay estates. It was a characteristic of the endowment of the Augustinian houses in particular that grants of advowsons, glebes, and tithes formed an appreciable proportion of the total. Many manors which were component parts of church estates had originally consisted only of the glebe and tithes of appropriated rectories. By endowments and purchases the glebe was expanded to a considerable demesne farm, hay tithes were commuted for meadow in severalty, and a subject tenantry was also acquired from lay donors or vendors.[91] But however the different types of estate were accumulated, by the end of the 13th century their likenesses were of more weight than their differences. The manor with its demesne farm and attached tenants was the basic unit of the estate. In the case of ecclesiastical estates a network of tithe-barns for the collection of grain tithes (as well as demesne corn) was added.

The manor itself, of course, varied from estate to estate. As in the 11th century village and manor did not necessarily coincide. Some manors could consist of a demesne farm only, others of tenants only, or could combine land and tenants—the more normal form of organization. In 1279, out of 134 villages in the hundreds of Guthlaxton and Gartree in only 37 did manor coincide with village. In 34 villages there were 2 manors, but in 63, more than 2. Two-fifths of the total number of peasants in villages in these 2 hundreds (where details are adequate) belonged to forms of manorial organization where there was no demesne farm.[92] The remainder were implicated in some degree in demesne farming. We must now turn, therefore, to the organization of the demesne in Leicestershire at the height of the second period of predominance of this type of landlord enterprise.[93]

---

[90] The figure for the honour of Leic. must not be taken as representing normality, as the accounts are rendered by royal officials after confiscation, and therefore under abnormal conditions.

[91] Grants of land often include the villein tenants of the land. For example, see Nichols, *Leics.* ii, App., 5, 91, 108. For a more detailed description of the way in which eccl. estates were built up, see Hilton, *Econ. Development of Some Leics. Estates*, 33–47, 107–15.   [92] Ibid. 9, and Hilton, in *Studies in Leics. Agrarian Hist.* 20.

[93] As in France, Engl. demesne farming after the 11th century had begun to disintegrate. Demesnes were leased out and labour services commuted. Unlike France, however, this trend was held up and even reversed in Engl. from about the middle of the 13th century. Evidence for the 12th-century trend away from demesne farming is unfortunately lacking for Leics.

Just as the peasant's messuage or cottage was the focal point of his holding, so the manor hall, courtyard, and outbuildings were the focus of demesne farming. Fortunately, the landlords' houses are described more adequately than those of the peasants. A good example of a working demesne farm without any of the elaborations which would be provided for a resident lord is that belonging to the Yorkshire abbey of Selby in Queniborough, described in a survey of 1320.[94] The living-quarters were modest, for they would probably house only a bailiff. They consisted of a hall, a small room attached to it on the north, and a kitchen.[95] The outbuildings, however, were more extensive. In one block[96] was a granary, a bakehouse, a brewhouse, and a dairy. Then there were two barns, a cowshed, a stable, a sheepcote with a piece of land attached, and a dovecot. Such were the buildings of the manor demesne. But in addition to the buildings there were at the manorial centre two apple orchards, three small inclosures (*curtilagia*) which would probably be vegetable gardens, and three stewponds. The rest of the demesne property consisted of arable, meadow, and common pasture. There were 245 acres of arable distributed amongst 34 furlongs. Compared with some cases already quoted, consolidation of strips was comparatively advanced. There were two complete furlongs owned by the abbey. For the rest, in one furlong there were as many as 22 acres grouped together. The smallest single lot was of nearly 2 acres on some headlands by the village. As a general rule, in each furlong in which there was abbey demesne land there were between 5 and 15 acres of it. There were 35 acres of meadow in 8 different places. There was no separate pasture, but the common rights appurtenant to the demesne were sufficient for 16 oxen, 16 cows, and 300 sheep.

This survey tells us nothing of the livestock and equipment indispensable for the farming of the demesne. Some idea of what stock would be found on a similar demesne farm can be gained from an indenture in 1309 by which the keeper of the chattels of the Rothley estate of the dissolved Templars handed them over to another official.[97] There was first the equipment of various domestic offices—hall, kitchen, brewhouse, bakehouse, pantry, and buttery. The livestock was housed in four establishments—the cowshed, the sheepcote, the pigsty, and the cart-shed. There were 24 oxen, 1 bull, 11 cows, 9 steers, and 4 calves in the cowshed; 342 sheep and 123 lambs in the sheepcote; 33 pigs (including 2 boars) and 12 suckling pigs in the pigsty; 5 cart-horses, 5 draught animals, and a mule in the cartshed. Ploughs, curiously enough, are not mentioned, though at the smaller manors of Baggrave and Gaddesby there were 1 and 2 respectively. To supplement what is clearly an incomplete list we may mention an inventory of the goods of Edmund of Appleby, a west Leicestershire squire, at Appleby. They included, in the cowshed, 3 ploughs, 3 iron and 2 wooden harrows.[98] At Lyndridge in 1323 the ploughing costs of the year's account tell us that 7 new ploughs, 4 new ploughshares, and 4 new harrows had been bought.[99] At Rothley there were 2 iron-bound carts and a wagon,

[94] B.M. Add. MS. 36579.

[95] Compare Sir Robert Swyllington's manor house at Kirby Bellars in 1420, which had 14 chambers in addition to the hall. Inq. p.m. printed in Farnham, *Leics. Notes*, ed. iii, 126.

[96] I assume this because they are valued together.

[97] E 142/105. Rothley manor demesne in 1338 contained 217 acres of arable and 58 acres of meadow: *The Knights Hospitallers in Engl.* (Camden Soc. lxv), ed. L. B. Larking, 176.

[98] Nichols, *Leics.* iv, 429.

[99] S.C. 6/1147/8. The inventory of dead stock was valued at 32s.

but beyond this no agricultural equipment. In the granary there were 26 qr. of wheat, 29 of rye, 26 of dredge, 12 of beans, 26 of peas, and 85 of oats. In the barn there were 10 qr. of maslin. The grain in the granary was threshed, that in the barn probably not.

If the scale of demesne farming, in the sense of the number of manors per estate, was moderate in Leicestershire, so also was the actual cultivated area in demesne. Only a minority of demesne farms (about 35 per cent.) at the end of the 13th and the beginning of the 14th centuries had arable land of more than about 150 acres. Only about 15 per cent. of demesnes were greater than 250 acres in arable area.[1] These figures have an important bearing on the problem of labour on the demesnes, and consequently on the problem of rent also. The lords of manors were the main employers of labour, for the great majority of peasant holdings were cultivated by the labour of the peasant family. In a relatively undifferentiated peasant society there tends to be a shortage of wage-labour, and consequently where landlords hold political power they exact forced unpaid labour in the form of rent from the peasants dependent upon them. But where manorial demesne farming was not on a large scale, and where the estates themselves were neither large nor old-established, we should not be surprised to find that labour service as the principal form of rent had not been successfully imposed upon the peasantry.

This was so in Leicestershire. The only known case of peasants performing 'week work' occurs on the Leicester Abbey manor of Stoughton. Here the yardlanders owed 2 days a week for the greater part of the year and 4 days a week between 20 July and 29 September (10 weeks), that is, 124 days' work a year. In addition, the yardlanders owed ploughing, mowing, reaping, and carting services. The number of these depended on the needs of the demesne and were therefore unfixed, but were unlikely to involve less than 10 extra days' labour. There were 24½ yardlands held from the Abbey in 1341 by villein tenants, so that there would be available annually for the cultivation of the demesne some 3,280 days' labour. On all other manors for which there is evidence labour services were on a much smaller scale, consisting of ploughing, harvest, and haymaking services at the peak periods of the agricultural year. In c. 1300 a half-yardlander at Kibworth Harcourt owed annually 23 fixed days' work and some uncertain services, principally carrying, when demanded. Even this level of labour services was high, and on most manors villein tenants owed fewer than 15, many fewer than 10 days' work a year.[2]

Though Leicestershire manorial demesnes were moderate in size, agricultural labour was still necessary, and the small number of imposed labour services was supplemented by wage labour. There are even cases where wage labour was preferred to labour services which were claimable. At Broughton Astley in 1322 labour services to the value of £5. 9s. 3d. were commuted. The demesne was being fully exploited with the help of wage labour. Wage labour was of two sorts. First there was that of the permanent farm servants (*famuli*), paid an annual wage; secondly, there was seasonal labour provided by the rural (sometimes even urban) population, paid by the piece or by the day. The *famuli* were the backbone, as it were, of the demesne labour force. Their numbers normally varied with the size of the demesne farm. At Cold Overton in 1257

[1] Hilton, *Econ. Development of Some Leics. Estates*, 9–10.
[2] Ibid., 12–15, 73–76, 139; Hilton, in *Studies in Leics. Agrarian Hist.* 34.

the permanent staff comprised 6 ploughmen (3 to guide the plough, 3 who drove the team), and 1 carter. In the same year, on the smaller manor of Barton-in-the-Beans, there were only 2 ploughmen and a hayward who supervised the fields, meadows, and buildings. At Lindridge in 1323 there was a carter, 6 ploughmen, and 1 foreman, a park-keeper, and a helper for making the food of these hired hands.[3] These permanent farm servants must be presumed to have been recruited from younger sons of peasant families who had no hopes of succeeding to a holding. The recruitment may even have been compulsory in some cases. The Abbot of Selby claimed by customary right to be able to take *famuli curie* from among the sons of villeins at low rates. The survey of 1320 tells us that he need only pay ploughmen, carters, or shepherds so recruited 4s. 3d. a year as compared with 8s. paid to an outsider; or 3s. 6d. to the driver of the plough-team instead of 6s. 8d.; or 2s. 6d. for a carter working in the autumn instead of 4s.

These permanent hired servants increased in number and variety during the 14th century. Meanwhile, their labours were supplemented by those of the second category of wage labourers: those who were too inadequately endowed with land to subsist on their own holdings; the sons (and daughters) of established yardlanders; and such vagrants of town and country as existed even in under-populated medieval England. At Cold Overton in 1257 the total wage bill was £7. 17s. 3½d., equivalent very roughly to between 1,600 and 1,700 days' work.[4] At the smaller manor of Barton in the same year, with a demesne of 52 sown acres and 7 acres of meadow, compared with the Cold Overton demesne of 210 sown acres and 63 acres of meadow, the total wage bill was £1. 16s. 4½d. The wage bill for the manor of Stretton (9½ sown acres and 3½ acres of meadow), in the same year, was £2. 13s. 6d. On the first two manors, very little unpaid labour service was used, on the last, more. Seventy years later, in Edward II's time, we find the same predominance of the labour of the permanent hired servants and of seasonal labour on the manors of Broughton Astley, Lutterworth, Lindridge, and Newbold Verdon—all manors of powerful lay lords.[5] We have seen something of the *famuli*. The provenance of the casual labour is not hard to seek when we remember that more than one-third of the peasant family holdings on the Rothley soke in the middle of the 13th century contained fewer than 12 acres of arable—many of them mere acre holdings.[6] A century later, in three of the more important Leicester Abbey manors (Stoughton, Lockington, and Thurmaston) over half the tenants were mere cottagers or crofters.[7]

Labour supply, responsible for the bulk of agricultural costs on the landlord estate, was undoubtedly one of the main problems of the owners and their administrators. Marketing must have been another. For while we have hitherto stressed the predominantly subsistence character of medieval Leicestershire agriculture, it nevertheless contained important sectors which were producing for the market—sectors no doubt of qualitative rather than of quantitative significance. Reference has already been made to grain sales in 1257 on the Lord Edward's three Leicestershire manors. In that year £49 worth of grain was put

---

[3] S.C. 6/1094/11 and 1147/8. Note the absence of herdsmen. Demesne beasts may have gone with those of the village.

[4] Valued at 1d. each for five-sixths (winter and summer) and 2d. each for one-sixth (autumn).

[5] Hilton, *Econ. Development of Some Leics. Estates*, 14–15.   [6] Above, pp. 169–70.

[7] Hilton, *Econ. Development of Some Leics. Estates*, 100–5.

on to the market from these manors.[8] It is true that a few years earlier (1254) Leicester Abbey stored most of the grain from its Leicestershire manors, and only sold grain from outlying manors in other counties. This may have been due to a purely temporary decision to hold up sales for that year. By the end of the century (1297–8) there were some grain sales from the Leicestershire manors, though once again most grain sales were from the outlying parts of the estate. On the other hand, sales of wool in Leicestershire were very large, amounting to £220, or 35 per cent. of the year's income. This was somewhat more than the value of the Leicester Abbey wool (c. £180) which the Florentine merchant Pegolotti considered the abbey could produce annually in the early 14th century, and about the same as he expected from the smaller Premonstratensian abbey of Croxton.[9] Income from sales, including grain sold from manors outside Leicestershire, and some minor items, amounted to 64 per cent. of the total income of the estate as recorded in the Treasurer's Receipt Roll of that year. By 1341 the income from grain sales was £573, more than all other sources of income together.[10] There is no other Leicestershire evidence so comprehensive as that from Leicester Abbey at this period.[11] That other big landlords were relying on sales of demesne produce for an appreciable part of their income is indicated by some accounts for the Lancastrian manors in 1314. At Desford, corn and hay was sold for £10, more than a quarter of total receipts. At Earl Shilton the grain was sold in bulk for £33, nearly one-third of total receipts.[12]

The development in the 13th century of production for the market, especially on the demesnes, naturally had as its by-product the development of market centres. Our principal evidence for country market towns at this period is no reliable guide to the volume of commercial transactions that actually took place there, but only whether feudal lords managed to get market privileges from which they hoped to profit. Since lords of manors usually had to pay for the privilege of establishing a weekly market and often, in addition, an annual two- or three-day fair on their manors, we assume that they anticipated some return from tolls, stall rents, and similar market profits. Of the 37 towns and villages with official markets in medieval Leicestershire 25 had been given the privilege before 1300. Only 2—Melton Mowbray and Belvoir—are recorded as having acquired markets before 1200.[13] Most of these medieval market-towns lay on the main routes which radiated from the central market of Leicester.[14] The east and west-central areas of the county do not seem well served;

[8] Grain prices were average this year. The wheat was sold at about 5s. a quarter.

[9] F. B. Pegolotti, *La Pratica Della Mercatura* (ed. Evans), 259–69. The only comparable monastic wool producer was the Cistercian abbey of Garendon, whose crop was expected to be 20 sacks at 9 to 20 marks a sack (say £190). The houses of Launde and Langley produced only 5 sacks a year.

[10] Hilton, *Econ. Development of Some Leics. Estates*, 21–33, 79–88.

[11] The accounts of the keepers of contrariants' manors for the year 1322–3 which have been used as evidence, e.g. for the proportion of crops sown on demesne, cannot be had as evidence for sales, as the custodians may well have pushed up sales as a policy of short-term exploitation.

[12] D.L. 29/1/3.

[13] Medieval towns and villages with market privileges were: Arnesby 1292, Ashby-de-la-Zouch 1219, Bagworth 1270, Belton 1244, Belvoir 1100–23, Breedon 1330, Castle Donington 1278, Croxton Kerrial 1246, Gaddesby 1306, Goadby Marwood 1319, Glen Magna 1272, Cosby 1338, Hallaton 1284, Hinckley (first mentioned 1313, no grant known), Kegworth 1290, Kibworth Beauchamp 1223, Leicester 1229, Lowesby 1301, Loughborough 1227, Lubenham 1327, Lutterworth 1214, Market Bosworth 1285, Market Harborough 1203, Melton Mowbray 1077, Mountsorrel 1292, Narborough 1219, Odstone 1263, Packington 1257, Rothley 1284, Scalford 1304, Seale 1310, Stapleford 1308, Twyford 1250, Waltham on the Wolds 1227, Whitwick 1292, Wymeswold 1338, Wymondham 1303. The dates given are those of the first known grant of market and/or fair privilege.   [14] See map.

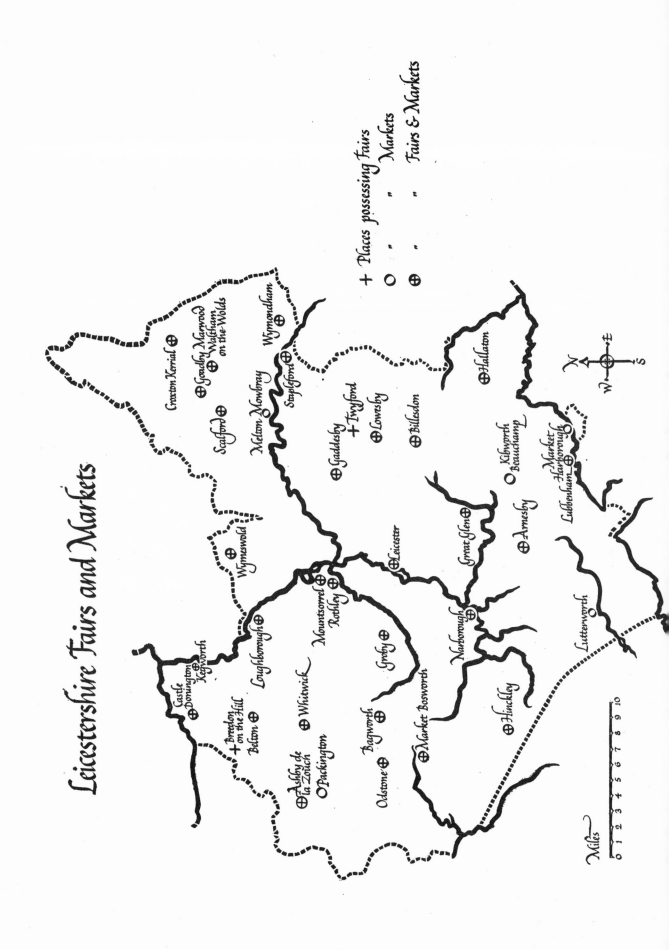

Leicestershire Fairs and Markets

Places possessing Fairs   +
     "   "   Markets   O
     "   "   Fairs & Markets   ⊕

Croxton Kerrial
Goadby Marwood
Waltham on the Wolds
Wymondham
Scalford
Melton Mowbray
Stapleford
Twyford
Gaddesby
Lowesby
Billesdon
Hallaton
Kibworth Beauchamp
Market Harborough
Lubbenham
Arnesby
Great Glen
Leicester
Narborough
Lutterworth
Hinckley
Market Bosworth
Groby
Bagworth
Odstone
Whitwick
Packington
Ashby de la Zouch
Belton
Breedon on the Hill
Castle Donington
Kegworth
Loughborough
Wymeswold
Mountsorrel
Rothley

N
W   E
S

Miles
0 1 2 3 4 5 6 7 8 9 10

but as we see from 14th-century evidence, villages could well be centres of buying and selling without being official market-towns.

There is evidence for the existence of boroughs in regard to four places (besides Leicester itself) in Leicestershire. The 'borough' of Hinckley is first mentioned in 1209,[15] and 'burgesses' at Hinckley are referred to at the end of the 13th century.[16] The *firma burgi* of Hinckley is mentioned in 1209,[17] but it is doubtful whether this should be taken to mean that the borough revenues were being farmed by the burgesses.[18] Under Thomas, Earl of Lancaster (d. 1322), the profits of the tolls, market, and fair of Hinckley borough were farmed by an individual.[19] No charter establishing a borough at Hinckley is known. At Lutterworth, twenty-five burgesses are mentioned in 1279,[20] and burgages there are mentioned in 1364–5[21] and in 1595.[22] Burgages at Ashby-de-la-Zouch are mentioned in 1330, 1347, and in the 16th century.[23] No borough charter is known for either Lutterworth or Ashby, but a royal grant of the right to hold a market at Lutterworth was obtained in 1214,[24] and Ashby obtained a grant of both a fair and a market in 1219.[25] The information regarding Castle Donington, the fourth of the boroughs in the county, is rather more extensive. The first reference to burgesses and burgages at Donington occurs in 1311, and burgages there are mentioned at various times until the 17th century.[26] A rental of 1462, which lists forty-three burgesses in all, shows that some, though not all, of the Donington burgesses at one time owed labour services.[27] No borough charter for Donington is known, but the right to hold a market and annual fair there was granted to the Earl of Lincoln, the lord of the manor, in 1278.[28] The boroughs at Hinckley, Ashby-de-la-Zouch, and Castle Donington were all presumably brought into existence in the hope that they would develop into markets for the agricultural products of the surrounding areas.

ESTATE ADMINISTRATION

The administration needed for running a landlord estate varied according to the size and structure of the estate. By the end of the 13th century administration had become complex, largely owing to the increasing supervision exercised by the estate-owners in the interests of increased yields, especially in cash. The honour of Leicester had probably the most complex (and the best known) organization in the county.[29] Its manors were supervised by reeves chosen from amongst the customary tenants. These men had not only to control the agricultural activities of the demesne farm but to represent the lord before the other peasants, especially in the exaction of rent and services. The immediate

[15] *Pipe R. 1209* (Pipe R. Soc.), n.s. xxiv, 24.   [16] H. J. Francis, *Hist. of Hinckley*, 35.
[17] *Pipe R. 1209* (Pipe R. Soc.), n.s. xxiv, 25.
[18] The *firma villenagii* of Hinckley is also mentioned in 1209 (ibid.). The position in 1209 was exceptional, as Hinckley, normally part of the possessions of the earls of Leic., was then in the king's hands.
[19] L. Fox, 'Mins. Accts. of the Honour of Leicester', *T.L.A.S.* xix, 233, 239.
[20] Nichols, *Leics.* i, p. cxv.   [21] A. H. Dyson, *Lutterworth*, 25.
[22] *Cat. Anct. D.* v, A13463.
[23] Farnham, *Leics. Notes*, vi, 34; Hist. MSS. Com., *Hastings*, i, 4, 352.
[24] *Rot. Chart. 1199–1216* (Rec. Com.), 201.   [25] Nichols, *Leics.* iii, 562.
[26] G. F. Farnham and A. Hamilton Thompson, 'The Castle and Manor of Castle Donington', *T.L.A.S.* xiv, 49, 55–58, 65–66, 76.
[27] Ibid. 56–58. It is not clear whether the services were being actually performed in 1462, or whether they had then been commuted for money payments.
[28] *Cal. Chart. R., 1257–1300*, 207.
[29] Fully described by L. Fox, *The Administration of the Honour of Leic.*

superior of the reeve was the bailiff, usually a professional administrator, who had to collect all those rents and feudal dues which were not collected by the reeves in the demesne manors. These bailiffs were responsible for the general supervision of the lord's rights within a considerable area. The bailiff of the Carlton Curlieu bailiwick had to look after the affairs of the honour in twenty-three villages.[30] Other local officials were mainly concerned with Leicester Forest. At the centre of the administration was a clerical receiver whose main function was the receipt of money from local officials. The steward, the senior official of the honour, was usually a local gentleman. He supervised the honour, particularly in its feudal aspects, and presided over the courts. The financial side of the whole organization was finally checked by the auditors. They were trusted lay or clerical administrators, usually high up in the counsels of the lord of the honour.

Other lay estates followed much the same pattern. The three manors of the Lord Edward in 1257 were supervised by one bailiff, but under him was a villein reeve for each manor (clearly a local tenant) who was associated with the bailiff in rendering the annual account. The reeve, as was common on many manors, was assisted by a hayward (*messor*), another customary tenant who had a variety of duties, most important of which were protection of the lord's crops and hay and supervision of the harvest work. But the bulk of the administrative apparatus of the Lord Edward's vast estates was, of course, outside the county.

The ecclesiastical estates were somewhat differently organized. At the manorial level the organization was usually the same as on the lay estates, though the accountant for the Owston Abbey land (mainly glebe) at King's Norton in 1358 was probably one of the canons[31] instead of a lay bailiff or reeve. Centrally the monastic administration differed in so far as the income of the estate was allotted to purposes peculiar to ecclesiastical corporations. There were two main ways of doing this. Each obedientiary could be allotted manors and rents which he would administer and whose revenue he would spend upon his office. Thus in most monasteries the cellarer had most revenue allotted to him. Alternatively the revenues could all be concentrated into the hands of a central receiver or treasurer, who would allot money to the obedientiaries for their expenses. To prevent the waste of resources through inefficiency or dishonesty, this second system was generally replacing the first by the end of the 13th century. By 1286 Leicester Abbey's financial administration seems to have been fully centralized, for we find that in a treasurer's expenses roll of that year the expenses of the cellarer and under-cellarer at the great fairs were accounted for as part of general expenses. The 1297 receipt account of the two treasurers can be seen by comparison with rentals to include all the revenue of the estate. The only other Leicestershire religious house for which we have accounts is Owston Abbey. By the end of the 14th century most of the estate revenue was accounted for by a receiver, though the existence of a number of rentals showing rent appropriated to the pittancer indicates the survival of elements of the old system.[32]

The aim of the increasingly complex administration of the big estates was to make them more profitable to the owners, and in particular to increase the

[30] Fox, *The Administration of the Honour of Leic.* 74.
[31] S.C. 6/908/36. The accountant's title was *Dominus*.
[32] S.C. 6/1108/23 (Receivers' account for 9 and 10 Ric. II); S.C. 12/3/2, 10/19 and 20 (Pittancers' rentals of reign of Ric. II).

owners' cash income. This was done both by increasing money rents and other monetary exactions, and by increasing labour services so as to permit an augmentation of demesne production for the market.[33] Between 1254 and 1341 the money rents from the Leicestershire estates of Leicester Abbey doubled. This increase may have been due in part to rent from newly acquired lands, but other evidence shows that the movement to increase rents was general. The mid-13th-century survey of the Rothley soke shows that since they received it from the Crown, the Templars had imposed an all-round rent increase of 15 per cent., which in the case of individual holdings often amounted to a 20 per cent. increase. A survey of Croxton Kerrial manor made in 1251 shows that even greater increases had been demanded at an earlier period. Philip Basset, who in the early 1230's had been given the manor by Hubert de Burgh, had raised the rents of customary yardlands from 5s. to 8s. and of cottages from 1s. to 1s. 6d. A mid-13th-century survey of the Abbot of Croxton's manor of Waltham in the Wolds also refers to a rent increase without specifying its amount: the rent totals given are qualified *olim, hodie plus*.[34] It should not cause surprise that as a reaction to this demand for more rent came a refusal by the peasants to pay it. Leicestershire was not different from other parts of England as the scene of sporadic agrarian unrest, an inevitable by-product of lord–peasant relations at this time.[35]

Clashes between lords and peasants cannot all have been recorded. In most cases they cannot have got as far as the King's court, to be described for posterity. Those that are recorded inevitably assume the form of a dispute about status, for that was the only way in which royal courts could interest themselves in the case. But the root cause was clearly an attempt by lords to increase rents and services. The only legal way peasants could resist was by claiming to be of free or privileged status, and so to be exempt from increases of rent beyond a previous customary level. The earliest recorded Leicestershire case concerns Withcote. This was a royal manor acquired by exchange by King John. In 1268 its peasants, claiming to be sokemen, not villeins, complained that the keeper of the manor, Peter de Neville, had tried to get them to perform unwonted customs and services, and upon their refusal had evicted them and confiscated their property. The jury of Framland hundred which was sworn to tell the facts of the case (and which may well have been subject to seigniorial pressure) confirmed that the complainants were villeins, that they could be tallaged at will, should pay merchet, and should obtain permission to sell livestock. But the jury also confirmed that the keeper had raised the money rent beyond the customary level of 4s. a yardland (we are told nothing of labour services). He was instructed by the court not to try to gain his aims by eviction and destruction,[36] but the real upshot of the case was a defeat for the peasants.

Two cases ten years later have similar features. Villeins of the Abbot of Leicester at Stoughton attempted in 1278 to resist an increase in rents and services, pleading that they were sokemen, not villeins, and as such not subject to the lord's arbitrary will. They too were defeated on the question of status by the judgement of a jury in the King's court, and (since villeins could have no case there against their lord) had to return to their village to submit to their

---

[33] This second method, though used, was probably of inconsiderable importance in Leics.
[34] *Archaeologia*, xlvii. Nichols, *Hist. of Leics.* ii, App., 80–81, 97.
[35] Cf. R. H. Hilton, 'Peasant Movements in Engl. before 1381', *Econ. Hist. Rev.* (Second Ser.), ii, 2.
[36] *Abbrev. Plac.* (Rec. Com.), 161.

lord in the manor court. A year later, at Garthorpe, a number of tenants of Bennet of Rolleston impleaded their lord for having forced them to do extra customs and services, in spite of their being free sokemen of the king. Bennet claimed them as his villeins, and as such without right against him. A jury was summoned but the result of the dispute is not known.[37] Other cases illustrate the lord's pressure on the peasants in their need for extra labour services. At Narborough in 1286 a neighbouring lord who was the guardian of the lord of Narborough (a minor) was accused of amercing Narborough tenants for not reaping his corn, putting them in the stocks for not carrying his wood, and extracting extortionate entry fines to tenements. Two years later a tenant of Sutton Cheney accused a landowner of distraining him of £5 of goods in order to force him to do villein services. Here once more the defence became one of status, or rather of tenure, for the plaintiff denied holding in villeinage.[38]

Another form of social conflict in the countryside arose from the attempt by lords of manors to increase the profit of their estates by extending arable cultivation at the expense of the common pastures. There is much more evidence for conflict over this than for conflict over rent, because freeholders who had access to the royal courts suffered as much from encroachment on the commons as did customary tenants. They also had a case at law, since the Statute of Merton of 1236, which confirmed the rights of lords over the 'waste', also said that free tenants (not villeins) should be left sufficient common pasture. Many lawsuits resulted, especially in the expansive years of the 13th century; fewer in the 14th century, when lords were contracting their agricultural interests; then more again in the 15th century, which saw the beginning of large-scale inclosure for pasture.[39] The lawsuits more frequently reveal conflict between lords and peasant freeholders, but also very often between two lords in one village, competing for pasture rights. This aspect of the situation should not, however, be allowed to conceal an important social aspect of seigniorial expansion of the arable area, that it sharpened the existing conflict between lords and peasants.

The approvement of the waste resulting in the creation of inclosed severalties was on the largest scale in the most heavily wooded areas, that is, principally in the west of the county. An early-13th-century grant of land in Quorndon included 128 acres of assart land, and evidence for clearance on this scale is abundant throughout the century.[40] Waste land was often granted, especially to monastic houses, specifically for the purpose of reduction to arable cultivation. A landowner in Ibstock who made a grant to Garendon Abbey, in addition to transferring land in the open fields, confirmed to the abbey *quicquid monachi fregerunt de brueria*. In 1301 the Abbot of Croxton was accused of inclosing and ploughing up 80 acres of a moor in Skeffington township on which the tenants had rights of common pasture. Others besides the monks were, of course, doing the same. In 1284 it was the Prior of Belvoir who accused another landowner in Stockerston (William Murdak) of breaking up

[37] R. H. Hilton, 'A 13th-century Poem about Disputed Villein Services', *E.H.R.* lvi, 90–97; Farnham, *Leics.* ii, 284.

[38] Farnham, op. cit. iii, 249; v, 203.

[39] See below, pp. 191–3. It should also be added that a minor, though important, cause of complaint in the 13th as in the 15th and 16th centuries was the inclosure of woodland in order to make parks.

[40] Hist. MSS. Com., *Hastings*, i, 67. For later evidence see R. H. Hilton, *Econ. Development of Some Leics. Estates*, 61.

(*frussura*) for arable cultivation land subject to rights of common pasture. These two came to an agreement that they should only break up land for arable by mutual consent. They added that this would be done without damage to Stockerston township and the neighbouring township of Horninghold.[41] Lords were not usually so scrupulous, even on parchment. The Statute of Merton was frequently invoked by them to justify their right to approve the waste, rather than by free tenants (in the first place) to protect their rights of common. A free yardlander of Kirkby Mallory in 1293 complained that the lord of the manor had robbed him of common pasture in 30 acres of pasture by converting it to arable. The lord claimed his right to do this by the Statute and said he had left the tenant enough common. The tenant lost the case. A similar case occurred at Barlestone between a free yardlander, who claimed common in 36 acres of pasture, and Theobald de Verdon. Theobald's steward invoked the Statute with partial success, since the assize only recognized that the tenant had been deprived of right in 6 acres. Sometimes a predatory landowner came up against more powerful opponents. In 1286 the prioress of Gracedieu accused Alan of Thringstone of disseising her of common pasture by inclosing 80 acres of wood in Thringstone. Alan said he was lord of the township and that according to the Statute he could approve his waste; but the prioress argued that he was not the sort of magnate in a great manor intended by the Statute, and that she and other free tenants had just as much right to the waste. This plea was successful, for the destruction of Alan's inclosure was ordered.[42]

AGRARIAN CHANGE IN THE LATER MIDDLE AGES

In the preceding pages the description of some of the main features of medieval Leicestershire rural life has been attempted. The documents used have been principally of the 13th and early 14th centuries, yet much of what has been said is valid for the later period. Although there were important changes in agrarian life in the 14th and 15th centuries, much remained unchanged. For example, important as was the 15th- and early-16th-century movement for inclosure for sheep and cattle pastures, open-field agriculture was still predominant, not merely at the end of the Middle Ages but until the later 17th century. As has been shown, open-field agriculture had a most important social aspect in addition to its special features as a technique of farming. An open-field village community, with its concern for innumerable communal routines, could not be the same as a village of individual inclosed farms. Even at the end of the Middle Ages, although the old system was being seriously undermined, the powerful influence of traditional ways was still felt.

The most important changes in the agrarian life of the county which occurred in the later Middle Ages were common to most of England. These changes were the consequence of profound economic and social developments which were transforming the whole life of Europe. Even before the middle of the 14th century the expansion of the economy of the big estates, which had been continuous (if uneven) since the 11th century, had ceased. There are many signs of crisis in both agriculture and industry, whilst at the same time an increasing proportion of society's resources was consumed in warfare and other

[41] Nichols, *Leics.* iii, 806; Farnham, *Leics. Notes*, v, 133; Hist. MSS. Com., *Rutland*, iv, 138–9.
[42] Farnham, op. cit. iii, 152; v, 26; vi, 97.

forms of unproductive expenditure. Social struggles increased in intensity. Old ways of social and political life and old forms of economic organization were no longer adequate. Naturally the forms of change varied considerably from county to county and from region to region. In Leicestershire we can study three aspects of these changes: the decline of demesne farming on the bigger estates; the development of further class divisions among the peasants; and the inclosure movement for cattle and sheep farming.

As elsewhere, the abandonment of demesne farming by lords of manors was an uneven process, spread over at least a century and a half. Manorial lords whose most important estates lay outside Leicestershire would be more inclined to lease those demesne lands which lay away from the main centres of their activity to their tenants or to single farmers. When Merton College in 1270 acquired Kibworth Harcourt manor from the founder of the college, it abandoned the cultivation of the demesne within a few years.[43] Although the honour of Leicester was an important enough part of the Lancastrian estate, it was only one of the many component baronies. An inquiry of 1322 tells us that even in the days of Edmund of Lancaster the demesne lands of the honour were in the hands of farmers. This is confirmed by bailiffs' accounts of 1314. At Desford and Earl Shilton we find the villein tenants holding the demesne arable on terms somewhat unusual in England—*ad campipartem*, that is, for a proportion of the crop. The demesne at Hinckley in the same year was held by a farmer for life (*per scriptum*). Subsequent accounts for the old Lancastrian manors show that while the woods and parks were still kept in hand, the demesne arable continued to be leased out.[44]

Other lay lords of the county seem to have kept their demesnes in hand for a longer period. The evidence is somewhat scattered, consisting of isolated surveys, inquisitions, and accounts. Using some of these, we find that before the Black Death of 1349, out of 24 manors, in only 7 (including the Lancastrian manors) were the demesnes leased out. The evidence for the part played by the Black Death as a determining factor in the trend towards leasing is uncertain enough for England as a whole. That the dislocation it caused was an important contributory factor cannot be denied. There is very little accurate evidence for Leicestershire. The Leicester Abbey chronicler, Henry Knighton, speaks of it as a real catastrophe. The court rolls of Kibworth Harcourt certainly confirm that the ravages of the plague were considerable. At the courts held in the years immediately preceding the plague only one or two holdings are recorded as falling into the lord's hands through death. But at the court held at the end of April 1349 12 tenants were reported dead, and by the court held at the end of July following 26 had died. By the court held in the middle of August the number was back again to 1, and likewise at the subsequent court.[45] After the catastrophe the evidence from lay estates shows that the trend towards the leasing of demesnes speeded up. On 12 out of 22 manors held by lay lords between the middle of the century and 1427 demesnes had been leased out.

The progress of events in one ecclesiastical estate more or less conforms to that seen on the lay estates.[46] The small abbey of Owston before the middle of

---

[43] R. H. Hilton, 'Kibworth Harcourt', in *Studies in Leics. Agrarian Hist.*, ed. W. G. Hoskins, 32.

[44] Except for the De Lacy manor of Castle Donington; *Cal. Inq. Misc.* ii, pp. 138–9; D.L. 29/1/3; 198/3111, 3112; S.C. 6/1146/9.

[45] Hen. Knighton, *Chron.* (Rolls Ser.), ii, 63; Merton Coll., Oxf., MS. 6405.

[46] Though the scantiness of the evidence from lay estates must preclude any firm conclusions.

the century was working 9 small demesnes, 2 of which were leased out by 1348. By 1363 another 4 had been leased out, so that by the turn of the century the abbey was relying on demesne production only in Owston itself and 2 other manors. Leicester Abbey, on the other hand, was slower in adopting this policy. In 1408 a number of demesnes and rights to tithe in parts of the country remote from Leicester—in Derbyshire, Buckinghamshire, Northamptonshire, and Warwickshire—were leased out, but in Leicestershire only two demesnes. It was some time between 1408 and 1477 that the large-scale leasing out of the demesne lands and tithes (even more lucrative than the demesnes) took place. According to a rental of 1477 16 demesnes and 24 groups of tithe were by then in the hands of farmers. Only the home farm at the abbey itself and 3 other nearby demesnes were still kept in hand.[47]

A process spread out over so long a period cannot have one single explanation. The leasing out of demesnes in outlying manors might result from a rational administrative decision in a number of different circumstances. It is clear, however, that the general trend must have been closely connected with the declining profitableness of large-scale farming as carried out on the feudal estates. It has long been realized that lords of manors did not take once-for-all decisions to lease out their demesnes and to commute the labour services necessary for their cultivation. In the first stages only a portion of the demesne was leased out. Sometimes this resulted in a permanent contraction of the demesne area, sometimes policy fluctuated over a number of years. A rental of Leicester Abbey of 1341 shows that while most abbey demesnes were still kept in hand, portions of them had been let out to the manorial tenants, while such demesnes as were entirely abandoned from the point of view of manorial production were leased among many small tenants rather than to a single lessee. In some cases quite large areas were involved—82 acres at Theddingworth and 87½ acres at Thurmaston, for instance. In the last case we are told by the rental that this land was arrented, 'quia inde nullum profectum habuimus per ballivos'.[48] These facts from Leicester Abbey are confirmed from other 14th-century Leicestershire evidence which shows rather more cases of demesnes leased out piecemeal to a number of tenants than of individual farmers taking on the whole demesne.[49] Normally we only know of this piecemeal leasing from evidence reflecting one year's activities. But a series of account rolls from Kirby Bellars (1384–1406) and Castle Donington (1377–1441) shows how a core of demesne land was kept in hand (as at Kirby Bellars) or leased to a big farmer (as at Castle Donington), while the rest of the demesne was leased for short terms in small pieces to manorial tenants, the shortness of the term obviously being determined by the reluctance of the tenant to take demesne arable on lease when it lay fallow.[50]

By the period of the large-scale leasing of demesnes, that is, in the 15th century, two things had happened. First, demesne cultivation by the big estate owners had mostly been abandoned, so that demesnes were farmed out *en bloc*. Secondly, there now existed men who were willing and able to pay the rent and meet the risks of this considerable economic enterprise. Leicester Abbey

[47] R. H. Hilton, *Econ. Development of Some Leics. Estates*, 91–93.

[48] Ibid., 89–91.

[49] Cf. Barwell, 1392, demesne leased to tenants (D.L. 43/14/3, ff. 69–70); Nailstone, 1392, demesne land valued per acre, *secundum tenuram tenencium* (ibid. ff. 54–55).

[50] Hilton, *Econ. Development of Some Leics. Estates*, App. iv, pp. 157–162.

by 1477, as has been shown, had withdrawn from active participation in farming in most villages where it had had demesne land. The lessees of the demesnes were no longer the middling peasantry of the days of piecemeal leasing, for not only were the complete demesnes taken on lease, but in many cases the farmer also took on the tithes, of which the abbey, as appropriator of many churches on its estate, had many. This often involved the payment of annual rents of £10 or more—considerable sums when one thinks of the average peasant rent of 10s. to 15s. a yardland. Yet the 15th- and early-16th-century demesne lessees were mostly peasants, often those whose original holdings (or whose ancestors' holdings) had been only of average size. What new process of social differentiation had taken place in the 14th century? How different was the social structure of the village from that of the 13th century, when there was already a distinct stratification of the peasantry? What were the causes of change?

In peasant communities relative equality of holdings can normally only disappear where there are both freedom of and grounds for alienation—in fact, a market in land. The market in land depends in turn on the existence of a market for the products of the land. In the 13th century there was such a market, in which not only the big and medium estate owners but the peasants also participated. Yet in spite of some signs of the breaking up of tenements under special circumstances (e.g. on the Rothley soke) the traditional oxgang or yardland holding seems to have generally remained, until the mid-14th century, the characteristic unit of cultivation. The principal stabilizing feature was undoubtedly the power of the lord, with his demand for rent and services assessed on the traditional holding, reinforced by the prohibition of illegal transfers of land amongst the peasantry.[51] But since the régime of labour services was light in Leicestershire, it is not surprising that even before the general leasing out of demesnes the seigniorial pressure to stabilize the tenurial situation should be relaxed.

In the 14th and early 15th centuries there was a decline in the prosperity of the big estates. In 1341 the Leicester Abbey rent roll in the county totalled £266. It had fallen to £207 in 1408 and to £177 in 1477. Comparisons of the rents of individual holdings in 1341 and 1477 show that this fall was due to a fall in rents per acre. The same fall in the landlords' rent revenues can also be observed in other estates. Certain rents of Owston Abbey had fallen between the 13th century and a date before the Black Death. Merton College rent revenues in Kibworth Harcourt show the same decline.[52] A decline in seigniorial fortunes is reflected also in numerous inquisitions *post mortem* of the period. A statement in a Belvoir inquisition of 1353 that 3 ploughlands were worth only 60s. on account of the plague and for lack of tenants is not surprising only a few years after the Black Death, but the castle was already in ruins ten years earlier. An inquisition held at Whitwick in 1427 shows an even worse situation. The castle and manor site were in ruins, 12 out of 31 holdings in the lord's hands for lack of tenants, and nearly 300 acres of demesne arable in use as waste and valued (presumably for pasture) at 2d. an acre.[53] Not all manors by any

[51] As there are no 13th-century Ct. R. we have no direct evidence for this in Leics. But it was normal elsewhere, and it is found in Owston Abbey Ct. R. of the late 14th century. Hilton, op. cit. 126. (Note that the Rothley soke was exceptional in this respect, as in others: above, p. 169.)

[52] Hilton, op. cit. 86, 100–5, 123; Hilton, in *Studies in Leics. Agrarian Hist.* 38–40.

[53] *Leics. Notes*, ed. Farnham, vi, 108–9; Nichols, *Leics.* iii, 114.

means were in this condition, but taken with the evidence of declining rents they suggest that the economic situation of the lords of manors at any rate was critical.

SOCIAL CHANGES IN THE LATER MIDDLE AGES

These signs of declining economic activity, reflected in documents of the landlord estates, provoke the question: Why did not the same stagnation affect peasant farming and thus hold up the process of class differentiation which was becoming increasingly apparent? The answer involves not one but many factors. For various reasons land was becoming available on terms freer than the customary terms governing the traditional holdings. First there was land taken in from waste and wood. This was almost always leased out for a money rent only, and at rents which were (as far as this is conceivable in a society where production was still to a great extent for subsistence) of a 'competitive' or 'economic' character. On a number of Leicester Abbey manors, by 1341, many pieces of assarted land were held by tenants at the lord's pleasure. In other words, the leases were terminable when the abbey wished, and could therefore be leased out at the best rent currently obtainable. At the same time the demesne land which was being leased out piecemeal was also held by lessees at money rents of a non-customary character. Finally, even before the Black Death, peasant tenements were being divided up and taken piecemeal by other peasant lessees, again at money rent. After the Black Death there was normally a great (if temporary) increase in the ratio of land to lessees. More demesne land was available, and the holdings of the peasants who had died of plague and had no heirs swelled the available supply. The 14th-century rentals of Kibworth Harcourt manor show a remarkably rapid circulation of land amongst lessees in the middle of the century, as well as a complete disintegration of certain types of holding (especially free holdings). Portions of a free yard-land varying between one rood and 6 acres in area were held at two successive dates by 15 and 13 lessees. Only 2 of the 13 who followed the 15 seem to have succeeded by inheritance to their portion. Contemporary Leicester Abbey surveys and terriers illustrate the same phenomenon. Nor was this social mobility, inseparable from a freer market in land, simply the temporary consequence of the plagues of the mid and later 14th century. Considerable changes in landholding families between the end of the 14th century and the early 16th century can be deduced from a comparison between family names in the 1377 and 1381 tax lists and those of 1524 and 1525, implying, if not a continuous movement during the intervening century and a half, at any rate periods of upheaval not yet datable.

It seems, then, that there was much land available at something like competitive rents—and from the middle of the 14th century until the end of the 15th this meant lower rents. It was in these conditions that a new social stratification of the peasantry took place. Those peasants who were already richer than their fellows could take advantage of the economic embarrassment of both lords and poor peasants. If in addition they held an official position in the manorial community, such as that of reeve, their opportunities would be greater. The reeve of Kibworth Harcourt, Roger Polle, was accused in 1349 (before the Black Death arrived) of a succession of misdeeds by which he sought to enrich himself. He took bribes from the tenants that he should not collect their rents or exact due services. He also took bribes from demesne lessees, presumably as a condition for their having the land. He took, from successors to tenements, entry fines which should have gone to the lord, and in one instance took the large fine of 4 marks and failed to record on the court roll the entry of the tenant into the land in question. He himself took over the land which lapsed into the lord's hand without conducting the transaction in the lord's court and therefore without paying a fine. The family of Polle (of which there appear to have been 4 branches, 2 of free tenants and 2 of villeins) continued to give trouble, for there exists an elaborate document of the reign of Henry IV which attempts to prove by quotations from court rolls and other records the villein status of those Polles who were attempting to escape from it. It was characteristic that economic expansion should be accompanied by attempts to escape from the restriction of villein tenure.[54]

It has been suggested[55] that the 14th-century population decline resulted in the elimination or considerable reduction in numbers of the landless labourers and smallholders, since the survivors were able to move into vacant peasant tenements. Immediately after the Black Death there was plenty of land available in certain areas. At Kibworth Harcourt, at the first court held after the worst of the plague was over, 5 new tenants had to be chosen by their fellow tenants to take over vacant tenements. At the following court 3 new tenants had to be forced to take land, and one of those chosen by the homage to take over a tenement at the previous court succeeded in surrendering it on the ground that he was unable to work it.[56] But if there was a surplus of land available, and large numbers of wage-earners and smallholders became at least full yardlanders, this should have resulted in a more homogeneous peasant population than before rather than the development of class divisions. Even if this were true of some parts of the country, it does not seem to fit in with other Leicestershire evidence.

The evidence of the great 1477 rental of Leicester Abbey shows that on most manors of the abbey peasant land-holders, and especially smallholders, had fallen considerably in number. Holdings seem to have increased in size, so that at the top of the scale we find tenants holding as much as 3 yardlands, containing, say, 60 to 90 acres in all. The rental naturally contains no information about the landless, and this is the crucial problem. Have the smallholders of the 13th and early 14th centuries moved up into the class of yardlanders, or have they been reduced to the condition of wage labourers? Other evidence about the growth of big holdings is scanty, but what there is suggests that it was on a sufficient scale to presuppose as a counterpart an appreciable quantity of wage labour. The accounts of the Lancastrian manor of Castle Donington contain many details about leasing. They show tenants taking portions of demesne and of lapsed tenements on lease for short terms. The amount rented by one man in any given year therefore varied, but in 1421 the manorial bailiff had 215 acres of arable on his hands. At the same time there was a demesne farmer cultivating 270 acres. Since it is doubtful whether even 50 acres (that is, 2 yardlands) could be worked by the labour of one family alone, it is clear that these big holdings could not have been kept going without wage labour.

[54] Merton Coll., Oxf., MSS. 6405; 6365; 6464.
[55] M. M. Postan, 'Econ. Evidence for Declining Population', *Econ. Hist. Rev.* (Second Ser.), ii, 3.
[56] Merton Coll., Oxf., MS. 6405.

The evidence for wage labour in late-14th-century Leicestershire is not lacking. Its importance in the 13th and early 14th centuries has already been shown.[57] By the end of the 14th century the demesne lands of Owston Abbey were exclusively cultivated by wage labour, the cost of seasonal labour (paid by the day or task) being about equal to the costs of the permanent farm servants (wages reckoned by the year, partly in money and partly in grain). Wages paid in money at King's Norton manor in 1358 came to a third of the money spent.[58] A piece of evidence contemporary with the accounts of Owston Abbey is the Poll Tax return of 1381. It reinforces the impression, derived from the accounts and from the evidence of large holdings needing wage labour, that wage workers could not have been a negligible element in the population. The tax lists are notoriously unreliable for total population figures, for as many members of families as possible were concealed. However, the lists are unique in stating the occupations of the persons taxed, and since wage earners without property could obviously conceal themselves more easily than agriculturalists, the proportion of labourers to the total population is more likely to be under- than overestimated. It is interesting, therefore, to find that in seventy-one villages in Framland and Guthlaxton hundreds,[59] the proportion of the population described in such a way as to imply that they were wage earners was 28 per cent.; craftsmen and other self-employed persons, 10 per cent.; husbandmen, 57 per cent.; cottagers, 2 per cent.; and unspecified, 3 per cent.

Besides confirming the stratification of rural society these figures show that the existence of a large number of wage earners (even if they received as little as half of their wages in money) is an important element in the formation of the home market for commodities. For just as the labour of the landless peasant becomes marketable, the payment made for that labour in the form of wages is used to purchase the means of subsistence, thus stimulating production for the market. It is interesting to compare figures for wage earners in 1524 and 1525, a period when the progress of class stratification among the peasantry is usually thought to have been well advanced, and when, too, the post-medieval economic revival was well under way. According to the subsidy assessments of these years, 30 per cent. of the taxed population were assessed either on wages or on goods of the same value as the wage earners' wages.[60] The figures are not strictly comparable with those of 1381, for they do not cover quite the same area and are based on a different type of assessment. Nevertheless, even a rough indication that the proportion of wage earners in Leicestershire was not much less at the end of the 14th century than in the third decade of the 16th century is of some significance. On the one hand it emphasizes the importance of wage labour in the medieval Leicestershire village, even though there are no satisfactory indications whether there was a proportional increase as compared with a century earlier. On the other hand it hints at a slowing down of the tempo of social change, between 1381 and 1524.

Changes in the social structure were not confined to the peasants or to ecclesiastical dignitaries and the nobility. Often bigger landlords were replaced as agricultural producers by the wealthier peasant demesne-lessees, whose

---

[57] Above, pp. 173–4.   [58] S.C. 6/908/36.

[59] Market towns have been excluded so as not to overweight the number of wage earners.

[60] In the 1524 list all wages are assessed at 20s. Counted as wage earners are those assessed in goods at 20s. Lists for 1381 and 1524 are printed in *Leics. Notes*, ed. Farnham, *passim*; cf. W. G. Hoskins, *Essays in Leics. Hist.*, 129–30, for a discussion of the 1524–5 assessment.

emergence by the end of the 14th century has been referred to. Nor must we forget that even in the 13th century the lesser landlord was an important element in the social structure. Unfortunately our knowledge of the methods employed by lesser landlords in managing their estates is scanty. Yet the evidence of land sales, especially in the 15th century, suggests that properties were being re-grouped. In consequence a prosperous gentry, led by representatives of old families of the lesser nobility but reinforced both from below and from outside, was to emerge. The sales of complete manors as well as of much land in the villages are obscured by the intricacies of the 15th-century feoffments to uses. The results of the process, however, by the end of the 15th century were the emergence of a substantial if not yet numerous gentry[61]—the Villierses, Hasle-riggs, Shirleys, Kebells, Pulteneys, and many others found in the inquisitions *post mortem* of the reign of Henry VII, and who were active in economic and social life as the old aristocracy was ceasing to be.

While many of these gentry were descendants of the old knightly class, a few had been considered as only substantial yeomen at the beginning of the 15th century. An example is to be found at Twycross. The designation in the legal records of the social status of Thomas Kendale at the beginning of the 15th century was a matter for doubt. In 1417 he was described as a husband-man, a year later as a gentleman. But by the middle of the century the Kendales are always called gentlemen, even though at the beginning of the 16th century the widow of Bartholomew Kendale, gentleman, may have lapsed from that estate or (to put it more exactly) had by marrying a yeoman (Richard Hewes) demonstrated the fluid line between the two social groups. By 1549 William Kendale on his death was possessed of much land in Twycross, Snibson, Swith-land, Sheepy Parva, and Lutterworth.[62]

A further addition to the landed class came from the ranks of commerce, sometimes (not surprisingly in view of Leicestershire's wool) from merchants of the Staple. William Wyggeston, the founder of Wyggeston Hospital in Leicester, was (like his father) a Stapler. The foundation deeds of the hospital show how he bought up land in the county, often from other merchants. Humphrey Bannister, who later became Mayor of the Calais Staple, bought Swannington manor in 1499 from Humphrey Markham for £250—to be paid ·in wool—and sold it twenty years later to Wyggeston for 500 marks. A London vintner named Baraby had inherited land in Barkestone from his father and sold it to another vintner who in turn, in 1524, sold it to Wyggeston.[63]

Wyggeston's accumulation of lands might from the very beginning have been prompted by the charitable aims which he fulfilled. But the conversion of merchant capital into rents and land could as easily have had as object its owner's settlement as a member of the landed gentry. The co-plaintiffs (feoffees to use, no doubt) of Sir Stephen Jenyns, citizen and alderman of London, in a fine of 1513 by which Lubbesthorpe manor was transferred from the Hastings family to Jenyns and his heirs, are a mixture of town and country types. Headed by Robert Brudenell, a Justice of Common Pleas (and an inclosing Leicestershire

---

[61] Many Leics. villages at the beginning of the 16th cent. were without a resident squire. This was also the case at the end of the 14th cent. More than ⅔ of the villages for which we have tax returns in 1381 had no resident squire. In some a rich 'frankleyn' probably played the same role. Leland, in his itinerary, mentions the following gentlemen as being 'most of reputation': Villiers, Digby, Brokesby, Neville of Holt, Shirley, Skeffing-ton, Purefey, Vincent, Turville, and Hazlerigg. *Itinerary in England*, ed. L. Toulmin Smith, i, 21.

[62] *Leics. Notes*, ed. Farnham, iii, 288–9.   [63] *Wyggeston Hosp. Rec.*, 142, 447–8.

landowner), they include a Sacheverell, two Shirleys, and a Kebyll, a London alderman and other citizens, namely an ironmonger, a fishmonger, a merchant, and a salter. The will of Hugh Noble, described as a gentleman of Scalford, in 1513, expressed the dead man's desire to be buried in St. Sepulchre's, London, and amongst the surveyors of the will were three London citizens—a skinner, a baker, and a corviser.[64] Such was the social milieu of the Leicestershire gentry, new and old, at the end of the Middle Ages. It was not, of course, that the acquisition of land by merchants as a gilt-edged security was a new phenomenon. The Pulteney family who headed the 1524 subsidy list for the depopulated village of Misterton[65] probably originated in the nearby hamlet of Pulteney; but the John de Pulteney who acquired the manor and half of the advowson of Misterton in 1331 was described as citizen of London, and must have made the purchase with city money. Pulteney's commercial habits were brought to Leicestershire, for the legal records show a succession of pleas of debt from 1380 until the end of the 15th century in which a Pulteney is almost invariably the plaintiff—usually against husbandmen or squires, and for sums up to £40.[66]

Merchants did not always negotiate for complete manors. Simon Hauberk, mercer of London, bought a group of lands in Scalford in 1350, and by the end of the century his family seems to have been established as members of the local gentry. William Brett (d. 1496), a London draper but a member of an old Leicestershire family, had lands in 7 villages, but nowhere more than 3 yardlands, except in Rotherby. Here he had a messuage, a cottage, 2 tofts, and 3 virgates which he had bought for £5 from Bartholomew Brooksby. Rotherby had apparently been the home of William's father, and by 1516 his heir George Brett was referred to as a 'gentleman' of Rotherby.[67] Not all the merchants who settled down as landowners were Londoners, of course, though the proportion occurring in our evidence is high. The occupations of the taxed population of rural settlements in 1377 and 1381 include an occasional merchant or chapman assessed at more than his fellow villagers, such as John de Langton, 'merchant of wool', at Kegworth in 1377, who paid 12d. to everybody else's 4d.; or Thomas Milner, merchant, of Lockington, who paid 3s. 8d.; or William Dalby of Tilton, who paid 40d. These men may have owned land as well, but their role in bringing money made in trade to the countryside should not be exaggerated. There were more substantial merchants in the market towns like Market Harborough, Market Bosworth, and Melton Mowbray, but none of these places produced men rich enough to emulate the Londoners. Leicester, of course, was in a different category—witness Robert Oxton, bailiff of Leicester, to whom Evington manor was leased in 1500 for forty years at £50 a year.[68]

MEDIEVAL INCLOSURES FOR PASTURE

These social changes are inseparable from economic developments during the same period. Land was probably not at more than 10 years' purchase in the 13th century, and was being sold at 16 years' purchase in Leicestershire in

[64] Farnham, *Leics. Notes*, iv, 32–33; v, 266.
[65] They also had the largest assessment in the county. Hoskins, *Essays in Leics. Hist.* 128 n.
[66] Farnham, *Leics. Notes*, iii, 222–30.   [67] Ibid. iii, 341; iv, 29.
[68] Ibid. ii, 201.

the early 16th century.[69] The stagnation of the old agrarian organization was being disturbed in the later 15th century by a lively movement towards inclosure for sheep and cattle pastures, part of that movement whose social consequences so worried the Tudor government.

Sheep farming, as has been seen, had been moderately important on the estates of Leicestershire in the 12th, 13th, and early 14th centuries.[70] Although sheep could be found in most parts of the county the densest concentrations were on the north-eastern wolds (especially on the lands of the religious houses), and to a lesser extent in the west (the Charnwood Forest area) and in the southeast (the Leighfield Forest area). It will be noticed that in these districts there were stretches of wold or woodland pasture on which sheep could be grazed when the common fields were under crop and in numbers beyond the stint imposed for pasture on the fallow. Consequently inclosure for pasture was not yet an economic and social problem.

The religious houses were the principal sheep farmers. Charters of the period show such houses as Garendon and Croxton to have been gathering pasture rights in villages where they were able to put up sheepcotes. Such grants implied a considerable total flock. We find, for instance, grants of pasture to Garendon Abbey for 300 sheep at Easton, for 500 at Gaddesby, for 300 at Waltham-on-the-Wolds, and for 200 at Welby. Lawsuits show that Croxton Abbey had pasture for 200 sheep at Bottesford, and for 100 at Eaton during the same period.[71] According to a list drawn up by an Italian exporter, the amount of wool which could be expected annually from Croxton and Garendon Abbey estates in the early 14th century was 25 and 20 sacks respectively. At 250 fleeces a sack this implies flocks of at least 5,000 to 6,000 sheep. Leicester Abbey flocks, also mentioned in the list, were reckoned to produce as much as those of Garendon. The only other Leicestershire religious houses mentioned in the list are Launde and Langley Priories, with an expected yield of 5 sacks a year.[72] But there were other Leicestershire producers not on the list. The Hospitallers' inquest of 1338 tells us that whilst only 100 sheep were then kept in Dalby bailiwick, there had once been 1,100. The keeper of the Templars' estate in 1309 accounted for 402 sheep and 123 lambs on Rothley manor.[73] Owston Abbey towards the end of the century had a small flock varying between 400 and 700 sheep.

Religious houses were not the only wool producers in this period. References in deeds and lawsuits to sheepcotes show that such lords as Roos of Belvoir and Picot of Burton on the Wolds were engaged in sheep farming. Reynold of Ibstock disputed the possession of 100 sheep at Ibstock with the Abbot of Garendon in 1369. The bailiff of Lutterworth manor in 1361 accounted for 641 sheep in his annual account. Most spectacular of all, we find that in 1340, when all the English wool available was being mobilized to pay for the French war, Lord Ferrers of Groby was licensed to transport 20 sacks

---

[69] Hilton in *Studies in Leics. Agrarian Hist.* 23 (Sale of manor of Kibworth Harcourt); *Wyggeston Hosp. Rec.*, 197 (purchase of land in Breedon, 1532).

[70] Above, pp. 164–5, 172, 175. Cf. Hilton, *Econ. Development of Some Leics. Estates*, 67–68, for Leic. Abbey flocks, and p. 134 for Owston Abbey flocks.

[71] Hist. MSS. Com., *Rutland*, iv, 4 (12th century); Nichols, *Leics.* ii, App., 133, 138; *Doc. Illustrative of the Soc. and Econ. Hist. of the Danelaw*, ed. F. M. Stenton, p. 251 (12th century); Farnham, *Leics. Notes*, ii, 192 (early 13th century), vi, 187 (early 13th century).

[72] F. B. Pegolotti, *La Pratica Della Mercatura* (ed. Evans), 259–69.

[73] *The Knights Hospitallers in Engl.* (Camden Soc., lxv), ed. L. B. Larking, 65; E. 142/105.

of wool from his Leicestershire estates. Since on his death in 1340 he only possessed one manor (Groby) in demesne in the county it is difficult to believe that all the wool came from his own flocks. It is more probable that he was also buying it from smaller producers, including his tenants. The same may, of course, have been true of monastic wool. We have already seen that in many villages the common pasture available to the yardlander allowed him to keep a flock of 30 to 40 sheep. Not all yardlanders kept flocks of this size, but peasant flocks could reach a respectable number. In 1359 at Kimcote, among those prosecuted at the view of frankpledge for trespass, was the owner of 80 sheep. His flock was the largest, but he himself was not the only transgressor. Others charged at the same court had flocks of 15, 16, 22, and 30.[74]

The big flocks of the landlord estates in the 13th and early 14th centuries were producing mainly for export. The decline in the Dalby flocks suggests that a decline in numbers may have already set in before the middle of the century. The recovery in sheep farming did not come until the later 15th century, as a result of the expansion of the home cloth industry. By this time, and in the early 16th century, the squires were perhaps the most important of the sheep farmers, although some of the religious were re-expanding the pastoral side of their estates also. George Boyvile (d. 1519), member of a family which succeeded the Thomas Palmer of Holt who had inclosed the township of Keythorpe in c. 1456, used to keep 600 sheep on his lands there. The lessee of the Hospitallers at Dalby on the Wolds in 1537 had farmed the manor house and demesne for the past 15 years and had a flock of 700 sheep and 160 cattle. A lawsuit of 1530 shows that Richard Cave reckoned his flock at Stormsworth at at least 500. Thomas Bradgate, a wealthy yeoman of Peatling Parva, at his death in 1539 had (besides his other livestock) 400 sheep. Launde Priory before the Dissolution had kept 2,000 sheep at Whadborough, while Ulverscroft Priory had 1,000.[75] The most striking evidence for the extension of sheep farming at the end of the Middle Ages lies, however, not so much in the details of the sheep flocks themselves as in the movement of inclosure for pasture, which has left considerable traces in the records.

The inclosure by manorial lords of land taken in from waste for arable cultivation, which had roused some resentment in the 13th and early 14th centuries, had slackened with the decline of seigniorial agriculture. Yet the inclosure of arable still went on, though more slowly. It has been shown that lords and wealthy freeholders always tended to maintain arable cultivation in severalty, especially of land assarted by themselves from the forest. Then the disintegration and regrouping of tenements during the 14th and 15th centuries made possible a consolidation of scattered strips, so that eventually a large enough block of land could be made into an inclosure. Exchanges with the aim of such regrouping can often be traced. In the early 14th century strips in or adjacent to the furlong called Kirkwong in Lockington took place. This led to an agreement between Leicester Abbey, lord of Lockington, and the tenants that the abbey could inclose the whole wong and cultivate it in severalty.[76]

---

[74] Nichols, *Leics.* ii, App., 12; iii, 811; Farnham, *Leics. Notes*, iii, 8; *Cal. Close, 1339–41*, 577; *Cal. Inq. p.m.*, viii, pp. 315–19; B.M. Egerton R., no. 1911; S.C. 6/908/33.

[75] G. F. Farnham, 'Prestwold and its Hamlets', *T.L.A.S.* xvii, 77–81; Farnham, *Leics. Notes*, iii, 89; v, 149; Hoskins, *Essays in Leics. Hist.* 154; Nichols, *Leics.* iii, 318, 1091.

[76] Hilton, *Econ. Development of Some Leics. Estates*, 46. The inclosed wongs at Eaton in 1396 (see above, p. 159) may always have been in severalty, or have been inclosed after a similar consolidation.

A similar inclosure by agreement was made in the 1330's at Breedon. The Prior of Breedon arranged for the inclosure with hedges and ditches of a place in Breedon called Skalakre. The principal obstacle to doing this seems not to have been the arrangement of land exchanges but the satisfaction of those who thereby lost rights of common pasture. That the obstacle was overcome is shown by a series of charters in the Breedon cartulary by which lords of the neighbourhood and free tenants quitclaimed to the priory in perpetuity their rights to common pasture.[77] There were less harmonious episodes, of course. A lay lord of Breedon, John of Driby, inclosed a green outside his manor house and was challenged by the prior. A local jury supported John, and the prior, not wishing to be accused of negligence, appealed to the parent house of St. Oswald, Nostell (Yorks.), for legal aid. But he was refused, since the canons of Nostell did not think the expense worth so little gain.[78] From all the evidence, however, we can conclude that a slow and piecemeal inclosure movement, mainly for arable, was going on throughout the period preceding the more dramatic inclosure movement for pasture of the late 15th and early 16th centuries. It should not be assumed that the two movements were unconnected. The ease with which arable could be converted to pasture would largely depend on the extent to which common pasture rights had been weakened and open-field cultivation undermined, as it were from within, by the creation of arable severalties.[79]

At a certain stage the expansion of demesne inclosure led to the almost complete inclosure of whole villages.[80] This involved the eviction of the peasantry with all the social consequences that followed the disruption of a deep-rooted traditional way of life. The later depopulation movement was anticipated in some places in the middle of the 15th century. In some cases the object of inclosure was the creation of a park. William, Lord Hastings, was licensed in 1474 to inclose and impark 2,000 acres of demesne land and wood in each of his two manors of Bagworth and Kirby Muxloe.[81] But the creation of even very large parks was not of great economic significance. In the forest areas of the county since the 13th century there had been imparking which resembled the approvements of waste and wood already referred to. In other cases the conversion of arable farms to sheep-runs was involved. A number of villages, of which Keythorpe is a classic example, were depopulated of arable farmers in the middle of the 15th century. The depopulation and inclosure of Keythorpe led to much litigation at the end of the century. This litigation illustrates the turbulent character of these economic changes, not merely because of clashes between arable farmers and inclosing pastoralists, but because of the ambitions of rival sheep farmers.[82] Keythorpe appears to have been largely inclosed by Thomas Palmer of Holt in c. 1456. In 1469 Leicester Abbey

[77] John Rylands Libr., Latin MS. 222, ff. 28b, 29a, 64 et seq., 68 et seq.

[78] Ibid., f. 65b.

[79] An undated terrier of South Croxton entitled 'The terre belonging to the Cottys Close' shows that this close had consisted of 24 small pieces of land (between 1 r. and 4 a.) once lying in 15 separately named wongs. Leics. E. 303/35.

[80] It may be noted that the inclosure of demesne could reach an advanced stage, as at Stoughton at the end of the 15th century, whilst the tenant land had not yet been encroached upon.

[81] *Cal. Chart. R., 1427–1516*, 242.

[82] *T.L.A.S.* xvii, 77–81; S. H. Skillington, 'The Skeffingtons of Skeffington', *T.L.A.S.*, xvi, 92–98; L. A. Parker, 'Enclosure in Leics., 1485–1607' (unpublished thesis, Univ. Coll., Leic.). Much of what follows on Leics. inclosure is based on Dr. Parker's unpublished work; see also his 'Agrarian Revolution at Cotesbach', in *Studies in Leics. Agrarian Hist.* 41–76.

AERIAL VIEW OF THE SITE OF THE DESERTED VILLAGE OF HAMILTON

inclosed its demesnes in Ingarsby for pasture in order to maintain its manorial flock of 400 sheep.[83] The land inclosed was surrounded by a ditch and fence at a cost of £74. 11s. 9d. Such abbey lands in Ingarsby fields as lay outside the inclosed pasture were rearranged so that the abbey's carts could go in with materials for hedging and ditching without disturbing other farmers. Moreover, before the inclosure was carried through, an agreement with representatives of eight neighbouring villages was made for the division of the pasture, presumably in settlement of claims for common. Yet even if the records of this agreement reflect what really happened, it cannot be assumed that matters were always settled so amicably.

For the progress of conversion is indicated, too, by the reaction of the arable farmers. It was not only in the middle of the 16th century that peasants broke down hedges and attempted to restore the old forms of husbandry. In 1448 a husbandman of Hoton was charged with breaking down the inclosure of Richard Neel, a Justice of the Common Pleas, and ploughing up the ground. It was the Neel family which was involved in the fierce litigation (to which reference has already been made) over inclosed sheep pasture in the nearby village of Keythorpe. At Oadby in 1463 four husbandmen and a Leicester merchant broke into the inclosure of John Brooksby, lord of Frisby-on-the-Wreak, and pastured their cattle there. In 1490 William Brabason, lessee of the Abbot of Garendon, sued James Huddleston, gentleman, and others for ploughing up 360 acres of his land at Eastwell. This was not a simple case of reaction to inclosure since Huddleston had claims by marriage on the land. But it is probable that he used social discontent to further private ends. Another rich farmer, George Kyngston, seems to have been an inclosing sheep farmer whose activities caused much friction at Illston-on-the-Hill, a manor of Christ's College, Cambridge. In 1511 he was suing a husbandman for breaking into his inclosure and pasturing his sheep and other cattle there during August. Next year he was involved in a quarrel with the lessee of the manor. Kyngston and his supporters accused the lessee of the unjust distraint of 160 head of stock and of attempting to rob tenants of their title to land. But the lessee accused Kyngston of occupying certain inclosures in severalty on which the lessee and the College tenants had common pasture rights. These and other cases suggest that villages where inclosure was gradually encroaching on arable must have been the scene of continual squabbles culminating in violence and legal action. Thus was the ground prepared for the larger protest movements of 1549 to 1553.[84]

By the end of the 15th century the inclosure and conversion movement had gathered momentum, reaching its peak in the two decades 1490 to 1510. During this period the movement involved large-scale inclosure, leading in many cases to the almost complete depopulation of entire villages. There was a slackening of activity in the next decade and in spite of a fresh spurt between 1521 and 1530 the inclosures henceforth tended to be on a smaller scale. In those villages where inclosure was most complete, the incloser was, as might be

---

[83] It is usually assumed that the whole lordship (*dominium*) was inclosed, but the rental of 1477 speaks of 17½ yardlands in villeinage and 18 yardlands in free tenure. If it was not depopulated in 1469, this fate certainly overtook it; Hoskins, *Essays in Leics. Hist.* 75–79; Nichols, *Leics.* iii, 292.

[84] *T.L.A.S.* xvii, 43; Farnham, *Leics. Notes*, ii, 183, 262; iii, 24–26. The cases of inclosure-breaking cited by Farnham are numerous, especially towards the end of the 15th century. In some cases they have no connexion with protest against conversion, but in many they clearly have.

expected, the owner of the lordship.[85] Hence peers and squires were the largest inclosers.[86] The squirearchy in particular stands out as the social group from which the leaders of this economic transformation came, just as it was the same class which was the ultimate beneficiary in the share-out of monastic property after the Dissolution. And yet it must be remembered that only a minority of the class promoted inclosure, just as we must remember that, catastrophic as inclosure may have been where a whole village was turned over to sheep farming, the county as a whole remained an arable, open-field county.[87]

Since the inclosed village represented what was new and emergent in the agrarian life of Leicestershire, whilst the traditional open-field system was to disappear within a couple of centuries, it is worth considering in detail what the change involved. The village of Knaptoft is a good example. A more than usually detailed survey of the village was drawn up in 1301 by the escheator on the death of the lord of the manor, Richard Gobion.[88] Gobion's manor comprised the whole village. There was a manor house with an inclosed garden, two fishponds, a few parcels of demesne pasture in severalty, and two small spinneys. There were 360 acres of demesne arable and 9 acres of meadow. There were 26 tenants in the village. Of the three free tenants one held a ¼ knight's fee, but the size of his holding is not stated. The two others held 2 and 1 yardlands respectively, at 20 acres to the yardland. There were 21 villeins, each of whom held a yardland. We are given their names and the rents and services which they owed. It is characteristic of the county that they owed no week work, but in addition to a money rent of 13s. 4d. and a rent in kind valued at 8d. did 23 days' work of various sorts during the year for each

[85] Dr. Parker's figures (given in his unpublished thesis: see p. 192, n. 82) for 1485–1550 show the following distribution:

	1485–90	1491–1500	1501–10	1511–20	1521–30	1531–40	1541–50
Places where inclosure occurred .	2	13	12	15	3	5	..
Percentage of total acreage inclosed, 1485–1550 . .	12·3	33·3	28·2	6·6	15·9	3	0·7

Dr. Parker gives evidence of inclosure in 20 villages besides those given in *Domesday of Enclosures*, ed. I. S. Leadham, i, 226–42. They are: Lowesby and Quenby (1485–9), Bittesby (1494), Whatborough (1495), Lindley and Elmsthorpe (1500), Mowsley and Husbands Bosworth (1496–1502), Wigston Parva, Knaptoft, Misterton and Pulteney (1507), Newbold Verdon (1509), Hallaton and Cole Orton (1510–12), Thurlaston (1511), Normanton Turville (1511–15), Chadwell and Wycombe (1516), Thorpe Acre (1517).

[86] Dr. Parker's figures (given in his unpublished thesis, p. 83) are as follows:

Inclosures	Average inclosed	%
Crown . . .	303	2·1
Monastic . . .	2,420	17·6
Nobility . . .	1,668	12·1
Squirearchy . . .	8,067	58·4
Unknown . . .	1,354	9·8
Totals . . .	13,812	100·0

The 'unknown' group should probably be included with the squirearchy, giving a total of 67·5 per cent. for that class in all.

[87] E. F. Gay, basing his remarks on figures from the inclosure inquisitions of 1517–19, is inclined to underestimate the early-16th-century inclosure movement. (E. F. Gay, 'Enclosures in Engl. in the 16th century', *Quarterly Jnl. of Econ.* xvii, 576–9). Dr. Parker's revised figures of acres inclosed (13,812 as compared with 5,780½) bring the total to something less than 3 per cent. of the county area. The proportion of the new inclosures to the incalculable total of arable, meadow, and pasture would, of course, be greater.

[88] C. 133/101/2.

yardland. The works owed clearly indicate that this was a village of arable farming, for they were ploughing, harrowing, weeding, haymaking, and harvesting services. Finally, there were two cottagers, one of whom was the miller, the manor being served by a windmill. There can be little doubt that Knaptoft at this time was a normal open-field village of about the average size. But by 1507, when so many neighbouring villages were still carrying on the old open-field routine, Knaptoft was completely transformed. In the later 15th century the manor had come by marriage to the Northumberland family of Turpin, who were to be prominent inclosers and sheep farmers. As early as 1482 we find John Turpin suing a chaplain of Knaptoft for taking 50 of his steers and 100 of his sheep.[89]

The process of inclosure at Knaptoft is not known, but the results are revealed in a series of inquisitions. The greater part of the village was by 1507 divided into three great inclosed fields of 340, 500, and 700 acres. The rest of the village land was occupied by the orchard and grounds attached to the manor house, and by five other inclosed fields. These were smaller than the three main inclosures, though still of considerable size, the smallest being 60 acres. By 1524, according to the subsidy assessment, the only inhabitants of the village were the lord and five propertyless labourers, taxed on their wages. These, however, were not the only persons who were concerned with sheep-farming at Knaptoft. In 1507 the three big inclosures were held by lessees, one of whom, Thomas Bradgate of Peatling Parva, was the richest yeoman in the county—richer, indeed, than any of the gentry except for Sir Thomas Pulteney of Misterton. For we must not imagine that the rich peasant leaseholders, whose emergence has been noted from the late 14th century, in all cases simply followed the old methods of the seigniorial demesne farmers. The aged witnesses in the Keythorpe lawsuit of 1541 make it clear that it was not only the successive (or rival) lords in Keythorpe—Palmer, Boyvile, and Neel—who were engaged in sheep farming. George Boyvile (d. 1519) had leased out his pastures to at least three farmers for terms of years (probably successively rather than concurrently), for whom three witnesses or their fathers had been shepherds. It was as shepherd to Boyvile's farmers rather than to Boyvile that the oldest witness had had to keep his flocks from the pastures where Christopher Neel's shepherd was tending his master's sheep.[90]

THE DISSOLUTION

The upset to the old economic and social structure which the inclosure movement caused was carried farther by the Dissolution. The effects of the redistribution of the monastic lands was felt after the period dealt with in this article, but the Dissolution itself symbolizes the end of an epoch in the agrarian history of the county. For in spite of some considerable monastic adventures in sheep farming the religious houses represented a conservative influence in the agrarian structure, just as the release of their possessions on to the land market quickened the tempo of developments of which the elements were already present. On the whole the monasteries as estate-owners were rentiers, and unenterprising

[89] Nichols, *Leics.* iv, 217; Farnham, *Leics. Notes*, v, 392.
[90] Parker, unpublished thesis (p. 192, n. 82), citing C. 142/49/2 and E. 150/1133/13. I quote Dr. Parker's figures rather than those in the abbreviated version in Farnham, op. cit. v, 393 et seq.; Hoskins, *Essays in Leics. Hist.* 87, 128; *T.L.A.S.* xvii, 79–81.

rentiers at that. Most of their demesnes and tithes were leased out to farmers on traditional terms of tenure. Those terms usually involved a division of responsibility for the maintenance of the buildings. In 1535 the farmer of the Leicester Abbey manor of Kirkby Mallory was Thomas Dylke, a yeoman, who was also one of the abbey's receivers for the estate outside Leicestershire. He was obliged by the lease to provide for the upkeep of all buildings outside the manor house and its attached premises; but the abbey maintained the manor house and found all the heavy timber for the purpose.[91] Dylke's lease was a long one—41 years. At a period of increasing competition for land, when 'economic' rents were aimed at by landowners, these long monastic leases seem not to fit into the general picture. Certain landlords were at this time seizing any opportunity to abolish customary terms of tenure and to let out land on short or terminable leases so as to be able to adjust rents rapidly to changing market conditions. It has sometimes been held that long monastic leases were connected with anticipation of the impending dissolution. They should rather be associated with the conservative outlook of the monasteries, the last bulwarks of the old feudal estate organization. The great collection of leases taken over from monastic archives after the Dissolution shows that long leases were common before there can have been any fear of dissolution. The apparent lengthening of terms as time went on was probably due to the increased pressure of lessees as well as to the financial difficulties of the monasteries. On the whole it seems to have been the small peasant lessees who took land on the shortest terms (say 20 years), while the gentry and rich yeomen had the longer leases of 40 years and more.

A study of monastic leases confirms the conclusions drawn from other evidence such as wills.[92] In many cases the social condition of the lessee is described, in others it can be guessed. The gentry and the yeomen were already taking over. Antony Smalley, gentleman, had Diseworth parsonage from Leicester Abbey from 1526 for 30 years. John Uvedale, gentleman, receiver general of Croxton Abbey, took the lease in 1535 of Waltham on the Wolds for 61 years. John Turvile, esquire, had the rich Leicester Abbey parsonage and tithes of Billesdon for 42 years from 1536. John Boyer, gentleman, had Shepshed parsonage for 40 years from 1539. We find yeomen or husbandmen renting from Croxton Abbey the granges of Nether Broughton and Skeffington and Croxton Kerrial parsonage; from Leicester Abbey the manors of Horsepool, Stoughton, and (as we have seen) Kirkby Mallory, and Weston and Bagworth rectories. These examples could doubtless be multiplied were we to track down the social position of lessees whose occupations are not stated in the leases. Yeomen and husbandmen are also to be found in some strength taking on long lease what must once have been customary tenements. Yardlands were rented often at less than 20s., an indication that monastic lessors were failing to push rents up. These facts should be read side by side with the incontrovertible evidence of the eviction of other peasant farmers by inclosers. The two phenomena are not contradictory. They show that while sections of the peasantry were rising in society, others, as part of the same economic processes, were being pressed down.

[91] E. 303/Leics. 216; *Valor Eccl.* (Rec. Com.), iv, 148. Dylke is described as a yeoman in another lease.
[92] The main source used by Hoskins for his 'Leics. Farmer in the 16th Century', *Essays in Leics. Hist.* 123–83.

MEDIEVAL AGRARIAN HISTORY

The situation in the Leicestershire countryside at the end of the Middle Ages was full of contrasts whose implications were not yet fully worked out. The county was still fundamentally one of arable farming. In most villages the old open-field system was still working. It is true that it was by no means like that of two centuries before. Whilst many small peasant holdings were even further fragmented into uneconomic units composed of scattered arable strips of less than one acre, larger holdings tended to be consolidated into larger units. In particular, much of the manorial demesnes, whether in the hands of the lord or of a farmer, was inclosed. This was so even where arable farming still predominated. The juridical position of most of the peasants was still medieval in character, for they held by customary tenure, of which 'copyhold' was but the contemporary description. Villeinage was by no means forgotten, at any rate by the lords of manors on the lookout for means of extorting money to make up for their declining rent rolls. Attempts by lords to claim men who had escaped from bondage are not uncommon in the 15th century. As late as 1532 Thomas Sherard, esquire, of Stapleford, tried to claim a wealthy yeoman of Burton Lazars, Richard Hartopp, as a bondman. He imprisoned him, threatened his life, and (no doubt bitterest of all for the wealthiest inhabitant of Burton) prevented him from going about his business and making profit.[93]

And yet there were many changes, some fully, others partially completed. The technique of arable farming had not stood still. The increasing use of legumes, already noticed in the 14th century, was maintained. The average Leicestershire farmer was so employing nearly half his crop acreage. Evidence begins to accumulate that ley-farming, by the temporary conversion to grass of open-field strips, was not uncommon at this time.[94] Most revolutionary, of course, was the development of large-scale sheep farming, with its localized but dramatic disruption of complete communities of arable farmers. Where an increase in sheep farming did not bring about inclosure and depopulation, it would still have its effect on arable farming, for there is a close connexion between an increase in stock, the elimination of fallow from rotation, and inclosure for arable.

The social structure of the county had acquired striking new features which were to develop farther. It has already been shown that even at the height of the Middle Ages class differentiation amongst the peasantry, as well as between peasants and lords, was very marked. This differentiation was even greater on the eve of the Dissolution. In 1524–5 the proportion of the population wholly or partly dependent on money-wages for a livelihood may have been as high as 30 per cent. In addition, amongst those cultivating their own land or otherwise self-employed, great social differences existed. The 1524 tax assessments show that 4 per cent. of the rural population owned one quarter of the personal estate, and 15½ per cent. owned half of it. The inequalities in landed property cannot be statistically expressed but were probably even greater.[95] These inequalities were not simply the (somewhat exaggerated) inheritance of the medieval village; they resulted from the breakdown of the old village structure. We have seen beginnings of the breach in customary tenures in the 14th century. The break-up of demesnes and of traditional

---

[93] Farnham, *Leics. Notes*, v, 374.

[94] See Hoskins, *Essays in Leics. Hist.* 138 et. seq., for these 16th-century developments. Leys are referred to in the 1425 Wymeswold by-law, but this appears to be the only 15th-century evidence.

[95] Ibid. 129–31.

tenements meant the growth in importance of the various forms of leasehold tenure. It was from this more fluid reserve of lands, especially those which had been converted from arable to pasture, that the bigger peasant farms were created. Leasehold tenure was in fact not only, not even primarily, the symbol of the lost security of the customary tenant. It was also the characteristic tenure by which men who were shortly to enter the ranks of the gentry held their land.

Movement and change had always been more significant in Leicestershire medieval agriculture than immobility and stability. But the tempo varied. Undoubtedly it was vastly increased in the late 15th century and the first four decades of the next. That is why the period marks a turning-point between old and new, even if the decisive transformation was not to come for two centuries.

We may end this survey of the agrarian history of Leicestershire by a brief analysis of the tax yields from the various hundreds of the county in 1524–5. The lay subsidy levied in these two years formed the most comprehensive assessment for taxation since the poll taxes of the late 14th century. The accounts for Leicestershire[96] may be tabulated as follows:

Hundred	1st Payment (1524)			2nd Payment (1525)			Total		
	£	s.	d.	£	s.	d.	£	s.	d.
Framland	202	13	8	200	1	4	402	15	0
Gartree	173	1	7	163	15	0	336	16	7
Goscote*	377	1	2	356	5	6	733	6	8
Guthlaxton	124	5	6	128	15	3	253	0	9
Sparkenhoe	159	16	8	147	0	2	306	17	0
Borough of Leicester . . .	109	19	8	83	10	4	193	10	0
Totals	1,146	18	3	1,079	7	9	2,226	6	0

* East and West Goscote hundreds are not distinguished in the record.

Reckoning the total area of the hundreds at 510,204 acres,[97] the subsidy in Leicestershire (excluding the borough) produced almost exactly 80s. per 1,000 acres. This may be compared with the average yield of rather more than 87s. per 1,000 acres from the generally more fertile county of Rutland. There were, however, great variations in the yield from the Leicestershire hundreds: the ancient distinction between the west and the east of the county, clearly marked as far back as the 11th century, was still very apparent. The western hundred of Sparkenhoe yielded only 55s. 4d. per 1,000 acres; that of Framland, in the north-east, about 90s. 2d. The tax yields reflect closely the agricultural wealth of the various hundreds, for outside the borough of Leicester the county was exclusively agrarian in its interests and occupations. The only industries it supported—coal-mining and quarrying—were on a very small scale, of no significance in the national economy. Well into the 17th century it was still possible to say that tillage was 'the great manufacture' of Leicestershire.

[96] E. 359/41.
[97] W. White, *History, Gazetteer, &c.* (1863), 18.

AGRARIAN HISTORY, 1540–1950

I. 1540–1640. II. 1640–1660. III. 1660–1760. IV. 1760–1860. V. 1860–1950

PRECISE dates fit clumsily into the jigsaw of agrarian history. The date 1540, therefore, has no great significance, but it serves as a signpost to two events of national importance which shaped Leicestershire history for the next century. It opened a decade in which the coinage was debased, and the consequent sharp rise in prices dealt the first serious blow at the economic structure. It marked, moreover, the first considerable sales of monastic land, which followed the dissolution of religious houses in 1536 and 1539. The transfer of so much valuable land to new owners was important both as an agent and an index of social change. But its significance was heightened when the Crown and lay landlords, embarrassed by rising prices, were driven to the same expedient. The sales of monastic land were but the prologue to a century of exceptional land-market activity, which affected all ranks of property-owners.

In an almost purely agricultural county like Leicestershire, the impact of these changes was sharp. The upward trend of prices, which had begun almost imperceptibly in the 1530's with the influx of precious metals from the New World into Europe, and which was accelerated in England by the debasement of the coinage between 1542 and 1547, sent the price index of wheat soaring from 100 in the decade 1531–40 to 222 in 1571–82, and to 466 by 1612.[1]

The immediate effect on the Leicestershire farmer was to yield him far more profit from the sale of his crops and stock than it cost him in increased expenses. In the three generations before 1540 the expanding market for wool had produced in Leicestershire the first serious wave of inclosure—an attempt largely initiated by the great landowners, the nobility, the squirearchy, and the heads of monastic houses in order to screw greater profit out of their estates by converting them into cattle and sheep farms.[2] In the new circumstances, in which the value of all farm produce was increased, opportunities for gain were no longer reserved to the upper strata of society. They were grasped by the peasantry, and in particular by the free tenants, who enjoyed that security in the tenure of their land which encouraged them to improve and expand their farming enterprise when opportunity offered.

Out of this situation came efforts in many different directions to improve the use and the yield of the land. The reappearance in the 16th century, after a long pause, of literature recommending new methods of husbandry was a sign of the times. It is impossible to discover how far scientific farming, modest though its pretensions still were, was translated from the pages of these books into the practice of Leicestershire farmers. But it is not difficult to trace certain other improvements that were made with similar ends in view.

[1] D. Knoop and G. P. Jones, 'Masons' Wages in Medieval Engl.', *Econ. Hist. Supplement to Econ. Jnl.* (Jan. 1933), ii. 485.
[2] L. A. Parker, 'Enclosure in Leics., 1485–1607' (Lond. Univ. Ph.D. thesis), 82–83.

Of these, the most spectacular was undoubtedly the inclosure of the open fields. It was a movement that faithfully mirrored economic trends, for it responded to the stimulus of price changes and throve upon a quickening rate of land transfer. Ultimately the movement held the stage for more than 400 years. From a county of compact villages, each surrounded by its broad open fields, and each pursuing a system of co-operative mixed husbandry, Leicestershire became a county of pasture farms worked in severalty. The movement was slow to reach completion, and in its course involved all ranks of society. But it was in the century after 1540 that it passed through its most significant phase, since it was in these years that the peasantry gradually came to participate in a movement which had earlier threatened them with ruin.

1540–1640

Inclosure. Inclosure before 1540 had left indelible marks on the countryside in the depopulation and physical decay of many hitherto flourishing villages.[3] Its seemingly rapid pace from 1485 had been set by the more substantial landowners, the lords of manors who were wealthy and powerful enough to buy out, or in the worst cases to evict, tenants who stood in the way of inclosure. Since inclosure on this scale almost invariably meant the conversion of arable land to pasture, many peasant families lost at one stroke their land and all chances of local employment. It was not surprising that, faced with the evidence of such distress, and with the knowledge that the county was renowned for the richness of its tillage,[4] neither the victims of inclosure nor the Government, which had to deal with the ensuing problem of poverty, were reconciled to the argument that inclosure was a sound business proposition.

Local outbreaks of violence, when hedges were thrown down and ditches were filled in, recurred throughout the century. But only on three occasions between 1540 and 1640 did they take on a threatening character: in 1549 and 1553 after a commission had been appointed by Protector Somerset to investigate inclosure and depopulation; and in 1607 when the movement had again gathered momentum. Details of the first outbreaks in 1549 and 1553 are meagre. Their location is unspecified, and the only recorded punishments are those of ten men who acknowledged 'their faulte comitted of late in plucking upp of a hedge', and were ordered 'at their commyng home to make upp the saide hedge agayne at thier costes and charges'.[5] It was perhaps impatience and disappointment at the ineffective measures taken by the Government against inclosing landlords rather than anger at a new wave of inclosure that promoted the disturbances. The early movement had reached its peak between 1490 and 1500, and by the end of the forties had declined to its lowest point since 1485.[6] Long-standing grievances were not, therefore, inflamed by recent experience of large-scale inclosure, and it was no doubt for this reason that the demonstrators, though not without sympathizers in Rutland, failed to muster any considerable support in their own county. In 1607 the situation was different, and will be best understood when some account of the character of inclosures in the second half of the century has been given.

---

[3] W. G. Hoskins, 'Deserted Villages of Leics.', *Essays in Leics. Hist.* 67–107.
[4] W. G. Hoskins, 'Leics. Farmer in 17th century', *Agric. Hist.* xxv, 9.
[5] Parker, 'Enclosure in Leics.' 81–82.
[6] Ibid. 29–30.

By means of legislation prohibiting the conversion of arable land to pasture, and through the active supervision of local affairs by the Privy Council, a more spirited attempt was made by the Government in the second half of the century to prohibit all inclosures that were likely to cause evictions and unemployment.[7] These measures were not without their deterrent effect, but they ran counter to the self-interest of every improving landlord and farmer, and were not likely for long to stem the rising tide. A more promising solution of the problem, as it turned out, lay in another direction, in a broadening of the social basis on which the movement was built. By 1640 the participation of the peasantry in inclosure schemes was to prove more effective in mitigating distress than government interference. But it was only very slowly that inclosures by agreement between lord and tenants gained ground, and even at their height they did not eliminate entirely the hardships to the poor with which Elizabethan legislation had been most concerned.

Peasant farmers came to play an increasingly important part in schemes of inclosure in the years after 1550, a fact that is not difficult to understand when seen against the background of rising agricultural prosperity. The rise in prices and the quicker rate of land transfer wrought a noticeable change in the scale of their farming enterprise and their standards of living—a change that affected the husbandman no less than the well-to-do yeoman. It has been calculated that the average farmer with some 40–50 acres of land, who in 1531 had possessed personal estate worth only £14. 8s., expected to leave goods worth £46. 17s. in 1588, or better still in 1603, goods worth nearer £67. 2s.[8] These figures reflected a substantial increase in personal wealth, for whereas food prices by 1588 had rather more than doubled, the value of personal property had trebled.[9] On closer analysis, moreover, these figures disclose the important fact that household goods, as distinct from farm tools, crops, and livestock, had become a relatively more important item. In the period 1500–31 the value of household goods of all kinds represented usually less than a fifth of all personal property. By 1600 the Leicestershire farmer took considerably more pride and interest in the comforts of his dwelling. The small cottage in Galby in which Robert Smalley, husbandman, had died in 1559, with its hall, kitchen, and parlour and its simple furniture—a board for a table, a form and two stools for seats, a bedstead and a coffer[10]—had in 1596 given place to the more spacious dwelling of Robert Coulson of Wigston Magna. Though he left goods worth only £22. 13s., he had a house with a living-room, three bedrooms, a buttery, 'an entree', and furniture that included a table, a chair, two forms, a bench and two trestles, four stools, a cupboard, a wheel, fire-irons, and hangings on the wall.[11] The prosperity indicated by these material comforts was even more in evidence forty years later, on the eve of the Civil War, when the personal property of the husbandman was valued on an average at £74. 8s. 6d., and that of the yeoman at £176. 10s.[12]

There was every encouragement to the enterprising farmer in these years to take on new land, and to improve the efficiency of his cultivation. Evidence as to the former is plentiful. As to the latter, it is as yet meagre, but valuable indirect evidence may be gathered from a study of the farm implements in use

[7] R. H. Tawney, *Agrarian Problem in 16th century* (1912), 353–7.
[8] Hoskins, *Essays in Leics. Hist.* 145, 135.   [9] *Econ. Hist. Suppl. to Econ. Jnl.* ii, 485.
[10] Hoskins, *Essays in Leics. Hist.* 133–4.   [11] Ibid. 179–80.
[12] *Agric. Hist.* xxv, 12.

on the average Leicestershire farm. Some light has been thrown on the subject by a preliminary survey of the material available in farmers' inventories. The stock-in-trade of every farmer, save the very poorest husbandman, included one or two carts, two or three harrows (made of wood, not of iron), and usually a plough. The poor peasant who lacked the latter borrowed or hired one from a bigger farmer, or had a share in the 'town plough', a piece of communal property bought and maintained by contributions from the villagers who used it. It was among the less usual implements that technical advance was to be measured. Draw-rakes were becoming common in the second half of the 16th century and rollers by the beginning of the 17th. Wagons were rare in 1550, and remained so after 1600, when many gentry and yeomen still managed without. But where wagons or carts shod with iron strakes were found, they represented a considerable advance in the value and utility of a farmer's equipment.[13]

On the whole, no doubt, the use of new implements spread as slowly as the new machinery of the 18th and 19th centuries. In contrast, the inclosure movement, which was the forerunner of many innovations in farming technique, made rapid strides. Owing to the steadily expanding market for meat, particularly in London, and the fact that wool continued to command a high price, the stimulus to inclose and convert to pasture lost none of its vigour. A small number of peasants began to take the initiative in inclosing their land, and by 1607 had been responsible for 19 per cent. of the inclosures carried out in the previous fifty-seven years.[14] They had become, in fact, the second largest class of inclosers, even though they lagged a long way behind the squires. At the same time those farmers who had become men of consequence in their villages found that their goodwill and co-operation had become an essential ingredient in the inclosure schemes of their overlords. At Buckminster and Sewstern, for example, Sir Alexander Cave appears to have gone to some lengths to secure the co-operation of 31 tenants before inclosing the two lordships in 1597.[15] At Tilton on the Hill, Sir Everard Digby inclosed some 1,335 acres of his estate with the consent of 16 of his tenants.[16] Agreements gradually became more common. At least 15 (and possibly a further 3) were completed between 1540 and 1640, while 20 years later they were regarded as the usual method of inclosing a whole lordship.[17] In the early days, no doubt, they dealt out a rough kind of justice to tenants, but this was an improvement on the old system, which guaranteed no compensation for lost land or rights. By the second half of the 17th century, when the machinery of agreement had become formalized, it compared favourably with that of later Parliamentary Acts, while the practice of securing agreements by a collusive suit in Chancery, and enrolling such agreements, helped to safeguard the interests of the weak against the strong.[18] From the point of view of the lord, the increased value of his estate after inclosure fully compensated for the concessions he made to his tenants.

Contemporary accounts of the long negotiations that sometimes preceded

---

[13] Hoskins, *Essays in Leics. Hist.* 149–50. [14] Parker, 'Enclosure in Leics.' 149.
[15] Ibid. 125–6. [16] Ibid. 142–3.
[17] Ibid. 94, for agreements between 1551 and 1607. Agreements between 1607 and 1640 are recorded for Broughton Astley, Donington-le-Heath, Higham on the Hill, Thurnby, Willoughby Waterless, Market Bosworth, Loddington, and Nailstone.
[18] E. M. Leonard, 'The Inclosure of the Common Fields in the 17th Cent.', *Trans. R. Hist. S.*, N.S. xix, 114. For an example of an enrolled agreement, see that for Laughton, C 78/669, no. 18.

agreement point the contrast between the old situation and the new. William Brocas was prepared in about 1582 to grant to his tenants at Theddingworth 'diverse gratuities and leases of good value' to secure their consent to the inclosure of a seventh of the lordship.[19] The Earl of Newport inclosed his estate at Loddington shortly before 1631 on the understanding that a third of the land of all tenants holding 30 acres and more should remain in tillage for twenty-one years (a provision that appeased the Privy Council), and that those who refused to accept the terms of the new leases should receive from him an annuity of £10 a year for twenty-one years when they left the village to work elsewhere.[20] Some so-called inclosure agreements merely concealed the coercive powers of the squire over his tenants. This was the charge levelled by the tenants against Maurice Berkeley at Edmondthorpe and Wymondham.[21] But it was at least a tribute to the growing prestige of voluntary agreements that more ruthless landlords cultivated the pretence.

Inclosures by agreement, however, are not sufficient to explain entirely the advance of the movement in the 16th and 17th centuries. There was more than one weapon in the armoury of the movement, and it was only with the aid of them all that it ultimately conquered Leicestershire. Agreements were important because they anticipated the Acts of Parliament which finally killed open-field farming in the 19th century. But the final conquest depended just as much on small victories in scattered places. Some of these were carried out by the gentry who inclosed a whole township within the century, but who contrived it in slow stages. The Hastings family inclosed Braunstone in two moves separated by an interval of 17 years.[22] At Halstead the lord of the manor began to inclose in 1559; his work was carried on by his family and two tenants; but in 1605 a fifth of the township still lay in open fields.[23]

Small farmers who had managed to consolidate their strips by purchase or exchange joined forces with the squirearchy. They hedged a hundred acres or less, reduced the size of the common fields, but did not put an end to open-field farming by the remaining inhabitants of the village. It was probably men such as George Villiers, squire of Hoby, who inclosed and converted 100 acres of arable in 1578, and John Ruding and Leonard Danet, yeomen of Bromkinsthorpe, who agreed on the same day in July 1561 to inclose 28 acres, who made the greatest inroads in Leicestershire's open fields.[24] Inclosure figures bear witness to the importance of piecemeal encroachments, for, whereas some 75 villages saw the first appearance of hedged fields between 1540 and 1607, at most only 19 were entirely inclosed.[25] In the next generation, however, owing to the partial progress made in earlier years, there was a notable increase in the number of townships completely inclosed. In 19 places where inclosures and open strips had lain side by side, the open fields finally disappeared. In another 14 places, including Leicester Forest, inclosure was begun and completed by 1640. Piecemeal inclosure proceeded in a further 12 places.[26]

[19] Parker, 'Enclosure in Leics.' 113–14.   [20] S.P. 16/187, no. 83.
[21] Parker, 'Enclosure in Leics.' 106.   [22] Ibid. 122–4.
[23] Ibid. 94, 101–3.
[24] Ibid. 110, 97.
[25] Ibid. 93. Dr. Parker lists 72 places affected by inclosure, and a further 10 probably affected, between 1540 and 1607. Seven of these had already undergone partial inclosure between 1485 and 1540. The figure of 19 places completely inclosed is a modification of Dr. Parker's 18, arrived at by adding Lockington and Syston (though inclosure here is not finally proved), and subtracting Stoke Golding. See App. I for further details.
[26] For fuller details on which these figures are based, see App. I.

The pace had steadily quickened, and yet in the years after 1607 only two villages, Foston and Sysonby, were depopulated. Another two, Ilston and Cold Newton, only survived in a shrunken form.[27] This is not to say that inclosure had ceased to evoke opposition. Disturbances took place at Garendon in 1603, and at Grimston in 1611. At Hallaton, the inclosure of 20 acres of common in 1617 provoked a riot, led by Thomas Bleivepusse, a weaver, 'whoe was a principall stirrer and agent in pulling downe inclosures in the last commotions in Leicestershire'.[28] Inclosure was never a painless process, but its grosser injustices were being moderated, and by 1640 opinion was beginning to swing slowly in its favour.

In 1607, when the last midland revolt against inclosure broke out, this change of viewpoint was not yet evident. The Government had consistently maintained a hostile attitude towards all inclosures that threatened to cause depopulation. Yet after a comparative lull between 1510 and 1570, the movement had been steadily gathering momentum again, reaching a peak in the period 1600–7, when almost as much land was inclosed as in the previous fifty years.[29] This was enough to explain the alarm that the revolt inspired among local administrators. But in one sense it was contradicted by the revolt itself, for it did not affect more than the southern tip of Leicestershire in the neighbourhood of Cotesbach. Here the persistent attempts at inclosure by the new landlord, John Quarles, had been the cause of bitter disputes ever since 1602.[30] When disturbances broke out in Northamptonshire in the spring of 1607, and spread thence into Warwickshire, 'men, women and children to the number of full five thousand' assembled at Cotesbach to 'level and lay open inclosures'. Prompt measures were taken by the lord lieutenant, and the revolt did not spread. Nevertheless it is clear that although the disturbance had been localized, the tide of popular sympathy had been running strongly in favour of the rioters. It was feared that the citizens of Leicester—who must have been among the least affected by the inclosure—would march out to assist the rioters. And although this did not occur, a gallows erected in the town on 6 June was torn down by irate citizens on the 8th. The restricted scope of the Leicestershire revolt was not an accurate measure of the sympathy which it evoked. And although the alarm was over within a month, it resulted in the appointment in August of a commission to inquire into the extent of inclosures since 1578 in six midland counties, including Leicestershire.[31]

On the basis of present evidence it is possible to estimate that by 1607 at least 25 per cent. of the county was inclosed. This was an impressive area. More than 1 in every 3 villages of Leicestershire had experienced the effects of inclosure. By 1640 nearly 1 in every 3 villages was entirely inclosed.[32] These figures give a fair idea of the swift advance of the movement, and indirectly some inkling of its accompanying social effects.

A map of inclosure in the century after 1540 would show its first deep penetration into the Wolds north of the Wreak. Elsewhere, on the eastern uplands,

[27] Hoskins, *Essays in Leics. Hist.* 87, 101, 107.

[28] Parker, 'Enclosure in Leics.' 148; D. G. C. Allan, 'Agrarian Discontent under the early Stuarts, and during the last decade of Elizabeth' (Lond. Univ. M.A. thesis), 69.   [29] Parker, 'Enclosure in Leics.' 94.

[30] Ibid. 147–8. For a full account of the Cotesbach inclosure, see L. A. Parker, 'The Agrarian Revolution at Cotesbach, 1501–1612', in 'Studies in Leics. Agrarian Hist.', *T.L.A.S.*, xxiv, 41–76.

[31] Allan, 'Agrarian Discontent', 51, 54, 57.

[32] These figures are calculated from the list in App. I. They are based on an estimate that, in parishes affected by inclosure, one-quarter of the land was, on an average, inclosed.

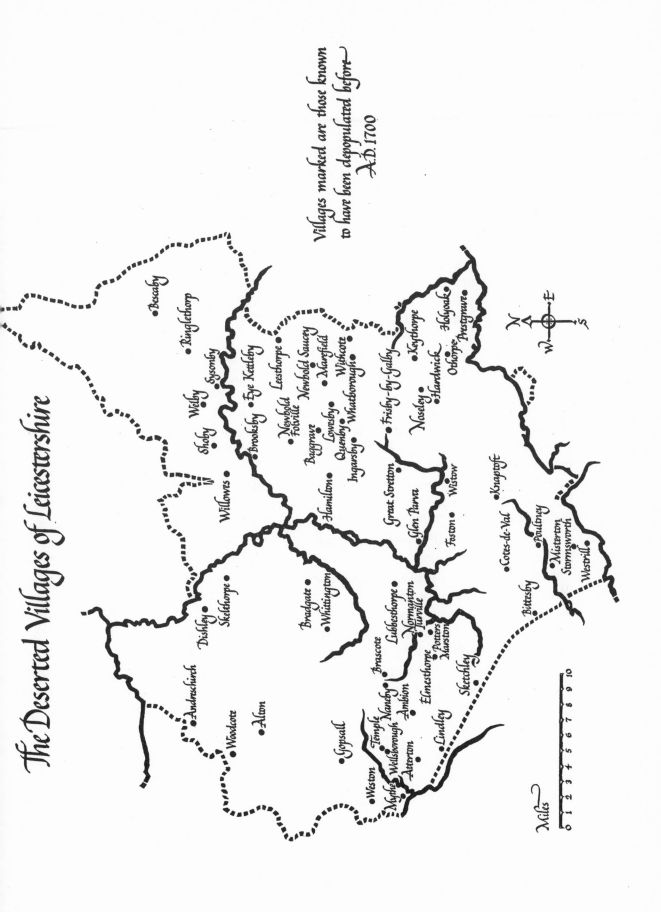

The Deserted Villages of Leicestershire

Villages marked are those known
to have been depopulated before
A.D. 1700

Bescaby
Ringlethorp
Sysonby
Welby
Shoby
Eye Kettleby
Brooksby
Leesthorpe
Newbold
Folville
Newbold Saucey
Mawfield
Withcott
Baggrave
Lowesby
Whatborough
Quenby
Ingarsby
Frisby-by-Galby
Keythorpe
Noseley
Hardwick
Holyoak
Othorpe
Prestgrave
Willows
Hamilton
Great Stretton
Wistow
Knaptoft
Dishley
Skeffthorpe
Glen Parva
Foston
Cotes-de-Val
Poultney
Bradgate
Whittington
Lubbesthorpe
Mistron
Swinnsworth
Westrill
Andreschurch
Brascote
Normanton
Turville
Bittesby
Woodcott
Alton
Gopsall
Temple
Nanby
Ambion
Elmesthorpe
Potters
Marston
Skeffley
Weston
Mythe
Wellsborough
Atterton
Lindley

N
W E
S

Miles
0 1 2 3 4 5 6 7 8 9 10

205

and on the fringes of the highland in the south and south-west, inclosures spread across countryside already partially hedged before 1540.[33] The pattern is an untidy one, in which students of soil and climate may one day detect a logic that will give better satisfaction than the simple accidents of ownership. To the 17th-century peasant, however, there was less to explain than to wonder at. How was the imagination of the peasant affected who was born into the village of Somerby on the eve of the Civil War? There is no evidence to show that any part of Somerby had been inclosed by that time. Yet there was scarcely a village within a radius of four miles which did not bear the imprint of inclosure. Little Dalby, Pickwell, Cold Overton, and Knossington on the north and east sides of the parish, and Owston and Cold Newton on the south and south-west had all been completely inclosed by 1640.[34] Tilton had been entirely inclosed, and Halstead next door almost entirely by 1610. Whatborough, Marefield, and Lowesby on the south and west, Withcote on the south-east, and Lees-thorpe on the north, were deserted villages. Considerable inclosure had taken place at Burton Lazars,[35] Dalby-on-the-Wolds, Great Dalby, and Burrow-on-the-Hill, and probably some encroachments at Launde. By 1648 there was some inclosure, though it may have been only small, at Twyford.[36] It was only at Thorpe Satchville[37] that inclosure had not apparently gained any firm hold. In areas like this, where inclosure had achieved its greatest triumphs, the cause of open-field farming seemed in 1640 to be long since lost.

Social structure. The outline of the social structure of the county that has emerged from the preceding pages can now be filled in. At the apex of the pyramid stood those noble families who not only owned land in the county but lived there. Their fortunes tended to fluctuate with political and regnal changes rather than with tides of economic prosperity. In 1540 there were three principal noble families resident in the county. The Greys of Groby and Brad-gate were created dukes of Suffolk in 1551, but owing to the treason of Henry, the 1st duke, in 1554, the dukedom was immediately extinguished. They were created earls of Stamford in 1628.[38] The Hastings family of Ashby-de-la-Zouch were created earls of Huntingdon by Henry VIII in 1529.[39] The Manners family of Etal (Northumb.) came to Belvoir as the only surviving heirs of Edmund, 10th Lord Ros, who died in 1508. Thomas Manners was created Earl of Rutland in 1525, and at the Dissolution acquired much valuable land, including the site and lands of Croxton, Garendon, and Owston Abbeys, and Belvoir Priory.[40] These families kept splendid households, the Earl of Rutland's being described as 'like a Prince's Court'.[41]

The largest group in landowning society was the gentry, who owned the bulk of the land, and who bore on their shoulders the weight of the county's administration. In the 16th century there was a less sharp social division between them and their tenant farmers than that which characterized rural society in the

[33] Parker, 'Enclosure in Leics.' 189–90.
[34] The evidence for Cold Overton is open to revision. See App. I.
[35] Burton Lazars was probably completely inclosed. It was by 1649. C 54/3402, no. 3.
[36] C 54/3402, no. 3.
[37] Thorpe Satchville, however, is listed by John Monk as old inclosure: G. Slater, *Engl, Peasantry and the Enclosure of the Common Fields*, 198–9.
[38] *Complete Peerage*, iv, 420–1. [39] Ibid. vi, 370–6.
[40] Ibid. xi, 106–8; W. G. Hoskins, *Midland Engl.* 52.
[41] Gervase Holles, *Memorials of the Holles Family, 1493–1656*, ed. A. C. Wood (Camden Soc., 3rd ser., lv), 215.

19th century. They did not live on a lavish scale, and they were content, like the parents of George Villiers of Brooksby and William Faunt of Foston, to send their sons to the village school.[42] But in the social life of most Leicestershire villages they did not play a conspicuous part, for only one village in seven had a resident squire.[43]

Thus in many places it was the yeomen—the descendants of the free tenants of the manor—who were the most substantial inhabitants of the village. Their numbers were larger than in most English counties, but this fact was not immediately noticeable except in certain places like Wigston Magna where their ranks had not been much thinned by time.[44] Everywhere the title of yeoman commanded due social respect, and conferred on its owner recognition of his dignity and standing. At the same time, gradations of wealth within the class of yeomen were many. Thomas Bradgate of Peatling Parva, whose goods were valued at £110 in 1525—the second highest assessment in all Leicestershire[45]—was ranked alongside a host of modest men, tilling a hundred acres or less, who boasted no comparable wealth save that which lay in the esteem of their neighbours. In general, however, the yeomen were distinguishable as a class by the extent of their property in land and goods. The Hortons of Mowsley were an outstanding example, for they were assessed on three-quarters of the personal estate of their village.[46] On an average, members of their class owned some 25 per cent. of the personal estate taxed in their parishes.[47] This was enough to distinguish them from the husbandman, who farmed at most 40–50 acres,[48] the craftsman who earned a living by his trade but supplemented it with produce from a smallholding, and the cottagers and labourers, who had insufficient land to keep them but who relied on their earnings from casual farm work. This last group, with some 1–5 acres apiece, numbered about one in three of the population.[49]

These broad categories remained the same throughout the 16th and 17th centuries, but it was one of the wonders of the age that men were able to pass so rapidly from one class to another. More is known of the successful husbandmen and yeomen than of the unsuccessful gentry who gave place to them. The reasons for failure, however, have become well known. The gentry, who depended on rents for their income, were unable, or unwilling, to raise them to meet the increased cost of living. The benefits of appreciating land values fell into the lap of farmers paying customary rents on a long lease, whose chief expenses were therefore fixed, while their farm produce yielded increasing profit. The fact that the old-established gentry were the promoters of 72·5 per cent. of the inclosures between 1550 and 1607[50] was proof that many were trying to keep abreast of economic trends, and to make their estates pay. Sir Basil Brooke spoke on their behalf in 1608, when he defended his inclosure of Lubenham as a desperate expedient for increasing his inadequate income. Yet the Brooke family was compelled to sell out before 1642.[51] The Berkeleys of Coston, having tried unsuccessfully to introduce twenty-one-year leases and

[42] Hoskins, *Essays in Leics. Hist.* 127 n.
[43] Ibid. 127.
[44] Ibid. 128.
[45] Ibid.
[46] Ibid. 127.
[47] Ibid. 129, 146.
[48] Ibid. 146.
[49] This figure represents the number of persons listed in the 1524 subsidy assessment who were taxed on wages or goods worth 20s. only.
[50] Parker, 'Enclosure in Leics.' 149.
[51] Ibid. 136–7; Nichols, *Leics.* ii, 698–9.

heavier fines in order to raise their revenues, fell back on inclosure as a remedy, but still had to sell out in about 1620.[52] Perhaps the most pitiful description of the plight of the lesser gentry is that given of Edward Charnell, gentleman of Snarestone, who died in 1620. He had owned some 216 acres of land and leased a further 120 acres. His land was charged with an annuity of £10, while other debts amounted to £120. 'The house is soe ruynous', it was reported, 'that it is underpropped in eight severall places without which it could not stand, and besides it is so uncovered that it rayneth into most places thereof.' Of personal estate Edward Charnell possessed nothing 'save only one cowe, and scarce a bedd to lye uppon. Naye the widowe hath scarce cloathes to cover her nakednes, her husband entring upon the land but at Crispinmas (25 October) and dyed at Whitsontyde and being before for preservation thereof (not having any other meanes at all) enforced to worke daie labour at the Colepitts as a Collyer'. Part of their land had already had to be sold by Edward Charnell's father and grandfather, so that the impoverishment of the family was clearly the outcome of many years' struggle. His widow had to charge this shrunken estate with a further debt in order to secure the wardship of her son and the meagre profits that accrued from the property until his coming of age.[53] It was upon the decayed fortunes of such families as these that men from the lower ranks were able to make their way up into the class above.

The land market was the meeting-place of all men who were doing well and wanted to do better, and its activities afford a background to the social advance of many of them. A rough impression of the quickening pace of land transfer may be gathered from the final concords levied in the Common Pleas. Fourteen transactions were the annual average in Leicestershire in the late 1550's; they increased sharply in the sixties to as many as 60 in 1564, to 48 in 1565, and 32 in 1566. The average figure over a decade, which levels out the fluctuations between different years, shows a steady increase from 30 in the sixties to 45 in the seventies, 60 in the eighties, 80 in the nineties, 100 in the first ten years of the new century and 138 in the second. Thereafter the number of transactions diminished slightly to 111 in the 1620's and 113 in the thirties.[54]

The background to these sales was an already high rate of mobility among the rural population. In 1525 it was rare to find more than one in ten families who had been settled in a village for five generations. Even in a relatively stable community of peasants, as at Wigston Magna, only a quarter of the subsidy-paying families had been settled there for a century or more.[55]

In terms of social change the significance of these sales may be seen in the striking career of John Bale, yeoman, who bought two farms in Carlton Curlieu in 1549, 400 acres in Burton Overy eight years later, and several hundred more in the same district between 1562 and 1563. He left to his nephew enough property to enable him to assume the title of gentleman, to buy the manor of Carlton Curlieu in 1575 and Saddington in 1606, and to acquire a knighthood in 1622.[56] Nor was this an isolated success story. The Bent family of Cosby, who in 1524 paid as much in taxation as most gentlemen, consolidated their position in the next generation by buying over a period of eight years Cosby

---

[52] Parker, op. cit. 121; Nichols, *Leics.* ii, 143.   [53] Wards 5/23.

[54] Figures taken from the P.R.O. Index to Notes of Fines. Although they include trusts and leases as well as sales, it is probable that the proportions did not vary greatly. But it is possible that part of the increase was due to the growing habit of levying fines.

[55] Hoskins, *Essays in Leics. Hist.* 131.   [56] Ibid. 156–7.

manor, together with 660 acres of land and numerous houses.[57] The Hartopps of Burton Lazars, who paid the highest assessment in their village in 1524, managed, by buying 100 acres in Braunston-by-Belvoir in 1552, the whole manor in 1564, and land in neighbouring parishes over the next generation, to rise from yeomen to gentlemen and from gentlemen to baronets by 1642.[58]

Clearly the foundation of these successes was the acquisition of land, but when once these thriving families had surmounted the first social barriers, rich marriages and royal recognition followed in their wake. The process of consolidation can be seen at its best in the case of the Bradgates of Peatling Parva, for Thomas Bradgate, yeoman, married one of the Wards of Carlton Curlieu— a family which paid the highest assessment in the parish in 1545—while his son, Richard, married the sister of William Jervis, likewise the wealthiest yeoman in Peatling Magna. By 1567 both the Bradgates and the Jervises were the lords of their villages.[59]

Behind them stood a throng of smaller yeoman families who on a less spectacular scale invested their wealth in land. Some of it they bought outright, the rest they leased. Their farming enterprise expanded, and they entrenched themselves more firmly in Leicestershire society. Such were the Freers of Wigston, who were represented there by a husbandman in 1504, and who shared in the purchase of the principal manor of Wigston in 1606.[60] Such also were the Hortons of Mowsley, who were its wealthiest inhabitants in 1524, who bought 180 acres there between 1546 and 1573, but who were not styled gentlemen until shortly before 1660.[61]

The story of the more successful yeoman families captures the imagination and tends to obscure the parallel advance of the well-established gentry who accepted them into their ranks. Beyond the glare of spectacular success they built up their estates by the same methods as their lesser neighbours. They suffered casualties, it is true, for difficulties lay in wait for all those who followed the fashion of extravagant spending on their houses without any corresponding rise in income. According to contemporary accounts, there were always vultures waiting to devour them—outsiders from London, merchants from the towns, who sought in distant places the country seat on which to spend the profits of their trade. Yet to focus attention on the casualties and the new-comers is to give a false impression, for they were comparatively few, fewer than those in the counties immediately surrounding London. And there was a hard core of indigenous squires whose accumulation of riches was just as impressive as the incursions of the vigorous and ruthless business man.

An illustration of this point may be found in the sales of monastic land. The peasantry took almost no part in them; their turn came later. Some 60 per cent. of Leicestershire's monastic land (calculated by value, not acreage) was sold by the end of Henry VIII's reign, and only 20 per cent. remained to be disposed of by 1552. Those who gained most were the nobility and gentry of the county, who secured 28 and 15 per cent. respectively—a percentage, moreover, that included all the most valuable estates. Speculators, usually London tradesmen, and less often lawyers, formed the third largest group, taking a small share of 12 per cent., made up of scattered parcels. The only other groups

[57] Ibid. 155–6. [58] Ibid. 157.
[59] Ibid. 128.
[60] W. G. Hoskins, 'Leicestershire Yeoman Families and their Pedigrees', *T.L.A.S.* xxiii, 50.
[61] Parker, 'Enclosure in Leics.' 89–90; L. G. H. Horton-Smith, 'The Hortons of Leics.', *T.L.A.S.* xxiii, 5.

taking any appreciable part in the sales were religious bodies, who obtained 6 per cent., and officials of the Court of Augmentations, who bought 4 per cent. The full figures are set out in the following tables.

The Distribution of Monastic Land between Local Interests and Strangers

	per cent.
Property granted to religious bodies	6
„ „ „ local persons	35
„ „ „ persons without known local connexions	30
„ for which no grant is known	13
Uncertain items	16
	100

The Distribution of Monastic Land between Different Classes

	per cent.
Property granted to the nobility	28
„ „ „ „ gentry	15
„ „ „ speculators	12
„ „ „ officials of the Court of Augmentations	4
„ „ „ religious bodies	6
„ for which no grant is known	13
Uncertain items	22
	100

These figures show the considerable financial capacity of the gentry to absorb additional land. It was not exhausted when those speculators who had bought indiscriminately—men such as Henry Herdson, a skinner and alderman of London, John Johnson, a London fishmonger, and Thomas Reve, gentleman, who together bought eight parcels of land, besides operating individually in other syndicates—began to sell again. By 1563 27 per cent. of their purchases had been put into the market again, compared with the resale of only 7 per cent. of monastic property as a whole.[62] Although there are no figures to show the exact results, small samples and comparable experience in other counties suggest that it was among the local families, the gentry, and to some extent the peasantry also, that the more permanent gains were made. Isolated examples point to this conclusion. The Wigleys of Scraptoft, who leased the tithes of corn and hay from the Prior of St. Mary 's, Coventry, bought the manor outright at the Dissolution and were the largest landowners in Scraptoft by the beginning of the 17th century.[63] The Caves of Stanford bought the manor of Stanford, forfeited by Selby Abbey, in 1540.[64] At second hand, Richard Bradgate, yeoman, acquired two manors in 1567–70 by purchase from Sir Walter Devereux, Lord Ferrers of Chartley, the first recipient of all the Leicestershire lands of Merevale Abbey.[65] William Jervis of Peatling Magna, yeoman, already mentioned for his marriage alliance with the Bradgates, followed their example by buying the manor of Peatling Magna in 1550 from the first purchaser, William Villiers.[66] Only a detailed study of resales would tell whether these samples were a faithful miniature or a distortion of the true picture.

Other signs pointing to the prosperous condition of many of the gentry

[62] Figures collected by Mr. R. A. McKinley. All percentages are calculated from the valuations given in the *Valor Eccl.* (Rec. Com.).

[63] Parker, 'Enclosure in Leics.' 135.

[64] Nichols, *Leics.* iv, 350–1.

[65] Hoskins, *Essays in Leics. Hist.* 155.

[66] *Cal. Pat., 1549–51,* 244.

were to be found in the fabric of their houses. The Bent family of Cosby, after a generation of spending on the purchase of land, turned their attention to the building of 'a mansion house' in the fifties, an elaborately styled timber dwelling which stands today in the main street of Littlethorpe.[67] The Bents were to have many imitators. The Ashbys, who reigned alone in the deserted village of Quenby, built a splendid and lasting house, 'the finest Jacobean house in Leicestershire', between 1620 and 1630.[68] At Edmondthorpe, where the impoverished Berkeleys had sold out to Roger Smith by 1620, a new manor house was built in the following year.[69] At Goadby the manor house was rebuilt by Sir George Villiers in the following decade.[70] When at the Restoration some of these large estates were put up for sale, the architecture of their houses was deemed a principal attraction. Seekers after social prestige could not fail to be tempted by the description of the manor house at Blaston, lately built at a cost of more than £1,000, or the mansion 'well and fashionably built' at Belgrave.[71]

Land use. Turning from the gentry, whose wealth was derived as much from rents and trade as from the produce of the land, to the farmers whose sole source of income it was, it is important to know to what use the land was put, what crops the Leicestershire farmer found most suitable to the soil and most profitable at the market. One of the changes affecting the use of land, namely inclosure, has already received attention. But even in 1640 the majority of farms still lay in open fields; the majority of farmers lived in houses ranged along the village street with their gardens, orchards, and crofts adjoining.[72]

The average peasant farm was some 40–50 acres in extent, of which between two-thirds and three-quarters lay in tillage. The rest consisted of pasture, which lay intermixed with the arable, and meadow land, apportioned to each farmer according to the number of his strips, but lying outside the boundaries of the three fields. The allocation of meadow and pasture allowed farmers to keep about 1¼ sheep for every acre of land, and a few cattle according to their stint.[73] At Wigston Magna the stint was 8 kine and 40 sheep for every yardland (32 acres in this case) in the open fields. At Glen Magna in 1605 it was the same. At Cotesbach the allowance per yardland of 20 acres was 2 horses, a 'breeder', 3 beasts and a breeder, and 30 sheep. Pasture rights for these animals were exercised in the fallow field all the year round; in the pease field after the gathering of the crop until 25 March next following; in the corn field and in the meadows from harvest until the following 2 February.[74]

Few parishes except those on the fringes of Charnwood had any waste land by the 16th century, and fewer still had woodland of any size. The county was in fact one of the most highly cultivated areas in the kingdom, the barren lands of Charnwood occupying about 3½ per cent. of the total area, and other waste land perhaps an additional 1½ per cent.[75] Even in the first half of the 16th century this dearth of waste gave rise to a considerable fuel problem. The districts of Charnwood and the eastern uplands around Launde and Owston were well timbered. So also was Leicester Forest until it was disafforested by the Crown in 1628.[76] But in the southern half of the county only 1 acre in 200

---

[67] Hoskins, *Essays in Leics. Hist.* 156.
[68] Hoskins, *Midland Engl.*, illus. facing p. 48.
[69] Nichols, *Leics.* ii, 176.
[70] Ibid. ii, 195.
[71] Leic. City Mun. Room, Clayton MSS. 35'29/59, 58.
[72] Hoskins, *Essays in Leics. Hist.* 136.
[73] Ibid. 145.
[74] Ibid. 144.
[75] *Agric. Hist.* xxv, 10.
[76] Levi Fox and Percy Russell, *Leic. Forest,* 107.

lay in woodland. Most villages had to rely for their fuel on coal carried long distances from the coalfields, or, in the case of the poor, on dried cow-dung, bean haulms, and furze.[77]

Open-field farming took for granted the willingness of every villager to cultivate his land in broad conformity with his neighbours. Farming was more of a co-operative enterprise than it was in inclosed parishes, even though the harvest of every man's land was his own. But it was by no means an inflexible system, incapable of adapting itself to changing needs or differing soils. At Lutterworth in 1607 the amount of pasture on three farms of 3 virgates each (about 54 acres) ranged from 4¼ to 11½ acres.[78] On three small farms in Wigston Magna, of 47 roods, 60½ roods, and 56½ roods, the proportion of land under 'leys' was 17, 21½, and 10 per cent. respectively.[79] In short, no farmer was prevented by open-field husbandry from having twice as much pasture as his neighbour if he wished, even when their farms were of much the same size. The limiting factor was the amount of arable needed for food for his family and his animals. The larger farmer could afford to leave a larger acreage, perhaps a quarter or a third of his farm, in grass, while the smaller farmer could leave only a fifth.[80]

This flexibility of practice, which allowed the temporary and sometimes permanent conversion of arable strips to pasture, probably gave a longer life to open-field farming than it might otherwise have had. For the condition of the market throughout the 16th and 17th centuries encouraged concentration on sheep and cattle rather than on crops. But so long as the individual farmer could alter the balance of his arable and pasture without upsetting the whole basis of open-field cultivation, he was not at once driven to inclose. At Foston it was reported that about half the land in the fields was 'antient grasse ground' long before it was inclosed in 1575.[81]

In spite of considerable variations from farm to farm in the amount of land devoted to different crops, the general pattern of crop-growing was uniform. It gave pride of place to peas, second place to barley, and third place to wheat. Peas were eminently suited to Leicestershire's heavy soil, and had become by 1588 the most stable crop, occupying 45·9 per cent. of the arable area.[82] Most villages had three open fields, of which one lay fallow every year; of the two fields under cultivation, therefore, one was given over almost entirely to peas. Next in importance came barley, a crop which occupied 35·8 per cent. of the sown area in 1558, 38·6 per cent. in 1588, and 40 per cent. in the first half of the 17th century.[83] The labour problem involved in leaving most of the sowing until spring was in fact no problem at all, for peas and beans were usually in the ground by early February.[84] The acreage under wheat was more variable: it occupied 13·8 per cent. of the sown area in 1531, only 8·6 per cent. in 1558 and 1588, and 14 per cent. in 1608.[85] That these changes signified variations in the consumption of wheaten bread is suggested by William Lilly, who came of good yeoman stock, but who was agreeably surprised by the white bread which he ate in London in 1620 'contrary to our diet in Leicestershire'.[86]

[77] W. G. Hoskins, *Essays in Leics. Hist.* 145–6.
[79] Ibid. 141.
[81] Hoskins, *Essays in Leics. Hist.* 142.
[83] Ibid.; *Agric. Hist.* xxv, 12.
[85] Ibid. 169; *Agric. Hist.* xxv, 12.
[86] Hoskins, *Essays in Leics. Hist.* 169.

[78] Ibid. 140.
[80] *Agric. Hist.* xxv, 16.
[82] Ibid. 172.
[84] Hoskins, *Essays in Leics. Hist.* 167.

AGRARIAN HISTORY, 1540–1950

Rye and oats were grown in the same field as wheat, but the cropping of these was very irregular, and the total yield was small. The soil did not favour rye, though some was grown and replaced wheat for bread. But on an average the acreage dropped from 8·6 per cent. in 1558 to 4 per cent. in 1588, and by the 17th century had become insignificant.[87] Oats showed an increase in 1558 to 8·5 per cent. compared with 5 per cent. in 1531, perhaps because of the increased use of horses for work on the farms after 1530. But by 1588 it occupied only 3 per cent. of the land, and had become rare by the next century.[88]

Fluctuations over the years in the amount of land devoted to different crops were not large, and were probably due to changes in the numbers of stock kept from year to year. Peas were grown for animal as well as human consumption;[89] winter wheat was fed to the stock in late winter and early spring, and possibly rye also, as it was in the 18th century. This enabled the farmer to keep a large proportion of his cattle alive through the winter, for it was not the practice, as has often been contended, to kill off the bulk of the stock in winter.[90] The number of animals kept on the average (median) farm in 1588 was 30 sheep and 9 head of cattle. Through inclosure the number of sheep had increased by 1603 to 52, but it was only among the squirearchy that sheep-farming on a large scale was practised. Sir William Turpin of Knaptoft, who died in 1617, had 3,100 sheep; Anthony Faunt of Foston had 1,300; but among the yeomen 200–300 sheep was a good-sized flock in the 16th century.[91]

1640–60

The land market. By 1640 the tide of rural prosperity showed signs of receding. Prices continued to move upwards,[92] but the curve was gradual, and already, as the figures of land sales showed, the period of frenzied land purchase had passed. The biggest fortunes had already been made. The outbreak of the Civil War in 1642 turned this gentle decline in agricultural prosperity into a steep fall. The immediate effects differed from county to county and from place to place, for the effects of war spread slowly. Leicestershire as a whole was not the worst ravaged of counties. But apart from the destruction of property, which was strictly localized in Leicestershire, the heavy burden of taxation necessary to pay for the war, and the fact that men were called away from the land to join the forces of Parliament or the king, brought acute depression to the countryside.

Those social questions which had absorbed the attention of the Privy Council in the period of Charles's personal rule (1629–40), and which had become still more urgent because of the war—inclosure, poor relief, food supply —were thrust into the background. A new set of problems, those concerned with raising money to pay for the war, and with identifying and punishing the enemies of Parliament, took their place. Rural distress inevitably received only cursory attention from a Parliament troubled throughout the Interregnum by problems of internal and external security.

[87] Ibid.
[88] Ibid. 170, 177; G. E. Fussell, 'Four Centuries of Leics. Farming', *T.L.A.S.* xxiv, 156.
[89] Hoskins, *Essays in Leics. Hist.* 172.   [90] Ibid. 174.
[91] Ibid. 175–6.
[92] Knoop and Jones, 'Masons' Wages in Medieval Engl.', *Econ. Hist., Supplement to Econ. Jnl.* (Jan. 1933), ii, 485.

The economic tug of war between impoverished tenants and impoverished landlords was naturally embittered by political differences between the parties. Fragmentary details emerge from the case-histories of royalists whose lands were seized by Parliament, but they tell the story of one group of landlords, and only occasionally permit a glimpse of the condition of the poorer classes. In the course of administering the estate of Sir Charles Smith, the sequestration commissioners disclosed that his tenants at Ashby Folville were so impoverished that they had defaulted on their rents. On his lands in Warwickshire, recently inclosed, the closes were 'daily endeavoured to be thrown open'.[93] The plight of both rich and poor was genuine enough. The experience of Ferdinando, Earl of Huntingdon, whose Leicestershire estates brought in only £900 in 1646 compared with their pre-war value of £1,808, was common among landlords.[94] Yet it was impossible to raise rents. Even the local sequestration commissioners, who were constantly urged as a matter of principle to lease forfeited lands 'at the utmost improved yearly values that any man will give for the same',[95] were obliged to make reductions to tenants to take account of taxation and the agricultural depression.

To the moneylender and the land speculator, however, these were years of golden opportunity. Of all their victims royalists were the richest and lay most at their mercy. It had been the policy of both Parliament and the king from the earliest days of the war to seize the property of their opponents in the areas which they controlled. Leicestershire early fell within the orbit of Parliament's authority, and yielded no land to the king. But by April 1648 Parliament had confiscated the property of about 280 gentry and 45 clergy in the county, together with all the lands of the Crown and Church.[96] These estates were taken over ('sequestrated' in contemporary terminology), and administered by local sequestration commissioners for the benefit of the State. In October 1650 it was stated that the annual revenue from the land of royalists and recusants had amounted formerly to £7,580.[97] But Leicestershire's total contribution cannot be measured since the rents derived from Crown and Church lands have never been calculated.

The quantity of private land in the hands of the commissioners, unlike that forfeited by the Crown and the Church, varied constantly. For royalists were encouraged from 1643 onwards to compound for their estates by paying to Parliament a fine, assessed according to the nature of their offence. By April 1648 about 28 per cent. of Leicestershire's delinquents had recovered their land in this way.[98] The fine paid was sometimes considerable. Sir Henry Hastings of Braunstone had to pay the sum of £2,072, representing one-tenth of the capital value of his land.[99] Mountjoy, Earl of Newport, who held the two manors of Allexton and Loddington, paid £4,579 at the same rate for the offence of joining the king at Oxford.[1] But the advantage of recovering their property induced most royalists to adopt this expedient. By 1651, when the monarchy had been abolished and the Commonwealth seemed securely established, the majority of Leicestershire royalists had compounded with Parliament.

It is not difficult to see why the chapman and the moneylender flourished

---

93 *Cal. Committee for Compounding*, iii, 1916.
94 Ibid. ii, 1043.
95 *Harl. Misc.* ix, 548.
96 *Cal. Committee for Compounding*, i, 84, 108–12.
97 Ibid. i, 325.
98 Ibid. i, 108–12.
99 Ibid. iii, 1760.
1 Ibid. ii, 1244.

AGRARIAN HISTORY, 1540–1950

in these years. All royalists, whatever their financial position, were compelled in greater or less degree to pledge their future income to pay their composition. The less drastic method was to raise a loan from a friend or moneylender; the more desperate remedy was to sell part of the land in order to save the rest. Henry Nevill of Holt, who sent his sons with money and arms to fight for the king, and whose estates in Leicestershire, Northamptonshire, and Essex were sequestrated, survived the Interregnum by employing both devices. Regular sums of £300–£500 a year were borrowed from a neighbouring landowner in Essex, and the family estates in that county sold. Yet in 1664 Henry Nevill owed £6,000 to his neighbour and £5,000 to his eldest son, whose inheritance had been pledged as security.[2]

Debts traceable to the same cause brought Ferdinando, Earl of Huntingdon, to the Fleet Prison, and finally made necessary the sale of the manor of Loughborough.[3] Sir John Pretyman, whose star had been in the ascendant in the first half of the century, but whose estate was sequestrated during the Interregnum, sold considerable lands in Allexton in the fifties, and in 1670 finally had to sacrifice his chief estate at Loddington to meet a Crown debt of £19,864.[4]

Many similar experiences were described in Chancery at the Restoration, when long-standing accounts were brought before the judges for settlement. Royalists had met the situation in many different ways. Some had achieved complete financial recovery through a careful administration of their property. Others were on the brink of bankruptcy. It was not that parliamentary fines had imposed an insupportable burden on the land, but that most estates were already charged with mortgages and annuities necessary to finance estate improvements and further land purchases, or to provide pensions and marriage portions for other members of the family. In those cases in which the unexpected burden of sequestration dealt a crushing blow to family fortunes it was rarely the first and only cause of collapse.

The experience of William Staresmore, who owned a small estate at Frolesworth alleged to be worth only £50 p.a., bears out this point. In 1649 Staresmore was obliged to pay a fine for delinquency of £400, but the real root of his later difficulties lay in the fact that the land was already encumbered with debts, the charges of educating his two sons at boarding school at Nuneaton had to be met, and his mansion at Frolesworth was in bad need of repair. Staresmore decided to sell a part of his estate, but this did not end his troubles, for in the course of a generation after 1660 his family, which had been settled at Frolesworth since the late 16th century, had sold out entirely.[5]

Richard Turpin of Knaptoft suffered a similar eclipse because the burden of a parliamentary fine of £566 was imposed on an estate already mortgaged to provide portions for his five daughters. When in 1648 Lady Grace Manners foreclosed on the mortgage, Knaptoft, which had been the ancestral home of the Turpins for two centuries, passed out of their hands into those of the earls of Rutland.[6] This transaction revealed one thread in the web of financial obligations which, like marriage alliances, bound so many Leicestershire families together. But money opened the door to more than one new-comer. It was

---

[2] C 78/1277, no. 8.
[3] Hist. MSS. Com., *Hastings*, iv, 351.
[4] Leics. City Mun. Room, Clayton MSS. 35'29/15.
[5] *Cal. Committee for Compounding*, ii, 1167–9; Nichols, *Leics.* iv, 183.
[6] W. G. Hoskins, *Midland Engl.* 49–50.

through the financial troubles of another royalist, Sir Henry Skipwith, that the Packe family, who still live in Leicestershire, first formed their connexion with the county. Sir Henry Skipwith, in order to provide for his stepchildren, had mortgaged Prestwold manor to Christopher Packe, a London draper and later lord mayor, and when during the Civil War Skipwith was impoverished by sequestration, the property came into Packe's full possession.[7]

From the beginning of the Civil War until 1647 the land market lay stagnant. Political uncertainty was a deterrent to both buyers and sellers. In 1647, however, two years after the first Civil War had ended, the market revived. More and more royalists took advantage of the opportunity to compound with Parliament. The first Church lands, forfeited by the bishops and archbishops, were put up for sale in order to raise money to pay off the army. In 1649 the lands of deans and chapters and of the Crown were offered for sale, followed in March 1650 by the sale of fee-farm rents. Three Acts in 1651 and 1652 ordered the sale of the lands of those remaining royalists who had refused to compound, or who, on account of their high position in the royalist party, were not permitted to do so.

Land sales in Leicestershire, therefore, were as numerous in the years between 1647 and 1660 as they had been in the two decades up to 1640, but with an important difference. They now included many transactions forced on landowners not by business incompetence but by political misfortune, and they were inflated by the Commonwealth sales, which, although the outcome of financial necessity, were shaped to serve political ends.

Commonwealth sales suggested to contemporaries a parallel with the earlier sales of dissolved monastic property, for both were measures of financial expediency and both served as a mirror to accompanying changes in the social structure. But again there was a decisive difference. The sales of monastic land were far more astutely managed than those of Parliament could afford to be. The former were spread over more than twenty years, when the demand for land was insatiable; those of Parliament were compressed into the short period of about eight years, between 1646 and 1654, when money was tight and great suspicion attached to the legality of the sales. Parliament never succeeded in allaying fears that the sales were only a temporary measure and would one day be reversed. This view was expressed by Sir Arthur Hazlerigg, Member of Parliament and head of the Hazlerigg family of Noseley, when he declared in the Commons in February 1658: 'I know not how long after I shall keep the Bishops' lands. For no King no Bishop, no Bishop no King: we know the rule.'[8]

Doubts of this kind did not prevent people from buying forfeited land. Indeed, Hazlerigg himself had been an assiduous purchaser, particularly of the estates of the bishopric of Durham, and for that reason had earned himself the nickname of 'Bishop of Durham' among the members of the Commons. But they prevented Parliament from getting a high price for the land. When the administrative costs were deducted, it is to be doubted whether the net profit on forfeited land in Leicestershire represented much more than half the gross revenue of £17,000.[9]

Forfeited estates in Leicestershire were in any case small in extent. They

---

[7] Nichols, *Leics.* iii, 354.
[8] *Diary of Thomas Burton*, ed. J. T. Rutt, ii, 423–4.
[9] This is the total sum mentioned in the indentures of bargain and sale, enrolled on the Close R.

amounted to no more than 10,000 acres—less than 2 per cent. of all the land in the county—and four-fifths of this was made up of land forfeited by four royalists, the Duke of Buckingham (offspring of the Villiers family of Brooksby), Rowland Eyre of Hassop and Thomas Coke of Melbourne (Derbys.), and Walter Fowler of St. Thomas (Staffs.). Only Buckingham could be said to have had long ancestral connexions with the county. The Church forfeited seven estates, which together covered less than 2,000 acres, and the Crown four properties in Leicester, Garthorpe, and Newbold which extended over only 100 acres. Compared with the great tracts of territory surrendered by the monastic houses a century earlier these were trifles. Moreover, the most valuable prizes, Buckingham's four manors, were not put up for public sale, but were granted away as gifts. Dalby-on-the-Wolds and Nether Broughton were bestowed on Oliver Cromwell, and Garendon and Shepshed on Bridget Ireton, daughter of Cromwell and relict of Henry Ireton, the parliamentary commander who had died during the Irish campaign in 1651.[10] These four manors formed the lion's share of royalist land, and left only 1,680 acres out of 8,000 acres for public sale.

By a geographical accident most forfeited estates in Leicestershire were distributed along the fringes of the county, except for a few Crown and Church estates in Leicester and the neighbourhood. But fee-farm rents, which consisted mainly of rents reserved to the Crown when monastic land was sold, were scattered in every corner of the county. As the value of many of them was no more than a few shillings, they were sold in great lots irrespective of location and county boundaries.

When Parliament's enemies inveighed against these sales, their wrath was spent on the upstarts, careerists, and money-grabbers who, but for the war, it was alleged, would have remained obscure men of mediocre fortune. Examples of their activity in Leicestershire explain why they earned so much obloquy. A few were nothing short of dealers drilled to a regular routine of buying up large properties and selling them off in small lots. Andrew Sparrow, secretary to the Generals of the Fleet, John Sparrow, a colonel in the parliamentary army, and William May formed a ring for this purpose, buying land in the midland and eastern counties and fee-farm rents in the Home Counties and in Leicestershire.[11] The scale of their enterprise naturally attracted attention and obscured the more modest purchases of local people. But in fact the gains in land made by the local gentry and craftsmen at the first sales were roughly equal to those of the dealers, while among the 17 purchasers of fee-farm rents, 5 came of local families, to compete with 8 confirmed speculators. Malicious reports and idle rumour magnified the share of the latter and ignored entirely the share of the former. But it was to Sir Thomas Hartopp, who already held a lease of the estate from the Bishop of Ely, that Burton Lazars was sold;[12] it was to Charles Byerley, squire of Belgrave, that the parsonage of Belgrave was sold;[13] and it was the Earl of Rutland who purchased the lands in Eastwell and Hose, forfeited by Rowland Eyre.[14]

Smaller items were bought by craftsmen: a tenement, called 'The Greyhound', in Hinckley became the property of Underwood Palmer, a plumber of

[10] C 54/3668, no. 19; C 54/3673, no. 11.
[11] C 54/3667, no. 8.
[12] C 54/3402, no. 3.
[13] C 54/3669, no. 19.
[14] C 54/3725, no. 18.

that place;[15] and a house in Leicester High Street was sold to Richard Dann, a jerseycomber and probably the tenant, for £27. 7s. 8d.[16] Mention must also be made of two purchases by William Lilly, the astrologer. In legal documents of the period he was described as a gentleman of St. Clement Danes, although he had already bought an estate at Horsham (Surr.). But it was in Leicestershire also that he chose to invest some of his wealth, in the purchase of fee-farm rents at Leicester Frith and at Castle Donington near his native Diseworth.[17]

Lands bought by local people remained in the possession of the first purchasers until the Restoration, but those which had been sold to speculators were but at the beginning of their journey. Unfortunately it has not been possible to trace their later passage, but it is fair to assume that in Leicestershire, as in southern England, resales tended to increase the proportion of local owners. Nevertheless the properties forfeited here were so few—only one manor remained after the Duke of Buckingham's four manors had been granted away— that there was little scope for any subdivision of land or broadening of the basis of landownership. For the same reason it is misleading to speak of any class as the chief beneficiaries of these sales. Rather it should be said that the land came into the hands of a few local gentry and one or two townsmen. The sales were too limited in extent to have made any deep impression on the county.

Inclosure. That continuous thread in the fabric of agrarian history formed by the inclosure movement was weakened but not broken by the Civil War. Only three villages, Shenton, Galby, and Twycross,[18] appear to have been inclosed in the sixteen-forties. But with the end of the war the movement gathered strength again, and in the fifties at least seven, and possibly a further three, places were inclosed. During the lull the practical arguments in favour of inclosure had, if anything, gained in cogency, for all landlords had been hard hit by the war. At least two royalists, whose lands had been sequestrated, were among those who proceeded to inclose: Francis Needham, a clerk of Rotherby, who co-operated in the inclosure of Gaddesby;[19] and Rowland Eyre, who inclosed his lands in Eastwell and Hose in strange alliance with the Parliamentary Committee.[20]

Although inclosures by agreement were becoming more usual—agreement preceded at least six out of the thirteen inclosures in these two decades—they were not yet universal practice, nor had they achieved a perfection that eliminated subsequent disputes. At Holwell the settlement of 1654 was the subject of an apparently genuine grievance in 1656.[21] A tithe dispute arose in the sixties out of the inclosure agreement at Belgrave,[22] and a disagreement about a right of way at Catthorpe in 1694.[23]

The poorer peasants remained inarticulate, but it is unlikely that they drove a better bargain than their richer, litigious neighbours. Their hardships were observed in Leicestershire by John Moore, minister of Knaptoft, and formed the central theme of his slashing attack on inclosures in *The crying Sin of England of not caring for the Poor*, printed in 1653.[24] Battle was joined by Joseph Lee,

---

[15] C 54/3833, no. 39.
[16] C 54/3790, no. 17.
[17] C 54/3534, no. 15; C 54/3633, no. 26.
[18] Galby is quoted by Dr. Hoskins as completely inclosed by 1630, but Nichols states that the common field was not inclosed until 1642: *Agric. Hist.* xxv, 17; Nichols, *Leics.* ii, 569. Shenton is listed by John Monk, see G. Slater, *Engl. Peasantry*, 198–9.
[19] C 54/3898, no. 7.
[20] C 78/1335, no. 2.
[21] C 78/526, no. 8.
[22] C 78/1214, no. 5.
[23] Nichols, *Leics.* iv, 76.
[24] Ibid. 83.

the rector of Catthorpe, who defended inclosure by compiling in 1654 a list of villages in the county and on its borders which from his own knowledge in the previous fifty years had been inclosed without depopulation and without the decay of tillage.[25] Once again the old controversies were being fought out, with Leicestershire still forming a principal battleground.

A petition from the county against inclosure was considered by the Council of State in November 1655, and was followed in 1656 by a Bill to regulate inclosure, presented to the Commons by Edward Whalley, Major-General for Leicestershire and four other midland counties.[26] Both petition and Bill met with a display of neglect and indifference which seemed at the time of little significance but which in later years were recognized as marking a turning-point in the history of government policy towards inclosure. Whalley's Bill was the last of its kind to be introduced into Parliament, and no attempt was subsequently made to revive the old inquisitions and restrictions on inclosure.

The thirteen inclosures of the Interregnum already mentioned were inclosures of entire villages. But the parliamentary surveys of forfeited land afford a fleeting glimpse of many small encroachments on the common fields and minor adjustments in the layout of closes. These are the finer details of the process which are usually beyond the vision of the historian but which to the Leicestershire peasant were as familiar a background to his daily life as the more spectacular scenes enacted before it. The sale of a small estate of the Bishop of Oxford at Orton-in-Twycross discloses the fact that 58 of its 88 acres were inclosed.[27] At Nether Broughton, where the glebe land was still open in 1674, 970 acres out of 1,050 acres had been inclosed, apparently without disturbance. In other places the large closes of 200 acres and more, into which the fields had first been divided, were in process of being broken up into smaller units. At Nether Broughton a close of 213 acres had been divided into 6 parts, and another of 281 acres into 10 parts.[28] At Garendon a close of 38 acres was divided among 4 tenants, and one of 165 acres between 5 tenants.[29] At Easton, on the other hand, 3 closes amounting to 26 acres had been thrown 'all open to one'.[30] These readjustments may have been due to the difficult conditions of farming during the forties, when the labour on which the large farmers depended was scarce, and when land that was confiscated from its owners had to be leased to others. But it may be that farmers were already beginning to realize that the small pasture close was more convenient for controlling the grazing of animals than the vast Tudor inclosure, and that the additional hedges afforded valuable shelter for stock as well as a supply of timber. By the end of the 18th century a pasture of between 8 and 12 acres was considered to be the most convenient size. Robert Bakewell, with characteristic exactitude, asserted that a 50-acre pasture divided into 5 would go as far as 60 acres all in one piece, and according to Monk his view was widely accepted. Yet in practice the size varied enormously in the 18th century, from 5 to 40 acres for recent inclosure, and anything up to 100 acres for old inclosure.[31] By the middle of the 19th century opinion had not hardened in favour of the 10-acre pasture. It was evidently a little on the small side, for the majority were between 10 and 20 acres, while a

25 Slater, *Engl. Peasantry*, 111–12.
26 *Cal. S.P. Dom.*, 1655–6, 9; *D.N.B.* sub Edw. Whalley.
27 C 54/3801, no. 25.
28 C 54/3668, no. 19.
29 C 54/3673, no. 11.
30 C 54/3496, no. 14.
31 J. Monk, *General View of the Agric. of the County of Leic.* 45–46.

grazier of Market Harborough favoured 24 acres—a pasture that would carry
20 head of cattle and 30 sheep in the middle of May.[32]

1660–1760

Crops and Stock. The economic dislocation caused by the Civil War did
not affect the steady transformation of Leicestershire from a predominantly
arable to a predominantly pastoral county. When Gabriel Plattes looked across
the Vale of Belvoir in the 1630's and deemed it the best corn land in Europe,
he was surveying a long chapter of farming history that was steadily approach-
ing its close.[33]

Nevertheless, open-field husbandry remained characteristic of about half
the county until the end of the 17th century, though this did not mean that on
all farms the arable acreage exceeded the pasture. Cropping after 1660 continued much as before, peas and beans continuing to occupy about 45 per cent.
of every farmer's sown arable, while barley and wheat were sown roughly in the
proportion of five to one in the second field. Beans gradually came to supplant
peas, as William King's jingle suggests ('Leicester beans and bacon, food of
Kings!'), and on some farms by 1700 more wheat was being grown at the
expense of barley. Rye and oats were rare.[34]

The most significant developments in farming in the period between 1660
and 1760 took place on inclosed pasture farms. Although nothing occurred to
challenge the supremacy of the pasture farmer, the secret of his continuing
prosperity lay in the fact that he was steadily adapting his husbandry to satisfy
a new market. The farmer who specialized in raising sheep alone was giving
ground to the grazier who specialized not only in wool but in producing meat
for the towns and in particular for London.[35]

Already in Elizabeth I's reign there were signs that the 'all-devouring
sheep' was being displaced. The wool merchants and mercers, who supplied
from their ranks thirteen mayors of Leicester between 1485 and 1550, were
represented by only six mayors between 1550 and 1603.[36] Their place was
being taken by butchers, tanners, and glovers, among whom John Freake,
freeman of Leicester, was typical. His father, Philip Freake, had come as a
stranger to the town in the middle of the century, but he rapidly built up a
prosperous business as a butcher and grazier and became mayor in 1581. His
personal estate was valued at £627. 13s. 6d. in 1589 and included livestock
worth £236. 6s. 8d.; his leaseholds covered several hundred acres of pasture.
Philip Freake and his son, who likewise became mayor in 1611, stood for a
small group of traders and farmers who had developed into an important class
by the end of the 17th century.[37] Just how important they were may be judged
from Defoe's impressions in the 1720's. 'The whole county seems to be taken
up in country business . . . particularly in breeding and feeding cattle; the
largest sheep and horses in England are found here, and hence it comes to pass
too, that they are in consequence a vast magazine of wool for the rest of the

[32] W. J. Moscrop, 'Report on the Farming of Leics.', *Jnl. Royal Agric. Soc.*, 2nd ser. ii, no. 4, 293, 298.
[33] *Agric. Hist.* xxv, 9.   [34] Ibid. 12–15.
[35] The market for north Leics. was Birmingham, but by the 1780's some stock from this district was being
driven to Rotherham (Yorks.) for sale in the manufacturing towns of Yorks. and Lancs.: W. Marshall, *Rural
Econ. of Midland Counties*, i, 229–30 and n.
[36] Hoskins, *Essays in Leics. Hist.*, 114.   [37] Ibid. 108 et seq.

nation; even most of the gentlemen and grasiers, and in some places the grasiers are so rich, that they grow gentlemen: 'tis not an uncommon thing for grasiers here to rent farms from 500l. to two thousand pounds a year rent.'[38]

As a hurried traveller Defoe's attention was naturally drawn to the large graziers, to men such as Samuel Bickerston of Beeby, whose corn and malt were worth only £23 at his death in 1670, while his livestock were valued at £427; or to Richard Cranwell of Stockerston, who possessed nearly 1,100 sheep and lambs and 71 cattle at his death in 1703, worth in all £700.[39] But on smaller open-field farms also much arable was being converted to ley for the rearing of livestock. At Asfordby George Austin had only 4 acres of his strips under crops in 1700, while his animals accounted for £100 of his total personal estate of £146. 10s.[40]

The open-field farmer who had been able in the 16th century to turn some of his arable over to sheep pasture without disturbing the three-field husbandry of the village was still not obliged to inclose when he turned to the rearing of livestock. If he left the bulk of his land under grass, he simply tethered his animals for grazing. If his strips were to be kept for hay, he fenced them off with hurdles. It was not usual for the open-field farmer to abandon mixed farming entirely, but in the county as a whole, and more particularly in the south-east and east, where the heavy clay soil was most suitable for fattening cattle, the proportion of land under leys in the open fields increased as the century wore on.[41] In detail this system of convertible husbandry was probably not dissimilar from that described by William Marshall on inclosed farms in the 1780's. The routine then was to plough up land that had been under grass for between six and seven years for a rotation of oats, wheat, and barley (sometimes with a turnip crop before the barley to clear the land more thoroughly), and then to lay it to grass again.[42]

The expanding trade in livestock gave a new importance to towns possessing cattle markets. Camden had observed the business done at Market Harborough, where cattle were brought from as far away as the Vale of Belvoir. By the end of the century the graziers of the south and east of the county had another market on their doorstep, at Uppingham, to which, wrote Celia Fiennes, came 'such a concourse of people that my Landlord told me he used to have 100 horses set up at his inn'.[43]

The widespread interest in farming improvements, on which Robert Houghton had made some general comments in the 1680's, was naturally directed in Leicestershire towards improving the quality of livestock.[44] It is difficult to identify all the individuals who in the early days were the pioneers in improved stock-breeding. Robert Bakewell won the highest reputation and secured the most publicity, but on the evidence of William Marshall, who did most towards advertising his activities, he had his predecessors as well as a distinguished group of disciples.[45] Hugo Meynell, the first master of the Quorn Hunt, was already breeding foxhounds in the 1760's on the same principles as Bakewell with his sheep and cattle. Quorn Hall lies only six miles

[38] D. Defoe, *Tour Through England and Wales* (Everyman ed.), ii, 89–90.
[39] *Agric. Hist.* xxv, 18–19.
[40] Ibid. 14.
[41] Ibid. 16–17.
[42] *T.L.A.S.* xxiv, 165–6.
[43] *Agric. Hist.* xxv, 19.
[44] R. Houghton, *Husbandry and Trade Improv'd*, iv, 56.
[45] Marshall, *Rural Econ.* i, 294–5.

from Dishley Grange, where Bakewell worked, and it is an open question whether Meynell learnt from Bakewell, or the other way round.[46] As to Bakewell's success, it was the evident achievements of his collaborators as well as his own efforts which enhanced his fame in the outside world.

By experimenting with the inbreeding of local types, and, to a lesser extent, by crossing them with non-local types, Bakewell and his colleagues led the way in the production of fine meat-yielding animals. According to William Marshall, who between 1784 and 1786 studied farming methods in north-west Leicestershire from Statfold over the border, the pioneer work on sheep had been done by Joseph Allom of Clifton, a self-made farmer, who bought his breeding stock from Mr. Stone of Goadby Marwood. Allom took the first step towards improving the long-wooled Leicestershire variety, though it was Bakewell who developed it to perfection.[47] In contrast with the old Leicestershires, admired by Gervase Markham in the early 17th century as 'a large boned Sheep of the best shape and the deepest staple',[48] these new Leicestershires were small-boned animals, carrying in consequence a much higher proportion of meat, possessing good fattening qualities, and a finer fleece.[49] Some comparatively progressive farmers, such as Mr. Frisby of Waltham near Melton Mowbray, still pinned their faith on the Old Leicestershires, but Bakewell's new breed was vastly superior as meat, and was being developed by at least seventeen farmers known to Marshall, including Mr. Paget of Ibstock, Mr. Stone of Quorndon, and Mr. Henton of Hoby.[50]

When once the elementary principles of controlled breeding were understood, they were applied to all forms of livestock. Experiments with cattle were carried out on the Longhorn variety, then the most common in the county. Before Bakewell's day it produced a fine draught ox and a fair dairy cow, but Bakewell, rearing from a herd belonging to Mr. Webster of Warwickshire, transformed it at the expense of its milking qualities into an early maturing beef steer of much superior quality.[51]

The Leicestershire horse called for less drastic improvement. It was a black horse, already renowned for its toughness and endurance, and, at the end of the 17th century, was being bred by graziers for use on the farm and, when fully grown, for service as a coach horse on the streets of London. Even arable farmers who did not go in for the breeding of horses bought colts at two years, working them in the plough until they sold them two years later. Bakewell, who was at his best when improving breeds for meat, wrought little change in the species, though he followed the lead of others in developing a shorter, stocky horse of greater strength. Of these he was said to have much superior specimens.[52]

Bakewell's pre-eminence as a breeder led him to foster the practice of hiring out his male stock for breeding. The business developed its own methods of advertisement, private shows being held in the spring, and the beasts hired out

---

[46] Cf. Arthur Young's account in 1801 of the experience of Mr. Crowe of Ashwicken (Norf.) in the selective breeding of sheep. 'It was breeding greyhounds which gave him the idea, to conviction, that he could breed, with attention, so as to transfer any point desired without taking the bad ones: and (he) has observed that he can do the same thing with sheep': Arthur Young, *Annals of Agric.* (1801), xxxvii, 439.

[47] Marshall, *Rural Econ.* i, 381, 382.   [48] *T.L.A.S.* xxiv, 159–6.

[49] Marshall, *Rural Econ.* i, 388–91.

[50] Ibid. 380, 385–6. The Old Leicestershires lingered longest in the Melton Mowbray district: Monk, *General View*, 33.   [51] Marshall, *Rural Econ.* i, 315, 318–20.

[52] *T.L.A.S.* xxiv, 161; W. Pitt, *General View of Agric. of the County of Leicester*, 243; Marshall, *Rural Econ.*, i, 306 et seq.

ROBERT BAKEWELL

DISHLEY GRANGE

for a season that lasted usually from April to August. Public shows like the Market Bosworth show for bulls, the Leicester show for rams, and the Ashby-de-la-Zouch show for stallions, although designed principally as markets, also did service as hiring-places.[53]

Horses, cattle, sheep, and pigs (in which Bakewell also excelled) earned Leicestershire men a high reputation as stock farmers. Bakewell ranked deservedly as their leader, because he surpassed them in the range of his improvements. Every branch of his farming seems to have been the subject of experiment, whether it was a species of cabbage, a device for floating turnips down stream to save carting them across the farm, or a method of improving the quality of his pasture by watering.[54]

Bakewell's contemporaries, who were equally receptive to new ideas but inventive in less spectacular ways, went on the whole unnamed. But their training was probably not very different from his—all learning the farming lore of their forebears and augmenting it with observation and instruction gathered from farther afield. Marshall was impressed by the education which the sons of yeomen received in Leicestershire and neighbouring counties.[55] Of its content he said little, but its practical side is suggested in the statement that Bakewell spent some days with Mr. Boswell in the west country learning his method of watering grassland before he adopted it himself.[56] How much Bakewell owed of wisdom and experience to his father it would not be difficult to guess, even without the explicit statement of William Pitt.[57] The Bakewells had farmed at and near Normanton-le-Heath for several centuries before one of them removed to Dishley, and Robert Bakewell's grandfather still held land at Swepstone, near Normanton, when he died in 1716. That his farming preferences were transmitted to his son and grandson is evident from his will, for 66 per cent. of his personal estate was composed of cattle, horses, sheep, and pigs. A further 11 per cent. was made up of wool and cheese in store, making a total of £602. 10s. out of his estate of £793. 10s.[58]

Inclosure. The extension of pasture farming in this period is a clue to the progress of inclosure. In the fifty years from 1660 to 1710 some forty-one places, and by 1760 another thirty-two, were entirely inclosed. Further evidence is needed to indicate how much piecemeal inclosure had taken place, but already there is information enough to show that 47 per cent. of the county had been inclosed by 1710. The data for the period 1710–30 are too scanty to show any change. In 1730 the parliamentary Acts began; but inclosures without Act before 1760 accounted for 48 per cent. of the area of the county. Judging by the acreage affected by parliamentary inclosure after 1730, this figure should be nearer 61·8 per cent.[59] The deficiency no doubt lies in the unknown amount of piecemeal inclosure after 1660, and outright inclosure after 1700. By 1730 it would probably be true to say that more than half the county was inclosed.

The inclosure movement had advanced over a period of 300 years in three distinct waves. Until 1550 it was characterized by spasmodic and violent outbursts of activity, which caused acute social distress. In the next century it spread out over the whole county, but by enlisting the support of all classes

[53] Marshall, op. cit. i, 334–5, 302–3.
[54] Ibid. 261, 286, 284.
[55] Ibid. 116–18.
[56] Ibid. 284–5.
[57] Pitt, *General View*, 217.
[58] Probate Inv. of Robert Bakewell of Dishley, 1716, in Leics. County Rec. Off.
[59] Slater, *Engl. Peasantry*, 196. See p. 204, n. 32, above for method of calculating these percentages.

weakened the force of its enemies' strongest criticisms. After 1660 it encountered no effective opposition, and proceeded steadily towards its goal of complete inclosure of the county. The distinctive feature of the 17th century movement was that it did not spread so rapidly into new parishes as in the 16th century, but pushed piecemeal inclosure to completion. Only 66 places are known to have been affected by inclosure for the first time between 1607 and 1700, compared with 140 between 1485 and 1607. But whereas 49 places were entirely inclosed in the early period, 91 were wholly inclosed between 1607 and 1700.

Settled political conditions no doubt account for the crop of inclosure agreements in the five years after 1660, when Ashby Parva, Cossington, Laughton, Peatling Parva, Shawell, Long Whatton (pasture only), Woodhouse, and Woodthorpe underwent inclosure. The absence of official attempts at regulation after 1660 left the situation entirely in the hands of local landowners. Progress was determined by local conditions—by the unanimity of the freeholders, the length of tenants' leases, and the crop preferences of the district.

Crop preferences had a special bearing on the question, not because they placed positive obstacles in the way of inclosure but because they sometimes diminished the urgency of the problem. This was demonstrated in the area west of the Soar, where the lighter clay lands were more friable to the plough, and pasture farming never made such headway as in the east.[60] Wherever crop husbandry persisted, the arguments against open-field cultivation, at least from the farmer's point of view, were less cogent. The system was, after all, adaptable enough. Its most intractable problem was a growing shortage of pasture as more of the common pasture was brought under the plough to support a bigger population. It could be overcome by a revision of the rules governing the open fields, involving usually a reduction in the stint and sometimes the laying down of more arable strips to grass.[61] This had been done at Thurcaston in 1600,[62] at Cosby in 1668,[63] and at Wigston Magna in 1707,[64] and in each case the consideration of inclosure was postponed for many years. In the south-east of the county the difficulties of ploughing the heavy liassic and boulder clays underlined the economic incentives to stock rearing, and helped the conversion from arable to pasture. Nevertheless a study of the Leicestershire inclosure map warns us to beware of overstressing the importance of soil variations.[65] There were too many other factors involved to allow of any tidy geographical pattern.

Although conflicting interests delayed complete inclosure in many places, there was no doubt on which side the interests of landlords lay. The particulars of sale, circulated by the renowned scrivener Sir Robert Clayton to his clients after the Restoration, never failed to emphasize the attractions of inclosed land. In selling recently inclosed land at Gaddesby and Peatling Magna he assured his client that the land was 'very much improvable without further charge'.[66] In selling open land at Drayton and Sapcote he enticed a buyer by forecasting

---

60 R. Auty, *Leics.* (Rep. of Land Utilization Surv.), 253–4.
61 *T.L.A.S.* xxiv, 158–9; W. G. Hoskins, 'Midland Peasant' (Unpublished hist. of Wigston Magna).
62 C 78/368, no. 21. Thurcaston was inclosed under an Act of 1798.
63 C 78/669, no. 6. Cosby was inclosed under an Act of 1767.
64 Hoskins, 'Midland Peasant' (see n. 61 above). Wigston Magna was finally inclosed in 1766.
65 M. W. Beresford, 'Glebe Terriers and Open-Field Leics.', *T.L.A.S.* xxiv, 77.
66 Leic. City Mun. Room, Clayton MSS. 35'29/293, 411.

imminent inclosure,[67] which would double and even treble the value of the property. Land at Medbourne promised to be worth thrice as much, at Holwell and Sapcote twice as much.[68] Nor were these calculations fanciful optimism. When the Parliamentary Commissioners surveyed Cromwell's lands at Dalby-on-the-Wolds they valued the open arable at approximately 3s. 6d. an acre and the inclosed pasture at between 9s. 8d. and 11s. an acre.[69]

Inclosures in the 1660's and 1670's reflected in part the determination of landlords to recover some of their losses of the Interregnum. But the agreements which preceded them did not deal unfairly with the claims of tenants. The Ashby Parva agreement, for example, was implemented by five referees and two surveyors chosen by all parties to the inclosure.[70] At Cossington a majority of the freeholders appointed five commissioners to apportion the land and to appoint surveyors. Land was allotted with due regard for 'the quantity, quality, and convenience of every man's land'; ancient freehold cottagers with common rights received land in compensation; the poor received provision at the discretion of the commissioners.[71] The procedure was not unlike that of the later parliamentary awards.

Inclosure Acts did not begin in Leicestershire until 1730, when an Act was passed to complete (or more probably to confirm) the inclosure of Horninghold. Great and Little Claybrooke obtained an Act in 1734, and Norton-juxta-Twycross another in 1748 to confirm an agreement of the previous year. Growing interest in agricultural improvements swelled the river, and the floodgates opened. Twelve Acts were passed in the fifties and no fewer than 11 in 1760. By that date at least 197 out of 396 places in Leicestershire (50 per cent.) were fully inclosed.[72]

Social structure. At the Restoration the royalists had high hopes of recovering their property and receiving full compensation for their losses. In the event they were disappointed, for those of the king's supporters who had sold some of their land in order to compound with Parliament were given no legal or financial help in recovering it. But the property of the Crown, the Church, and private royalists which had been compulsorily sold was restored to its former owners. Opposition from the dispossessed was forestalled by a promise to give compensation, usually in the form of leases, to those purchasers who could prove undue hardship, though this concession applied only to purchasers of Church and Crown land. That it did not remain a dead letter is seen in the fact that Underwood Palmer retained an interest in the house he had bought at Hinckley, originally forfeited by the Dean and Chapter of Westminster.[73]

The scrutiny of estate accounts in 1660 resulted in a further reshuffle of landowners and the sale of some important Leicestershire properties. The London scrivener, Sir Robert Clayton, who had a hand in the real-estate transactions of almost every English county, handled the most important of those

---

[67] Ibid. 35'29/281, 447.

[68] Ibid. 35'29/383, 447; P.R.O. C 78/526, no. 8; in spite of Clayton's statement that the freeholders had agreed to inclose Sapcote, it does not appear to have been inclosed until the Act of 1778.

[69] C 54/3668, no. 19.

[70] Ashby Parva inclosure agreement (MS. copy in possession of H. Goodacre, Esq., at Ullesthorpe Court, Leics.).

[71] Florence and S. H. Skillington, *Hist. of Cossington*, 162–3.

[72] *C.J.* xxi, 514. Other evidence suggests that Horninghold was fully inclosed by 1620. See App. I and table on p. 229, below.

[73] Leics. County Rec. Off., Wills of 1663, no. 46.

in Leicestershire. He was responsible for the sale of all the Leicestershire lands of the Duke of Buckingham, and for the mortgages and sales negotiated by the old gentry families—by the Hartopps of Burton Lazars, the Nevills of Holt, the Burtons of Lindley, the Pretymans of Loddington, the Ortons of Peatling Magna, and the Smiths of Ashby Folville.[74]

This concentration of business in the hands of Clayton inevitably deprived the land market of such localism as it still possessed. Clayton sought his purchasers and moneylenders among the merchants of London and the gentry of any and every county. His business, confined as it was to the great estates, was but one small token of the widening gulf between the large and small landed proprietors.

These transfers of land were, however, insufficient to alter radically the composition of the landowning class, which remained remarkably stable for the next century. Even the sequestrated royalists, who had complained of the meagreness of royal charity at the Restoration, showed in some cases unexpected qualities of endurance, their prophecies of bankruptcy remaining unfulfilled a century later. The Nevills of Holt, who shouldered apparently crippling debts in 1660, were among the first dozen of the county's wealthy gentry in 1780, while royalist families like the Palmers of Carlton Curlieu,[75] the Noels of Dalby,[76] and the Brudenells of Stonton Wyville,[77] who received titles from Charles II, reached the same harbour on calmer seas.

Even the collapse of the South Sea Company in 1720 does not appear to have dealt any serious blow to the Leicestershire gentry. The number of final concords levied showed no marked fluctuations until 1727, when they shot up by 47 per cent. above the average for the previous five years. This sharp and temporary increase, lasting until the spring of 1731, remains to be explained, but unless the time-lag was unusually long it can have had little to do with the South Sea Bubble. The subject, however, deserves more research than has so far been devoted to it. The conventional story of sudden bankruptcies and the shattering of family fortunes overnight is a simple theme that was probably disentangled from many more intricate and subtle variations.[78]

On the whole, economic conditions in the period 1660–1760 favoured the older gentry and handicapped their less deeply rooted fellows. Because prices remained comparatively stable, purses did not fill half as readily as they had done in the preceding century.[79] This fact, combined with the triumph of conservatism in politics, had a solidifying effect on the social structure. Promotion from one class to another became more difficult, and the frontiers between the classes more pronounced. There were not wanting writers who were anxious to rationalize these sharpening class divisions into a legal system of class stratification.[80]

It would be easy to exaggerate this social immobility, simply by virtue of the contrast it afforded with the previous century. It was most noticeable among the large landowners, shading off down the social scale until among the

74 Leic. City Mun. Room, Clayton MSS., *passim*.
75 Nichols, *Leics.* ii, 540.
76 Ibid. iii, 252.
77 Ibid. ii, 864.
78 This problem was posed by Dr. Hoskins in his introduction to 'Studies in Leics. Agrarian History', *T.L.A.S.* xxiv. It is open to question how far the Fines at this late date are a reliable index to the activity of the land market.
79 E. V. Morgan, *The Study of Prices and the Value of Money* (Helps for Students of History 53), 21–22.
80 *Social Engl.*, ed. H. D. Traill, iv, 473.

smallest peasants it lost any meaning. But the conclusion to be drawn from an analysis of landowners in 1780 who paid more than £200 a year in land tax is inescapable. Only three out of the sixteen in this class, Ralph Franks of Misterton and Poultney, Charles Boothby of Tooley Park, and the Earl of Aylesford of Ashby Magna, had no long ancestral connexions with Leicestershire. Of the rest the Duke of Rutland, the Earl of Huntingdon, the Earl of Harborough, and the Earl of Stamford, to mention four out of the first six, all came of families which were in the front rank of Leicestershire gentry in the early 16th century—some years before the small farmers threatened to invade their positions. The same was true of five out of the last ten families in this list— the Noels of Dalby, the Pochins of Barkby, the Nevills of Holt, the Caves of Stanford Hall, the Brudenells of Stonton Wyville, and the Hazleriggs of Noseley. The Palmers of Carlton Curlieu, who held third place, were an old and distinguished Northamptonshire family, more recently absorbed into Leicestershire society through their purchase of Carlton Curlieu manor in the mid-17th century. The Hartopps, who held fourth place in this scale of landed wealth, were an old county family whose social position was founded on the purchases of the enterprising yeoman, Thomas Hartopp, in the mid-16th century. Only Viscount Maynard and Charles Boothby had not such deep roots in the county, the first having inherited land there through a marriage alliance with the Banasters of Northamptonshire in 1641, and the second being descended from a London merchant who settled at Tooley in the mid-17th century.[81]

The strength of these families was manifest in the period 1660–1760, not in the purchase of new lands, but in the consolidation and improvement of those they already had. No small part of their success may be ascribed to the growing habit of entailing land. When capital was needed it was raised by mortgages rather than sales, and although these involved intricate transactions, and the piling of debt on debt, they preserved the estate itself from slow dismemberment.[82] Sometimes rapidly, sometimes slowly, wealth, reputation, and service to the Crown brought titles in their wake. Bennet, Lord Sherard, was promoted Earl of Harborough in 1719,[83] Charles, Lord Maynard, took the title of Viscount Maynard in 1766,[84] and Sir Edward Noel the title of Viscount Wentworth of Wellsborough in 1762.[85] The Brudenells became earls of Cardigan in 1660, and by marriage dukes of Montagu in 1776.[86] In 1780 seven of these sixteen families had been linked together by marriage alliances in the previous three generations.[87]

For want of evidence about the way of life of nine-tenths of the population, it is from the recorded habits of the nobility and gentry that the historian is usually obliged to reconstruct the social and cultural history of a period. The small numerical importance of this class can only be measured in the occasional tax assessments which affected the bulk of the population. These afford a brief glimpse of the otherwise forgotten majority who lived on the fringe or entirely outside the range of economic opportunity. The hearth-tax return of 1670 shows that poverty and near-poverty were as conspicuous a feature of Leicestershire

81 Leics. County Rec. Off., Land Tax Assessments; Nichols, *Leics.*, *passim*.
82 H. J. Habakkuk, 'English Landownership, 1680–1740', *Econ. Hist. Rev.* x, 7.
83 Nichols, *Leics.* ii, 335.   84 *Complete Peerage*, viii, 602.
85 Nichols, *Leics.* iv, 768.   86 Ibid. ii, 804.
87 Ibid. *passim*.

villages as they had been in the first half of the 16th century. The 30 per cent. of the population which in 1524 depended wholly or partly on wage labour for a livelihood was deemed in 1670 too poor to pay the hearth tax. If the outward signs of industrial poverty were anywhere apparent, it was in areas where the early framework-knitters were being recruited. But the problem of poverty was of much the same dimensions throughout the countryside. West Goscote hundred, a region of poor soil and precocious industrial development, had the highest percentage of poor, 36·5 per cent., and Framland hundred, on the richer farming land, the lowest rate of 25 per cent. But in the county as a whole the proportion of poor households was 31 per cent. One in every three families lived in poverty or destitution. The towns do not seem to have been consistently worse off in this respect than the villages. Indeed, Leicester had the surprisingly low proportion of 27·4 per cent. of its population granted exemption from payment of the tax. At Market Harborough (though the total population of 158 households is suspiciously low) the proportion of poor was 22 per cent., at Ashby-de-la-Zouch 23 per cent., and at Hinckley 26·5 per cent. But Loughborough, with 43 per cent. of its households counted poor, Melton Mowbray with 40 per cent., and Lutterworth with 38 per cent., already nourished the seeds of a poor-relief problem that was to become acute a century later.

The numbers of hearths per house, as recorded in the tax returns of 1670, give a rough guide to the size of the different classes of the population. Families living in houses with only one hearth—roughly three out of every five families—comprised the bulk of the labouring population. In Framland hundred the exact proportion was 59 per cent., in East and West Goscote it was the highest anywhere—66 per cent. The average for the county was 62 per cent. Two households in every 5 occupied houses with more than 1 hearth. This group included most of the better-off yeomen and tradesmen and all the gentry. Between one-fifth and one-quarter of Leicestershire households lived in houses with 2 hearths, and 1 in 10 in houses with 3 and 4 hearths. The wealthiest families, who occupied large mansions of more than 10 hearths, represented less than 1 per cent. of the population.[88]

1760–1860

Industrialization. Urban influences, which had for long been seeping into the countryside, gathered the force of a torrent in the century after 1760. They inundated those areas of the county which, because of their proximity to the growing towns, were defenceless, and laid the rest of the county open to the more or less disturbing effects of their long-range currents. In the eastern half of the county these were least disruptive, chiefly because of the absence of any important mineral deposits to stimulate the settlement of industries there. But an important auxiliary factor later on was the absence of a railway line between Melton Mowbray and Market Harborough, due to the steadfast opposition of local landowners and particularly hunting interests.[89] The eastern uplands were thus preserved from colonization by the town, and the chances of reviving a countryside which had been depopulated by old inclosure defeated.[90]

[88] E 179/240/279.
[90] Ibid. 259.

[89] Auty, *Leics.*, 259, 261.

An 18th-century Yeoman's House at Kibworth

A 16th-century Yeoman's House at Littlethorpe

AGRARIAN HISTORY, 1540–1950

Through the growth of Leicester as an important manufacturing centre at the heart of the county, and of Derby and Nottingham on its northern edges, the loose ties of dependence that had always linked these towns with the surrounding villages were forged into chain fetters. The old market-towns of Hinckley and Loughborough became satellite industrial towns, but they were only the more obvious conquests of an industrial empire which gained far more from the subtle infiltration into the villages of urban ways of earning a living. The canals in the 18th century, the railways in the 19th, and the hosiery industry throughout both, attracted an ever-increasing number of landless peasants into jobs that finally severed their lives from deep roots in the land. It was no accident that the hosiery industry began to develop in the west of the county from the mid-17th century onwards, for it was West Goscote hundred that had the highest percentage of poverty-stricken households in 1670, as we have seen, and here that the cheap and abundant labour was to be found by those with knitting-frames to rent out.

Inclosure. Through the rapid growth of population in this century a large labour force was made available for the development of industry. The final inclosure of the county, by reducing the amount of labour needed on the land, further augmented its numbers. Although the last bastion of the open-field system, Medbourne, did not fall until 1842, John Monk, nearly fifty years before, rightly deemed Leicestershire an inclosed county.[91] Between 1761 and the end of the Napoleonic War 123 inclosure acts were passed, leaving only four places to be finally inclosed between 1815 and 1842.[92]

The number of Inclosure Acts in Leicestershire, 1730–1850

1730–40 .	. 2	1781–90 .	. 16	1831–40 .	. 1
1741–50 .	. 1	1791–1800	. 21	1841–50 .	. 1
1751–60 .	. 23	1801–10 .	. 11		—
1761–70 .	. 41	1811–20 .	. 1	Total	. 153
1771–80 .	. 33	1821–30 .	. 2		

In consequence of these changes agrarian history forfeited much of its territory. The amount of farming land which was devoured by the towns was not large. The greater loss was the loss of people, whom the land could no longer employ and whose numbers rose steadily throughout the next two centuries. Whereas agrarian history had long resembled a closely woven fabric, in which farm routine threaded the lives of every country dweller, these tightly knit threads were now gradually loosened and separated. By 1861 the proportion of the population, both male and female, engaged in agricultural occupations, amounted to only 13 per cent. of the whole.[93]

Farming improvements. Set against a background of industrialization, which wrought such rapid change in the lives of individuals, the pace of farming improvements was slow. The most important trends in stock-breeding and crop husbandry have already been described, for the first pioneers belonged to an earlier generation. But much of their work was being done in the seventies, eighties, and nineties. Bakewell himself lived until 1795, while his successors watched a steady improvement in the quality and quantity of his harvest for another half-century.

[91] J. Monk, *General View of Agric. of the County of Leic.*, 45; Pitt estimated in 1809 that no more than 10,000 acres still lay in open fields: W. Pitt, *General View of Agric. of the County of Leic.* 68.

[92] Typescript list of inclosure acts compiled by Mr. W. E. Tate, at the Leics. County Rec. Off.

[93] *1861 Census* [3221], p. 79, H.C. (1863), liii (1); [3221], pp. 556–9, H.C. (1863), liii (2).

It is easy, however, to overestimate the rate at which ideas of improved farming spread.[94] Contemporary writers unwittingly fostered this optimism, because they concentrated attention on the most progressive farms, not on the inefficient ones. Monk's and Pitt's reports to the Board of Agriculture in 1794 and 1809 agreed in portraying Leicestershire as a county that was as progressive as any in its methods, but if some of their enthusiasm were not discounted it would be difficult to explain the pessimism of James Caird in the next generation or so. Investigating the low state of agriculture in 1850, he concluded of Leicestershire 'that hitherto the large proportion of landlords in Leicestershire have given little attention to the improvement of their estates'.[95]

Outside the small circle of improving farmers already mentioned the new methods spread in a haphazard way. The explanation did not lie simply in the inherent conservatism or obstinacy of farmers. The most important obstacle was undoubtedly the shortage of capital. Bakewell's own career—for he was once bankrupt and often in financial difficulties[96]—afforded the best proof of both the costs and the risks of innovations. He had embarked on a programme of reorganization which affected every field, every animal, and every tool he possessed; not everyone's ambitions ran as high as this. But improvements in the initial stages could not help but be expensive. Drainage, for example, was still experimental in Monk's day, and experience was bought at disproportionate expense. Nor were the mistakes always due to ignorance—though this was the chief reason for the drains being sunk sometimes at insufficient depth—for experience carefully gained in one soil might prove to be folly when applied to another.[97]

Moreover, in the realm of stock-breeding, over which Bakewell reigned as king, it was he who was responsible for the policy of keeping prices for hiring animals high. His purpose was understandable enough—to maintain the quality and the reputation of his breeds.[98] It was accepted by members of the Ram Society and Associated Breeders—a club formed by Bakewell and his friends to promote the exchange of information between members.[99] But it evoked much hostility among outsiders, for it placed pedigree stock out of the reach of all but the well-to-do farmers. It is not, therefore, surprising to find that most of the distinguished improving farmers singled out for mention by William Marshall were men of more than average property. Some were the owners of their land, such as Robert Burgess of Hugglescote, who at his death in 1810 left £1,446. 12s. 4d. worth of personal estate—and one share in the Ashby-de-la-Zouch canal 'considered valueless';[1] or William Knowles of Nailstone, grazier, who paid the highest contribution to the land tax in the parish in 1780, and bequeathed legacies totalling £3,350 to be raised by the sale of his property;[2] or Edward Green of Normanton, who owned the manor and most of the lands in his native parish;[3] or George Moore, who received a gold medal for land drainage from the Society of Arts in 1794, and who was lord of the manor of Appleby Parva.[4] The rest were tenant farmers, and included Robert

---

[94] Coke of Holkham calculated that his improvements travelled at the rate of a mile a year: R. E. Prothero, *Engl. Farming Past and Present* (1936), 220.

[95] J. Caird, *Engl. Agric. in 1850–51*, 220.

[96] *D.N.B.* sub Robert Bakewell.

[97] *Jnl. Royal Agric. Soc.*, 2nd ser. ii, no. 4, 292–3.

[98] Monk, *General View*, 29.

[99] Pitt, *General View*, 255.

[1] Leics. County Rec. Off., Land Tax Assessments; Will of Robert Burgess, 1810.

[2] Leics. County Rec. Off., Will of Wm. Knowles, 1784.

[3] Nichols, *Leics.* iv, 812.

[4] Ibid. iv, 440.

Bakewell, whose farm at Dishley was held on a lease at an easy rent;[5] Richard Astley of Odstone, who rented more than 500 acres of the family estate of his brother, and built up a good market for his pedigree stock in Ireland;[6] and Thomas Parkinson of Quorndon, less affluent than the rest, for he rented land taxed at only £12. 9s. 1d., and left £520 in bequests at his death, but whose confidence in the future of farming was readily expressed in his wish that his son be 'put to the farming business'.[7]

The close personal ties that existed between these farmers is one of the incidental items of information emerging from their wills. Robert Bakewell, senior, was apparently connected with the Pagets of Ibstock by ties of kinship as well as those of business;[8] Thomas Paget was the executor of William Knowles of Nailstone; and Robert Burgess was the executor of another improving farmer, John Stone of Quorndon, who left a competence of £1,065. 15s.[9]

Judging by the size of their farms and the value of their property, the economic status of these 'improvers' was high. From this group of gentry and independent yeomen, and from the aristocracy who adopted their methods, were recruited the members of the various farmers' clubs that came into existence. The Agriculture Society was one of these, presided over by the Earl of Moira, with William Pochin as one of its vice-presidents, and Richard Weston, an agricultural bibliographer, as its secretary. It met annually in October at Leicester, and when Monk was writing in the 1790's had just decided to set up an experimental farm in Queniborough lordship.[10] Of its subsequent work nothing is known, but it was the forerunner of many another society founded in the 19th century with similar objectives.[11]

The most notable experiments and improvements of these years were carried out not on the average-sized farms of 100–200 acres but on those of 200–500 acres.[12] Monk's statement to this effect has been lost sight of, though its truth was heavily underlined by the fact that successive writers drew their illustrations from the estates of the biggest landowners, the Duke of Rutland, the Earl of Moira, and Lord Berners.[13] Even on these estates, apart from the home farm, expenditure on capital improvements, such as land drainage, was cautiously undertaken, for all classes of rural society were hard hit by the long years of depression that followed the end of the French wars. It was not until the 1830's that the strong land on the Duke of Rutland's estate began to be drained and much-needed farm buildings erected.[14]

Machinery, for which the farmer shouldered entire financial responsibility, was sufficiently costly to put it out of the reach of most small farmers. Drilling machines were an exception, but in Pitt's day they were in general use only on the larger arable farms.[15] The same was true of steam-driven machinery by the middle of the 19th century. On Lord Berners's lands it effected drastic economies, being used for threshing, grinding, sawing, and for work in the fields

---

[5] Pitt, *General View*, 217. [6] Nichols, *Leics.* iv, 916.
[7] Leics. County Rec. Off., Land Tax Assessments; Will of Thos. Parkinson, 1784.
[8] Leics. County Rec. Off., Will of Robert Bakewell.
[9] Leics. County Rec. Off., Will of John Stone, 1783.
[10] Monk, *General View*, 63; G. E. Fussell, *More Old Engl. Farming Books, 1731–93*, 85–86.
[11] *Jnl. Royal Agric. Soc.*, 2nd ser. ii, no. 4, 336.
[12] Monk, *General View*, 9.
[13] *Jnl. Royal Agric. Soc.*, 2nd ser. ii, no. 4, 303.
[14] Ibid. 304.
[15] Pitt, *General View*, 59.

hitherto performed by horses.[16] But who could have justified such elaborate equipment on less than 500 acres?[17]

Farming progress, however, cannot be measured by machines alone. Increasing regional specialization was a significant stride forward in the use of land. That it had already proceeded some way by the end of the 17th century is made clear by the observations of William Camden and Richard Blome, and has been confirmed by evidence gathered together since then to show the predominance of the grazier in the eastern half of the county and his rarer appearance in the west.[18] But it was not until the 19th century that the broad differences already observed between the husbandry prevailing on the Keuper marls of the west and the boulder and lias clays of the east were accentuated so as to bring out the finer local variations.

In the north-west of the county the cold clay was interspersed with outcrops of sandy, free-working soil, which, owing to their proximity to the towns of Nottingham and Derby, provided ideal conditions for market-gardening. In the Charnwood area the soil was almost invariably poor in quality, while in the south-west it again formed a mixture of stiff and light clay. Both districts north and south of Charnwood were still fairly evenly divided between grassland and tillage in the mid-19th century, conversion to pasture never having followed consistently on inclosure. At Thurlaston 1,310 acres were divided almost equally between arable and grass in 1801 and 1851. At Norton-juxta-Twycross, where in 1801 there were only 394 acres under the plough, farmers came to lean more heavily towards tillage, and in 1844 the arable area had grown to 1,064 acres. In other places the balance struck between crops and grass was nearer two to one in favour of grassland. At Desford in 1845 there were 1,400 acres under grass and 549 acres under crops, but even so the arable area had increased since 1801, when it was reported as 398 acres. At Twycross there were 924 acres of grass and 542 acres under the plough in 1850, but here again the arable had been extended from 320 acres in 1801.[19] Grazing farms in the west were not common, the more usual being dairy farms with some 20–30 cows, specializing in the production of milk and cheese.[20]

In the eastern half of the county, the liassic clay was stiff in the south and more friable in the north.[21] The stiffer soils, because they were intractable to the plough, were being steadily turned over to pasture, and in the region of Market Harborough more than repaid the care devoted to improving the quality of the grass. Towards the north and particularly in the Belvoir district, because of the poorer quality of the pasture compared with the south, dairy and sheep pastures were the most common. But, because of the lighter texture of the soil, a larger acreage was still kept in tillage.[22] Dairy farms, which were usually smaller than grazing farms, were particularly numerous on the eastern uplands, in the Melton Mowbray, Kettleby, and Nether Broughton area.[23] This was the district in which the famous Stilton cheese had first been made, and on which Leicestershire's reputation as a dairying county chiefly rested. It first attracted

---

[16] *Jnl. Royal Agric. Soc.*, 2nd ser. ii, no. 4, 309–13.

[17] Arthur Young put forward the same argument. See Prothero, *Engl. Farming*, 206.

[18] *Agric. Hist.* xxv, 17.

[19] W. G. Hoskins, 'Leics. Crop Returns of 1801', *T.L.A.S.* xxiv, 127–153; Leics. Co. Rec. Off., Tithe Awards.

[20] *Jnl. Royal Agric. Soc.*, 2nd ser. ii, no. 4, 314, 316; Auty, *Leics.*, 253, 250, 248.

[21] Auty, op. cit. 253.   [22] Pitt, *General View*, 154.

[23] *Jnl. Royal Agric. Soc.*, 2nd ser. ii, no. 4, 302.

attention in the early 18th century when it was made by Mrs. Elizabeth Orton of Little Dalby, a lady who had learned the art before her marriage when she worked as a housekeeper to the Ashby family. The cheese was then called Quenby cheese, though the recipe used by the Ashbys was always known to them as 'Lady Beaumont's recipe' and must have originated with the Beaumont family of Coleorton or Stoughton. It did not acquire its nation-wide reputation or its accepted name of Stilton cheese until Mrs. Orton began to supply it to the landlord of the Bell Inn at Stilton.[24] Then, when the recipe became known in the neighbourhood, its manufacture spread to almost every village in north-east Leicestershire. Dalby, in fact, was said to pay its rents with the profits of its cheese.[25] Southern Leicestershire produced many good varieties of red cheese, which some preferred to Stilton, but they never attained the popularity of the latter.[26] In the first half of the 19th century it was calculated that 1,500 tons of cheese were sent out of the county each year—the produce of 7,500 cows.[27]

Whereas in the west husbandry was more evenly balanced between grass and arable, it was not unusual to find some grazing farms on the richest land of the south and east without any arable at all. In 1801 only 30 out of 1,378 acres in Carlton Curlieu were under crops. By 1850 little appreciable change had taken place: 140 acres were under crops and 1,148 acres in grass.[28] In the course of the century, however, circumstances combined to shake the convictions of those who regarded tillage as a mere nuisance on the grazing farm. It was in part due to the fact that not all the grassland turned out to be of first-rate quality. Monk's opinion that the restrictions which landlords had placed on the breaking up of pasture for tillage had ceased to serve their own or their tenants' interests had won general acceptance among thoughtful farmers and writers by the 1860's.[29] Then, too, store stock gradually became scarcer and dearer, and the grazier who relied on buying his stock every spring began to find himself at a financial disadvantage. The risks of bringing in livestock from elsewhere were manifested by several outbreaks of disease. As a result grazing farms without arable, which had fetched £3 an acre, became less desirable than those with sufficient land under crops to enable cattle to be kept through the winter. Moscrop in the mid-1860's spoke of this change of front as 'tending somewhat towards a revolution'.[30]

The effects of inclosure and agricultural depression. Greater specialization in land use during this hundred years was accelerated by the final inclosure of the county, and marked a further step forward in the direction of productive efficiency and labour economy. Looked at from the social aspect, however, inclosure seemed at the time to be the principal instrument in tearing the age-old fabric of rural society asunder. The fall in the demand for wage labour was attested and lamented by many observers, but its extent cannot, at this distance of time, be satisfactorily measured. The impact of inclosure on the owners of land, however, is a less obscure aspect of its history. Many accounts have been given of inclosure procedure, underlining the hardships which it inflicted on

[24] W. G. Hoskins, *Midland Engl.*, 95–96. Dr. Hoskins favours Mary Ashby of Coleorton as the author of the recipe. She was the dau. of Sir Erasmus de la Fontaine, who was born at Kirby Bellars, only 7 miles from Quenby.   [25] Marshall, *Rural Econ.* i, 356.

[26] W. G. Hoskins, *Midland Engl.*, 96.

[27] Pitt, *General View*, 228.

[28] *T.L.A.S.* xxiv, 139; Leics. Co. Rec. Off., Tithe Awards.

[29] Monk, *General View*, 58; *Sel. Cttee. on Agric. Customs*, H.C. 461/0.119, para. 3772 (1866), vi.

[30] *Jnl. Royal Agric. Soc.*, 2nd ser. ii, no. 4, 295, 299.

the small owner. The truth of these criticisms has been borne out by random illustrations from different counties, showing how the precarious situation of the small peasants after inclosure was aggravated by the growing need for expenditure on capital improvements, and by the costs of stocking land that was being turned over to pasture for the first time; and that, although agricultural prosperity during the Napoleonic War arrested their decline, the sharp depression that followed after 1815 was enough to thrust many small owners off the land within two or three generations from the time of inclosure.

In investigating the more restricted area of one county, contradictory evidence tends to blur the firm outlines of these generalizations, without, however, obscuring their central truth. It would in any case be surprising, bearing in mind the distinctive characteristics of Leicestershire agriculture in 1800 and today, to find outstanding evidence of the classic kind. In the first place the county was predominantly pastoral by 1815, and it was generally agreed that the depression, which lasted without noticeable intermission from 1816 to 1837, reacted less severely on the pastoral than on the arable farmer. Moreover, in tracing the decline of the small owner, it is important to remember that in 1939 holdings of less than 50 acres still represented 48·1 per cent. of all holdings in the county.[31] This figure represents a considerable reduction on the figure of 82 per cent. that was average at the time of inclosure in the second half of the 18th century,[32] but it shows that the smallholder is even now far from extinction. The principal problem, therefore, is to decide whether the decline in the number of small owners was especially rapid in the hundred years after the first inclosure acts, or whether it was a slower and less dramatic development that has still not yet reached its close.

The statistical material for solving this problem is imperfect. Official agricultural statistics do not begin until 1866, and then supply only sum totals for the whole county. Before that date the inclosure awards and the land-tax assessments of 1780–1832 alone provide comparable material, but they have serious shortcomings. It is extremely doubtful whether the valuations placed on land when the land tax was first introduced in 1692 were consistent as between one parish and another. By 1780, when the assessments first become available to the historian, they had certainly fallen out of step. The grossest disproportion was that prevailing between rural and newly urbanized parishes, but the whole structure of the tax valuation was by that time outmoded. For the purpose of tracing changes in land distribution, therefore, these assessments serve only as a rough and ready guide. They can be turned to some use only if their deficiencies are constantly borne in mind, and care is taken to choose as comparable samples only those parishes that remained until 1832 predominantly agricultural.

The results of this analysis show many zigzag threads in the pattern of development, with certain overriding regularities. The immediate effect of inclosure was in nearly all cases to increase the number of proprietors, since land was granted to cottagers who had previously had only common and pasture rights. In some pastoral parishes like Sharnford and Sileby inclosure, far from causing gradual depopulation, led instead to a steady increase in the number of owners until 1832. At Sharnford their numbers rose from 36 in 1765 to 49 in

[31] Auty, *Leics.*, 269.
[32] Average taken from a sample of holdings at the time of the inclosure awards.

1781 and 57 in 1830, and at Sileby from 65 in 1760 to 75 in 1781 and 102 in 1832. At Stathern the 37 proprietors in 1791 had more than doubled by 1832.

There were examples of a reverse kind, however, at Houghton-on-the-Hill, Gumley, and Desford, where the decline in numbers was constant after 1780. Here the vacant land was becoming concentrated in the hands of the medium and large landowners, those who paid £2 and more in tax. At Desford 9 people paid 64 per cent. of the tax in 1830 compared with 13 who paid 55 per cent. in 1781. At Gumley 8 people paid 89 per cent. in 1781, while in 1832 there were 7 paying 91·7 per cent.

But in spite of these contradictory trends there was in most places a regular increase in the number of small owners paying 10s. and below. At Billesdon, where the total number of proprietors had been constantly fluctuating (though in 1781 and 1832 it stood at 53 and 55 respectively) there were 29 smallholders in 1781 paying 9·25 per cent. of the tax, and in 1832, 33 paying 10 per cent. At Sileby, a parish where the landowning population had grown steadily, there were 34 paying 5·9 per cent. in 1781 and 60 in 1832 paying 6·7 per cent. At Desford, where the population was falling, the number of those paying 10s. and less fell from 52 in 1781 to 43 in 1830, but the number of people paying 4s. and less rose from 20 to 25. Only at Houghton-on-the-Hill were they being steadily driven out of existence, 25 remaining in 1832 where there had been 35 in 1780, or, among those paying 4s. and less, 9 remaining out of 22.

There were, in short, few signs of a decline in the number of small owners in the years up to 1832. But what was equally significant was that the amount of tax paid per head was falling. Among those who paid 10s. and less, the average amount paid fell from 5s. to 3s. at Sileby, from 4s. 7d. to 3s. 9d. at Billesdon, and from 5s. to 4s. 6d. at Desford. If the tax can be used as a very rough guide to the size of holdings, it suggests that individual allotments were being reduced in size rather than in number. While the smallholding was tending to be eaten away by the depression, the larger owners, paying £2 and more in tax, were enlarging their individual holdings without suffering any striking diminution in their numbers.

When these conclusions are set beside the evidence of witnesses to the Parliamentary Committees and Royal Commissions on agriculture in the twenties and thirties, there is little to suggest the dramatic disappearance of the small peasant either at the time of the inclosure or in the course of the long depression after 1815. On the first point, indeed, it is likely that the profits which the peasant owner had enjoyed during the war years had enabled him to pay off these old liabilities, for none of the later witnesses to government inquiries considered inclosure debts to be a source of worry. What they emphasized was that small owners had been encouraged by high prices during the war to embark on expensive improvements, thereby charging their land with interest payments which became a heavy burden when prices fell.[33] From their personal experience, they testified to the fact that owner-occupiers only kept their heads above water by drawing on their capital. They cut their expenditure on labour and maintenance to the minimum, but long years of unprofitable farming relentlessly drained away their reserves.[34] At Great Easton eleven out of the twenty-five proprietors who owned 10 acres and less

[33] *Sel. Cttee. on Agric.*, H.C. 612, pp. 398–9 (1833), v.
[34] Ibid., p. 403.

at the time of the inclosure in 1804 disappeared between 1820 and 1827. This example of heavy casualties revealed the effects of the depression in a dramatic way.[35] More often they were concealed by the determination of owners to retain their land as long as possible. The situation was best described in the words of Farmer John Buckley, who stated in 1833: 'They may not have sustained a visible loss, but the value of their estates has fallen very considerably.'[36] This assessment of the situation endorses the statistical conclusions reached above. The exhaustion of capital among small landed proprietors was an insidious disease, the progress of which could not be measured in statistical terms until long after 1832. Spokesmen before governmental commissions in the thirties pointed to this hidden factor as of greater significance than the more flagrant evidence of ruined yeomen.

Among tenant farmers the situation was simpler to analyse. The rate at which farms changed hands in the mid-twenties spoke for itself.[37] At the beginning of the war rents had been adjusted to a wheat price of 80s. a quarter.[38] When wheat reached a peak price of 126s. 6d. a quarter in 1812, tenants enjoyed a substantial margin of profit. But when it fell from 74s. 4d. in 1814 to 65s. 7d. in 1815 and 56s. 1d. in 1821, rents did not fall correspondingly.[39] Not until after 1824, and then only in certain districts, was any reduction allowed. Tenants clung to their land as long as they could, but the effects of a steady shrinkage of capital were not so long concealed as was the case with owner-occupiers, particularly as leases in Leicestershire were granted for a short term of one year and could therefore be quickly terminated.[40]

The distinction drawn between owner-occupiers and tenants takes account of only one aspect of the agricultural depression. The burden was unevenly distributed between arable and pasture and between dairying and grazing farms. Arable land was the first to be hit, since corn prices fell before other prices, and because the outgoings on labour were higher. Moreover, any attempt at a reduction of labour costs merely increased the poor rate.[41] On the heaviest clay lands, where farmers were usually those with least capital, farms were being allowed to go out of cultivation by the thirties.[42]

After 1821 meat prices took the same downward path,[43] ruining graziers in some areas where outbreaks of disease occurred, but benefiting others when the temporary shortage increased prices again. John Buckley, a mixed farmer, who thought that graziers were no better off than arable farmers, gave evidence in 1833 that he had 60 per cent. fewer orders for the hire of ram tups than before the war and paid two-thirds less to hire bulls.[44]

Dairy farms, particularly those situated near the large towns, were protected from the keener winds of depression, for their market was assured even in the worst times.[45] John Ellis of Beaumont Leys near Leicester, who since

[35] Analysis of Inclosure Award and Land Tax Assessments for Great Easton, furnished by T. Hughes.
[36] *Sel. Cttee. on Agric.*, H.C. 612, p. 398 (1833), v.
[37] Ibid., H.C. 465, p. 77 (1836), viii (2).
[38] *Sel. Cttee. on Pets. relating to Agric. Distress*, H.C. 668, p. 199 (1821), ix.
[39] Prothero, *Engl. Farming*, 489.
[40] *Sel. Cttee. on Agric.*, H.C. 465, pp. 75, 77 (1836), viii (2); *Sel. Cttee. on Agric.*, H.C. 612, p. 395 (1833), v; Monk, *General View*, 59; Caird, *English Agriculture*, 219.
[41] *Sel. Cttee. on Agric. Distress*, H.C. 668, p. 197 (1821), ix.
[42] *Sel. Cttee. on Agric.*, H.C. 465, p. 78 (1836), viii (2); *Sel. Cttee. on Agric.*, H.C. 612, p. 399 (1833), v.
[43] *Sel. Cttee. on Agric. Distress*, H.C. 668, p. 198 (1821), ix.
[44] *Sel. Cttee. on Agric.*, H.C. 612, pp. 395, 397 (1833), v.
[45] *Sel. Cttee. on Agric.*, H.C. 465, pp. 72–73 (1836), viii (2).

1828 had paid £650 a year for a dairy farm of 374 acres, which his father had rented in 1807 at £370, had no complaint to make of agricultural conditions in 1836.[46] His remarks on dairy farming earned general agreement among his colleagues. But was this John Ellis the gentleman of the same place who in 1846 had £475,800 invested in railway shares?[47] If so, his farm was established on such a financial basis as to make his experiences of the depression a rather special case. Had he had less capital and fallen on evil days, he would have found himself squeezed out more quickly than impoverished farmers in more exclusively rural areas.[48] At Wigston Magna, where townspeople created keen competition for farms, the small owners were being rapidly dispossessed by the larger. The number of small owner-occupiers paying less than £2 in land tax fell from 33 to 22 between 1781 and 1831, while the total number of proprietors fell from 94 to 64.[49] This trend of events was not usual in rural parishes that were not so exposed to urban influences.

Of the condition of agricultural labourers more was implied than directly stated in parliamentary inquiries. It was generally agreed, in spite of the fact that no investigation into the state of agriculture took place between 1821 and 1833, that conditions had deteriorated most noticeably after 1824. From then until after 1837 wages fell from between 13s. and 15s. to 10s. The subsidizing of wages, intended as a remedy for this distress, only aggravated it and produced widespread unemployment every winter, between November and March.[50] The 1834 Poor Law brought to an end the worst abuses to which the agricultural labourer was exposed, but a general revival of agriculture after 1837, leading to a boom period between 1853 and 1863, did more than anything else to improve wage-rates.

The extent of the revival after 1837 is indicated in the renewed interest shown in farming improvements. A reduction in the costs of transport, made possible by the coming of the railways, enabled manures and artificial fertilizers to be much more widely used. The costs of delivering lime to Leicester, to take but one example, were lowered from 10s. to 5s. 6d. a ton.[51] A cheaper system of drainage with straw, introduced to the county by John Ellis of Beaumont Leys, and known as the Essex method, led to improvements which many landlords for financial reasons could not otherwise have contemplated.[52] The Government gave assistance from 1846 by granting loans for drainage improvements, and by enlarging the scheme in 1864 to include grants for the construction of buildings, roads, railways, and canals. These measures resulted in Leicestershire in the expenditure of some £35,344 between 1864 and 1901, principally by the larger landlords. Edward Frewen of Cold Overton spent £22,154 of this on drainage, fencing, buildings, roads, and watering-places for cattle. Sir Arthur Hazlerigg spent £4,464 on the restoration and improvement of his house at Noseley. Earl Howe in 1901 spent £4,428 on improvements to his mansion and the installation of electricity at Gopsall and on his estates in the neighbourhood.[53]

46 Ibid., p. 72.
47 *Railways Subscription Contr.*, H.C. 473, p. 94 (1846), xxxviii.
48 *Sel. Cttee. on Agric.*, H.C. 612, pp. 399, 402 (1833), v.
49 W. G. Hoskins, 'Midland Peasant' (unpublished hist. of Wigston Magna).
50 *Sel. Cttee. on Agric.*, H.C. 612, p. 398 (1833), v; Prothero, *Engl. Farming*, 525.
51 *Sel. Cttee. on Agric.*, H.C. 465, p. 73 (1836), viii (2).
52 Ibid. 72.
53 Ministry of Agric., Land Division, *Reg. of Loans.*

Another government measure intended to help landlords and farmers to their feet again after the depression was the Tithe Commutation Act of 1836. The antiquated burden of the tithe of produce in kind was replaced by a money payment which varied according to the current price of corn. Tithe-redemption awards for Leicestershire do not relate to the whole county, however, for in many places the opportunity had been taken at the time of the inclosure to redeem the tithe payment.[54]

The economic and social problems which beset agriculture in the period 1760–1860 have been described above in isolation from their setting, but they cannot be fully understood until they are set once more against their proper background, and considered in relation to the problems created by the growing industrialization of the towns. Social dislocation in the countryside was not the restricted problem of the landowner, the farmer, and the agricultural labourer. It affected that increasing army of country-born people who could find no employment on the land. Already in 1765 at Wigston Magna this was no trivial matter, for 70 per cent. of the population were without land and had to get their living from wage labour.[55] Yet their chances of finding agricultural work were fast diminishing, as more inclosed land was laid down to grass. On the Duke of Rutland's estates, which remained almost untouched by inclosure until 1766, all the richest land that was valued at more than a guinea an acre was laid down to permanent grass, and the poorer land, formerly used for sheep-walks, broken up for arable.[56] An anonymous pamphleteer had calculated in 1772 that 1,000 acres of good open-field arable would employ only five families after inclosure and conversion compared with twenty families before.[57] George Kilby of Queniborough testified to this fact two generations later when he estimated the cost of labour on grassland at 4s. an acre per year. On a comparatively large farm of 200 acres the labour bill amounted to the trifling sum of £40 p.a.[58]

Industrial employment. Economy became a doubly effective argument in favour of conversion to pasture when industry began to compete seriously with agriculture for labour in the 18th century. From the second half of the 17th century, when the hosiery trade established itself firmly in Leicester and Hinckley, the industry had been spreading quickly to the villages, especially in the western half of the county. Already in 1760 it is probable that the population was more densely concentrated there than in the east. But the growth of industry in the western half finally sealed the distinction. In 1861 the thickest area of settlement was in Leicester and the Soar valley, where 102,139 people lived, but apart from this concentration in the centre of the county there were 84,478 living in the west compared with only 43,447 in the east.[59]

Industry absorbed the landless rural population and by 1801 gave employment to almost twice the number of people engaged in agriculture.[60] It attracted labour by appearing to offer higher wages. Pitt estimated in 1809 that a family with four children needed about 16s. a week to maintain it. The highest farming wage was 15s., the industrial wage nearer a guinea.[61] But figures like this,

[54] W. Pitt, *General View of the Agric. of the County of Leic.*, 46–47.
[55] W. G. Hoskins, 'Midland Peasant'.
[56] Pitt, *General View*, 14–15.
[57] G. Slater, *Engl. Peasantry and the Enclosure of the Common Fields*, 96.
[58] *Sel. Cttee. on Agric. Customs*, H.C. 461/0.119, para. 3820 (1866), vi.
[59] Moscrop, 'Rep. on the Farming of Leics.', *Jnl. Royal Agric. Soc.*, 2nd ser. ii, no. 4, 289.
[60] Forty-two thousand engaged in industry compared with 24,000 in agriculture in 1801: Pitt, *General View*, 323.   [61] Ibid. 327.

far from suggesting that an increasing proportion of the rural population was enjoying a rising standard of life, only underlined the more heavily its precarious nature. For industrial workers were exposed to recurring periods of unemployment; their claims on poor relief rose relentlessly. To the Duke of Rutland the connexion between industry and poverty in the countryside was simple and direct. It was one of his boasts that because he had forbidden the introduction of stocking manufacture on his estates he had thereby kept the poor rates low.[62] The explanation was in fact more complex than this, but it contained much truth. At Barrow-on-Soar in 1801 poor rates reached a figure of £2,000, representing an annual charge of 13s. 4d. on every acre of land in the parish. Woodhouse rates had risen within living memory from £100 to £1,200 and cost landowners 20s. per acre. In the whole county between 1776 and 1803 the poor rate (of which a fifth was devoted to purposes other than maintaining the poor) had increased from £26,360 to £107,568.[63]

The poor rate bore principally on owners of land and allowed the captains of industry to get off almost scot free. Inevitably it became increasingly difficult to find tenants for farms, and at one time it was stated by William Pochin that the whole of Wigston Magna was thrown out of cultivation for that reason.[64] The new Poor Law of 1834 had the merit that it saved the farmer from extinction.

Social structure. The effects of industrial development in the towns reached out to touch every social class in the countryside. The monopoly of social prestige hitherto enjoyed by the owners of land was for the first time effectively challenged by the manufacturers and merchants, whose wealth was measured in terms of factory buildings, machinery, stocks, and capital. On the whole these two social groups remained tolerably distinct. Those who invested the largest sums in railway shares in 1846, for example, were not at the same time the biggest landowners in the county. There were, of course, exceptions like the Hazleriggs, who owned 2,162 acres of land and had between them some £25,250 invested in railway shares.[65] More usual were the families whose younger branches had ventured into business while the older preserved their ancestral estates in land. The Pagets of Ibstock, who in the 18th century earned a solid reputation as improving farmers, and whose land in Leicestershire, vested in Thomas Paget, ran to 3,950 acres in 1873, had been launched into banking in 1800, when Thomas Paget's father, at the age of 21, became a partner in the new Leicestershire bank. His marriage in 1807 to Anne, the daughter of John Pares, another grazier turned banker, consolidated this advance into new territory. From the same family was descended George Byng Paget of Sutton Bonnington, whose principal source of income certainly did not lie in the ownership of land, for his son inherited only 47 acres in Leicestershire and Nottinghamshire, but who possessed £525,740 worth of railway shares in 1846.[66] Few of the big landed gentry boasted large-scale investments in industrial property as well.

---

[62] Ibid. 15.

[63] Ibid. 48–49.

[64] Hoskins, 'Midland Peasant'.

[65] *Return of Owners of Land*, C. 1097, H.C. (1874), lxxii (1); *Railway Subscription Contr.*, H.C. 473 (1846), xxxviii.

[66] *Ret. of Owners of Land*; *Leic. Advertiser*, 14 May 1932, 12; Burke, *Landed Gentry* (1871), ii, 1042; *Railway Subscription Contr.* Paget's Bank was sold in 1894. Geo. Byng Paget's son was Sir Ernest Paget, Chairman of the Midland Railway Co. for many years: *Leic. Advertiser*, 4 June 1932, 3.

Where land was concerned the gentry had little competition to fear, for business men were content to invest the bulk of their capital in other enterprises. The large estates in Leicestershire, therefore, tended to remain in the hands of the older gentry. In 1780 21 per cent. of the land tax of the county was paid by only 73 individuals, each paying £50 and above. A further 700 people, each paying £7 and above, were responsible for another 19 per cent. of the tax. This indication of the concentration of landownership may count for little when all the reservations necessary in using the land-tax assessments are made. As one would expect, it proves to be an extremely conservative estimate when compared with the results of the more accurate, though still incomplete, Return of Owners of Land of 1873, a century later. At that date 86 families alone owned half the total area of the county and 16 families owned one-quarter. Whereas 773 people had been assessed for 40 per cent. of the land tax in 1780, 801 persons owned 98 per cent. of the land, judged by acreage, in 1873.[67]

It is impossible to estimate with any precision the rate at which land accumulated in fewer and fewer hands in the century after 1760. The pace of change is clearly exaggerated by setting figures taken from an antiquated land tax in 1780 beside a distribution of acreage in 1873. But there need be little doubt on the main issue that the currents flowed in the same direction as in the 18th century. The majority of the great landed families were unshakeably rooted, and but for the accidents of birth, marriage, and death their position in the county was exposed to few hazards. Only the families of the Earl of Harborough and the Duke of Montagu had died out for want of heirs, and the Boothbys of Tooley Park through extravagance and dissipation.[68]

Of the families with more than 4,000 acres each, who occupied the front rank in 1873, 8 had occupied the same position among the county magnates a hundred years earlier. The 5 families who had been displaced since 1780 were still substantial Leicestershire gentry, owning more than 1,000 and usually more than 2,000 acres. That this was no mean estate is evident from the fact that only 84 people in the county possessed more than 1,000 acres, and only 39 more than 2,000 acres.[69] The Nevills with 1,657 acres, the Hazleriggs with 2,162 acres, and the Frankses with 2,725 acres, therefore, remained distinguished landowners, while the disappearance of the other two names from among the county's first dozen and a half families merely meant that they had extended their estates in neighbouring counties. The Palmers of Carlton Curlieu owned 1,692 acres in Leicestershire but had another 2,429 acres in Northamptonshire. The Caves of Stanford Hall had 2,896 acres in Leicestershire and another 1,065 acres in Northamptonshire.[70]

The new names among the biggest landowners in 1873 included several notable families long entrenched in Leicestershire and on its borders. The Pochins of Barkby and Edmondthorpe and the Curzons of Breedon were examples of families who had advanced by slow stages. By 1873 they owned 8,000 and 4,753 acres respectively. Henry Keck with 6,530 acres was the surviving heir of the Beaumonts of Stoughton Grange. The Earl of Denbigh, head of the Fielding family, which had been seated at Newnham Paddox

[67] Leics. County Rec. Off., Land Tax Assessments; Ret. of Owners of Land.
[68] Complete Peerage, vi, 295 ff.; ix, 110 ff.; J. B. Firth, Highways and Byways in Leics., 407.
[69] Summary of Ret. of Owners of Land, H.C. 335, p. 9 (1876), lxxx (1).
[70] Ret. of Owners of Land.

(Warw.) since the early 17th century, continued to hold 5,176 acres in Leicestershire as a reminder of the family's early home at Lutterworth.[71]

Marriage alliances brought several new names to the head of the list. The Earl of Dysart with 8,421 acres was connected by a marriage a century before with the Manners family, though 18,025 acres of his total estate in 1883 of 27,190 acres lay in Lincolnshire.[72] The De Lisles with 6,857 acres held land in Garendon and Gracedieu by right of inheritance from the Phillipps family.[73] Lord Berners was the owner of Keythorpe Hall and 5,586 acres, his connexions with Leicestershire being derived from his kinship with the Wilsons of Allexton.[74]

The Duke of Rutland remained by far the largest property-owner, with 30,109 acres in Leicestershire and 40,000 acres in six other counties, chiefly in Derbyshire. Second to these were the lands of the Hastings family, vested in 1873 in the Countess of Loudoun, and amounting to 10,175 acres, one-third the size of the Rutland estate. The Earl of Stamford owned 9,013 acres, the Hartopps 7,194 acres, the Dixies of Market Bosworth 5,491 acres, and the Herricks of Beaumanor, whose ancestors had been mayors of Leicester in the mid-16th century, 5,004 acres. The three families descended from Viscount Wentworth, Lord Maynard, and the Earl of Aylesford each possessed more than 4,000 acres.[75]

Through trade and good business Lord Howe attained eminence enough to be ranked third to the Duke of Rutland and the Countess of Loudoun. His career illustrated the golden opportunities that were opened to the enterprising industrialist by the flourishing conditions of industry in the late 17th century, for the estate at Gopsall was built on the profits of Humphrey Jennens, a great ironmaster of Birmingham, whose father, John, had been an ironmonger there until he died in 1651. Humphrey's business grew until he owned furnaces in many places in Warwickshire, Staffordshire, Shropshire, and at Whitwick on the edge of Charnwood. Many family histories through four generations have followed the same course as that of the Jennenses. Humphrey's son, Charles, studied at the Middle Temple, and was the first to live on the estate at Gopsall, but he did not go into the iron business. Nor were the business qualities of Humphrey Jennens revived in Charles's son, though the family tradition of great public generosity survived. He built the great mansion at Gopsall (demolished in 1951), maintained a magnificent household there, and was a collector and renowned patron of the arts. The estate at his death passed to Penn Assheton Curzon, who had married his niece, Lady Sophia Howe.[76]

The mansion at Gopsall emulated the grandeur of the stately homes of the nobility, which reached their apogee in this century. The great estates, with their spacious parks and gardens, first laid out in the early 18th century, emphasized more than anything else the gulf that now yawned between the richest landowners and the merely well-to-do gentry. Their houses resembled palaces, their lands petty kingdoms with well-marked frontiers of brick and stone. Both pride and good taste were manifest in many fine buildings and in enormous expenditure devoted to taming and beautifying the countryside.

Schemes of afforestation were undertaken in the 18th century which bore

---

[71] Ibid.; *Leic. Advertiser*, 16 July 1932, 10.
[72] *Complete Peerage*, iv, 562 et seq.
[73] Burke, *Landed Gentry* (1871), i, 340.
[74] *Complete Peerage*, ii, 153 ff.
[75] *Ret. of Owners of Land.*
[76] Nichols, *Leics.* iv, 856–7.

full fruit in the 19th. Thomas Hitt, the author of a treatise on fruit-trees published in 1755, first learned his trade at Belvoir, where it was one of his duties in 1724 to plant a warren with oaks.[77] These plantations were steadily enlarged until by 1866 the Duke had 1,700 acres of woodland.[78] At Donington Park at the beginning of the 19th century Lord Moira had 400–500 acres.[79]

In the south of the county a larger scheme was undertaken when the Revd. William Hanbury, rector of Church Langton, planted a nursery ground of 50 acres with the seeds of many different trees, mainly from North America, in order to foster the art of tree-planting. By selling young trees, and gradually extending his plantations (they were estimated to be worth £10,000 in 1758), he earned enough money to devote the proceeds of a trust fund to decorating the church at Langton, providing an organ, and supporting an organist and schoolmaster. But from a modest plan, 'conducive to the Glory of God and the advantage of society', it grew to a mammoth enterprise earmarking revenues for centuries ahead. It envisaged profits that would pay for the building of a village hospital, a minster, a public library, and a choral college at Oxford. None of these more ambitious dreams was realized, but the trees which Hanbury planted have remained a fine and lasting memorial to him. He had been responsible for some of the plantations at Gumley Hall, where Joseph Cradock later spent lavishly on its buildings and gardens, and traces of his work still survive in neighbouring villages like Laughton.[80]

Most of the fine buildings erected in this period exist today, though they have often been put to new uses. Georgian residences like Prestwold Hall, where John Nichols declared in 1800 that probably more trees had been planted within the previous thirty years than anywhere else in the county;[81] Belvoir Castle, which was rebuilt between 1801 and 1816 at a cost of more than £60,000;[82] Donington Hall, the home of the Hastings family after Ashby Castle was demolished in the Civil War, and which was rebuilt at the end of the 18th century:[83] these are the silent witnesses to that elegant-mannered life which was one aspect of the social history of the 18th and 19th centuries.

Land use. Crop selection in a county where dairying and grazing held pride of place, where, according to Monk's rough estimate, the population grew less than half the corn which it consumed, was principally a matter of satisfying the needs of livestock.[84] Normally some 15–20 per cent. of a 200-acre farm was given over to arable,[85] and of the crops of the normal rotation (oats, wheat, turnips, barley, and clover) only wheat was not fed to animals. Barley, which had at one time been used for bread, was exclusively devoted to brewing and livestock-feeding by the beginning of the 19th century,[86] and, although it was less important than it had been in the 16th century, in 1801 it still occupied some 26 per cent. of the arable area.[87] Rye, in the few places where it continued to be grown (in 1801 only 100 acres in the county were sown with rye), served as early spring pasture for sheep.[88]

[77] G. E. Fussell, *More Old Engl. Farming Books*, 29.
[78] *Jnl. Royal Agric. Soc.*, 2nd ser., no. 4, 332.   [79] Pitt, *General View*, 171.
[80] *D.N.B.*; Firth, *Highways and Byways*, 223.   [81] Nichols, *Leics.* iii, 355.
[82] W. G. Hoskins, *Midland Engl.*, 59. The estimate of cost was given in 1809, before completion: Pitt, *General View*, 21.
[83] Firth, *Highways and Byways*, 118.   [84] J. Monk, *General View*, 58.
[85] Ibid. 10.   [86] Pitt, *General View*, 109.
[87] W. G. Hoskins, 'Leics. Crop Returns of 1801', *T.L.A.S.* xxiv, 137.
[88] Ibid. 141; Pitt, *General View*, 104.

AGRARIAN HISTORY, 1540–1950

The most important change in cropping was the decline in the production of peas and beans. In the 16th century they had occupied 46 out of every 100 acres of arable, but by 1801 the percentage was only 8½,[89] new feeding-stuffs such as turnips and cabbages having by then displaced them. Marshall in 1790 had regretted the fact that in the district with which he was familiar turnips did not occupy one in a hundred acres.[90] But in 1801 they were being grown on 11½ per cent. of the arable in the county. In ten parishes in Sparkenhoe hundred this figure rose to 13·6 per cent., and in eight parishes in Framland hundred to 17·9 per cent.[91] By the first decade of the 19th century, in fact, turnips could be found in all parts of the county, although they were gradually being displaced by another variety, the Swedish turnip, particularly in the good lands of the Soar valley between Leicester and Loughborough.[92]

Potatoes were not yet common in the fields at the turn of the century, but were reserved for odd patches of ground and gardens. Pitt, however, spotted some growing in the new inclosures of the Wolds, where from being reserved for table use they were coming to be fed to cattle.[93]

Carrots, which Bakewell had recommended because their green tops could be used for hay, made little headway because of the unsuitability of the soil, but among green vegetables cabbages were gaining ground because they provided nutritious food for ewes and lambs in spring and for milking cows.[94]

The factors that had conspired to turn so much of Leicestershire into pasture operated with reduced force in the years of the French Revolutionary and Napoleonic Wars. Owing to the deficiency of the wheat harvests and the uncertainty of oversea supplies, England was unusually dependent on her own agricultural resources. Wheat prices were high throughout the years 1794–1815, and there is little doubt that they acted as a direct stimulus to the growing of corn. Indeed in 1814 it was estimated that the corn-production of the kingdom as a whole had increased by 25 per cent. in the previous ten years.[95]

Crop returns for the years 1793, 1794, 1795, and 1801,[96] though incomplete, suggest that Leicestershire made a significant contribution to this increase in corn production, for a remarkably steady rise took place in the total acreage in tillage, and also in the acreage of each of the main crops, namely wheat, barley, oats, beans, and peas. A table of results will illustrate this trend most clearly (see p. 244).

In the county as a whole wheat was the largest single crop by 1801, covering some 15,832 acres. If the parishes missing from the crop returns were allowed for, the total would probably be nearer 20,000 acres. Wheat, in short, covered 28 per cent. of all the arable land compared with 26 per cent. devoted to barley.[97] But in the course of the war wheat had not consistently gained

[89] *T.L.A.S.* xxiv, 137.
[90] W. Marshall, *Rural Econ. of Midland Counties*, i, 253.
[91] *T.L.A.S.* xxiv, 137.
[92] Pitt, *General View*, 117.
[93] Ibid. 133; Monk, *General View*, 14.
[94] Pitt, *General View*, 128–30.
[95] R. E. Prothero, *Engl. Farming Past and Present* (1936), 269, 319.
[96] The crop returns for 1793, 1794, and 1795 came to light at Leicester Castle after Dr. Hoskins wrote his article on the 1801 returns. They are incomplete, relating only to Sparkenhoe and Framland hundreds and to a few parishes in Guthlaxton hundred. The most complete series is for the year 1795. The returns were apparently first asked for in November 1795 by the Home Secretary in order to assist a Select Committee of the House of Commons in its task of accounting for the high price of grain (*C.J.* li, 19, 85). Since the parishes appearing in the 1793–5 returns do not in all cases reappear in the 1801 returns, it has been necessary in the following table of acreages to reduce the number of parishes used for comparison in 1795 and 1801.
[97] *T.L.A.S.* xxiv, 136, 140.

ground at the expense of other crops. Taking the acreage in 1795 as 100, the wheat lands in 1801 in 8 parishes in Framland hundred had increased to 118, in 7 parishes in Guthlaxton hundred to 134, in 10 parishes in Sparkenhoe hundred to 144, and in another 10 parishes in Framland hundred to as much as 208. But in 3 out of 5 samples peas and oats had increased more than wheat. Only barley was a consistent loser, showing the smallest increase in 4 cases out of 5.

Crop Acreages in Leicestershire between 1793 and 1801

Year	*Wheat*	*Barley*	*Oats*	*Beans*	*Peas*	*Rye*	*Maslin*	*Turnips*	*Potatoes*	*Total*
	(1) GUTHLAXTON HUNDRED: TOTALS FOR 9 PARISHES									
1793	459	534	403	125½	..	..	2	..	..	1,523½
1794	518	566½	503	129½	3½	..	2½	..	..	1,823
1795	558	586	517	165	4½	11	36	..	..	1,877½
1801	705¼	818	749½	24	40½	5	..	445	26¾	2,814 (2,342¼ excl. turnips and potatoes)
	(2) SPARKENHOE HUNDRED: TOTALS FOR 25 PARISHES									
1793	1,670½	1,563	1,219	265	1	..	..	..	..	4,718½
1794	1,802¾	1,601½	1,324	370	3	..	..	..	..	5,101¼
1795	1,933½	1,785½	1,378½	381¾	6½	½	..	..	..	5,486¼
	SPARKENHOE HUNDRED: TOTALS FOR 6 PARISHES									
1795	695½	589	395½	188½		..	..	..	..	1,868½
1801	734¼	541½	466½	196		..	..	91	11¾	2,041 (1,938¼ excl. turnips and potatoes)
	(3) FRAMLAND HUNDRED: TOTALS FOR 12 PARISHES									
A year preceding 1794*	205	429¼	692¼	68	6	..	..	..	..	1,400½
1794	307	655¼	980	158	54¾	..	..	..	..	2,155
1795	434¼	825	988¾	69¾	30	..	..	..	..	2,347¾
	FRAMLAND HUNDRED: TOTALS FOR 8 PARISHES									
1795	388¼	740	787¼	88¼		..	..	..	..	2,003¾
1801	457	825½	1,030	120		..	..	536	21	2,989½ (2,432 excl. turnips and potatoes)

* The crop return was called for in autumn 1795, and was intended to relate to the years 1794, 1795, and to one year preceding 1794. In most cases the year taken was 1793. In the returns for Framland hundred the precise year to which the returns related was not specified.

Further research will have to be done to determine how the impressive increase in land in tillage, indicated by the table above, was achieved; whether it was, indeed, as great as it on paper appears, or whether the constables of the hundreds and the incumbents who collected the figures, and the farmers who gave them, were simply becoming more efficient. The problem is not a simple one, for there was little waste land in Leicestershire, and most of the arable increase must have been achieved at the expense of pasture. Yet many landlords strictly forbade the ploughing up of grass. Until further work is done on the subject, the problem can only be stated without being solved.

Stock-rearing. Of the work of the Leicestershire stock-farmers in the late 18th century in establishing the principles of pedigree breeding something has already been said. Yet the breeds that were being perfected by 1860 were not theirs. John Monk, who had expected that Bakewell's New Leicester sheep would shortly supersede all others, would have been perplexed to find that in the 1860's they had become quite rare.[98] Their disappearance was due chiefly to a change in taste, for the public grew to dislike the excessive fat of the New Leicester mutton. Bakewell had already countered criticisms on this score at the beginning of his career, arguing that fat mutton met the needs of the poor, because it went farther and provided a cheap substitute for bacon.[99] The next hundred years turned these arguments against him. By 1866 the sheep that was most common in the east was a cross between a Lincoln ram and a Leicester ewe (or vice versa). Its tendencies to run to fat were arrested, its mutton was improved in quality and its wool in quantity. In the western half of the county the native breed was being crossed with Shropshire Downs.[1]

Bakewell's Longhorn cattle suffered a similar fate, but for different reasons. Monk's verdict in 1794 that on the whole graziers were not very particular about their breeds augured little success for Bakewell's variety.[2] If graziers were not well disposed towards them, dairy farmers were even less so, as their milking qualities suffered at the expense of their meat. Dairy farmers turned their attention to Shorthorns, while the bigger farmers experimented with several different breeds—Lord Berners with the Herefords, Lord Moira and Mr. Cheney of Gaddesby Hall with the improved Durhams. By 1866 the order of preference in eastern Leicestershire was the Shorthorn, the Hereford, the Devon, the Scot, the Welsh Runt, and the Kerry cow.[3] None of these breeds outshone the rest, and farmers were content to differ in opinion on which was superior.

1860–1950

Economic conditions. Farming history in Leicestershire since 1860 has reproduced in brighter tones the picture of English agriculture as a whole. It has passed through the same periodic booms and slumps and has undergone the same mechanical revolution. As in other counties machinery and other scientific improvements have enabled fewer hands to till the land, and have turned an industry which until the 18th century engaged the majority of the population into the specialized occupation of a minority.

Between 1860 and 1874 farming enjoyed a prosperity parallel with that of industry. There was even a tendency in Leicestershire for pasture to be ploughed up for corn, so favourable were the market conditions.[4] But the advantages of new techniques of husbandry were not exclusive to Britain, and in the late seventies and eighties farmers began to experience the serious effects of foreign competition. From 1875 until the First World War threw into sharp relief the vulnerability of food-supplies from abroad, agriculture became more and more of an orphan industry in the nation's economy.

The depression which overtook farming after 1874 followed much the same course as that of 1816–37. Grain prices fell before meat prices, and farmers took immediate steps to convert their arable into pasture. The situation of Leicestershire differed from that of other counties only in so far as more than half the cultivated area was already under grass. This fraction increased in the course

[98] Monk, *General View*, 24.
[1] *Jnl. Royal Agric. Soc.*, 2nd ser. ii, no. 4, 329, 321.
[3] Pitt, *General View*, 234; *Jnl. Royal Agric. Soc.*, 2nd ser. ii, no. 4, 313, 327.
[4] *Royal Com. on Agric.* [Cmd. 45], p. 148, H.C. (1919), ix.
[99] Marshall, *Rural Econ.*, i, 400.
[2] Monk, *General View*, 36.

of the depression, but the county was from the beginning insulated against the worst effects of the slump.

Witnesses to the Richmond Commission, which sat between 1879 and 1882, reiterated the explanations given in similar circumstances more than forty years before. Leicestershire was a county of many small pasture farms. The market for dairy produce was not seriously affected by the slump, and good prices kept the graziers in business.[5] Cattle diseases, particularly an outbreak of rinderpest in 1865, and recurrent outbreaks of sheep-rot, which reduced the number of sheep in the county from 462,953 in 1867 to 357,757 in 1880,[6] exposed the pasture farmer to serious hazards. But there was no doubt that he was better off than the arable farmer.

The Richmond Commission ascribed the depression primarily to poor harvests and secondarily to foreign competition.[7] Subsequent events were to prove the faulty balance of this judgement, but at the time it did not seem unreasonable. Leicestershire, indeed, supplied convincing evidence of the ravages of bad weather. The average yield per acre of wheat, barley, and oats before 1878 had been 4, 5, and 6 quarters respectively. In 1879 it stood at $1\frac{1}{2}$, 2, and 4 quarters, while the turnip and mangold harvest on the clay and loam soils had been a failure for two years in succession.[8]

Following the recommendations of the Richmond Commission, attempts were made to remove some of the minor causes of the depression, including the weight of local taxation and the scourge of disease. Improved weather conditions between 1883 and 1890 gave temporary relief, but another run of bad harvests between 1891 and 1894 brought renewed crisis.[9] A second Royal Commission disclosed how fragile were the foundations on which this interval of apparent prosperity had rested. Farmers had had no chance to build up their reserves of capital; costs had been cut to the bone; improvements had been at a standstill. The condition of the land was deteriorating in consequence. In one year, between 1892 and 1893, 1,035 more acres in Leicestershire had been laid down to pasture and yet there had been no increase in the number of live-stock. On the contrary there were 1,842 fewer cows in milk and calf, 7,206 fewer cattle of other kinds, 257 fewer horses, and 658 fewer pigs. Capital was being drained away in current expenditure. Few farmers brought up their sons to follow the same occupation.[10]

The areas of worst depression were those where high rents had been obstinately maintained. Better conditions obtained in the Belvoir and Melton Mowbray districts, where more far-sighted landlords like the Duke of Rutland had cut rents by as much as 25–30 per cent.[11]

The total picture, however, was far from being unrelievedly gloomy. Dairy farming, in particular milk production, was still considered to be a most profitable business. Mr. Nuttall of Beeby, the biggest dairy producer in Leicestershire, calculated that on 20 acres a farmer with 6 cows could make £120 a year from the yield of Stilton cheese, butter and milk, and an annual calf. His colleagues preferred to give a more conservative estimate of £12–£15

[5] *Royal Com. on Agric. Depression* [C. 3096], p. 35, H.C. (1881), xvii.

[6] Prothero, *Engl. Farming*, 375; *Agric. Stats.*; *R. Com. on Agric. Depression* [C. 2778—II], p. 371, H.C. (1881), xvi.   [7] Prothero, *Engl. Farming*, 380.

[8] *R. Com. on Agric. Depression* (1881), Pt. 2, p. 371.   [9] Prothero, *English Farming*, 383.

[10] *R. Com. on Agric. Depression* [C. 7400—II], pp. 256–7, H.C. (1894), xvi (2).

[11] Ibid., pp. 255, 257.

a cow, but even this was a fair return, and Nuttall himself had made £28 in the best years.[12] At Worthington, the home of one of the witnesses to the 1894 Commission, where half the inhabitants earned their living from the land, all were engaged in milk production. Forty churns were dispatched daily to Newcastle-upon-Tyne and London, and business prospered because the financial returns were quick.[13]

Smallholders could manage to keep their heads above water by working hard and relying exclusively on family labour,[14] and since 69 per cent. of agricultural holdings in 1880 were of this kind,[15] there was far less acute poverty than that familiar in the eastern counties. But the living was hard and precarious. The only farmers who were apparently undismayed were tradesmen bent on retiring to the country, who continued to pay competitive prices for the land.[16]

Conditions were at their worst in 1894–5, when wheat recorded its lowest price for 150 years.[17] Thereafter a slow upward climb began, which lasted until 1914. In the meantime, foreign competition, which lay at the root of the depressions after 1874, began to invade the meat and dairy market as well as the grain market. Shipments of frozen meat from countries where the costs of production were lower began to arrive in the nineties, together with Danish factory-made butter and American factory-made cheese.[18] This did not diminish the rate at which arable was turned over to grass. By 1910, 373,270 acres out of the cultivated area of 473,610 acres (78 per cent.) were under permanent grass, showing an increase of 61,157 acres over the grass area of 1880.[19] But competition forced farmers to make some adjustments to the balance of their pasture farming. Dairying and milking began to expand at the expense of grazing—a trend clearly illustrated in the rising proportion of pasture cut for hay.[20]

The constantly widening gap between the arable and pasture acreages meant that Leicestershire farmers were feeding fewer and fewer people. This was of little importance in one county, but in the kingdom as a whole it involved grave risks when war broke out in 1914. Not until December 1916, however, when shipping losses became serious, was any official attempt made to redress the balance.[21] Then for the first time the Government used compulsory powers to extend the arable area, and by 1919 had persuaded farmers to plough up 40,000 acres in Leicestershire—some 10·7 per cent. of permanent pasture.[22]

The policy of increasing corn production was abandoned at the end of the war, but a price guarantee for wheat and oats lasted until 1921, and kept some 27,594 acres more under the plough than in 1910. But depression in the twenties had restored the grass area by 1930 to its 1910 level, and between 1930 and 1939 added a further 3,495 acres, making a total of 378,120 acres, with another 3,334 acres of rough grazing.[23]

[12] *Royal Com. on Labour* [C. 6894—I], p. 134, H.C. (1893–4), xxxv.
[13] *R. Com. on Agric. Depression* (1894), pt. 2, p. 255.
[14] Ibid. 256.   [15] *Agric. Stats.*
[16] *R. Com. on Agric. Depression* (1894), pt. 2, pp. 256, 260.
[17] Prothero, *Engl. Farming*, 385.
[18] *Departmental Cttee. on Agric. and Dairy Schools* [C. 5313—I], p. 34, H.C. (1888), xxxii.
[19] *Agric. Stats.*
[20] R. Auty, *Leics.* (Rep. of Land Utilization Surv.), 265, 274.
[21] Prothero, *Engl. Farming*, 400.
[22] *Royal Com. on Agric.* [Cmd. 24,] p. 145, H.C. (1919), ix.   [23] *Agric. Stats.*

Land use. The comparatively small acreage of arable (98,091 acres in 1879, 127,934 acres in 1920, and 67,618 acres in 1939) continued to be devoted principally to the needs of livestock, with the result that the wheat acreage between 1860 and 1931 was reduced by more than 70 per cent. Only the Wheat Subsidy Act of 1931 broke the pace of this decline, but at the expense of oats, not of grass.[24] It was not until the outbreak of war in 1939 that the trend was temporarily reversed, with results that were evident to any traveller through Leicestershire familiar with its previous history. In many places pasture land was ploughed up for the first time since inclosure. Since 1945 much of it has again reverted to grass. The demand for increased meat production had reduced the arable area by 1950 to rather less than that attained in 1941. The scale of the change is seen in the following table:

Changing Arable and Pasture Acreage in Leicestershire, 1939–50

Year	Arable acreage	Pasture acreage (excluding rough grazing)	Year	Arable acreage	Pasture acreage (excluding rough grazing)
1939	67,618	378,120	1944	238,006	203,256
1940	95,392	351,569	1946	178,578	261,138
1941	171,681	276,859	1948	159,886	280,012
1942	188,570	256,645	1950	156,075	285,614
1943	224,537	217,931			

Barley, which was the second largest crop until the mid-19th century, was reduced to insignificance by the disappearance of sheep-with-barley farming—a system which became uneconomic because of the increased imports of mutton and the growing preference for smaller joints. The decline was most rapid between 1876 and 1910, when barley fell from a peak of 37,000 acres to 9,670 acres. By 1939 it occupied only 2,625 acres. Its usefulness increased with the war, and since 1943 it has never fallen below 10,000 acres, nor risen beyond 17,000 acres.[25] Until 1939 the place of barley as fodder was taken by oats. At that date, when the oats subsidy of 1937 had reversed the tendency for this crop to be sacrificed on account of the subsidy for wheat, it occupied 15·9 per cent. of the sown area. In 1950 it had advanced to 18·3 per cent.[26]

Root crops other than mangolds never occupied any large amount of land. The turnip and swede acreage declined with the decline of sheep farming, a trend that was particularly noticeable in the period between 1880 and 1910. The 12,650 acres of 1880 had fallen to 7,396 by 1910, to 2,281 acres by 1939, and stood at 1,292 acres in 1950. The corresponding fall in the number of sheep was from 462,953 in 1867 to 357,757 in 1880, and to 195,223 in 1920. A slight increase to 266,649 was recorded in 1939, but this gain was lost in the course of the war. Since then there has been a small but steady rise in numbers, from 116,843 in 1946 to 150,415 in 1950. Owing to the 40 per cent. increase in the number of cattle between 1870 and 1939, mangolds became a slightly more important crop, though they rarely exceeded 7,000 acres.[27] Sugar-beet occupied 677 acres in 1939, and was concentrated in the north and north-west, near the factory at Colwick near Nottingham. A campaign to raise production during the Second World War produced a temporary increase in 1942 to 2,037 acres, a level which has not been attained since.[28]

[24] Auty, *Leics.*, 271.
[25] Auty, op. cit. 278; *Agric. Stats.*
[26] Auty, op. cit. 275, 277–8; *Agric. Stats.*
[27] Auty, op. cit. 279, 283; *Agric. Stats.*
[28] Auty, op. cit. 279; *Agric. Stats.*

Scientific farming. A brighter side of farming history since 1860 has been the steady spread of education and the growth of more effective methods of collaboration between those engaged in scientific research and practical farming. The depression of the eighties and nineties stimulated some hard thinking on this subject, and one of the more hopeful signs emerging from the evidence of Leicestershire witnesses to the Royal Commissions was the emphasis laid on the need for technical education parallel with that developing in industry.

Leicestershire farmers were alleged to be some of the most obstinate in accepting instruction, yet the deficiencies in their theoretical knowledge were having glaring financial consequences. No dairy was capable of producing either butter or cheese of the same quality twice over. As a result cheeses at the Leicester fair might range in price from 40*s.* to 90*s.*, and yet no producer could account for his success or failure. Buyers were beginning to turn to Danish butter, because its quality was uniform and could be relied on.[29]

No technical training was available in Leicestershire, and only a few students received scholarships from the County Council to go to Cambridge. The Church schools at Hinckley stood alone in submitting students for the agriculture examination at South Kensington in 1888.[30] By the first decade of the new century, however, Leicestershire was able to take advantage of the Agricultural College established on Lord Belper's estate at Kingston-on-Soar in Nottinghamshire (now the Midland Agricultural College, Sutton Bonnington), the chief purpose of which was to serve the needs of Midland farmers by improving the methods of dairy work, butter- and cheese-making, and stock-feeding.[31]

The diffusion of theoretical knowledge was the more important because of the rapid progress made in the science of agriculture. The range of improvements in the last century has been so enormous that it would be impossible to give an adequate account of them in this short space. It is sufficient to say that agriculture has now become such a highly specialized branch of science that no farmer can be content to rely alone on the practical experience which satisfied his father and grandfather. Agriculture now calls to its aid a whole army of scientists and engineers who are constantly experimenting with and improving old methods of cultivation. Whereas machine-driven threshing-drums, steam cultivators, and steam ploughs, corn-cutters, and binders seemed to have revolutionized agriculture by the beginning of this century,[32] they have been left far behind by the new tractor-driven implements, and particularly by the combine harvester, which has simplified a series of processes, carried out at the mercy of the weather, into a single operation. No farmer in the last twenty years has been able to pursue his course unaffected by these far-reaching changes.

Distribution of holdings. The effect of mechanization and economic depression has been to drive more and more people away from work on the land in the last hundred years. The process, inevitable though it doubtless was, did not go unlamented. Public concern was reflected in the attention paid to the provision of allotments and smallholdings from the eighties onwards.

[29] *R. Com. on Agric. Depression* [C. 7400—II], p. 267, H.C. (1894), xvi (2). *Departmental Cttee. on Agric. and Dairy Schools* [C. 5313—I], pp. 33–34, H.C. (1888), xxxii.

[30] Ibid. p. 33; *R. Com. on Agric. Depression*, p. 261.

[31] John Harrison, unpublished article on Leics. Agric. in the 19th century, written 1907 for V.C.H. (Inst. Hist. Research, London).   [32] Ibid.

A campaign, based on the argument that they helped to retain labour on the land and that their output per acre was higher than that of ordinary farm land, engaged the sympathy of several landlords, who were prepared to take the financial risks of letting land on this basis. By 1891 the provision of allotments in Leicestershire was not ungenerous, averaging as it did one allotment to every 15·9 people, compared with 21 in Nottinghamshire and 10·7 in Bedfordshire.[33] Some, it is true, were held on restrictive covenants that detracted from their value. The Duke of Rutland, for example, insisted that the land be cultivated only with the spade, that no occupiers should sell the produce without his permission, and that half the land should be cropped with barley and the other half with potatoes and other roots.[34]

Whereas allotments only supplemented an agricultural labourer's weekly earnings, smallholdings of up to 50 acres were a livelihood in themselves, and were in much greater demand. The Duke of Rutland had 1,034 holdings of less than 30 acres on his estate in 1893, and the whole of Mrs. Cheney's estate of 1,500 acres at Gaddesby was successfully turned into smallholdings. In the Melton Mowbray district, where they were devoted to the making of Stilton cheese and other dairy produce, the small unit proved to be extremely profitable.[35]

The end of the First World War marked a period of revived interest in smallholdings. In Leicestershire the scheme was energetically encouraged by the Clerk to the County Council, and 3,281 acres were bought up by the County authority for this purpose, and another 287 acres leased. They were situated mainly in the south and south-west, around Hinckley, Market Harborough, and Blaby, though there were some at Melton Mowbray also.[36] These were in addition to the holdings provided by private landowners like the Earl of Dysart, who had allocated 500 acres in lots of 40–50 acres.[37]

The provision of smallholdings and allotments, however, acted only as a gentle brake on the decline of population in the rural areas. Between 1871 and 1881 the number of agricultural labourers fell by 11·5 per cent., in the next decade by 15·94 per cent., and between 1891 and 1901 by 25·6 per cent.[38] At the same time the flow of Irish labourers, making annual visits at harvest time, dried up for lack of demand.[39] In 1939 the labour force of regular workers was just under 6,000, or one worker for every 74·3 acres of farm land. In 1851 it had been over four times as great—nearly 25,000 workers.[40]

Small farmers with less than 50 acres suffered a similar reduction in numbers as the long years of precarious living took their toll and their land was delivered into the hands of bigger competitors. The pace at which their numbers fell between 1880 and 1944 is indicated in the table below. Some of the responsibility lay with the high rents prevailing on dairy land, particularly in the west. It was not unusual for rents of £2 an acre to be paid here, compared

---

[33] *Royal Com. on Labour* [C. 6894—I], p. 141, H.C. (1893–4), xxxv.
[34] Ibid. 153–4.
[35] Ibid. 142.
[36] *Royal Com. on Agric.* [Cmd. 24], p. 152, H.C. (1919), ix.
[37] Ibid. 152.
[38] *Royal Com. on Labour* [C. 6894—XXIV], p. 165, H.C. (1893–4), xxxvii (2).
[39] *Rep. on Decline in Agric. Population* [Cd. 3273], p. 90, H.C. (1906), xcvi; *Royal Com. on Labour* [C. 6894 —I], p. 134, H.C. (1893–4), xxxv.
[40] Auty, *Leics.*, 272–3; *1851 Census* [1691—II], pp. 547, 550, H.C. (1852–3), lxxxviii (2). The 3,933 persons classed as farmers' wives and daus. are not included in this total as they were not presumably in regular employment. One thousand three hundred and seventeen farmers' sons and male relations living in the house are, however, included.

with only 25s. an acre for grazing pastures.[41] But the principal reason was the unfavourable condition of the market, which rendered the larger unit more economic. It was only during the Second World War that the need for more intensive cultivation and a guarantee of sale increased the number of small farms from 2,523 in 1940 to 2,663 in 1944.[42]

Holdings of 51–100 acres, which are usually devoted to dairy farming, represented 21·5 per cent. of all holdings in 1939, and those of 101–300 acres— usually grazing farms—27·3 per cent. Large units of 301–700 acres represented only 2·7 per cent. of all farms in the county. It is clear, therefore, that the small farms of 50 acres and less, representing 48·1 per cent. of the total, still play an important part in Leicestershire agriculture. Nevertheless it would not be true to say that Leicestershire was a county of small farms, for the average percentage in England as a whole in 1939 was 60 per cent.[43]

Table[44] showing Changes in the Size of Agricultural Holdings in Leicestershire, 1880–1950

Year	1–50 acres	51–100	101–150	151–300	301–500	501–1,000	Above 1,000	Total
1880	5,833	896	1,407		189	36	2	8,363
1910	4,788	2,483			188			7,459
1920	4,018	1,067	655	769	187			6,696
1930	3,396	1,139	688	765	155			6,143
1940	2,523	1,137	688	778	132	29	4	5,291
1944	2,663	1,066	697	750	139	41	4	5,360
1950	2,675	1,049	655	768	150	43	5	5,345

Regional specialization. Only slight modifications have to be made to bring the account of land specialization up to date. Except on the marlstone around Belvoir dairying preponderates in the north-east of the county. Indeed, the Vale of Belvoir carries a larger proportion of dairy cattle than any other district in the county.[45] Cheese-production, which in the rest of the county fell off in the first part of the 20th century owing to the shortage of skilled dairymaids, has not yet been completely displaced by milk in this area, for the pull of the urban market is weaker than elsewhere. Nevertheless there were only four farmers and thirteen factories in the whole county in 1939 making Stilton cheese. Two of the factories, at Harby and Long Clawson, were run on co-operative lines, the shares being held by local farmers.[46]

Graziers in the south-east, around Market Harborough, have continued to concentrate on prime beef production, since their pastures are good and they can compete on fairly even terms with foreign producers. But the first-class grass land is less extensive than is commonly supposed, and because of the growing public preference before the Second World War for small joints there was, at least until 1939, a steady movement of conversion to dairy farming. This is a change that involves heavy outlay, for Leicestershire has always been a county

[41] Auty, *Leic.*, 270. [42] *Agric. Stats.* [43] Auty, *Leics.*, 269–71.
[44] The table is compiled from *Agric. Stats.* Figures for 1950 are not strictly comparable with the rest as the holdings are classified as follows: 1–49¾ acres, 50–99¾ acres, 100–149¾ acres, &c.
[45] Auty, *Leics.*, 287.
[46] Ibid. 293, 300; *Royal Com. on Agric.* [Cmd. 24], p. 146, H.C. (1919), ix.

with meagre farm buildings.[47] It is probable that the trend was arrested by the Second World War.

In the western half of the county, where cattle stocking on mixed farms was particularly heavy in the mid-19th century, grazing has been superseded by dairying to a very large extent. This is due in part to the poorer quality of the pasture compared with the south-east, and to the fact that milk finds a ready market in the neighbouring towns. The extent of the change that has taken place is seen in the figures for dairy cattle, which in the county as a whole increased from 23 per cent. of all cattle in 1874 to 38 per cent. in 1939. The total number of cattle since 1874 has increased by 40 per cent., whereas beef cattle have declined by 25 per cent.[48]

In contrast with the trend towards a larger farming unit in agriculture, the history of the great estates of the nobility and gentry over the last century suggests that the distribution of landownership has proceeded in the opposite direction—that the owners of land have steadily multiplied. The same conclusion might not emerge from a more complete study of land sales in the county. But in the case of the larger family estates, where the financial burden of maintaining great households, and of meeting heavy death duties with every succeeding generation, has reduced the size of most of them and dismembered some of them entirely, the dispersal of the property has usually been carried out by the sale of parcels to small farmers and tenants.

The passing of the old social pattern of landownership strikes the imagination more than the coming of the new, though both aspects of the change deserve equal attention. The Hastings family, which ranked as one of the three noble families in Leicestershire in the 16th century, have parted with most of their lands in the county. They were already seriously impaired by the extravagances of the 4th Marquess Hastings, who, before his death in 1868, had gambled away two estates and a fortune of £30,000 a year, but they were not finally sold up until after the First World War—the estate at Ashby-de-la-Zouch in 1921 and the Donington estate in 1923.[49] Among the lands of the younger nobility the 10,000-acre estate of Lord Howe at Gopsall was sold to Mr. Samuel Waring, later Lord Waring, in 1919,[50] and of the lands of the older gentry, those of the Dixies at Market Bosworth were sold up in 1931.[51]

Those families who have preserved their ancestral estates have done so only by selling outlying portions. Three thousand, seven hundred acres of the Cave family estates at Stanford, with a rent-roll of £4,400 p.a., were sold in 1924, though the mansion and park were retained.[52] The dukes of Rutland, who in 1883 drew a gross rental of nearly £100,000 from their 70,000 acres in Leicestershire and elsewhere, possessed in 1940, when the 9th duke died, only 18,000 acres—barely a quarter of the former estate.[53]

The parcelling of these lands, so long in the possession of one family, is a social process which deserves more attention than has yet been accorded it. Who, for example, were the beneficiaries of the 6,230 acres of the Gopsall estate which were put into the market in 1927 and were divided into 239 lots? How many tenants took advantage of the sales of the Horninghold estate, with its 1,788 acres, in 1931, and of the Goscote Hall estate, with its 875 acres, in

[47] Auty, *Leics.*, 286, 288.
[48] Ibid. 282–5.
[49] J. B. Firth, *Highways and Byways in Leics.*, 121; *Leic. Advertiser*, 20 Jan. 1923, 8; 29 Sept. 1923, 8.
[50] Ibid. 2 June 1923, 5; 26 Feb. 1927, 5.
[51] Ibid. 2 May 1931, 1.
[52] Ibid. 5 Jan. 1924, 12.
[53] W. G. Hoskins, *Midland Engl.*, 60.

1933?[54] Have these sales, indeed, broadened the basis of landownership, or merely transferred land from the older gentry to the newer mercantile and industrial aristocracy? How much of the land is being absorbed by real-estate companies and by large organizations such as the Co-operative Wholesale Society, which farms roughly 3,000 acres in Leicestershire?[55] Much of the economic and social history of this century would no doubt be reflected in the answers to these questions.

Another equally significant aspect of recent developments is already familiar. Several estates with their great mansions have been bought by public bodies for social purposes, and have so been preserved from the fate of Ragdale Hall, which has been allowed to fall into ruin. On the other hand the mansion of the Tollemache family at Buckminster Park has been dismantled for its building materials. Bradgate Park was bought from the Grey family—the house itself having been allowed to fall into decay after about 1740, when the Greys moved to Staffordshire—and presented to the community for use as a public park; the home of the Dixie family at Market Bosworth, bought by the County Council, is now a hospital.[56]

The breach of continuity in the ownership of Leicestershire's old estates, however, is by no means complete. The Fieldings are still lords of Lutterworth manor, where they lived in the 15th century. The Caves, who bought dissolved monastic land at Stanford in the 16th century, still live in the village. The Hartopps are still lords of the manor of Burton Lazars, and the Hazleriggs of Noseley. The Martins of Anstey can trace their descent through twenty generations of their family, through freeholders of Anstey in the 16th century, freemen of Leicester in the reign of King John, back to John Martyn who was living in the 12th century. The Pochins are the heirs of Matthew Pochin, who became the squire of Barkby in the early 17th century, and whose forebears had been seated there in the reign of Edward III.[57]

It is rarely that broken threads are picked up and re-knotted again as they were when Ambrose March Phillipps De Lisle, the descendant of a family which had acquired some of the lands of the dissolved abbey of Garendon, helped to lay the foundation of the new Cistercian house by granting lands for the site of Mount St. Bernard.[58] But although the manifold social and economic changes of the last four centuries have transformed the landscape and the way of life of Leicestershire people, both bear indelible marks of their history. Not only have families retained their attachments to villages in which their medieval ancestors were buried, but their houses, churches, and lands preserve to this day the evidence of their activities. The grass in the fields of Cold Newton and Ilston cannot entirely conceal the remains of the streets and houses wherein a larger population flourished before the 17th century.[59] The ridges of the old open fields can still be seen in the pastures of Lindridge, though they have lain under grass for 600 years, and in the large fields at Foston and Knaptoft survives a fragment of the history of the early inclosure movement, when farmers carried over into the new husbandry the old notions of large fields that had prevailed for centuries before them.[60]

[54] *Leic. Advertiser*, 15 Jan. 1927, 1; 26 Feb. 1927, 5; 8 Aug. 1931, 1; 13 May 1933, 1.
[55] *Ex inf.* Mr. J. Brooks, Leics. County Sec., Nat. Farmers' Union; see also Hoskins, *Midland Engl.*, 48.
[56] *Leic. Advertiser*, 16 Apr. 1932, 12; Firth, *Highways and Byways*, 62.
[57] *Leic. Advertiser*, 13 Aug. 1932, 10.   [58] Ibid. 4 June 1932, 12; 29 Oct. 1932, 10.
[59] W. G. Hoskins, *Essays in Leics. Hist.*, 107.   [60] Ibid. 106, 88 n.

APPENDIX I

Inclosure in Leicestershire without Parliamentary Act

EXPLANATORY NOTE

THE sources of information listed in column 3 are cited in abbreviated form as follows:

M. W. Beresford, 'Glebe Terriers and Open Field Leicestershire', *Studies in Leics. Agrarian Hist.*, is cited as *Beresford.*

W. Burton, *The Description of Leics. . . .*, is cited as *Burton.*

W. G. Hoskins, *Essays in Leics. Hist.*, is cited as *Hoskins.*

J. Lee, *A Vindication of a Regulated Inclosure*, is cited as *Lee.*

J. Monk, *General View of the Agriculture of the County of Leicester*, is cited as *Monk.*

J. Nichols, *The Hist. and Antiquities of the County of Leicester*, is cited as *Nichols.*

L. A. Parker, 'Enclosure in Leics., 1485–1607' (Ph.D. thesis, Lond. Univ. 1948), is cited as *Parker.*

For the sake of completeness, all depopulated villages are included in this list even though a few were deserted before inclosure. Places about which no information has been found are not mentioned in the list.

A period rather than an exact date given in columns i and ii signifies that inclosure took place at an unknown date within the period, not that it was prolonged over the whole span.

The abbreviation 'Ch.' is used for 'Chapelry'.

Place	(i) *Date of first inclosure evidence*	(ii) *Date of full inclosure*	*Sources for* (i) *and* (ii)
Aldeby	..	By end 12th cent.	Depopulated village 'if there ever was a village there': *Hoskins*, 104.
Allexton	1509	1555	*Parker*, 60.
Alton	..	..	Depopulated village: *Hoskins*, 72.
Ambion	..	2nd half 14th cent.	Depopulated village: *Hoskins*, 104.
Andreschirch . . .	..	late 14th cent.	Depopulated village: *Hoskins*, 102.
Appleby	..	*c.* 1778–80	Marshall, *Rural Econ.* ii, 39.
Ashby-de-la-Zouch . .	1514	by 1601	(i) *Parker*, 67. (ii) *Beresford.*
Ashby Folville . . .	..	*c.* 1651	*Cal. Cttee. for Compounding*, 1916.
Ashby Magna . . .	1600	by 1653	(i) *Parker*, 133. (ii) *Lee.*
Ashby Parva . . .	..	1665	MS. agreement at Ashby.
Aston Flamville . . .	1579	1601–25	(i) *Parker*, 112. (ii) *Beresford.*
Atterton	..	..	Depopulated village: *Hoskins, T.L.A.S.* xxii, 242.
Aylestone . . .	1581	..	*Parker*, 112.
Baggrave	..	1500–1	Depopulated village: *Hoskins*, 80.
Barkby	..	by 1601	*Beresford.*
Barkestone . . .	1597	by 1612	(i) *Parker*, 125. (ii) *Beresford.*
Barleston Ch. . . .	1595	by 1674	(i) *Parker*, 122. (ii) *Beresford*; *Monk*, 'old inclosure'.
Barrow-on-Soar . .	..	by 1605	*Beresford.*
Barwell	1596	1625–74	(i) *Parker*, 122. (ii) *Beresford*; *Monk.*
Beaumanor . . .	1542	..	*Parker*, 76.
Beaumont Leys . . .	..	'old enclosure'	*Monk.*
Beeby	..	1605–29	*Beresford*; *Nichols*, 'old enclosure'.
Belgrave	1516	1654	(i) *Parker*, 67. (ii) C 78/1214, no. 5, articles of agreement.
Belton	1595	by 1625	(i) *Parker*, 124. (ii) *Beresford.*
Belvoir	..	by 1734	*Nichols*, ii, 82.
Bescaby	..	by 1538	Depopulated village: *Hoskins, T.L.A.S.* xxii, 242.
Billesdon	..	by 1653	*Lee.*
Bittesby	..	1494	Depopulated village, *Hoskins*, 93 n.
Bitteswell	..	by 1674	*Beresford.* But see *Nichols*, iv, 43, for evidence that in 1754 it was still open.
Blaby and Countesthorpe .	1627	..	Wards 5/23, Thos. Saville.
Blackfordby . . .	1514	..	*Parker*, 67.
Blaston Ch. . . .	1630	*c.* 1650	(i) *Nichols*, ii, 449. (ii) *Beresford.*

Place	(i) Date of first inclosure evidence	(ii) Date of full inclosure	Sources for (i) and (ii)
Bosworth, Husbands. . .	1496–1502	..	*Parker*, 48.
Bosworth, Market . . .	1592	by 1625	(i) *Parker*, 117. (ii) *Beresford*; 1631 inclosure commission: S.P. 16/183/17.
Bowden, Great . . .	..	1703	*Beresford*.
Bradgate	..	1499	*Parker*, 45.
Bradley	by 1539	..	*Parker*, 74.
Brascote	..	1499	Depopulated village: *Parker*, 46.
Braunstone . . .	1579	1596	*Parker*, 111, 122.
Bredon	1541	..	*Parker*, 74.
Brentingby Ch. . . .	1587	by 1674	(i) *Parker*, 116. (ii) *Beresford*.
Bromkinsthorpe . . .	1536	probably by 1620–8	(i) *Parker*, 73. (ii) Wards 5/23, John Dannett.
Brooksby. . . .	1378	1492	Depopulated village: *Parker*, 36.
Broughton Astley . .	..	probably by 1631	*Cal. S.P. Dom. 1631–3*, 54–5, but 1637 acc. to *Nichols*, iv, 60.
Broughton, Nether . . .	1651	..	C 54/3668, no. 19.
Buckminster . . .	..	1597	*Parker*, 125.
Burbage Ch. . . .	1603–4	by 1625 ?	(i) *Parker*, 140. (ii) *Beresford*.
Burrough-on-the-Hill . .	1606	1601–84	(i) *Parker*, 147. (ii) *Beresford*.
Burton Lazars . . .	1539–45	by 1649	(i) *Parker*, 80. (ii) C 54/3402, no. 3.
Cadeby	..	1597	*Parker*, 130.
Carlton Ch. . . .	..	1625–74	*Beresford*. Possibly by 1642 because tithes compounded for by then: Clayton MS. 35'29/231.
Carlton Curlieu . . .	1599	by 1601	(i) *Parker*, 128. (ii) *Beresford*.
Catthorpe . . .	..	1655	*Nichols*, iv, 76.
Chadwell . . .	1516	..	*Parker*, 67.
Charley	1618	..	Wards 5/23, Sir Rich. Waldram.
Claybrooke, Great . .	..	1694	*Nichols*, iv, 104.
Claybrooke, Little . .	..	1681	*Nichols*, iv, 103.
Coleorton	1511	by 1638	(i) *Parker*, 63. (ii) *Beresford*. But acc. to Nichols inclosure without Act, 1799: *Nichols*, iii, 740.
Cossington . . .	..	1663	*T.L.A.S.* xx, 6.
Coston	1591	1634–7	*Parker*, 120.
Cotes	1513	probably by 1637	*Parker*, 67. (ii) Wards 5/23, John Poultney.
Cotesbach . . .	1503	1603	*Parker*, 51, 155.
Cotes de Val . . .	..	..	Depopulated village: *T.L.A.S.* xxii, 242.
Coton	1604 ?	..	*Parker*, 145.
Countesthorpe, *see* Blaby			
Cranoe	1598	..	*Parker*, 128.
Croft	1545	..	*Parker*, 76–77. Agreement for inclosure of half the fields, 1630: S.P. 16/192/24.
Croxton Kerrial . . .	1538	..	*Parker*, 73.
Dadlington . . .	..	1625 ?–74	*Beresford*. 1671 acc. to *Nichols*, iv, 714.
Dalby Magna . . .	..	c. 1601	*Beresford*. But acc. to Nichols inclosure without Act, 1753: *Nichols*, iii, 242.
Dalby-on-the-Wolds . .	1543	..	*Parker*, 240.
Dalby Parva . . .	..	probably by 1634	Wards 5/23, Geo. Hartopp. 1612–79 acc. to *Beresford*.
Dishley	..	c. 1529	Depopulated village: *Hoskins*, 72.
Donington, Castle . .	1482	..	*Parker*, 97.
Donington-le-Heath . .	..	by 1631	S.P. 16/183/17.
Donisthorpe . . .	1655	..	See C 54/3838, no. 33 (1655), where lands lie 'dispersedly in several inclosures'.

Place	(i) Date of first inclosure evidence	(ii) Date of full inclosure	Sources for (i) and (ii)
Drayton, Fenny . . .	1511	by 1674	(i) *Parker*, 64. (ii) *Beresford.*
Easton Ch.	1650	..	C 54/3496, no. 14.
Eastwell	1653	1656	(i) C 54/3725, no. 18. (ii) C 78/1335, no. 2.
Eaton	..	*c.* 1575	*Beresford.*
Edmondthorpe. . . .	1563	by 1607	*Parker*, 104, 107.
Elmesthorpe . . .	..	temp. Hen. VIII	Depopulated village: *Parker*, 48.
Enderby	..	1604	*Parker*, 143.
Eye Kettleby . . .	..	..	Depopulated village: Hoskins, *T.L.A.S.* xxi, 242.
Foston	1575	by 1622	(i) *Parker*, 107. (ii) *Hoskins*, 88.
Freeby	1587–97	by 1735	(i) *Parker*, 122. (ii) Different periods up to 1735: *Nichols*, ii, 281.
Frisby-by-Galby . .	1631	1638–79	(i) S.P. 16/187/80. (ii) Depopulated village: Hoskins, *T.L.A.S.* xxii, 242. Glebe terrier of 1638 shows open fields, contradicting the inclosure *c.* 1628. S.P. 16/191/10, i–ii; *Beresford.*
Frolesworth . . .	..	by 1622	*Burton.*
Gaddesby . . .	1580	1650	(i) *Parker*, 111. (ii) Leics. County Rec. Off. copy of Chan. decree 28 Nov. 1670; articles of agreement, 17 Apr. 1650.
Galby	1614	by 1642	Hoskins, 'Short history of Galby and Frisby', *T.L.A.S.* xxii, 190, gives 1630 as date of final inclosure but acc. to Nichols the common field was inclosed in 1642: *Nichols*, ii, 569.
Garendon	1559	..	*Parker*, 97.
Garthorpe . . .	1631	1674	*Beresford.*
Glen Parva . . .	..	by 1653	Depopulated village: *Lee.*
Glooston	1511	..	*Parker*, 63.
Goadby Ch. . . .	1511	1625–90	(i) *Parker*, 54. (ii) *Beresford.*
Goadby Marwood . .	1595	1638–74	(i) *Parker*, 124. (ii) *Beresford.*
Gopsall	..	..	Depopulated village: Hoskins, *T.L.A.S.* xii, 242.
Hallaton	1510	..	*Parker*, 62.
Halsted	1559–69	..	*Parker*, 102. 80% inclosed by 1605.
Hamilton . . .	..	mid-15th century	Depopulated village: *Hoskins*, 74.
Hardwick . . .	..		Depopulated village: *Hoskins*, 72.
Heather	1574	'old inclosure'	(i) *Parker*, 107. (ii) *Monk.*
Higham-on-the-Hill .	1564	1632	(i) *Parker*, 99. (ii) *Beresford.* Date given in 1806 Inclosure Act.
Hinckley. . . .	1510–12	..	*Parker*, 62.
Hoby	1578	..	*Parker*, 110.
Holwell	..	1654	C 78/526, no. 8.
Holyoak	..	1496	Depopulated village: *Hoskins*, 86.
Horninghold . . .	1598	by 1620	*Parker*, 127; Wards 5/23, Geo. Turpin.
Hose	1605	..	*Parker*, 145.
Huncote	..	'old inclosure'	*Monk.*
Husbands Bosworth, *see* Bosworth, Husbands			
Ilston	..	*c.* 1615	C 78/669, no. 13. But acc. to Nichols it was partly inclosed by 1663, and completed 1788: *Nichols*, ii, 552.

Place	(i) Date of first inclosure evidence	(ii) Date of full inclosure	Sources for (i) and (ii)
Ingarsby	..	1469	Depopulated village: *Hoskins*, 76.
Keythorpe	..	1450–60	Depopulated village: *Hoskins*, 85.
Kilby	1609	..	Wards 5/23, Hen. Wyett.
King's Norton	..	by 1656	*Nichols*, ii, 732.
Kirby Bellars	1536	'old inclosure'	(i) *Parker*, 73. (ii) Monk.
Kirby Muxloe	1590	by 1634	*Parker*, 118.
Knaptoft	..	c. 1500	Depopulated village: *Parker*, 56.
Knossington	c. 1597	1601–25	(i) *Parker*, 126. (ii) Beresford.
Laughton	..	1663	C 78/669, no. 18.
Launde	1538	..	*Parker*, 42–43.
Leesthorpe	..	..	Depopulated village: Hoskins, *T.L.A.S.* xxii, 242.
Leicester Forest	..	1627	*Nichols*, iv, 785.
Lindley	..	1500	Depopulated village: *Parker*, 47.
Lockington	..	1601–6	Beresford.
Loddington	1539	by 1631	(i) *Parker*, 43. (ii) S.P. 16/187/83.
Lowesby	..	c. 1487	Depopulated village: *Parker*, 33.
Lubbesthorpe	..	1471–1550	Depopulated village: *Parker*, 78.
Lubenham	1600–1	..	*Parker*, 136.
Marefield, North	..	by 1502	*Parker*, 74.
Market Bosworth, *see* Bosworth, Market			
Melton Mowbray	1550	..	(i) *Parker*, 79. (ii) Beresford gives full inclosure by 1601, but see Wards 5/23, Wm. Holt, Peter Bingley, and Wm. Hickson, for open fields, 1605–37.
Misterton	..	by 1507	Depopulated village: *Parker*, 58.
Mowsley	1496–1502	..	*Parker*, 48.
Muston	..	1629	Beresford.
Mythe	..	..	Depopulated village: *Hoskins*, 72.
Nailstone	1604	1628	*Parker*, 145.
Naneby	..	1499	Depopulated village: *Parker*, 46.
Nethercote	1595	..	*Parker*, 122.
Nevill Holt	..	by 1572	*Parker*, 99.
Newbold Folville	..	..	Depopulated village: Hoskins, *T.L.A.S.* xxii, 242.
Newbold Saucey	..	..	Depopulated village: *Hoskins*, 72.
Newbold Vernon	1509	by 1674	(i) *Parker*, 60. (ii) Beresford.
New Parks (by Leicester)	1538	..	*Parker*, 76.
Newton Burgoland	1594	1611–25	(i) *Parker*, 122. (ii) Beresford.
Newton, Cold	1578	by 1641	(i) *Parker*, 110. (ii) *Nichols*, iii, 349.
Newtown Linford	..	'old inclosure'	Monk.
Normanton-le-Heath	1506	1629	(i) *Parker*, 55. (ii) *Nichols*, iv, 812.
Normanton Turville	..	1512–15	Depopulated village: *Parker*, 65–66.
Norton, East	..	1652	*Nichols*, iii, 490.
Norton-juxta-Twycross	1606	1747	(i) *Parker*, 145. (ii) Inclosure Act of 1748 confirmed articles of agreement of 1747.
Noseley	1504	1509	Depopulated village: *Parker*, 51–52.
Orton-on-the-Hill	c. 1587	..	*Parker*, 117.
Othorpe	..	..	Depopulated village: Hoskins, *T.L.A.S.* xxii, 242.
Overton, Cold	..	by 1631	*Cal. S.P. Dom. 1629–31*, 497. But acc. to Monk it was partly open in 1794.
Owston	1536	by 1604	*Parker*, 74.

Place	(i) Date of first inclosure evidence	(ii) Date of full inclosure	Sources for (i) and (ii)
Packington	1499	c. 1609	(i) *Parker*, 46. (ii) *Beresford*.
Peatling Magna . . .	1561	by 1659	(i) *Parker*, 98. (ii) Leicester Mun. Room, Clayton MSS. 35'29/411, 412.
Peatling Parva	..	1665	Copy of agreement in Leics. Co. Rec. Off.
Peckleton	1663	by 1675	(i) C 78/669, no. 15. (ii) *Beresford*.
Pickwell	1590	1615	*Parker*, 120. Monk gives date of full inclosure as 1628.
Plungar	..	by 1612	*Beresford*.
Potters Marston . . .	..	..	Depopulated village: Hoskins, *T.L.A.S.* xxii, 242.
Prestgrave	..	..	Depopulated village: Hoskins, *T.L.A.S.* xxii, 242.
Prestwold	..	by 1633–4	*Beresford*.
Poultney	..	by 1507	Depopulated village: *Parker*, 58.
Quenby	..	1485–9	Depopulated village: *Parker*, 31.
Ragdale	1495	1628	*Parker*, 44, 119.
Ravenstone	1610	..	Wards 5/23, John Shenton.
Rearsby	1625	..	Wards 5/23, Thos. Noble.
Ringlethorp	..	..	Depopulated village: *Hoskins*, 72.
Rollestone	..	'old inclosure'	*Monk*.
Rotherby	..	1625–74	*Beresford*. 'Late general inclosure' mentioned in 1674.
Rothley	1579	..	*Parker*, 111.
Sapcote	1638	..	Wards 5/23, John Cooper, John Bent, Edw. Wright. Projected inclosure referred to in Clayton MS. 35'29/447, mid-17th century.
Saxby	1628	1674–1736	(i) Wards 5/23, John Thompson. (ii) *Beresford*.
Scraptoft	..	1601	*Parker*, 135.
Sewstern	..	1597	*Parker*, 125.
Shangton	..	1638	*Nichols*, ii, 791.
Shawell	1653	1665	(i) C 54/3757, no. 29. (ii) C 78/669, no. 4.
Sheepy Magna . . .	1639	..	*Beresford*. Glebe Terrier refers to inclosure in 1639, but 1679 terrier shows open fields. Nichols gives date as 1659: *Nichols*, iv, 925.
Shenton Ch. . . .	1603	1646	(i) *Parker*, 140. (ii) *Monk*.
Shilton, Earl, Ch. . .	1599	..	*Parker*, 130.
Shoby	..	by 1530	Depopulated village: *Parker*, 72.
Sibstone	1679	..	*Beresford*.
Skeffington	1591	..	*Parker*, 120.
Skelthorpe	..	..	Depopulated village: Hoskins, *T.L.A.S.* xxii, 242.
Sketchley	..	c. 1597	*Parker*, 132.
Snarestone	..	1638–90	*Beresford*.
Snibston	1590	..	*Parker*, 119.
Stapleford	1603	..	*Parker*, 141.
Stapleton	1581	by 1653	(i) *Parker*, 112. (ii) *Lee*.
Staunton Harold . .	1506	'old inclosure'	(i) *Parker*, 55. (ii) *Monk*.
Stockerston	1579	1601–78	(i) *Parker*, 111. (ii) *Beresford*.
Stoke Golding . . .	1601	by 1604	(i) *Parker*, 138. (ii) *T.L.A.S.* xiv, 217. Burton in 1622 wrote of 'inclosure 20 years since'. But see Wards 5/23, Edw. Richardson, for evidence of open fields in 1622.
Stonesby	1579	..	*Parker*, 111.
Stonton Wyville . . .	..	1638–79	*Beresford*. Acc. to Nichols, date is c. 1650: *Nichols*, ii, 804.

Place	(i) Date of first inclosure evidence	(ii) Date of full inclosure	Sources for (i) and (ii)
Stormsworth	..	by 1500	Depopulated village: *Hoskins*, 105.
Stoughton	1592	..	*Parker*, 122.
Stretton-in-the-Fields	..	'principally old inclosure'	*Nichols*, iii, 1029.
Stretton Magna	..	'largely inclosed by end of 17th century'	Hoskins, 'Leics. Farmer in the 17th century', *Agric. Hist.* xxv, 17.
Sutton Cheney Ch.	..	by 1674	*Beresford*.
Swepstone	1583–97	1625–90	(i) *Parker*, 115. (ii) *Beresford*.
Sysonby	..	first half 17th century	Depopulated village: *Hoskins*, 101.
Syston	..	by 1601	*Beresford*.
Temple	..	..	Depopulated village: *Hoskins*, 72.
Theddingworth	c. 1582	'old inclosure'	(i) *Parker*, 114. (ii) *Nichols*, ii, 285.
Thorpe Acre	1517	..	*Parker*, 67.
Thorpe Arnold	1600	1601–1700	(i) *Parker*, 133. (ii) *Beresford*.
Thorpe Satchville	..	'old inclosure'	*Monk*.
Thrussington	1601?	..	*Parker*, 133.
Thurcaston	1600		C 78/368, no. 21.
Thurlaston	1511	1638–99	(i) *Parker*, 65. (ii) *Beresford*.
Thurnby	..	1616	Hoskins, 'Leics. Farmer in 17th century', op. cit. 17.
Tilton-on-the-Hill	1496	1603	*Parker*, 44, 142.
Twycross	..	1647	Lord Howe family papers, *penes* (1952) Messrs. Trower, Still, and Keeling, Lincoln's Inn.
Twyford	1649	..	C 54/3402, no. 3.
Ullesthorpe	..	1725	*Nichols*, iv, 118.
Ulverscroft	1540	..	*Parker*, 74.
Upton	1513	..	*Parker* 67.
Walton-on-the-Wolds	1614	..	Wards 5/23, Libbeus Darby.
Wanlip	..	'old inclosure'	*Nichols*, iii, 1097.
Welby	..	1605	Depopulated village: *Parker*, 146.
Welham	1597	1601–6	(i) *Parker*, 127. (ii) *Beresford*; *Monk*.
Wellsborough	..	1529–30	Depopulated village: *Parker*, 69.
Weston	..	early 14th century	Depopulated village: *Hoskins*, 103.
Whatborough	..	c. 1495	Depopulated village: *Parker*, 40.
Whatton, Long	1664	..	C 78/1581, no. 5. Agreement to inclose pasture only.
Whittington	..	..	Depopulated village: Hoskins, *T.L.A.S.* xxii, 242.
Whitwick	1587	by 1704	(i) *Parker*, 117. (ii) *Beresford*.
Wigston Magna	1588	..	C 78/73, no. 7.
Wigston Parva	..	1507	*Parker*, 55.
Willoughby Waterless	..	1637	*Nichols*, iv, 393.
Willowes	..	1495	Depopulated village: Hoskins, *T.L.A.S.* xxii, 242.
Wistow	..	..	Depopulated village: Hoskins, *T.L.A.S.* xxii, 242.
Withcote	..	by 1538	Depopulated village: *Parker*, 75.
Witherley	..	'old inclosure'	*Monk*.
Woodcote	..	by 1468	Depopulated village: *Hoskins*, 105.
Woodhouse Ch.	1656	..	*Nichols*, iii, 111.
Woodthorpe	..	1662	*Nichols*, iii, 911.
Worthington	1506	..	*Parker*, 55.
Wycomb	1516	..	*Parker*, 67.
Wyfordby	1587	1612–74	(i) *Parker*, 116. (ii) *Beresford*.
Wymeswold	1578	..	*Parker*, 110.
Wymondham	1563	probably by 1607	*Parker*, 104, 107. But Nichols gives date of full inclosure as 1596: *Nichols*, ii, 401.

APPENDIX II

List of Parliamentary Inclosure Acts and Awards for Leicestershire

P.R.O. = Public Record Office.   L.R.O. = Leicestershire Record Office.

N.B. Only one location is given, although other copies of the Acts and Awards are known to be in existence—e.g. with Parish Councils or Solicitors.

Parish	Date of Act	Date of Award	Location Act	Location Award
Anstey	1 Geo. III (1761)	19 July 1762	..	L.R.O.
Appleby	11 Geo. III (1771)	29 July 1772	L.R.O.	L.R.O.
Arnesby	34 Geo. III (1794)	29 May 1795	L.R.O.	L.R.O.
Asfordby	1 Geo. III (1761)	26 May 1762	..	P.R.O.
Ashby-de-la-Zouch	8 Geo. III (1768)	27 May 1769	L.R.O.	L.R.O.
Ashby Woulds	40 Geo. III (1800)	25 June 1807	..	L.R.O.
Aylestone	7 Geo. III (1767)	16 Dec. 1768	..	L.R.O.
Bagworth, *see under* Thornton				
Barkby	19 Geo. III (1779)	3 Feb. 1780	..	L.R.O.
Barkestone and Plungar	31 Geo. III (1791)	20 Feb. 1796	L.R.O.	L.R.O.
Barrow upon Soar (*see also under* Charnwood Forest and Rothley Plain)	32 Geo. II (1758–9)	29 July 1761	..	L.R.O.
Barsby and South Croxton	34 Geo. III (1794)	9 Aug. 1798	L.R.O.	L.R.O.
Beaumanor, *see under* Charnwood Forest				
Belton, *see also under* Charnwood Forest	52 Geo. III (1812)	Award not traced	L.R.O.	..
Billesdon	4 Geo. III (1764)	31 July 1765	..	L.R.O.
Birstall	32 Geo. II (1758–9)	20 May 1760	..	L.R.O.
Bitteswell	27 Geo. III (1787)	14 Mar. 1788	L.R.O.	P.R.O.
Blaby	6 Geo. III (1766)	3 Dec. 1766	..	L.R.O.
Bottesford, Easthorpe, and Normanton	10 Geo. III (1770)	1772	..	Duchy of Lancaster Office
Bowden, Great	16 Geo. III (1776)	1777	L.R.O.	P.R.O.
Bowden, Little	19 Geo. III (1779)	15 Apr. 1780	..	L.R.O.
Branston	6 Geo. III (1766)	19 Nov. 1767	..	L.R.O.
Breedon-on-the-Hill, Newbold, and Worthington	42 Geo. III (1802)	1806	L.R.O.	P.R.O.
Breedon-on-the-Hill, Tonge, and Wilson	32 Geo. II (1758–9)	1762	..	P.R.O.
Bringhurst, Easton Magna, and Drayton	44 Geo. III (1804)	3 Mar. 1810	..	L.R.O.
Broughton, Nether	4 Geo. III (1764)	1765	..	P.R.O.
Bruntingthorpe	16 Geo. III (1776)	1777	..	P.R.O.
Burton Overy	5 Geo. III (1765)	11 Aug. 1766	..	L.R.O.
Caldwell, *see under* Wycombe and Caldwell				
Charley, *see under* Charnwood Forest				
Charnwood Forest and Rothley Plain (including parts of Barrow-upon-Soar, Beaumanor, Belton, Charley, Groby, Hugglescote and Donington-le-Heath, Knightthorpe, Loughborough, Maplewell, Maplewell Longdale, Markfield, Newtown Linford, Ratby, Roecliffe, Rothley Plain, Shepshed, Stanton-under-Bardon, Swithland, Thringstone, Ulverscroft, Whitwick, and Woodhouse)	48 Geo. III (1808)	4 Dec. 1829	L.R.O.	L.R.O.
Clawson, Long	19 Geo. III (1779)	1780	..	P.R.O.

Parish	Date of Act	Date of Award	Location Act	Location Award
Claybrooke	7 Geo. II. (1734)	Articles of agreement quoted in Act	..	..
Congerstone	4 Geo. IV (1823)	17 Jan. 1826	L.R.O.	L.R.O.
Cosby and Littlethorpe . . .	7 Geo. III (1767)	30 Dec. 1767	..	L.R.O.
Countesthorpe	6 Geo. III (1766)	1767	L.R.O.	P.R.O.
Cranoe, see Glooston and Cranoe				
Croft	19 Geo. III (1779)	10 Mar. 1780	L.R.O.	L.R.O.
Cropston	21 Geo. III (1781)	18 Jan. 1782	..	L.R.O.
Croxton Kerrial	6 Geo. III (1766)	4 Nov. 1767	..	L.R.O.
Croxton, South, see under Barsby				
Croxton, South (Nether End) .	No Act: Award made pursuant to Articles of Agreement made 9 Feb. 1756	11 Apr. 1757	..	L.R.O.
Desford and (part of) Peckleton .	32 Geo. II (1758–9)	7 Aug. 1760	..	L.R.O.
Diseworth	34 Geo. III (1794)	1804	..	P.R.O.
Donington, Castle . . .	18 Geo. III (1778)	12 May 1779	L.R.O.	P.R.O.
Donington-le-Heath, see under Hugglescote				
Drayton, see under Bringhurst				
Dunton Bassett	36 Geo. III (1796)	25 May 1797	L.R.O.	L.R.O.
Easthorpe, see under Bottesford				
Easton, Great, see under Bringhurst				
Eaton	9 Geo. III (1769)	1771	..	P.R.O.
Evington and Stoughton . .	1 Geo. III (1761)	21 Apr. 1761	..	L.R.O.
Fleckney	9 Geo. III (1769)	1770	..	P.R.O.
Foxton	10 Geo. III (1770)	1771	..	P.R.O.
Frisby on the Wreak . . .	33 Geo. III (1759–60)	9 Oct. 1761	..	L.R.O.
Frolesworth	45 Geo. III (1805)	7 Jan. 1808	..	L.R.O.
Gilmorton	17 Geo. III (1777)	13 Mar. 1778	..	P.R.O.
Glenfield	49 Geo. III (1809)	1809	L.R.O.	..
Glen, Great (Nether or South End Fields)	32 Geo. II (1758–9)	6 June 1760	..	L.R.O.
Glen, Great (Upper or North End Fields)	31 Geo. II (1757–8)	29 Jan. 1759	..	L.R.O.
Glooston and Cranoe . . .	6 Geo. IV (1825)	11 June 1828	..	L.R.O.
Grimston	5 Geo. III (1765)	12 Mar. 1766	..	L.R.O.
Groby (see also under Charnwood Forest)	29 Geo. III (1789)	30 Jan. 1790	..	L.R.O.
Gumley	12 Geo. III (1772)	6 July 1773	..	L.R.O.
Hallaton	10 Geo. III (1770)	11 Mar. 1771	..	P.R.O.
Halstead	6 & 7 Will. IV (1836)	9 July 1839	..	L.R.O.
Harby	30 Geo. III (1790)	28 Dec. 1793	..	L.R.O.
Harston	29 Geo. III (1789)	11 Apr. 1791	..	L.R.O.
Hathern	17 Geo. III (1777)	1778	L.R.O.	P.R.O.
Hemington	29 Geo. III (1789)	1791	L.R.O.	P.R.O.
Higham on the Hill . . .	41 Geo. III (1801)	4 Oct. 1810	..	L.R.O.
Hinckley	33 Geo. II (1759–60)	21 May 1761	..	L.R.O.
Hoby	33 Geo. II (1760)	21 May 1761	L.R.O.	L.R.O.
Horninghold	3 Geo. II (1730)	Award not traced	..	..
Hose	31 Geo. III (1791)	19 Feb. 1796	..	L.R.O.
Hoton.	32 Geo. II (1758–9)	8 Jan. 1760	..	L.R.O.
Houghton on the Hill . . .	5 Geo. III (1765)	5 Aug. 1765	..	L.R.O.
Hugglescote and Donington-le-Heath (see also under Charnwood Forest)	14 Geo. III (1774)	12 Apr. 1775	..	L.R.O.
Humberstone	28 Geo. III (1788)	19 Feb. 1789	L.R.O.	L.R.O.
Hungarton	2 Geo. III (1762)	1 July 1763	L.R.O.	L.R.O.
Husbands Bosworth . . .	4 Geo. III (1764)	4 May 1765	..	L.R.O.

Parish	Date of Act	Date of Award	Location Act	Location Award
Ibstock	14 Geo. III (1774)	8 May 1775	L.R.O.	P.R.O.
Kegworth	18 Geo. III (1778)	1780	L.R.O.	P.R.O.
Kettleby, Ab	1 Geo. III (1761)	16 Dec. 1761	..	L.R.O.
Keyham	11 Geo. III (1771)	23 Mar. 1772	..	L.R.O.
Kibworth Beauchamp, Kibworth Harcourt, and Smeeton Westerby	19 Geo. III (1779)	14 June 1779	L.R.O.	L.R.O.
Kilby and Newton Harcourt in the Parish of Wistow	11 Geo. III (1771)	1771	L.R.O.	P.R.O.
Kilworth, North	5 Geo. III (1765)	12 Mar. 1766	..	L.R.O.
Kilworth, South	29 Geo. III (1789)	1792	..	P.R.O.
Kimcote and Walton in the Parishes of Kimcote and Knaptoft	18 Geo. III (1778)	12 Mar. 1779	..	P.R.O.
Kirby Mallory	13 Geo. III (1773)	Award given in Act		
Knaptoft, see under Kimcote				
Knighton	28 Geo. II (1754–5)	19 Feb. 1756	..	L.R.O.
Knightthorpe and Thorpe Acre (see also under Charnwood Forest) .	19 Geo. III (1779)	1 Oct. 1779	L.R.O.	L.R.O.
Knipton	37 Geo. III (1797)	21 June 1803	..	L.R.O.
Langton, East, West, Church, and Thorpe	17 Geo. II (1743–4)	13 Sept. 1743 Articles of Agreement quoted in Act	L.R.O.	
Langton, West, East, Thorpe, and Tur	31 Geo. III (1791)	6 Dec. 1792	L.R.O.	L.R.O.
Leicester (St. Margaret), see St. Margaret (Leicester)				
Leicester (Southfields), see Southfields (Leicester)				
Leire	19 Geo. III (1779)	18 Mar. 1780	..	L.R.O.
Littlethorpe, see Cosby and Littlethorpe				
Loughborough (see also under Charnwood Forest)	32 Geo. II (1758–9)	5 Feb. 1762	..	L.R.O.
Lubenham	6 Geo. III (1766)	1767	..	P.R.O.
Lutterworth.	30 Geo. III (1790)	1792	..	P.R.O.
Maplewell, see under Charnwood Forest				
Markfield (see also under Charnwood Forest)	9 Geo. III (1769)	27 Dec. 1769	..	L.R.O.
Marston, Potters, see Stanton, Stoney				
Medbourne	5 Vict. (1841–2)	24 Sept. 1844	..	L.R.O.
Melton Mowbray. . . .	33 Geo. II (1759–60)	16 July 1761	..	P.R.O.
Misterton, see under Walcote in the Parish of Misterton				
Mountsorrel	21 Geo. III (1781)	20 Dec. 1781	..	L.R.O.
Mowsley	28 Geo. III (1788)	19 Dec. 1788	..	L.R.O.
Narborough	25 Geo. II (1751–2)	10 Nov. 1752	..	L.R.O.
Newbold, see under Breedon-on-the-Hill				
Newbold Verdon	50 Geo. III (1810)	2 Dec. 1820	L.R.O.	L.R.O.
Newton Burgoland in the Parish of Swepstone . . .	No Act: Award made pursuant to Articles of Agreement made 9 Apr. 1772	31 Aug. 1772	..	L.R.O.
Newton Harcourt, see under Kilby				
Newtown Linford, see under Charnwood Forest				
Normanton, see under Bottesford				
Norton, see under Stretton, Little				
Norton-juxta-Twycross. . .	22 Mar. 1748	29 Sept. 1748	L.R.O.	L.R.O.

Parish	Date of Act	Date of Award	Location	
			Act	Award
Oadby	32 Geo. II (1758–9)	20 June 1760	..	L.R.O.
Orton-on-the-Hill . . .	22 Geo. III (1782)	1783		P.R.O.
Osgathorpe	25 Geo. III (1785)	30 Apr. 1786	L.R.O.	P.R.O.
Peatling Parva . . .	Pursuant to Articles of Agreement for inclosure	27 Mar. 1665	..	L.R.O.
Peckleton, *see under* Desford				
Peggs Green, *see under* Whitwick				
Plungar, *see under* Barkestone				
Queniborough	33 Geo. III (1793)	27 Aug. 1794	L.R.O.	Parish Council
Quorndon	2 Geo. III (1762)	9 July 1763	L.R.O.	L.R.O.
Ratby (*see also under* Charnwood Forest and Rothley Plain)	10 Geo. III (1770)	15 Aug. 1771	..	L.R.O.
Ratcliffe Culey	6 Geo. III (1766)	2 Apr. 1767	..	L.R.O.
Ravenstone	10 Geo. III (1770)	1771	..	P.R.O.
Rearsby	1 Geo. III (1761)	16 June 1762	..	L.R.O.
Redmile	32 Geo. III (1792)	16 Mar. 1797	..	L.R.O.
Roecliffe, *see under* Charnwood Forest				
Rothley	21 Geo. III (1781)	23 Feb. 1782	L.R.O.	P.R.O.
Rothley Plain, *see under* Charnwood Forest				
Saddington	10 Geo. III (1770)	30 Jan. 1771	..	L.R.O.
St. Margaret (Leicester) . .	4 Geo. III (1764)	20 Dec. 1764	..	L.R.O.
Saltby	11 Geo. III (1771)	1772	..	P.R.O.
Sapcote	18 Geo. III (1778)	1779	..	P.R.O.
Scalford	5 Geo. III (1765)	7 Jan. 1766	..	L.R.O.
Seagrave	33 Geo. II (1759–60)	1761	..	P.R.O.
Shackerstone	9 Geo. III (1769)	11 May 1774	..	L.R.O.
Sharnford	4 Geo. III (1764)	8 Mar. 1765	..	P.R.O.
Shearsby	13 Geo. III (1773)	25 Feb. 1774	..	L.R.O.
Sheepy Magna	50 Geo. III (1810)	1820	..	P.R.O.
Sheepy Parva	8 Geo. III (1768)	8 Feb. 1769	..	L.R.O.
Shepshed, *see under* Charnwood Forest and Rothley Plain				
Shilton, Earl	18 Geo. III (1778)	14 Apr. 1779	..	L.R.O.
Sibson	43 Geo. III (1803)	1 June 1804	..	L.R.O.
Sileby	32 Geo. II (1758–9)	30 June 1760	..	L.R.O.
Skeffington	12 Geo. III (1772)	4 Jan. 1773	..	L.R.O.
Slawston	33 Geo. III (1793)	12 June 1794	L.R.O.	L.R.O.
Smeeton Westerby, *see* Kibworth Beauchamp, Kibworth Harcourt, and Smeeton Westerby				
Somerby	33 Geo. II (1759–60)	12 June 1761	..	L.R.O.
Southfields (Leicester) . .	44 Geo. III (1804)	30 May 1811	..	L.R.O.
Sproxton	11 Geo. III (1771)	1772	..	P.R.O.
Stanton, Stoney and Marston, Potters	4 Geo. III (1764)	1765	..	P.R.O.
Stanton under Bardon in the Parish of Thornton (*see also under* Charnwood Forest)	19 Geo. III (1779)	1780	..	P.R.O.
Stathern	32 Geo. III (1792)	12 June 1799	..	L.R.O.
Stonesby	20 Geo. III (1780)	1780	..	P.R.O.
Stoughton, *see* Evington and Stoughton				
Stretton, Little, in the Parish of Norton	10 Geo. III (1770)	17 Jan. 1771	L.R.O.	L.R.O.
Sutton Cheney	34 Geo. III (1794)	1798	..	P.R.O.
Swepstone, *see* Newton Burgoland in the Parish of Swepstone				

Parish	Date of Act	Date of Award	Location	
			Act	*Award*
Swinford	20 Geo. III (1780)	1783		P.R.O.
Swithland (*see also under* Charnwood Forest and Rothley Plain)	38 Geo. III (1798)	27 June 1799	L.R.O.	L.R.O.
Syston and Barkby . . .	17 Geo. III (1777)	26 June 1778	..	L.R.O.
Thornton and Bagworth (*see also under* Stanton-under-Bardon)	34 Geo. III (1794)	29 Sept. 1797	..	L.R.O.
Thorpe Acre, *see under* Knightthorpe				
Thringstone, *see under* Charnwood Forest				
Thrussington	29 Geo. III (1789)	20 May 1790	..	L.R.O.
Thurcaston	38 Geo. III (1798)	26 July 1799	..	L.R.O.
Thurlaston	9 Geo. III (1769)	14 Dec. 1769	...	L.R.O.
Thurmaston	2 Geo. III (1762)	27 June 1763	..	L.R.O.
Tonge, *see* Breedon-on-the-Hill, Tonge, and Wilson				
Tugby	24 Geo. III (1784)	1785	..	L.R.O.
Twyford	36 Geo. III (1796)	9 July 1798	L.R.O.	L.R.O.
Ulverscroft, *see under* Charnwood Forest				
Walcote in the Parish of Misterton	36 Geo. III (1796)	30 June 1797	L.R.O.	L.R.O.
Waltham	6 Geo. III (1766)	23 Dec. 1767	..	L.R.O.
Walton, *see under* Kimcote and Walton				
Walton-on-the-Wolds . . .	32 Geo. III (1792)	13 July 1796	..	L.R.O.
Wartnaby	4 Geo. III (1764)	12 Dec. 1764	..	L.R.O.
Whatton, Long	18 Geo. III (1778)	27 May 1779	L.R.O.	P.R.O.
Whetstone	4 Geo. III (1764)	6 Apr. 1765	L.R.O.	L.R.O.
Whitwick, Thringstone, and Peggs Green (*see also under* Charnwood Forest and Rothley Plain)	43 Geo. III (1803)	3 Dec. 1807	L.R.O.	L.R.O.
Wigston Magna	4 Geo. III (1764)	17 Nov. 1766	..	L.R.O.
Wilson, *see under* Breedon-on-the-Hill				
Wistow, *see under* Kilby				
Woodhouse, *see under* Charnwood Forest				
Worthington, *see under* Breedon-on-the-Hill				
Wycombe and Caldwell . .	17 Geo. III (1777)	6 July 1778	..	L.R.O.
Wymeswold.	30 Geo. II (1756–7)	21 Feb. 1759	..	L.R.O.

THE FORESTS OF LEICESTERSHIRE

URING the Middle Ages there were in Leicestershire three regions known as forests. To the west of the Soar lay Charnwood Forest and Leicester Forest, while on the eastern border of the county there was a royal forest which, though lying mostly in Rutland,[1] at one time included a part of Leicestershire. Of these three regions, only the king's forest of Leicestershire and Rutland was subject to the forest law and the royal machinery of forest administration. Neither Leicester Forest nor Charnwood Forest was ever subject to the special code of forest law, although during the Middle Ages both contained large areas of woodland.[2]

THE ROYAL FOREST OF LEICESTERSHIRE AND RUTLAND[3]

The royal forest of Leicestershire and Rutland owed its origin to Henry I. A 13th-century inquisition describes how King Henry, while travelling through Leicestershire, saw five hinds in a wood,[4] and left one of his retinue, a certain Pichard, to take charge of them. It is implied that Pichard was thus entrusted with the custody of a forest in Leicestershire and Rutland. Subsequently Pichard associated with himself a man of those parts, Hasculf of Allexton. When the king returned to Leicestershire, Pichard asked that the functions previously entrusted to him might be transferred to Hasculf, and to this the king agreed.[5] These events must have taken place before Michaelmas 1130, when Hasculf was already in charge of the forest.[6] The extent under Henry I of the royal forest thus established is unknown, but a document of 1227 shows that at that date the king's forest in Leicestershire consisted of a strip of territory running north from the Welland as far as Cold Overton, stretching west to the neighbourhoods of Somerby, Tilton, Skeffington, and Rolleston, and on the east extending to the Rutland border.[7]

Hasculf remained the keeper of the royal forest in Leicestershire and Rutland until he was murdered during Stephen's reign.[8] The royal forest ceased to exist under Stephen,[9] but it was re-created by Henry II before 1160.[10] The wardenship of the forest was given by Henry II to Hasculf's son Peter, who married one of the Nevilles, a family prominent in connexion with the king's forests during the 13th century.[11] Peter's descendants remained wardens

[1] The Rutland part of the forest is described in *V.C.H. Rut.* i, 251.
[2] G. F. Farnham, *Charnwood Forest and its Historians*, 3–10.
[3] Sometimes known as Leighfield Forest.
[4] Described as *boscum qui vocatur Riseberwe.* Its locality is unknown. Nichols, *Leics.* ii, 516, identifies it with a certain Reresby wood, but this seems to be merely a conjecture.
[5] *Select Pleas of the Forest* (Selden Soc. xiii), ed. J. G. Turner, 45; C. Petit-Dutaillis, *Studies and Notes Supplementary to Stubbs' Constitutional Hist.* (1915), i, 170.
[6] *Pipe R. 1130* (Rec. Com.), 87.   [7] *Rot. Litt. Claus.* (Rec. Com.), ii, 207.
[8] *Select Pleas of the Forest*, ed. Turner, 45.
[9] Turner, op. cit., pp. xcix–c; *Cal. Pat.*, 1225–32, 110; *Rot. Litt. Claus.* (Rec. Com.), ii, 169.
[10] *Pipe R. 1160* (Pipe R. Soc. ii), 36.
[11] *Select Pleas of the Forest*, ed. Turner, 44–46; *Complete Peerage*, ix, 479–81, and p. ii (following p. 502).

of the forest until after the Leicestershire portion of it was disafforested.[12] How much woodland the afforested region contained during the 12th and 13th centuries is unknown. When the Domesday Survey was made, the area of the later royal forest in the south-east corner of Leicestershire was densely wooded.[13]

The issue of the Charter of the Forest in 1217 was apparently not followed by any disafforestation in Leicestershire, though a perambulation of the royal forest in the county seems to have been made in 1218.[14] After the forest charter had been reissued in 1225, the whole of the king's forest of Leicestershire seems to have been disafforested, after a perambulation, on the grounds that since the forest had been created by Henry II it should be disafforested in accordance with the terms of the charter of 1217.[15] When Henry III came of age in 1227 he challenged the validity of these proceedings, stating that districts afforested by Henry I, disafforested under Stephen, and reafforested by Henry II, ought not to be disafforested under the terms of the charter. The king therefore ordered that the royal forest in Leicestershire and Rutland should be maintained as it had been before the recent disafforestation.[16] The royal forest in Leicestershire continued to exist until 1235, when it was disafforested by a royal charter.[17] After 1235 the only part of Leicestershire which remained part of the king's forest was a royal demesne manor at Withcote.[18]

LEICESTER FOREST[19]

Domesday records the existence in Leicestershire of an area of woodland called 'Hereswode', 4 leagues in length and 1 in breadth.[20] It is probable that 'Hereswode' was the area later known as Leicester Forest, though the identification cannot be considered quite certain. In Domesday the 'Hereswode' is described as 'the woodland of the whole sheriffdom', and it does not seem to have been held by any lord. In the 13th century it was stated that Leicester Forest had been held by Robert, Count of Meulan and Earl of Leicester[21] (d. 1118). The forest was certainly in possession of the earls of Leicester before 1168,[22] and it remained in their hands until 1265, when it passed to the earls of Lancaster. After 1399 the forest formed part of the Duchy of Lancaster estates.[23] Little is known of the administration of the forest in the 12th and 13th centuries, though the Earl of Leicester's foresters and other ministers in Leicester Forest are mentioned in a document which is not later than 1168.[24] Amercements were being levied in the forest in 1206, when it was temporarily in the king's hands.[25] In the 14th century the forest was in charge of a master forester,

---

[12] *Select Pleas of the Forest*, ed. Turner, 44–46; G. F. Farnham, 'Hist. of the Manor of Withcote', *Assoc. Arch. Soc. Rep.* xxxvi, 140–1.

[13] See p. 149.

[14] *Select Pleas of the Forest*, ed. Turner, p. xcvi; Nichols, *Leics.* ii, 516, where the date 1217 is assigned to the perambulation in error.

[15] *Rot. Litt. Claus.* (Rec. Com.), ii, 26, 80, 169; *Cal. Pat.*, 1225–32, 110.

[16] *Select Pleas of the Forest*, ed. Turner, p. xcvii; *Rot. Litt. Claus.* (Rec. Com.), ii, 169; *Cal. Pat.*, 1225–32, 110.

[17] *Cal. Close*, 1234–7, 51; *Cal. Chart. R.*, 1226–57, 193.

[18] *Cal. Close*, 1234–7, 304–5. King John had obtained the manor by exchange; *Assoc. Arch. Soc. Rep.* xxxvi, 131. The Forest Charter of 1217 provided that disafforestation was not to extend to the royal demesne.

[19] For a full account of the history of Leic. Forest, see L. Fox and P. Russell, *Leic. Forest*.

[20] *V.C.H. Leics.* i, 306.

[21] *Leic. Boro. Rec.*, 1103–1327, 43.

[22] Ibid. 3.

[23] Fox and Russell, *Leic. Forest*, 67–68.

[24] *Leic. Boro. Rec.*, 1103–1327, 3.

[25] *Rot. Litt. Claus.* (Rec. Com.), i, 68.

who had under him a receiver[26] (for financial matters), several foresters, and a number of inferior officials.[27] In 1285 Edmund, Earl of Lancaster, was empowered by the king to hold pleas of the forest and to determine trespasses done in his parks and chases.[28] Trespasses against the vert and venison in Leicester Forest appear to have been dealt with under the powers thus granted.[29]

From the 12th century onwards the burgesses of Leicester were allowed to gather firewood in the forest, which was heavily wooded.[30] Leicester Forest extended in the 13th century to the south and south-west as far as the neighbourhoods of Desford and Earl Shilton.[31] Early in the same century the forest seems to have stretched as far northwards as the vicinity of Thurcaston,[32] but Simon de Montfort, while Earl of Leicester, alienated large areas in the northern part of the forest.[33] In the south-west part of the forest parks belonging to the earls of Lancaster were in existence by 1296 at Desford and Earl Shilton. Some further inclosures were made at various times during the Middle Ages in the forest, but a large part of it was still open at the beginning of the 16th century.[34] In 1523 a commission inspected Leicester Forest and reported that although it was well stocked with deer, it was greatly lacking in timber.[35] The forest must, however, still have contained a good deal of woodland, for in 1526 it was stated that nine score trees had been cut down in the part of the forest called Leicester Frith.[36] In 1526 a considerable area in the northern part of the forest was transformed into inclosed pasture, and rented out by the Duchy of Lancaster.[37] The inclosed portion was cleared and drained during the 16th century.[38] In 1605 it was reported that in the uninclosed remnant of the forest much wood had been cut, that many sheep were kept there, and that rabbit warrens and burrows had greatly increased. Evidently the area was being gradually converted into pasture.[39] Little timber was left by the early 17th century.[40]

In January 1627 Sir Miles Fleetwood, Receiver of the Court of Wards, was empowered to survey the forest, and later he was authorized to negotiate concerning its disafforestation with the various interested parties. As a result of these negotiations the Exchequer issued in 1628 an award providing for the inclosure of that part of the forest which was still open.[41] The numerous persons who owned land within the forest, or who claimed rights of common in it, were compensated by grants of land, totalling about 2,700 acres, in the area to be inclosed. The remainder of the land, amounting to nearly 1,600 acres, was almost all sold by the Crown, for a price of £7,760. A yearly ground-rent of 1s. an acre was payable to the Crown from the land thus sold.[42]

---

[26] For an account of a forest receiver, see L. Fox, 'Mins. Accts. of the Honour of Leic.', *T.L.A.S.* xix, 223–5.

[27] *Leic. Forest*, 35–43, 126.

[28] Ibid. 48–49. [29] Ibid. 49–50.

[30] *Leic. Boro. Rec., 1103–1327*, 43–44; Fox and Russell, *Leic. Forest*, 23.

[31] Fox and Russell, op. cit. 26; Hist. MSS. Com., *Hastings*, i, 341–2.

[32] Hist. MSS. Com., *Hastings*, i, 342.

[33] *Cal. Chart. R., 1226–57*, 408; *Rot. Hund.* (Rec. Com.), i, 238.

[34] Fox and Russell, *Leic. Forest*, 30–31, 64–66; *Cal. Inq. p.m.* iii, p. 289.

[35] Fox and Russell, op. cit. 77–78.

[36] Ibid. 80.

[37] Ibid. 82–84. For a list of the pastures existing after 1526, with acreages of each, see ibid. 134.

[38] Ibid. 85.

[39] Ibid. 93–97.

[40] Ibid. 97.

[41] Ibid. 106–15. The award is printed in Nichols, *Leics.* iv, 785–95.

[42] Fox and Russell, *Leic. Forest*, 136–8; Nichols, *Leics.* iv, 782.

CHARNWOOD FOREST

Charnwood Forest is a large and geologically interesting region,[43] formerly wooded, in the north-west part of Leicestershire. It has been suggested that the existence during the Middle Ages of courts or assemblies called swanimotes in three of the manors bordering on Charnwood Forest shows that it was before the Conquest an area subject to the royal forest law,[44] but it seems unlikely that any special code of law for the royal forests existed before 1066,[45] and there is no evidence that Charnwood was ever a royal forest. Charnwood Forest is not mentioned in Domesday,[46] but in 1086 the region was probably an uninhabited waste; the only place recorded in Domesday which can be stated with certainty to have been within the area of Charnwood Forest is Charley, where there were 4 carucates lying waste in 1086.[47] The only land in Charnwood mentioned in the Leicestershire Survey of 1124–9 is 6½ carucates at Charley.[48] According to a charter printed by Nichols,[49] Charnwood,[50] with Charley and Alderman's Haw[51] and all the woods around Charnwood formerly held by the Earl of Chester (except one unnamed park), was granted to Robert, Earl of Leicester, by Henry I, to whom the lands had been surrendered by the Earl of Chester.[52] By a second grant,[53] drawn up between 1139 and 1147, Ranulf, Earl of Chester, enfeoffed Robert, Earl of Leicester, with Charley[54] and with all Earl Ranulf's woods lying adjacent to Charnwood Forest except the park of Barrow.[55] The effect of these two charters should have been to transfer the whole of Charnwood Forest, except Barrow Park, to the Earl of Leicester, who under Henry I already possessed the manors of Shepshed, Whitwick, and Groby, adjoining the forest.[56] It is uncertain whether the Earl of Leicester ever in fact obtained possession of Charnwood Forest as a whole, for early in the 13th century the Earl of Chester possessed a considerable area in the eastern part of the forest.[57] The greater part of Charnwood Forest was divided from the 13th century onwards between the lords of several manors adjacent to the forest, each manor

[43] *V.C.H. Leics.* i, 3–5.

[44] G. F. Farnham, *Charnwood Forest and its Historians*, 6–7.

[45] C. Petit-Dutaillis, *Studies and Notes Supplementary to Stubbs' Constitutional Hist.* (1915), i, 166.

[46] The 'Hereswode' mentioned in Dom. Bk. (*V.C.H. Leics.* i, 306) may possibly be Charnwood, but it is more likely to be Leic. Forest.

[47] *V.C.H. Leics.* i, 336.

[48] Ibid. 349. The extant part of the Survey does not cover all Leics.

[49] Nichols, *Leics.* iii, 120.

[50] 'Cernewoda.'

[51] Both in Charnwood Forest as it later existed.

[52] The MS. from which Nichols printed the charter is not now available; Farnham, *Charnwood For.*, 17.

[53] Printed Hist. MSS. Com., *Hastings*, i, 66–67, from the original. See also Farnham, op. cit. 17.

[54] 'Cernelea.'

[55] The existence of these 2 charters, one printed by Nichols, and one in Hist. MSS. Com., *Hastings*, i, 66–67, has given rise to difficulties: (1) It is said that the 2 charters conflict. It is certainly true that while in the first charter (printed by Nichols) Charley and other woods were granted to Robert, Earl of Leic. by Hen. I, in the second charter (printed *Hastings MSS.*), drawn up later, Charley and the other lands were granted to Earl Robert by the Earl of Chester. But it is quite possible that in the reign of Stephen, Earl Robert thought it advisable to obtain a grant of the property from the Earl of Chester. Under Stephen there were at one time close political connexions between the Earls of Leic. and Chester (see above, pp. 80–1). The second charter implies that at the time when it was granted Charnwood Forest was being held from the king by the Earl of Leic. (2) The forest with which the 2 charters deal is described in both as the forest of Leic. The reference in the *Hastings MSS.* charter to the park of Barrow as being adjacent to the forest shows that the forest in question must have been Charnwood, and not the woodland generally known as Leic. Forest, for Barrow, while on the edge of Charnwood Forest, does not border on Leic. Forest at all.

[56] Farnham, *Charnwood For.* 16; *V.C.H. Leics.* i, 350–1.

[57] Farnham, op. cit. 15; Farnham, *Leics. Notes*, vi, 349; Hist. MSS. Com., *Hastings*, i, 67.

possessing a portion of the forest as part of the manorial waste.[58] In the manors of Whitwick, Shepshed, and Groby courts or assemblies called swanimotes were held.[59] The first mention of a swanimote in Charnwood occurs in 1371,[60] and swanimotes were still being held in 1512.[61]

Encroachment upon Charnwood Forest began before the middle of the 12th century. The hamlet of Quorndon, in the eastern part of the forest, is not mentioned in Domesday Book, and therefore probably did not exist in 1086, but before 1153 it was established with a chapel of its own.[62] Within the forest religious houses were founded at Ulverscroft before 1153,[63] at Charley before 1190,[64] and at Alderman's Haw before about 1220.[65] A settlement had been established at Swithland, in the south-east part of the forest, by the early 13th century,[66] and the hamlet of Mapplewell, also in the forest, is first mentioned in 1284.[67] Newton Linford, a village in the southern portion of the forest, is first mentioned in 1293.[68] A park existed at Barrow-on-Soar, on the edge of Charnwood Forest, before the middle of the 12th century,[69] and other parks were in existence within the forest at Bradgate by 1247,[70] at Quorndon by 1232,[71] at Bardon by 1270,[72] at Burgh (in the manor of Groby) by the same date,[73] at Groby itself by 1288,[74] and at Whitwick by 1289.[75] Many small encroachments were made on the forest during the Middle Ages and subsequently.[76] Though much land must have been cleared, Charnwood Forest still contained plenty of timber in the 16th century.[77] In the middle of the 17th century it was usual for the livestock in the forest to be rounded up twice a year, presumably to ensure that animals were not pastured in the forest by those who had no right to do so.[78] There is some evidence to show that as early as the 14th century it was already customary to collect the livestock at intervals.[79]

The amount of timber in the forest was greatly reduced during the 17th and 18th centuries. The disappearance of the woodland must have been accelerated by the activities of the great ironmaster, Humphrey Jennens, who in the late 17th century set up forges at Whitwick, and purchased large quantities of timber from the forest, presumably to be made into charcoal.[80] In the 18th century much wood from the forest was sold to the ironfounders at Melbourne (Derbys.).[81] The extensive rabbit warrens which existed in the forest, until largely destroyed during riotous proceedings in 1749, perhaps also contributed to the destruction of the trees.[82] By the end of the 18th century the forest was largely without woodland, though some fine plantations existed on the eastern

[58] Farnham, *Leics. Notes*, vi, 352–4, 356, 361, 367; Farnham, *Charnwood For.* 165–6; Nichols, *Leics.* i, p. cxvi.
[59] Farnham, *Leics. Notes*, vi, 367–8, 370; Farnham, *Charnwood For.* 6, 7, 105, 110, 131, 137.
[60] Farnham, *Charnwood For.* 105.
[61] Ibid. 110.
[62] Ibid. 15; Dugd. *Mon.* vi, 467.
[63] See p. 19.
[64] See p. 23.
[65] See p. 1.
[66] Farnham, *Charnwood For.* 91; *Rot. Hugonis de Welles*, ed. W. P. W. Phillimore, i, 254.
[67] Farnham, op. cit. 71, 85.
[68] Ibid. 101.
[69] Nichols, *Leics.* iii, 120; Hist. MSS. Com., *Hastings*, i, 66–67.
[70] Farnham, *Leics. Notes*, vi, 351.
[71] i.e. before the death of Ranulf de Blundeville, Earl of Chest.; Nichols, *Leics.* ii, App. 114.
[72] Farnham, *Leics. Notes*, vi, 352.
[73] Ibid.; Farnham, *Charnwood For.* 100.
[74] Farnham, *Charnwood For.* 100.
[75] Ibid. 134.
[76] See, for some examples, Farnham, *Leics. Notes*, vi, 348–95.
[77] *Leland's Itin.*, ed. Lucy Toulmin Smith, i, 17–18.
[78] Farnham, *Leics. Notes*, vi, 390.
[79] Ibid. vi, 367; Farnham, *Charnwood For.* 14.
[80] Nichols, *Leics.* iii, 130.
[81] Ibid. iii, 135. For a map of the forest drawn in 1754, showing inclosures and woods, see ibid. iii, 131.
[82] Ibid. iii, 131.

edge, and the greater part of the area was covered with gorse, fern, and grass. About 1750 it was established after litigation that the forest was a free common for the inhabitants of certain adjacent towns and villages, and in the late 18th century the uninclosed parts were used as pasture, chiefly for sheep.[83]

In 1808 an Act was passed providing for the inclosure of Charnwood Forest.[84] The open land in the forest was then about 11,000 acres in extent.[85] Allotments of land were made to the lords of the manors bordering on the forest, and to those who had common rights in it. Tithe-owners were also compensated, and the Act provided that 200 acres should be set aside for the building and endowment of one chapel or more in the forest.[86] After the inclosure many of the smaller allotments were bought, and several estates were formed.[87] A chapel, known as the Oaks Chapel, was built in the forest in 1815,[88] and two more chapels were built, at Copt Oak and Woodhouse Eaves, in 1837.[89]

With the destruction of the trees in Charnwood Forest the last considerable area of woodland in Leicestershire disappeared. In 1809 Leicestershire was described as 'by no means a woodland county'.[90] There was at that time plenty of young timber on the Duke of Rutland's estate, around Belvoir, and there was a plantation covering 400 or 500 acres at Castle Donington. There were also woods of some size at Burbage, Aston Flamville, and Beaumanor, but generally there was little timber in the county, except in the hedgerows.[91] Since that date no important area of woodland has come into existence in Leicestershire, and forestry has never been an industry of any importance in the county.

---

[83] Nichols, *Leics.* iii, 131–5; W. Pitt, *General View of Agriculture of . . . Leics.* 169, 174–6; Curtis, *Topog. Hist.* 41; Farnham, *Charnwood For.*, p. vi.

[84] Nichols, *Leics.* iv, 795.

[85] T. R. Potter, *Charnwood Forest*, 34, gives the area as 11,500 acres, but this figure includes Rothley Plain (inclosed at the same time), which covered about 500 acres (W. Pitt, *General View*, 174).

[86] Nichols, *Leics.* iv, 796. For details of claims made at the inclosure, see Potter, op. cit. 31–34.

[87] Curtis, *Topog. Hist.* 42. [88] Ibid.

[89] T. R. Potter, *Charnwood Forest*, 39.

[90] Pitt, *Gen. View*, 169. [91] Ibid. 169–71.